Wyoming Revisited

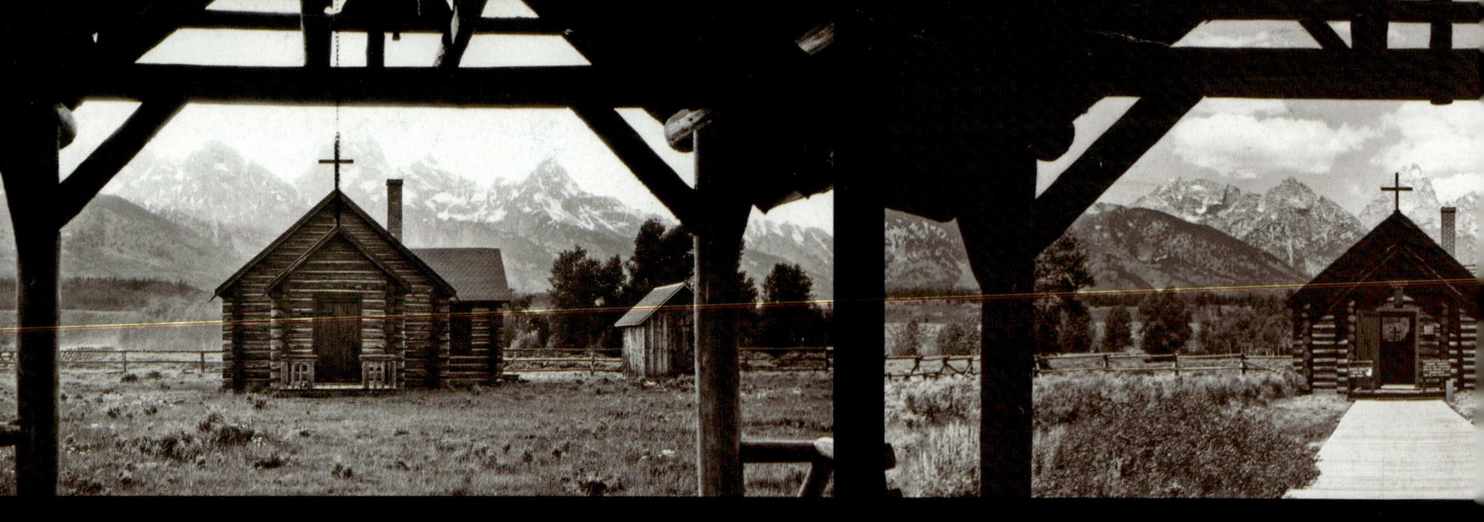

Wyoming Revisited

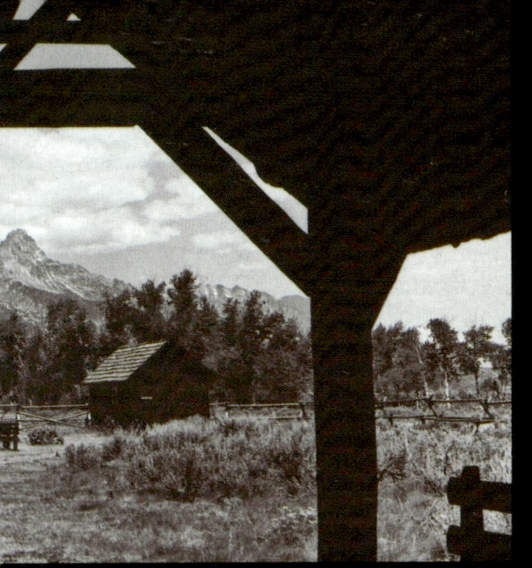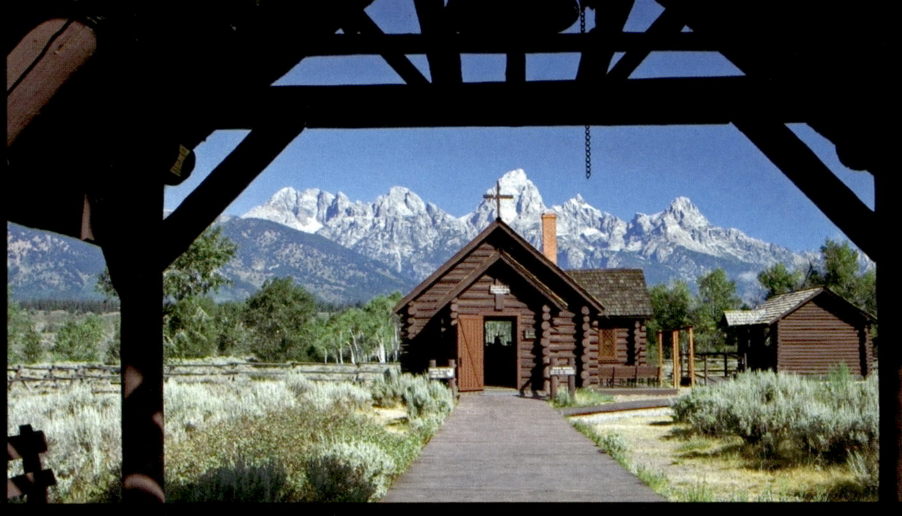

Rephotographing the Scenes of Joseph E. Stimson

Michael A. Amundson

University Press of Colorado
Boulder

Published by University Press of Colorado
5589 Arapahoe Avenue, Suite 206C
Boulder, Colorado 80303

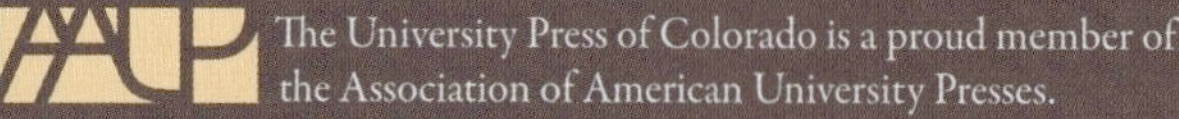 The University Press of Colorado is a proud member of the Association of American University Presses.

The University Press of Colorado is a cooperative publishing enterprise supported, in part, by Adams State University, Colorado State University, Fort Lewis College, Metropolitan State University of Denver, Regis University, University of Colorado, University of Northern Colorado, Utah State University, and Western State Colorado University.

♾ This paper meets the requirements of the ANSI/NISO Z39.48-1992 (Permanence of Paper).

The publication of this book is supported in part by the Wyoming Cultural Trust Fund.

Library of Congress Cataloging-in-Publication Data

Amundson, Michael A., 1965–
 Wyoming revisited / Michael A. Amundson.
   pages cm
   ISBN 978-1-60732-304-4 (hardback) — ISBN 978-1-60732-305-1 (ebook)
1. Wyoming—Pictorial works. 2. Repeat photography—Wyoming. 3. Stimson, J. E. (Joseph Elam), 1870–
1952. 4. Wyoming—History, Local. I. Title.
 F762.A57 2014
 978.7—dc23
                                2013050476

23   22   21   20   19   18   17   16   15   14   10   9   8   7   6   5   4   3   2   1

Dust jacket and text design by Daniel Pratt

Front-cover photograph credits: Chapel of Transfiguration, Moose Wyoming; 1930 photograph by Joseph E. Stimson (top left); 1988 and 2007 photographs by Michael A. Amundson (top right, bottom).

Contents

Acknowledgments

In many ways, this book serves as a window into my professional life as a historian over the last three decades. It began in the spring of 1987 as my collegiate basketball career was winding down at the University of Wyoming in Laramie (though it was never really wound up) and continued through graduate school and the publication of *Wyoming Time and Again* in 1991 while I was in a PhD program at the University of Nebraska. I re-hatched the project a dozen years into my tenure as a history professor at Northern Arizona University and am seeing it come to publication in my twentieth year of university teaching.

Along the way, the American Studies Program, Department of History, Journalism Department, and College of Arts and Sciences at the University of Wyoming (UW) all provided support and funding for fieldwork. Thanks to the Wyoming Council for the Humanities for the first opportunity to present my work around the state and to Pruett Publishing in Boulder, Colorado, for publishing *Wyoming Time and Again* and later relinquishing those rights so I could reuse those images in this work. At UW, I was fortunate to have great teachers of photography, including Robert C. Warner and Paul Jacque. I was even luckier to experience the teaching of a number of western historians who all went on to bigger places, including Robert Righter, Peter Iverson, Colin Calloway, and Mary Murphy. Thanks as well to my American Studies professors John Dorst and Eric Sandeen who supported my interest in history but encouraged me to think in an interdisciplinary way. Likewise, thanks to Pete Maslowski, Ken Winkle, Gary Moulton, Fran Kaye, and especially John Wunder and Fred Luebke at the University of Nebraska.

Mark Klett's rephotography has inspired my work from the beginning. His book *Second View: The Rephotographic Survey Project* introduced me to the subject twenty-five years ago; since then, Klett has rephotographed much of the American West. More important, though, his books on Yosemite, the San Francisco earthquake, and the Grand Canyon are provocative studies of place and time. *Yosemite in Time* especially, with its foldout pages and interesting essays by writer Rebecca Solnit on modernity and postmodernity, has inspired this work. I urge anyone interested in "then and now" photography to read *all* of Mark Klett's books.

The re-start of the Wyoming Project began in the summer of 2007 when the Cody Institute for Western American Studies awarded me a summer scholarship to rephotograph a number of sites two decades after I first photographed them. Thanks especially to former curator Juti Winchester, as well as Lynn Houze, Bob Pickering, Rebecca West, and Marguerite House. The following summer, Northern Arizona University's (NAU) Internal Grants Program provided me with a summer salary to finish the project, part of which culminated in the 2013 publication of *Passage to Wonderland*, which focused on rephotographing J. E. Stimson's 1903 trek along the newly opened Cody Road to Yellowstone. Thanks as well to NAU's Office of the Vice President for Research, and College of Arts and Letters Dean Michael Vincent, who helped me purchase photo rights for this project. Finally, a sabbatical in the fall of 2011 provided the time to concentrate on writing, as well as to travel back to Laramie where my 1987 UW basketball team was inducted into the University of Wyoming Sports Hall of Fame. During that visit, I had the opportunity to present research to the American Studies Program. That juxtaposition reminded me of what a special place my alma mater could be.

Throughout the twenty-seven years I have been working on Stimson, the Wyoming State Archives in Cheyenne, home to the Stimson collection of more than 7,500 images, has been totally supportive of my work. Thanks to Paula Chavoya and LaVaughn Bresnahan back at the beginning and Suzi Taylor of late. These photo curators have been amazing supporters of this project. Thanks, Suzi, for all the scans. Thanks also to Richard Collier for his discussions on Stimson photography.

Mark Junge, former Wyoming state historian, photographer, and J. E. Stimson biographer, deserves a special thank you. Mark first brought Stimson prints for me to look at in the Wyoming locker room following a basketball game my junior year, assisted me with fieldwork in 1987–88, and then, after his retirement, supported my ongoing work with several long telephone conversations that provided the encouragement I needed.

Thanks also to Stimson's daughter, the late Josephine Love of Dayton, Wyoming, who allowed me to tape an interview with her back in 1988 that I still have and that

I listened to while preparing this book. Also thanks to Stimson's grandson, the late Richard A. Patterson of Cheyenne, for talking with me.

Librarians and archivists also assisted me admirably on this project. Thanks especially to Erin Kinney at the Wyoming State Library in Cheyenne, who is spearheading the Wyoming Newspaper Project to digitize the state's newspapers between 1849 and 1922. This amazing project allowed me to track Stimson's life across the state from my home computer in Flagstaff. Thanks also to Tamsen Hert, Hebard Collection librarian at the University of Wyoming, and Rick Ewig, associate director of UW's American Heritage Center, for their many years of friendship and support. At my home institution, Northern Arizona University, the staff of the Special Collections and Archives not only helped me find relevant materials but also provided friendship and a home department feeling. Thanks especially to Karen Underhill, Sean Evans, and Jess Vogelsang. Thanks especially to my friend Todd Welch at Special Collections for making the wonderful maps in this book.

I owe a special thanks to the Wyoming Cultural Trust Fund for its generous support of this project's publication and to the Wyoming State Historical Society for partnering with the University Press of Colorado to make it happen. The cost and quality of this book are a result of these wonderful institutions. Along the way, thanks to Rick Ewig, Tamsen Hert, Marguerite House of the Buffalo Bill Center for the West, Judy Musgrave of the Sheridan County Historical Society, and Eric Sandeen of the American Studies program at the University of Wyoming for their last minute letters of support. Thanks also to everyone at the Press for your help!

My colleagues in the history department at NAU have made it a special place to work. Former chair George Lubick wrote letters of support for me and read and re-read the manuscript. Thanks, George. Thanks as well to Cynthia Kosso, Eric Meeks, Linda Sargent Wood, and Leilah Danielson for their support. English professors Steven and Laura Gray Rosendale always gave me their support by getting me away from history during hikes in northern Arizona's forests and mountains. I appreciate as well the many conversations about history, geography, and trains with Thomas Paradis, professor of geography at NAU. Thanks to NAU provost Laura Huenneke for the great support, especially during her previous job in the Office of Research.

As I discuss in the text, the move to digital photography is fraught with computer issues. Tim Darby, NAU's IT guy for my college, has three times saved my crashed computer with all its files and urged me to back up, back up, and back up my information. Thanks, Tim, for your dedication and support.

I dedicated *Passage to Wonderland* to my dog Nellie, who passed away at age fifteen and a half while I was writing that book. Nellie had been with me for ten years and accompanied me on several of the field work trips for this book. I am pleased to report that a new dog, a beautiful border collie named Tessa, is filling my life with walks and playing ball in the park. Sweet dogs make such a difference.

In the time since the publication of *Wyoming Time and Again*, both of my Wyoming grandparents, Al and Frances Zakotnik of Kemmerer, have passed on. My grandmother was born to a coal mining family in 1913 in the small town of Sublet. My grandfather came to Wyoming during the Great Depression and became a coal miner in Kemmerer. My grandpa had accompanied me back in 1987 on several photo trips in southwestern Wyoming, and I thought about both of them a great deal while I was writing this book. My other Wyoming relatives, Doug and Rozanne Reachard of Cody and Gary and Joanne Zakotnik of Eden, put me up and fed me both in the 1980s and again in 2007–08 while on photo trips. Thanks for your help.

Across Wyoming, locals in Cheyenne, Laramie, Rawlins, Rock Springs, Green River, Evanston, Diamondville, Kemmerer, Cokeville, Chugwater, South Pass City, Atlantic City, Douglas, Fort Laramie, Hartville, Newcastle, Sundance, Buffalo, Sheridan, Big Horn, Beckton, Wolf, Ranchester, Worland, Thermopolis, Lander, Cody, Yellowstone, Moose, Jackson, and many places in between took time out of their lives and helped me locate sites and sources in both 1987–88 and 2007–08. Thanks especially to Jack and Gerry Brinkers for showing us their beautiful home in Ranchester, Randy Farella for taking us to Cambria, Federal Magistrate Stephen Cole of Mammoth for showing us his home, Cici Ives of the Madison Fork Ranch in West Yellowstone, Montana, for her knowledge about Dwelle's Inn, and Tim Travis of Dome Lake for his wonderful hospitality.

At the University Press of Colorado, I have enjoyed great relationships with the staff and thank them for their hard work on my behalf. Thanks especially to Director Darrin Pratt, Acquisitions Editor Jessica d'Arbonne, copyeditor Cheryl Carnahan, and designer Dan Pratt. Thanks also to two anonymous reviewers whose suggestions made this a better book.

My immediate family—parents Arlen and Joan Amundson of Loveland, Colorado, sister Kathy Amundson of Denver, and in-laws Britt and Mary DeMuth and brother-in-law Eric DeMuth, all of Flagstaff—have been amazingly supportive of my work. Lauren's grandparents, Barb and Don DeMuth of Cornville, Arizona, were always interested in what I was doing as well. Don, a terrific photographer, has been an inspiration. Sure, everyone teased me about finding a real summer job, but they were always interested in what I was doing. Most of all, thanks Mom and Dad for watching Nellie those two summers and for all of your support in everything I've ever wanted to do.

I met my wife, Lauren, playing softball for the Lowell Observatory Infrared Sox. She accompanied me during both summers of fieldwork in 2007 and 2008 as we put more than 10,000 miles on the car and barely left Wyoming! Now the head librarian and archivist at Lowell, Lauren contributed ideas about photo selection, aided me in the field with finding camera stations and selecting lenses, helped me with file storage and metadata, read all of my written work, and listened to me talk about Stimson and Wyoming repeatedly over the last five years. Along the way, she put up with a four-hour stopover in Chugwater to shoot one rephotograph, eating lunch at Pahaska Teepee for a week, dining on gas station mac and cheese in Sundance when we learned that the only restaurant in town had closed, taking a side trip to the wrong town of Colony, Wyoming, being scratched by a mean barbwire fence in Wolf, Wyoming (and enduring a subsequent tetanus shot in Sheridan), playing late night "badminton" on Cody tennis courts, putting up with my incessant need to play an Alabama CD over and over one summer, and experiencing enough hours in the Wyoming sun and wind to make her practically a native. And all this before we became engaged! Thanks, Lauren, for all your help and especially for your good humor and patience. This book is dedicated to you.

Wyoming Revisited represents almost thirty years of my life and work. If I have forgotten or misplaced anyone who has helped along the way, please forgive me. I assume full responsibility for any errors herein.

Wyoming Revisited

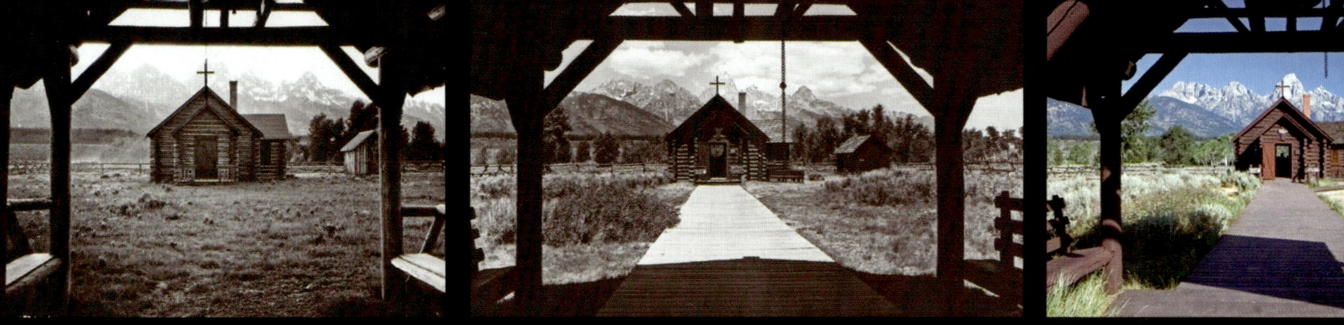

Revisiting *Wyoming Time and Again*

DOI: 10.5876/9781607323051.c000

Between 1890 and 1952, Cheyenne, Wyoming, photographer Joseph Elam Stimson produced more than 7,500 promotional images of Wyoming and the West. He made many of these photographs for his two main employers, the State of Wyoming and the Union Pacific Railroad. During the summer of 1903, he prepared views of the state for the 1904 St. Louis World's Fair. That year, Stimson traveled throughout Wyoming's then thirteen counties as well as Yellowstone National Park, documenting townscapes, mines, ranches, farms, oil wells, tourist sites, and other places that could help sell the state to would-be investors and settlers. His images, preserved at the Wyoming State Archives in Cheyenne, are stunning. Made with an 8 × 10-inch view camera on glass plates, the photographs are artistically composed and incredibly sharp. They contain a great deal of visual information and can be enlarged over and over to bring out the smallest detail. Many are also one-of-a-kind color pictures Stimson hand painted in an era before color film. Although he made most of his photographs for promotion, their detail means we can also read them as documentary photographs to better understand Wyoming, early photography, and Stimson the artist.

Twice during the last twenty-five years, first as an undergraduate history major at the University of Wyoming in the late 1980s and then again as a history profes-

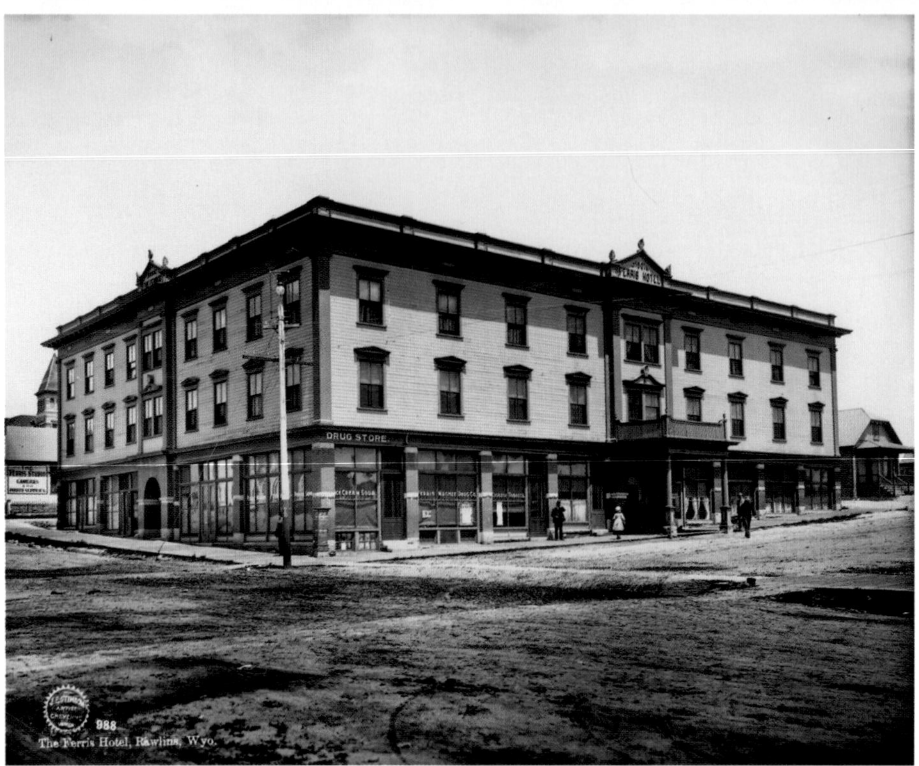

sor twenty years later, I have explored Stimson's work and Wyoming by repeating his images from the same vantage point he used more than a century earlier. This process, called repeat photography or simply rephotography, is a historical tool used to better understand the places, processes, and people who made photographs at an earlier time. Viewed side by side, such before-and-after images illustrate the essence of history—change over time. Like multiple frames of a motion picture, the then-and-now scenes not only illuminate what's in front of the lens—the effects of nature and human action over the course of a century— but also provide hints as to why Stimson composed his original views and how those vantage points fit into today's landscape. Indeed, in many ways rephotography is a personal adventure; as one repeatedly stands in the footsteps of an earlier photographer and repeats scene after scene, the intimate relationships between subject and artist become clearer. We see not only glimpses of another time but also personal expressions of how the photographer understood and tried to relate his views to his audiences.

Rephotography in Wyoming can also suggest broader cultural ideas about the American West over the last century. By looking closely at the images and the processes that created them, a viewer today can see hints of both the Old West and the New West as they play out through history. Along the way, we can discern broader ideas about ecology, historic preservation, photography, urban planning, industrialization, and modernism and postmodernism.

For example, examine the trio of photographs made at the site of the Ferris Hotel in Rawlins. Like many of Stimson's images, this one captures one of the com-

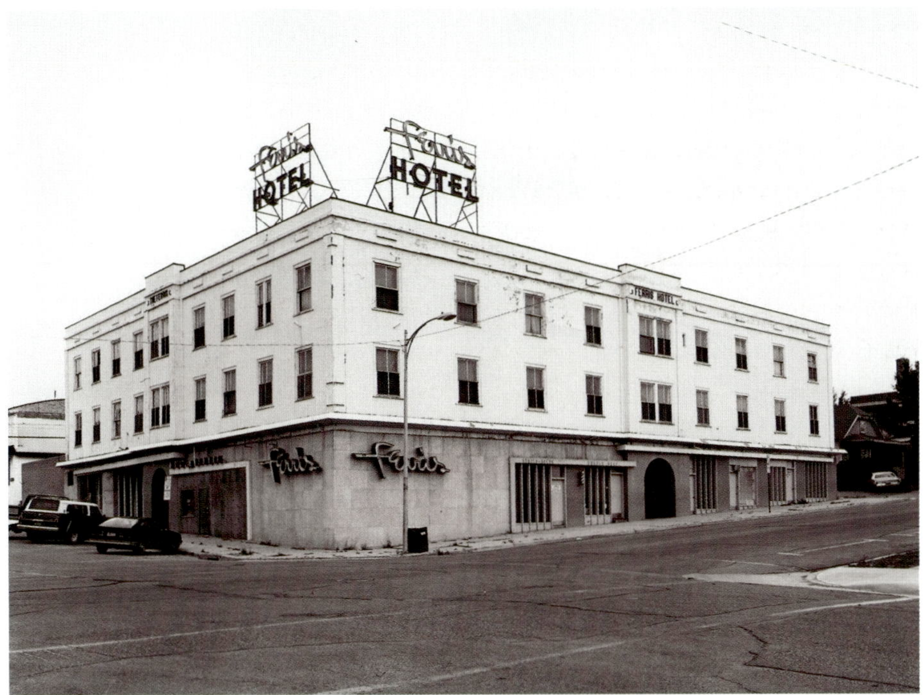

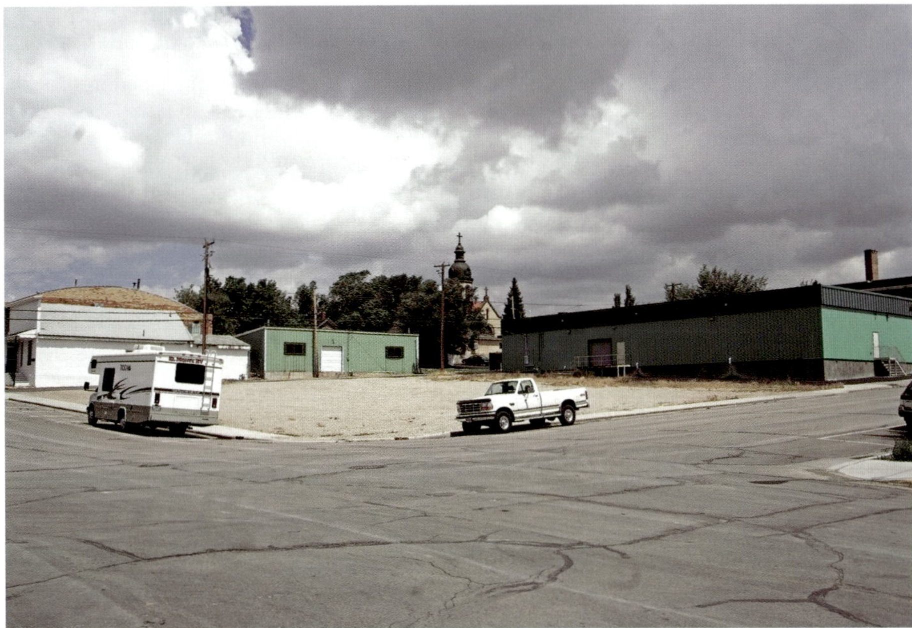

FIGURES 1.1, 1.2, 1.3. Discovering the changes to, and demolition, of the Ferris Hotel in Rawlins, 1903, 1987, 2007.

munity's leading businesses. Named for local entrepreneur George Ferris, the hotel was constructed in 1902 primarily to serve railroad passengers. Stimson visited it in 1903 while photographing Wyoming for the St. Louis Fair the following year. He chose a vantage point diagonal from the hotel, looking northwest, enabling him to capture both sides of the building in what could be called a commercial por-trait style—a common technique Stimson often employed when photographing

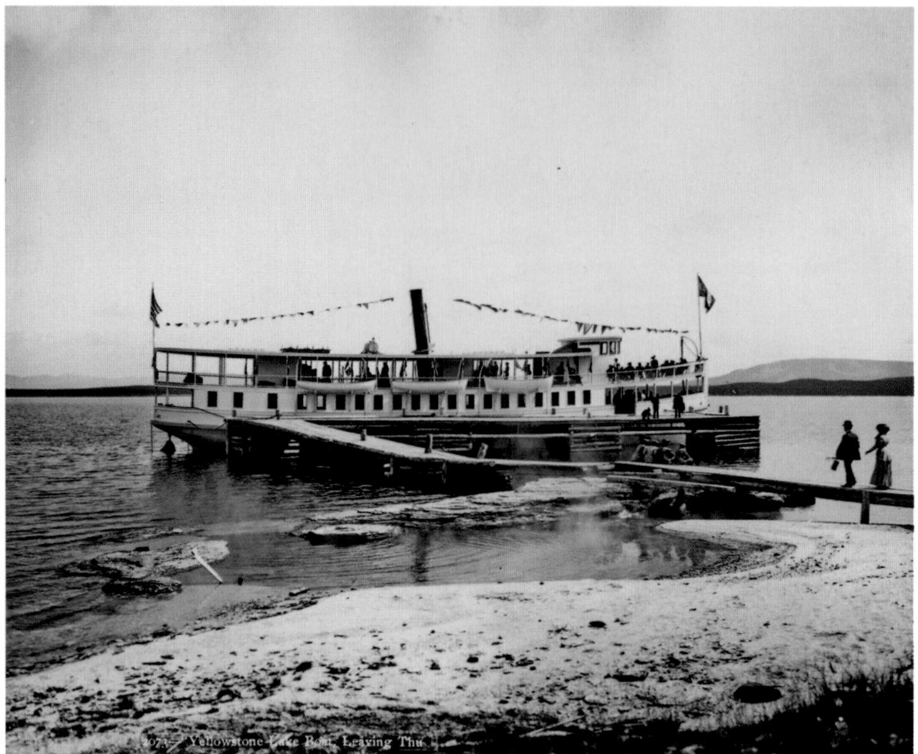

FIGURES 1.4, 1.5, 1.6. The West Thumb dock site on Yellowstone Lake, photographed in 1907, 1988, and 2008.

businesses. The right front of the building is bathed in sunlight, highlighting the Victorian-style wood siding and the small shops along the street. Zooming in, we can see four people looking at the photographer.

Jump ahead to the second photograph, one I made in the summer of 1987. This view, also from across the corner, shows a dramatic change. Although the Ferris Hotel remained, in 1956 its owners tried to "modernize" the structure by covering it in stucco. When I visited it thirty years later, the small shop windows remained covered. Though no one was present at the site, the automobiles to the left are probably the best hints as to what had happened. With the decline in railroad passenger traffic, the hotel had to appeal to those traveling on the nearby state highway. The large neon sign on the roof shows the attempt to attract such travelers.

Although the changes from 1903 to 1987 were dramatic, when I returned to the site in 2007 I encountered an even more drastic change: the Ferris Hotel was gone! Unable to compete in the new Rawlins featuring interstate travel and too expensive to remodel for other purposes, in the late 1990s the city demolished the structure, leaving an empty lot in its place.

A comparison of these three images serves as a good introduction to this book. Stimson's original photograph is clearly a promotional image, composed to capture the building in its best light to sell Rawlins as a modern community ready to receive railroad passengers. My first rephotograph suggests the changes from train

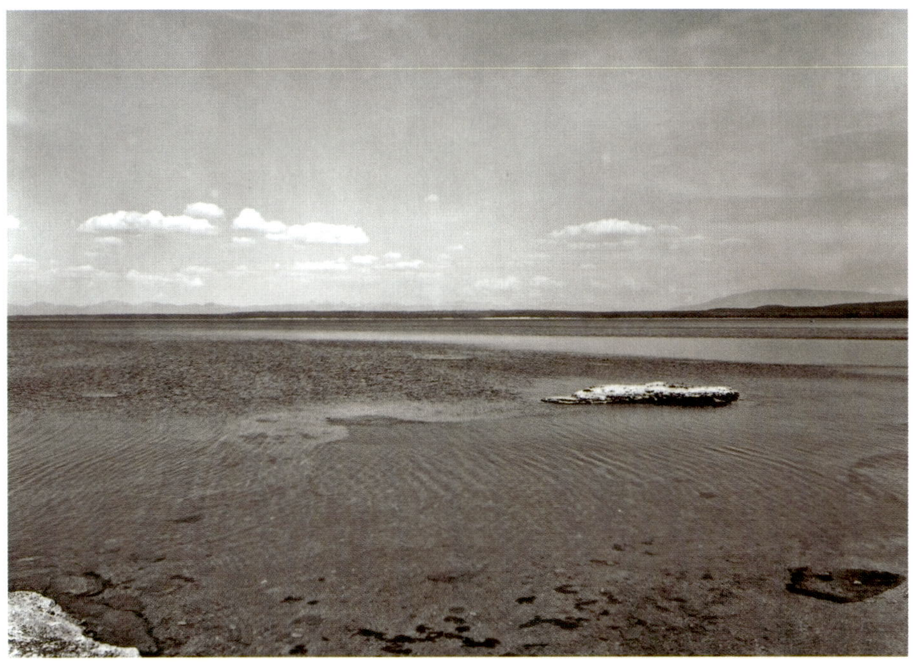

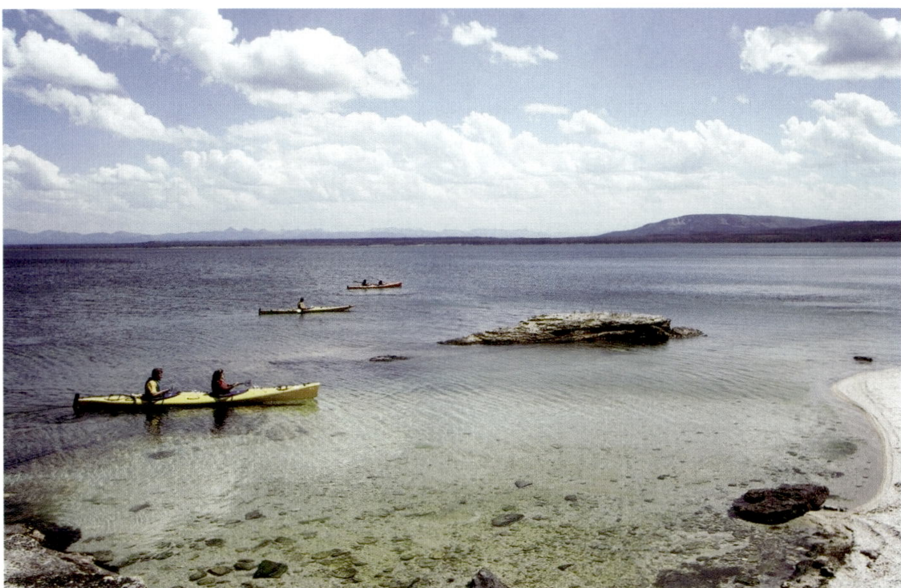

to car tourism, the attempts to adapt the old railroad landscape to the new one of the automobile, and the legacy of "modernization" three decades later. My final image made another twenty years later, showing the empty lot, reminds us that the historic built environment of our cities and towns is under constant threat. Moreover, its demise hints at bigger issues, including changing economies and transportation networks and the costs and difficulties of historic preservation.

Another set of images, across the state in Yellowstone National Park, further helps to introduce this book's concepts. When Stimson visited the park in 1907, he photographed the small steamboat *Zillah* at the thermal features at West Thumb,

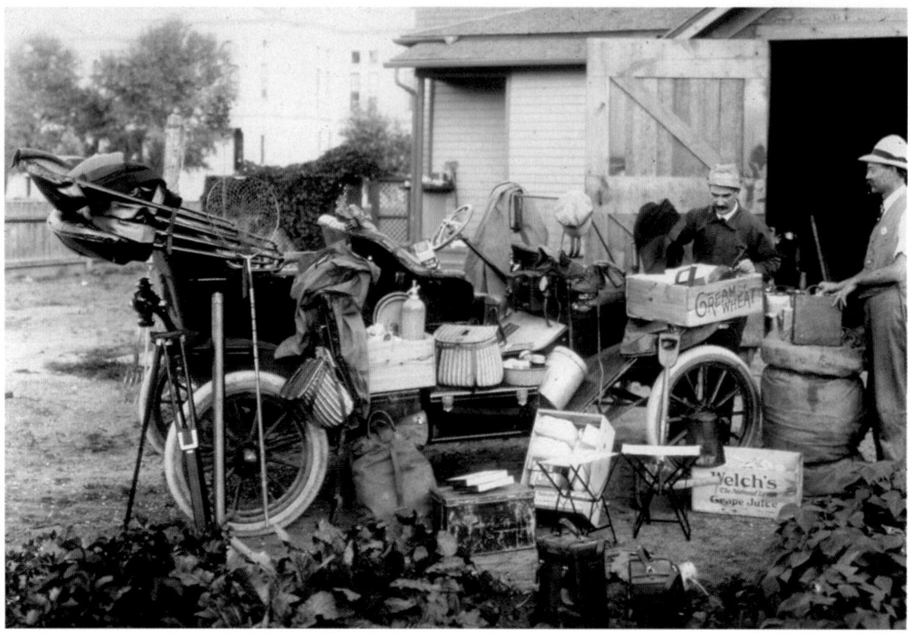

FIGURES 1.7, 1.8, 1.9. Preparing for travel, Stimson in 1912 and me in 1987 and 2007.

on the western shore of Yellowstone Lake. This boat, owned by concessionaire E. C. Waters, was not a pleasure boat but actually part of the transportation system in the park's early years. Although most of the familiar Grand Loop road network was in place by this time, actual transportation by stagecoach was very hot and dusty. Travelers going north toward the Lake Hotel could exit the coaches in favor of a smooth, clean boat ride.

In many ways, Stimson's image at this site is also a commercial portrait of an important transportation business in the park. His composition is tight. He placed the boat in mid-frame with the dark waters of the lake offset by the whiteness of the thermal feature on the shore. The passenger ramp slices out of the picture to the right, with a man and a woman on the edge of the picture walking toward the boat, leading the viewer in as well. Steam rises in the foreground, suggesting the wildness of Yellowstone while at the same time the boat and ramp above it hint at human control of that same feature.

My 1988 image suggests a very different meaning for this place. After automobiles were introduced into the park in 1915, tourists quickly lost interest in the stage and boat services. Communal travel gave way to individual car trips, and the West Thumb dock reverted to nature. At the same time, the changing water levels of Yellowstone Lake submerged this feature so that only a portion of it remained to be seen. In short, what had once been a very popular tourist locale no longer existed.

When I returned twenty years later, the scene had changed again. Although the thermal feature remained partially submerged, the site had become a popular access point for water-based tourism. But instead of a passenger boat, individuals paddled kayaks through the scene. Once again, the surface changes suggest deeper

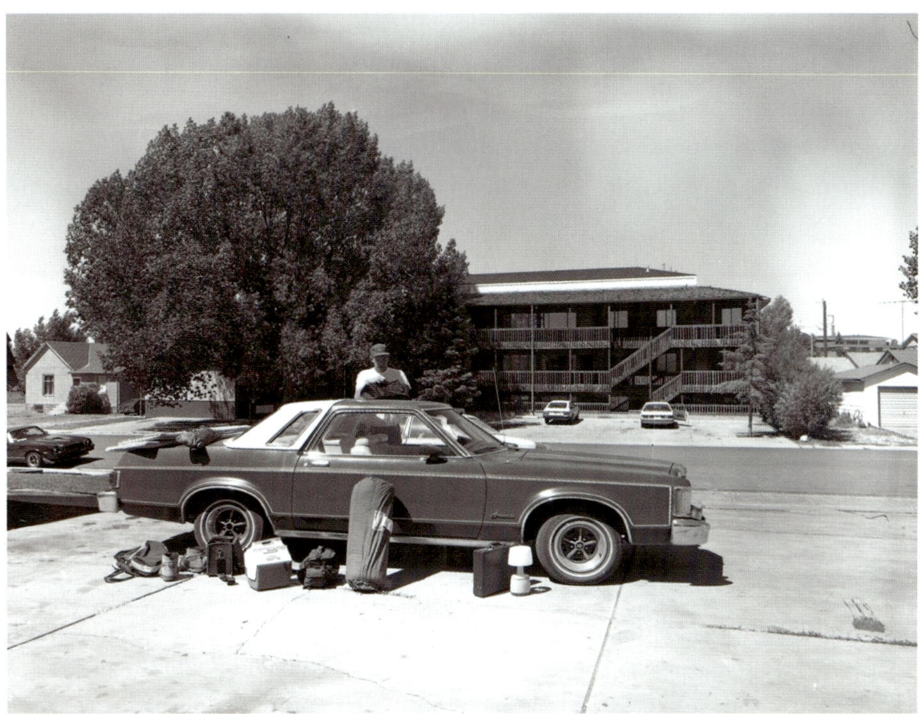

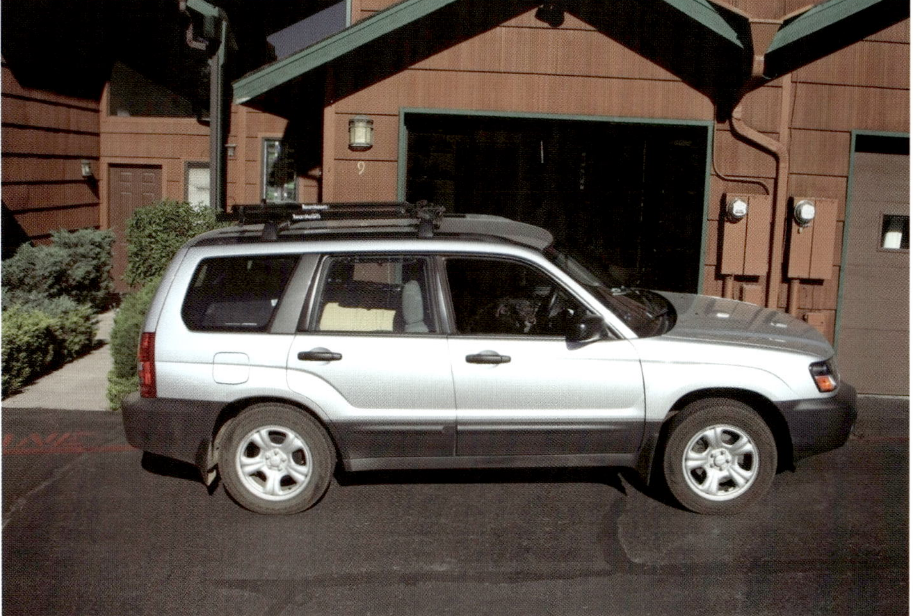

meanings, including the transformation from group to individual tourism as well as the rise of recreation-based experiences.

The final set of pictures to consider here includes self-portraits made by Stimson and myself. The first, taken by Stimson in 1912, shows the photographer and his friend Lem Ellis readying his car for a fishing tip. The view clearly dates the image, with the old Model T–style car strewn with fishing equipment, camping supplies, and what looks like a camera case. The setting is behind Stimson's garage, with the Wyoming capitol building in the distance.

The second view features me packing my car for a 1987 rephotography trip. My 1976 Ford Granada clearly dates this image, and, upon closer examination, photography equipment and camping gear can also be seen scattered about my Laramie apartment parking lot.

The final image, taken in 2007, shows my 2005 Subaru Forester outside my Flagstaff townhouse. Because digital equipment is so much smaller than previous gear, everything is packed away inside the car, including my dog Nellie in the passenger seat.

In addition to the cars and the equipment, which clearly date each image, this triad of photographs serves as an important reminder that photography and rephotography are *personal* endeavors. Although Stimson had paying clients suggesting where he should go or what he might photograph, it remained within his own expertise and personal taste to decide exactly where he wanted to shoot, at what time of day, and how he wanted to frame each image. Likewise, although I had financial support for my research on Stimson, I decided which images I wanted to rephotograph and when I wanted to do them. In both cases, although the final images represent many things about their subjects, each is fundamentally an artistic and cultural expression created by the photographer and thus reflects ideas about how that person conceived and executed his photograph. An old adage suggests that what is behind the camera—the photographer—is as important as what is in front of the camera: the subject. This is especially true in rephotography because the modern images of the same locales offer new hints as to what the original photographer saw and how he made each photograph.

Repeat photography is thus an important tool for exploring history because it provides insight into both places and processes. First, it reminds us of what today's scenes look like and gives us glimpses of what those same places looked like in the past. Second, exploring those places anew helps us see the processes of representation at work both then and now. Combined with historical research and artistic analysis, rephotography can also point to broader understandings of place, image, and history. In these respects, rephotography is a form of visual history akin to oral history. Just as followers of the latter seek out witnesses to past events to record and preserve historical information through recorded interviews, rephotographers hunt for the vantage points of earlier photographers to record and preserve visual information about how landscapes have endured over time.

To accomplish this, this book is organized into three sections. The first, J. E. Stimson, Wyoming, and Me, includes two chapters that describe the history of this project. Chapter 1 begins this process by exploring a detailed professional biography of J. E. Stimson as a Wyoming photographer. Chapter 2 dives into the history of photography and rephotography, explaining the details of how the process worked for me in the 1980s and again in the first decade of the twenty-first century.

Part II is called Seeing Anew because it focuses on critical examinations of what this rephotographic project created. Chapter 3 begins at an alpaca ranch south of

Laramie and then explores the global connection the state has always had with the rest of the United States and the world. Chapter 4 starts with the obvious sacred landscape of Yellowstone but then expands on this notion to look at historic preservation throughout the Cowboy State. Chapter 5 takes an intimate look at a beautiful home near the Montana border in Ranchester and shows the relationship between the modernity presented in Stimson's views and the postmodern world represented in my own. The epilogue looks back at the process of rephotography in the digital world before looking ahead to future projects. Throughout the first two sections, references to rephotographic sets are indicated with parentheses, such as (15) for number 15, Castle Dome, Red Buttes Country. A master list of images can be found in the appendix.

The final section of the book presents Stimson's photographs and my rephotographs along with detailed captions and GPS locations. It is broken into seven geographic subsections: the Union Pacific, Fort Laramie Country, the Black Hills, the Big Horns, South Pass, the Bighorn Basin, and Yellowstone and Grand Teton National Parks.

J. E. Stimson, Wyoming, and Me

J. E. Stimson, Wyoming, and Me

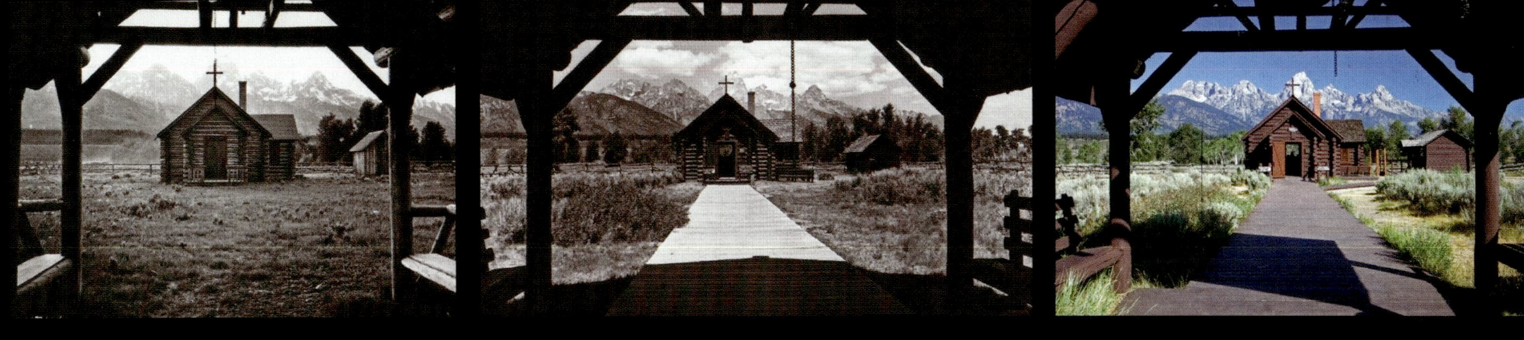

CHAPTER 1

J. E. Stimson, Wyoming Photographer

DOI: 10.5876/9781607323051.c001

Between 1889 and 1948, Joseph Elam Stimson of Cheyenne photographed Wyoming and the American West, producing more than 7,500 images of scenic landscapes, mining, railroads, community life, ranching and farming, and tourism. Most of these shots were made on 8 × 10-inch glass plates and are artistically composed and incredibly sharp. They are not a cross-section of the Progressive Era West but instead are promotional photographs, specifically composed and created for Stimson's various employers, including the Union Pacific Railroad, the Wyoming State government, and the Bureau of Reclamation. On many of the images, Stimson placed a small stamp, circumscribed by the boundaries of a sun, that proclaimed "J. E. Stimson, Artist, Cheyenne, Wyo." He was indeed an artist, as he carefully composed and then often hand-colored his prints in an era long before the advent of color film.

J. E. Stimson was born in Virginia in 1870 and spent most of his childhood in the southern Appalachian Mountains of South Carolina. At age thirteen he moved with his family to Pawnee City, Nebraska, southeast of Lincoln, near the Missouri and Kansas borders. Three years later he left for Appleton, Wisconsin, to work as an apprentice for his cousin, photographer James Stimson. While in

Appleton, he learned the requisite skills of portrait photography and the details of both the wet-plate and the newer dry-plate negative processes. In 1889, J. E. Stimson left Wisconsin and moved to Cheyenne, Wyoming, probably at the suggestion of two brothers who worked for the Union Pacific Railroad. He was only nineteen. Wyoming became a state in July 1890, and by that October, Stimson had made a deal to purchase the studio and equipment of Cheyenne photographer Carl Eitner. He renovated the studio and within two weeks began running advertisements in the *Cheyenne Daily Leader* that read "Go to Stimson the Photo Artist for Pictures." Four years later he married Anna Peterson, and in 1895 they had the first of what would be three daughters.[1]

Throughout the 1890s, Stimson worked primarily as a studio portrait photographer. According to biographer Mark Junge, his clients included the area's earliest citizens, as well as folks from outlying farms and ranches. An early account ledger indicated that Stimson often scheduled up to six sittings in a single day and sometimes traveled to patrons' homes to photograph them. Although most of these glass plates were accidentally broken in the 1930s when a shelf collapsed, the small surviving sample shows the usual small-town portrait assortment, including individuals, families, and groups such as cowboys on roundups, politicians, fraternal organizations, athletic teams, and social clubs.[2]

Although George Eastman had introduced his flexible-film, handheld Kodak to the masses in 1888, professional photographers like Stimson relied on a large-format, 8 × 10-inch view camera that captured images on dry-emulsion glass plates. For Stimson, this meant a wooden camera mounted on a heavy tripod. To take a picture, he would set up the camera, select the lens, open the diaphragm to a wide aperture to let in the most light, and then step under a black cloth behind the camera to compose and focus the image on the 8 × 10-inch ground glass. Once the composition was secure, he would slide a holder containing two covered sheets of unexposed glass into the camera's back, stop down the diaphragm and set the shutter speed for the correct exposure, remove one of the glass plate covers, and trip the shutter. He would return the plate's cover to protect his latent image, remove the plate holder, and then start the whole process over for the next image. The process was slow and deliberate. All exposures were more or less staged.

No records describe Stimson's exact development and printing processes, but standard practices of the time are basically the same ones used by generations of black-and-white photographers right up to the digital era. After making his exposures in the field, Stimson carried his glass negatives back to Cheyenne and developed them in his studio darkroom. After mixing his chemicals to a predetermined temperature and pouring them into large tanks, he would have had to turn off all his lights to work in total darkness. Development began by removing the exposed glass plates from their holders and securing them into hangers. He then set about ten hangers in the first tank that contained developer. After a set amount of time, he would have removed the hangers and plates from the first tank and placed them for a brief time into a second tank containing water that halted the development process. He then moved the hangers and plates into a third tank that contained sodium hyposulfite, or "hypo," which "fixed" the image onto the glass. At this point Stimson could turn on the darkroom lights and finally inspect the images he had made sometimes weeks prior. After a wash in a fourth tank containing water, Stimson would have let the plates dry, removed them from their hangers, and prepared them for printing.

Printing glass plates would also have been remarkably similar to the black-and-white film printing process still used today. The one main difference was that because Stimson shot with 8 × 10-inch glass plates, he did not have to use an enlarger for 8 × 10-inch prints but could simply "contact print" his images by setting his negative plate on top of a piece of photographic paper, exposing it to light for a predetermined period, and then developing it. At that time, printing paper came in different contrast grades, so to increase the contrast he would have had to select a different sheet of paper. When he wanted larger sizes, Stimson would have placed a plate into an enlarger and projected the negative onto a big piece of photographic paper, exposed it, and then developed the print.[3] Either way, once the photographic paper was exposed, Stimson, working under red safelights, would have dipped the paper through a series of trays containing once again a developer, water, hypo, and a wash bath. He would then have hung the paper to dry.

Select images were colored by hand. This process involved taking the final dried print and applying oil- or water-based paint onto the image, using either fine brushes or a hand-pumped airbrush. This process was based on Stimson's recollection of what the particular place looked like in real color, and he could either make "lifelike" images or purposely change the color palette of an image to suggest a different season. Stimson then mounted and framed the final prints and hung them in his shop on display.[4]

Properly exposed images thus made contained a great deal of visual information stored in the large-format light-sensitive plates. Although extremely fragile, the images were exceptionally sharp at 8 × 10, and Stimson often enlarged his images to 30 × 44 inches without losing resolution.

Such a format was perfect for capturing the new State of Wyoming. Its previous life as a territory, starting in 1868, had been one of booms and busts, including railroad construction, cattle, and—on a smaller scale—gold mining. To balance its economy, the territory had distributed its government institutions—and their assured payrolls—all along the railroad, with Cheyenne getting the capital, Laramie the university, Rawlins the penitentiary, and Evanston the asylum. To the north, the end of the Plains Indian wars in 1877 opened lands for settlement, although the native Shoshone and Arapahos were placed on a central reservation along the east side of the Wind River Range. The federal government designated Yellowstone National Park in the northwest corner of the territory in 1872 and created an adjacent forest reserve east of the park in 1891. Further east, to the Big Horn Mountains and beyond, coal mining, ranching, dry-land farming, and eventually the tourist trade, including dude ranching, became the lifeblood of the region.[5]

When Stimson set up shop in 1890, Wyoming's population was only 60,000; its largest city, Cheyenne, had just over 11,000 residents. Laramie and Sheridan were the only other towns with more than 8,000 citizens. The state's economy focused on the railroad, government, ranching, and coal mining in the south and cattle ranching, farming, and tourism in the north. Of these, the Union Pacific Railroad and its coal mining subsidiary had the largest impact, especially in the southwest corner of the state. Irrigated farming had also begun, with small community-based efforts in the Mormon communities in the state's western areas and a few state-federal projects, such as in Eden Valley, just under way under the Carey Act, named for Wyoming senator Joseph Carey. According to longtime state historian T.A. Larson, the period between the end of the Spanish American War in 1898 and the start of World War I in 1916 was one of "optimism, belief in progress . . . and eagerness for economic development [that] possessed Wyoming citizens as never before nor since." Wyomingites had reason for optimism. During this time, the sheep industry tripled in size and soon matched the state's booming cattle production. Dry-land farming and irrigated agriculture expanded, with the number of farm units doubling. The miles of railroad track increased as the Union Pacific double-tracked its main line and other railroads such as the Burlington entered Wyoming. Coal mining grew, and a small copper boom developed in the southeastern part of the state. Oil production was just beginning around Casper. Overall, the state's population grew by more than 50,000, from 92,000 in 1900 to 146,000 ten years later. Of this number, most of the new citizens settled in the northern half of the state. The federal government's influence also expanded with the creation of Teton Forest Reserve in 1897 and, in the first decade of the twentieth century, the designation of Devil's Tower as the country's first national monument and Shoshone Dam as one of the first federal reclamation projects.[6]

Other historians see a more complex place. Journalist Samuel Western views this period as one in which large cattlemen cemented their standing against small ranchers and farmers, creating an unsustainable economy. Western further suggests that through promotional literature and images, including some of Stimson's, Wyoming promoted itself as a place of rugged individualism—expressed especially through its bucking bronco logo—at the same time that its failed economy became increasingly dependent on federal largesse in the form of national parks, forest reserves, and reclamation projects. Similarly, University of Wyoming history professor Phil Roberts, in his "Readings in Wyoming History" and "A New History of Wyoming," identifies ten "organizing concepts" for understanding the state's history, including its continued boom-and-bust economy, federal control, environmental debates, water development, its role as a route to someplace else, diversity and women's rights, intra-state sectional debates between the southern and northern parts of the state, and its relationship to the world. Finally, through all of this, Roberts looks more deeply at Wyoming's seemingly simplistic cowboy logo, which symbolizes individualism and freedom in an increasingly complex world.[7]

Regardless of how historians see it, Wyoming's first decade of statehood offered a photographer such as Stimson an exciting array of progress, development, and federal largesse to document beyond his studio. Several events during this period moved Stimson's career path from studio portraiture to landscape photography. In 1894, Wyoming state engineer Elwood Mead, later commissioner of the Bureau of Reclamation and for whom Lake Mead was named, came into Stimson's studio asking if some glass plates he had made on a recent irrigation study in the Big Horn Mountains could be developed. When Stimson obliged, he was impressed with the scenery and was surprised to learn that such beautiful landscapes existed in his adopted state. The following summer, Mead brought Stimson along on another excursion to the Big Horns. The twenty-five-year-old photographer loved the scenery, but his first pictures were overexposed. Four years later Albert Nelson, Wyoming's first game warden, took Stimson to visit the Jackson Hole area and the picturesque Teton Range, a place that came to be Stimson's favorite.[8]

These last images of the Tetons were better and were marketable, and they led Stimson to pursue more scenic photography. In 1898 the *Sheridan Post* ran a small ad for Stimson's "beautiful pictures of Mountain Scenery" in sizes from 8 × 10 to 30 × 40 inches. The photographer then traveled to nearby Wheatland and to the Shoshone Indian Reservation in central Wyoming to make portraits. He also photographed the beginnings of Cheyenne's famous rodeo, Frontier Days. By the turn of the century, Stimson had begun presenting magic lantern slide shows of his images and selling small portfolios and albums based on his growing collection of negatives. Newspaper announcements describing "Stimson's Indians" appeared in Cheyenne papers around Christmas 1900 and described the work as a "fine collection." They also reported that the photographer was receiving album orders from "all over the country for his celebrated photographs of the Grand Teton mountains and other scenics in the vicinity."[9]

Around this time, a Union Pacific Railroad agent obtained one of these albums and hired Stimson as a publicity photographer for the railroad. Reorganized in 1897 by Edward H. Harriman, the Union Pacific (UP) was in the midst of rebuilding and modernizing the nation's first transcontinental railroad by operating bigger trains, straightening its many curves, and double-tracking the entire route. The UP needed an energetic photographer to document its efforts and contracted Stimson to photograph the line not just in Wyoming but throughout the West. Under the open-ended terms, the railroad paid Stimson four dollars for the first 8 × 10-inch print, one dollar each for the next ninety-nine, and seventy-five cents apiece for every print thereafter. He had no restrictions placed on the subjects he photographed or on the number of images he made as long as they promoted the railway. Further, any negatives made for the UP could also be printed and sold for his own gain. In addition, the railroad provided Stimson with free transportation either by train or, more often, through the use of a small gas-powered one-seat rail motor car.[10]

Over the next decade, Stimson photographed such railroad landscapes as depots, train wrecks, bridges, tunnels, and new lines from Omaha to California. More important, he captured adjacent UP cities and towns, as well as farms, ranches, timber outfits, dams, and mines nearby. Stimson also shot Wyoming's beautiful scenery, including Yellowstone National Park, for the developing tourism industry.[11] As an artist, Stimson often enlarged his prints and then hand-colored them using paints to produce beautiful, one-of-a-kind color prints. The Union Pacific agreement provided the young photographer with the means to travel the West, as well as a ready buyer for his photographs. It also exposed his work to others. The June 1903 issue of *Leslie's Weekly* magazine featured six of his images. The magazine stated that Stimson had a "keen eye for the picturesque and an artistic sense of position and proportion" and called him "one of the best scenic photographers in the United States."[12]

The State of Wyoming soon discovered Stimson and began a relationship with the photographer that would last nearly fifty years. In June 1903 the Wyoming Commission of the Louisiana Purchase Exposition hired Stimson to photograph the state for display at the 1904 St. Louis World's Fair. Under this agreement, the commission paid the photographer $875 to produce 182 hand-colored prints from across Wyoming. More specifically, he was to make a dozen 8 × 10-inch images from each of the state's twelve counties plus another twelve scenes from Yellowstone National Park. In addition, Stimson would provide one 30 × 40-inch print of the state and another of the park. Although the contract called for the photographer to cover all of his own expenses for travel, printing, coloring, framing, labeling, and boxing the images, Stimson felt the pay was reasonable because, as with the UP agreement, he would retain ownership of all negatives so he could print and sell them for himself while working on the state contract.[13]

The 1904 Louisiana Purchase Exposition in St. Louis commemorated the 100th anniversary of the acquisition of much of the American West, including most of Wyoming. The official guidebook for what has been called the 1904 World's Fair proudly stated that "this Exposition has already rendered an inestimable public service by awakening a universal popular interest in the story of the Louisiana Purchase and its glorious results." Like previous such fairs, the 1904 expo featured elaborate grounds and promotional displays from nearly every state and many foreign countries. The exposition also hosted the 1904 Olympics.[14]

Although the Wyoming Commission of the Louisiana Purchase Exposition hired Stimson to promote the state through his photographs, it did not construct its own state building at the fair. Instead, its $25,000 appropriation was devoted entirely to exhibits in the Palaces of Mines and Agriculture. Stimson's photographs, like his work for the Union Pacific, would promote the state through photography. To do this, Stimson was to "travel all over the state, consult with boards of county commissioners and local industrial committees, and make views best calculated to show [the state's] varied resources and magnificent scenery."[15]

The summer and fall of 1903 turned into a whirlwind of photographic fieldwork for Stimson. In late June, just three weeks after getting the contract, he began the project by traveling to the irrigated farming community of Wheatland and the nearby iron mining town of Sunrise. He then spent five days at Newcastle in the northeast corner of the state. Two weeks later, the *Buffalo Voice* reported in a story titled "A Busy Day for Mr. Stimson" that the photographer had captured images around that northern Wyoming community. He then photographed ranches in nearby Big Horn and Beckton. A week later, the *Sheridan Post* recorded that Stimson had photographed that city and the coal mining town of Dietz to the north. At about the same time, the *Crook County Monitor* in Sundance reported the photographer at work there, as well as at nearby Devil's Tower. He then traveled to Cody and Yellowstone National Park before turning east to capture Meeteetse and the Pitchfork Ranch during the first week of August. Stimson traveled next to the Shoshone Indian Reservation, Lander, and the Popo Agie River Valley and by the end of August had photographed Evanston and Kemmerer. He returned to Cheyenne at the end of that month. Cheyenne's *Wyoming Tribune* summarized his hectic summer when it reported in an article titled "Some Fine Views" that the photographer had spent six weeks in the field and was "very busy these days developing" the hundreds of exposures he had made. Stimson then went back on the road to Douglas and Converse County during the first week of September, Laramie in mid-month, and then west to the Sierra Madre Range where the *Dillon Doublejack* reported that he photographed the famous Ferris Haggerty Copper Mine in late September. The first week of October found him in Casper, and a month later he was finally back home in Cheyenne.[16]

Stimson worked for the next eight months on his portfolio of Wyoming views for the St. Louis Fair and included more than 500 images in his *Catalogue of Wyoming Views,* published in 1903. In the brief introduction, Stimson stated that "these views comprise the full set made for the World's Fair Commission, and many other views from plates made for the Union Pacific and B. & M. [Burlington and Missouri] Railroads." He offered standard 8 × 10-inch prints, "tinted in natural colors" and matted for framing. Enlargements up to 30 × 40 inches were also available. In a section he called the "St. Louis Fair Series," Stimson offered 29 images from Natrona County, 35 from Uinta County, 21 from Sweetwater County, 12 from Albany County, 35 from Weston County, 33 "General Views," and 44 "Views along Cody Gateway to National Park" in Big Horn County. The catalog boasted 67 images of Sheridan County, 27 from Johnson County, 22 showing Crook County, 43 of Laramie County, 28 of Carbon County, 39 from Fremont County, and another 23 depicting Converse County. In another section labeled "Yellowstone Park Series," Stimson included 65 images of the park, most of which were taken in 1902. Throughout the catalog, Stimson provided each entry with his original index number and a one-line description that was often included on the negative and print. These identifiers are the same ones used by the Wyoming State Archives today.[17]

For the St. Louis Fair, Stimson selected 182 hand-colored images, 12 from each county plus another dozen from Yellowstone, for display in two buildings: the Palace of Mines and the Palace of Agriculture. Some of the views were grouped together as an individual exhibit, while others simply illustrated Wyoming's economy. All of them were used to promote the new state. Expo judges awarded Stimson a silver medal for his photographs of mines and machinery, and two other exhibits containing his images also received silver medals.[18]

The following year, the state moved its exhibits to the Lewis and Clark Centennial American Pacific Exposition and Oriental Fair in Portland, Oregon. This fair, though not an "official World's Fair," commemorated the explorers' 100-year anniversary of arriving at the Pacific Ocean and also marked the twentieth-century arrival of the United States as a Pacific Rim power. Twenty-one countries and nineteen US states and territories participated, attracting more than 1.6 million visitors over the four months of operation. In contrast to the St. Louis Fair, the State of Wyoming created its own exhibit, including Stimson's 1903 set of photographs.[19] Stimson and his family made the trip to Portland and were noted in newspapers as among the "seventy-one Wyomingites" to attend the fair.[20] Stimson won two bronze medals for his photos of Wyoming scenery and for images of mines and machinery. Stimson biographer Mark Junge suggests that his work from these two fairs gained the artist "national and international recognition" and placed him at the peak of his career. Stimson then displayed his images and catalog in several Wyoming towns, drumming up business and solidifying his reputation as the state's premier photographer.[21]

Although he continued to photograph the Union Pacific until World War I and the State of Wyoming for the remainder of his life, Stimson never again concentrated as much time and energy on traveling and photographing the state as he had done in 1903. Instead, the photographer worked mostly along the railroad from Omaha to Sacramento, capturing towns and farms, mines, and ranches throughout the corridor. In 1904–05 he photographed the Lucin Cutoff, a trestled shortcut across the Great Salt Lake.[22] He also documented new industries that sprang up along the line, including the Nevada gold rush towns of Goldfield and Tonopah as well as the copper boomtown of Encampment, Wyoming.[23] Ever the booster, Stimson photographed farms and towns across Nebraska in 1905, as well as scenes in Ogden, Utah, and Los Angeles and Pasadena, California, on the initial run of the Los Angeles Limited train.[24]

In 1906, by automobile and railroad car, Stimson embarked on his most ambitious photographic journey for the Union Pacific, dubbed a "Journey across the Continent." Stimson took his brother Ben as an assistant and joined a Southern Pacific photographer, his wife, and an assistant, "taking views along the two systems of railroad from Omaha to San Francisco." The *Laramie Republican* reported that the group left that city with its equipment loaded onto a special railcar, while the photographers followed in a motor car. A week later, Evanston's *Wyoming Press* noted that the photographers had arrived in "photograph car No. 2297, and carrying a four wheeled gasoline motor, with a seating capacity of four persons." The photographers spent several hours "taking views and securing data for a joint publication to be issued by the Union Pacific, Oregon Short Line, and the Southern Pacific." All in all, Stimson captured more than 250 images of the railroad, adjacent towns and cities, farm, ranches, mines, and other industries on this trip. Aside from his 1903 World's Fair project, it was his largest, most concentrated photographic effort to date.[25]

Around this time, Stimson also promoted his adopted hometown of Cheyenne for both the Union Pacific and various organizations in the state. The June 1907 edition of the *Wyoming Industrial Journal* focused on Cheyenne and Laramie County and included many Stimson images, including a pair of rephotographs of Capitol Avenue made from the UP Depot tower in 1904 and again in 1907, showing the city's "wonderful improvements." In 1910 the Union Pacific included fifteen Stimson images in a promotional brochure it produced on Cheyenne's Frontier Days rodeo.[26]

Beyond the capital, Stimson worked for the Wyoming Department of Immigration and other agencies promoting the state's dry-land and irrigated farms, ranches, mines, tourism, and other industries. In 1909 Stimson shipped sixty images of the Sheridan area to that city's chamber of commerce for promotional purposes.[27] The following year the *Riverton News* reported that "Mr. Stimson took a large number of pictures of our alfalfa and grain fields, which will be used in illustrating the advertising pamphlets to be prepared by Immigration Agent W. Y. Judkins."[28] Other efforts took him to Rawlins, Granite Springs, Sherman Hill, Newcastle, Hartville, Buffalo, Sunrise, Saratoga, Encampment, the Big Horn Mountains, Wheatland, Worland, Riverton, Powell, and Superior.[29]

For most of these images, Stimson made outstanding black-and-white photographs. Often, he sought out aboveground vantage points to make "bird's-eye" images and multiple negative panoramas that helped bring order to the clutter of a frontier urban setting or expose the state's natural grandeur on a large scale. For the former, Stimson most famously and repeatedly climbed to the top of the Union Pacific's clock tower, where he made views looking down on the city. But the photographer also climbed to the dome of the state capitol and to the top of the UP's water tower and produced a 4-foot by 15-inch panorama of the city that he sold by subscription.[30] Beyond the capital city, Stimson produced bird's-eye panoramic views of Newcastle, Sheridan, Rock Springs, Green River, and Evanston, to name a few, as well as multiple frame panoramas of such places as the Carissa Mine at South Pass City, Forbes Ranch in Beckton, the Natural Bridge near Douglas, and Sylvan Lake in Yellowstone National Park.

In other cases, he produced unique, hand-colored images that reflected his artist's skill in reproducing Wyoming's beauty. From his 1903 survey of the state, color images exist of Yellowstone scenes, Devil's Tower, and the Tetons. In 1908 the photographer experimented with an expensive new German technique that produced one-of-a-kind color positives, similar to modern slides. No known images survive from this process.[31] The following year, Stimson shipped fifteen traditionally hand-colored, 25 × 40-inch Wyoming prints to Union Pacific headquarters in Omaha. When I interviewed his daughter Josephine Love in 1988 as part of my research for *Wyoming Time and Again*, she told me that she remembered helping him by hand-pumping the mechanism for airbrushing images and that he could take one basic scene of some aspen trees and make it look like different seasons depending on what colors he chose to use.[32] In the winter of 2012, the State of Wyoming placed a traveling exhibit of images at the Fort Caspar museum called *Stimson Colors Wyoming*, which featured two dozen hand-colored images.[33] One of my most cherished purchases on eBay is a small original Stimson hand-colored scene of a pack train in the Wind River Mountains.

As busy as he was, Stimson also lived a full life beyond photography. He maintained an active, physical lifestyle, not only traveling throughout the West doing scenic photography but also joining friends on fishing trips. He and his wife, Anna, raised two daughters and were active members of Cheyenne's social scene.[34] Stimson also owned one of Wyoming's first automobiles, sold tires and cars on the side, and became a leading booster of the state's Lincoln Highway and the Good Roads Movement.[35] He was active in the Masonic Lodge and served in public office just prior to World War I, when Laramie County appointed the photographer to serve as a county commissioner. The county then reelected Stimson in his own right. In office, Stimson was best known for championing better roads.[36]

Although Stimson continued to be productive through World War I, the postwar economic depression in Wyoming, combined with changing tastes regarding his images at Union Pacific headquarters, brought what biographer Mark Junge called a "decline in the scope of his work" following the war.[37] Nevertheless, Stimson continued to photograph the State of Wyoming throughout the rest of his life. He made images for the Wyoming Department of Immigration, sold scenic photographs and postcards from his downtown Cheyenne studio, returned to portrait work, and did occasional commissions for a Cheyenne business or a nearby ranch. After he lost nearly everything in the stock market crash in 1929 and the ensuing Great Depression, his old friend Elwood Mead, then commissioner of the Bureau of Reclamation, hired the fifty-nine-year-old photographer to document bureau dams and irrigation projects throughout the West.[38] Three years later Stimson ventured out on a ten-day pack trip into the alpine country of the Wind River Mountains. He photographed Civilian Conservation Corps camps in the 1930s and often took his camera with him on automobile trips throughout the state.[39]

His wife, Anna, died of a heart attack in 1938, but Stimson remained active in his retirement years. He still received and fulfilled orders for black-and-white as well as hand-colored images from his extensive portfolio. In February 1939, Stimson and his brother Benjamin, who had accompanied J. E. on his "Trip across the Continent" in 1906, made an automobile trip. They pulled a small trailer to Mexico and returned by way of their boyhood home in South Carolina. After returning to Cheyenne, Stimson remained active and in 1948 was hired by the Wyoming Department of Commerce and Industry, successor to the Department of Immigration, to photograph the Tetons and Yellowstone. He was seventy-eight. Four years later, Stimson died of a heart attack while visiting his daughter in Connecticut. The State of Wyoming purchased his collection of more than

7,500 negatives for $2,000 in 1953, and it remains at the Wyoming State Archives, Museum and Historical Department in Cheyenne.[40]

Stimson's images have been described as the work of a skilled photographic craftsman. As biographer Junge notes, Stimson "avoided abstractions or photo-journalistic statements . . . and understood how to form light and shadow into patterns." He had strong compositions, often with clear vanishing points that gave his images perspective and interest. Although many of his images were made in the "golden hours" of early morning and late afternoon light, his travel require-ments, clients' needs, and the sensitivity of his glass plates meant that he worked throughout the day. He often used above-the-eye vantage points from rooftops, water towers, and high rocks and made panoramic views that included multiple plates. He understood exposure and edge-to-edge focusing. In addition, he often enlarged his 8 × 10-inch negatives into much larger prints and tinted many of them to better represent nature.[41]

Stimson's work can also be analyzed as industrial portraiture. Trained to present people in their best light, Stimson took the skills of the portrait photographer to the outdoors to record for his employers the progress and development the Union Pacific Railroad and the State of Wyoming wanted to show. In that sense, his images of Wyoming ranches, farms, mines, roads, railroads, and communities are products of a concerted effort to always present the best that Wyoming had to offer.[42]

But things are not always what they are presented to be. In a fascinating study of Buffalo Bill and his Wild West Show's European tours, historians Robert W. Rydell and Rob Kroes explain the difference between cultural production and con-sumption. In their example, Buffalo Bill Cody formed his famous Wild West Show by collecting icons of the American frontier—such as cowboys, Native Americans, and trick shooters—into a circus and exhibiting them across the Atlantic to show Europeans what the American West was like. But when the show came to Prussia, army officers took note not of the frontier icons but of the organization and effi-ciency with which Cody fed, housed, and transported his cast. Simply put, while Buffalo Bill *produced* images of the frontier West, the Prussian army *consumed* an image of Chicago and the industrial East.[43]

For Stimson, this analogy means that although his images were *produced* to rep-resent progress and development, they can also be *consumed* as documentary pho-tographs representing a slice of Wyoming life. Ultra-sharp images on 8 × 10-inch glass negatives contain huge amounts of visual data. When scanned and viewed on a computer monitor, the photographs can be enlarged again and again without los-ing resolution and thus reveal minute details not noticed at first glance or possibly intended by the photographer when he made the image. For this reason, Stimson's images must be reconsidered not only as promotional images but as documentary photographs as well.

As such, Stimson's work fits into the broader spectrum of Western photogra-phers who followed a few decades after the exploration surveys of William Henry Jackson and Timothy O'Sullivan. For this "second generation," photographers like Stimson and Denver's Louis C. McClure shifted their focus from images of discovered canyons, mountains, and ruins to pictures that promoted the region's railroads, mines, ranches, farms, and burgeoning tourist industry.[44]

Examined in this manner, Stimson's photographs can be viewed not simply as promotional or even documentary images but as symbols of the complexity raging in Wyoming among a multitude of forces, including traditionalism, modernity, individualism, federalism, economic development, environmental protection, diversity, and identity. In other words, Stimson's photographs, like any other primary source, have been interpreted in their own time and then reopened time and again for revision and new meaning.[45]

J. E. Stimson spent a lifetime photographing and selling his images of Wyoming to the Union Pacific and other railroads, to the state for promotion at world's fairs and exhibitions, and to immigration bureaus, reclamation bureaus, newspapers, chambers of commerce, city governments, and local ranchers, businessmen, and everyday people who hired him. In all, he produced more than 7,500 8 × 10-inch glass plates, a startling number in an era when a good photographer might take no more than a handful of images in a day. Further, Stimson often enlarged and then hand-colored each image with oils and water colors to make each view more realistic and then framed the images in beautiful oak frames that presented them not as mere snapshots. Indeed, Stimson viewed them not as mere records of what he saw but as his own vision of how he composed, captured, and reproduced the places and people he was hired to represent. Like Ansel Adams a generation later, Stimson saw his views not simply as visual stenographic records of the "decisive moment" but as works of art.[46] After all, in the corner of each image, Stimson did more than simply sign his name and list his occupation as "photographer": he marked each print with a stylized sun logo and placed within it "J. E. Stimson, Artist, Cheyenne, Wyo." With any work of art, it is imperative to learn as much as we can about the artist and his or her settings as we understand and revise that understanding of what the artist's work means over time.

One of the best ways to get to know Stimson's images is to rephotograph them. Rephotography—also known as repeat photography or before-and-after photography—is the process of finding and duplicating photographs from the same vantage points used by earlier photographers. It has been popular for more than a hundred years. For that, we turn to the process and history of rephotography.

Notes

1. Mark Junge, *J. E. Stimson: Photographer of the West* (Lincoln: University of Nebraska Press, 1985); *Cheyenne Daily Leader*, October 5 and 21, 1890.

2. Junge, *Stimson*.

3. Ansel Adams, *The Camera* (Boston: Little, Brown, 1980).

4. The basic process for developing film is discussed in Ansel Adams, *The Negative* (Boston: Little, Brown, 1980) and the printing process in Ansel Adams, *The Print* (Boston: Little, Brown, 1980).

5. Taft Alfred Larson, *A History of Wyoming*, 2nd ed., rev. (Lincoln: University of Nebraska Press, 1978), remains the cornerstone of Wyoming history.

6. Ibid. The quote is from Larson's introduction to Stimson in Junge, *Stimson,* x.

7. Samuel Western, *Pushed off the Mountain, Sold down the River: Wyoming's Search for Its Soul* (Moose, WY: Homestead, 2002). Phil Roberts's "A New History of Wyoming" and his "Readings in Wyoming History" are available online at http://www.uwyo.edu /robertshistory [accessed January 14, 2013].

8. Junge, *Stimson.*

9. Ibid.; *Sheridan Post*, October 27, 1898; *Wheatland World*, January 14 and 21, 1898; *Cheyenne Wyoming Tribune*, December 12, 1900; *Cheyenne Daily Leader,* December 14, 21, and 25, 1900.

10. Maury Klein, *Union Pacific*, vol. 2: *1894–1969* (Minneapolis: University of Minnesota Press, 1989); Junge, *Stimson.*

11. I recently purchased a rare album of Stimson's Yellowstone photos from a bookstore in Germany. The album contains twenty-five black-and-white scenes and was published by Stimson with the Albertype Company of Brooklyn, New York. The *Cheyenne Daily Leader* ran a small ad for this album on August 21, 1903, which described it as a "beautiful collection of views of the most striking features of the National Park in Wyoming" and listed the price as $1.50. The images were made using a new photo-mechanical process that allowed inexpensive photographic reproductions as postcards and portfolios. See J. E. Stimson, *Yellowstone Park* (Brooklyn, NY: Albertype, 1903). For information on the Albertype Company, see the Historical Society of Pennsylvania's website: http://www.hsp.org/sites/default/files/migrated/findingaidv18albertype.pdfQ1 [accessed July 19, 2011].

12. Junge, *Stimson.* The *Laramie Daily Boomerang,* March 12, 1901, is one of the first accounts to identify Stimson as "the Union Pacific photographer," although it incor-rectly names him as "W. E." rather than "J. E." See also, "Curious Bits of Western Scenery," *Leslie's Weekly* 95, no. 2493 (June 18, 1903): 611, 623.

13. Junge, *Stimson*; "For the St. Louis Fair," *Cheyenne Wyoming Tribune*, June 3, 1903.

14. M. J. Lowenstein, comp., *Official Guide to the Louisiana Purchase Exposition* (St. Louis: Louisiana Purchase Exposition Company, 1904), 7. This and other documents about the exposition can be found at the website hosted by the 1904 World's Fair Society home page at http://www.1904worldsfairsociety.org/index.htm [accessed July 20, 2011].

15. *Official Guide to the Louisiana Purchase Exposition*, 115; "For the St. Louis Fair," *Cheyenne Wyoming Tribune*, June 3, 1903; "Magnificent Collection," ibid., February 17, 1904.

16. Thanks to the ongoing Wyoming Newspaper Project, which is in the process of digitizing all of the state's papers, following Stimson around the state in 1903 has become much easier. See http://www.wyonewspapers.org/ [accessed July 20, 2011]. By simply doing a search for Stimson or in some cases "Stimpson," one can follow his photographic exploits week by week all over the state. This brief overview is culled from the following newspapers: *Wheatland World*, June 26, 1903; "A Busy Day for Mr. Stimson," *Buffalo Voice*, July 18, 1903; "Making Fine Views," *Cheyenne Wyoming Tribune*, July 19, 1903; *Sheridan Post*, July 23, 1903; "Mr. Chase Home Again," *Cody Wyoming Stockgrower and Farmer*, July 28, 1903; "For the St. Louis Fair," *Cheyenne Wyoming Tribune*, August 5, 1903; "Stimson at Lander," ibid., August 10, 1903; "Some Fine Views," ibid., August 18,

1903; ibid., September 8 and 18, 1903; *Grand Encampment Herald*, September 28, 1903; *Bill Barlow's Budget* (Douglas, WY), September 30, 1903; *Cheyenne Wyoming Tribune*, October 8, 1903; *Laramie Boomerang*, October 10, 1903; "Photographer Stimson's Work," *Cheyenne Wyoming Tribune*, November 6, 1903; "Wyoming Will Make Hit," ibid., December 18, 1903.

17. J. E. Stimson, *Catalogue of Wyoming Views* (Cheyenne: J. E. Stimson), 1903, 1.

18. Junge, *Stimson*, 9.

19. http://www.oregonencyclopedia.org/entry/view/lewis_clark_exposition/Q2 [accessed February 27, 2014].

20. "Seventy One Wyomingites," *Cheyenne Daily Leader,* September 28, 1905. The same paper had reported eight days earlier that "Mr. and Mrs. J. E. Stimson and little daughters will leave soon for Salt Lake City and Portland for [a] month's visit"; ibid., September 20, 1905.

21. Junge, *Stimson*; 1904–05 newspapers.

22. *Along the U.P. Line: A Listing of the J.E. Stimson Photographs in the Collection of the Wyoming State Museum* (March 1977); "Salt Lake View for the Salt Lake Route," *Laramie Republican,* December 28, 1905.

23. The *Grand Encampment Herald,* June 2, 1905, noted that Stimson's images appeared in a promotional booklet for the nearby Penn-Wyoming copper smelter and tramway.

24. *Along the U.P. Line*, 30.

25. Ibid., 35–40. The Trip across the Continent is mentioned in the *Laramie Republican,* June 29 and 30, 1906, as well as the *Evanston Wyoming Press,* July 7, 1906.

26. *Cheyenne Wyoming Industrial Journal*, June 1, 1907; "Frontier Folder," *Cheyenne Wyoming Semi-Weekly Tribune*, July 15, 1910.

27. The *Sheridan Daily Enterprise,* November 27, 1909, reported that sixty Stimson pictures taken in the vicinity of Sheridan were "extremely well executed and very beautiful, and each member of the Chamber expressed himself as believing they could be most effectively used in advertising the city and surrounding country."

28. Junge, *Stimson*. See also the *Riverton News*, August 13, 1910.

29. For an overview of Stimson's work during this time, see Junge, *Stimson,* and the Stimson index, *Along the U.P. Line*. The following newspapers also contain short descriptions of Stimson photography outings in Wyoming: *Cheyenne Wyoming Tribune*, July 23, 1908; "Mr. Stimson Returns," ibid., March 10, 1909; *Cheyenne Daily Leader,* April 1, 1909; *Buffalo Bulletin,* August 18, 1910; *Laramie Daily Boomerang*, August 26, 1910.

30. *Along the U.P. Line*; "Large Pictures of Cheyenne Are Out," *Cheyenne Daily Leader*, May 13, 1905.

31. The article "In True Colors," *Cheyenne Wyoming Tribune,* March 20, 1908, explained that Stimson had been experimenting with an expensive German process that made color positives, like modern slides.

32. May 4, 1909, *Cheyenne Wyoming Tribune*; Josephine Stimson Love, interview with author, August 3, 1988, Ranchester, WY.

33. "Casper: 'Stimson Colors Wyoming,'" *Casper Star Tribune*, December 28, 2012. http://trib.com/weekender/casper-stimson-colors-wyoming/article_36d643d7-d850 -5965-9fe1-98b5a5227796.html [accessed February 27, 2014].

34. Wyoming newspapers, especially those in Cheyenne, bustle with little society news stories regarding Stimson and hint at his growing popularity in the city and the

state. They include the *Laramie Republican*, February 27, November 29, December 1, 4, 17, 1905; August 13, 24, 1906; July 10, September 23, 1908; June 23, 26 1909; December 15, 1910; September 14, March 27, 1912; June 19, 1913; *Cheyenne Wyoming Tribune*, May 6, October 7, 1905; January 6, 15, 1909; October 15, 1914; April 12, 1918; *Cheyenne Daily Leader*, May 9, 10, 1905; June 2, 1907; May 3, September 28, 1908; March 24, 1909; *Cheyenne State Leader*, January 12, 1909; July 27, September 15, 1911; August 25, 28, 1912; July 12, September 9, 1914; May 5, 1915; March 25, 1919; *Evanston Wyoming Times*, September 12, 1912; *Laramie Daily Republican*, February 7, 1912; *Sheridan Daily Enterprise*, March 28, 1912.

35. Stimson's advocacy of roads and cars is discussed in my 1988 interview with Stimson's daughter and is also described in "Motorists Have Club," *Cheyenne Daily Leader*, March 9, 1909; "Is Blazing the Trail," *Laramie Republican*, April 16, 1909; "Pathfinder Goes West," *Cheyenne Daily Leader,* April 16, 1909. Cheyenne's *Semi-Weekly Wyoming Tribune,* June 11, 1909, included a front-page map of Wyoming's automobile roads and an article titled "Club Is Accomplishing Results" that mentioned that J. E. Stimson was on the board of managers for the Cheyenne Motor Club. See also "State Auto Club and Road Sign Posts," *Cheyenne Wyoming Tribune*, May 27, 1909; "Consistory Members Out in Automobiles," ibid., June 16, 1910; "Sleeper Is the President," *Worland Grit*, February 27, 1912; "Thirteen Autos and No One Hurt; Have Great Time," *Cheyenne State Leader*, July 7, 1914. Stimson also apparently did more than boost automobiles. The *Laramie Republican* on July 28, 1910, included an advertisement for "Standard Tire Protectors" and listed J. E. Stimson as the "Distributor, Cheyenne, Wyo.," while the *Cheyenne Wyoming Tribune* for May 6, 1911, in a story called "Whirling with the Automobiles," described Stimson as a "local agent and one of the best drivers and all around automobile men in Cheyenne." The following month, in its June 18, 1911, edition, the *Cheyenne State Leader,* in an article titled "Some Recent Sales of Automobiles," mentioned the sale of "a Model T Ford through the local agent, J. E. Stimson." This reputation was tested the following year when Stimson, while photographing near Wheatland, ran into a mud hole and he and his passenger were ejected from the car, with Stimson suffering a broken leg. See "J. E. Stimson Injured at Bordeaux Yesterday," ibid., August 25, 1912; *Evanston Wyoming Times*, September 12, 1912. The *Laramie Republican*, September 15, 1912, reported that the photographer "is able to be up and about a little on crutches."

36. Josephine Stimson Love, interview with author, August 3, 1988. Stories about his political involvement can be found in the *Laramie Republican*, April 19, 1913; "Commence Work on South Road," *Cheyenne State Leader*, August 10, 1913, "J. E. Stimpson [*sic*] Candidate," *Cheyenne Wyoming Tribune*, October 15, 1914; "Why Joe Stimson Should Be Re-Elected," ibid., November 6, 1915; "Reasons to Vote for Joe Stimson," *Cheyenne State Leader*, January 15, 1916; "For 2-Year County Constable," *Cheyenne Wyoming Semi-Weekly Tribune*, August 8, 1916; "Political Announcements," *Cheyenne Wyoming Tribune*, August 21, 1916.

37. Junge, *Stimson*, 14.

38. In my August 3, 1988, interview with Stimson's daughter Josephine, she stated that her father "lost everything" in the Great Depression.

39. See Junge, *Stimson*, 168–69; J. E. Turner, *Summer of 1932 Incorporating also Top Country* (Silver Springs, MD: WRybolot, 1999). The latter publication was written by a

man sixty-seven years after Stimson had photographed him as a young boy during this pack trip.

40. Junge, *Stimson*.

41. Ibid., 19. An understanding of what time of day Stimson shot his photographs and from what vantage point can be best ascertained through a rephotography project such as this one.

42. Mark Junge, telephone interview with author, August 24, 2010.

43. Robert W. Rydell and Rob Kroes, *Buffalo Bill in Bologna: The Americanization of the World* (Chicago: University of Chicago Press, 2005), 114–15.

44. Louis C. McClure of Denver is probably the best comparison to Stimson because he worked for railroads and photographed similar subjects between 1890 and 1935 in neighboring Colorado. His collection is located at the Denver Public Library and is highlighted in William C. Jones, Elizabeth B. Jones, and Louis C. McClure, *Photo by McClure: The Railroad, Cityscape, and Landscape Photographs of L. C. McClure* (Boulder: Pruett, 1991). William Henry Jackson's work during the early twentieth century for the Detroit Publishing Company compares as well. See Peter B. Hales, *William Henry Jackson and the Transformation of the American Landscape* (Philadelphia: Temple University Press, 1988).

45. Samuel Western includes several Stimson images of small agriculture as symbols of the small rancher and farmers' fight against the growing power of large cattlemen in *Pushed off the Mountain, Sold down the River*. Interestingly, Western does not analyze these images and their photographer as illustrations of the complexity he argues for in the book's text. See ibid., 23, 38, 56.

46. Several recent works have reexamined Adams's works and their—and his—multiple meanings. See especially, Jonathon Spaulding, *Ansel Adams and the American Landscape: A Biography* (Berkeley: University of California Press, 1998); Andrea G. Stillman, *Looking at Ansel Adams: The Photographs and the Man* (New York: Little, Brown, 2012).

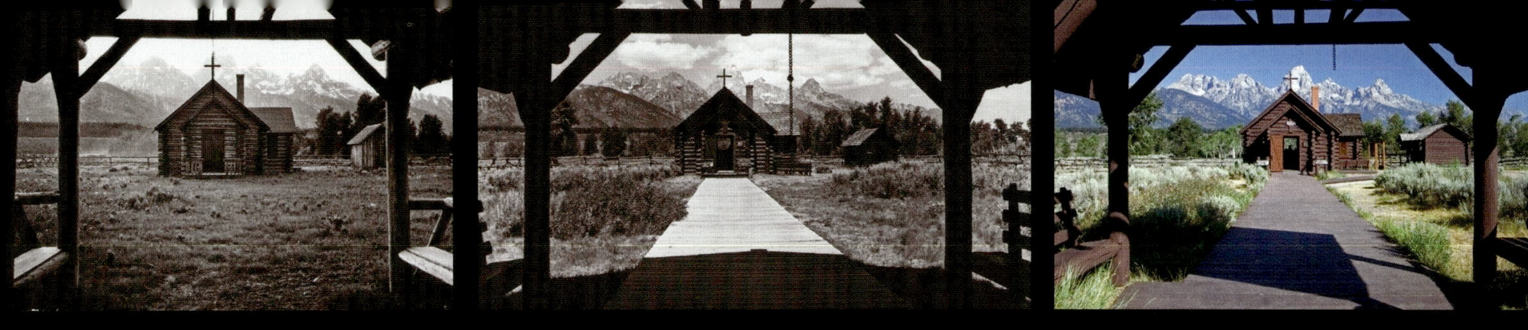

CHAPTER 2

Four Summers with Stimson

Rephotographing Wyoming in 1987–88 and 2007–08

DOI: 10.5876/9781607323051.c002

Twice over the last three decades I have conducted two-year rephotography projects tracing J. E. Stimson's work in Wyoming. Like many other repeat photographers,[1] I have carried out extensive archival work to select potential views, spent months in the field taking pictures, and expended even more hours perfecting the images, researching their subjects, analyzing their content, and making the photographs available for presentation. Over those twenty-five years, I have learned not only about J. E. Stimson's history, as described in chapter 1, but also about how the processes of photography and rephotography have changed. An examination of how I spent that time, both in the late 1980s and again in the early 2000s, should reveal such changes and what they tell us about J. E. Stimson the photographer.

My first exposure to the process in Wyoming was the small book *Rediscovering the Big Horns*, a Bicentennial Project of the Wyoming State Historical Society that retraced the images made by an eastern scientist throughout turn-of-the-century northern Wyoming. The best-known effort, and the one that became the standard, was photographer Mark Klett and colleagues' *Second View: The Rephotographic Survey Project* (RSP), which used precise arithmetic formulas, large-format cameras, and instant Polaroid film to make subtle camera shifts that expertly zeroed in on the classic photographs made by nineteenth-century exploration photographers across the West, including Timothy O'Sullivan and William Henry Jackson. As part of this project, Klett's team rephotographed several sites in Wyoming, including Yellowstone National Park and the Green River area.[2]

Finding Klett's work coincided with my discovery of Mark Junge's wonderful biography/portfolio titled *J. E. Stimson: Photographer of the West*. Beautifully illustrated with exquisite duotones, Junge's book sparked an interest that perhaps I could start my own rephotography project in Wyoming, in essence applying Klett's techniques to Junge's material. I had met Junge sometime before because he often photographed Cowboy basketball games at the University of Wyoming (UW) in Laramie. As a seldom-used player occupying one of the last seats on the bench, I had often seen Mark snapping pictures under the basket. During the spring of 1987, I contacted Junge at the Wyoming State Historic Preservation Office in Cheyenne. To my delight, he agreed to bring a couple of folders of Stimson's pictures to the next home basketball game and share them with me afterward. I don't remember anything about the game, but I do remember sitting at my locker and looking through Stimson's pictures and starting to piece together the idea of rephotographing them. After more talks with Mark and several visits to the Wyoming State Archives in Cheyenne, I decided to focus my project on the Union Pacific Railroad.

After securing a small research grant from UW's College of Arts and Letters, I borrowed a 4×5 camera, was given darkroom access by the Journalism Department, in which I was a major, and set out to retake pictures. The first year I captured images in Cheyenne, Laramie, Rawlins, Rock Springs, Green River, and Evanston, as well as Kemmerer, Diamondville, Cokeville, Hartville, Sunrise, and Fort Laramie. The following year I concentrated on the northern half of the state, rephotographing Douglas, Newcastle, Sundance, Sheridan, Buffalo, Worland, Thermopolis, Cody, Yellowstone, and Grand Teton National Park. The project was amazing for a twenty-two-year-old, as not only did I find about 150 vantage points but also because the whole process served as sort of a photographic apprenticeship. I traveled throughout the state, planned my own fieldwork, made pictures in far-off places, and developed and printed final images.

At that time, I made photographs very similar to the way Stimson had made his images eighty years earlier. I used a large-format 4×5 Crown Graphic press camera on loan from the Journalism Department. To use it, I had to pre-load 4×5 cut sheet film into holders while standing in a darkroom in total darkness with no red lights. It was a tedious process. Like everyone else in 1987, I was used to loading film cartridges into a camera but had never experienced cut sheet film. To do it, I had to take my ten film holders and the box of sheet film into the darkroom. I turned off the lights and opened the film box. After removing the lid and opening another box inside, I tore open the pouch containing the film and ran my index finger along the top, looking for the little notches along the top left that indicated the light-sensitive emulsion side of the sheet. Finding this, I removed one piece of film, slid out the cover of the holder, slid the film inside, and replaced the cover—making sure the small raised dots on the handle always faced outward, indicating unexposed film. I then repeated the process on the back side of this film holder—each held two sheets—and did the same for the remaining nine holders. Interestingly, I often performed this procedure with my eyes closed, probably because that is how I had always practiced the maneuver, even though in the darkroom it did not matter. When all ten holders were filled, I put the remaining film back into the storage pouch, placed it in the box within the box, and turned on the lights. I was ready to go.

In the field, I had a changing bag that performed as a very small portable darkroom. This contraption looked like a small black shirt with no neck or waist holes, just a body with two elasticized sleeves coming off it and a zipper on the bottom. To load film, one simply unzipped the bag, loaded the film holders and film box into it, and zipped it shut. To load, I pushed my hands into the two sleeves and felt for the materials. Using this bag, I could load the holders in bright sunshine, though I still tended to close my eyes out of habit. After repeating the same process I used in the darkroom, the holders were ready to go and I could unzip the bag.

With the equipment ready, I began my search for Stimson's location or vantage point. This was not a haphazard procedure. I used topographic maps, the 1940s Works Progress Administration's *Guide to Wyoming*, and other local history books and maps to narrow my search. I often asked locals as well. I drove around looking at my images and comparing them to my surroundings. This search for the exact location where an earlier photographer made an image is the very essence of repeat photography. It is a fascinating, sometimes exhilarating feeling knowing that you have somehow broken history's secrets and are actually standing in the footsteps of someone who decided a century earlier that this very spot was the ideal one in which to take the photograph you are holding in your hand. It's an amazing place to be.

It's also a curse. Finding the exact location from which someone a century earlier made an image can be very difficult. You might also find yourself in a difficult spot: high atop a tower or in a forest with grizzly bears. The fundamental difficulty is that a photograph depicts what a place looked like *from* that vantage point, not what a particular vantage point looked like more than a century earlier. That's a lot of time for things to change, and change they do. As discussed often in the descriptions of individual images, retaking photographs often meant sacrificing original vantage points for ones nearby simply because trees or new buildings blocked the original view.

I also had to exclude some seemingly obvious locations from my project because Stimson did not photograph them a century ago. For Stimson, this mainly involved the city of Casper, one of the two largest towns in the state. As much as I would have liked to rephotograph images of the "Oil City" to appeal to one of my largest potential audiences, the fact is that Stimson did not shoot images of the community. He shot ranches and nearby towns but not Casper itself. Apparently, this absence was not a mistake but a matter of respecting other photographers who were vying their trade there.[3]

I was also limited to recapturing what Stimson originally photographed, not what might have seemed interesting or exciting in my time. For example, this meant that images of Wyoming's oil industry were limited to small fields at Spring Valley or along the Popo Agie rather than including today's booming Overthrust Belt. Similarly, I knew that mining scenes meant Sheridan-area coal mines rather than post–World War II uranium mines or the modern Trona mines. In rephotography, access is determined by a context created a century ago, not the one that exists today.

These problems aside, over the course of my four summers with J. E. Stimson I learned a great deal about the ways he took photographs, as well as the problems associated with getting back to that same space a century later and also problems one might encounter looking in the same direction with the camera once there. These latter problems include not having enough visual information in the original photograph to locate the original site, the destruction of the original camera station or one's ability to access it, being denied access to the original vantage point by the property's current owner, or having the original vantage point obstructed by a manmade or natural object.

The problem of having too little visual information to find the original vantage point is not evident in this book. All of those sites were discarded long ago. Each summer in which I started to do rephotography, I would select upward of 300 images I was interested in, but at least 100 each summer were not repeated because I could not find the original location. I remember spending almost a full day in the summer of 1987 with a friend from Laramie who was a Union Pacific Railroad expert and had been to the long-lost community of Tie Siding south of town. My Stimson photograph of the town showed a few false-front buildings sitting atop a mostly treeless plain. There were no mountains or canyons in sight. We looked and looked but could not find the location to duplicate the image. A similar story unfolded twenty-one years later while I was working on Stimson's images of the Cody Road to Yellowstone. I had successfully located 39 of his original 45 scenes by following the order in which he made them as he headed west from Cody to the park. On one image, Stimson simply recorded the phrase "Tremulo Pass," and the view depicted a bunch of aspen trees—the scientific name for aspen is *Populus tremuloides*. My uncle, who had hunted and traveled this road for years, was with me, but he had never heard the name of the pass and we were unable to find its location. As with Tie Siding two decades before, I could not access this vantage point because there was insufficient visual information to locate it.

The destruction of a vantage point or losing access to it occurred infrequently over the years. The best example took place at the site Stimson called the Irma Post Office west of Cody. When Stimson visited this location in July 1903, he was traveling with a guide up the newly opened Cody Road to Yellowstone. His view depicts the South Fork of the Shoshone River cutting across the scene left to right. In the middle, the small Irma Post Office, named for Buffalo Bill's daughter, sits as a small log structure. The road to the park moves from the left foreground to the middle background, crossing a small truss below a sagebrush-covered hill. Rattlesnake Mountain looms in the distance. When Lauren and I visited Cody in the summer of 2007, we discovered that this spot was now under more than 100 feet of water, inundated by Buffalo Bill Reservoir. We first considered hiring a boat to take out on the lake to duplicate the shot, but instead we found a small causeway and walked out on it to get close enough to effectively make my image.

Similar problems of destruction occurred in other locations, albeit on a smaller scale. Stimson labeled his view of the Green River depot park (30) as having been taken from the "Union Pacific Gate Tower." Such an elevated building was used to watch over the rail yard and to control access to the tracks. When I visited the location in 1987, the gate tower was no longer there and a black metal pedestrian bridge occupied the general location. Although the bridge did not give me precisely the same vantage point, it was elevated and close, and I could obtain the effect of the original shot. At Beckton, Stimson must have photographed his panorama of the Forbes Ranch (71) from a water tower. I had to make do by standing on a 10-foot ladder and hand-holding the camera for my rephotograph of the panorama.

The opposite of this problem, finding the original vantage point but then discovering that the original subject no longer existed, occurred far more frequently. The idea of returning to rephotograph scenes twenty years after I had first visited them began when I realized that many of my images in Yellowstone were taken early in July 1988, just as the infamous fires were beginning. Thus, many of my images show what the park looked like just before it was consumed by fire. A close look at views of Castle Geyser (102), Grotto Geyser (103), and Giant Geyser (104) attests to this. Not surprisingly, mines, smelters, and communities associated with such activities also represented this phenomenon, both in 1987 and again in 2007. Images made at the copper mining areas of Hecla (9, 10) and Grand Encampment (22) attest to this, as do those of the coal mining towns Cambria (50), Dietz (60, 61), and Kleenburn (62). More surprising was the demise of small-town hotels in Thermopolis (87), Kemmerer (36), Lander (84), and Rawlins (26).

At other sites, I was barred from even reaching the camera station. This first occurred in 2007 when I went to revisit Cheyenne's Union Pacific Depot Tower, now a museum, to climb back up into the tower. Along with my views of Yellowstone, I longed to get back to this spot to see how Cheyenne, Stimson's hometown, had endured over the last two decades. When I inquired at the museum, I was told that the City of Cheyenne now owned the depot and that it could not allow me to access the tower because of liability issues. After talking to another person who affirmed this position, I had to forgo access to this unique camera station. I instead made a new rephotograph from the arched doorway directly below the tower at street level (1).

I was also denied access to the former iron mining town of Sunrise. When Stimson visited this community in 1903, it was a company town owned by Colorado

Fuel and Iron and supplied Pueblo's steel mills with raw materials. His view shows the mine and several blocks of company housing. When I visited Sunrise in 1987, the mine had been closed for a few years. I was able to enter the town, climb up a hill to the site of a water tower, and duplicate Stimson's view. When Lauren and I left nearby Hartville in 2008 to visit Sunrise, we found a locked fence gate and warnings that trespassers would be arrested. We returned to Hartville and asked about crossing the fence. We were told sternly that if caught, we would indeed be arrested. Although I chose not to rephotograph Sunrise, I since have been encouraged to hear that a University of Wyoming folklorist has been allowed to take her class into the Sunrise town site for research purposes.

Of all the access problems, the most ubiquitous involved the issue of trees. In case after case, I was able to find the proper camera station and set up my equipment, only to find that trees had grown up into the view since Stimson's day and were blocking my rephotograph. This occurred both in the city and in the country, including the interior of the Hecla Mill (10), Vedauwoo (12), the state penitentiary in Rawlins (24), the Douglas hospital (44), the panorama of Newcastle (46), officers' quarters at Fort Mackenzie, outside Sheridan (59), Holdredge's Cabin at Dome Lake (76), Atlantic City (83), Menor's Ferry (115), and the former Bar BC dude ranch (116), the latter two near Moose. In nearly every one of these cases, simply moving a foot or two to one side allowed me to make a very similar photograph.

Once I had surmounted these difficulties, the actual process of taking photographs with a large-format camera in the 1980s required patience. After securing the camera to the tripod, I selected the most likely lens, either a "normal" 135-mm lens or a 90-mm wide-angle lens, and attached a cable release to the shutter. To ensure that enough light was present for sharp focusing, I opened the diaphragm to the largest aperture and draped a black cloth over the camera to block out ambient light. Standing beneath the cloth, I focused the camera and stood back to compare the image on the ground glass with my photocopy of Stimson's image. I then made basic left-right or up-down adjustments to replicate the original composition. Because the image on the ground glass was upside down, I held Stimson's original upside down for comparison. Although this process might seem odd, one benefit was that it helped break down the composition into elements that could be more easily compared to the original image than could a busy overall scene. At this point, the 4 × 5 allowed me to make minor camera movements to adjust the angle between the film plane in back and the lens board in front. These effects, including a front rise, an up or down lens tilt, or pivoting the lens left or right, could help control focus and image convergence. Generally, I avoided these minor adjustments except when photographing large buildings.

After all these adjustments were set, I locked in the focus, cocked the shutter, and calculated the exposure. Although I carried a light meter that allowed both reflective and incident light meter readings, I found that a simpler method for ensuring a basically good exposure was to follow the old "Sunny Sixteen Rule." This simple formula stated that if I used the f/16 aperture (a good choice because it provided very good depth of field), I should select a shutter speed at the reciprocal of my film speed. Because I generally used 400 ISO black-and-white film, this meant I could expose it at f/16 at 1/400th of a second or more likely f/16 at 1/500th of a second, the nearest speed on the camera. From this calculation, other combinations could be used if I wanted a greater depth of field, say f/22 at 1/250th or, for stop action, f/11 at 1/1000th of a second. I set the appropriate shutter speed, dialed the aperture to the correct size, and released and then re-cocked the shutter, effectively closing the light path onto the ground glass and making the camera ready.

With the composition and exposure set, I removed the black cloth, grabbed a film holder containing unexposed film, and loaded it into the back of the camera, being careful not to bump or move anything. I removed the film cover from the holder and pressed the cable release. As I did so, the shutter briefly opened and light passed through the lens and diaphragm, past the shutter, and onto the film sheet. I then replaced the film cover, with the little nubs turned around to indicate an exposed film, and removed the film holder. The entire process of taking one photograph usually took about an hour once the general vantage point had been secured. Given this time involvement, I often "bracketed" each shot by slightly changing the exposure combinations to allow a little less light in on one shot and a little more on the next. These next two photographs were made in just a couple of minutes, and then I unscrewed the camera from the tripod and put the equipment away until I was ready at the next vantage point. After I had completed twenty photographs, I grabbed my changing bag or found a darkroom, removed the exposed sheets from the front and back of my ten holders, and replaced them with fresh film, safely storing my shot film back in its original light-tight boxes.

Because film-based photography relied on a "latent image," I had no way to know whether what I had just done had produced a workable image until I developed the film later, back in the university darkrooms in Laramie. My only assurance was that I pretty much knew what I was doing, had practiced the skills of photography, and had bracketed my image, giving me at least three possible exposures.

Developing cut sheet film led me back not only into total darkness but also into a tedious process involving chemistry, temperature, and patience. Returning to Laramie after a week or two of rephotography work in the field, I often had several dozen sheets of film. The development process began by mixing chemicals, including developer that brought out the latent images, stop bath that halted the development process, fixer that solidified the image onto the film, water that washed the negative, and finally a wetting agent that improved drying. Each chemical had to be mixed from packaged powders at certain temperatures and then loaded into a series of small tanks, each about the size of a car battery. The temperature of the developer determined how long the film would be left in the developing bath, and I had to be sure every other tank was at about the same temperature.

When the preparations were done, I began the development process. I turned off the lights and opened my film holders, removing each sheet of film and placing it into a stainless steel hanger that supported it by its edges. After loading ten of these hangers with film, I immersed them in the developing tank and set a glow-in-the-dark timer to the time indicated by the temperature. Each minute, I would agitate the tank by tilting it from side to side, being careful not to spill any liquid. When the allotted time was up, I removed the ten hangers from the developer tank and plunged them into the stop bath, leaving them there for about thirty seconds. Composed of a concentrated acetic acid, the stop bath had a fairly strong vinegar smell. At this point the latent image was on the film, but I could not see it because it was still in total darkness. I could not turn on the light because the image was not yet permanent and any light would ruin it. Therefore, after the thirty-second stop bath, I removed the hangers and immersed them in fixer, a bonding agent that "fixed" the images to the film. After about eight to ten minutes, I could turn on the lights and inspect my images as I removed them from the fixer. This was the first time since taking the photograph several weeks earlier and several hundred miles away that I knew whether I had a successful image. After a quick glimpse, I moved the hangers into another tank located in the darkroom's sink that had running water coming into it for a fifteen-minute wash. After completion, I dipped the hangers into yet another tank containing a "wetting agent" that helped remove water in the drying process. Following this quick dip, I hung the hangers up to dry for about an hour and then removed the negatives and placed them in clear archival storage sleeves. I next inspected them on a light table. From start to finish, the entire process took about two hours. I then started on the next twenty sheets and repeated each step until all the negatives were developed and safely stored away. Sometimes this was done in one long day, more often over several days.

Except for the fact that I was using 4 × 5-inch film rather than 8 × 10-inch glass plates, I was essentially following the same developing processes J. E. Stimson had used eight decades earlier. I first went out into the field, found locations to photograph, exposed the plates, and returned home to develop them, trusting that my skill as a photographer had indeed secured the images I wanted. Recall that, at the end of his long 1903 summer of photographing all thirteen Wyoming counties plus Yellowstone National Park for Wyoming's World's Fair commission, Cheyenne's *Wyoming Tribune* recounted Stimson's six weeks in the field when it reported on August 18 that "Photographer J. E. Stimson is very busy these days developing the views of the state taken by him for the St. Louis Fair. The trip occupied six weeks and many hundreds of exposures were made."[4]

After my own hundreds of negatives were developed, like Stimson, I turned to printing. For many photographers, photographic printing is as much art as process. Indeed, Ansel Adams once claimed that while the negative was the score, the print was the performance, suggesting that each could be changed into a unique representation of the original piece. As with the development process, black-and-white printing in the 1980s was more or less the same as it had been eight decades earlier for Stimson.

The centerpiece of darkroom printing was the enlarger. Situated on the "dry side" of the darkroom and something akin to a vertical slide projector, the enlarger incorporated a light source, a negative carrier, and a diaphragm that controlled the amount of light that passed through the negative in a certain length of time. In some ways, the enlarger worked like a large camera: exposure was controlled by the amount of light allowed to pass through the diaphragm, the length of time that light was allowed to exist, and the sensitivity of the printing paper. Different-sized prints were made by raising or lowering the enlarger and placing appropriately sized paper into the easel below.

The paper came in two types. Traditional "graded" fiber-based papers were longer lasting but more difficult and time-consuming to use. Further, because each paper contained a different grade of contrast, a photographer had to have multiple grades of stock at all times to compensate for contrast issues in the negative. Variable-grade, resin-coated (VC, RC) papers were just coming into widespread use at that time. These papers, with a type of resin coating on the emulsion side, were faster and more flexible to use, though they required filters to be placed onto the enlarger to bring out different contrasts. Both types were orthochromatic, meaning they were not sensitive to red light and thus did not require total darkness; the familiar red "safelights" could be used.

The "wet side" of the printing darkroom was similar to the film development darkroom in that trays containing a developer, stop bath, fixer, and wash bath were also employed. Also relying on a "latent image" technique, black-and-white photo printing took white sheets of light-sensitive paper, exposed them to projected light from an enlarger at a certain intensity and time, then passed the papers through a series of baths that brought up the image and fixed it into onto the paper. The print was then washed, dried, and archivally stored.

The actual process of printing could also be tedious and time-consuming. After loading the 4×5 negative into the carrier and inserting it into the enlarger, I turned on the enlarger and projected the image down onto the easel where the light-sensitive paper was in place. Using a focuser that resembled a microscope, I examined the projected image and then finely focused the enlarger until the image was absolutely sharp. I turned off the enlarger and removed a single sheet of photographic paper to determine the proper exposure time with what was called a "test strip." Setting the timer to about five seconds, I covered all but an inch or two of the paper and turned on the enlarger. Light was projected through the negative onto the easel and exposed the uncovered inch of the paper for the selected time, then the enlarger was turned off. I uncovered another inch of the paper and repeated the process, so that now the first inch had been exposed for ten seconds and the second inch for five seconds. I repeated this process inch by inch across the paper so that, when completed and developed, I had a sheet of paper showing the image in five-second incremental exposures, from a light five seconds to a very dark fifty seconds on the ten-inch-long paper. This test strip allowed me to determine the rough time for the proper exposure. I then printed an entire sheet at that new time, developed it, and analyzed the exposure. If needed, dodging (covering an area during the exposure to lighten it) or burning (adding more light to an area to darken it) could be addressed for problem areas of the print. Often, printing a single image could take several hours of experimenting, developing, and drying.

As I concluded my darkroom work, I began to present my findings to wider audiences. In 1988 I joined the Wyoming Humanities Council's Speakers Bureau and was able to present my work to audiences across the state. Because scanners and PowerPoint did not yet exist, this required re-shooting all of my prints and the Stimson originals on slide film. For the Stimson images, Mark Junge allowed me use of his copy stand, which enabled me to quickly set up the 35-mm camera on one image, shoot it under appropriate lighting, and then replace the image and re-shoot. For my images, I borrowed a copy stand from the university, but since I did not have appropriate lighting, I used daylight slide film and copied all of my images outside. After completing the copying, I presented slide shows of my work over the next two years in Cheyenne, Laramie, Hanna, Sheridan, Buffalo, Douglas, Rawlins, and Big Piney. In 1991 I published a coffee table–style book, *Wyoming Time and Again: Rephotographing the Scenes of J. E. Stimson,* that featured 100 black-and-white pairs of images grouped into chapters on scenic landscapes, the built environment, and ghost towns. The book was well received, and copies from its 3,000-issue printing run were gone in a few years.[5]

After finishing the rephotographic project on Stimson, my focus turned to completing my master's degree in American studies in Laramie, getting a doctorate in the history of the American West at the University of Nebraska–Lincoln, and then working as a history professor at Idaho State University, Mesa State College, and Northern Arizona University (NAU). Throughout these years, I continued to be interested in researching and writing about Wyoming. I organized a *catalog raisonne* of an artist who was Stimson's contemporary, wrote an MA thesis on the polo-playing town of Big Horn, Wyoming, and completed a dissertation and book on uranium mining communities in the American West, including Jeffrey City, Wyoming.[6]

But I also remained interested in photography and rephotography. I continued to play with the 4 × 5 camera, and I learned to shoot with a 1950s stereo camera and then, around 1998, with a Sony Mavica digital camera owned by NAU that employed a fixed lens, shot 1.3 megapixels, and stored its images on 3.5-inch floppy discs. I soon purchased my own digital cameras, first a 3-megapixel Kodak point and shoot and then a 6-megapixel Canon digital SLR. I also followed rephotography projects conducted by others, including ones on the Colorado River, the Grand Canyon, Arizona, the Sonoran Desert, Route 66, Colorado, the Dust Bowl, Lake Tahoe, Estes Park, and Yellowstone.[7] Although most of these projects focused on the broader idea of landscape photography, others followed people over time or changes in grasslands. These books rekindled my interest in rephotography, and I first tried stereo rephotography and then eventually digital rephotographs of northern Arizona. But I kept thinking about Wyoming and J. E. Stimson.

Some photo historians suggest that a good way to think about a photograph is as a contract among what's in front of the camera, the technology of the camera, and what's behind the camera.[8] By that definition, everything about my first Wyoming rephotographic project had changed by the early twenty-first century. After all, Wyoming had gone through several important changes since my 1980s project, including a uranium bust, oil and gas booms, the Matthew Shepard incident, and Dick Cheney's rise to national power.[9] At the same time, the disciplines of both photography and history had changed. Digital technology was completely remaking imaging, allowing photographers instant access to what they captured through digital cameras, cell phones, and the Internet.[10] Simultaneously, the Internet and computers were making historical research increasingly accessible. For example, with the new Wyoming Newspaper Project, I could do a keyword search for Stimson articles in contemporary newspapers from my home computer in Arizona, in effect making more and more historical sources available. At the same time, new cultural and social theories were remaking the way we thought about history, moving away from the traditional "one damned thing after another" narrative to a more analytical, thought-provoking approach to the past. More specifically, my chosen field, the history of the American West—Wyoming included— was changing from the old-fashioned frontier school of Frederick Jackson Turner and its seeming progression of white civilization across the continent to the more inclusive, analytical New Western History of Patricia Limerick, Richard White, and Donald Worster. More western historians were studying the environment and looking more critically at the ways art and photography had shaped our views of the West.[11] Finally, I knew that as a tenured professor of history who needed to stay up to date with these various concepts through my own studies and teaching, I was much better prepared to think about what I was seeing than I had been as an undergraduate history-journalism major.

Nevertheless, basic questions lingered. Could I find the same locations I had visited more than twenty years earlier? Could I find new vantage points not visited during the first project? If I could find these spots, how would I reshoot them? Most important, would my new photographs tell me anything new about Wyoming or photography?

As I contemplated another rephotography project on Wyoming, the first place I turned to was the continuing rephotographic work of Mark Klett. After completing the RSP, Klett had published several more works that not only included stunning photography but also asked poignant questions about time, photography, and rephotography. His published work included an amazing set of panoramas of San Francisco, a follow-up to the RSP called *Third Views, Second Sites* that traveled back to many original RSP sites to rephotograph them more than twenty years later as well as to new sites added along the way, another on the 1906 San Francisco earthquake and fire that included color photos and foldout, before-and-after panoramas, and one more that focused on Yosemite National Park. All of Klett's work glowed with the precision of a master craftsman who still used Polaroid sheets in his 4×5 camera to zero in on his vantage point. His books used multiple original photographers and often employed essays by western writers and historians to help provide cultural context. Added to this mix was the book *View Finder: Mark Klett, Rephotography, and the Reinvention of Landscape* by William L. Fox that provided background biographical information about Klett and followed him and his team as they prepared images for *Third Views*. Leafing through these works fueled my fire to return to Wyoming and J. E. Stimson.[12]

I received a Cody Institute for Western American Studies summer research grant from the Buffalo Bill Historical Center (BBHC; now the Buffalo Bill Center of the West) in Cody, Wyoming, to start a new rephotography project on Stimson and Wyoming. My most immediate concern was getting back to Wyoming. In the 1980s, I was a University of Wyoming undergraduate student living alone in Laramie. This time around, I would have to uproot myself, my twelve-year-old dog Nellie, and my girlfriend, Lauren, from our homes in Flagstaff, Arizona, for a summer traveling around Wyoming. To complicate matters, I had agreed to teach the first session of summer school in Flagstaff in June, meaning I would have to cram a summer's worth of work into the six weeks between the Independence Day break and the start of the fall semester in late August.

I decided to make my parents' home in Loveland, Colorado—fifty miles south of Cheyenne—my home base for the summer. I could leave Nellie there safely and still access Wyoming for three or four big photographic sweeps through different parts of the state. The first would be a trip to the Wyoming State Archives in Cheyenne, where I could reacquaint myself with the photo archivists and once again work my way through the more than 7,000 images in the Stimson collection. Although I planned to focus on revisiting my 1980s locations, I was determined to also look for new sites to capture, especially panoramic views containing multiple images. After a long day at the archives, I decided to focus that summer on rephotographing western and southern Wyoming and spend the following summer east of the Big Horns and in the Black Hills of northeastern Wyoming. This plan meant making essentially three major trips: one to Cody, Yellowstone, Jackson, and the Big Horn Basin; a second focusing on southeastern Wyoming in Cheyenne, Laramie, Saratoga, and Encampment; and a final trip across southern Wyoming, basically following the Union Pacific from Cheyenne to Evanston. At the end of this excursion, I would turn north back to Cody, where I had to present my findings at a public lecture at the BBHC on August 9, a scant thirty days in the future.

This tight schedule began with a 450-mile drive to Cody. We wanted to get there quickly, so there were no planned stops other than for food and fuel. At least that was the plan. But as we drove north of Cheyenne toward the small ranching community of Chugwater, I was reminded that Stimson took a panorama of the Al Bowie Ranch at what later became Chugwater and thought that perhaps we should take a look around. The town has a population of only 244 and a town plat of only several streets, so this image should have been a quick and easy rephotograph to get my feet wet on the new project. We drove through the town and quickly figured out the location we needed. What Stimson called the Al

Bowie Ranch in 1903 had formerly been the home of the famous British-owned Swan Land and Cattle Company. The ranch, which controlled lands larger than Connecticut, had been organized from Scotland in 1883 to capitalize on the open range touted in James S. Brisbin's 1881 book, *Beef Bonanza: Or, How to Get Rich on the Plains,* which explained how ranchers could use the grasses of the West's public domain for enormous profits. The actual results varied. Initial prospects were good, but the infamous winter of 1886–87 decimated plains ranching and exposed the fact that the counts of western ranch cattle herds often deviated widely from their book counts. Despite these setbacks, the Swan Land and Cattle Company survived until the early 1950s.[13]

Standing at the site gave me goose bumps. In Stimson's 1903 scene (38), a large barn stands to the left, a false-front building is in the center, and a house is on the right. In the modern view, the barn and the house are still there, although large trees block the view of them, and the center building is gone. But the overall effect of the scene is strikingly similar. I was standing in basically the same spot and photographing a scene that had been visited more than a century earlier. As I unpacked my camera, it occurred to me how different this rephotography project would be. Instead of either Stimson's 8 × 10 camera with glass plates or my 4 × 5 press camera with cut sheet film, I had decided to go digital. Loaded on top of my tripod was an 8-megapixel Canon Digital Rebel XT DSLR camera with a 1.8-inch display.[14] I had an assortment of lenses, including a 24–105-mm zoom, a 10–22-mm zoom, a 70–200-mm zoom, and a 24-mm tilt shift lens that duplicated the movements of a large-format camera. The camera saved images in both JPEG and RAW formats onto compact flash cards. I had several flash cards, ranging from ½ gigabyte to 1 gigabyte. The camera used a lithium ion battery—I had two so a spare was always ready—and could also hold 6 AA batteries in its attached grip.

My jump to digital did not end with the camera. In addition, I brought along a Gateway laptop loaded with scans of all the Stimson images I hoped to rephotograph. I could also use this computer to back up my saved images. To view its screen in the sun, I had a small "tent-like" device that, when unfolded, could house the computer and shade the screen for better viewing. In addition, I carried an Epson P-2000, a battery-powered external hard drive with viewing screen and compact flash drive that I could use to both back up images and view those images without the use of the laptop. Finally, I carried an older Eagle Explorer handheld Global Positioning System (GPS) unit that provided latitude, longitude, and elevation readings for every site.

Taking a rephotograph using a digital camera was immensely easier than using the old large-format film camera. I first secured my camera to the tripod and attached a remote shutter release to ensure that I would not vibrate the camera while tripping the shutter. I then held an 8 × 10-inch photocopy of the original Stimson picture and scouted the approximate location of the vantage point. I looked through the camera's viewfinder and determined which lens best replicated the image. Exposure was simplified by using the "aperture priority" setting, which allowed me to set the diaphragm to a small aperture such as f/22 to maximize depth of field. ISO was set at 100 if possible, a bit faster if needed. The camera then set the appropriate shutter speed and I took a picture, compared the image on the camera's screen to the photocopy, and made the necessary adjustments to replicate the image. A simple push of a button on the camera allowed me to view the file's histogram, a tiny graph showing the distribution of lights and darks in each photo. After reading this display, I made appropriate corrections to allow more or less light to reach the sensor and snapped the shutter. During my second season in the field, in 2008, my new camera made this process even simpler by allowing me to see the scene directly on the camera's screen in what is called "live view" as I set up the shot. Now I could simply hold up the original image next to the camera's screen to compare images prior to making the image. Once taken, I always bracketed the photo by altering either the f/stop or the shutter speed, made duplicates of the image, and moved on to the next picture.

Backing up images in the field was crucial to preserve my work. Each night I opened that day's files on my laptop and copied the images to both the computer's hard drive and a portable hard drive attached to one of the USB ports. When this was not possible, I copied images onto the Epson P-2000 by inserting the camera's card into its built-in card reader. At the end of the second season, I added a portable DVD drive to the ensemble to allow me to back up all of my images by burning them onto DVDs.

Processing and printing digital is easy compared to using the chemical darkroom. Although Adobe Photoshop has been called a photo "manipulating" program and the phrase *to Photoshop* suggests fundamentally changing the elements of an image, the software has also brought photo processing to everyone's home office. Unlike the latent image system of film and prints, digital processing relies on the concept of WYSIWYG, or "what you see is what you get." Files are uploaded to the computer and viewed on monitors, with changes such as darkening or lightening an image immediately viewable on the screen. From there, a good inkjet printer will reproduce the image on the screen with a touch of a button.

For me, Photoshop has always been more of a digital processing program than an image manipulation one. I tend to follow a basic, minimally intrusive "workflow." I open my camera's RAW files in Adobe Bridge, an organizational software program that allows me to see the files as images, and then open them into Photoshop CS3. I make minor adjustments to the image's contrasts using levels, sharpen the image with the unsharpen filter mask, and save it as a .psd (Photoshop) file.

Printing images is also a WYSIWYG process. I have always used photo-quality Epson color printers, first an Epson 2200 that printed images up to 13 × 19 inches and most recently an Epson 3880 that prints larger 17 × 22-inch pictures. Each uses glossy or matte papers. For the 2200, I first loaded my completed psd files into a RIP software program called Imageprint, which provided better algorithms to my printer and made it print better black-and-white images. The 3880 prints directly from Photoshop. In either case, I print an image, compare its tone and contrast to the screen, make adjustments if needed, and print again until I have a satisfactory image. No darkrooms, no chemicals, no safelights; only the printer's inks have to be replaced.

All of these devices came about during the computer-digital revolution of the last twenty-five-plus years, and they both simplified and complicated rephotography. The benefits are obvious. First and foremost, the screen on the back of the camera, as well as the ability to plug that camera directly into the laptop for viewing on its large screen, allowed me to instantly see what the camera was seeing while at the camera station for the rephotograph. I immediately made adjustments and got a better rephotograph. Second, because I could save and view that digital file at the site on the camera, the Epson P-2000, or the laptop, I knew instantly that I had captured the scene. No more latent images to be developed later. Third, the built-in light meter and the camera's computer worked together to provide a small exposure graph, the histogram, that showed the distribution of lights and darks within the image, thus allowing me to make exposure corrections. Finally, the GPS unit pinpointed each camera station in the field for later upload to a digital map. Add to these cell phones, the Internet, and e-mail, and the digital revolution simplified the rephotography process by allowing me instant access to a quality image in the field and making vast research materials available at my fingertips.

The complications were less obvious or pressing. The biggest issue was one of optics. Both Stimson's 8 × 10 view camera and my 4 × 5 press camera produced negatives in relation to the other. By enlarging my negatives a simple twofold, I matched Stimson's format. But my Canon Digital Rebel produced a more rectangular image, sort of like a 35-mm camera, that did not, when enlarged, match either of the other formats. Although I could address this difference somewhat through zoom lenses, that choice meant I might compress scenes through the telephoto process. It also meant I could not match the tilt and shift camera movements of the large-format cameras. I could get around this issue by employing my 24-mm, fixed-focus, tilt-shift lens, but the lack of a zoom constricted my ability to match formats.

The second issue was the simple fact that the camera, laptop, GPS, and Epson all had computers that ran on batteries. I had to make sure I had multiple versions of each battery, multiple battery chargers, and access to electricity every night to recharge my batteries for the next day. I had used no batteries twenty-five years earlier.

Finally, I was operating each of these battery-powered computers in Wyoming's notorious wind and dust. Anytime I used an item, I had to be extra careful to protect it from the elements. This was especially true while changing camera lenses because that process exposed the very sensitive sensor to wind-driven dust particles that could embed themselves onto the sensor and mar every picture thereafter.

None of these complications, though, offset the wonderful advantages of digital photography. As I gazed through the lens at the Al Bowie Ranch in Chugwater and began snapping pictures, I looked to the camera's viewing screen and found color images at each click of the shutter. By pushing one button, histograms appeared, and I made subtle changes to shutter speed or aperture setting to compensate. After looking at the first few, I moved the tripod to the left and re-shot the scene. I then moved back a few feet and shot some more. Further viewing told me to move again, and I did this from spot to spot, taking and reviewing images at each, for the next two hours. It was both exhilarating and exhausting. On one hand, it was amazing to instantly see what I was getting; on the other, the overwhelming pressure to get it just right began to sink in. Lauren fired up the laptop, placed it in its little tent, set it on the top of the car, and had me reexamine Stimson's view compared with what I was getting on the camera. We removed the compact flash card from the camera and inserted it into the computer to compare my images with Stimson's on the bigger screen. Eventually, we found just the right spot and shot the panorama from left to right, matching each of the three parts of Stimson's panorama. Lauren recorded our location on the GPS unit, and I took down the camera and put everything away. The entire process had taken about four hours to rephotograph one location, and I realized that, despite the new technology, it was going to be a long, detailed project.

Over the next thirty-two days, Lauren and I put over 5,000 miles on my car as we followed Stimson around the entire State of Wyoming. From Chugwater, we went on to Cody, then to Yellowstone National Park. After shooting throughout the park at Canyon, Old Faithful, and West Yellowstone, we drove back to the Big Horn Basin and photographed Thermopolis, Worland, and Meteetsee. From there, we drove across the Big Horns to Sheridan and its hinterlands of Dietz, Kleenburn, and Big Horn. We went south to Buffalo, then finally back to my parents in Loveland. After a week recovering there, Lauren and I took my dog Nellie back north to Cheyenne, Vedauwoo, Hecla, Granite Springs Reservoir, Laramie, Saratoga, and Encampment. Lauren went back to Flagstaff and I made one more sojourn—up to Cheyenne, then westward across the state following the Union Pacific tracks and shooting Walcott, Rawlins, Green River, Evanston, Kemmerer, and Diamondville. From there, I drove back to Cody and presented my summer's work at the Buffalo Bill Center of the West in early August.

The following summer I received a research grant from NAU to finish the project, and we were back at our base camp—my parents' home in Loveland. We made trips back to Cody, where we concentrated on shooting the Cody Road to Yellowstone, which I spun off into its own book, *Passage to Wonderland*. We then traveled back to Yellowstone to shoot at Mammoth Hot Springs and other select points in the park that we had missed the first summer. We made a side trip back over the Big Horns to Sheridan and spent a wonderful day high in the mountains at Dome Lake before returning to Cody. From there, Lauren and I drove to Grand Teton National Park, Moose, Kelly, and Jackson Hole before going south to Cokeville and then on to my aunt and uncle's ranch in Eden, Wyoming. I photographed nearby South Pass City and Atlantic City, as well as Rock Springs, before we returned to Loveland. Our final trip of the project focused on capturing eastern Wyoming. We made a few images in Cheyenne, then traveled north to Wheatland, Douglas, and the nearby Ayres Natural Bridge. We turned east to shoot Fort Laramie and Hartville before heading north to Newcastle and the Black Hills. Using Newcastle as our base, we shot that town, the nearby ghost town of Cambria, then Sundance and Devil's Tower. With that, we were done and made our way back to our home in Flagstaff.

Over the course of the two summers, 2007 and 2008, I traveled almost 10,000 miles through Wyoming and rephotographed more than 180 sites Stimson had shot more than a century earlier. I had made it to nearly every one of the 150 places I visited in 1987 and 1988 with the exception of sites no longer accessible—such as the Union Pacific Depot Tower in Cheyenne—or ones I did not envision as much different from twenty years earlier, such as the abandoned Dale Creek Bridge site. In addition, I had rephotographed approximately 30 new sites, including about 20 panoramas.

The images were amazing. In describing Mark Klett's repeat photography in Yosemite, writer Rebecca Solnit suggested that she started to think about rephotography as a sort of Advent calendar, the Christmas paper calendars that show one grand scene but are punctuated by little doors that, when opened, reveal many smaller scenes within the bigger view.[15] I began to see Wyoming in many of the same ways. As I looked at the state in the early twenty-first century, I kept seeing little doors that opened up to Stimson photographs of the early twentieth century. They were almost like little time portals, peppering the landscape before me with small openings to an earlier time.

Moreover, after having now spent four summers with J. E. Stimson, I visualized a book that not only presented the many then-and-now images but that expanded on the photographs to think about the role of photography and rephotography in exploring landscapes, historic preservation, modernism and postmodernism, globalization, and the digital revolution as it has played out in Wyoming and the modern American West. In the next section I explore these ideas in three chapters, each of which identifies a particular theme and references photographic pairs or triads found in the last section of plates.

Notes

1. Robert H. Webb, Diane E. Boyer, and Raymond M. Turner, eds., *Repeat Photography: Methods and Applications in the Natural Sciences* (Washington, DC: Island, 2010); Garry F. Rogers, Harold E. Malde, and Raymond M. Turner, *Bibliography of Repeat Photography for Evaluating Landscape Change* (Salt Lake City: University of Utah Press, 1984), xii.

2. Wyoming State Historical Society, *Re-Discovering the Big Horns* (Cheyenne: Bighorn National Forest Volunteer Committee, 1976); Mark Klett et al., *Second View: The Rephotographic Survey Project* (Albuquerque: University of New Mexico Press, 1984).

3. For a beautiful portrait of Casper in historical photographs, see Mark Junge, *A View from Center Street: Tom Carrigen's Casper* (Casper: McMurray Foundation, 2003).

4. "Some Fine Views," *Cheyenne Wyoming Tribune*, August 18, 1903.

5. Michael A. Amundson, *Wyoming Time and Again: Rephotographing the Scenes of J. E. Stimson* (Boulder: Pruett, 1991).

6. My published work on Wyoming history includes "Through the Lens of Stimson: Past and Present," *Annals of Wyoming* (Spring 1988): 32–45; "The Rise and Fall of Big Horn City, Wyoming," *Wyoming Annals* (Spring-Summer 1994): 10–25; "No Longer a Home on the Range: The Booms and Busts of a Wyoming Uranium Mining Town, 1958–1985," *Western Historical Quarterly* 26, no. 4 (Winter 1995): 483–505; "Pen Sketches of Promise: The Western Drawings of Merritt Dana Houghton," *Montana: The Magazine of Western History* (Fall 1994): 54–65; *Yellowcake Towns: Uranium Mining Communities in the American West* (Boulder: University Press of Colorado, 2002); "The British at Big Horn: The Founding of an Elite Wyoming Community," *Journal of the West* 40, no. 1 (Winter 2001): 49–55; "These Men Play Real Polo: The History of an Elite Sport in the 'Cowboy' State, 1890–1930," *Montana: The Magazine of Western History* (Spring 2009): 3–22.

7. Hal G. Stephens, Eugene M. Shoemaker, and John Wesley Powell, *In the Footsteps of John Wesley Powell: An Album of Comparative Photographs of the Green and Colorado Rivers, 1871–72 and 1968* (Boulder, CO: Johnson Books, 1987); Robert H. Webb, *Grand Canyon, a Century of Change: Rephotography of the 1889–1890 Stanton Expedition* (Tucson: University of Arizona Press, 1996); Allen A. Dutton, *Arizona: Then and Now* (Englewood, CO: Westcliffe, 2002); Raymond M. Turner et al., *The Changing Mile Revisited: An Ecological Study of Vegetation Change with Time in the Lower Mile of an Arid and Semiarid Region* (Tucson: University of Arizona Press, 2003); Russell A. Olsen, *Route 66 Lost and Found: Ruins and Relics Revisited* (St. Paul, MN: MBI, 2004); John Fielder, *Colorado 1870–2000* (Englewood, CO: Westcliffe, 1999); John Fielder, *Colorado 1870–2000 II* (Englewood, CO: Westcliffe, 2005); Bill Ganzel, *Dust Bowl Descent* (Lincoln: University of Nebraska Press, 1984); Peter Goin, C. Elizabeth Raymond, and Robert E. Blesse, *Stopping Time: A Rephotographic Survey of Lake Tahoe* (Albuquerque: University of New Mexico Press, 1992); James H. Pickering, Carey Stevanus, and Mic Clinger, *Estes Park: Then and Now* (Englewood, CO: Westcliffe, 2006); Mary Meagher and Douglas B. Houston, *Yellowstone and the Biology of Time: Photographs across a Century* (Norman: University of Oklahoma Press, 1999).

8. John E. Carter, "Architecture, Photography, and a Quest for Meaning," *Exposure* (Fall 1987): 16.

9. Recent Wyoming history is best explained in University of Wyoming historian Phil Roberts's online book "A New History of Wyoming" and his "Readings in Wyoming History" page. They are accessible at his webpage http://www.uwyo.edu/robertshistory [accessed March 1, 2014]. See also the online "Wyoming Encyclopedia" project at http://www.wyohistory.org/ [accessed January 15, 2013].

10. Stephen Johnson, *On Digital Photography* (Sebastapol, CA: O'Reilly Media, 2006).

11. See especially, Patricia Nelson Limerick, *The Legacy of Conquest: The Unbroken Past of the American West* (New York: W. W. Norton, 1987); Richard White, *"It's Your Misfortune and None of My Own": A New History of the American West* (Norman: University of Oklahoma Press, 1993); Patricia Nelson Limerick, Clyde A. Milner II, and Charles E. Rankin, *Trails: Toward a New Western History* (Lawrence: University of Kansas Press, 1991); Donald Worster, *Dust Bowl: The Southern Plains in the 1930s* (New York: Oxford University Press, 1979).

12. Mark Klett and Eadweard Muybridge, *One City/Two Visions: San Francisco Panoramas, 1878 and 1990* (San Francisco: Bedford Arts, 1990); Mark Klett, Kyle Bajakian, William L. Fox and Michael Marshall, *Third View, Second Sights: A Rephotographic Survey Project of the American West* (Santa Fe: Museum of Santa Fe Press in association with the Center for American Places, 2004); Mark Klett, Rebecca Solnit, and Byron Wolfe, *Yosemite in Time: Ice Ages, Tree Clocks, Ghost Rivers* (San Antonio: Trinity University Press, 2005); Mark Klett and Michael Lundgren, *After the Ruins, 1906 and 2006: Rephotographing the San Francisco Earthquake and Fire* (Berkeley: University of California Press, 2006); William L. Fox, *View Finder: Mark Klett, Photography, and the Reinvention of Landscape* (Albuquerque: University of New Mexico Press, 2001).

13. http://tps.cr.nps.gov/nhl/detail.cfm?ResourceId=569&ResourceType=Building; http://www.wyomingtalesandtrails.com/swan2.html [both accessed September 21, 2011].

14. The following summer I upgraded to a 12.2-megapixel Canon Digital Rebel xsi with a 3-inch display.

15. Klett, Solnit, and Wolfe, *Yosemite in Time*, 27.

Seeing Anew

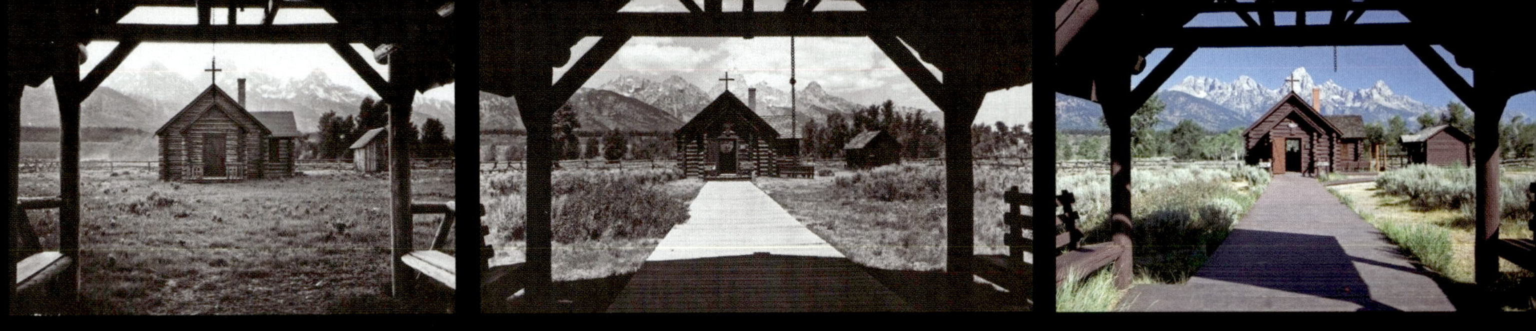

CHAPTER 3

Wyoming and the World

DOI: 10.5876/9781607323051.c003

In 1906, J. E. Stimson traveled east to Omaha, Nebraska, to photograph the Lane Cutoff, a massive, eleven-mile fill between South Omaha and the small community of Lane, Nebraska. The fill was part of Edward H. Harriman's plan to rebuild the Union Pacific to show that the railroad was an efficient, modern carrier. After capturing images of the work in progress, Stimson boarded a UP train and headed west, photographing the railroad all the way to California as part of what he labeled the "Journey across the Continent." As part of that project, the photographer disembarked from the train just south of Laramie, Wyoming, and made twenty photographs of the red, wind-eroded bluffs and rock formations known as the Red Buttes country. One in particular, an image of a singular small formation with a man clinging to its side that Stimson labeled "Castle Dome, Red Buttes Country" (15), is etched in my memory.

This area of sandstone formations had been described earlier by poet Walt Whitman in his 1871 ode to humankind's achievements in linking the world through the building of the Suez Canal, the laying of the Atlantic cable, and the completion of the transcontinental railroad across North America. Describing his trip across the continent in "Passage to India," Whitman wrote:

I see over my own continent the Pacific Railroad, surmounting every barrier;
I see continual trains of cars winding along the Platte, carrying freight and
    passengers;
I hear the locomotives rushing and roaring, and the shrill steam whistle,
I hear the echoes reverberate through the grandest scenery in the world,
I cross the Laramie plains, I note the rocks in grotesque shapes, the buttes.[1]

In 1987, as part of my first rephotographic project, I visited this area and found the rock formations virtually untouched since Stimson's day. Amazingly, one tree that grew out of sandstone rock looked basically the same as it had more than eight decades earlier. The only hints of any change were a small trailer and a split rail fence, barely noticeable in one of my rephotographs. My image of the Castle Dome (15) showed similar sparse vegetation at the base of the formation.

In the summer of 2007, Lauren and I again drove south from Laramie to the Red Buttes area to rephotograph the area. It is now a rural subdivision known as the Buttes. We captured four photographs of the area. Of these, only the one labeled "Sphinx Rock" (16) looked basically the same as it had twenty years earlier. In the other three, although that one tree remained eerily similar, more split rail fence running in and out of the rock formations denoted new property lines. The most obvious changes concerned the photograph labeled "Castle Dome." For this scene, I was unable to reach my vantage point because of a tall fence. I stepped back and found another split rail fence running directly from the side of the butte and none of the vegetation remaining in the foreground. In its place stood a small barn and about a dozen alpacas, residents of the Windy Ridge Alpaca Ranch. As I made my photograph the best I could, I began to think about how the global marketplace had finally come to Wyoming, in the form of a shaggy South American llama-like creature. But as I thought more about it, I began to make the connections among modern-day alpacas, Stimson's images of the Red Buttes, and Walt Whitman's "Passage to India." As I connected the dots, I realized that the world had always been coming to Wyoming.

I should have seen it in the wind, which, after all, is legendary in southern Wyoming. Those interested in wind power highlight the state as having great potential for electricity-generating wind farms. Locals joke about it, suggesting that Laramie is so windy because of Nebraska's inhaling power. Others wag that a Wyoming windsock is made of a heavy chain. It goes on and on. The power of the wind is what brought Stimson to the Red Buttes country in the first place. The many rock formations, like the Sphinx Rock and Castle Dome, are products of wind erosion. Over thousands of years, breezes carrying fine particles of dust have slowly carved the sandstone into interesting shapes. Of course, the wind is not simply a local event but the result of global forces. Areas of high and low pressure move about above the surface of the earth, creating pressure gradients that pull air molecules from areas of high pressure to areas of low pressure, thereby creating wind. Thus the winds of southern Wyoming are but a local effect of global processes.

Throughout the nineteenth century, Wyoming experienced other global connections. In 1807, John Colter, a member of Lewis and Clark's Corps of Discovery—the first American overland expedition looking for a Northwest Passage to Asia—explored much of the Yellowstone country after returning from the Pacific. Then in 1812, returning members of John Jacob Astor's trading enterprise in the Pacific discovered South Pass in central Wyoming. A decade later, mountain men used South Pass to cross the Continental Divide in search of beaver pelts and bison hides that were harvested in Wyoming and sold on the world market. When global fashions changed, these same adventurers became guides, escorting the first Protestant and Catholic missionaries—representatives of global religions—through the Wyoming wilderness to new posts in the Pacific Northwest. A decade later, hundreds of thousands of people passed through what became Wyoming on the Oregon Trail, part of one of the largest global migrations in the nineteenth century. Included in this movement were Mormons, members of the new Church of Jesus Christ of Latter-Day Saints, many of them recent converts who had immigrated to America from England and the Scandinavian countries, only to be pushed west to Utah in 1847. After gold was discovered in California, the world rushed in again, crossing Wyoming en route to new mines and cities.[2]

After the Civil War, Wyoming cemented its national and global connections through the construction of trade networks and the discovery and development of new natural resources and interests. In 1868, hundreds of Irish immigrants came to the area, constructing the new Union Pacific Railroad; building towns like Cheyenne, Laramie, Rawlins, Rock Springs, Green River, and Evanston; and necessitating the establishment of Wyoming from Dakota Territory that year. The railroad also developed new resources, including coal and timber, and integrated these local economies into national and international ones as raw materials left Wyoming and finished goods arrived via the rails. The jobs created in these new industries also enticed workers from around the globe to come to Wyoming. Rock Springs and Evanston boasted large Chinese populations until the 1885 Rock Springs Massacre drove many of them out of the territory. In their place, thousands of Europeans and Japanese were drawn to the area for jobs with the railroad, as well as in coal mining, the timber industry, and, at the end of the nineteenth century, the state's burgeoning oil industry. More than a half century later, the 1941 Works Progress Administration's *Guide to Wyoming* made special note of how Wyoming remained tied to the world, describing the state as the "home of many nationalities" and recording the presence of Italians, Greeks, Scandinavians, Basques, Chinese, Hungarians, Czechs, Slovaks, Danes, Englishmen, Irishmen, Estonians, and Japanese.[3]

The US Congress had also connected Wyoming to the world in 1872, when it created the world's first national park at Yellowstone. With extractive industries outlawed there, Yellowstone became Wyoming's first tourist destination, as visitors from across the country and eventually around the world flocked to the park to take in its geysers, waterfalls, canyons, and other scenic spots.

More than human workers and tourists came to Wyoming from throughout the world. Beginning in the 1860s, cowboys drove longhorn cattle from south Texas through the Great Plains to Wyoming's open ranges. These animals, which originated in Mexico, were brought north in the famous long drives after the Civil War on such routes as the Goodnight-Loving Trail, the Chisolm Trail, and the Western Trail. As exotics, they competed with overly hunted native bison, eventually conquering western ranges by the 1880s. During that decade, James Brisbin's *Beef Bonanza: Or, How to Get Rich on the Plains* enticed international investors from Scotland and England to invest in Wyoming cattle and ranches, including the Swan Land and Cattle Company in what became Chugwater. From a handful of cattle in the 1850s, Wyoming cows numbered more than 8 million by 1885. The disastrous winter of 1886–87 checked their growth and brought some control to the livestock industry.[4]

Sheep, too, became symbols of the world coming to Wyoming when they were imported to the area after the Civil War. Generally detested by cattle ranchers competing for the same resources, sheep adapted easily to Wyoming's rangelands and survived well in its harsh winters. By 1886 the state had more than 500,000 sheep; by 1906 the number had grown to more than 4.3 million. Around Sheridan, ranchers imported Rambouillet sheep from France and established trade networks that linked Wyoming to the European markets.[5]

My own historical research has also shown that Scottish and English immigrant ranchers who settled around the small village of Big Horn near Sheridan imported English polo ponies beginning in the 1880s and used those networks to establish an international horse market by the 1890s. During the 1890s' Boer Wars, William and Malcolm Moncreiffe started a firm that eventually purchased more than 50,000 horses from throughout the West, trailed them to Sheridan, and sold them to British cavalry officers who exported them to Africa.[6]

Exotic plants also migrated to Wyoming and the West from around the world. The ubiquitous tumbleweed, a native of Eurasia, probably traveled to Wyoming as an unintended volunteer, as seeds on the backs of livestock. It expanded in such numbers that it became the very symbol of the West. Sugar beets that originated in Prussia were brought to Wyoming and the northern plains in the early twentieth century, with processing plants built in Sheridan, Worland, Lovell, Wheatland, and Torrington. Likewise, hardy winter wheat originated in Russia but was brought to the Great Plains in the early twentieth century and soon spread to Wyoming.[7]

J. E. Stimson contributed to this expanding globalization through his work with the Union Pacific Railroad and especially as Wyoming's official photographer for two world's fairs. As the official publicist for the one major transportation link between the state and the nation, Stimson's work for the Union Pacific (UP) Railroad was important for documenting and promoting Wyoming to the rest of the country. In that capacity, he photographed everything that looked promising for business and always in the best light. His images suggest growth and opportunity, the very thing the railroad needed to sell.

For the St. Louis World's Fair, the Wyoming World's Fair Commission hired Stimson to continue the kind of industrial and tourist promotional work he was doing for the railroad. Cheyenne's *Wyoming Tribune* described the order as the "finest and largest collection of colored photographs ever gotten together illustrative of the scenery and industries of the state." To accomplish this, the photographer scoured every corner of every county of Wyoming, plus Yellowstone National Park, consulting with county commissioners and business leaders to "make views best calculated" to show Wyoming's "varied resources and magnificent scenery."[8]

In St. Louis, Stimson's images of Wyoming were presented to the world in small state exhibits in both the Palace of Agriculture and the Palace of Mines. All forty-seven states and three territories, as well as more than fifty foreign countries, participated in the fair. Judges awarded Stimson three silver medals for his images, suggesting how well-received his photographs were.[9]

The following year, Wyoming shifted its world appeal to Asia by moving Stimson's images to the Lewis and Clark Exposition in Portland, Oregon. Created to commemorate the centennial of the Corps of Discovery's winter at Fort Clatsop, Oregon, the expo also opened American trade to Asia. In fact, the official but seldom-used name for the exhibit was the "Lewis and Clark Centennial and American Pacific Exposition and Oriental Fair." Stimson again won prizes for his depictions of mines and machinery, suggesting the appeal of his photographs to would-be customers. As Stimson biographer Mark Junge suggests, as a result of these two fairs, Stimson gained "national and international recognition."[10]

When Stimson then embarked on his 1906 "Journey across the Continent," he was an internationally known photographer and continued to take pictures of the many farms and industries along the UP line that might appeal to the world. According to his catalog of images, the photographer began his journey in Omaha, snapping photographs of the gigantic fill on the Lane Cutoff as well as ones showing Buffalo Bill Cody and his internationally famous "Wild West."[11] He then made images across Nebraska, showing its many available resources to the world, including its wheat fields, cattle, sugar beet fields, and views of Cody's home near North Platte, the famous Scout's Rest Ranch. Stimson moved on to Cheyenne, capturing images of the depot and state capitol before stopping at Red Buttes. He stopped again in Laramie, photographing the University of Wyoming, the Laramie Depot, and the Carnegie Library. The rest of Wyoming included coal chutes at Wamsutter, the buttes around Green River, and the UP's Overland Limited train crossing the Hams Fork River at Granger. Evanston's *Wyoming Press* noted that Stimson joined a Southern Pacific photographer at that town to take pictures and record information for a joint publication to be issued by the Union Pacific, Oregon Short Line, and Southern Pacific. In Utah, Stimson continued to photograph his train at Echo Canon and then made views of Ogden and Salt Lake City, including ones of the Mormon Temple and Brigham Young's home. Further west, the photographer captured the copper smelter at Garfield, bathers at Saltair resort, pelicans on Bird Island, and the newly minted Lucin Cutoff across the Great Salt Lake. In

Nevada, he shot a reclamation dam on the Truckee River. Crossing into California, Stimson made scenic views of the Sierras, fruit orchards near Colfax, and historic sites in Sacramento, including Sutter's Fort and the California state capitol. All told, Stimson made more than 250 photographs on this trip.[12]

During the rest of his life, Stimson continued to photograph Wyoming to sell its products around the world and to entice people to move there to live. He made images for the Wyoming Department of Immigration and other state agencies showing the state's farms and ranches, mines, and especially its scenic wonders, including Yellowstone and Grand Teton National Parks.

Since Stimson's death in 1952, Wyoming has continued to work to integrate its economy into the national and international markets. The state exports coal, uranium, natural gas, trona, petroleum, beef, and farm products worldwide. Students from every corner of the world come to study at the University of Wyoming in Laramie. Tourists from all over the globe continue to visit the state's national parks, historic landmarks, and other scenic areas. State business associations, like the Wyoming Beef Council and the Wyoming International Trade Assistance Program, help small companies better position themselves in the global market. And yes, Wyoming ranchers bring alpacas to the state to live aside the more traditional exotic imports: cattle and sheep.

As I looked closer at my rephotography, I found more examples of the connection between Wyoming and the world. A comparison of Stimson's 1909 view of the Rawlins Depot (25) with both my 1987 rephotograph and my 2007 repeat image shows the ever increasing nationalization and, later, globalization of commerce. A close look at the left of the depot in Stimson's image shows a series of tracks with a single locomotive and tender idling by the station, as well as a string of boxcars and another group of tanker cars nearby. In short, Stimson's image shows a train of local origin: cars that would be filled in town and then connected to passing trains to take to national markets.

A similar look at the tracks in my 1987 rephotograph shows not local cars but instead flatbed cars loaded with semi-trailers that could be unloaded, connected to trucks, and moved across the country on interstate highways. The run-down depot and the seedy downtown hint at the growing importance of the highway and the automobile, as well as the diminished significance of the local station, in the national market.

Fast-forward another two decades, and another long train of flatbed cars carrying inter-modal containers shows the growing influence of the world economy on Rawlins and Wyoming more broadly. Inter-modals, a type of standardized shipping container that can be moved from ship to rail to truck without ever being unloaded, suggest efficiency and globalization. Bearing the name "K-Line," these compartments could have been stuffed with flat-screen televisions, diapers, or almost anything else. Packed in Asia, they moved across the Pacific Rim and could have been en route to anyplace in the United States. Their standardized size and shape suggest an ever increasing globalized, homogenized world.

This increasingly globalized world can also be observed in the many dead pine trees in my rephotographs along the Cody Road and in Yellowstone (95–98). Fueled by global warming, bark beetles have expanded their habitat into mountains traditionally too cold for their survival and infested millions of acres of Wyoming's pine trees. Foresters estimate that more than 3 million acres of the state's pine forests have been ravaged by the beetles and that the worst may finally be over, simply because there's little left to eat in their wake. This constitutes just one more example of how the world has come to Wyoming.[13]

All this talk about globalization fits into much of the thinking about the history of Wyoming and the American West over the last 120 years. Although historian Frederick Jackson Turner famously looked inward to examine the effects of the frontier in shaping the American character, Walter Prescott Webb complicated the story by taking more of a global approach to the relationship between what he called "the great frontier" and global history. Much like Turner, Webb saw the opportunity for "free" land as the crucible for Western civilization and worried that the 500-year history of that expansion ever westward was coming to an end.[14]

The New Western History that emerged in the 1980s brushed aside such sweeping generalizations but kept a focus on the relationship between the local and the global in the West. Removing the concept of the frontier as too ethnocentric, New Western History instead followed what historian Patricia Limerick defined as the four Cs: the conquest of the West by Euro-Americans and the legacy of that conquest, the convergence of many peoples in the West, the continuity of western history into the twentieth century, and the complexity of the discipline beyond Turner's simplistic frontier dichotomy. Embedded in this new way of thinking were comparative histories that examined how issues in the West, such as water development, mining, and politics, compared with those in similar places around the world.[15]

Still another line of thinking about the West and the world was promulgated by historian William G. Robbins in his examination of what has come to be called "World Systems Theory." Probably best explained by sociologist Immanuel Wallerstein, World Systems Theory looked beyond the political nation-state to examine the relationships between core areas with higher skills and capital-intensive production and periphery areas that relied on low-skill, labor-intensive production and the extraction of raw materials. Robbins built on these ideas to frame his study of the West as focusing on capitalism as a worldview and the history of the region as centered on neither the frontier nor the 4 Cs. Denying the exceptionalism of Turner, Webb, or New Western History, Robbins argued that the basic western narrative included (1) the penetration of market forces, (2) the subjugation and relocation of native peoples, (3) resettlement of their lands, and (4) integration of those lands into national and international markets.[16]

As I think back over Wyoming history, much of what Robbins argues makes a lot of sense to me. Wyoming has always been connected to global forces. Stimson's work for the Union Pacific Railroad integrated the state into the national market, and his presentation of promotional images at the St. Louis and Portland fairs brought photos of Wyoming to international markets as well. His 1906 Journey across the Continent furthered these endeavors, as his photographs commodified western landscapes and resources and helped incorporate them into the image of the West as an extractive periphery, or what writer Bernard DeVoto famously called the "plundered province." Even his seemingly benign image of Castle Dome at Red Buttes suggested a wild and scenic nature, not unlike Yellowstone, that tourists could visit and explore, like the climber clinging to the side of the rock formation.[17]

When I visited that same spot eighty years later and found it eerily similar to Stimson's landscape, I tended to think of the area as an isolated remnant of the frontier, forgetting that the same railroad that brought Stimson to this spot also linked it to the national market. But when Lauren and I returned in 2007 and found the Windy Ridge Alpaca Ranch had set up shop at Red Buttes, my immediate reaction was that the forces of globalization had recently transformed this little nook of Wyoming into a repository of exotic species. But after further thought about places such as the Rawlins Depot and the beetle-infested forests, I realized that this was not a unique situation in the history of the state but instead a variation on the constant theme of Wyoming and the world. From beaver pelts to global migrations to the importation and exportation of cattle, sheep, and polo ponies to the commodification of the state in promotional photographs for a national railroad or an international fair, Wyoming has always sought out the world, and the world has always sought out Wyoming.

Notes

1. http://www.bartleby.com/142/183.html [acccessed July 18, 2012].

2. A good western history textbook, such as Robert V. Hine and John Mack Faragher, *The American West: A New Interpretive History* (Lamar Series in Western History) (New Haven: Yale University Press, 2000) and Richard White, *"It's Your Misfortune and None of My Own": A New History of the American West* (Norman: University of Oklahoma Press, 1993), is a good starting point for all these topics. For Wyoming specifically, the standard remains T.A. Larson, *History of Wyoming*, 2nd ed., rev. (Lincoln: University of Nebraska Press, 1978).

3. Writers' Program of the Work Projects Administration in the State of Wyoming, *Wyoming: A Guide to Its History, Highways, and People* (New York: Oxford University Press, 1941), 123–25; hereafter WPA Guide. See also Gordon Olaf Hendrickson, *Peopling the High Plains: Wyoming's European Heritage* (Cheyenne: Wyoming State Archives and Historical Department, 1978).

4. James S. Brisbin, *The Beef Bonanza: Or, How to Get Rich on the Plains* (Philadelphia: J. P. Lippincott, 1881). The online version can be found at http://archive.org/stream/beefbonanzaorhow00bris#page/n5/mode/2up [accessed July 18, 2012].

5. Larson, *History of Wyoming*.

6. Michael A. Amundson, "These Men Play Real Polo: The History of an Elite Sport in the 'Cowboy' State, 1890–1930," *Montana: The Magazine of Western History* (Spring 2009): 3–22.

7. WPA Guide, 98–108. See also http://www.nass.usda.gov/Statistics_by_State /Wyoming/Publications/Crops/bull-08.pdf [accessed July 18, 2012].

8. "For the St. Louis Fair," *Cheyenne Wyoming Tribune*, June 3, 1906.

9. http://atthefair.homestead.com/States/Wyoming.html [accessed January 26, 2012]; Mark Junge, *J. E. Stimson: Photographer of the West* (Lincoln: University of Nebraska Press, 1985), 9.

10. Ibid.; http://www.oregonencyclopedia.org/entry/view/lewis_clark_exposition /Q3 [accessed January 26, 2012].

11. Buffalo Bill Cody's significance in international promotion is discussed in Louis Warren's excellent biography, *Buffalo Bill's America: William Cody and the Wild West Show* (New York: Knopf, 2005), and Robert W. Rydell and Rob Kroes, *Buffalo Bill in Bologna: The Americanization of the World* (Chicago: University of Chicago Press, 2005).

12. *Evanston Wyoming Press*, July 7, 1906; *Along the U.P. Line: A Listing of the J. E. Stimson Photographs in the Collection of the Wyoming State Museum* (March 1977): 35–40.

13. http://www.esa.org/esablog/ecologist-2/seeing-less-red-bark-beetles-and-global -warming/Q4; http://trib.com/news/state-and-regional/experts-pine-beetles-are-eating -themselves-out-of-wyoming/article_3af28c3d-2bde-5da8-9718-257f586000c8.html [both accessed January 15, 2013].

14. Frederick Jackson Turner, *The Frontier in American History* (New York: Dover, 1996); Walter Prescott Webb and William D. Rowley, *The Great Frontier* (Reno: University of Nevada Press, 2003).

15. Patricia Limerick, Clyde A. Milner, and Charles E. Rankin, eds., *Trails: Toward a New Western History* (Lawrence: University of Kansas Press, 1991).

16. William G. Robbins, *Colony and Empire: The Capitalist Transformation of the American West* (Lawrence: University Press of Kansas, 1994).

17. Bernard DeVoto, "The West: A Plundered Province," *Harper's Magazine* 169 (August 1934): 355-64; William G. Robbins, "The Plundered Province and the Recent Historiography of the American West," *Pacific Historical Review* 55, no. 4 (November 1986): 577–97.

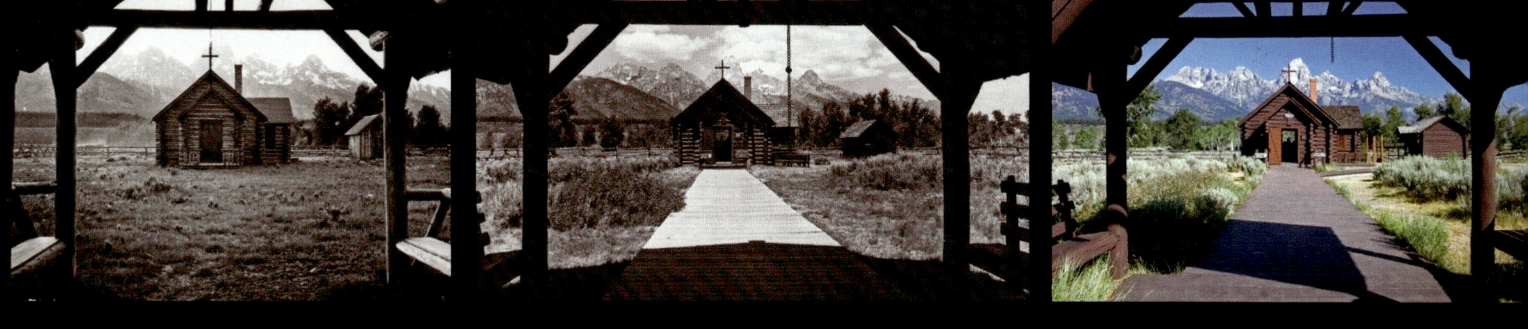

CHAPTER 4

Looking at Sacred and Profane Landscapes

DOI: 10.5876/9781607323051.c004

In his acclaimed book *Under Western Skies*, environmental historian Donald Worster examines the history of the Black Hills of South Dakota through the lens of sacred and profane landscapes. According to Worster, the Lakota Sioux held the Black Hills as sacred, their spiritual center that forever needed to be protected and preserved. In contrast, Worster argues that Euro-Americans saw the Black Hills as profane, an ordinary place where gold mining and other extractive industries could be carried out.[1] Worster's book is instructive as we examine my rephotography of Stimson's photographs because it helps us see how Wyoming's sacred and profane lands have endured over the last century.

It is important to better define what makes a landscape profane or sacred. Profane lands are probably easier to define and identify. In short, profane lands are part of the ordinary or vernacular landscape not protected in any way. In other words, such landscapes are open to the market and its conditions.[2]

Understanding the sacred is more difficult. In his book *Sacred Places*, John F. Sears identifies American sacred lands as those that provide "points of mythic and national unity." That could include anything from national parks like Yellowstone or Yosemite, more mundane places like the Hudson River Valley, or simply cemeteries, hospitals, and parks.[3] Others also make the connection between specific places on the land and the cultures that inhabit them. The International Union for Conservation of Nature, for example, defines sacred lands as "areas of land or water having special spiritual significance to peoples and communities."[4] The Gaia Foundation goes even further, suggesting that a sacred site is a "place in the landscape . . . which is especially revered by a people, culture or cultural group as a focus for spiritual belief and practice and likely religious observance." It suggests that such places must also have one or more of no fewer than nineteen characteristics under such headings as descriptive, spiritual, and functional, and they can be either natural or manmade.[5]

In short, we can think of sacred landscapes not as black-and-white ideas but rather as an entire spectrum of places ranging from national parks and monuments all the way down to historic neighborhoods and individual buildings. Indeed, the Secretary of the Interior's Standards for the Treatment of Historic Properties, including those on the National Register of Historic Places, serves as another definition of sacred sites, advising that its goals "are intended to promote responsible preservation practices that help protect our Nation's irreplaceable cultural resources."[6]

Wyoming has many different types of sacred "protected lands" that Stimson photographed, including nine types of federally managed areas that include national parks, national forests, national monuments, and places later designated as wilderness areas. Two types—state parks and state historic sites—are managed by the State of Wyoming, and another is managed by a county as a county park. Going even further, neighborhoods and individual buildings that have been designated National Historic Landmarks, placed on the National Register of Historic Places, or managed as part of a city's Main Street Program can be seen as smaller parts of the sacred built environment. In contrast, Wyoming's profane lands are all private properties managed by their owners.

Rephotography provides a tool for examining how these different types of lands and buildings have fared over the last century. By taking a good first look at Stimson's original images, we can establish a baseline for studying changes in the natural and built environments, as shown first in my 1980s rephotographs and again in my images from the early 2000s.

When Stimson arrived in Wyoming in 1889 and began shooting scenic landscapes a decade later, the state's only federally recognized sacred landscape was Yellowstone National Park. Yellowstone had been created by an act of the US Congress in 1872 when Wyoming was still a territory. Stimson first visited the park in 1902 and the following year produced a portfolio of views of Yellowstone for sale to the general public. This volume cost $1.50 and featured a view of the Lower Falls of the Yellowstone River on the cover and twenty-four albertypes of the park inside, including the original prints of the image from Grand View (109) used here.[7] Other images reproduced here from 1902 include Brink of Falls (110), Col. Meldrum's Residence (111), Mr. Meldrum's Office (112), and the Silver Gate (113). The following year, Stimson traveled to the park on the newly opened East Road from Cody, Wyoming. He made more than forty images of this route, including Index Mountain at Twilight (93), Scene on Cody Gateway to Y.N.P. (94), Cody Gateway to Y.N.P (95), Sentinel Rock and Shoshone River (96), "The Needle" (97), Hoyt's Peak (98), and Sylvan Lake Panorama (99). Four years later, the photographer returned to the park and produced more views, including exterior and interior views of Old Faithful Inn (100, 101) and views of geysers in the nearby Upper Geyser Basin, including Castle (102), Grotto (103), and Giant (104). He also made exterior and interior photographs of the Lake Hotel (105, 106), plus West Thumb (107) and Dwelle's Inn (108), just west of present-day West Yellowstone, Montana. At the time, this inn served as the transfer point for travelers entering from the west to board Yellowstone National Park coaches. Stimson traveled twice more to photograph the park, in 1910 and again in 1916.

Several of my rephotographs highlight important changes that have occurred in the park. My images from 1988 were taken just as the fires that ravaged the park later that summer and into the fall were getting started. With that in mind, my images show the park clearly thick with trees. The views of Castle, Grotto, and Giant Geysers present this most noticeably. In the images of Old Faithful Inn, the exterior image shows the influence of automobiles on the park, as the ground around the hotel has been transformed into a parking lot. Additional wings on the inn are also present. The interior view depicts the effects of the 1959 earthquake, as a large support beam has been wedged between the fireplace and the roof. At the Lake Hotel, the exterior was in the midst of a remodel in 1988, while the interior shows that updating had already occurred there. At West Thumb, the dock had been removed and the area restored to nature. For Yellowstone Falls, although the view from the brink looks strikingly similar, my rephotograph of Stimson's image from Grand View Point shows the slow growth of pine trees into the view over eighty-six years. Finally, my images near Mammoth Hot Springs of Colonel Meldrum's residence and office illustrate that the park's magistrate still lives in the home, although his office has been moved to another building. The final image of what Stimson called the Silver Gate, near Mammoth, is now a small side road in the area known as the Hoodoos.

Twenty years later, the effects of the 1988 fires are clearly visible in my 2007 views of Castle, Grotto, and Giant Geysers, where entire hillsides in the background have been cleared away. My views along the Cody Road of Hoyt's Peak and Sylvan Lake also show the signs of fire on distant hills. At the same time, my 2008 photograph of the intact exterior of Old Faithful Inn attests to the Herculean efforts to save that structure from the 1988 fires, as well as the extensive 2003 remodeling. The renovations of the interior are also clearly visible, including a new floor, removal of the chimney support pole, and renovation of the fireplace. The effects of the 1988 renovation of the Lake Hotel are also visible, although the interior view was mostly blocked by a National Park Service folding divider that contained a history of the hotel. The remodeling job is also visible in the view of the interior of the magistrate's house.

My 2008 views also show the devastation bark beetles have caused to Wyoming forests, especially within the greater Yellowstone ecosystem. Overall, foresters suggest that beetles have killed more than 3 million acres since the epidemic was first noticed in the early 1990s. In views along the Cody Gateway (95, 96, 97, 98) and in the Jackson Hole area (117), red and brown trees show the beetles' deadly effects. Although the beetles' spread has been linked to global warming—as temperatures rise, the mountains are no longer cold enough to keep the insects out—scientists believe the epidemic may be slowing, as the beetles are "running out of trees in the state to infest." Put another way, the beetles may have literally "eaten themselves out the state."[8]

My 2008 rephotographs also show the changes in the ways tourists visit Yellowstone. My views of West Thumb (107) and Dwelle's Inn (108) are perhaps the most interesting in this regard, as they contribute to the changing nature of visitor travel in the park. When Stimson visited Yellowstone in 1907, the current gateway town of West Yellowstone, Montana, did not exist. Instead, the Union Pacific Railroad came no closer to the western gate than Monida, on the Montana-Idaho border. From there, travelers boarded coaches that brought them to Dwelle's Inn, where around 200 tourists could clean up and spend the night before boarding Yellowstone Park coaches for the trip into the park. Just a couple of years after Stimson made his image, the UP built past the inn to the park's boundary and established West Yellowstone. Dwelle's Inn became a fishing club for a time and was eventually transformed into the private Madison Fork Ranch. Overnight, the key stopover spot was transformed from a place everybody went to a place no one went. Put another way, the railroad transformed Dwelle's Inn from a sacred landscape to a vernacular one. Today, only one small building remains, above the bridge on the left side of the picture.

The West Thumb story is similar. Beginning in 1891, tourists en route from Old Faithful to the Lake Hotel who were tired of the hot, dusty wagon ride could stop at the West Thumb lunch station and purchase a ticket on the *Zillah*, concessionaire E. C. Waters's forty-ton steamship, and then take a smooth, dust-free cruise to a dock near the hotel. When Stimson photographed the spot in 1907, a dock had been built over the geothermal feature in the foreground, and several dozen travelers can be seen crowded onto the boat while a handful rest on the planks and two more walk toward the boat. After automobiles were allowed in the park in 1915 and became the sole means of travel two years later, the *Zillah* became obsolete. Like Dwelle's, this site turned from sacred visitor spot to profane space virtually overnight.

During my 2008 revisit to the site, more than the geothermal feature was revealed by the fluctuating water level. As I started to take the photograph, ten kayakers paddled their way through my rephotograph, and I discovered that visitors could rent two-person sea kayaks nearby for about $100 for a three-hour guided tour. What is so remarkable is how well this represents the transformation in tourism over the last century. In 1907, when Stimson visited, tourism was a group activity in which travelers used public transportation (in this case the *Zillah*) to enjoy Yellowstone. A hundred years later, tourism had become a personal activity—like personal computers and iPods—so travelers now take small water craft on their own lake tour.

The final set of views in the park shows photographs taken near the Lower Falls of the Yellowstone River. Although the views taken in 1902, 1988, and 2008 at the site known as "Brink of Falls" look amazingly similar, the image taken at Grand View in 1902 and then hand-colored around 1915 shows an interesting problem developing. Stimson's original image shows a clean canyon with a clear view of the falls and the river below. But in my 1988 rephotograph, pine trees are growing into the photograph, already blocking the view of the river. Twenty years later, my 2008 photograph shows that those same trees have continued to grow and are not only blocking the river but have encroached on the view of the falls as well.

This finding raises important questions. In national parks, plants and animals are supposed to be protected and allowed to grow naturally. We also know, however, that tourist areas are often scripted—framed, staged, or somehow manipulated—to enhance the tourist experience. In other national parks, trees have been removed to improve vistas. Will the National Park Service perform similar work here? Will rangers march down into the canyon with chain saws and remove these trees to reopen the view from Grand View Point? Or will the trees be allowed to live out their lives, closing off this view for future generations?

My rephotographs of Yellowstone bring several conclusions to mind when considering the park as sacred space. First, it is clear that although *the way* we experience Yellowstone has changed over the last century, we still find the park a sacred place to visit and protect. Second, although the 1988 fires and later bark beetles ravaged parts of the park, other places were spared and even protected. Further, neither the fires nor the beetles destroyed Yellowstone but instead became part of the story, suggesting that our definition of sacred is no doubt changing as we learn to see these factors as part of the natural ecosystem of the West. Finally, Yellowstone remains increasingly popular, and we must be ever more vigilant in protecting it and making sure we do not love it to death.

Stimson's images of neighboring Grand Teton National Park reveal similar issues. Set aside in the nineteenth century as a forest reserve, Grand Teton became a small national park in 1929 when congress protected the Teton Range. After millionaire John D. Rockefeller Jr. secretly purchased ranches along the Snake River east of the park and donated them to the federal government, President Franklin Roosevelt combined that land with Teton National Forest and created Grand Teton National Monument in 1943. In 1950, the 1929 park and the 1943 monument were united into the park we have today.[9]

As all this land wrangling was occurring, J. E. Stimson visited the Jackson Hole area and the Teton Range and used his photographs of the area to publicize it and push for the creation of the enlarged national park. According to biographer Mark Junge, Stimson made his first successful attempts at landscape photography in the area during a visit with Wyoming's first game warden, Albert Nelson, in 1897. Stimson returned two years later and photographed Menor's Ferry across the Snake River near Moose (115). He returned in 1916 and again in 1924, when he photographed the Bar BC dude ranch (116), just downstream from the ferry. He came back to photograph again in 1925, 1927, 1928, and 1930, when he shot the Chapel of Transfiguration (114) just to the west of the ferry. He returned in 1931, 1933, and 1950, the latter date two years before his death at age eighty.[10]

Three of these locations—Menor's Ferry, the Bar BC, and the chapel—are located in what is today the southern end of Grand Teton National Park. Bill Menor homesteaded along the Snake River in 1894 to open his ferry, which became the "most important river crossing in Jackson Hole."[11] In 1923, the cabin served as the meeting place for National Park Service director Stephen Mather and local conservationists who worked to create a plan to preserve Jackson Hole from development. The ferry remained in service until a bridge was constructed nearby in 1927.

Rephotographs of the ferry show its significance. When Stimson visited the site in 1899, he positioned his camera across the river above some brush on the bank. A large tree frames the view. The ferry is just visible on the river, with the many barns of the homestead set against the backdrop of the majestic Tetons. When I visited the site in 1988, a large pine tree blocked much of the view, although the ferry landing can be seen, as well as several outbuildings. Twenty years later, that pine tree dominates the view from this spot, although the reconstructed ferry is visible on the river. In fact, Lauren and I were able to take a ride on the ferry back and forth across the Snake River that day as part of a living history program sponsored by the National Park Service.

The Chapel of Transfiguration, constructed by the Episcopal Church in 1925, is located just west of the ferry. Locals constructed it in the Western Craftsman style to serve nearby dude ranches. Although congress established Grand Teton National Park in 1929, this area remained in private hands until Franklin D. Roosevelt created the national monument in 1943. So when Stimson visited the site in 1930, it was still private. In his image, the photographer framed his view from the entrance just below the bell canopy. Benches are visible at left and right, with the chapel set against the distant mountains. A small storage shed appears to the right.

When I visited the chapel in 1988, the National Park Service controlled the site, although Sunday services were still held. My view shows that small changes had been made to the benches out front and that a wooden plank sidewalk had been constructed from the bell canopy to the chapel. Tourist signs are also visible in front of the chapel, explaining its history. When I went into the building, I found color postcards taken from Stimson's vantage point.

Twenty years later, the chapel remained a popular tourist stop in Grand Teton National Park. The small storage shed had been enlarged or replaced by a larger building, and a paved sidewalk connected it to the main path. A small information sign hangs in the bell canopy.

The Bar BC dude ranch is located on a shelf along the Snake River above Menor's Ferry. It was the second such operation in Jackson Hole and the first designed and created for that purpose. Established in 1912 by Struthers Burt and Dr. Horace Carncross, the ranch became famous when Burt described its operation in his 1924 book, *Diary of a Dude Wrangler*.[12] A few years later, the partners sold the ranch to Rockefeller's Snake River Land Company in exchange for a lifetime lease to run the ranch. Carncross died in 1928, but Burt and his new partner, Irving Corse, operated the guest ranch until 1937 when they had a falling out over its upkeep—Corse believed its authenticity was derived in part from keeping the ranch looking somewhat run-down—and Corse bought Burt out. Although Corse closed the ranch during World War II, he and his heirs kept the Bar BC in operation until 1988, when the property reverted to the National Park Service.[13]

Stimson's 1924 photo of the Bar BC captures it in its glory. Made the same year as the publication of *Diary of a Dude Wrangler,* Stimson's image was captured from across a small pond so the ranch, the distant pine trees, and the glorious Tetons could all be seen reflected in the water. About ten cabins are visible, and two guests can be seen walking away from the camera at right. The cabins exhibit the rustic dude ranch log style.

If Stimson's image marked the Bar BC in all its glory, my two rephotographs depict the dude ranch in its demise. In the 1988 image, taken the year the ranch changed hands from private ownership to the National Park Service (NPS), the pond is gone and the buildings look run-down and in disrepair. Twenty years later the scene remained basically the same, although a close look shows that the NPS has provided some basic maintenance. New red roofs appear on several buildings, and minimal signs of stabilization are present. Note as well the overgrown sagebrush and the slowly dying pine trees.

Menor's Ferry and the Bar BC dude ranch are important historic sites in the struggle to preserve the sacred lands of Jackson Hole through the expansion of Grand Teton National Park. In 1923, Struthers Burt and other local conservationists met with NPS director Stephen Mather at Maude Noble's cabin on the Bill Menor homestead and decided that a plan must be instituted to protect the area's natural features from development. Put another way, they worked to transform the valley from profane to sacred land. Burt later became one of the first landowners to sell out to Rockefeller's Snake River Land Company, which eventually turned over all its valley properties to the federal government for the creation of Teton National Monument in 1943 and the enlarged national park in 1950.

It is fitting that both Menor's Ferry and the Chapel of Transfiguration have been protected as sacred sites within Grand Teton National Park. They are immensely popular tourist stops, with many visitors snapping pictures of the beautiful range from the window of walls in the chapel and others like myself enjoying living history ferry boat rides across the Snake River. That said, the Bar BC also deserves more attention from the National Park Service. The site has received some maintenance and stabilization and the locale has been placed on the National Register of Historic Places, but more needs to be done.

Like Yellowstone and Grand Teton National Parks, Devil's Tower National Monument is a federally protected sacred site in the Black Hills of Wyoming. In fact, it is the nation's first national monument, set aside in 1906 by President Theodore Roosevelt. Similar in protection to a national park, national monuments are historically smaller in size, have geological or archaeological significance, and are created by presidential proclamation rather than an act of congress. An igneous intrusion that rises more than 1,200 feet above adjacent lands, Devil's Tower is not only sacred as a national monument but also serves as an important site for several Plains Indian cultures.

When Stimson visited the monolith in 1903 during his survey across Wyoming for the St. Louis Fair, the tower was not yet a national monument. The photographer made several views, including this one looking north from the banks of the Belle Fourche River (51). Taken in early morning light, Stimson placed the tower at the center of the picture and reflected in the river below. When I visited the tower in 1988, I snapped this image from nearly the same spot in warm evening light. The river had more water and the riparian grasses, protected from grazing for more than eight decades, had luxuriously returned. Twenty years later, I visited during the middle of the day, though the harsher sunlight did not detract from the image. The grasses remain thick and green and the view spectacular.

Yellowstone and Grand Teton National Parks and Devil's Tower National Monument represent the highest ideals of America's sacred landscape. Preserved for their aesthetic beauty, national parks and monuments are places where visitors come to enjoy the country's sacred lands. My rephotographs show that all three have endured well since Stimson's original images were made.

Also managed by the federal government, national forestlands are places where utilitarian, rather than aesthetic, preservation is practiced. Like national monuments, national forests were created by presidential proclamation, beginning with the first just east of Yellowstone National Park in 1891. Unlike national parks and monuments, though, national forests are managed to provide the most good for the most people. Characterized best by their slogan "land of many uses," national forests allow grazing, timber production, hunting, and other forms of recreation and industry not allowed in national parks. Still, all such activities are tightly regulated, so for many people, national forests seem to enjoy a status similar to national parks.

Wyoming is host to six national forests: Ashley, Bighorn, Bridger-Teton, Medicine Bow, Shoshone, and the Caribou-Targhee.

J. E. Stimson made photographs in two of Wyoming's national forests. His 1899 view of the Tetons from Gros Ventre Butte (117) was made east of Kelly in what is now Bridger-Teton National Forest but was then known as the Teton Forest Reserve. His view looks to the west, with the Gros Ventre River snaking through the valley floor and the Tetons rising majestically on the far horizon. The hills to the left are covered with pines, while those on the right are mostly grass. In 1925, just a few miles east of this vantage point, an entire hillside—an estimated 50 million cubic yards of rock—slid down Sheep Mountain, damming the river and creating Lower Slide Lake. Two years later the landslide dam failed and a massive flood washed down the canyon, taking much of the town of Kelly with it. Although my rephotograph of this site in 2008 does not show any of this, it does show a profusion of sagebrush on the foreground hillside and many new pine trees covering the river below. Distant hills also show new trees populated in what had once been meadows.

Stimson's views of the Cody Road to Yellowstone were made in July 1903, the week the road through the nation's first forest reserve opened. Originally called the Yellowstone Park Timber Land Reserve when it was created in 1891, the name was shortened to the Yellowstone Forest Reserve in 1903. Nearly all of Stimson's 1903 images and my 2008 rephotographs are reproduced in my book *Passage to Wonderland*; a select group of three is included here. His view called "Cody Gateway to Y.N.P" shows Sentinel Rock on the right and the silhouetted spires above the North Fork of the Shoshone River to the left (95). To access this vantage point in 2008, I had to climb up the side of a hill about 30 yards and position my camera in a small break along a rocky outcropping. My image shows the remains of a small fire in the foreground, the modern highway to the left, and the effects of bark beetle–damaged trees in the background. The second shot looks back at Sentinel Rock from the roadbed about a half mile further west (96). The newness of the road is evident from the lack of wagon wheel prints in the dirt. My rephotograph shows the enlarged modern road, complete with guardrail, and the reduced number of trees. Stimson's final shot in this forest featured the famous rock formation now known as Chimney Rock but labeled by the photographer as "The Needle" (97). In his view, the Cody Road cuts across the left side of the photograph and Stimson's guide, Fred Chase, is looking up at the rock formation. A hand-colored, four-foot-tall version of this image hangs in the Cheyenne Masonic Hall. In my 2008 view, the Cody Road has been moved down and to the left of the scene, and pine trees fill in that space. Lauren is gazing up at the formation.

Within national forests, the US Congress, following the passage of the 1964 Wilderness Act, set aside fifteen wilderness areas in Wyoming, another type of sacred land managed by the federal government more strictly than national parks. In such places, human activities are limited to non-motorized recreation, scientific research, and other noninvasive activities. The law prohibits logging, mining, mechanized recreation, road building, and other forms of development. Wyoming's wilderness areas include Absaroka-Beartooth, North Absaroka, and Washakie, near Cody; Bridger, near Pinedale; Cloud Peak, west of Sheridan; Encampment River, south of Saratoga; Fitzpatrick and Popo Agie, near Lander; Gros Ventre, Jedediah Smith, Teton, and Winegar Hole, near Jackson; Huston Park and Savage Run, near Centennial; and Platte River, south of Rawlins.

Although none of Wyoming's wilderness areas existed when Stimson was photographing, several of his images of profane lands (discussed later) along the Cody Road, including "Index Mountain at Twilight" (93) and "Scene on Cody Gateway to Y.N.P." (94), contain wilderness areas today. Perhaps the most evident feature of most of these sacred lands in the pairs of images is the *absence* of development in the distant hills. Likewise, Stimson's view of Black Tooth Mountain in the Big Horns (79), which the photographer called Elk Tooth Mountain, is today located in the Cloud Peak Wilderness Area. Interestingly, this photograph was taken from Dome Lake, one of the most picturesque privately held profane lands in the state.

One more type of sacred land under the federal umbrella is the Wind River Indian Reservation. By definition, the reservation is a sovereign piece of land managed by the Eastern Shoshone and Northern Arapahoe tribes under the US Department of the Interior's Bureau of Indian Affairs. Stimson first photographed on the reservation in 1903, when he made images around tribal headquarters at Fort Washakie. At that time, the reservation was larger than it is today because in 1906, a large portion of it was ceded to white settlers who founded the town of Riverton. My sole reservation photograph included here is one Stimson made in the Wind River Canyon (85) in the 1920s, while on an automobile trip. The view looks to the north and shows the tracks of what was then the Chicago, Burlington, and Quincy Railroad (now the Burlington, Northern, and Santa Fe) on the left, the Wind River (known as the Bighorn River off the reservation), and the new state road on the right. My 1988 view shows that, except for the expanded roadbed, the canyon looks essentially the same. Twenty years later, this sacred landscape remained remarkably similar.

As in Stimson's views of national parks and monuments, the sacred lands preserved in national forests, wilderness areas, and on the Wind River Reservation show that, for the most part, they have been well managed by federal and tribal governments since his day. That said, biologists might argue that the presence of roads in all of these federally managed lands has created problems beyond what might be visible at first glance, including too many people, more road kills, the introduction of lead and other pollutants from automobiles, plant destruction, and the entrance of invasive species.[14]

Beyond the federally and tribally preserved sacred lands, Stimson photographed in areas protected by the State of Wyoming today as state parks and historic sites. In 1911 he photographed the fountain at Thermopolis Hot Springs (88). Long a sacred site for the Arapahoe and Shoshone, the hot springs were deeded to Thermopolis in an 1896 treaty for use by the public and protected as Wyoming's first state park the following year. Stimson's image of the fountain shows what appears to be a manmade tepee of stone with a pipe sticking out of it, allowing the area's mineral-laden waters to flow over the formation. In the distance, tourists can be seen near large white tents. My 1987 image shows the effects of seventy-six years of that mineralized water: the formation of a large fountain where water merely trickled down its sides. Both in the foreground and in the distance, the improved groundskeeping is evident. My 2008 view is nearly identical, save for the growth of the distant trees.

Stimson's 1908 shot at Granite Springs Reservoir (11) and his 1910 view at Vedauwoo (12) are of protected places in what is now Curt Gowdy State Park between Cheyenne and Laramie. The State of Wyoming created the park in 1971 through a special lease agreement with the City of Cheyenne and the Boy Scouts and named it after the famous sportscaster and Wyoming native Curt Gowdy. The picturesque view at Granite Spring Reservoir shows a small party aboard a wooden boat named the *Lenore*. A forest surrounds the lake, with prominent rocks visible on the shore and in the background. My 1987 view, sans the boat, shows the same rocks and water, along what is a small arm of the reservoir near its inlet. Note the denser forest in the background. The 2007 view looks much the same, although the water level is a little higher. Surprisingly, little bark beetle damage is present. Also not seen in the most recent picture is the fine trail that enabled me to reach this site much more easily.

The Stimson view of Vedauwoo is actually not in the rock formation typically known as the Vedauwoo Glen but instead is north across Happy Jack Road, very near Hynds Lodge. In the original image, the trees in the foreground nicely frame the large rock formation. My 1987 view shows that the prairie in the foreground was used as the overflow parking lot for Hynds Lodge. This facility, constructed in 1922 by a prominent Cheyenne businessman as a recreational getaway for civic and religious groups, is just behind the rock formation to the right. The trees are taller, though the formation is still clearly visible. By 2007 the parking lot had been abandoned, and the foreground area was slowly returning to natural prairie. The road to the lodge was paved, and the trees almost blocked the view of the formation.

In addition to preserving sacred land as state parks, Wyoming also preserves South Pass City as a state historic park. Founded in 1867 as a gold mining boomtown, South Pass City soon boasted more than 1,000 residents. After Wyoming Territory was created in 1869 and women's suffrage had become law, Esther Hobart Morris of South Pass City was appointed the first woman to hold political office in the United States. Although the boom soon passed and the town became nearly empty, South Pass City hung on as a shadow of its former self for nearly a century until the entire town was purchased by the Wyoming 75th Anniversary Commission as a historic site in 1966. Since that time, buildings have been stabilized, and nearly the entire town serves as a walk-through museum of Wyoming history.[15]

When Stimson visited the area as part of his 1903 tour of the state, the town had seen better days. His view (81) shows no one in the streets, no clothes on the line, no one at work or play in the entire town. The place looks abandoned. In contrast, although only a couple of people can be seen in my 1987 view, the dozen or so cars present suggest that more people are around. What is most striking, of course, are the buildings. Seventeen of the existing twenty-three buildings have been restored, almost to the appearance shown in Stimson's image. In 2007, except for the removal of the parking lot, South Pass City appeared about the same.

Another clear sign that points to South Pass City's importance as a sacred space is the restoration of the Carissa Gold Mine above the town. As the first hard-rock mine in Wyoming, the Carissa owns a special place in the state's history. Opened in 1867, a year before Wyoming became a territory, the gold mine had a short boom until it closed in the 1870s. An infusion of capital reopened it in the early 1900s, and it had another wave of activity before closing for good in 1949. Over its lifetime, between 50,000 and 180,000 ounces of gold were extracted from the mine. The site sat abandoned for almost sixty years until the State of Wyoming purchased the property, mineral rights, buildings, and more than 200 acres of land for just over $300,000 in hopes of restoring the property and providing mine tours for visitors.[16]

Stimson's 1903 panorama of the Carissa (82) shows it if not hard at work, at least ready for work. The buildings are neat and organized, wood is stacked and ready, several people are posing outside one of the buildings, and a faint trace of smoke is coming out of one of the stacks. In contrast, my 2008 image shows the remains of a long-abandoned mine. Most of the original smelter buildings are gone, replaced by a larger operating plant on the right. It appears that only two structures remain from Stimson's image.

Like the federally controlled sacred lands, the state parks and historic areas also appear well managed and protected. South Pass City has been stabilized and is being rehabilitated. Hot Springs and Curt Gowdy State Parks are beautiful spaces with multiple recreational opportunities.

Another type of protected sacred land is Ayres Natural Bridge, a Converse County park near Douglas. Composed of red sandstone, the bridge is more than 30 feet high and 90 feet long and spans La Prele Creek. It is known as Ayres Natural Bridge for early resident Alva Ayres, who once owned the property. In 1923 his family donated the land to Converse County for a public park.

When Stimson photographed the natural bridge in 1903 (45), it was in private hands. He made several views that year, but this two-plate "panoramic view" is the most visually interesting, a classic Stimson portrait of a natural wonder. He framed the bridge to fill both of his plates while using the rock formation to do the same for his guide's horses and buggy. Although I rephotographed other views of the bridge in 1987, I did not take a panorama. My 2008 view, though, shows basically the same scene as Stimson's but with several children playing in the stream, suggesting that this sacred site is also used and well maintained.

Sacred landscapes can also include neighborhoods and individual buildings with such important historic significance that they are recognized as National Historic Landmarks, placed on the National Register of Historic Places, or included in Main Street Programs. Inclusion on the list of National Historic Landmarks signifies the highest achievement. Beginning in 1960, the secretary of the interior deemed these sites areas of national significance, places where people of national significance resided, or icons of ideas that shaped the nation. The National Register of Historic Places includes local sites self-nominated to be on the official list of the nation's historic places worthy of preservation. Created after the passage of the National Historic Preservation Act in 1966, the register serves as a national program to identify and protect the country's cultural heritage. Although inclusion on the list does not guarantee historic protection, it does suggest the significance of the property in local, state, and national contexts. Finally, Main Street Programs, part of an innovative approach that combines historic preservation with economic development, have revitalized downtowns and neighborhood business districts across Wyoming. Certified programs exist in Buffalo, Dubois, Evanston, Green River, Laramie, Rawlins, Rock Springs, and Sheridan. The Wyoming Main Street Program also recognizes affiliates in Douglas, Gillette, Glenrock, Guernsey, Kemmerer, Pinedale, and Torrington. Put another way, National Historic Landmarks, the National Register, and Main Street Programs further recognize America's sacred built environment.[17]

In Wyoming, the list of designated National Historic Landmarks found in Stimson images in this book is too long to allow much detail here, but it includes Green River's Expedition Island (28), where John Wesley Powell began his explorations of the Colorado River; Old Faithful Inn (100, 101); the J. C. Penney Historic District in Kemmerer (36); the Sheridan Inn (56, 57); the Swan Land and Cattle Company headquarters in Chugwater (38); and the Wyoming state capitol (1, 2, 3) and Union Pacific Depot in Cheyenne (1, 2). For details on the history of each of these landmarks, as well as an analysis of Stimson's photograph and my rephotographs, please see each individual photo and caption in part III.

The list of Stimson photographs that contain buildings and neighborhoods on the National Register is even longer and often coincides with sites in Main Street Programs for the cities and affiliates listed above. Going alphabetically by county, the list includes for Albany County Old Main (17), on the University of Wyoming campus in Laramie. Carbon County designees include the downtown Rawlins Historic District (23), the Rawlins Depot (25), the historic state penitentiary in Rawlins (24), the Grand Encampment smelter (22), and the Wolf Hotel in Saratoga (21). On the National Register in Crook County are the Devil's Tower entrance road (51), the Sundance school, and the Sundance State Bank (both 49). Fremont County boasts the Atlantic City Mercantile (83), the Lander historic district (84), and South Pass City (81, 82). Fort Laramie (40, 41) highlights Goshen County, and the Thermopolis downtown historic district is Hot Springs County's entry on the National Register (86, 87). Johnson County includes the Buffalo downtown historic district and its county courthouse (53, 54).

Laramie County has the most sites of any county in Wyoming, with Cheyenne alone boasting the Atlas Theater (8), the Capitol North District (3), the Downtown Cheyenne Historic District (5, 6), the Masonic Temple (7), the Nagle-Warren House in the Rainsford District (4), St. Marks Church, and the Union Pacific Depot (both visible in 2). Lincoln County had the Kemmerer Hotel, which has been torn down (36). Park County boasts the downtown Cody historic district (91), the Irma Hotel in Cody (92), and the Meeteetse National Bank (90).

Platte County highlights the Swan Land and Cattle Company in Chugwater (38). Sheridan County has a long list that includes Fort Mackenzie (59), the Bradford Brinton Memorial in Big Horn (72), the Sheridan Inn (56, 57), and Sheridan's Main Street (58). For Sweetwater County, Rock Springs boasts its city hall, the downtown Rock Springs Historic District, the First National Bank building, the Elks Lodge, and Our Lady of Sorrows Catholic Church (most of which are visible in 27); Green River includes Expedition Island (28), its Downtown Historic District (30), and the Sweet Water Brewery (29). Teton County boasts the Bar BC Ranch (118), Menor's Ferry (115), and the Chapel of Transfiguration (114). Uinta County highlights several Evanston properties, including the Downtown Historic District (32) and the Union Pacific Depot (33). Weston County includes several Newcastle sites: the commercial district, post office, and county courthouse (48). Finally, in Yellowstone National Park the list includes Fort Yellowstone at Mammoth and the Mammoth Hot Springs district (111, 112), the Yellowstone Grand Loop Road (113), the Old Faithful Inn Historic District (100, 101), and the Lake Hotel (105, 106).

Although such an extensive list—about 100 of the 117 photo sites included in this book—suggests that Wyoming has done an excellent job of preserving its sacred landscapes, it is not quite that simple. Obviously, most of the largest landholdings, the national parks and national forests, are federally managed. Less obvious are issues brought to light by this rephotography project. First is the simple fact that J. E. Stimson tended to photograph the "best and the brightest" places and structures Wyoming had to offer so he could sell the state for the Union Pacific Railroad, the two world's fairs, and other state bureaus. Such places were often well constructed and well loved and were therefore the first preserved landmarks. So the list is skewed in that way. Further, the rephotography process itself is at fault because, for the most part, I could only find and rephotograph places and structures that were fairly easily identifiable. In other words, those sacred places—such as the historic Canyon Hotel in Yellowstone—that Stimson photographed but I could not rephotograph remain separate from this list.

It is now time to turn to those profane spaces that have received no special government recognition. Cultural geographers also refer to such places as the everyday or "vernacular" landscape. That said, although such places are not officially recognized for their special features, such lands have histories and often contain unique characteristics. What is most telling about them, however, is that they are all private lands.

The most unusual profane lands documented by Stimson have to be at Dome Lake, west of Sheridan. Surrounded by Bighorn National Forest, the 1,040-acre Dome Lake Club got its start when railroad officials of the line that was building through Sheridan purchased the lands from the government in 1895, two years before the national forest was established. For the past 109 years, the club has maintained its property, including three lakes, as a private fishing resort. Not surprising given his railroad connections, Stimson visited Dome Lake several times during his photography career, during which he took his earliest extant scenic views in

1899 and others a decade later. In these images, which I rephotographed, Stimson made a "building portrait" of the clubhouse (73), a group portrait of visitors lined up on the porch of the same building (74), one looking off the porch down toward Dome Lake (75), another looking back to the clubhouse from the west (77), a view of another large log building owned by George Holdredge (general manager of the Omaha office of the Burlington and Missouri Railroad) (76), one shot from across the lake looking back to the cottages (78), and a photograph of three men fishing below the spillway of Dome Lake Reservoir (80). In two of these views, the effects of a recent forest fire are evident. Nevertheless, all of Stimson's photographs portray spectacular scenery and cabins that are rustic and certainly typical of the organic "parkitecture" style so famous in national parks.

When I visited Dome Lake in 1988, it was an exclusive and elusive place. At that time, a caretaker lived and worked year-round at Dome Lake and stayed in contact with Sheridan through mail and a short-wave radio. To reach the resort, I asked a friend I had met at the Sheridan KOA who had a four-wheel-drive truck to drive me and my camera to Big Horn, then up the Red Grade Road into the Big Horns, past the historic Spear O'Wigwam and Folly Dude Ranches to the locked gate of the Dome Lake Club, where I was told the caretaker would meet me. Finding no one at this spot, we climbed over the fence and hiked the three miles to the lake, where we met the current owner of the clubhouse, Timothy Travis, and several other club members. I learned that several of the members lived in Denver and flew private planes to Sheridan, then flew a helicopter up to the lake. We were treated to a gourmet lunch provided by their guest chef and beverages cooled by ice hand-cut from the lake and stored in an icehouse.

In rephotographing Stimson's views of Dome Lake, I found a profane landscape that very much typified the sacred landscapes of a national park or national forest. The lake was surrounded by tall trees, and the cabins looked basically the same as they had seventy or eighty years earlier. In fact, it all looked better than Stimson's images because everything had recovered so well after the fire visible in his views. But there had been absolutely no federal, state, or local protection of the land, the forest, the lake, or the buildings. How did this happen? Clearly, the Dome Lake Club's exclusiveness meant it had major private funding to protect these profane lands in a sacred manner. Indeed, everyone I talked to at Dome Lake described their trips to the lake as profound, sacred experiences.

Revisiting Dome Lake in 2008 was easier. I contacted Timothy Travis and made arrangements to meet him at the clubhouse. Lauren and I drove our Subaru Forester from Sheridan to the lake. Travis fed us a wonderful lunch, and we recounted our memories of meeting each other twenty years earlier. We then duplicated the views of the clubhouse, now the Travis Cabin, including Stimson's view of the guests lined up on the porch, with Travis appearing in both my 1988 and 2008 photographs. After that, I rephotographed the view down to the lake, learning that the club had clear-cut a path through the forest to provide a better view of the lake. While rephotographing the Holdredge Cabin, now surrounded by tall trees, we met the current owners who visited with us and offered their jeep for us to take to photograph the spillway into Dome Lake Reservoir. That view again showed the forest's magnificent recovery. All in all, my second visit to Dome Lake reaffirmed my belief that this private profane space was indeed a special and sacred place as well.

Another profane landscape seemingly untouched is that of the Red Butte, a lone red-rock formation in Weston County north of Newcastle. Stimson photographed what he called this "noted landmark" during his 1903 traverse of the state. In his view (52), the butte rises above a treeless meadow, its grasses clipped short from grazing. My 2008 image shows a scene strikingly similar, except for the presence of a few new trees that have popped up in the meadow.

No other profane space I rephotographed could match the preservation I observed at these two places. In fact, at the two other scenic lands not under some type of government protection, private development was beginning to chip away at the landscape's integrity. At another called Red Buttes, south of Laramie, what had been simply "Red Buttes country" in Stimson's images was now part of a real estate development known as "the Buttes." Although most of Stimson's images included here do not show the typical trophy homes, they do show subtle but important changes that have occurred.

To photograph Red Buttes, Stimson would have accessed all of his vantage points from the nearby tracks of the Union Pacific during his 1906 Journey across the Continent. His first view, "Scene in the Red Buttes Country" (13), shows a man standing amid red-rock formations with one large tree growing from one of the red rocks. In a view from a slightly different angle, "the Beehive Rocks" (14), the photographer has posed a railroad conductor in the middle of the view to give a sense of scale. In the Castle Dome view (15), that man is now perched aside another large rock. Finally, the Sphinx Rock (16) shows another, larger formation's eroded shapes.

When I visited the areas in 1987, I was dumbstruck at how little had changed in any of the scenes over the eighty-one years since Stimson made his photographs. The area was reached by a small country road and then a short hike to the rock formations. The very same tree shows up in several of the views, seemingly unchanged yet still alive after more than eight decades. Vegetation was noticeably sparser, no doubt because of the grazing of cattle. The only other visible difference was a small piece of split rail fence.

Two decades later, dramatic changes had taken place. To get to the area, I had to drive through the Buttes subdivision, then park my car at a fence and walk over to the rocks. As my rephotographs show, although no homes are visible in any of the images, split rail fence has been added through most of the scenes. This has subdivided the space into private lots and fenced out the cattle, allowing the native grass to re-develop. Although the Sphinx Rock looks essentially the same, the Castle Dome is now part of the Windy Ridge Alpaca Ranch. My rephotograph shows the impact of the imported animals on the environment and the relationship between Wyoming and the world.

A similar development of profane landscape can be found in Stimson's images of the Cody Road to Yellowstone taken west of Buffalo Bill State Park but east of Shoshone National Forest. When he captured his "Scene on the Cody Gateway" (94) in 1903, Stimson photographed the view looking north from the road across a prairie toward the trees along the North Fork of the Shoshone River. Beyond that, Jim Mountain rises from badlands into rugged, snowy peaks in the distance.

In my 2007 rephotograph, the scene's basic landscape seems practically unchanged. Looking north toward Jim Mountain, irrigated ranchlands spread north to a line of cottonwoods along the North Fork. Beyond the river, the same badlands are there, with similar vegetation patterns leading up to the same silhouette of Jim Mountain against a blue summer sky. Most of the background, including the mountain, is now within the North Absaroka Wilderness Area, an area of strict environmental protection where no machines are allowed.

But the visible differences in this pair are in the foreground. The barbwire fence running from left to right hints at the modern closed range, while the straight dirt road and my Subaru Forester offer hints of automobile tourism and the global marketplace. Most telling, of course, is the large white sign to the right (just in front of an old billboard framework) advertising a local realty company that is subdividing the ranch into smaller New West ranchettes. A Google search shows individual parcels of "raw land" selling for $850,000 and houses for more than $2 million.

Like so many beautiful places in the American West, the Red Buttes and Cody Road are no longer scenic profane lands but ones that have been commodified into parcels for "amenity migrants" seeking to own a beautiful piece of property in a unique part of the world. Globalization has transformed many parts of the West from local working lands to real estate developments selling viewscapes to newcomers importing their wealth into traditional economies.

Just as the built environment can be protected as sacred space, it can also be part of the profane or vernacular landscape. Although we have seen how many of Wyoming's historic buildings have been preserved as National Historic Landmarks and as entries on the National Register of Historic Places, rephotography also shows that many profane places in Wyoming's towns and cities remain but are not protected. As with my earlier discussion of the sacred built environment, the examples are too numerous to allow much detail here, but more will be said about them in their individual captions (see part III). Nevertheless, a few examples will show what I mean.

One of the places to look for the unprotected profane built environment is in a comparison of Stimson's 1903 image of Diamondville (34) with my 1987 and 2007 views. There are no National Register of Historic Places entries in this view, yet look at how many objects remain from the original view. The same can be said in comparing the cityscapes in the images of Sundance (49), Hartville (42), Wheatland (39), Worland (89), Douglas (43), and, if viewed closely, Cokeville (37).

Another set of comparison images of profane landscapes involves Wyoming's historic mining areas. If South Pass City and the Carissa Mine can be marked and preserved, then why not the sites of Hecla (10, 11), Cambria (50), Dietz (60, 61), and Kleenburn (62)? Each was once a bustling outpost of American capitalism; the last three were small communities of several hundred people. Of these, Cambria is the most interesting because its location, now mostly hidden by tremendous regrowth of forest, makes it appear to be part of the sacred lands of the nearby national forest, even though the town's site remains in private hands.

Finally, individual buildings and ranches in the profane landscape also need to be considered alongside the Bradford Brinton Memorial and the Nagle-Warren House. Certainly, the Hardin Ranch (63–70), an amazing symbol of both the modern and postmodern Wests, deserves recognition on the National Register of Historic Places, if not named a National Historic Landmark. The same can be said of the Forbes Ranch (71), another spectacular historic ranch in Sheridan County. Laramie's James Mathison residence (20) deserves recognition because as a small, single-family residence, it is the very *essence* of the profane built environment.

The concepts of the sacred and the profane provide useful introductions to analyzing Stimson's original photographs and my two sets of rephotographs. We can see how the sacred landscapes of national parks, monuments, forests, wilderness areas, Indian reservations, state parks, state historic sites, county parks, National Historic Landmarks, and places on the National Register of Historic Places have all contributed to preserving so much of Wyoming's history and culture.

At the same time, the profane landscapes show how private wealth can preserve places and how other unprotected spaces are threatened by development that will change their character forever. Finally, by comparing other rephotographic couplings of vernacular landscapes, we can clearly see that many historic areas remain and deserve government intervention to help preserve them as well.

Notes

1. Donald Worster, *Under Western Skies: Nature and History in the American West* (New York: Oxford University Press, 1994), 106–53.

2. John Brinckerhoff Jackson, *Discovering the Vernacular Landscape* (New Haven: Yale University Press, 1986), 27–33.

3. John F. Sears, *Sacred Places: American Tourist Attractions in the Nineteenth Century* (New York: Oxford University Press, 1989), 7.

4. http://www.sacredland.org/home/resources/tools-for-action/protection-strategies -for-sacred-sites/what-is-a-sacred-site/ [accessed August 1, 2012].

5. http://www.sacredland.org/media/Sacred-Sites-an-Overview.pdf [accessed August 1, 2012].

6. http://www.nps.gov/hps/tps/standguide/overview/choose_treat.htm [accessed August 1, 2012].

7. J. E. Stimson, *Yellowstone Park* (Brooklyn: Albertype, 1903); *Cheyenne Daily Leader*, August 21, 1903.

8. http://www.esa.org/esablog/ecologist-2/seeing-less-red-bark-beetles-and-global -warming/Q5; http://trib.com/news/state-and-regional/experts-pine-beetles-are-eating

-themselves-out-of-wyoming/article_3af28c3d-2bde-5da8-9718-257f586000c8.html [both accessed January 15, 2013].

9. Robert W. Righter, *Crucible for Conservation: The Creation of Grand Teton National Park* (Boulder: Colorado Associated University Press, 1983).

10. Junge, *Stimson*, 6. The dates of Stimson's visits to the Jackson Hole area are derived from *Along the U.P. Line*.

11. John Daugherty et al., *A Place Called Jackson Hole: A Historic Resource Study of Grand Teton National Park* (Moose, WY: Grand Teton National Park, 1999), 187.

12. Struthers Burt, *The Diary of a Dude Wrangler* (New York: Charles Scribner's Sons, 1924).

13. Daugherty et al., *A Place Called Jackson Hole,* 220–53.

14. Reed Noss, "The Ecological Effect of Road," at http://www.eco-action.org/dt/roads.html [accessed March 3, 2014].

15. http://wyoparks.state.wy.us/Site/SiteInfo.aspx?siteID=30 [accessed March 2, 2014].

16. Kelsey Dayton, "Official: Carissa Mine a Testimony to Wyoming's Mineral Heritage," *Casper Star Tribune*, September 3, 2011.

17. http://www.nps.gov/hps/tps/standguide/; http://www.wyomingbusiness.org/program/about-wyoming-main-street/3425 [both accessed August 12, 2012].

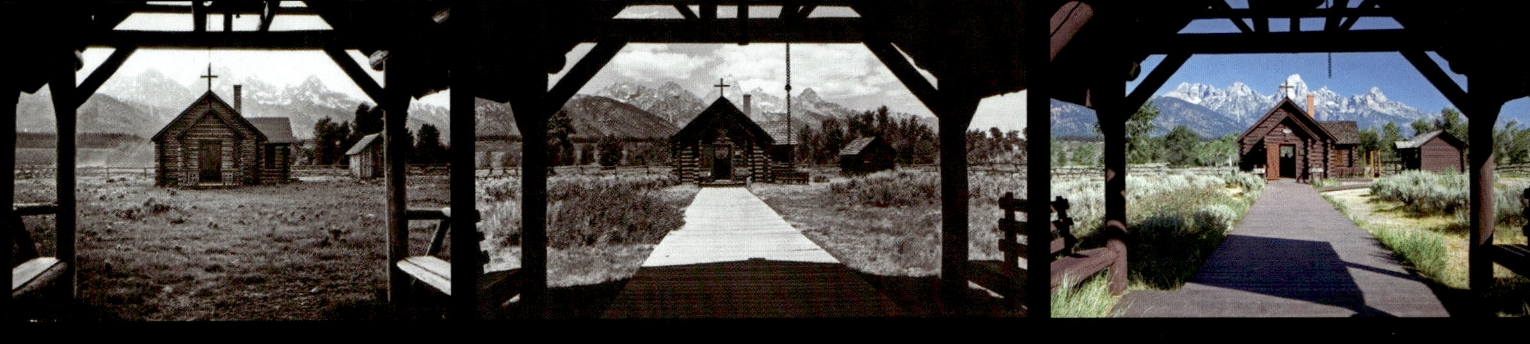

CHAPTER 5

The Modern and Postmodern in Wyoming?

DOI: 10.5876/9781607323051.c005

While waiting for dinner in a Perkins restaurant in Sheridan during our first summer of rephotography in 2007, Lauren and I did what we often do at dinner: scan local real estate magazines. I was living in a small townhouse in Flagstaff, and it was fun to investigate the real estate scene in other places and dream about owning a big house someday. As I sat looking through the listings, one image struck me. It depicted a large home in nearby Ranchester known as the Old Stone Inn bed and breakfast. I was certain that it looked like a Stimson image I had seen and copied for possible rephotography. We jotted down the address and phone number, then called and got directions. The next day, as we drove south out of Ranchester, we discovered that the Old Stone Inn was in fact the Samuel Howes Hardin ranch house, an Arts and Crafts masterpiece Stimson biographer Mark Junge described as "more opulent than many others in the West."[1] From the outside it looked to be in great condition. The owners let us in and showed us how they had restored the interior, using Stimson prints they had found at the Wyoming State Archives in Cheyenne. As we walked around the beautiful home, we found many Stimson images—even ones I had not seen—framed and hanging on the walls in the appropriate room pictured in the photograph.

That day I spent about five hours rephotographing all eight of Stimson's views, including two exterior panoramas and one very rare panorama of the interior's main room. On one level, the photographs and rephotographs present an unusual, detailed, and intimate portrait of one place. On another, they provide a portal to dig deeper into the role of photography as both a recorder and a shaper of history, as well as into the concepts of modernity and postmodernism.

First, though, let me begin with a little history about Samuel Howes Hardin and his ranch. According to the period 1908 book *Progressive Men of the State of Wyoming*, Hardin was born in Massachusetts in 1846 and raised in Chicago and Peru, Illinois, where his father ran a lumber and grain business. As a young man, Hardin worked in real estate and banking until 1878, when he decided to capitalize on the western cattle business by purchasing cows in Texas and driving them north. Two years later he founded the firm Hardin, Campbell, and Co., and located its range on the Tongue River in far northern Wyoming near the Montana line, in the former hunting lands of several Native American tribes. Over the next few decades, he built up his ranch in Wyoming and ran cattle on almost 400,000 acres of land he leased from the Crow Reservation across the state line in Montana. A colleague named the small town of Hardin, Montana, for him. He prospered as a rancher and "soon became prominent in all matters pertaining to the cattle industry." He organized the first livestock organizations in both Wyoming and Montana and served as their presidents. In 1895 he married Jessie Grieves McIlvain, a widow, and brought her son into partnership on his ranch. In 1902 he was nominated without his consent and elected to serve in the Wyoming legislature; two years later he was rumored to be a candidate for governor, though he never ran. He also served as president of the Old Settlers Club. He died while visiting his stepson in July 1921.[2]

Hardin's home, described in *Progressive Men of the State of Wyoming* as the "Hardin cabin," is anything but a cabin. According to a 1902 story in a Cheyenne newspaper, the house was one of the "most unique ranch buildings in the state." It was built from granite boulders taken from the Tongue River and was "large enough to hospitably entertain his friends who frequently visit him." *Progressive Men of the State of Wyoming* further stated that the house was "built on an eminence at the confluence of the Tongue River and Wolf Creek, commanding a grand view of mountains, hills, and valleys for miles in every direction. It is a most spacious and charming country home, having few if any equals in the Rocky Mountain Region." The book suggested that Mrs. Hardin's supervision of the "charming and hospitable home" constituted "a most delightful addition of cultured refinement."[3]

A closer examination of Stimson's images attests to the home's grandeur and modernity. In the first two-part exterior panorama (63), Stimson focused toward the southwest, showing the front of the home with its enclosed porch. Two men, presumably Hardin and his son-in-law and partner McIlvain, are wearing suits and standing to the right of the house. A square water tower is visible behind the home, and a barn can be seen further in the distance. Fenced pastures are visible as well, and the Big Horns rise on the horizon. Not a single tree is visible, and what appears to be a small irrigation ditch crosses in the foreground.

The second exterior (64) was taken from the south side of the house and looks north, confirming the home's position above the Tongue River Valley. The square water tower is clearly visible at the back of the house. A woman—presumably Mrs. Hardin—as well as three dogs, have joined the two men in front of the house. Inside the enclosed porch, two more women can be seen sitting on a free-standing porch swing. A rain barrel is visible at the southwest corner of the house below a downspout.

Stimson made the final exterior view (69) on the enclosed porch, looking to the north with two people—presumably Mr. and Mrs. Hardin—standing at the far end with a dog at their feet, framed by the porch's structure and silhouetted against the bright sky. A window to the house, at left, reflects the valley below.

With the exception of one view of the dining room and its stone fireplace (70), all of the other interior images focus on the great room. In this image of the fireplace, a clock sits on the right side of the mantel, with candleholders lined up all the way to the other side. Navajo rugs and pillows cover the adjacent nook benches. Three windows, one on each side of the fireplace and another placed interestingly above the mantel, flood light into the room through closed drapes. A wicker basket and what appears to be a Craftsman-style rug lie on the floor.

The views of the Hardin great room show an exquisite Craftsman-style home. A very rare interior panorama (65) looks northeast across the room, from the front porch on the right to the fireplace at left. In between, the room is filled with Craftsman furniture atop giant Turkish rugs. An animal skin and two spittoons are on the floor near the fireplace. A round table, with a Navajo rug atop it, holds a collection of books, including what appears on close inspection to be a first edition of Owen Wister's *The Virginian*. On the far wall, a large stone fireplace is draped with western mementos, including a Mexican sombrero and Native American pottery. Native American clothing, woven baskets, and beadwork adorn the dark panel walls on each side of the fireplace, while a European-style painting of a young boy and dog rests on the far wall.

The remaining interior photographs focus in closer on other parts of this room. One view (66) moves across the room from the previous vantage point and looks back south to where Stimson made his panorama. This image reveals another wicker rocker and an Aeolian player reed organ on the south wall with a large collection of rolls to its side. Like a player piano, when the pedals were pumped, this instrument played a pre-inscribed song from a scroll loaded into it.[4] On its top sit family photographs. Beyond the organ to the left is another side room, with what appears to be a large collection of family photographs on the wall. In the foreground, a detailed fireplace kit stands next to another animal hide.

The final image (68) moves back across the room to the corner by the fireplace and looks back toward the northeast side of the house, near where the last image was made. This angle reveals more detail, including several kerosene lamps, another

Craftsman rocker, a wicker chair, and a small desk and chair. Atop this desk sits a lamp and what appears to be a dial thermometer. An American flag is draped partially over a painting of George Washington on the wall behind it. Photographs of other men encompass the image of the first president. To the east, the opened windows provide glimpses of the enclosed porch and the lands beyond it. Below the windows, more bench nooks are visible. An ornate wooden chest rests below the painting of the small boy and dog.

Another photograph (67) is labeled "Interior of Hardin's Residence" and depicts Mr. and Mrs. Hardin in front of the fireplace. He is standing to the left, apparently reading something he is holding in his hands, and she is sitting in a rocker to the right. This view also provides a clearer picture of the Native American goods displayed on the wall to the right of the fireplace. Rebecca West, assistant curator of the Plains Indian Museum at the Buffalo Bill Historical Center in Cody, identified these goods as most likely of Lakota origin. The long beaded strip at the top is a blanket strip, an adornment added to buffalo hides and later to wool blankets. The tunic is a man's war shirt with images of horse hooves to represent stolen horses or battle exploits. The hair locks hanging with the shirt were most likely from women in his family who helped make the shirt. Below them hang a pair of men's moccasins and to the left a ceremonial pipe and beaded pipe bag of unknown origin.[5]

Before we look at these images within the framework of modernity, we need to better define modernity itself. The modern era generally refers to the period from about 1500 to the early 1900s and is characterized by the rise of capitalism and rationalism. Building on the Enlightenment, this worldview saw the rise of new modes of transportation that used inanimate power sources, new media (including photography), and new ways of looking at the world—including the scientific method, exploration and survey, the imposition of the national grid, and taxonomy.[6]

An analysis of these images in terms of modernity begins by recalling that Stimson's 1903 photographic survey of Wyoming's counties fits directly into the modern ideal to explore, survey, and record the world. Moreover, the fact that Stimson was producing these images for the State of Wyoming to exhibit at the St. Louis World's Fair, in effect to "sell" Wyoming, further strengthens their modern characteristics because Stimson's work was not simply for the sake of knowledge but rather was for capitalistic purposes. Thus Stimson's intense focus on the Hardin Ranch illustrates a modern sensibility to better know the world and bring it to the market.[7]

Cultural historians tell us further that one of the by-products of the rise of modernism was the increasing use of machines and, as a result, an increasing nostalgia for goods that were handmade and therefore more *authentic*. This *anti-modern* strain appeared throughout American culture at this time, ranging from Craftsman and Mission furniture to the rise of tourism—elites escaping the modern world for more authentic leisure activities in the anti-modern one. This nostalgia also surfaced in a growing fascination with the *primitive*, a culturally constructed idea that "pre-modern" peoples lived a life free of modern encumbrances and were therefore more real, more authentic. The fascination with Native American arts and crafts, regardless of the fact that official government policy at the time was one of forced assimilation into mainstream American culture, attests to this. At the same time, modern collectors fundamentally altered such items because they did not use them for their intended utilitarian functions but instead considered them ornamental "tokens" of their conquest of the primitive and their brush with primitive authenticity.[8]

A closer examination of Stimson's interior views of the Hardin Ranch shows a thoroughly modern "Hardin cabin" in the wilds of Wyoming. The Craftsman-style tables and chairs, as well as the player reed organ, were most likely delivered from Chicago by way of the railroad and then hauled by wagon to Ranchester. The idea even runs to the copy of *The Virginian* visible on the table because it was the first "Western," a new type of story that sought out anti-modern themes amid the post-frontier of Owen Wister's Wyoming.

The Lakota shirt and moccasins, pipe, and other artifacts hanging on the wall as artwork are considered modern as well because they have shed their original functions to become decorations on Samuel Hardin's wall. The same is true of the Navajo rugs and Southwestern pottery and basketry adorning the fireplace mantel. Moreover, in the era following the late-nineteenth-century Indian Wars, these functional items displayed as art also served as symbols of the conquest of the West. This is especially important in this section of the northern plains, just sixty miles south of the Little Bighorn battlefield. The Hardin home was also just a couple of miles south of the Connor battlefield, where General Patrick E. Connor of the Powder River Expedition attacked an Arapaho camp on August 29, 1865, along the Tongue River. The location is now a Ranchester city park.[9]

That said, research suggests that it is highly possible that these Indian goods were not trophies from Hardin's western exploits but merely items purchased locally as home decorations. Since 1900, Herbert Coffeen, son of Sheridan pioneer Henry Coffeen, had been advertising Indian crafts from his Sheridan store known as the Teepee Shop under the banner "Good Things from the West" in the highly stylistic *House Beautiful* magazine. The ad in the June 1900 issue included a photo of a Navajo rug accompanied by the statement that these rugs were "more durable than Turkish Rugs, and the richness of their coloring is just as decorative." The ad further stated that Coffeen had a "fine assortment of Indian baskets, pottery, and curios."[10]

All in all, Stimson documented the Hardin Ranch much the same way he surveyed and photographed Wyoming. In both cases, his images serve as hyperphotographs of modernity. Close examination reveals links to all kinds of symbols, from ones showing the rise of capitalism to others depicting modern transportation networks and national markets to the conquest of the West. Still others exhibit the quintessential anti-modern—and therefore quintessentially modern—tropes of handmade furniture, primitive arts and crafts, and the Old West. No wonder Stimson took so many images; he must have been utterly fascinated.

But as much as Stimson's images of the Hardin Ranch epitomized the modern, our visit to the Old Stone Inn in the summer of 2007 was indicative of the *postmodern*. Much of my thinking on this has been shaped by master rephotographer Mark Klett and colleagues' powerful book *Yosemite in Time* and its intriguing essays by Rebecca Solnit. For this book, Klett and co-photographer Byron Wolfe not only revisited and rephotographed classic images of Yosemite taken by such greats as Eadward Muybridge, Carleton Watkins, and Ansel Adams; they also took rephotography into new analytical realms. For example, in a rephotographic pairing with a Muybridge image of Grizzly Falls taken 131 years earlier, Klett first printed the before-and-after images, then printed another pair that isolated eighteen individual trees, seen in both images. He called these trees "time clocks." In her accompanying essay, "Ghost River," Solnit also isolated the concept of time as one link between photography and rephotography and reminded us that "photography does not record continuums, but moments; it is not the camera but our imaginations that construct narratives out of these moments."[11]

Solnit further suggests that rephotography can help us better understand what the original photographer was thinking. She believes rephotography can reveal " a lot about the initial photographer's sensibility, interpretations, and decisions." She adds that when "you return to the site of a photograph, you return to the site of creative decisions about what to include and exclude, you discover how far the artists went up a difficult slope, where a series of photographs were made in relation to each other . . . [and you can literally] map the movements of someone a century and more ago."[12]

At one point, she compares Klett's growing understanding of the placement of so many previous viewpoints within the frame of his current viewfinder as something akin to an Advent calendar. These paper calendars often show one big view but then have up to two dozen smaller openings that reveal additional images. Rephotographs can be like that, where the rephotographer observes the current view, knowing that there might be multiple "time portals" opening to previously made images.[13]

Solnit further explores this relationship between space and time by suggesting that rephotography is a "spectacularly postmodern exercise" because it does not seek original vantage points to make its own images but instead captures modern photographers' camera stations to see how the modern scene has held up over time. In other words, rephotography "turns its back on originality" by producing similar appropriated scenes rather than new underived views. In short, because rephotography seeks to replicate modern images exactly, it cannot be a modern exercise but instead falls into the theoretical framework of the postmodern.[14]

Solnit then expands the argument that Yosemite is also becoming a postmodern place because scientists and park rangers are consciously using historic images to replicate its historic natural features—for example, thinning forests or restoring plants in meadows—so the current park looks like pictures of it from 100 years ago. In other words, like rephotographers replicating historic images, park preservationists are replicating the actual landscape to appear as it did in modern-era images. Solnit writes, "The place is turning into its portrait, or into someone else's portrait, as though you were made up to resemble your great-grandmother."[15]

Pushing the idea further, Solnit argues that photography is thus not only a *recorder* of time but also a *shaper* of it. She suggests that we tend to look back nostalgically to the past—or the version of the past we remember through photographs—through a primitivist lens, imagining and projecting our own views and understanding onto our creation of history. In short, photographs help us create a concept of the past. Although we may like to think of that projected past as more authentic, it is not any more authentic—or inauthentic—than any other time.[16]

Returning to the actual landscape of Yosemite, Solnit notes that as scientists use historic images of the park to shape its landscape today, they are not restoring it to a more natural, authentic condition but to a version constructed to resemble photographs. The emerging, restored park is not authentic but a postmodern "simulacrum," or likeness of itself, based on photography.[17]

Like Klett, my rephotographs of the Old Stone Inn also represent postmodern views because they are not original renderings of this beautiful home but carefully fabricated images from modern vantage points established more than a century earlier. In other words, they are thoroughly postmodern images because, rather than deciding where I wanted to best depict these interiors, I purposely chose modern vantage points established by Stimson and then purposely moved my camera and tripod to those points to best capture how Stimson, the modern photographer, captured a modern home during the modern era. Most telling is the view where I posed the current owners to look somewhat like the original owners, albeit with the man wearing a T-shirt and jeans rather than a wool suit. Such repetitions of the modern are quintessentially *postmodern*.

Further, as with Yosemite, my postmodern images reveal the efforts of the current owners of the Old Stone Inn to restore the home, using Stimson's modern images as a basis for reconstructing its past look. Like postmodern ecologists in Yosemite, these "restorers" were in fact "restoring" the home not to its original modern condition but to a version that was represented in Stimson's thoroughly modern images. Simply put, restoration was a postmodern exercise to restore the home to its modern condition.

A closer look at my rephotographs furthers some of these ideas. Although the owners suggested restoring the house based on Stimson's images, my rephotographs reveal that the house was more likely restored *in the style* of the original rather than as a detailed duplicate. For example, the exterior images show that, as in Stimson's day, the home still commands a wonderful view back toward the Big Horns as well as down toward the Tongue River Valley. Further, the landscape remains mostly clear of big, overwhelming trees, although a few smaller bushes can be found around the home's foundation and nearby. The water tower and rain barrel have been removed, with an arbor now occupying the area behind the house. The home's chimney remains in place, as does the original barn, while a new metal garage is now located in the rear.

The more telling images are those of the interior where, once again, the current version of the house more closely reflects the style of the original Hardin home than a clear restoration of it. The house remains open, with a single great room with the same exposed beams and stone fireplace clearly evident, although the woodwork appears lighter in tone than in the original images. I wondered if this was simply the difference between Stimson's black-and-white originals and my color images, so I converted all of my digital images to grayscale black and white and the woodwork remained lighter in tone. The other notable difference is the introduction of electricity into the room, replacing the several kerosene lamps with electric chandeliers and a table lamp. That said, these light sources include several antler-based hanging lights and a stained glass table lamp. These are postmodern replicas, harking back to the handmade primitivism of the original home. Craftsman-style chairs, tables, bookcases, and rugs are also visible, postmodern homages to the original modern home. In the dining room, the oak table and the placement of the mantel clock, though smaller, shadow the items in the Stimson original. Even the basic layout of the furniture hints at the style of the Hardin home.

Only when one looks closely at the walls does the postmodern really come into light. On the big wall adjacent to the fireplace, the Native American clothing and arts and crafts, those quintessential primitive anti-modern pieces (and therefore the most modern ones), have been removed. In their place are framed original Stimson images obtained from the Wyoming State Archives and used as the guiding template images for restoring the house to its modern style. Located just to the left of the fireplace, one can clearly see the exterior panorama looking to the north and two, less clear interior views. To the right of the fireplace hangs the other exterior view looking to the southwest, flanked by two more interior scenes. In the same spots where Samuel Hardin hung his primitivist renderings of a conquered but authentic Native American past, the current owners have placed their own primitivist images of their own home. The modern constructs the primitive to justify its own modernity, just as the postmodern hangs its views of the modern to justify its own postmodernity.

The basic tenets of this analysis of the modern and postmodern can be extrapolated to the restoration of other modern structures and landscapes Stimson photographed in Wyoming. The two most obvious ones I rephotographed are the Old Faithful Inn and the town of South Pass City. As shown in both the exterior view of the Old Faithful Inn (100) but especially in the interior view of the massive fireplace (101), the postmodern renovation undertaken between 2001 and 2012 is evident, as the area around the fireplace was "restored" to its original sunken position seven inches below the surrounding floor. In addition, workers removed the extra beam to the right of the fireplace that had been placed there for support after the 1959 Hebgen Lake earthquake.[18]

Similarly, the entire town of South Pass City emulates this modern and postmodern condition. Ever since a group of citizens purchased the location in 1968 and donated it to the State of Wyoming as part of its centennial celebration, the town has been preserved as a museum piece depicting the modern community Stimson captured in his 1903 photograph (81). A close look reveals the historic restoration of its many buildings and the limiting of growth in the historic district (the right side of the image) compared with the independent part of town visible to the left. Although some might think time has seemingly stopped in South Pass City, a more accurate description would be that restorers, like the postmodern rephotographer who depicts the current view from the modern perspective, are thoroughly postmodern themselves as they deliberately turn back the clock to make South Pass City always look modern.

Similar discussions could occur regarding the Rawlins Frontier Prison (24), Fort Laramie (40, 41), the Lake Hotel (105, 106), and the Mammoth area (111, 112) in Yellowstone, as well as the Chapel of Transfiguration (114) and Menor's Ferry (115) in Moose. This analysis might even be extended to the many national forests, such as those depicted along the Cody Road (95–97) and near Jackson Hole (117), where forest rangers have employed fire suppression measures or controlled burns to maintain the look of the forest to resemble the modern view first encountered in the late nineteenth century. Such musings on entire landscapes might overstate the relationship between the modern and postmodern in Wyoming today, but the basics of some sort of relationship are probably there.

J. E. Stimson spent much of his career photographing modern Wyoming. During two different periods of my career, I have spent consecutive years rephotographing many of those same places, many of which have been restored to appear as they did a hundred or more years ago. Throughout this book, I have suggested that Stimson's images that were often used in promotion to "sell" the state and its products can now also be seen as documentary photographs, capturing both intended and unintended slices of life in early-twentieth-century Wyoming. Starting with his spectacular view of the Hardin cabin in Ranchester and moving to many more locations across the state, perhaps it is time to also consider them images of modernity and my rephotographs to be select slices of a postmodern Wyoming.

Notes

1. Junge, *Stimson*, 102-3.

2. A. W. Bowen, *Progressive Men of the State of Wyoming* (Chicago: A. W. Bowen, 1908), 221–22, quote from p. 222; http://www.bighorncountymuseum.org/Info.htm [accessed March 3, 2014]; "Samuel H. Hardin," *Cheyenne Daily Leader*, February 22, 1902; "A Gubernatorial Possibility," *Cheyenne Wyoming Tribune*, February 29, 1904; "Col. Sam H. Hardin Dies in Colorado," *Sheridan Enterprise*, July 14, 1921.

3. Bowen, *Progressive Men*, 222; "Samuel H. Hardin," *Cheyenne Daily Leader*, February 22, 1902.

4. Compare the organ in Stimson's image with one found on the Internet at http://vimeo.com/5706735 [accessed January 12, 2012].

5. Rebecca West, e-mail to author, January 12, 2012.

6. Chris Rodrigues and Chris Garratt, *Introducing Modernism* (n.p.: Totem Books, 2002).

7. William G. Robbins, *Colony and Empire: The Capitalist Transformation of the American West* (Lawrence: University of Kansas Press, 1994).

8. T. Jackson Lears, *No Place of Grace: Antimodernism and the Transformation of American Culture, 1880–1920* (Chicago: University of Chicago Press, 1994); Leah Dilworth, *Imagining Indians in the Southwest: Persistent Visions of a Primitive Past* (Washington, DC: Smithsonian Institution Scholarly Press, 1997); Thomas J. Harvey, *Rainbow Bridge to Monument Valley: Making the Modern Old West* (Norman: University of Oklahoma Press, 2011).

9. http://www.philkearny.vcn.com/connorbattlefield.htm [accessed January 17, 2013].

10. Dori Griffin, *Mapping Wonderlands: Illustrated Cartography of Arizona, 1912–1962* (Tucson: University of Arizona Press, 172), first alerted me to Coffeen's ads. The actual ad can be found in "Good Things from the West," *House Beautiful* (June 1900): 433. A brief biography of Coffeen can be found in "Progressive Stationers," *American Stationer*, August 13, 1913, online at Google Books. Coffeen later published a magazine of local and western history called the *Teepee Book*.

11. Mark Klett, Rebecca Solnit, and Byron Wolfe, *Yosemite in Time: Ice Ages, Tree Clocks, Ghost Rivers* (San Antonio: Trinity University Press, 2005), 17.

12. Ibid.

13. Ibid., 27.

14. Ibid., 18–20.

15. Ibid., 19.

16. Dilworth, *Imagining Indians*.

17. Klett, Solnit, and Wolfe, *Yosemite in Time*, 19; http://www.cla.purdue.edu/english/theory/postmodernism/terms/simulacrum.html [accessed March 3, 2014].

18. http://www.yellowstone-notebook.com/innrenovation.html [accessed January 17, 2013].

Plates and Captions

For Photographs and Rephotographs

DOI: 10.5876/9781607323051.c006

J. E. Stimson made the original photographs in this book over more than a thirty-year period and in no particular geographic order. His images range from 1898 to the 1920s and cover the entire state, from Cheyenne to Yellowstone and Evanston to Sundance. To make some sense of this, I have reconstructed them in a geographic arrangement, allowing location to take precedence over time.

Section A, the Union Pacific and Its Branches, begins in Stimson's adopted hometown of Cheyenne and follows his primary employer, the Union Pacific Railroad, and its subsidiaries, the Saratoga and Encampment Railway and the Oregon Short Line, as they moved east to west across the state. After reaching Cokeville near the Idaho border, the book comes back to Cheyenne before heading north. Section B focuses on the Fort Laramie country, including Douglas, Chugwater, Fort Laramie, and Hartville. Section C, the Black Hills, covers the northeastern corner of the state, including Newcastle, Sundance, the ghost town of Cambria, and Devil's Tower country. Section D, the Big Horns, ventures west to Buffalo, Sheridan, and their hinterlands, including the small communities of Big Horn, Beckton, and Ranchester, as well as the mining ghost towns of Dietz and Kleenburn. It also ventures up into the mountains at Dome Lake. Section E includes

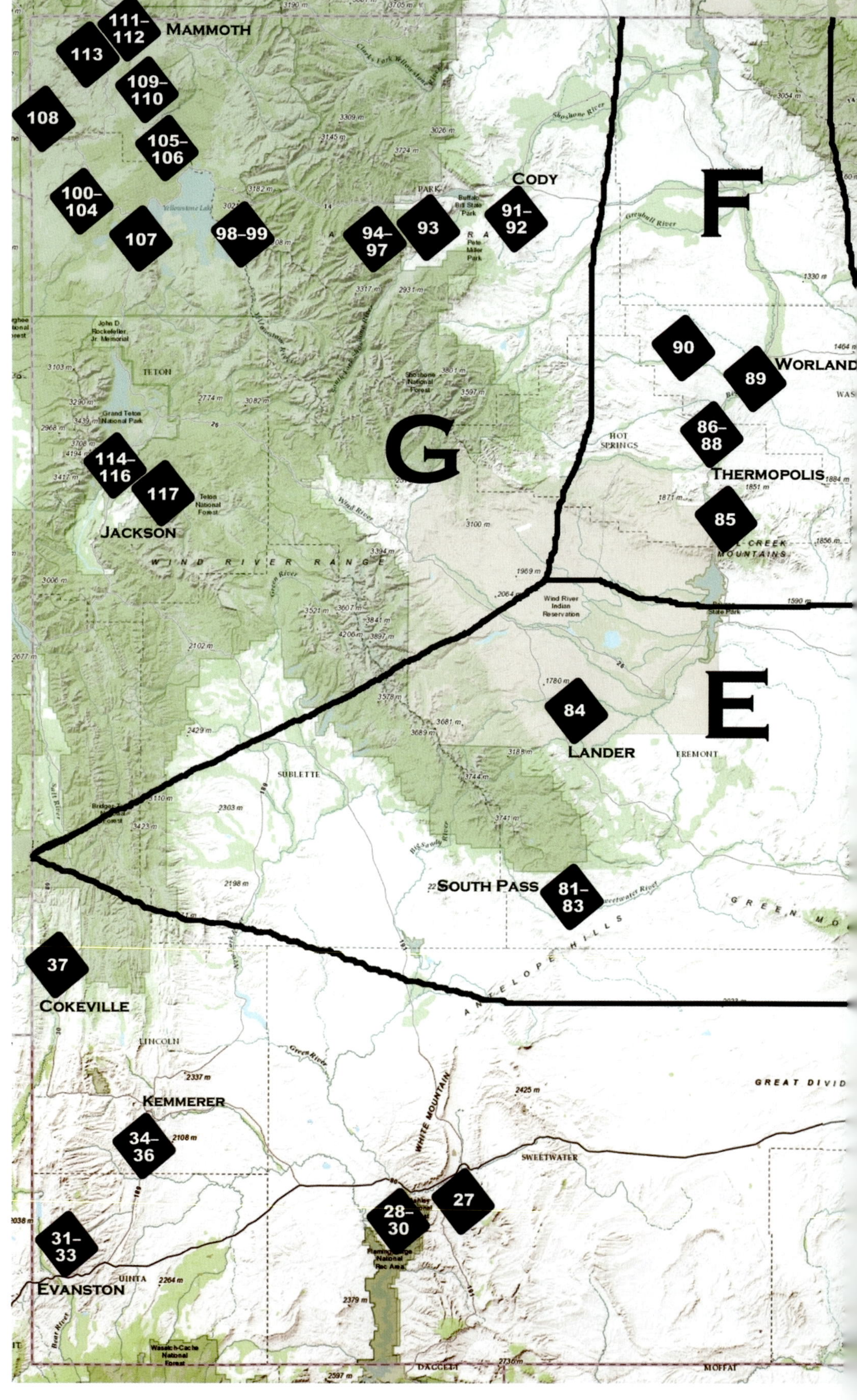

111–112
113
109–110
108
105–106
100–104
107
98–99
94–97
93
91–92
MAMMOTH
CODY
F
90
89
WORLAND
86–88
THERMOPOLIS
85
G
HOT SPRINGS
114–116
117
JACKSON
WIND RIVER RANGE
84
LANDER
E
81–83
SOUTH PASS
37
COKEVILLE
KEMMERER
34–36
27
28–30
31–33
EVANSTON

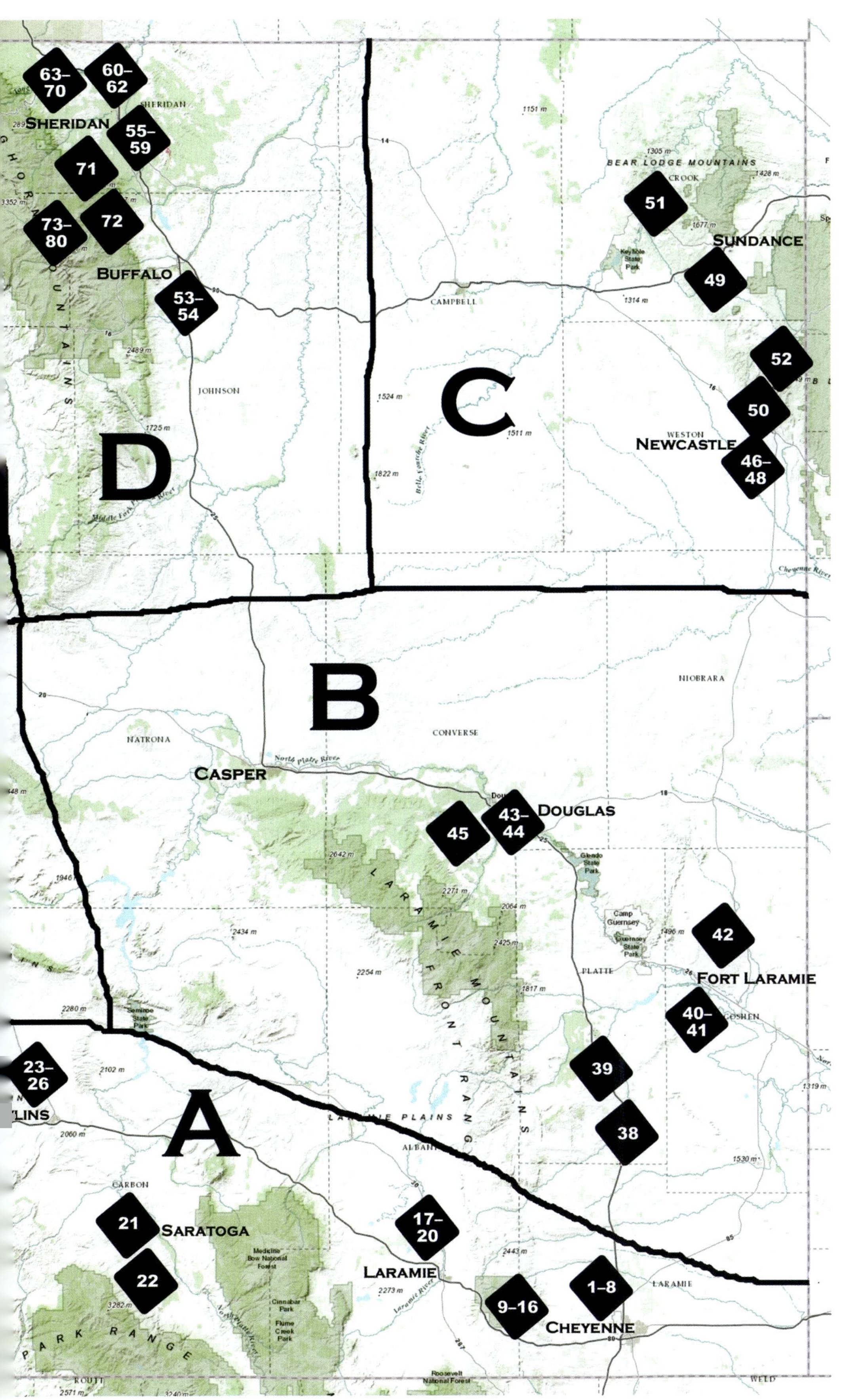

63–70
60–62
SHERIDAN
55–59
71
73–80
72
BUFFALO
53–54
51
SUNDANCE
49
52
50
NEWCASTLE
46–48
D
C
B
A
JOHNSON
CAMPBELL
WESTON
NIOBRARA
NATRONA
CONVERSE
CASPER
Douglas
45
43–44
42
FORT LARAMIE
40–41
39
38
CARBON
21
SARATOGA
22
17–20
LARAMIE
9–16
1–8
CHEYENNE
ROLLINS
23–26
PARK RANGE
LARAMIE FRONT MOUNTAINS RANGE
LARAMIE PLAINS
ALBANY
PLATTE
GOSHEN
BEAR LODGE MOUNTAINS
CROOK

the historic towns of South Pass City and Atlantic City as well as Lander. Section F, the Big Horn Basin, focuses on the area between the Big Horns and the road to Yellowstone and includes Wind River Canyon, Thermopolis, Worland, Cody, and Meeteetse. Section G, Yellowstone and Grand Teton National Parks, includes the Cody Road to Yellowstone, the park itself, and Grand Teton National Park.

I constructed the numbering system of the rephotographic pairs (1–117) for this book. The number that follows each of my numbers is Stimson's original index number. Those interested in viewing or obtaining copies of any original Stimson photograph can provide this number to the Wyoming State Archives.

The caption title provided is also Stimson's original photograph title and is often listed on the bottom of the original negative and print. This title is also included in the Stimson research guide, *Along the U.P. Line*, after the original number.

Following the caption are the dates of the original and the rephotograph(s). If images from my 1987–88 project are included, they will be noted.

The GPS information provided was either calculated in the field using a hand-held GPS unit or approximated on US Geological Survey (USGS) maps from known locations. Data are presented in degrees, minutes, and decimal minutes. Civilian GPS units are reportedly accurate enough to place one within an area about the size of a tennis court, so entering this information into a mapping system or Google Earth should take viewers very close to each camera station. To find exact vantage points, one must be on the site.

As noted, Google Earth provides an application called "Street View" with a small person-shaped icon called "Pegman." To get both a topographical view of the surrounding landscape and a 360-degree photographic panorama, enter the GPS coordinates and then drag Pegman to the site, making sure it is within the application boundaries marked in blue. After a computer-generated topographical view appears, if the site has been photographed by Google Earth, the application switches to the photographic image. Dragging the image to the proper direction should match the computer image to Stimson's original photograph and my rephotographs. Exiting "Street View" returns the viewer to a satellite image.

Several captions note that my rephotographs are not made from Stimson's original camera stations. Although each case is unique, natural obstructions such as tree growth facilitated moving from Stimson's vantage point to show the essence of the original image. In other cases, earth removal, dammed rivers, and controlled access have made it impossible to reproduce the exact Stimson location. Each of these occurrences is noted in its respective caption.

The text accompanying the photographs is not footnoted. Information from them was gleaned from sources provided in the bibliography.

Around 1901, the Union Pacific Railroad hired J. E. Stimson to take promotional photographs of the railroad. Eager to present itself in a new light after being reorganized by E. H. Harriman after bankruptcy, the railroad was modernizing with longer trains, fewer tunnels, and a double-tracked mainline. It needed an energetic photographer to promote itself and its customers. Under a flexible payment schedule, Stimson received four dollars for the first 8 × 10-inch print, one dollar each for the next ninety-nine, and seventy-five cents apiece for every print thereafter. He had no restrictions placed upon the subjects he photographed or on the number of images he made as long as they promoted the railway. Further, any negatives made for the UP could also be printed and sold for his own gain. And this agreement did not preclude Stimson from working for others at the same time. Finally, the railroad provided free transportation for him by train or, more often, through the use of a small gas-powered one-seat railcar. Overall, it was a lucrative arrangement for the young photographer.

Over the next two decades, Stimson photographed each of the major towns on the UP from Evanston in the west to Cheyenne in the east. He also shot on its two main branch lines, the Saratoga and Encampment Railway in those two towns, and the Oregon Short Line in Diamondville, Kemmerer, and Cokeville. In each of the places and many more nearby, Stimson photographed anything that promoted the railroad or its customers, including main streets, businesses, government, depots, houses, industries, mines, farms, ranches, and scenic areas.

I made the Union Pacific and its branch lines my initial focus on each of my rephotography projects. In 1987, I photographed every one of these sites. At the time, I was living in Laramie, so eastern Wyoming was never more than a day trip. For the western part, I stayed with my grandparents in Kemmerer.

In 2007, Lauren and I did one trip from my parents' home in Loveland to Cheyenne, Hecla, Granite Reservoir, Vedauwoo, Laramie, Saratoga, and Encampment. I then made another rephotography trip on my own, taking pictures in Rawlins, Green River, Kemmerer, Diamondville, and Evanston. Lauren and I then caught Cokeville and Rock Springs the following year while working on other sites.

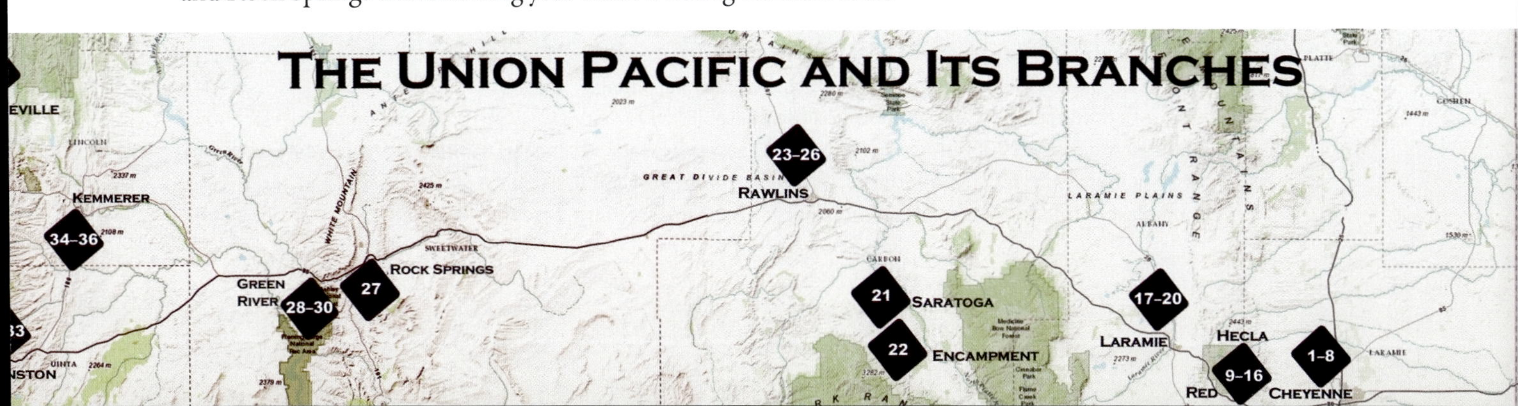

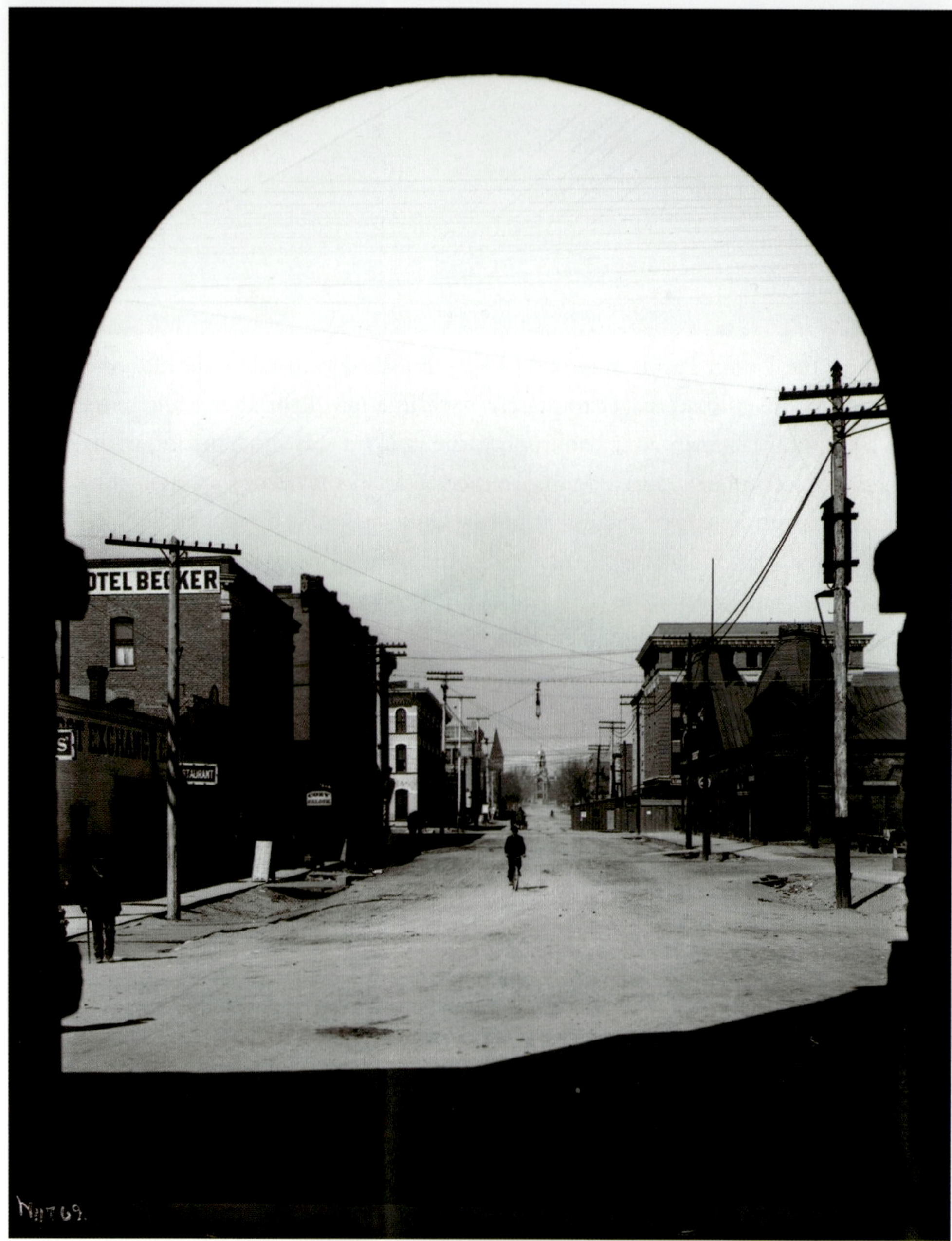

1. #1769

Union Pacific Depot Arch, Cheyenne, 1906, 2008
GPS COORDINATES: 41 7.9077N, 104 48.8815W

A view from Cheyenne's Union Pacific (UP) Depot is a fitting place to begin. Designed by Henry Van Brunt in the Richardsonian Romanesque style and constructed in 1887 by the railroad, the UP Depot serves today as the Wyoming Transportation Museum and is one of the landmarks of the Cheyenne skyline. Its placement at the south end of Capitol Avenue, with the Wyoming state capitol—constructed from 1868 to 1890—at the northern end, symbolizes the two major powers at work in early Wyoming.

J. E. Stimson used Cheyenne's railroad landscape often for city views. In 1904 he climbed the clock tower and photographed Capitol Avenue. The following year he made a 15-inch by 4-foot panorama from atop a water tower in the railyard. He made the image seen here from the Capitol Avenue Archway in 1906 and in 1907 again climbed the clock tower to repeat his image from three years previous to show the city's progress. Those photo-

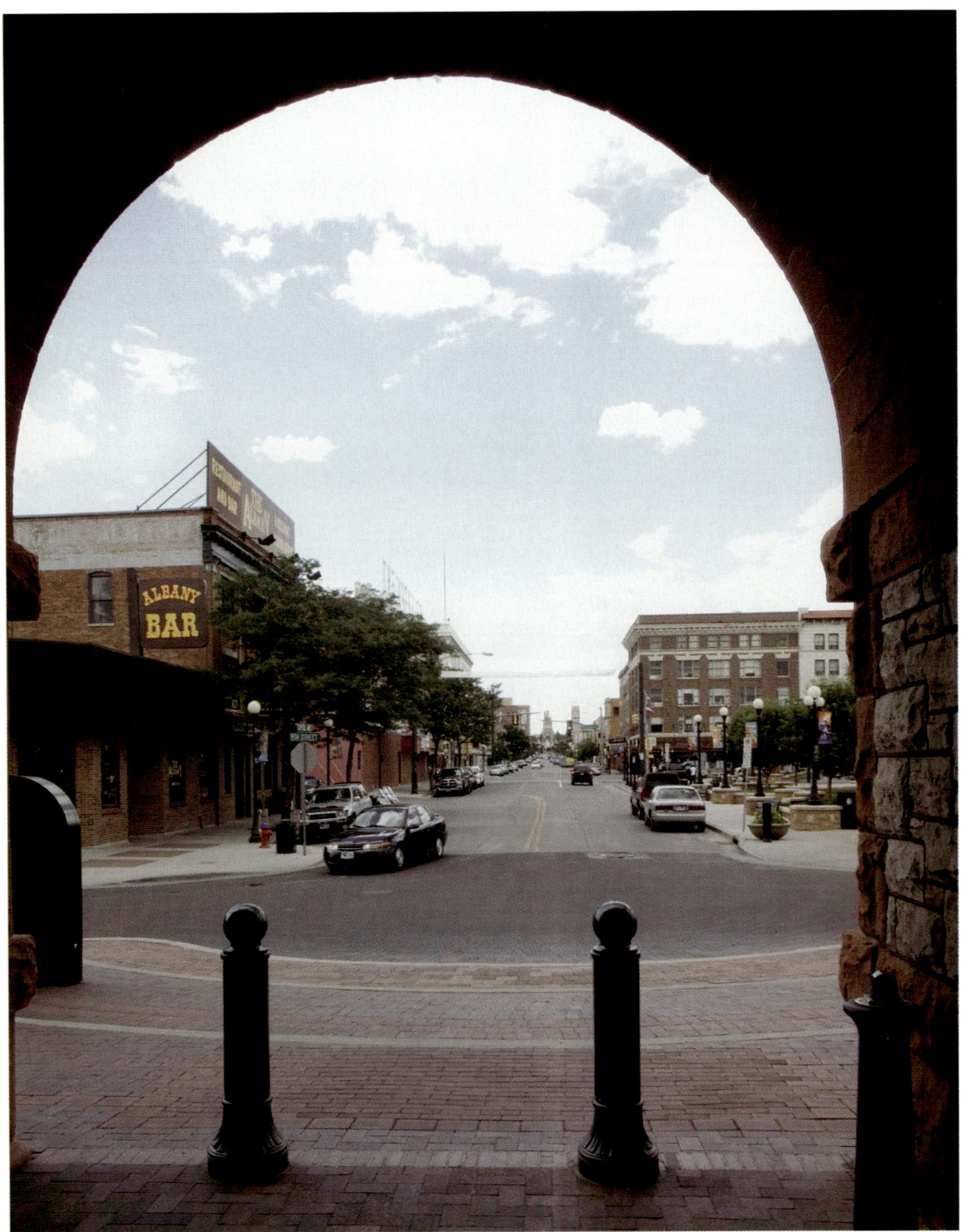

graphs appeared in a special Laramie County edition of the *Industrial Journal*. In 1910 Stimson returned to this site. I rephotographed those scenes for my book *Wyoming Time and Again*. Unfortunately, the railyard water tower no longer exists, and current liability issues make it impossible to reach the tower vantage point to repeat that series today.

Stimson artistically composed this view within the doorway, suggesting the railroad's view of Cheyenne. The Hotel Becker is visible at left, and the dark structure at right is the Chicago, Burlington, and Quincy Railroad Depot. Just north of the depot is the First National Bank building, still under construction. In the distance, the capitol's gold dome is clearly visible. Several pedestrians stroll on the board sidewalks, and a wagon and bicyclist ply the unpaved streets. Above them, the maze of telephone and electrical wires shows the city's many improvements.

My 2008 photograph could also be used as a publicity shot for a revived downtown Cheyenne. Paved streets, buried wires, and urban trees attest to this. At left, the Albany Bar occupies the site of the former Hotel Becker, and next door the Wrangler sells western-style clothes. The Cheyenne Depot Plaza now occupies the site of the Chicago, Burlington, and Quincy Depot, which was razed in 1928 and replaced by a bus depot that was removed in 1956 for a parking lot. The plaza now serves as an urban park for downtown events.

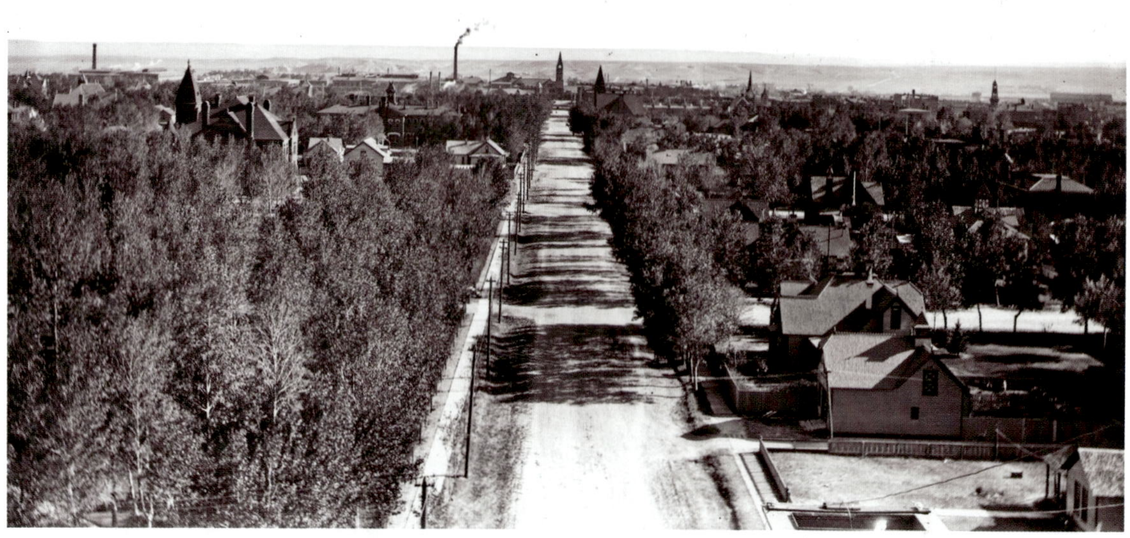

2. #5704

Capitol Avenue Looking South, Cheyenne, 1898, 1987, 2007
GPS COORDINATES: 41 8.41167N, 104 49.21517W

At the far end of Capitol Avenue and seemingly perched above the distant depot—symbolically presenting government's power over the railroad—sits the Wyoming state capitol. This view, made from a window just below its gold dome, looks south to the Union Pacific and beyond. My views, made in 1987 and again in 2007, show the reflections from that window.

Unlike his view from the depot, Stimson's early 1899 photograph depicts an almost pastoral Cheyenne, with its many trees rising from neat, orderly yards. At the same time, this flowering of deciduous trees and the imposition of the American grid onto the High Plains hint at man's mastery of nature. To the left looms the original Cheyenne High School. The Union Pacific's smokestack and depot in the distance remind viewers of the state's major industrial power.

My 1987 view depicts the growth of state government and business along Cheyenne's historic main street. The park at the left foreground lies in front of the Barrett Building, home of the Wyoming State Archives and Museum. On the right sits the Hathaway Building, named for the state's twenty-seventh governor. Beyond that building rises the American National Bank building, and across the street is St. Mary's Cathedral.

In my 2007 photograph, although there seem to be fewer trees, their green leaves stand out in stark contrast to the brown of the plains in the distance. Capitol Avenue has been decorated with bunting as it serves host to the annual Frontier Days parade in late July. Although this historic rodeo takes place north of the downtown, the presence of its daily parade down this street reminds us that the power of the Frontier myth must be placed alongside government and the railroad in Wyoming.

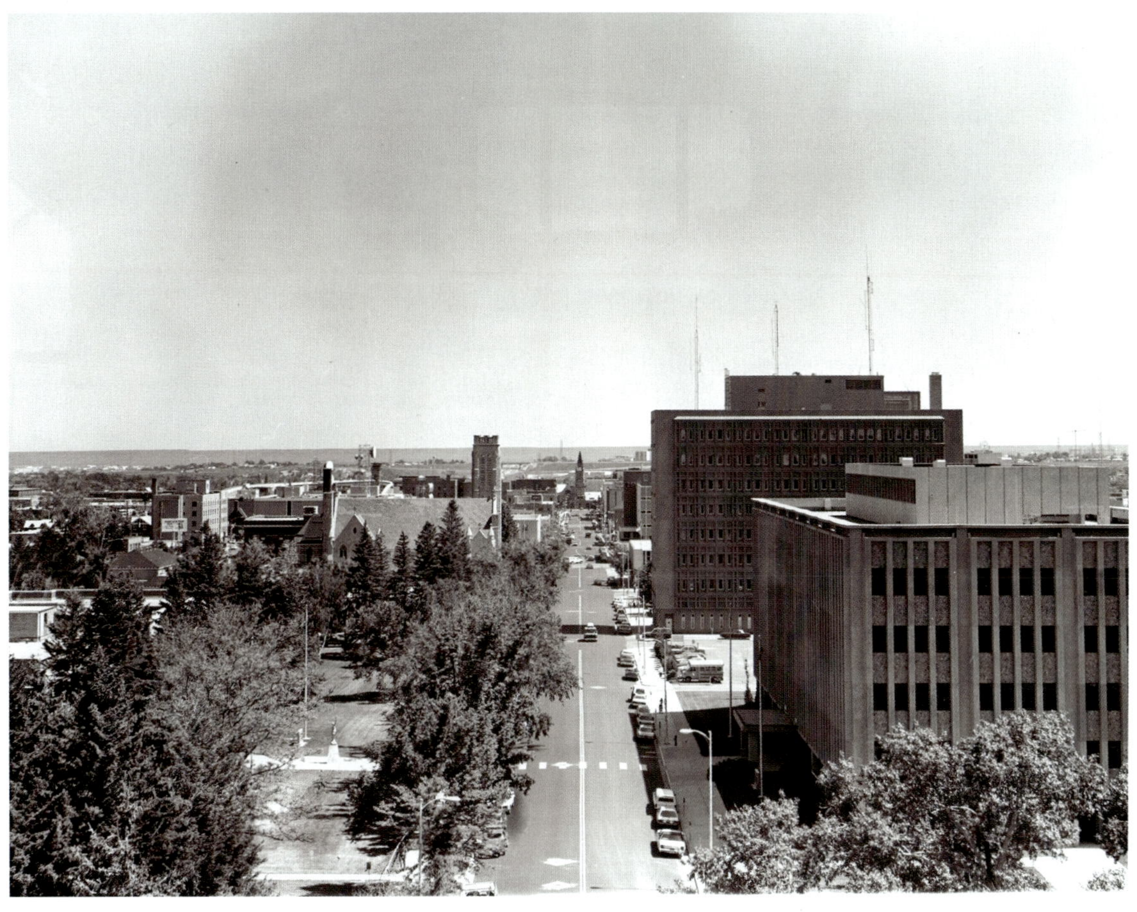

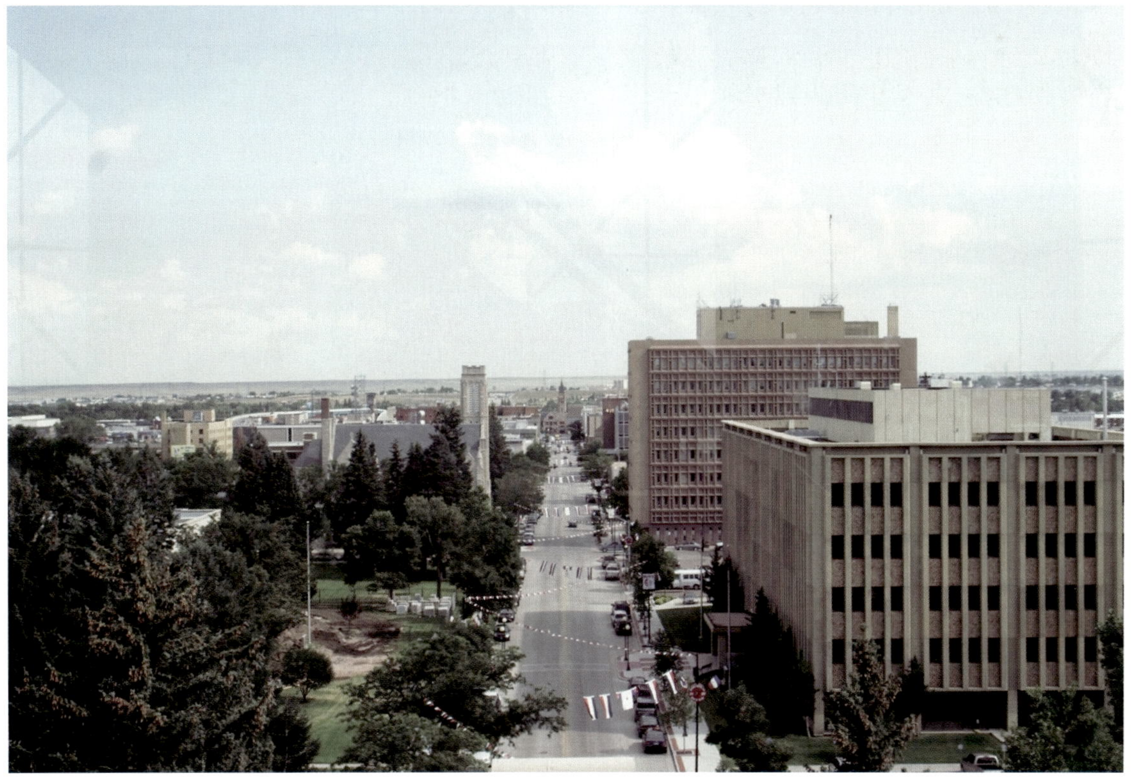

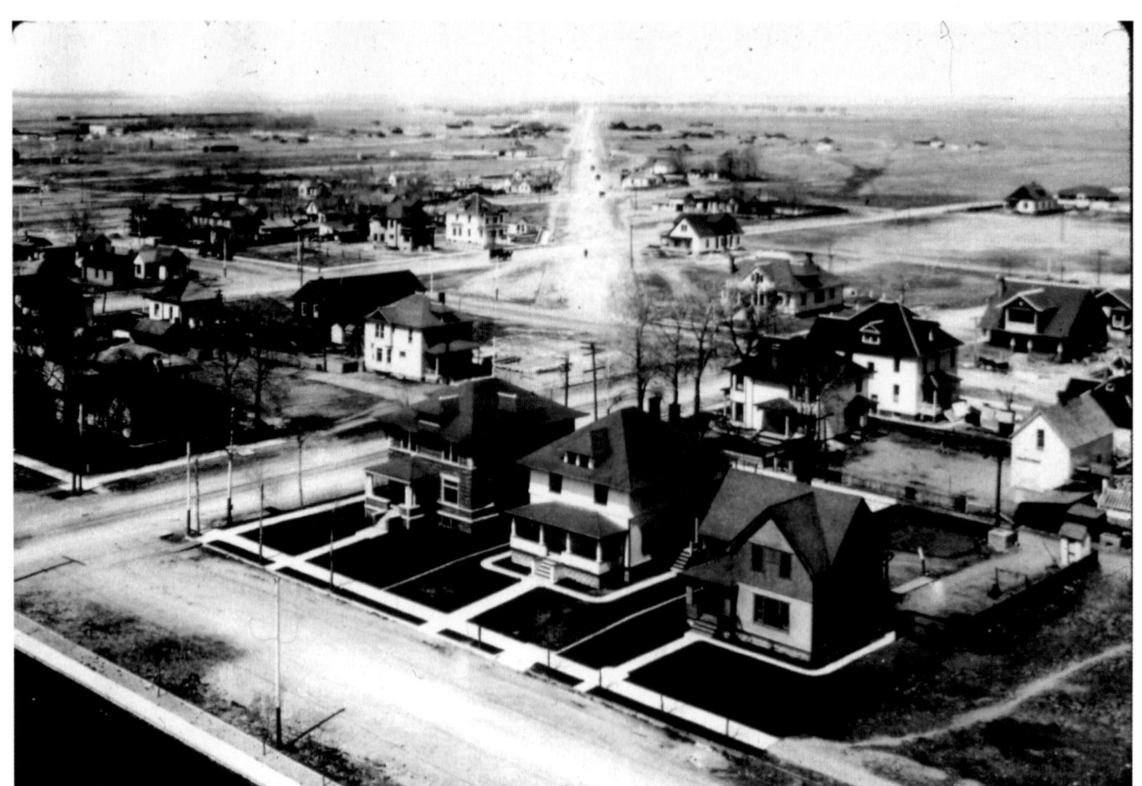

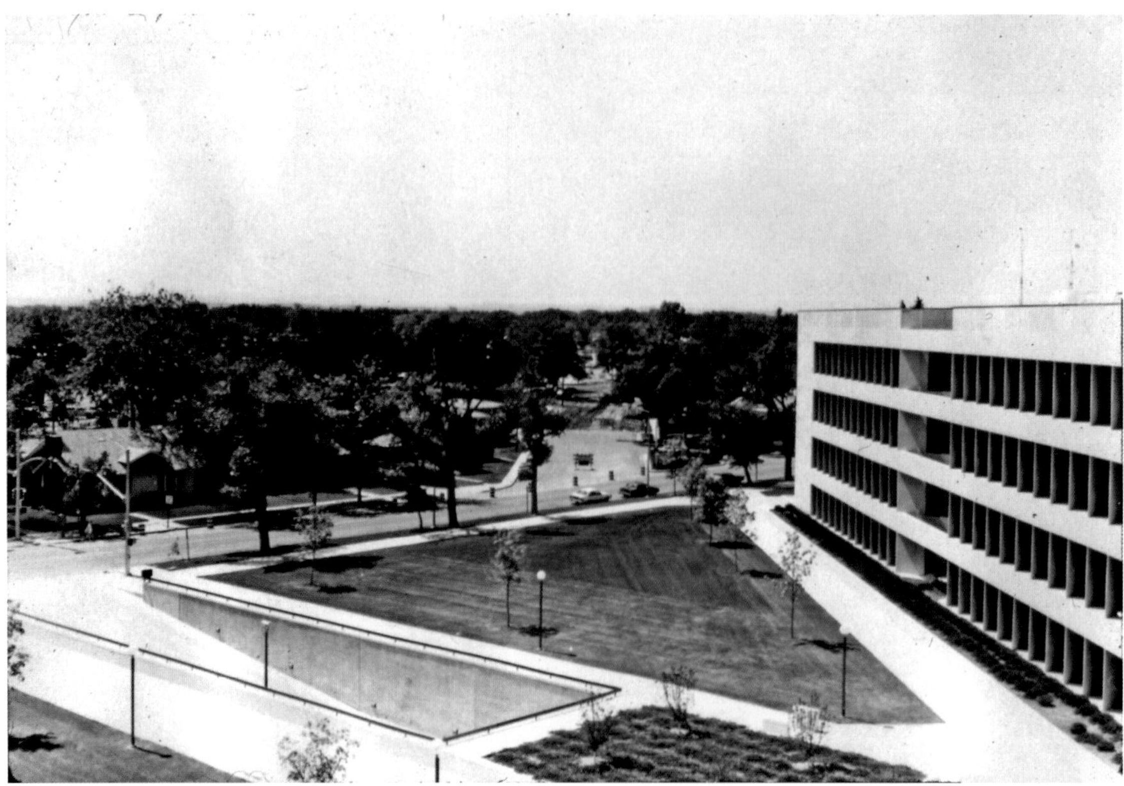

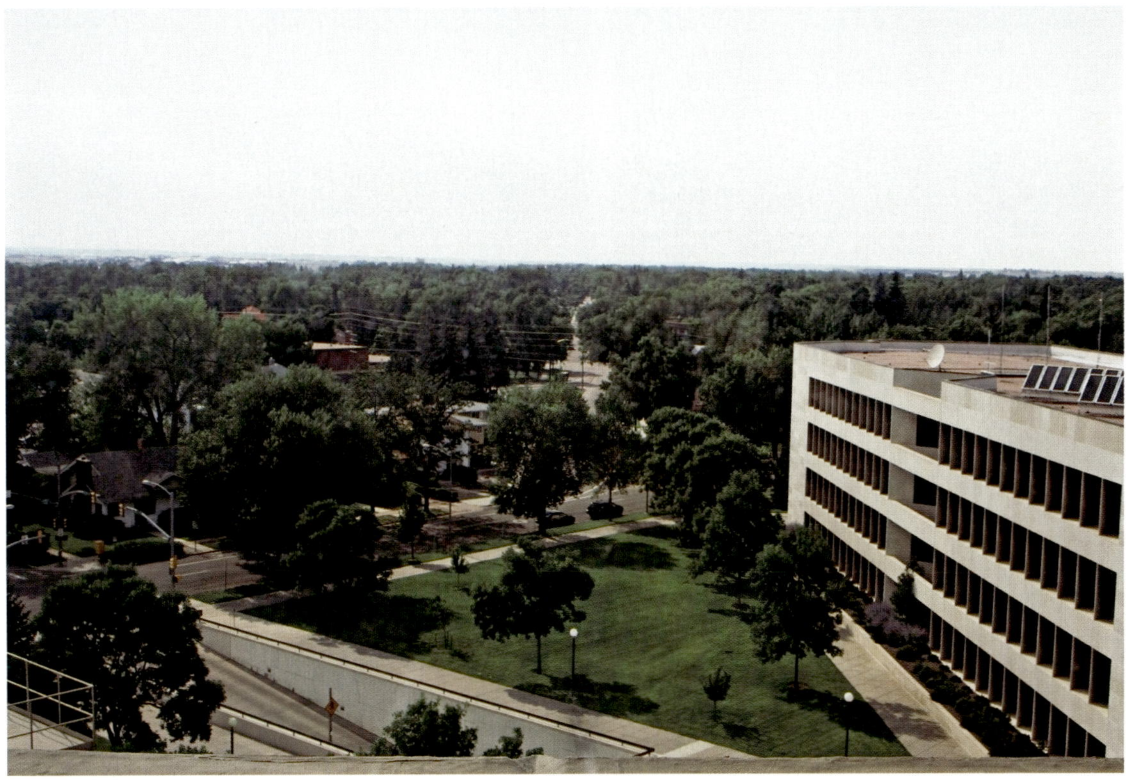

3. #2849

Looking up Randall Avenue from Capitol Dome, Cheyenne, 1910, 1987, 2007
GPS COORDINATES: 41 8.41167N, 104 49.21517W

Stimson's second view from the capitol dome looks northwest up Randall Avenue, with Fort Francis E. Warren (then called Fort D. A. Russell) on the far horizon. The house at the lower right belonged to Stimson. The rephotographs show that the Herschler Building, constructed in 1976 and named for former Wyoming governor Ed Herschler, has consumed the entire block behind the capitol building. Close inspection of my two photographs reveals that they were taken from slightly different vantage points. When I visited the site in 1987, a large satellite dish in the dome blocked views out of this northwest-facing window. Undeterred, a security guard who had guided me to the closed dome suggested that we could get a similar view from the building's roof below. We walked out on the roof and around the building to a spot directly below that window and took the photograph. When I returned twenty years later, the satellite dish was gone, so I repeated Stimson's actual vantage point. A comparison of all three views reveals that the Herschler Building with its solar panels and the complete transformation of the High Plains into a domestic forest of trees are the most noteworthy changes.

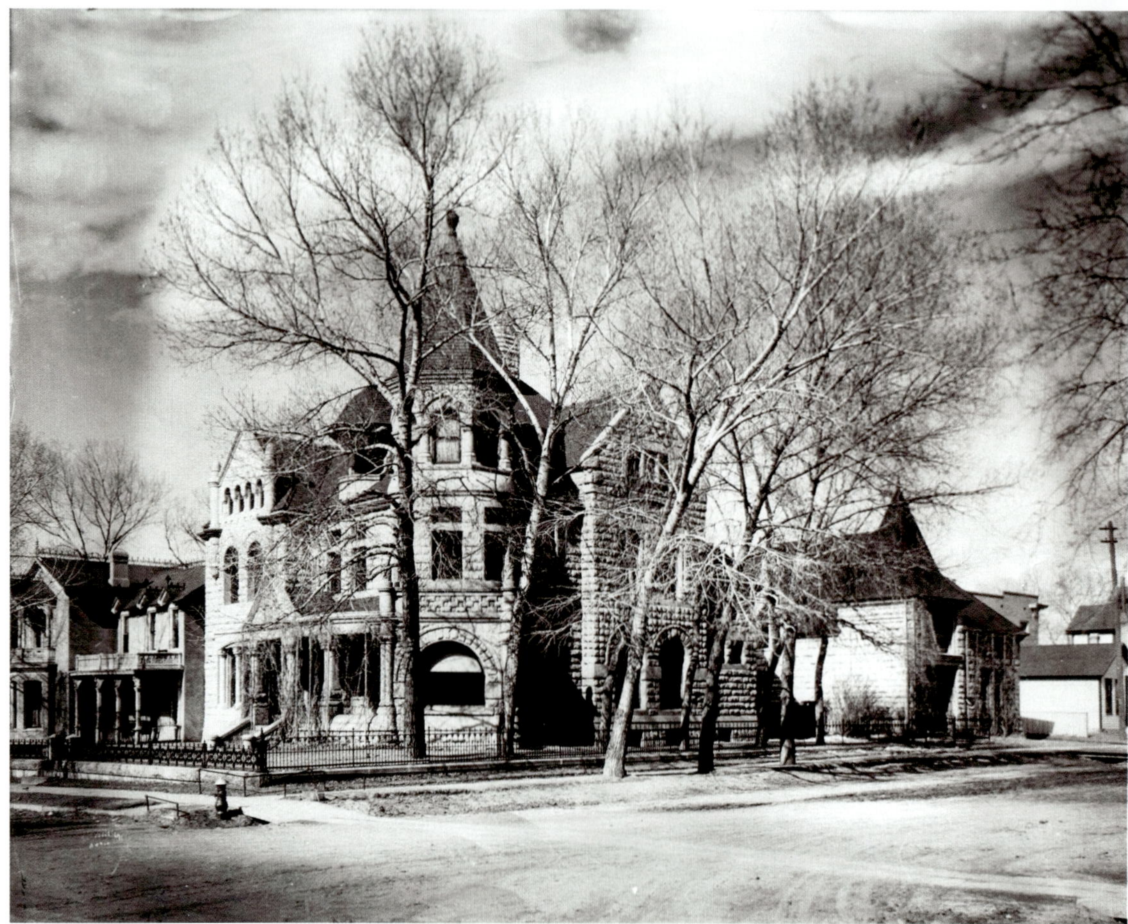

4. #6484

Nagle Residence, Cheyenne, ca. 1910, 1987, 2007
GPS COORDINATES: 41 8.0923N, 104 48.743W

Erasmus Nagle was chair of the first Capitol Building Commission and constructed this home in 1888 on what has been called "Cattle Baron's Row" at a cost of $50,000, including the use of stone rejected for use in the capitol. In 1910, former Wyoming governor and then senator Francis E. Warren purchased the house. After he passed away in 1929, his widow gave the mansion to the YWCA. By the 1950s the stone had begun to chip and crack, so the owners reinforced the entire house with concrete and covered most of it in stucco. Over the years, the mansion reverted back to a family home and now serves as the Nagle Warren Mansion Bed and Breakfast.

Only the carriage house, barely visible at right in the 2007 photograph, and portions of the front porch endure with the original stone intact. Both original iron fences, the cross-hatched one at left and the picket one on the right, remain as well. Also interesting are the adjacent third-generation trees. One of Cheyenne's few remaining nineteenth-century homes, the mansion was decked out in flags and bunting for the Frontier Days parade when I visited in 2007. Most interesting, though, was the fact that as I was setting up to take this photograph, Stimson biographer Mark Junge pedaled by on his bike.

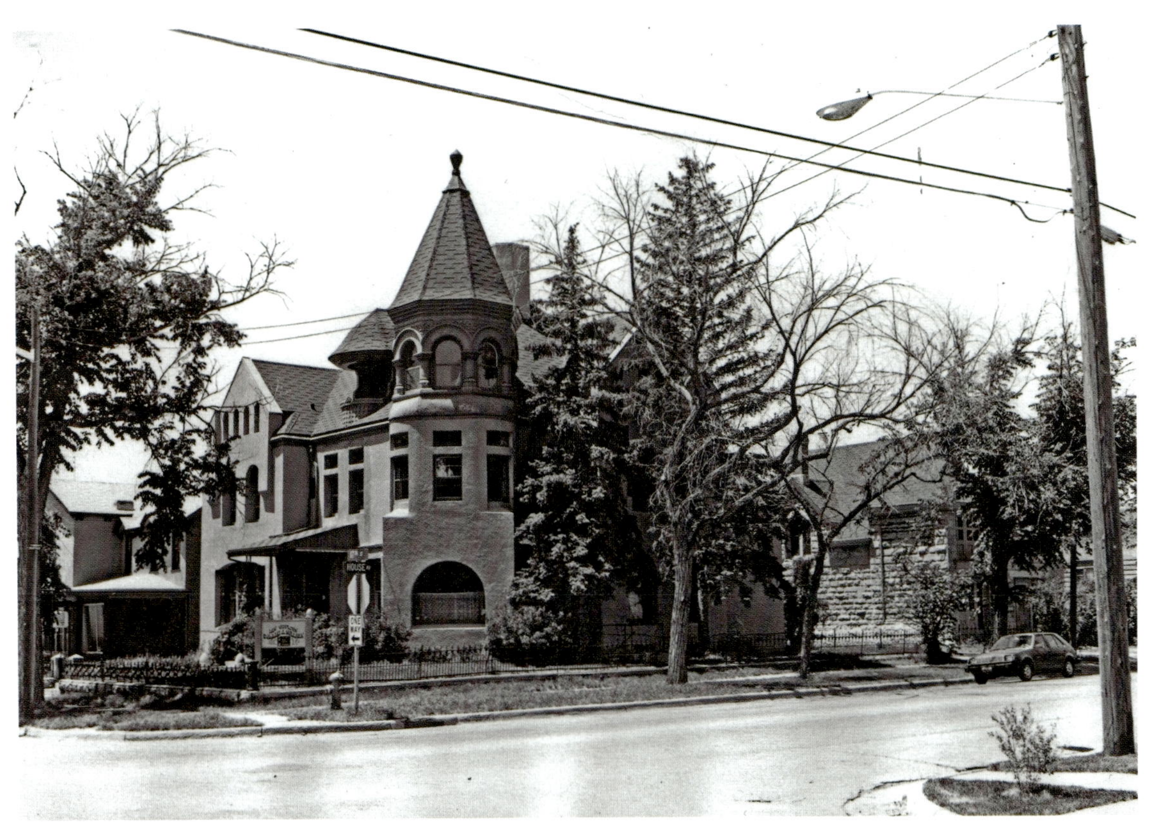

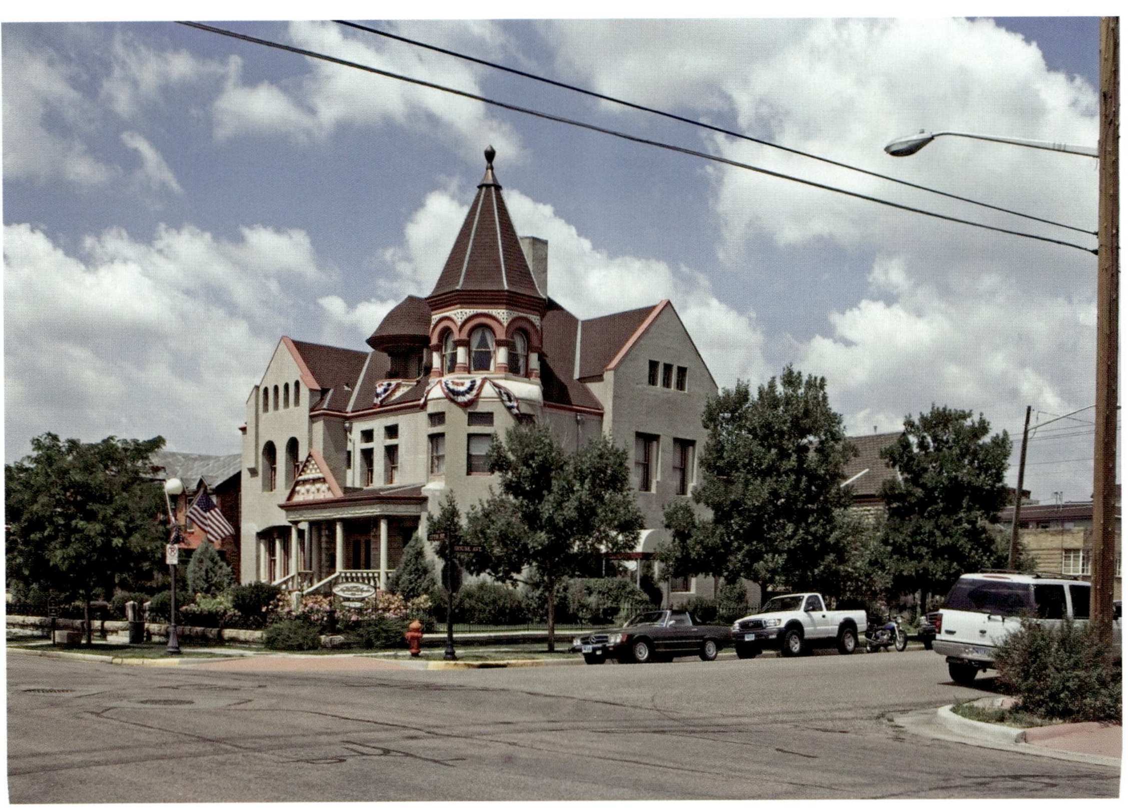

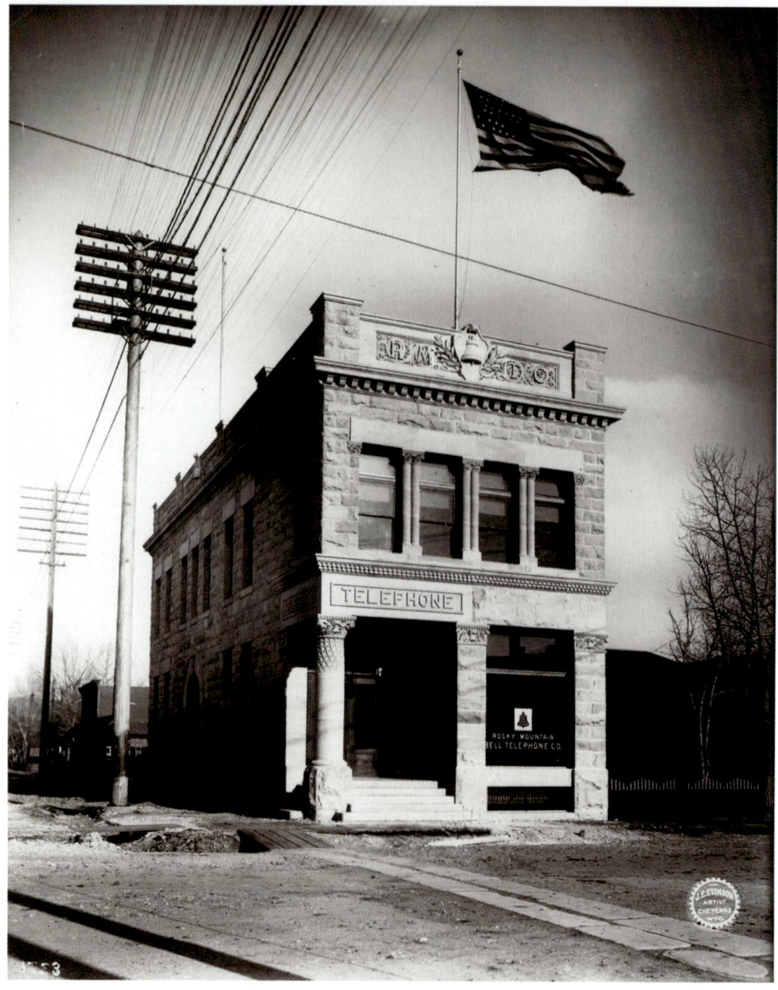

5. #1753

Telephone Building, Cheyenne, 1906, 1987, 2007
GPS COORDINATES: 41 8.018167N, 104 48.95983W

Located on the southeast corner of Seventeenth Street and Capitol Avenue, the original home of the Rocky Mountain Bell Telephone Company opened in 1906, the year Stimson made his original photo. It remained the company's home until the late 1920s. Sometime later, the building was converted to a hotel and a third floor was added. When I photographed the site in 1987, an art gallery occupied the building. Twenty years later, the building housed an architectural company. The original inscribed sign above the entrance that read "Telephone" was replaced with similar street signs for "Capitol Avenue" and, around the corner, "17th Street." Note also the remains of an old sign for the Cheyenne Business College slowly fading from the side of the building in the left background.

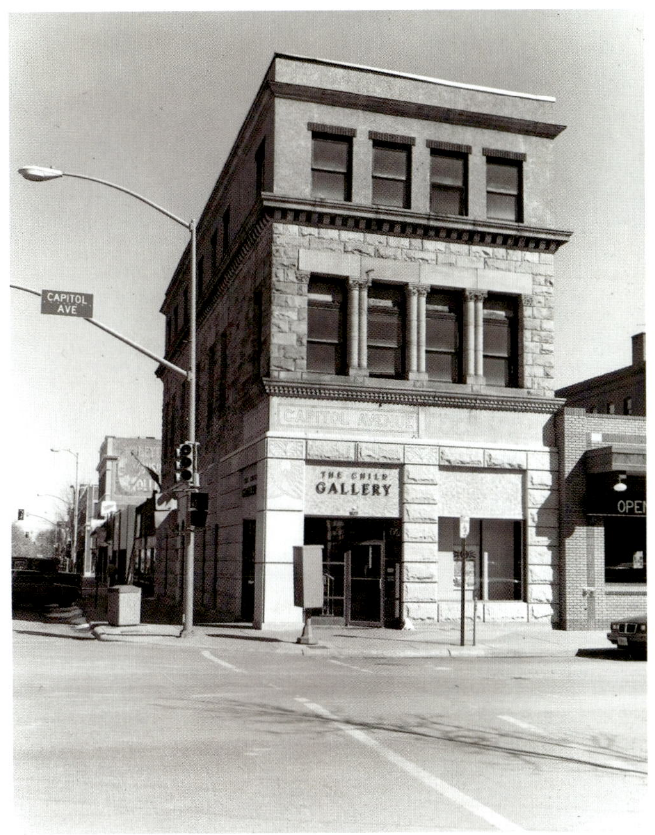

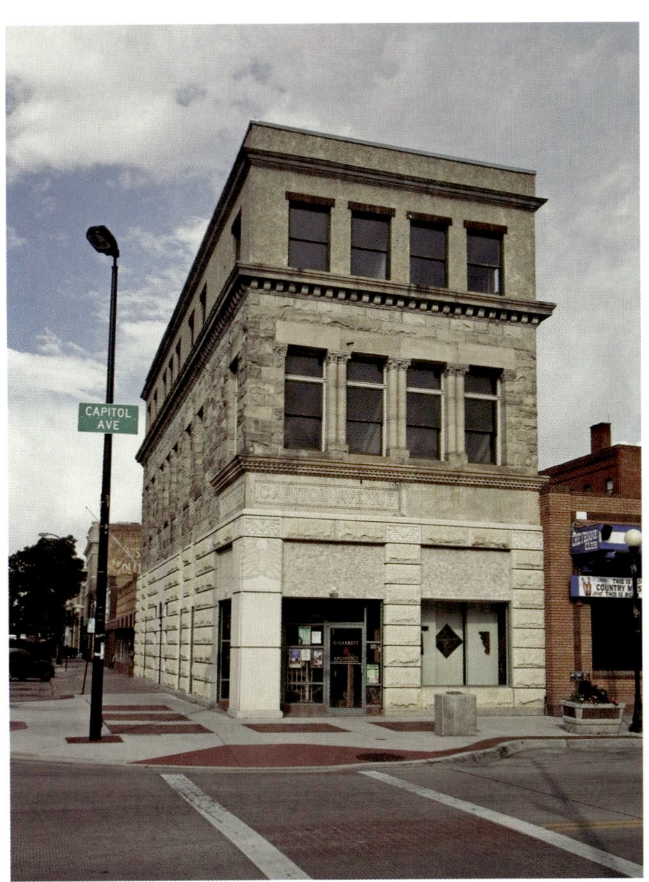

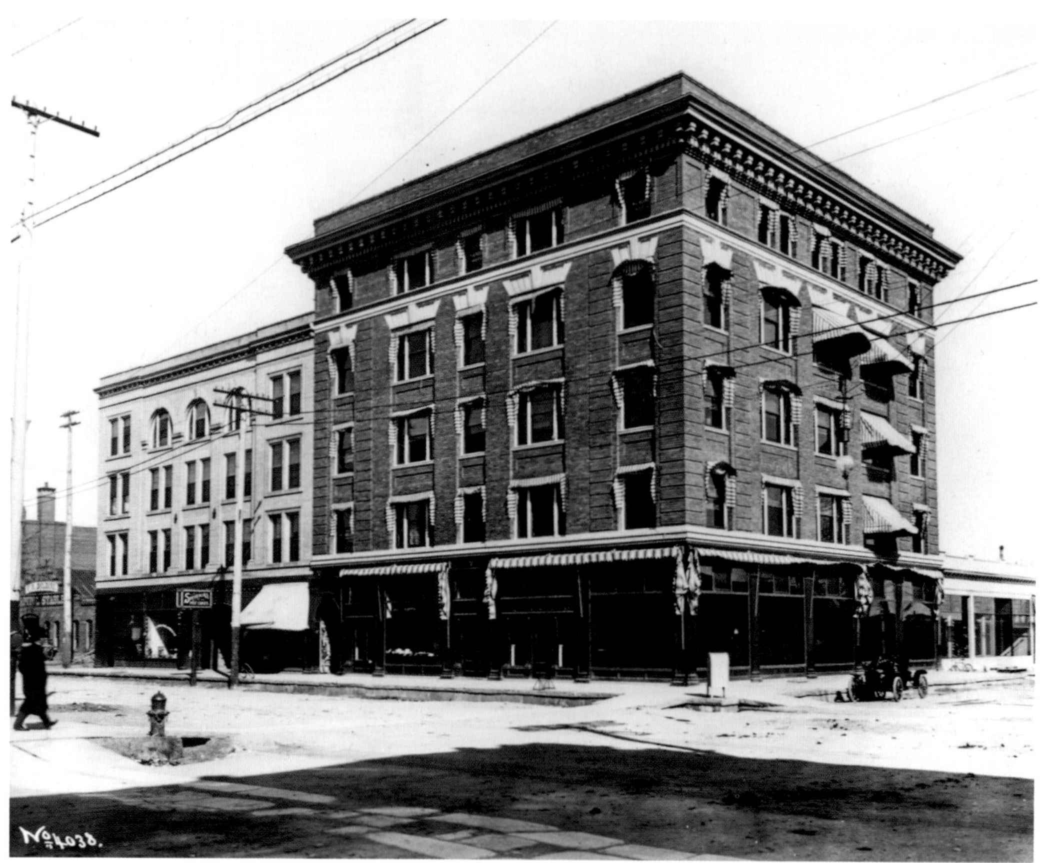

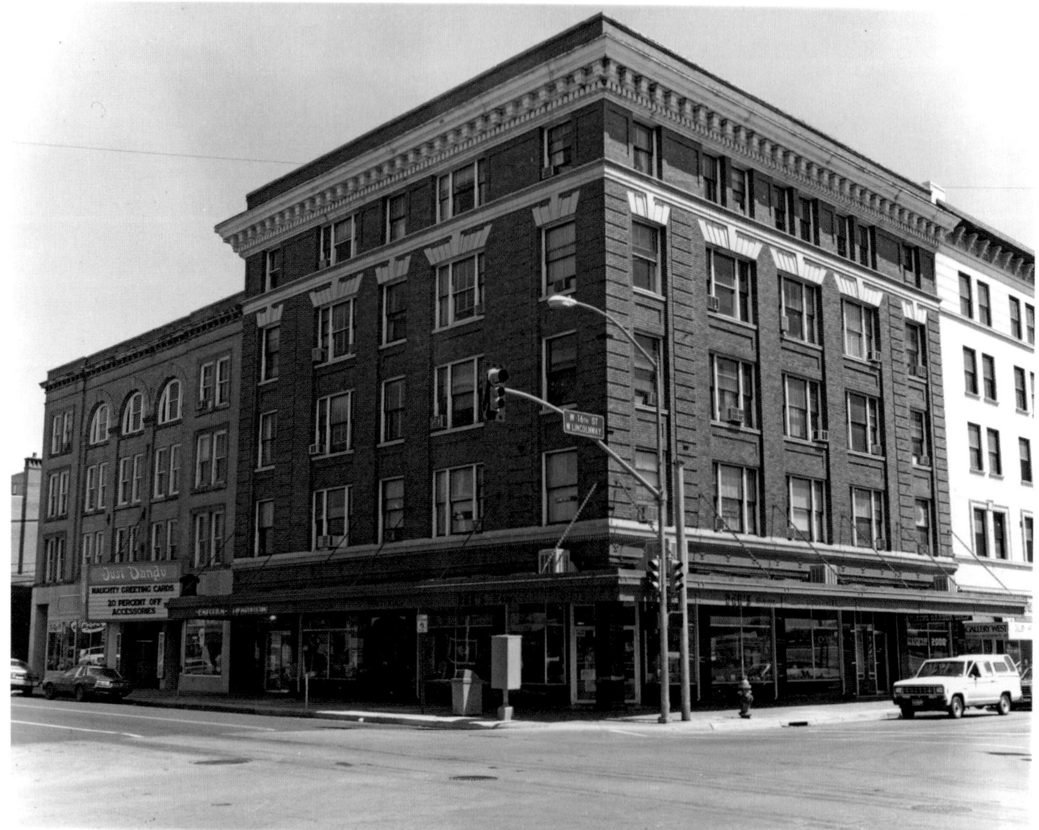

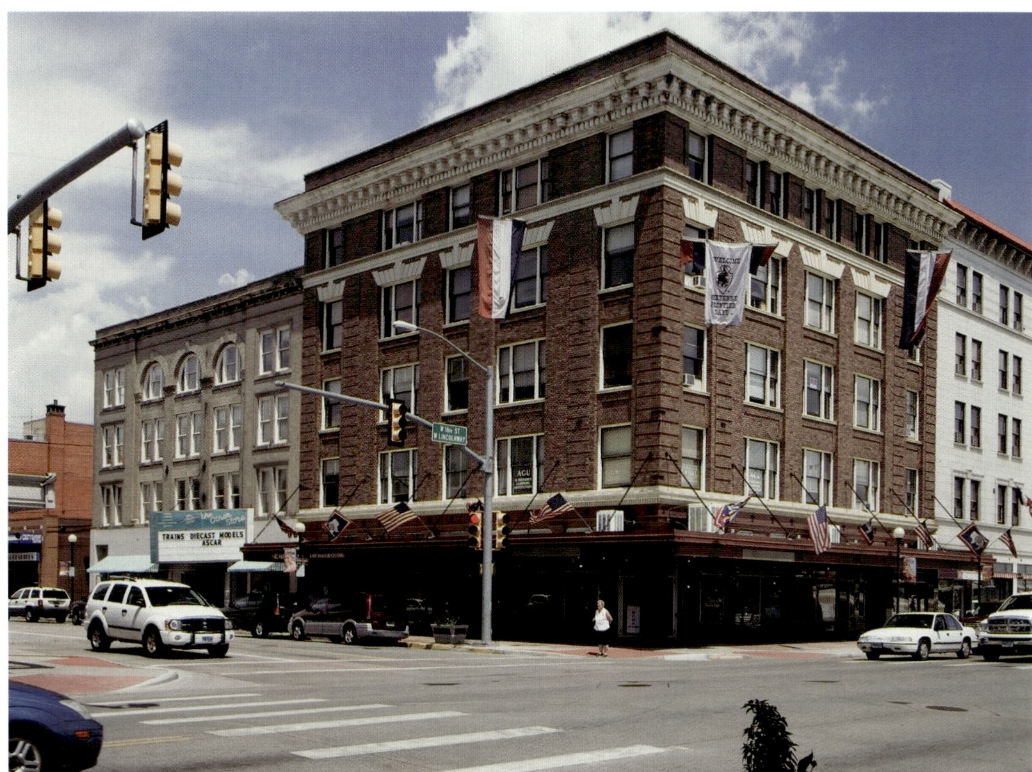

6. #4038

Majestic Theater and First National Bank Building, Cheyenne, 1908, 1987, 2007
GPS COORDINATES: 41 7.958N, 104 48.92367W

This classic Stimson building portrait features the northeast corner of the intersection of Capitol Avenue and Sixteenth Street in the heart of downtown Cheyenne. Both the theater and the bank represented progress for Wyoming's capital city and would have been important symbols of modernity for Stimson's employer, the Union Pacific Railroad, whose depot is just one block south. The photograph also displays the many awnings above the south-facing windows; the several sets of electrical, telephone, and trolley wires dangling above the street; and the presence of just a single automobile. The one sign visible in front of the building at left reads "Souvenirs/ Post Cards."

My 1987 view exhibits several interesting changes. The large building just to the right is the Plains Hotel, a Cheyenne landmark constructed three years after Stimson made his image. Window air conditioners have replaced the awnings, and many of the wires have been moved underground. The rise of the shopping mall and the accompanying decline of downtown Cheyenne are evident in the paucity of cars and pedestrians, as well as in the sign on the building to the left advertising "Naughty Greeting Cards!"

The 2007 photo also reflects a changing downtown. The presence of the many banners and bunting attests to the fact that I made my view during Frontier Days and might account for the increased number of cars and pedestrians. Then again, Cheyenne has made a concerted effort to revitalize its downtown, with the development of the Cheyenne Depot Museum one block south after the Union Pacific removed the last of its offices from that building in 1990. Then, in 2003 the city renovated a parking lot located between the depot and the bank building into Cheyenne Depot Plaza, a centerpiece for live music, arts and crafts, and history. The revitalization effort has breathed new life into this century-old urban landscape.

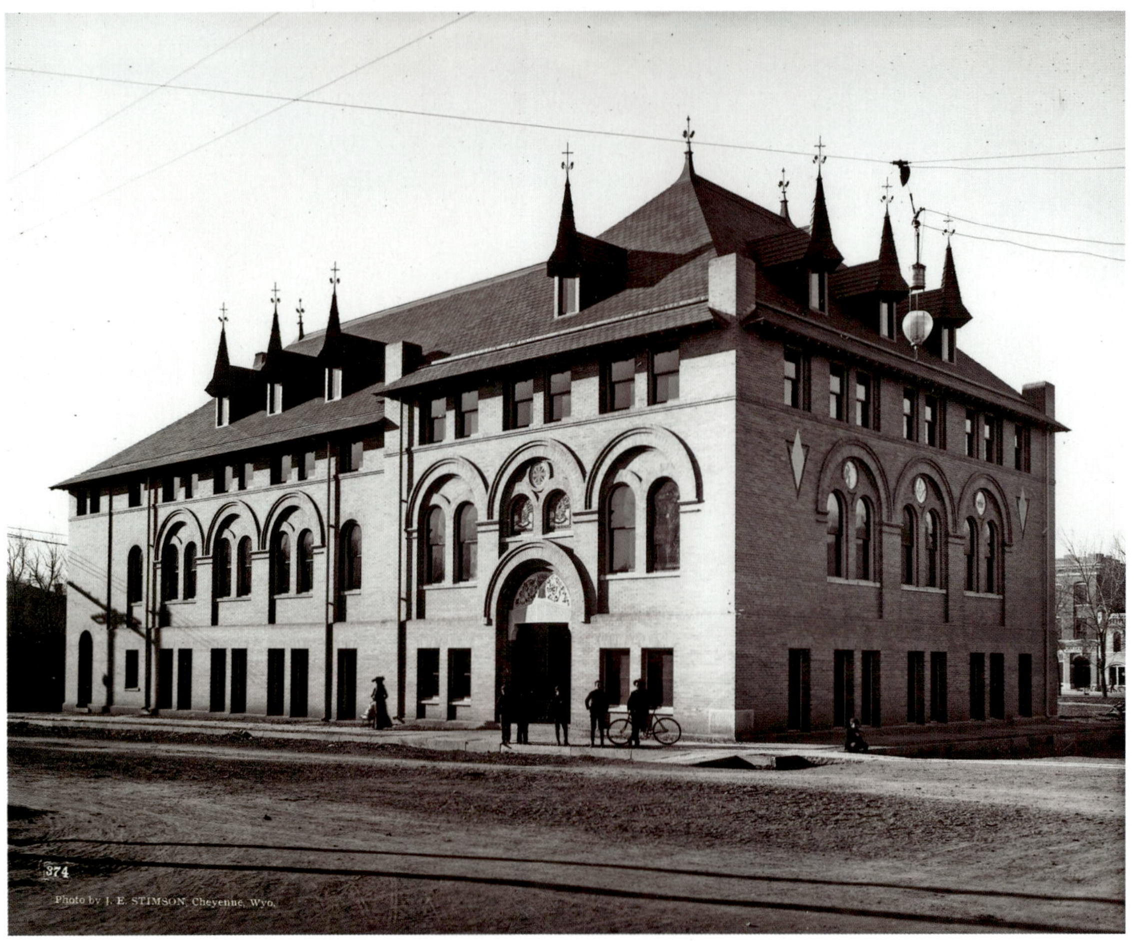

7. #374

Masonic Hall, Cheyenne, 1903, 1987, 2007
GPS COORDINATES: 41 8.129N, 104 49.0195W

Cheyenne Lodge Number One of the Masonic Order has a very special place in the Stimson story, not only because the photographer was a Mason but because it contains more than a dozen original Stimson hand-tinted photographs, the largest private collection outside the Wyoming State Archives. The lodge received its charter in 1868 and built its first temple on Sixteenth Street. The Masons laid the cornerstone for this new building in June 1901. Stimson photographed it in 1903, using a traditional building portrait style with the east wall, left, capturing the morning sun. A few pedestrians and a bicyclist are watching. Later that year, fire gutted the structure. When it was rebuilt around the original shell, the Gothic-inspired architectural style was gone, replaced with classical lines. The west wing, at right, was added in 1911.

Although the traffic lights have changed somewhat over the years, the temple's exterior remains the same, as can be seen in my two photographs taken in 1987 and twenty years later. The bunting and streamers were put up for Frontier Days. The interior of the building is also intact and contains a beautiful auditorium where ceremonies are conducted. The collection of Stimson color images includes shots of the Tetons, Chimney Rock on the Cody Road to Yellowstone, Buffalo Bill Dam, the Lower Falls of the Yellowstone, Devil's Tower, Elk Mountain, and the Big Horn River.

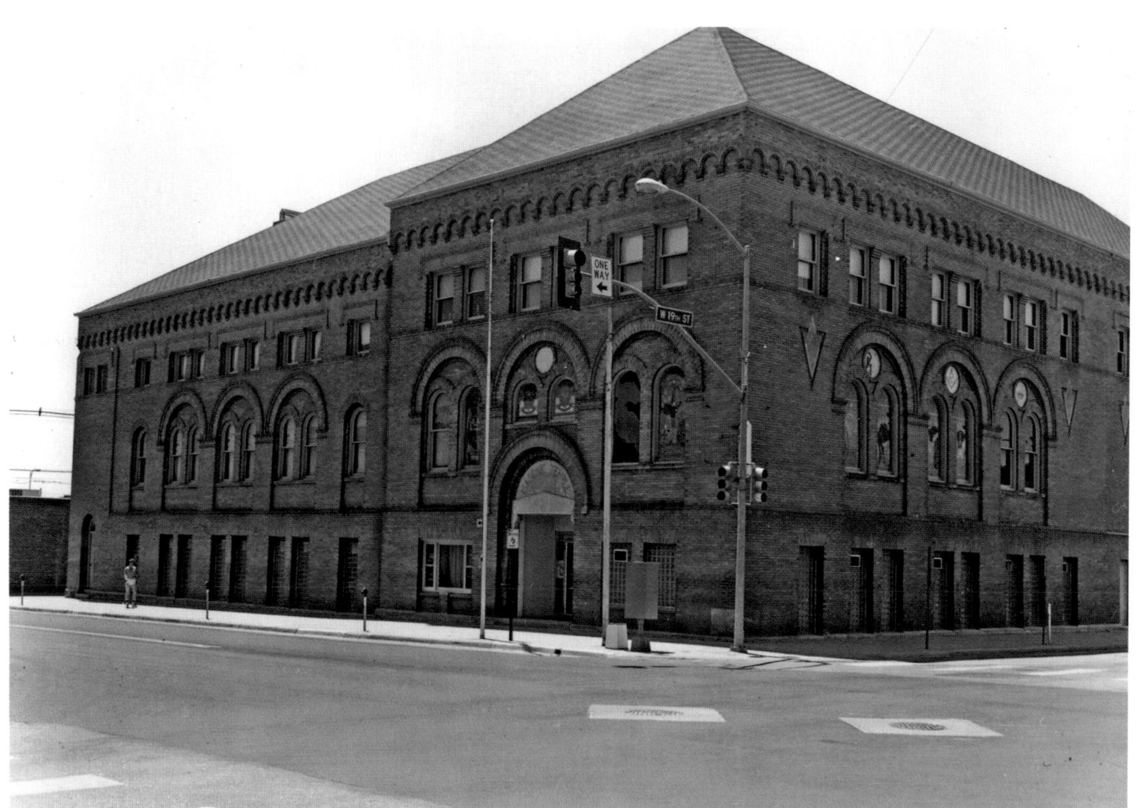

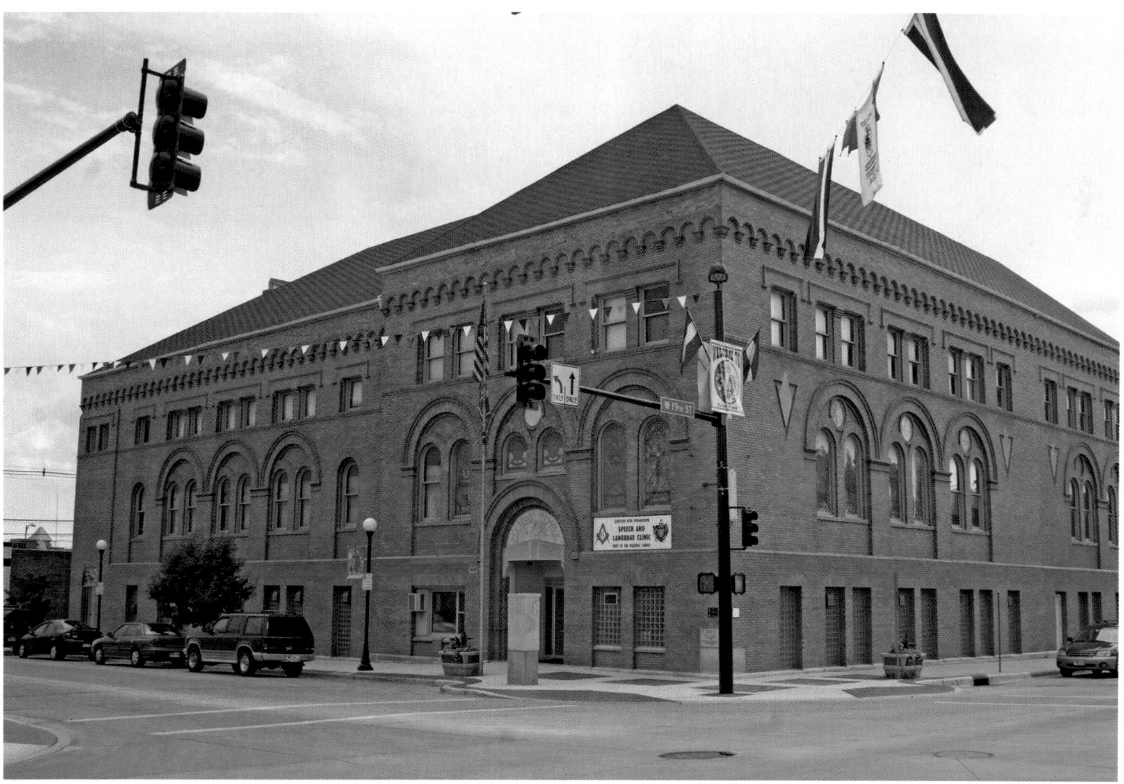

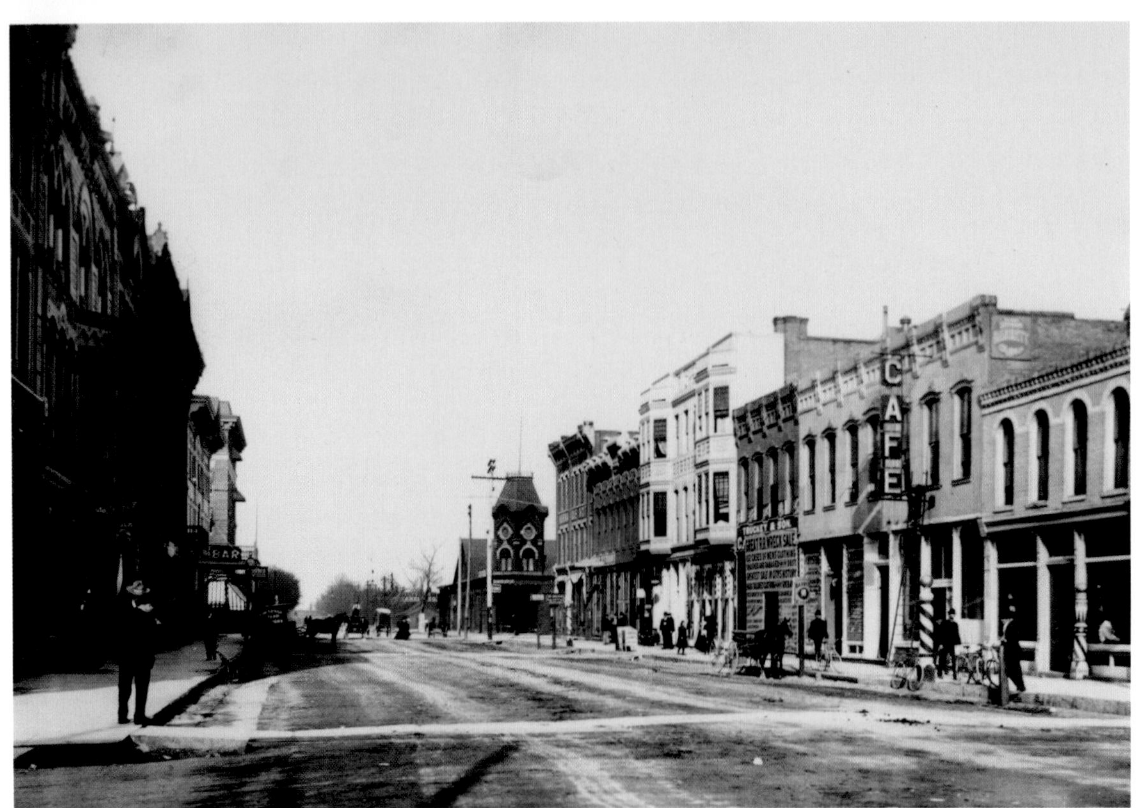
CAFE
BAR

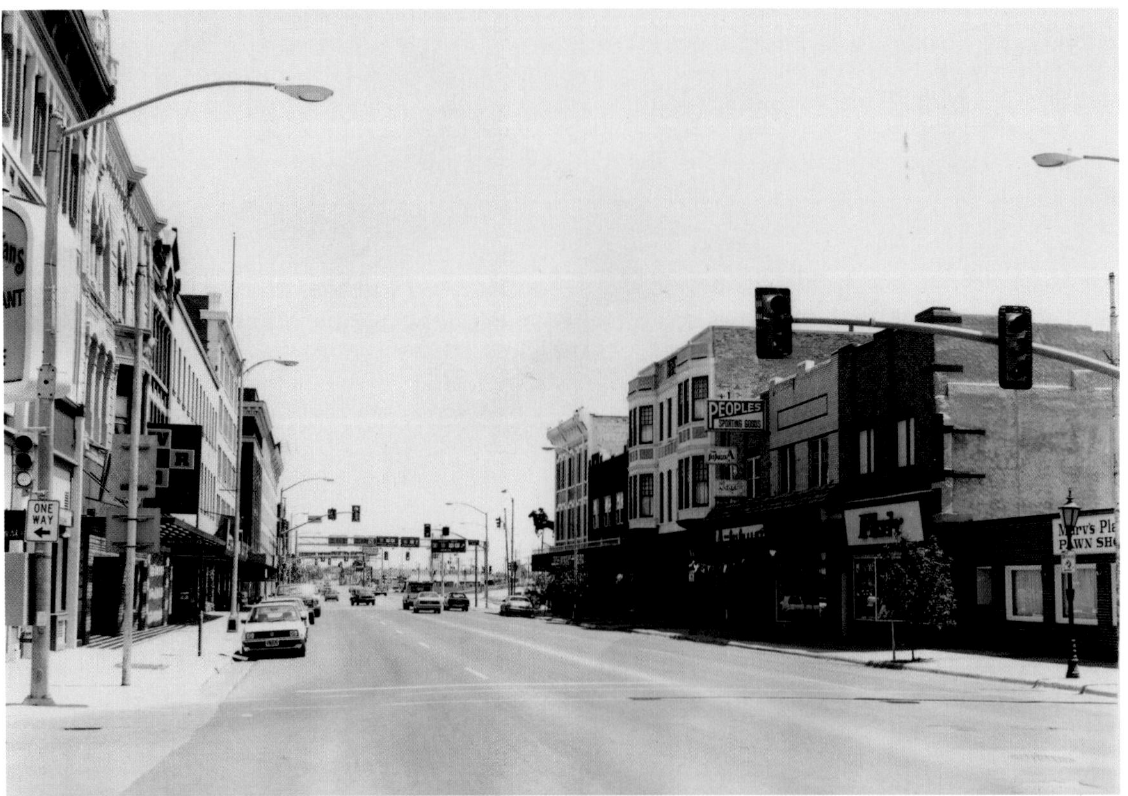
PEOPLES
SPORTING GOODS
ONE
WAY
Marv's Pla
PAWN SH

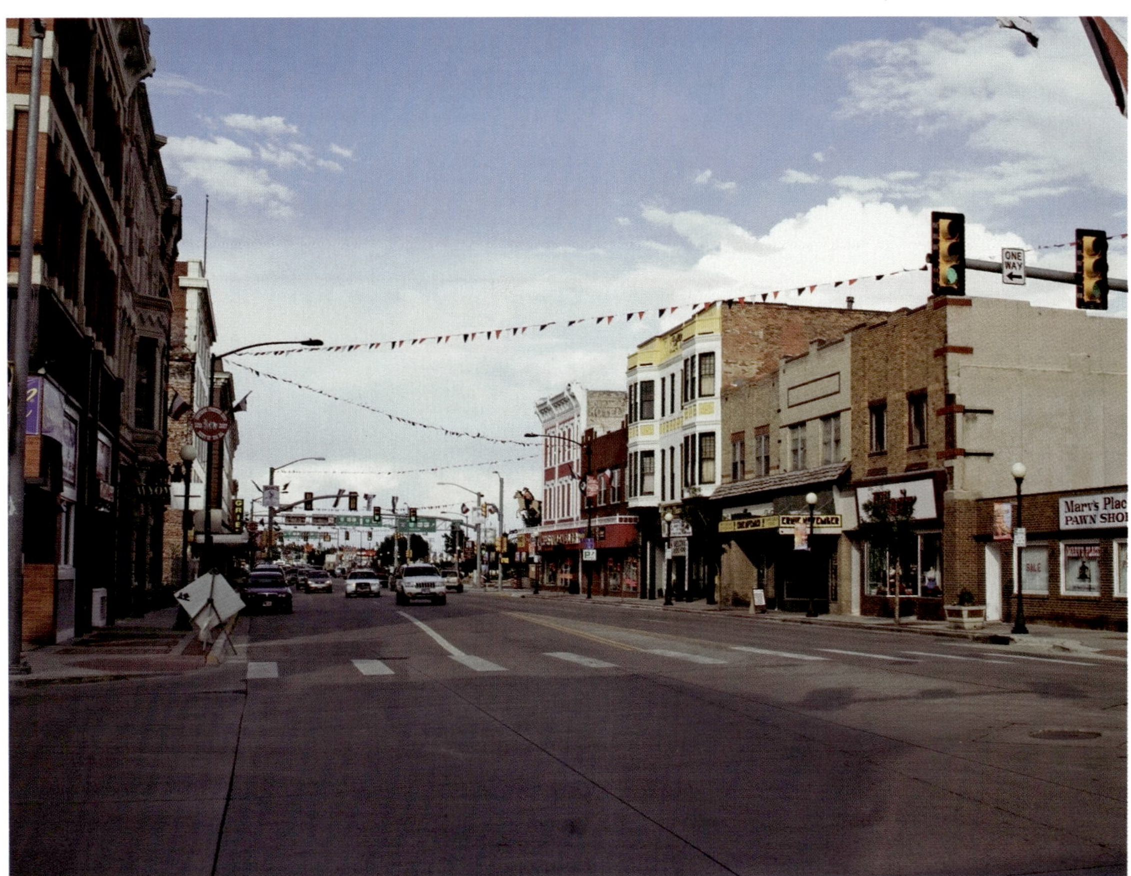

8. #4040

Sixteenth Street Looking East, 1908, 1987, 2007
GPS COORDINATES: 41 7.940167N, 104 48.99467W

Another classic Stimson street view, this one looks east from Carey Avenue onto Cheyenne's Sixteenth Street. The prominent building in the center-right is the Burlington Depot, constructed in 1882 and demolished in 1928. The light-colored building on the right with the two-story bay windows is the Atlas Theater, constructed in 1887 as a tea and confectionary shop and then remodeled into a theater the year before Stimson made his image. The tallest structure between the theater and the depot is the Phoenix Block, constructed in 1882. A barber shop, café, and men's clothing store can also be seen in Stimson's view of the bustling street. The latter boasts a large placard that reads "Great R.R. Wreck Sale—Greatest Sale in City's History."

In my 1987 shot, the absence of the Burlington Depot and the addition of streetlights, trees in the sidewalks, paved streets, and traffic signals are the most prominent differences. The street is still busy, though with cars rather than buggies. Clothing stores are still present, although the two pictured traded on Cheyenne's frontier image by selling "western wear." The most famous of these was Wrangler Western Wear, on the Phoenix Block, which featured a large electronic horse and rider sign out front.

Wrangler Western Wear remains a huge store and retail icon in downtown Cheyenne. The Atlas Theater endures as well, painted a warm yellow in the 2007 image. On the left side of the street, note the small, second-story bay window, visible in all three photos. The ever present streamers remind us that it is Frontier Days.

Although the Burlington Depot is gone, the presence of so many historic structures in this photo, as well as photos of the Nagle Warren Mansion, the Telephone Building, the Masonic Lodge, the state capitol and its surrounding neighborhoods, and the Union Pacific Depot Museum, are strong indicators of the efforts of the "Magic City of the Plains" to preserve its heritage.

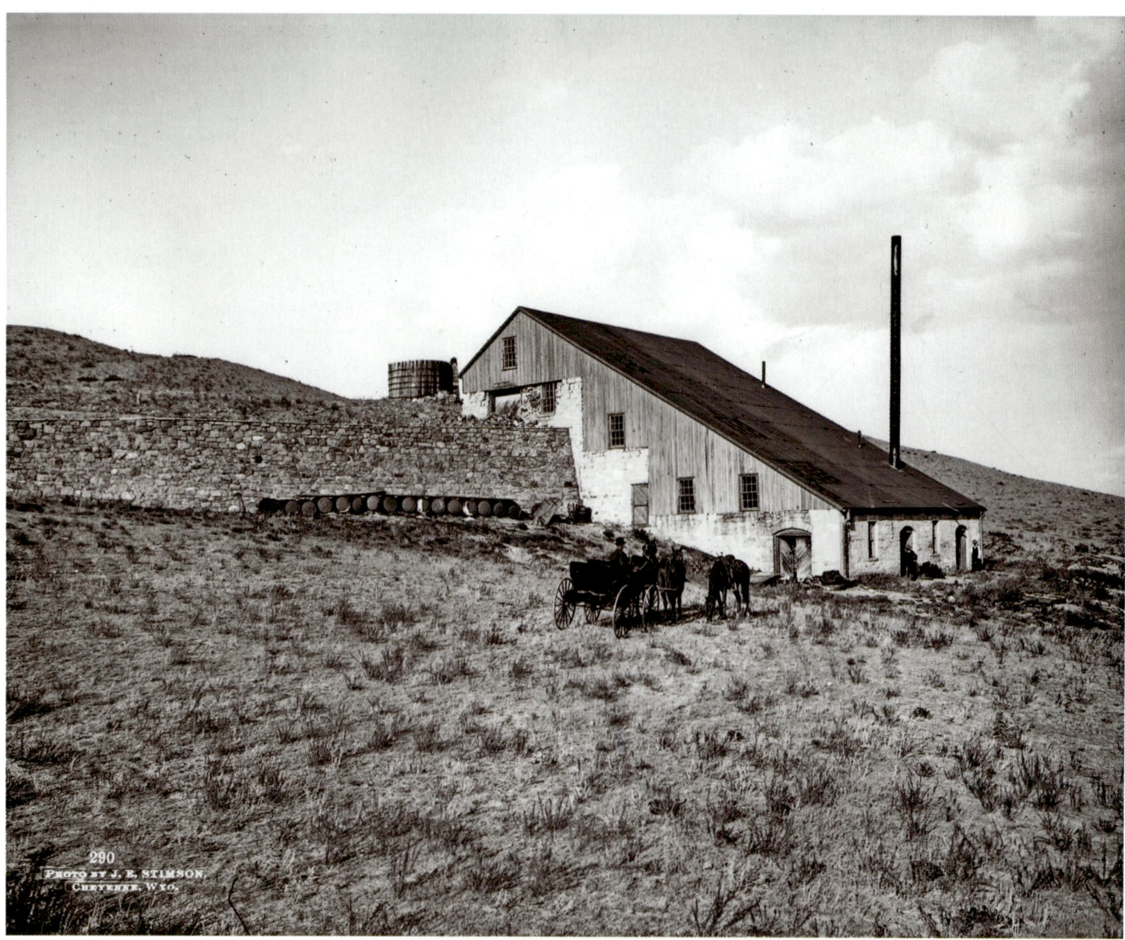

9. #290

Hecla Mill, 1902, 1987, 2007
GPS COORDINATES: 41 09.532N, 105 10.197W

Prospectors located the Hecla and Silver Crown mines about twenty miles west of Cheyenne in the early 1880s. They found deposits of gold, copper, and silver, producing a small rush to the location in 1886. When Stimson visited the site in 1902, another operation had built this small ore-crushing plant. Wagons brought ores along the top of the rock wall at left and dumped them into a bin inside the building. Gravity fed them through a steam-powered crusher, and the minerals were collected in small drums visible along the base of the wall. Although a small operation, the Hecla Mill served as another important site for Stimson because it represented Wyoming's developing economy, a link to national and international markets, and another potential customer for his boss, the Union Pacific Railroad. As with many of his business portraits, Stimson composed this image in the late afternoon so the western sun illuminated not just the building but its processes as well.

When I visited the site in 1987, I traveled west from Cheyenne on Happy Jack Road to the Crystal Reservoir turnoff and then headed west almost to the southern edge of the reservoir. The stone wall remained, as did the steam engine, rusting away in the open air. Remnants of a late spring snow were also present.

Twenty years later, Lauren, my dog Nellie, and I found that Hecla looked pretty much as it had twenty years earlier. The rock wall and the steam engine seem to defy scavengers looking for pieces of history.

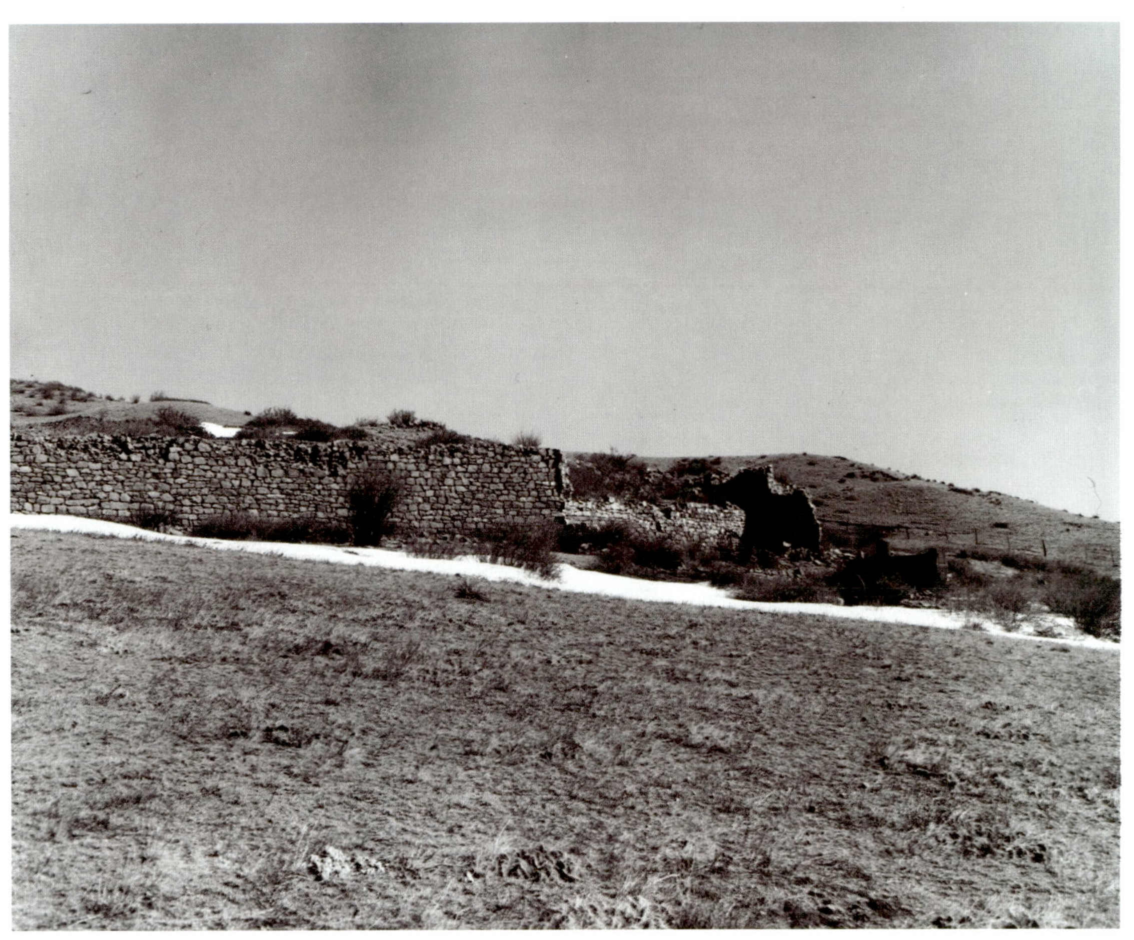

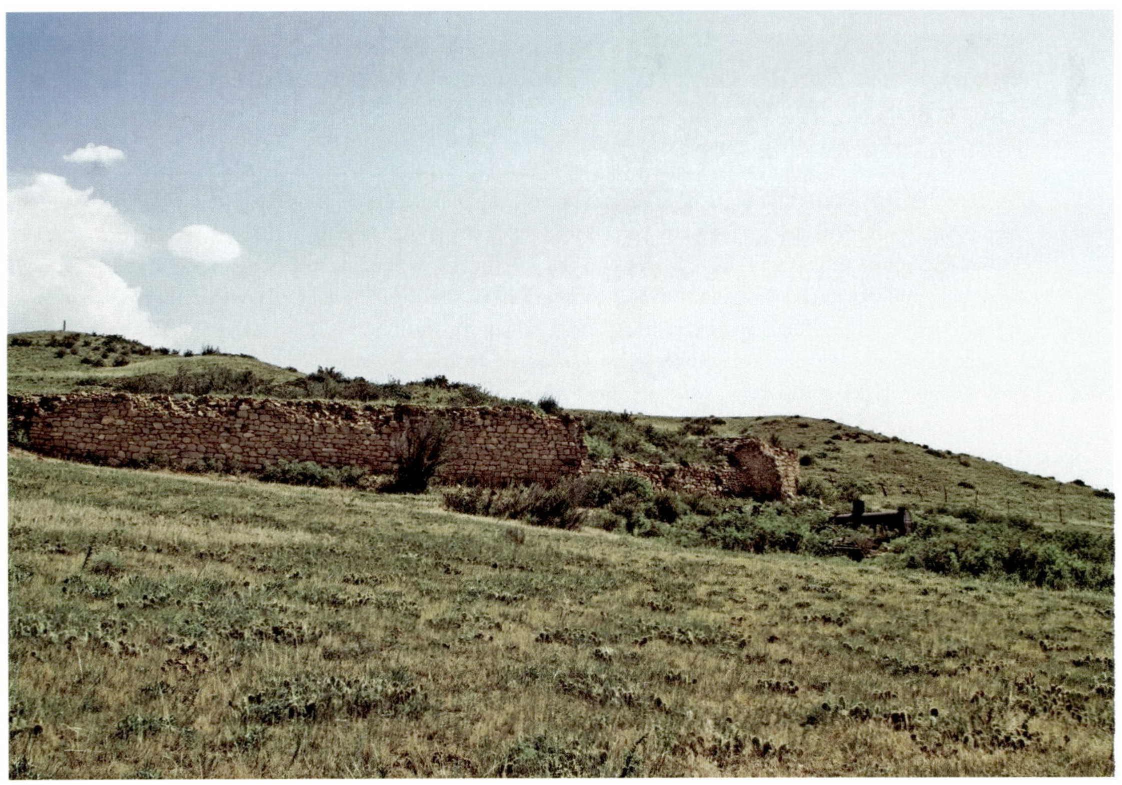

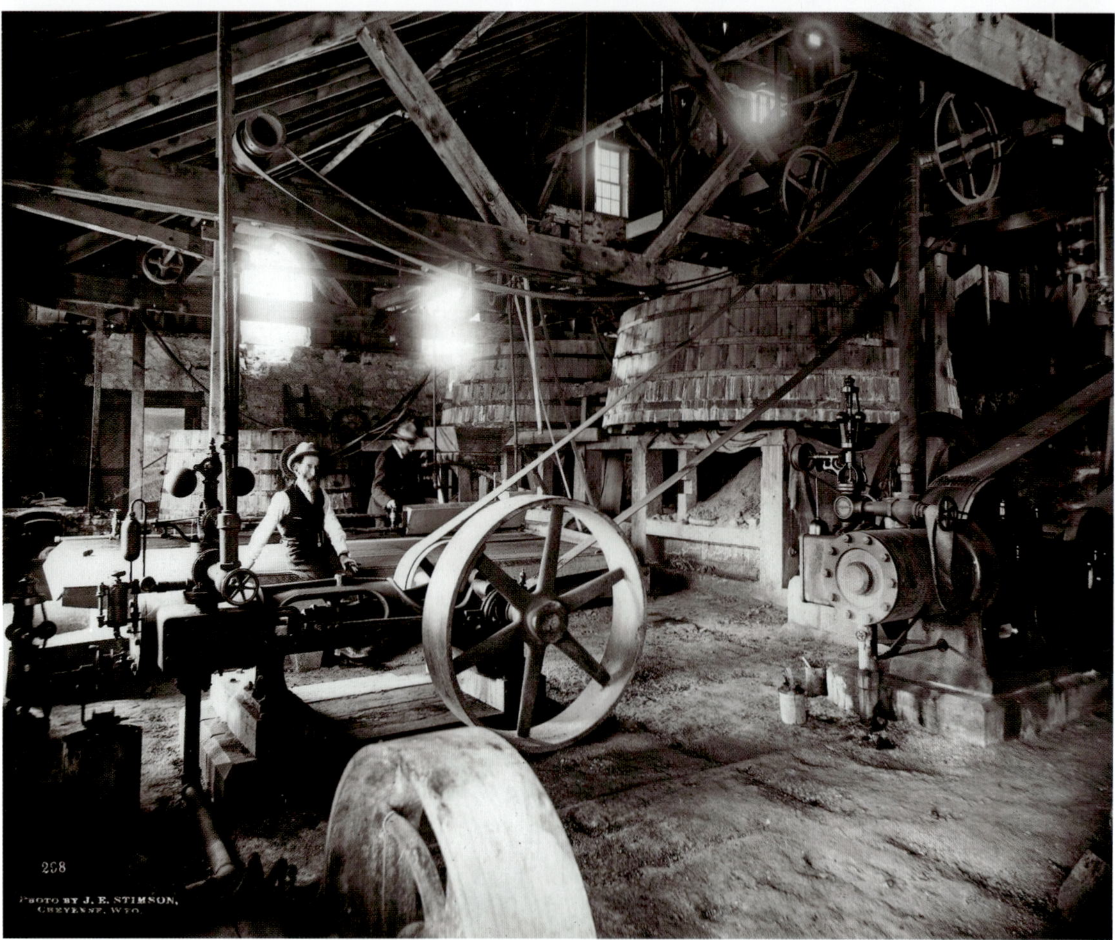

10. #298

Interior Hecla Mill, 1903, 1987, 2007
GPS COORDINATES: 41 09.546N, 105 10.148W

In Stimson's day, interior photographs were rare because of the necessity of using flash powders. To gain the correct exposure, the artist used a long exposure, evident by the sunlight pouring in through the western windows. His image shows various steam-driven, rock-crushing machines as well as the steam engine, right, and the various drive belts and flywheels needed to run machinery before electricity. No doubt taken the same day as the previous exterior view, this shot is an extraordinary image presenting the inner workings of a small factory.

Like its exterior partner, my 1987 photograph shows that although little of the structure remains, the heavy steam engine, right, is still there, although one bolt is gone. To show that detail, my friend at the back of the photo, Laramie photographer Paul Jacques, had to do a little pruning.

Twenty years later, Lauren stands at the back. The site looked essentially the same, although the bushes in the foreground seemed to have grown a bit. Perhaps in another two decades those bushes will have totally engulfed the steam engine, masking its existence and further protecting it from souvenir hunters.

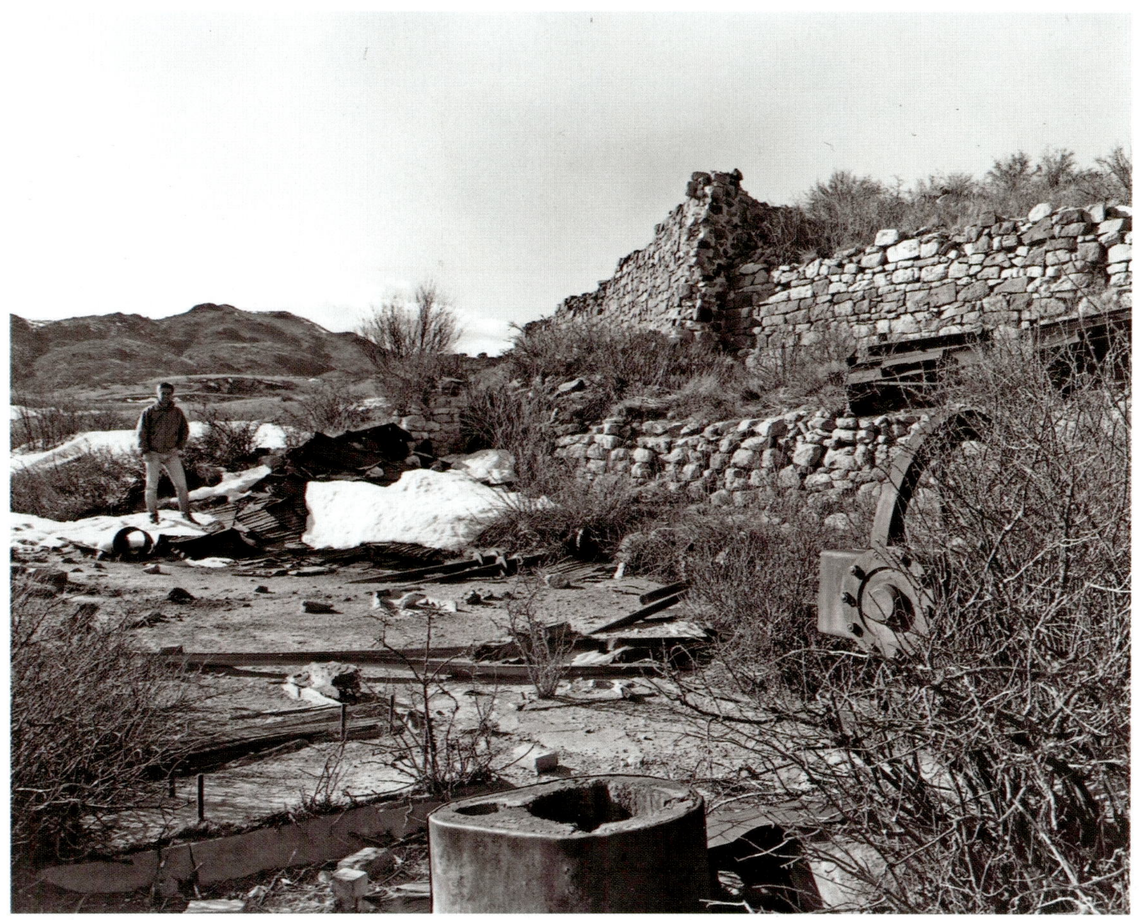

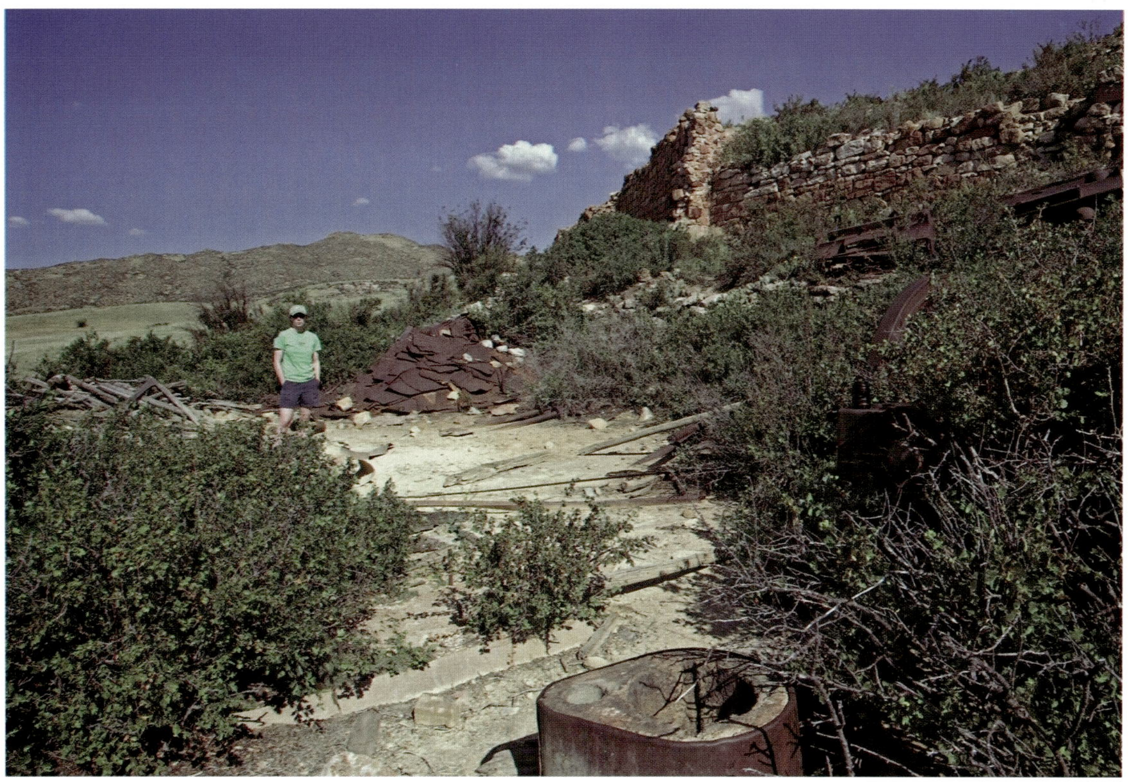

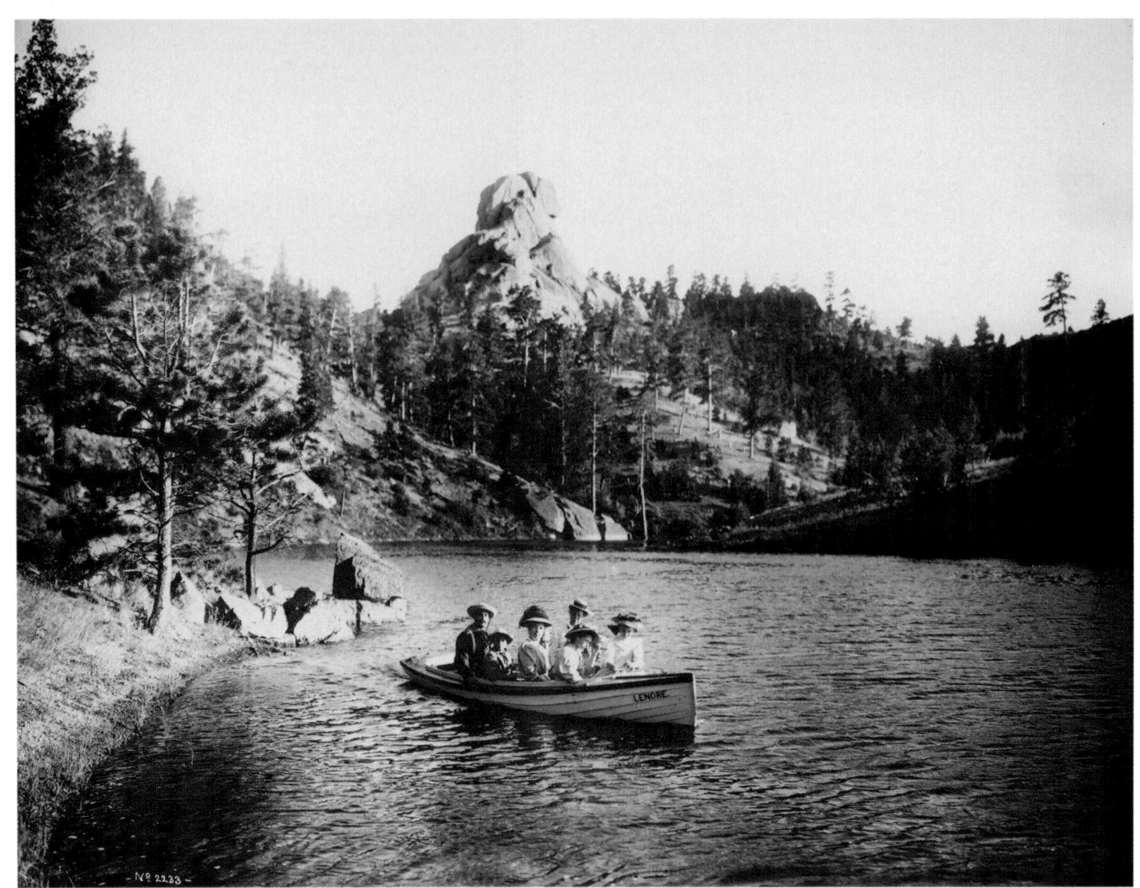

LENORE
Nº 2233

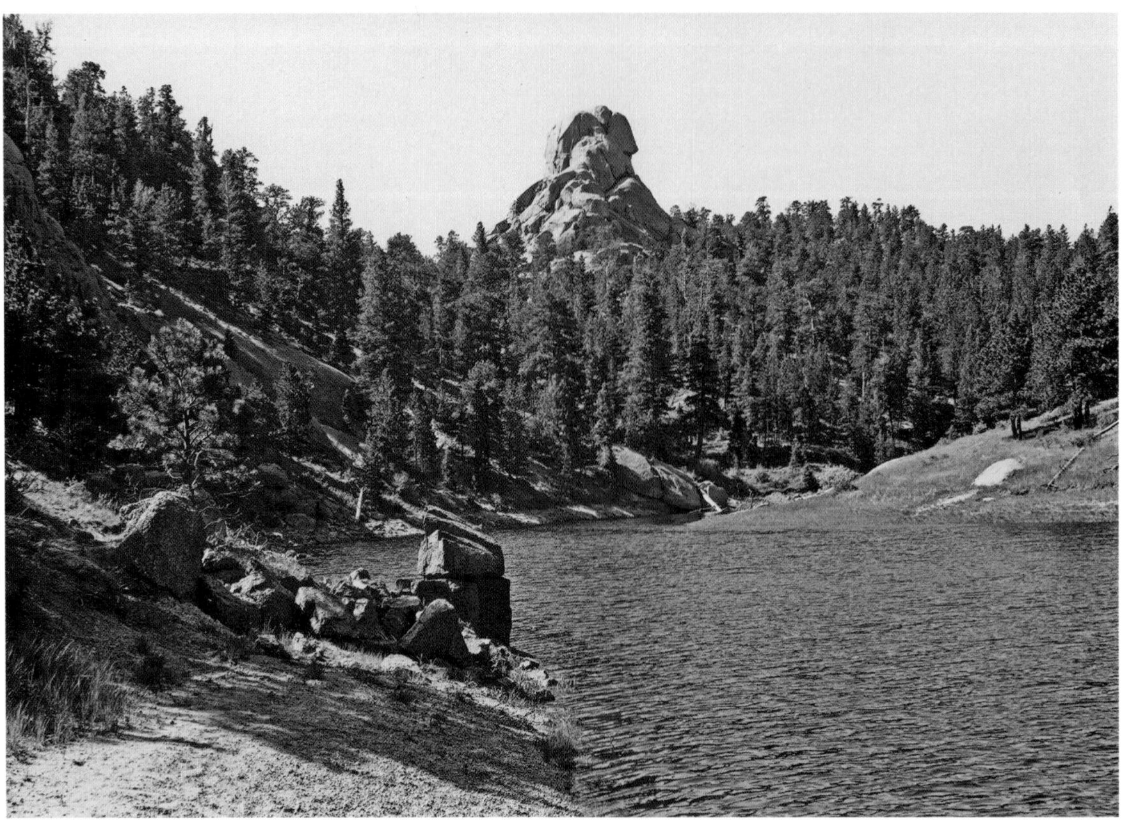

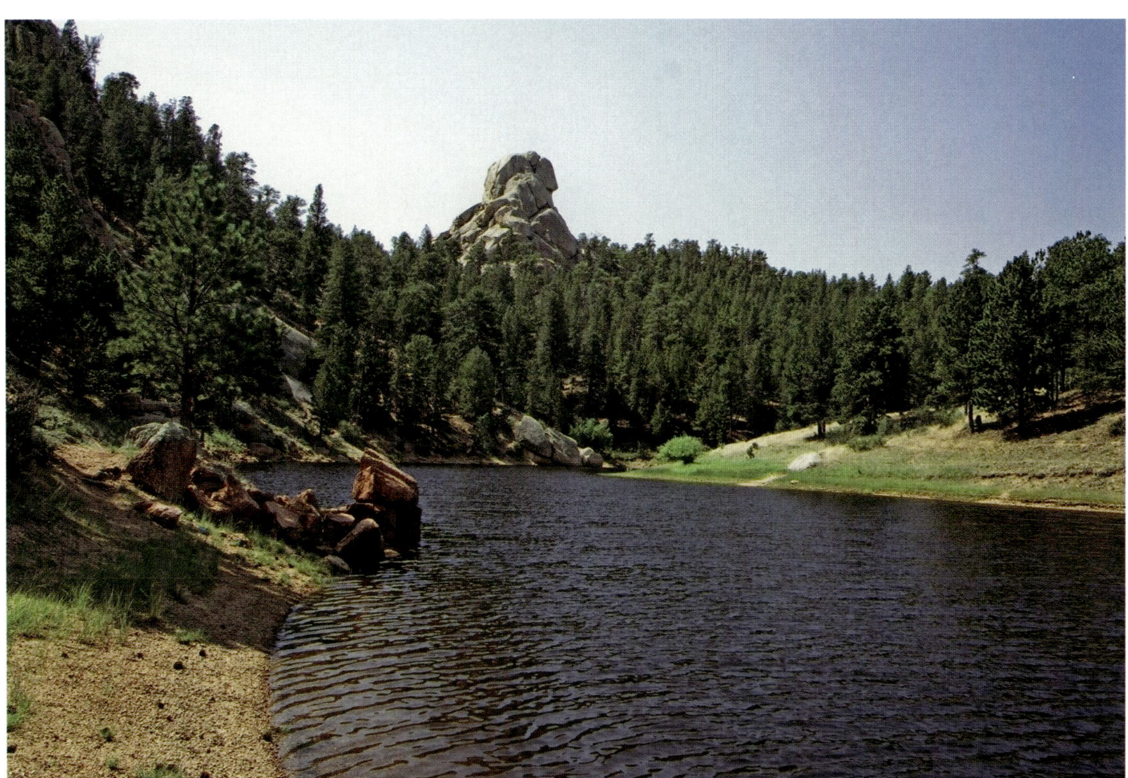

11. #2233

Outing at Granite Reservoir, 1908, 1987, 2007
GPS COORDINATES: 41 10.479N, 105 14.779W

Cheyenne's *Wyoming Tribune* reported in its "Personal" section on July 23, 1908, that "A. J. Vance and J. E. Stimson and their families have returned from a camping party at the Granite Spring reservoir. A .W. Darling and children, and James Hart, who were in the party, have also returned."

A close inspection of Stimson's original shows a man and two boys in the rear of the *Lenore* and two women and three girls toward the front. The young girl on the far right is steering the boat.

Granite Springs Reservoir is about twenty-five miles west of Cheyenne in what today is Curt Gowdy State Park. It was constructed by the City of Cheyenne in 1904 to provide water for the city. This view is just to the west of an access road near the inlet.

More of a family outing snapshot than a typical Stimson promotional photograph, this view of his family and friends at Granite Springs Reservoir could have been used to boost southeastern Wyoming tourism.

My rephotographs in 1987 and 2007 show a thicker forest and slightly higher water levels. It remains a picturesque spot.

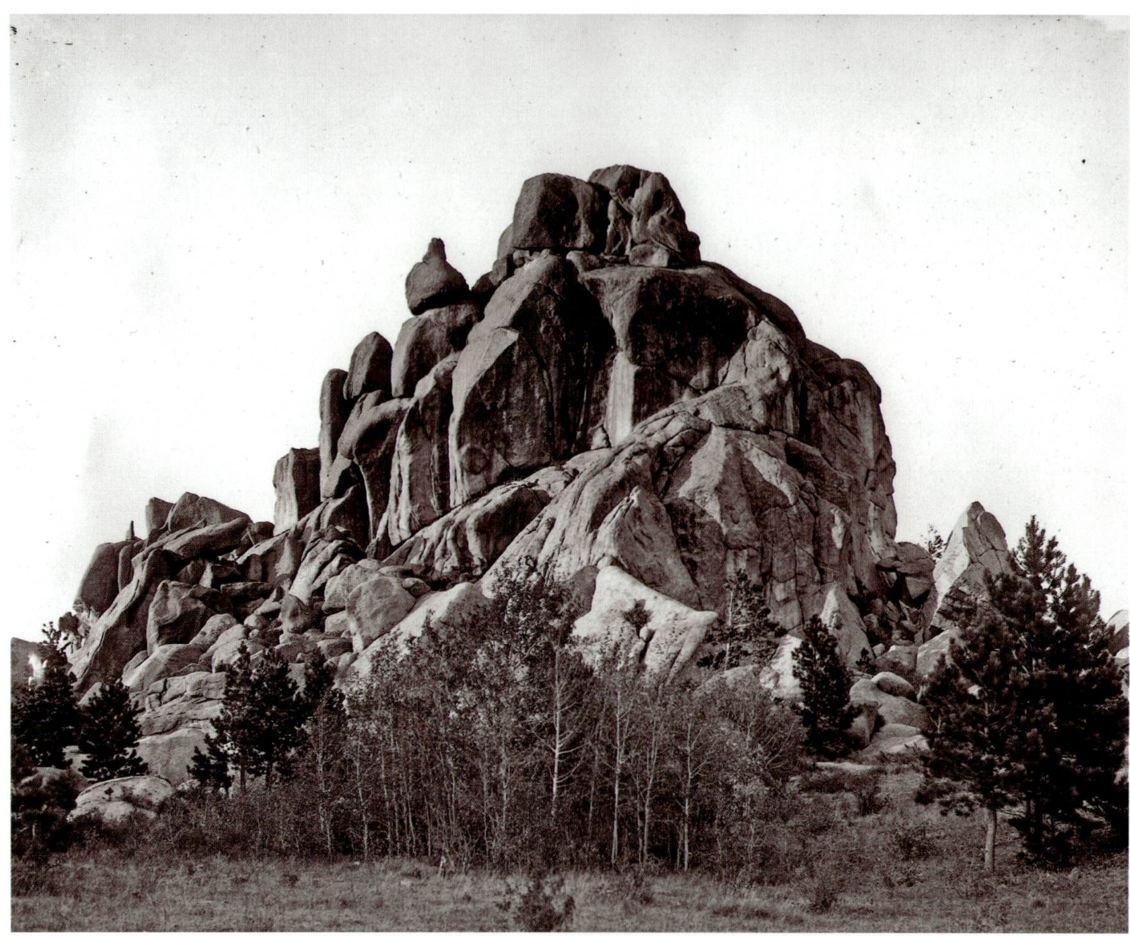

12. #6021

Vedauwoo, ca. 1910, 1987, 2007
GPS COORDINATES: 41 11.658N, 105 15.339W

Vedauwoo, between Laramie and Cheyenne, is an area of rocky outcrops of Sherman granite. It is a favorite area for rock climbing, hiking, mountain biking, cross-country skiers, and picnickers. The name *Vedauwoo* supposedly comes from the Arapaho word meaning "earth born." In 1924, the University of Wyoming Theater Department staged a play titled *Vedauwoo: A Pageant Based on Fact and Fancy* in a natural amphitheater in the area. The name caught on, and soon the entire area was being called Vedauwoo.

Stimson's photograph is not in the main section of what today is called Vedauwoo but instead is located off Happy Jack Road near the Hynds Lodge in Curt Gowdy State Park. Cheyenne businessman Harry P. Hynds, a contemporary of Stimson's and a founder of the Frontier Days Rodeo, constructed the lodge in 1922 for use by the Wyoming Boy Scouts of America as a recreational camp. In 1935, the City of Cheyenne took over operation until the state established Curt Gowdy State Park in 1971 and assumed control.

When I initially began looking for this vantage point in 1987, I was dumbfounded by the prospect of finding a specific rock formation among hundreds of square miles of outcrops. Only after traveling the backcountry highway called Happy Jack Road did I discover the site. In fact, it is only a couple of miles north of the previous photo at Granite Springs Reservoir.

Stimson's view of the rock formation is similar to his building portraits. He composed the shot straight on, with afternoon light both illuminating the front and providing shadows for depth. For my 1987 view, I had to move back from the Stimson vantage point because the aspen trees in his foreground had grown high enough to completely block the view. The vehicles in the foreground were parked in an overflow parking lot for the Hynds Lodge, located on the other side of the formation. For my 2007 view, I tried to duplicate my 1987 vantage point, showing that the parking lot has been removed although the road to the lodge is still visible at right. This view was one of the first "lucky finds" I made simply by knowing images and driving around looking at landscapes.

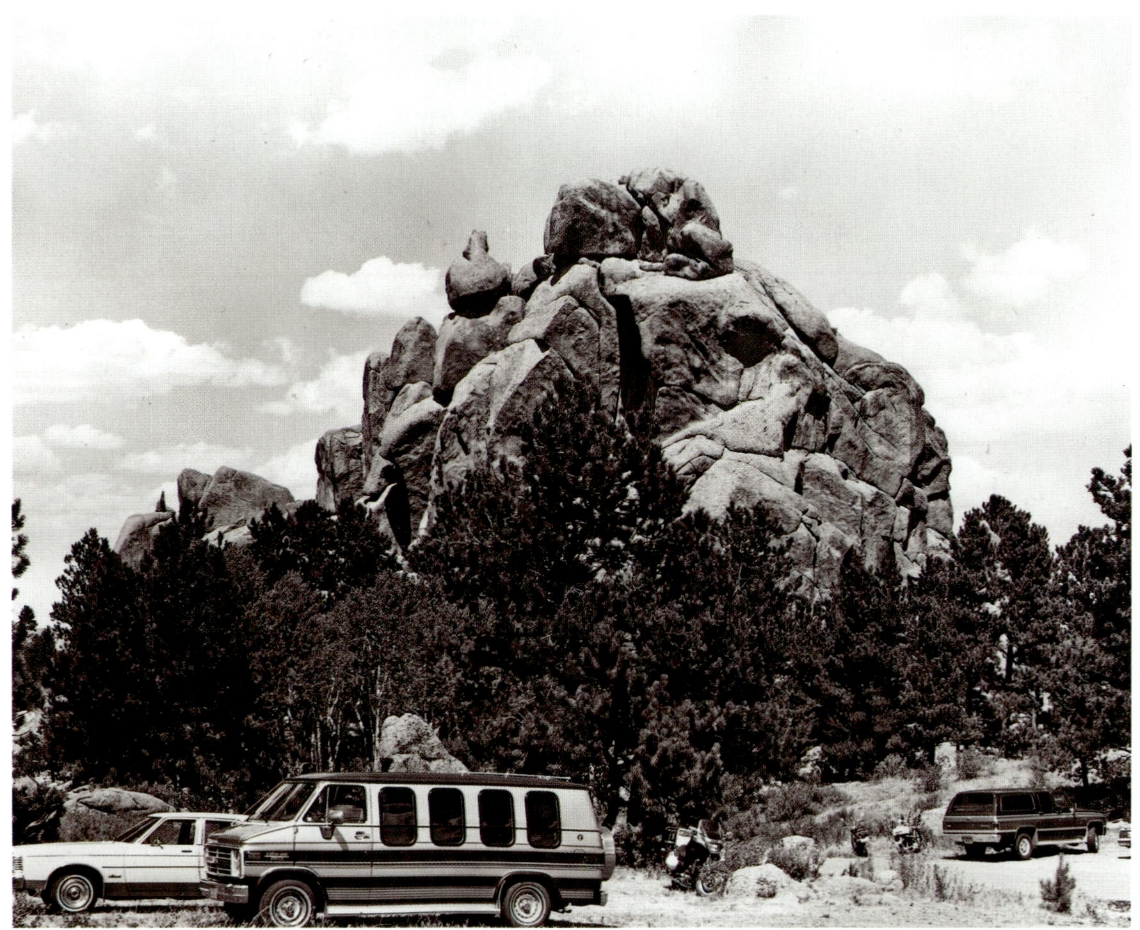

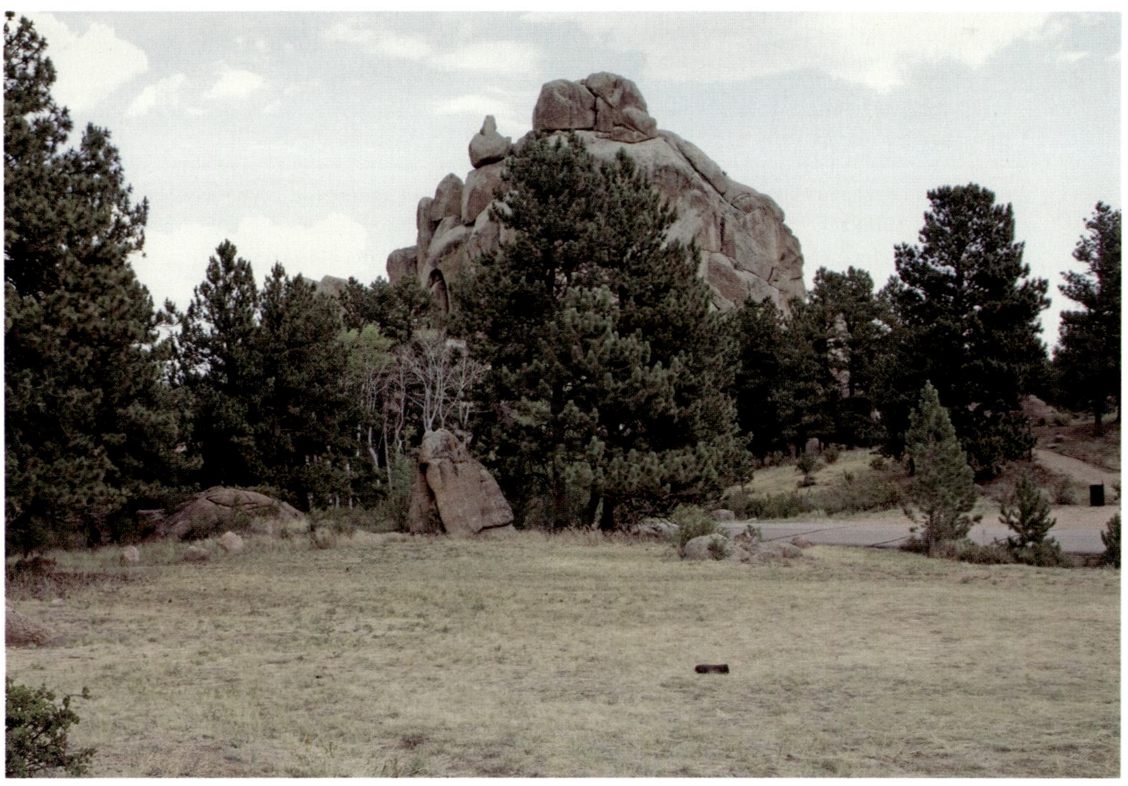

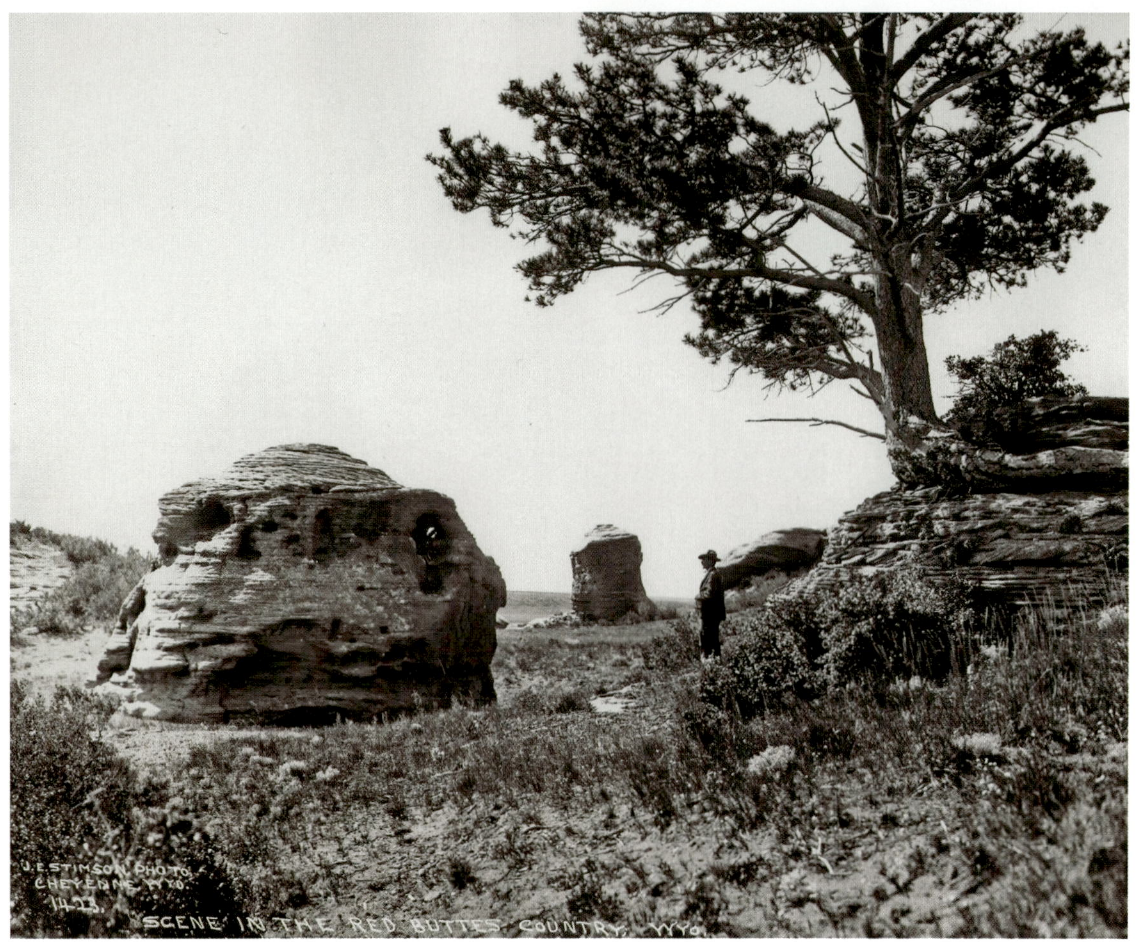

13. #1423

Scene in the Red Buttes Country, 1906, 1987, 2007
GPS COORDINATES: 41 10.21N, 105 33.324W

As discussed in chapters 3 and 4, the Red Buttes country south of Laramie had been identified for its unique scenery since at least the construction of the Union Pacific Railroad in the 1860s. Walt Whitman had included the area's wind-eroded rocks in that area in his 1871 ode to the completion of the transcontinental railroad, the Atlantic cable, and the Suez Canal, titled "Passage to India":

> *I hear the locomotives rushing and soaring, and the shrill steam whistle,*
> *I hear the echoes reverberate through the grandest scenery in the world,*
> *I cross the Laramie plains, I note the rocks in grotesque shapes, the buttes.*

Stimson visited the Red Buttes several times, including during his 1906 Trip across the Continent, and made these four photographs (nos. 13–16) of rock formations in the area. Never formally protected by any government, the Red Buttes country has always been a part of Wyoming's profane landscape, more or less left alone because of its remoteness. Since the late 1990s, however, a small rural subdivision called "the Buttes" has been created around the formations, offering small ranches for folks who work in Laramie.

In Stimson's 1906 photograph, he placed a person among the rocks to give the scene a sense of scale. When I first visited the site in 1987, I was struck by how similar the large tree at right appeared to be eight decades later. My rephotograph also shows a small piece of split rail fence just to the left of the tree in the mid-distance, the handiwork of a small rancher who lived in a trailer set amid the rocks. My 2007 photo, however, shows the intrusion of the new subdivision with its many split rail fences, the cordoning off of the profane landscape so common in the New West. The enduring tree at right, though, suggests that time here might best be measured in centuries.

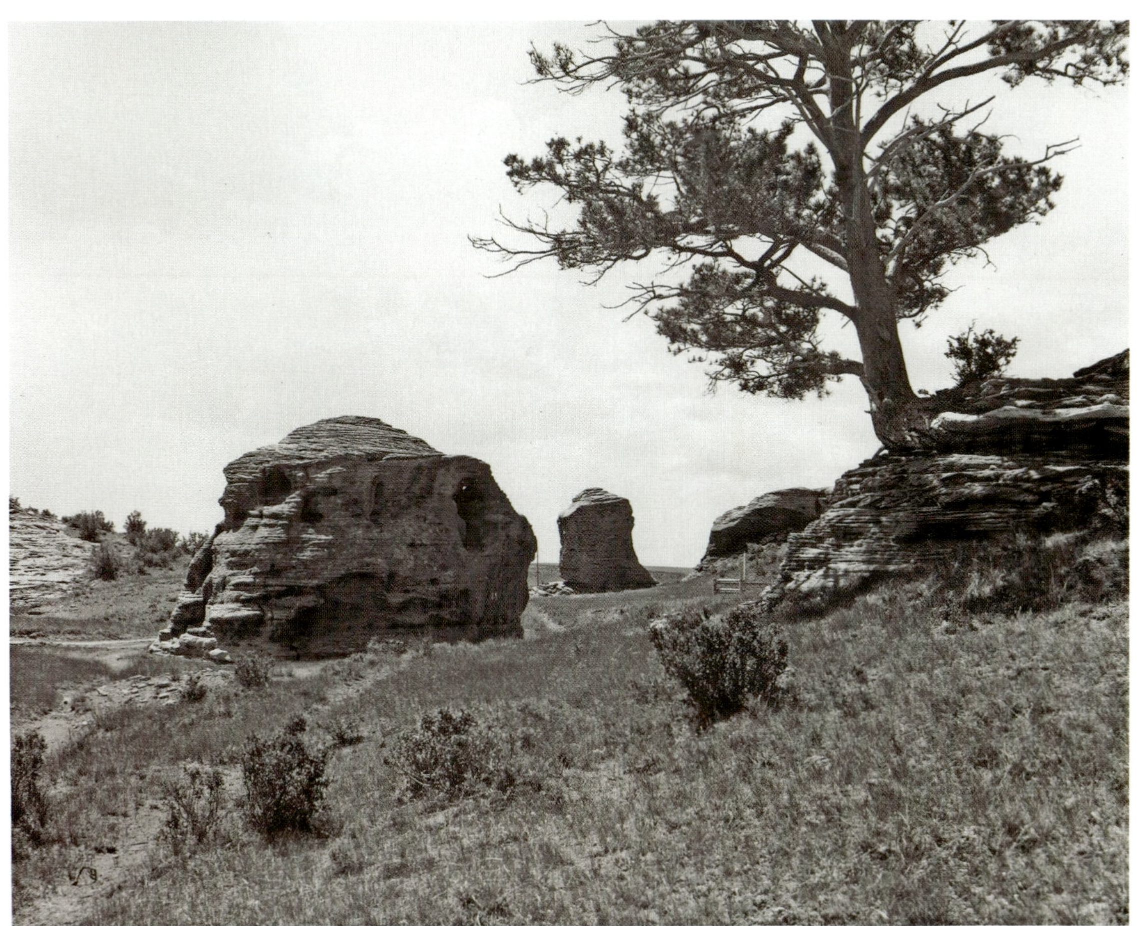

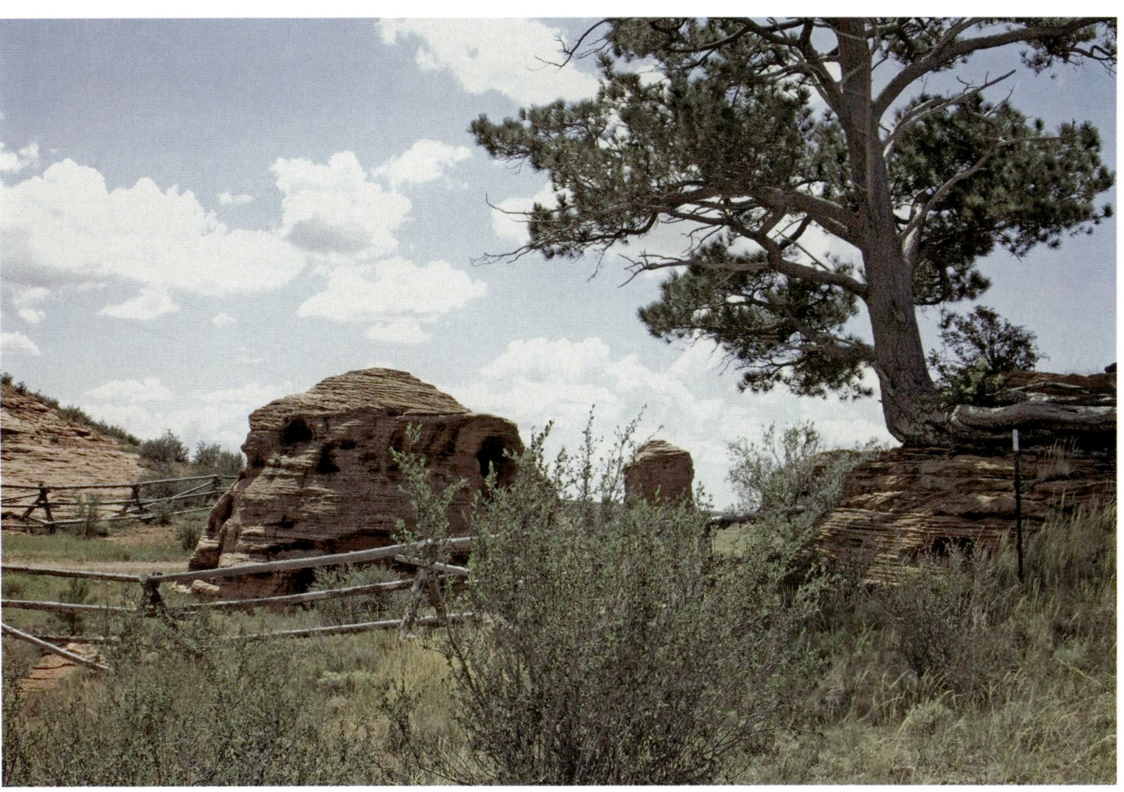

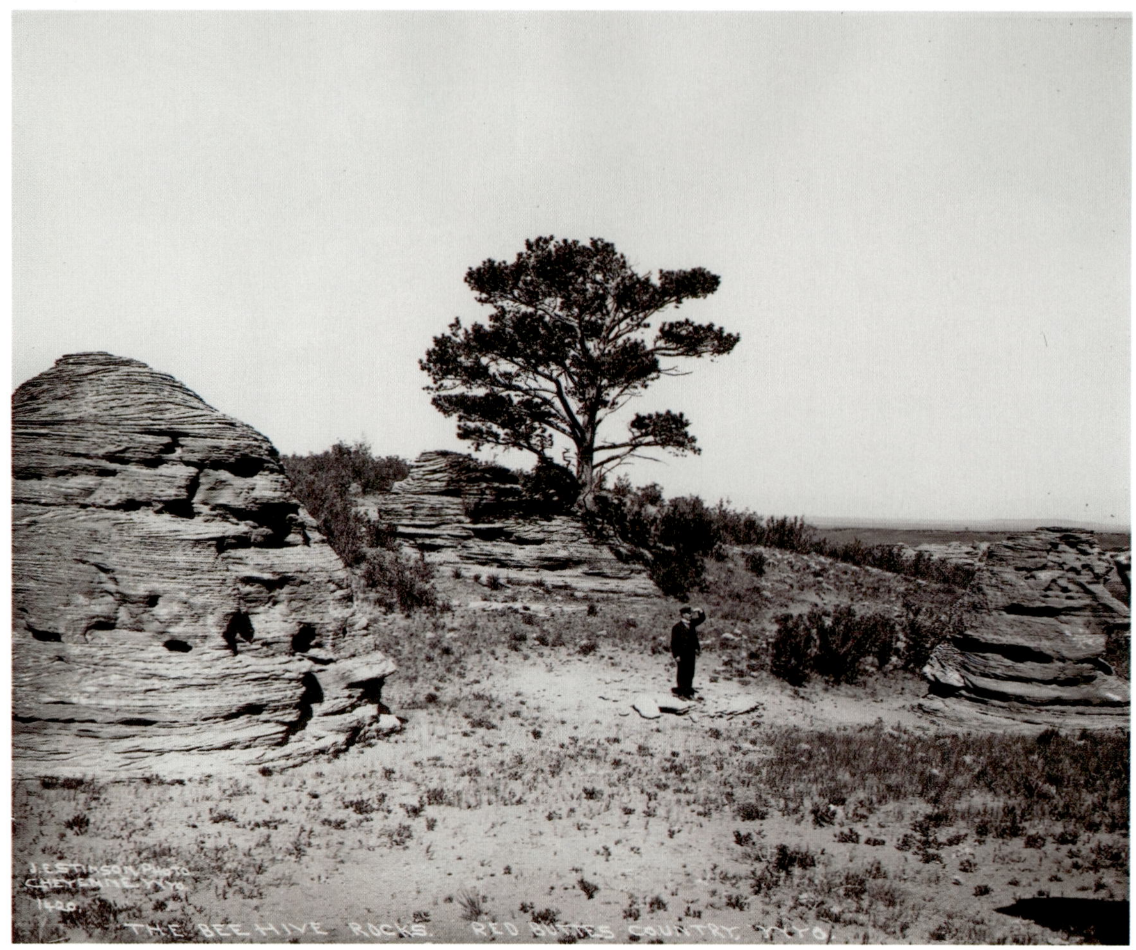

14. #1420

The Bee Hive Rocks, Red Butte Country, 1906, 1987, 2007
GPS COORDINATES: 41 10.222N, 105 33.353W

This second view shows basically the obverse view of the same location as the previous scene. Stimson has turned the camera around and is now looking back at the same tree growing out of a rock and the "Bee Hive Rocks" from the previous photograph. His model this time appears to be a train conductor, posed in the classic way looking off into the far distance. The effect is one of the sublime, the small man peering into the unknown, overwhelmed by the grotesque rocks and distances.

For my 1987 image, the scene looks basically the same as it had eight decades earlier. That tree, a bit fuller perhaps, looks more or less the same. The most obvious change is the rough path through the center, allowing the rancher to bring a four-wheel drive, high-clearance truck to the house trailer, hidden in this view. A single guy wire, planted in the ground at the base of the right-hand Bee Hive Rock, is also visible.

In my 2007 view, the scene looks fairly similar, with the enduring tree and the Bee Hive Rocks eerily the same. But it is fundamentally changed. A split rail fence has subdivided the land into a lot, and a gravel road has replaced the rough path, allowing passenger cars access. Like many places in the New West, the beautiful vernacular landscape has fallen prey to the developer, closing off scenes like this one.

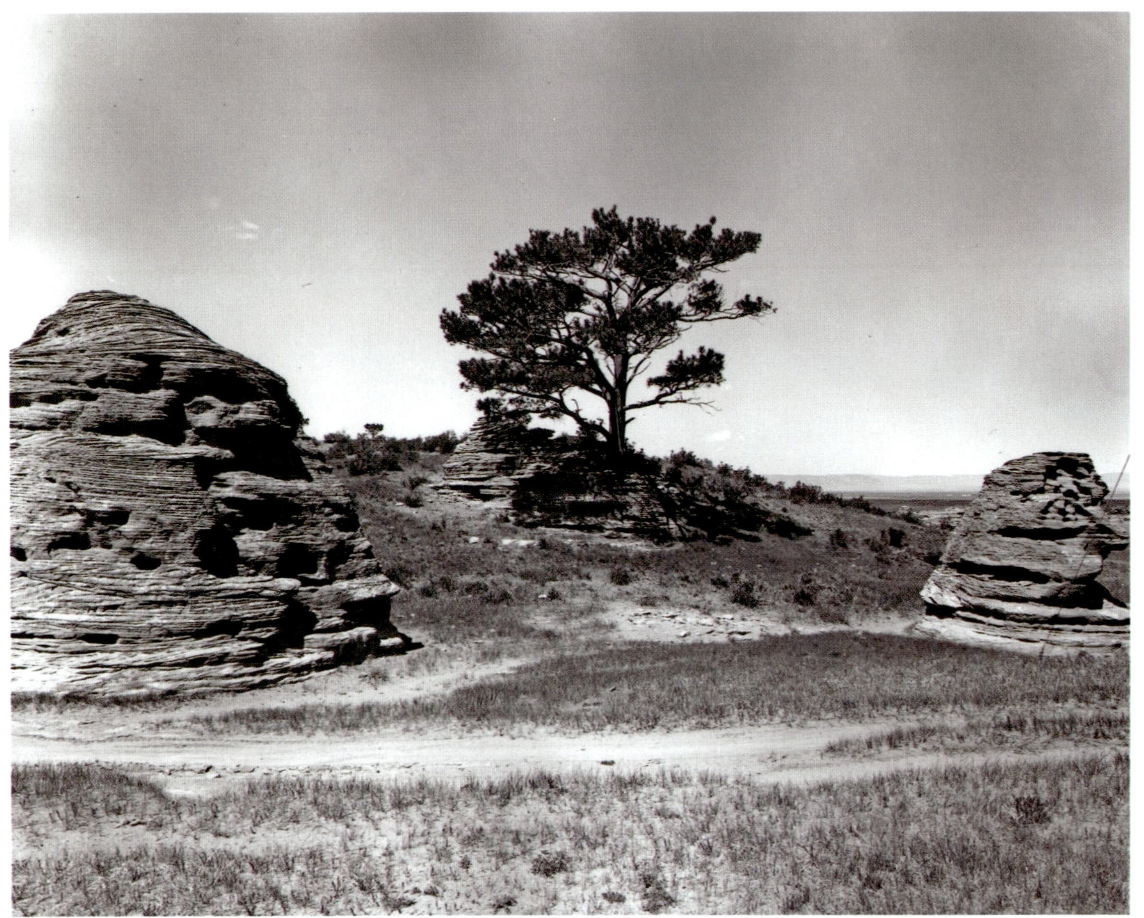

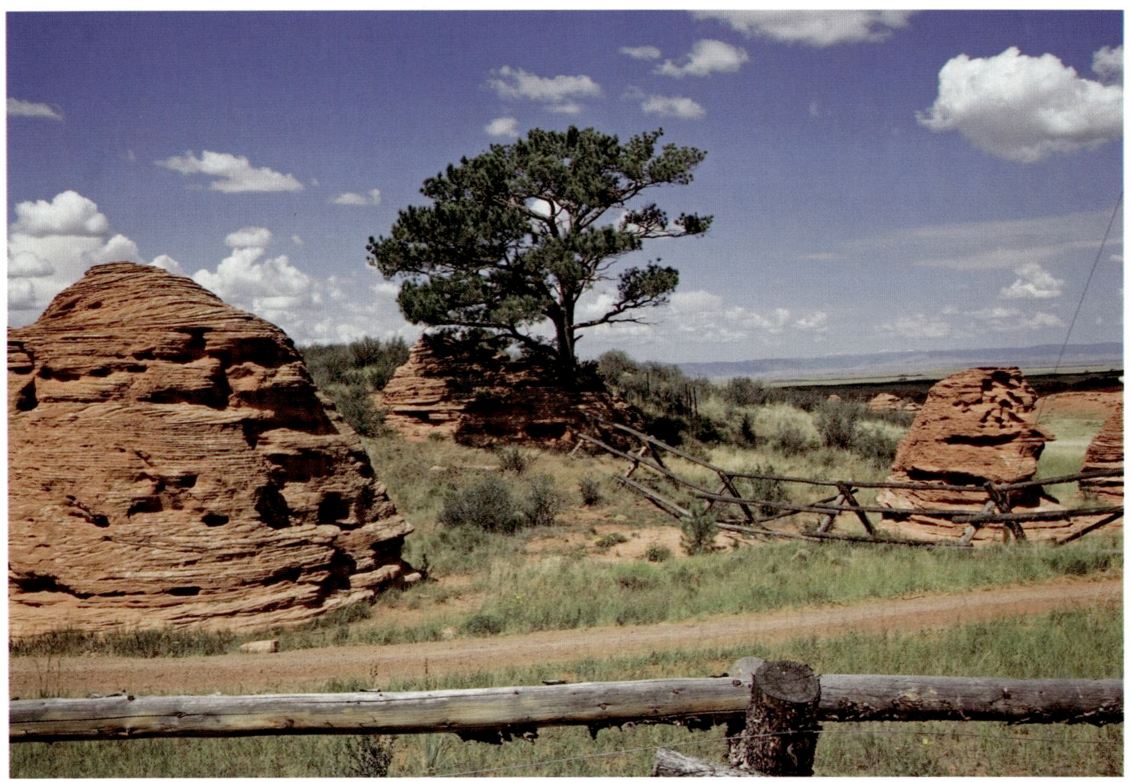

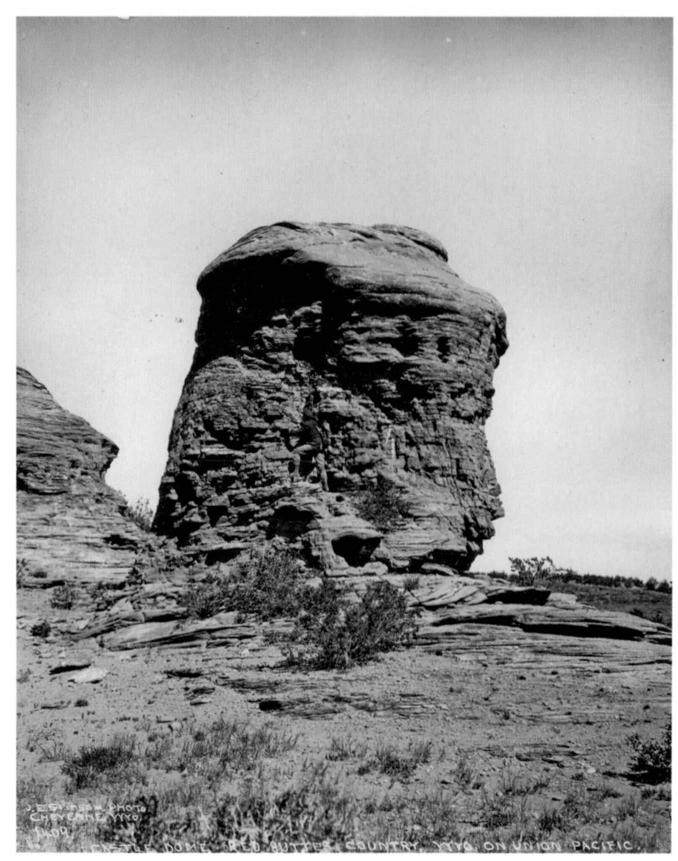
J. E. STIMSON, PHOTO
CHEYENNE, WYO.
1409
CASTLE DOME, RED BUTTES, COUNTRY, WYO. ON UNION PACIFIC.

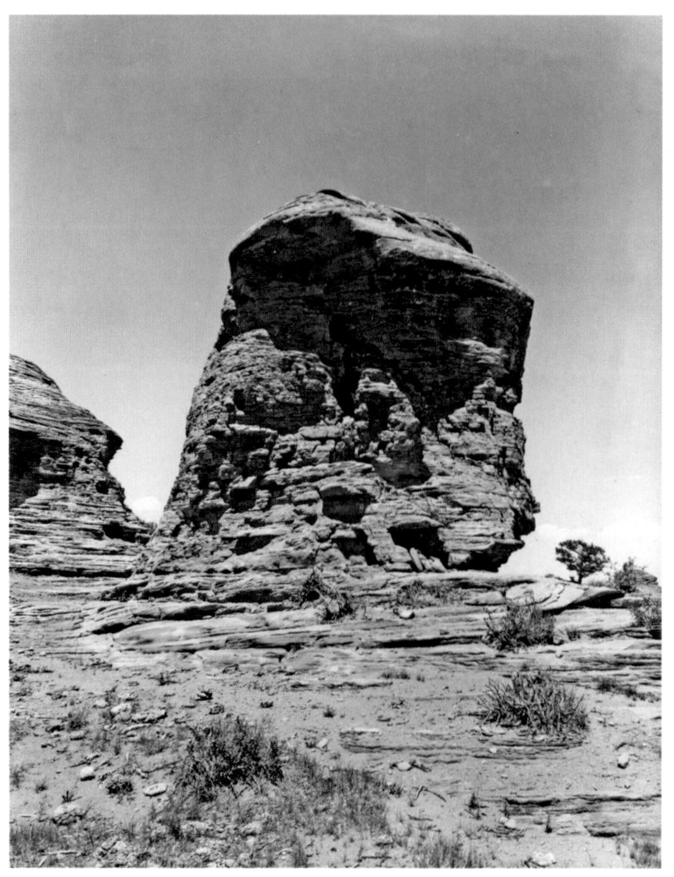

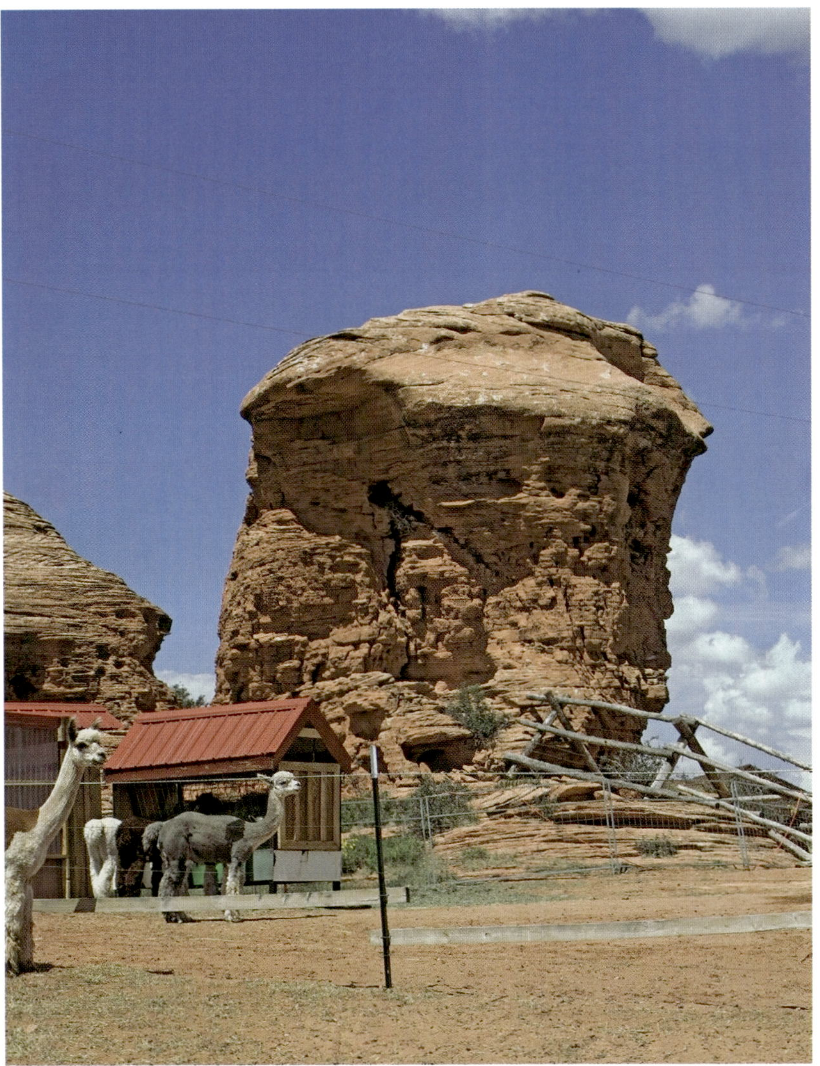

15. #1409

Castle Dome, Red Buttes Country, 1906, 1987, 2007
GPS COORDINATES: 41 10.143N, 105 33.274W

As discussed at length in chapter 4, Stimson's picture of the rock formation he called Castle Dome and my most recent rephotograph showing the Windy Ridge Alpaca Ranch occupying the same space depicts a lesson in the long history of Wyoming's relationship to the world. In his image, Stimson placed a man climbing on the side of the formation, as if exploring it. The composition is again one of portraiture, with the rock at the center of the image and the "explorer" at the center of the formation.

My 1987 view looks eerily similar. There is slight variation in the foliage at the base of the rock, but that's about it. The photo almost looks as though it could have been taken within a few years of the original, not more than eight decades later.

My 2007 image looks drastically different. The rock formation is still there, and it looks more or less the same. But the big difference is in front of the formation, where the Windy Ridge Alpaca Ranch has introduced a split rail fence on the side of Castle Dome and placed an alpaca holding pen and stable in the foreground. The land has been leveled and is devoid of vegetation. In the holding pen, non-native alpacas are eating and looking out across the landscape, somewhat reflecting the posture of the conductor two scenes back. Seemingly incongruous, the alpacas actually reflect a longstanding history of market capitalism, globalization, and the importation of exotics in Wyoming.

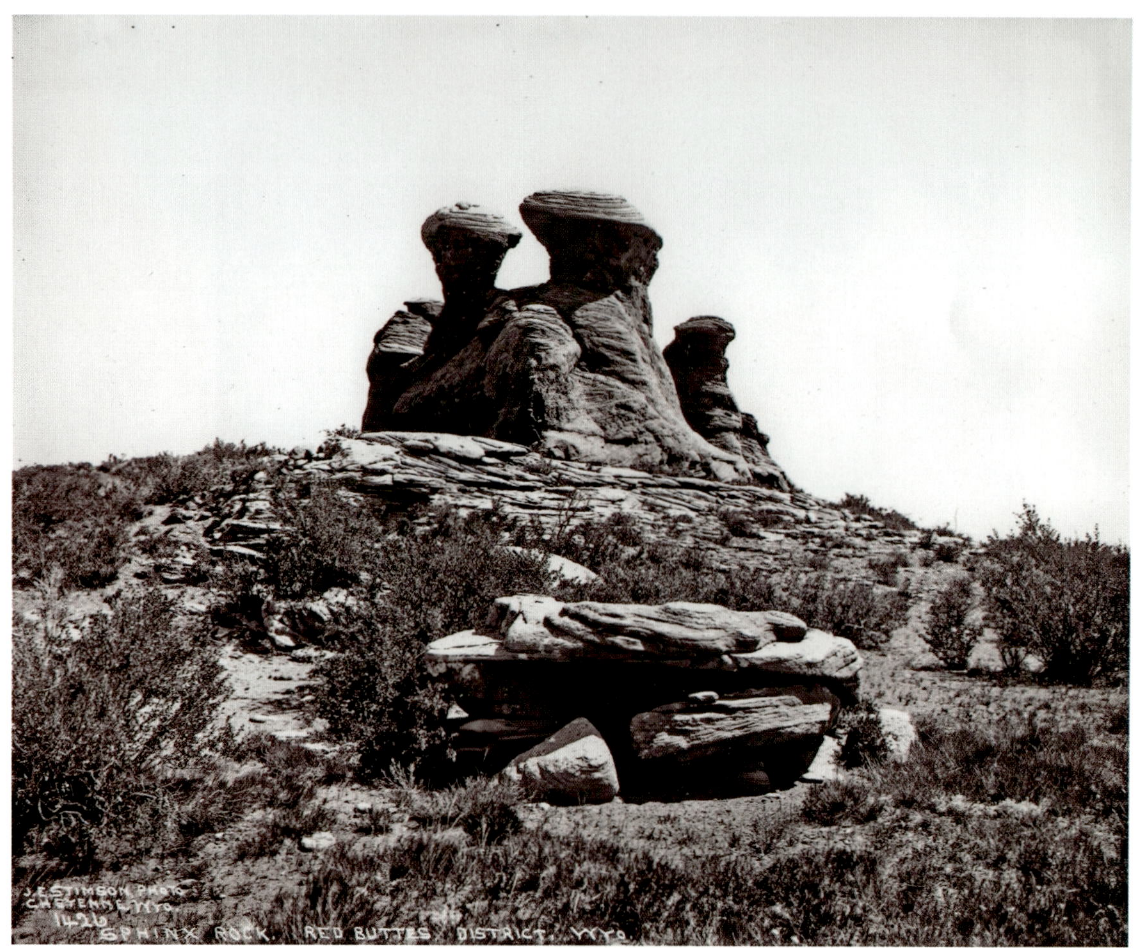

16. #1426

Sphinx Rock, Red Buttes District, 1906, 1987, 2007
GPS COORDINATES: 41 09.988N, 105 33.569W

Of the four images presented here that Stimson made in the Red Buttes area, only this one of the formation he called Sphinx Rock remains virtually untouched more than a century later. For his vantage point, Stimson set his camera to the west of the formation, down a slight hill and in front of another small horizontal set of rocks. The effect is one of looking up at Sphinx Rock, giving it a greater presence because of his low angle. Again, Stimson used a portrait-style composition, with Sphinx Rock centered in the image. The photograph was made midday to afternoon, allowing the light to illuminate the front of Sphinx Rock and cast shadows across its body.

Both my 1987 and 2007 rephotographs show that this formation has been basically untouched by the development going on behind it. The vegetation around the base of the formation has increased in terms of both area and size, perhaps because cattle have been removed since the creation of the Buttes subdivision. In 1987, several inscriptions could be found in the vicinity of Sphinx Rock, but when I visited twenty years later, I did not investigate them because the rock was now on private property.

This transformation from public lands somewhat protected by the reality of being out of the way to private lands at risk of development is a common occurrence in the New West. As the most scenic lands are set aside for protection, other places like the Red Buttes are developed.

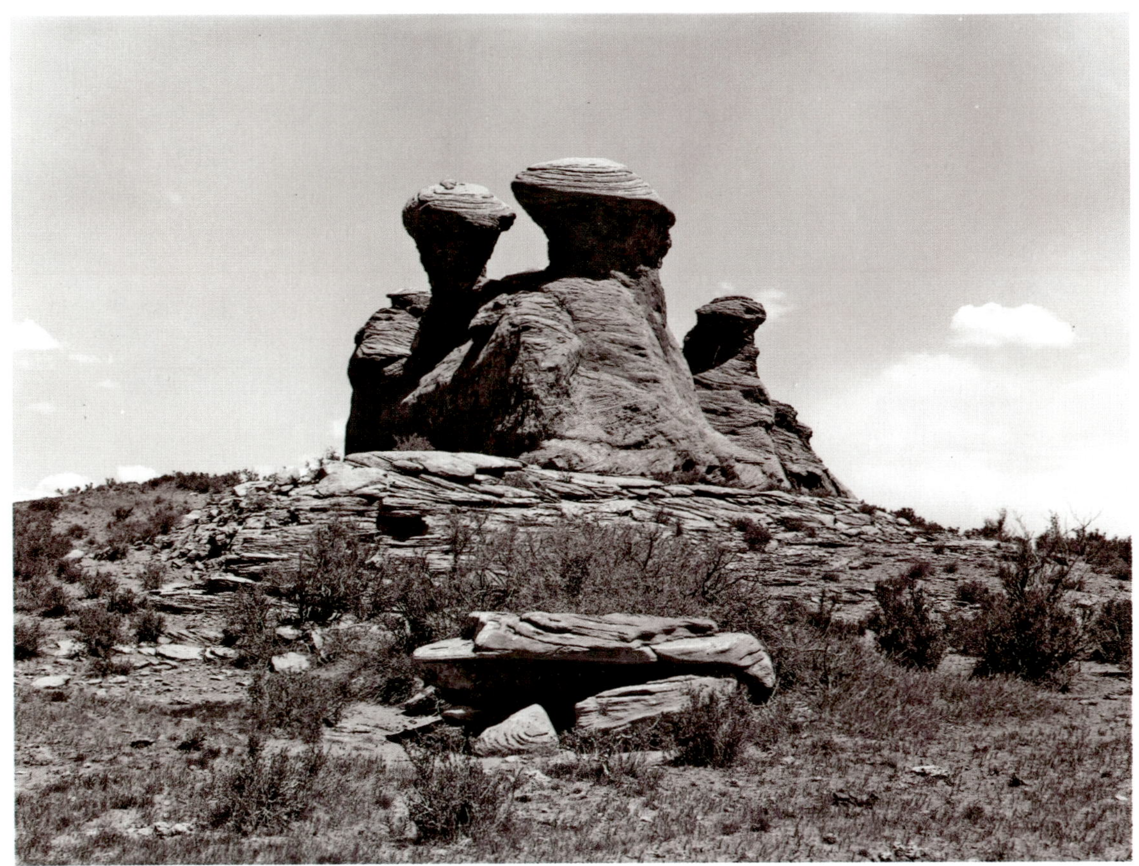

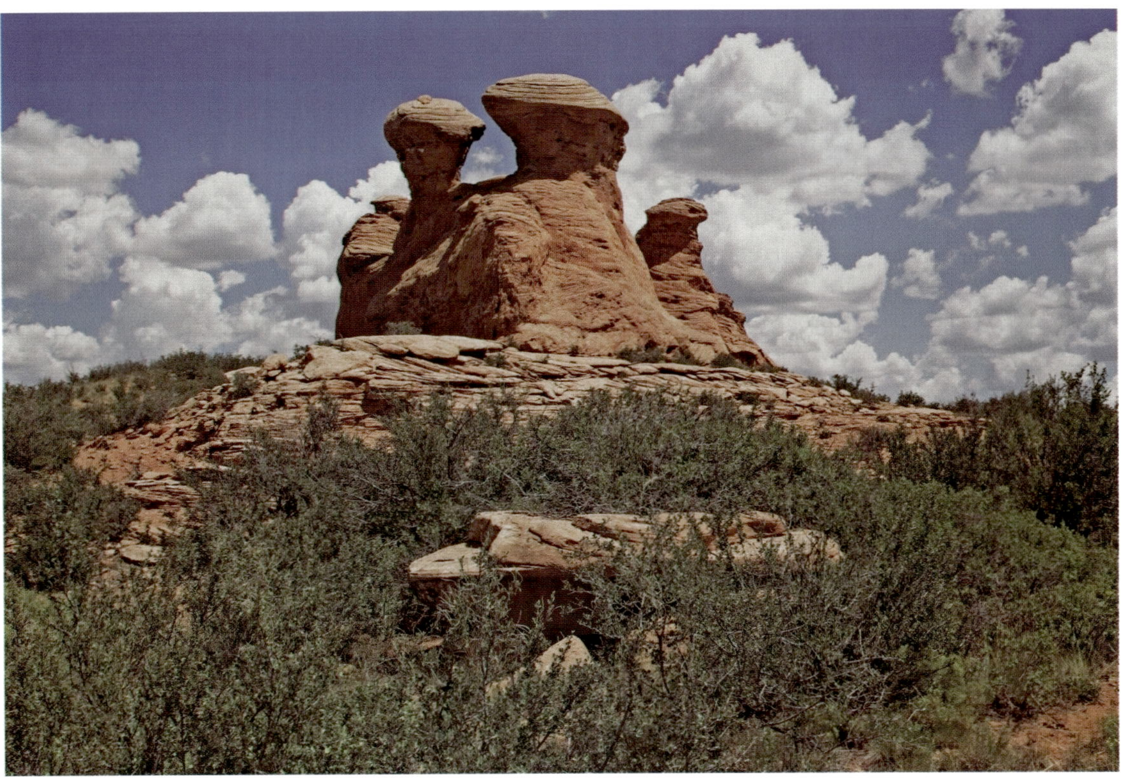

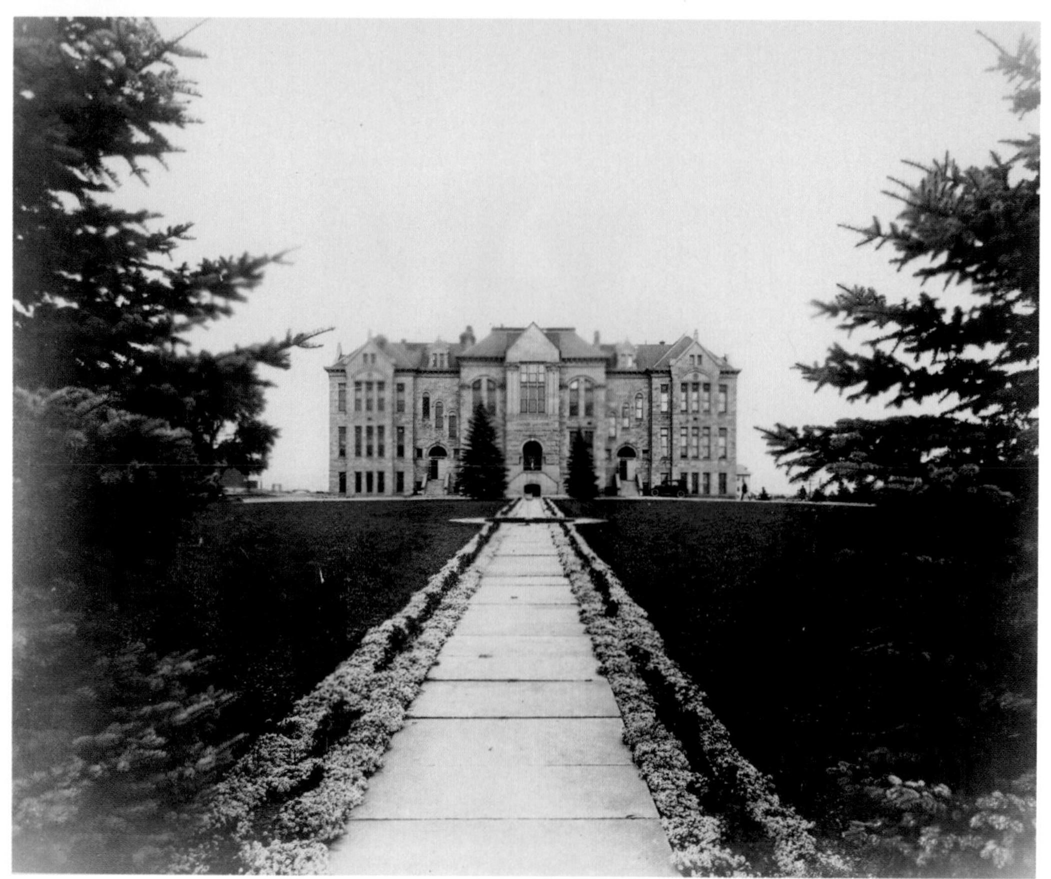

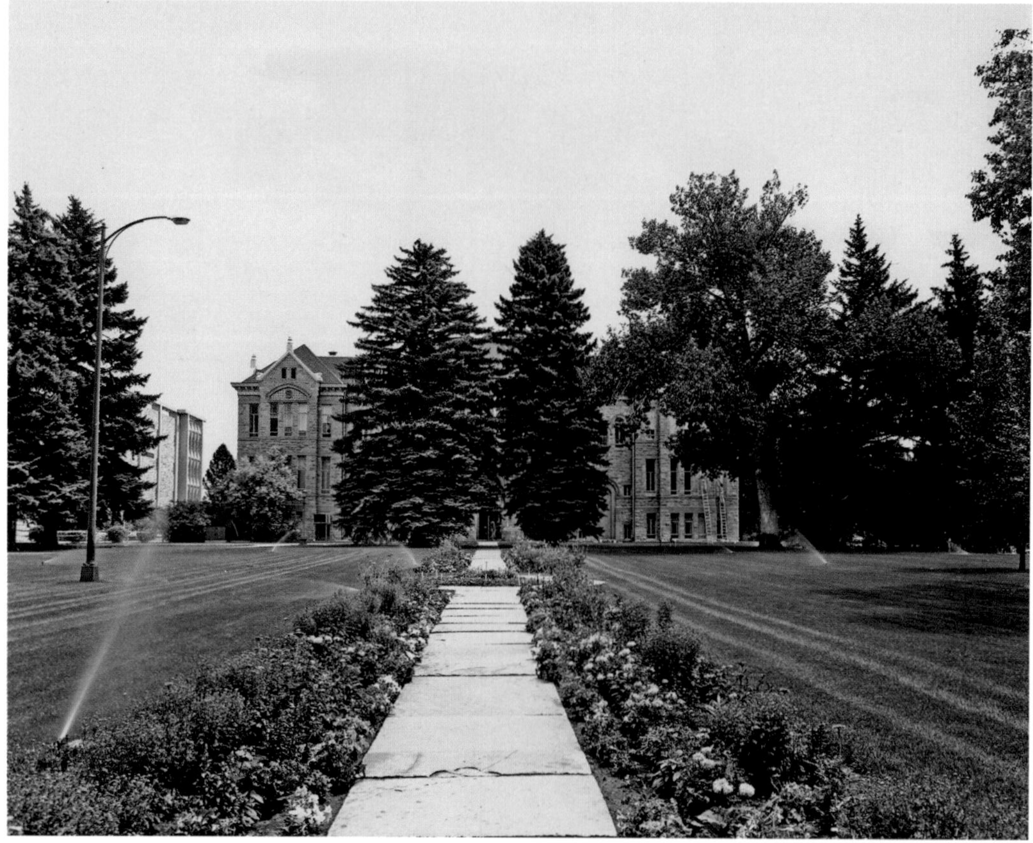

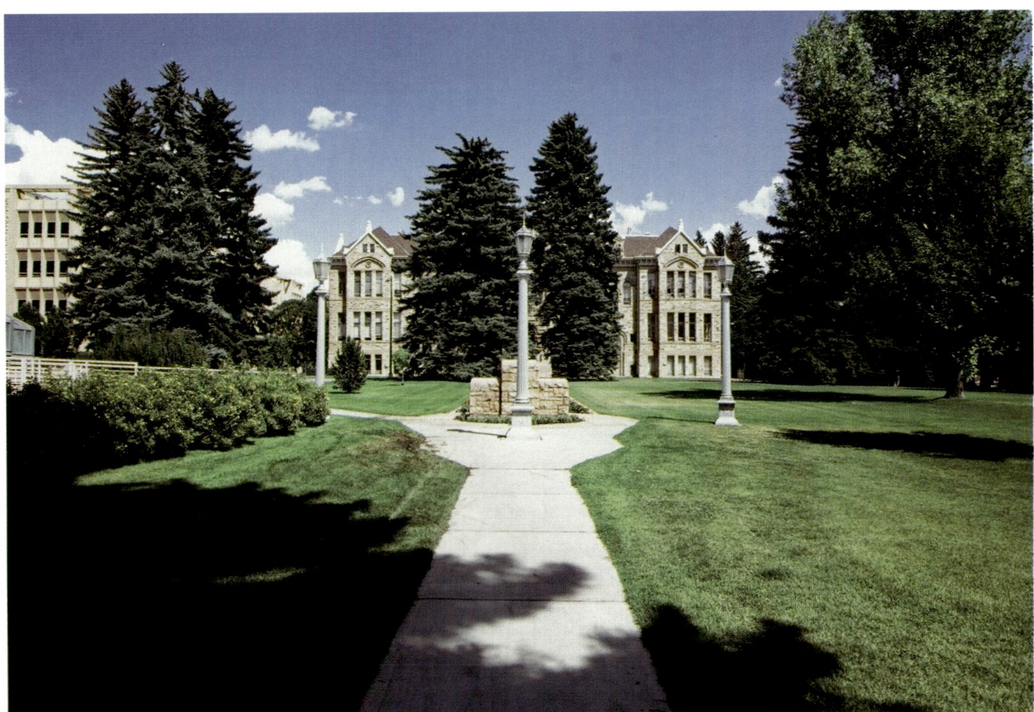

17. #7045

Old Main, University of Wyoming, Laramie, 1922, 1987, 2007
GPS COORDINATES: 41 18.7443N, 105 35.10783W

Old Main is the original building on the University of Wyoming (UW) campus. In fact, when it was constructed in 1886 in Wyoming Territory, Old Main *was* UW's campus. It housed all departments, the library, and a small auditorium and gym. The building also featured a tall tower rising from the center of its roof, though that feature was removed in 1917 for safety measures. In 1949, the entire structure was gutted and converted from classrooms to offices. Staircases were moved and floors rebuilt at different heights so that when inside, one still finds windows at odd heights. Nevertheless, like its 1880s Cheyenne contemporaries, the Wyoming capitol and the Union Pacific Depot, Old Main remains an important symbol of progress and endurance.

J. E. Stimson made several photographs of Old Main over the years. I liked a 1903 image made during his survey of the state because it featured the original tower but found it impossible to rephotograph because of the many trees surrounding the building. Instead, I chose this 1922 portrait. Composed like many of his architectural images, as a straight-on face view, Stimson framed his image with a pair of evergreens and used the stone sidewalk as a lead-in to the building.

I made my first rephotograph of Old Main by simply walking from my dorm room on the east side of campus a couple of blocks to this site. Because the two evergreens had completely overgrown the sidewalk, I had to move closer to Old Main to get the shot. I noticed the continued efforts to beautify the campus with flowers, including a sprinkler that almost soaked me, at left, and the fact that the right-hand evergreen in front of Old Main was now taller than the left one from Stimson's picture. The Biological Sciences Building can be seen at left.

Twenty years later, the flowers had been removed from along the sidewalk and a few vintage light posts installed, but Old Main still retained a sense of tradition and style for the university. True, UW had grown so far to the east that most visitors to campus for basketball or football games probably never saw Old Main. Still, its Richardsonian-style architecture with rough stonework has set a standard across the campus.

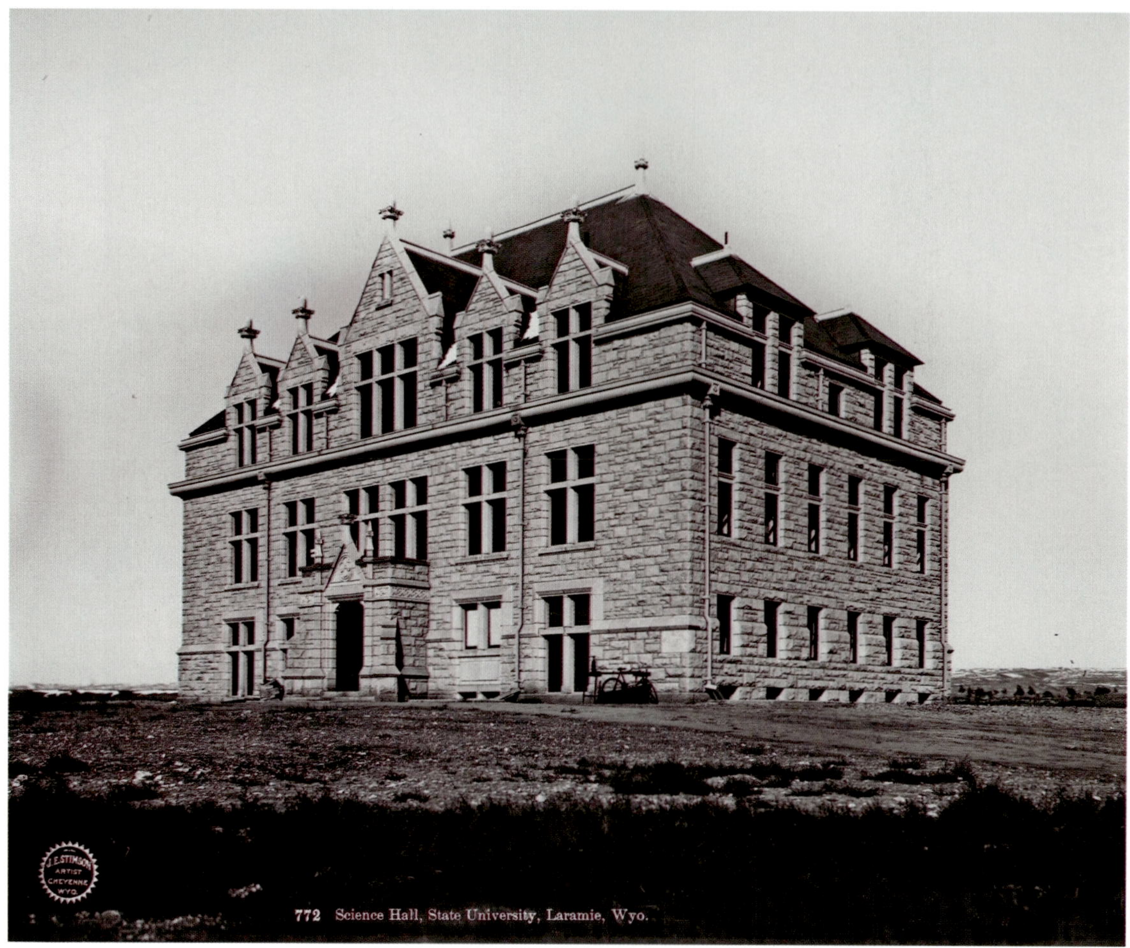

18. #772

Science Hall, University of Wyoming, Laramie, 1903, 1987, 2007
GPS COORDINATES: 41 18.84067N, 105 35.05083W

Science Hall, now the Samuel H. Knight Geology Building, was constructed in 1902 and is the second-oldest building on campus. Stimson photographed it in 1903 during his survey of the state for the 1904 World's Fair. Stimson's composition is beautiful. He took a low angle to give the effect of the building's power—and, in that, education—over the bleak prairie all around it. With its gothic spires and elaborate stonework, the building suggested a medieval cathedral, despite the presence of two bicycles parked outside.

My 1987 view showed a few more trees, bushes, grass, and a large sidewalk. The building itself remained basically intact. Twenty years later, it was still seemingly untouched. Indeed, I was tickled to see a new bike rack out front.

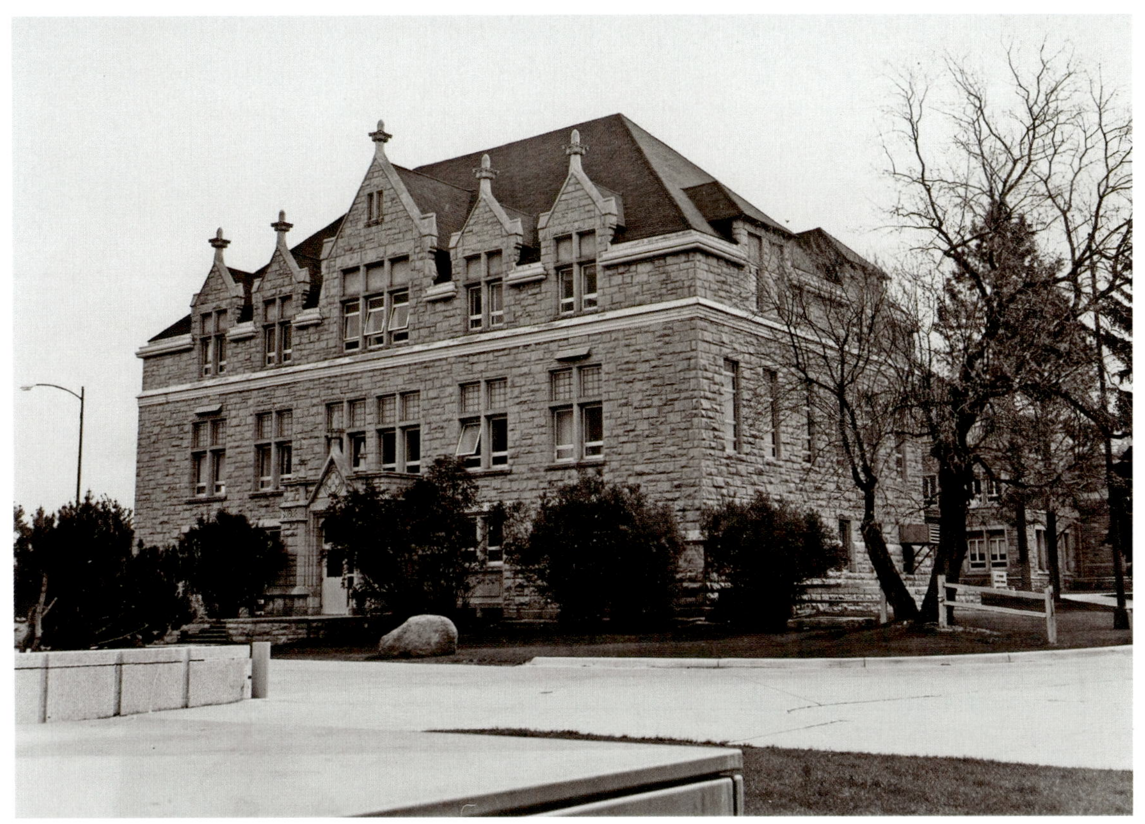

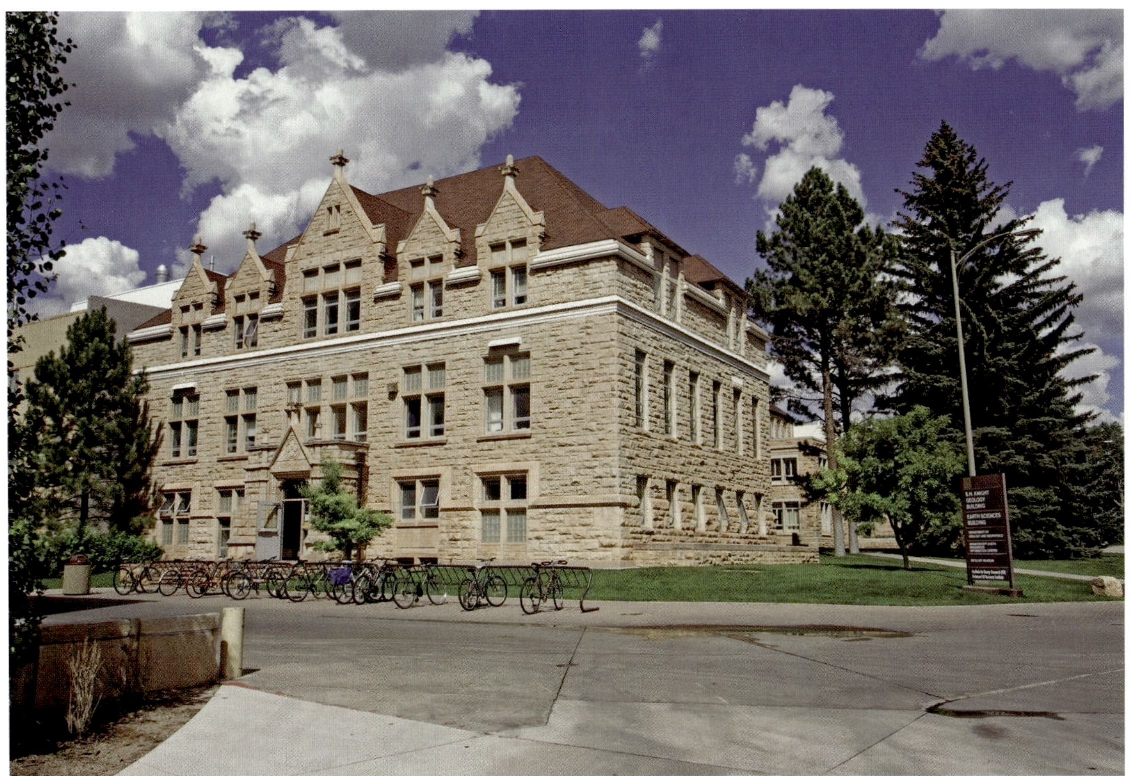

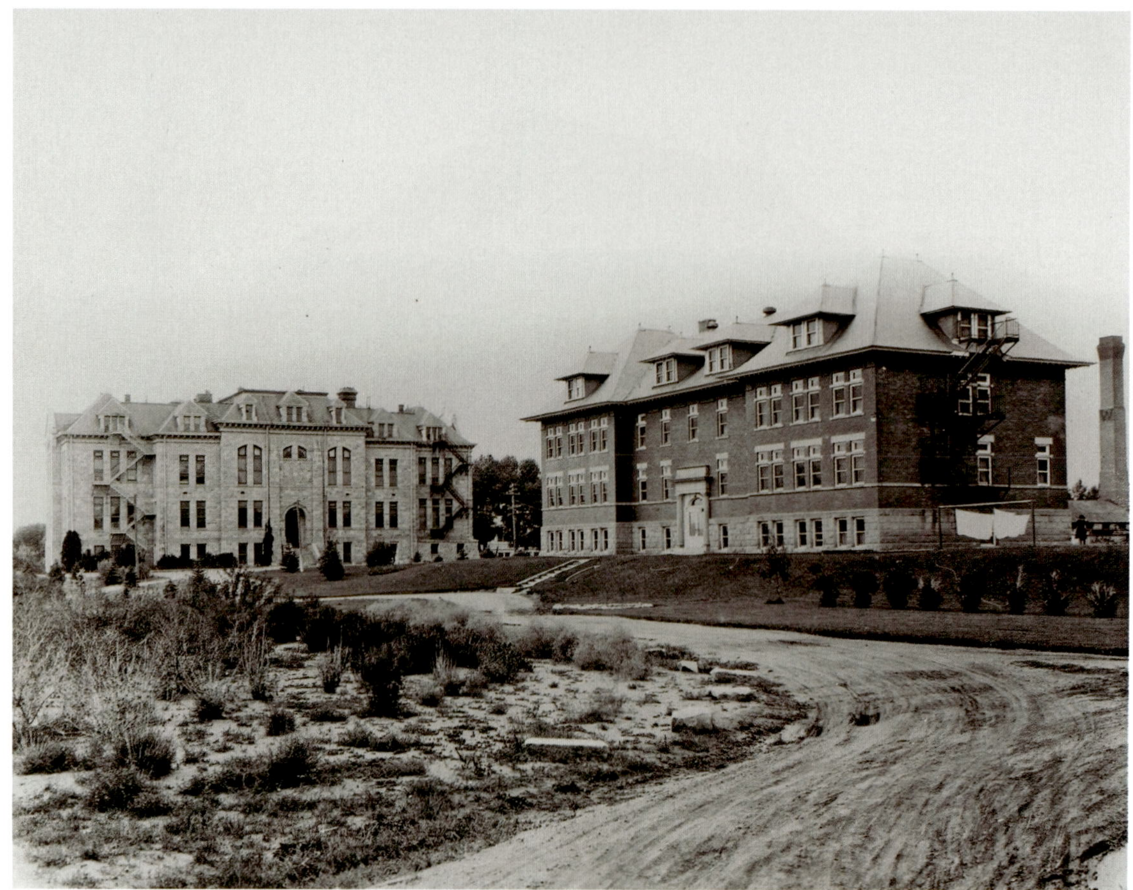

19. #7049

Merica Hall, University of Wyoming, Laramie, 1922, 1987, 2007
GPS COORDINATES: 41 18.715167N, 105 34.930167W

Photographed at the same time as his view of Old Main, Stimson's image of Merica Hall, the first women's dormitory on campus, also showed the back side of Old Main. The third-oldest building on campus, Merica Hall was built in 1908 and named for the eighth university president, Charles Merica. What makes Stimson's rather ordinary photograph so special is the presence of the sheets hung out to dry on the far right and the wild prairie seen to the left of the dirt road.

My 1987 rephotograph again shows the growth of trees and the spread of grass across campus. In fact, the wild prairie at left in Stimson's photo was by then referred to as the "campus green" for its plush grass. Also visible, at right, is part of the UW flower garden. By then, Merica Hall had been converted to offices.

Twenty years later, the continued growth of trees and the number of automobiles on campus is readily apparent, as the view of Old Main is completely blocked and part of the campus green has been turned into parking.

Despite the many changes to the University of Wyoming campus, these photos of its three oldest buildings—Old Main, the Samuel H. Knight Geology Building, and Merica Hall—show that the campus remains a well-kept, beautiful place.

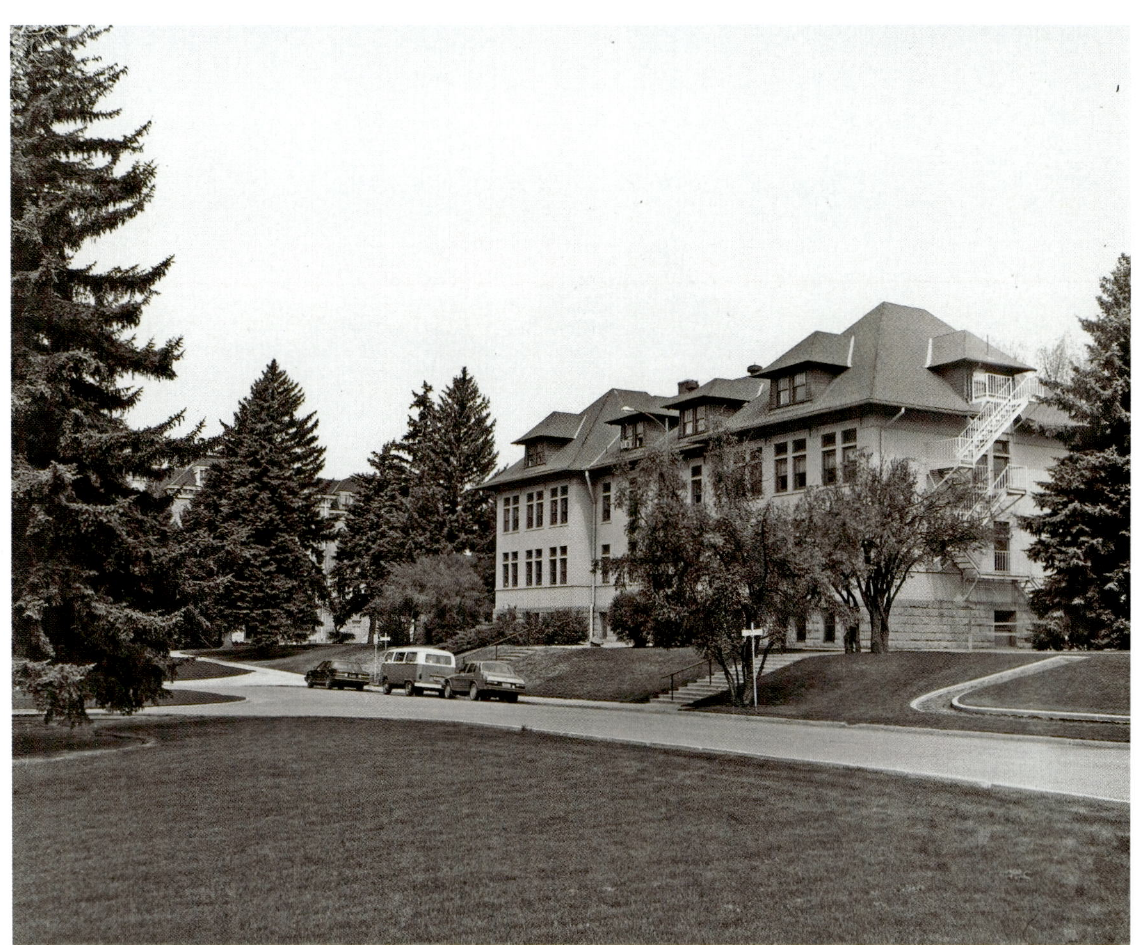

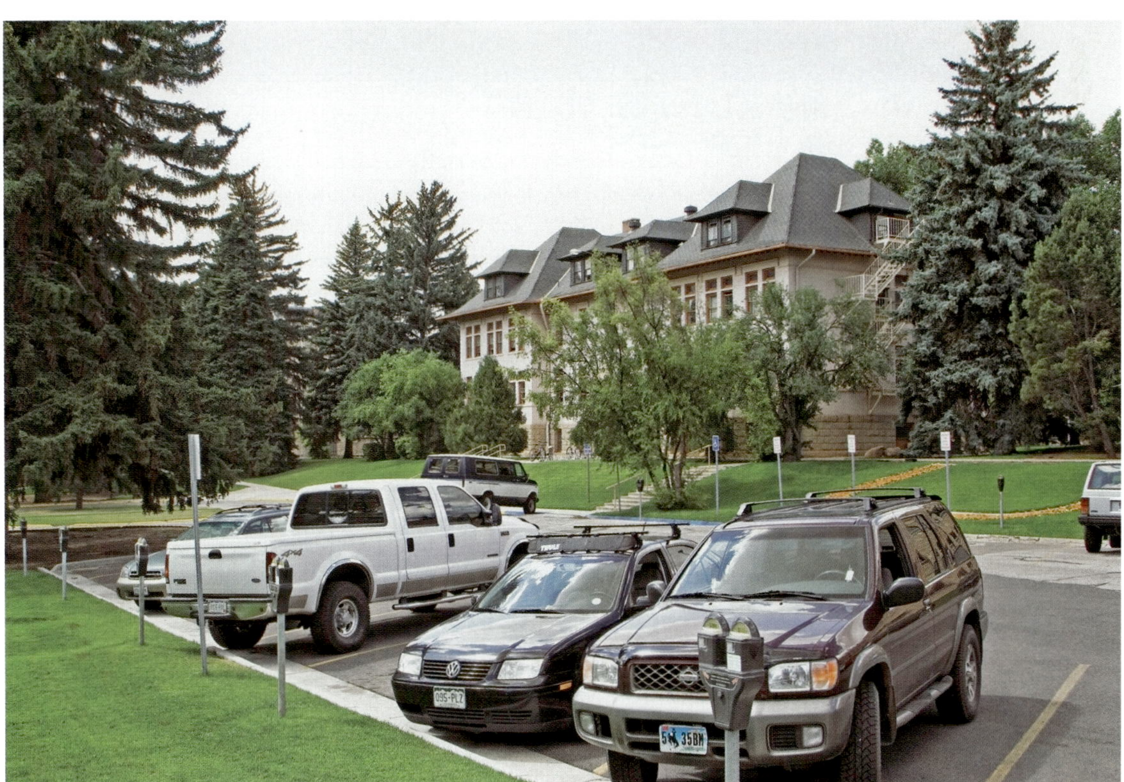

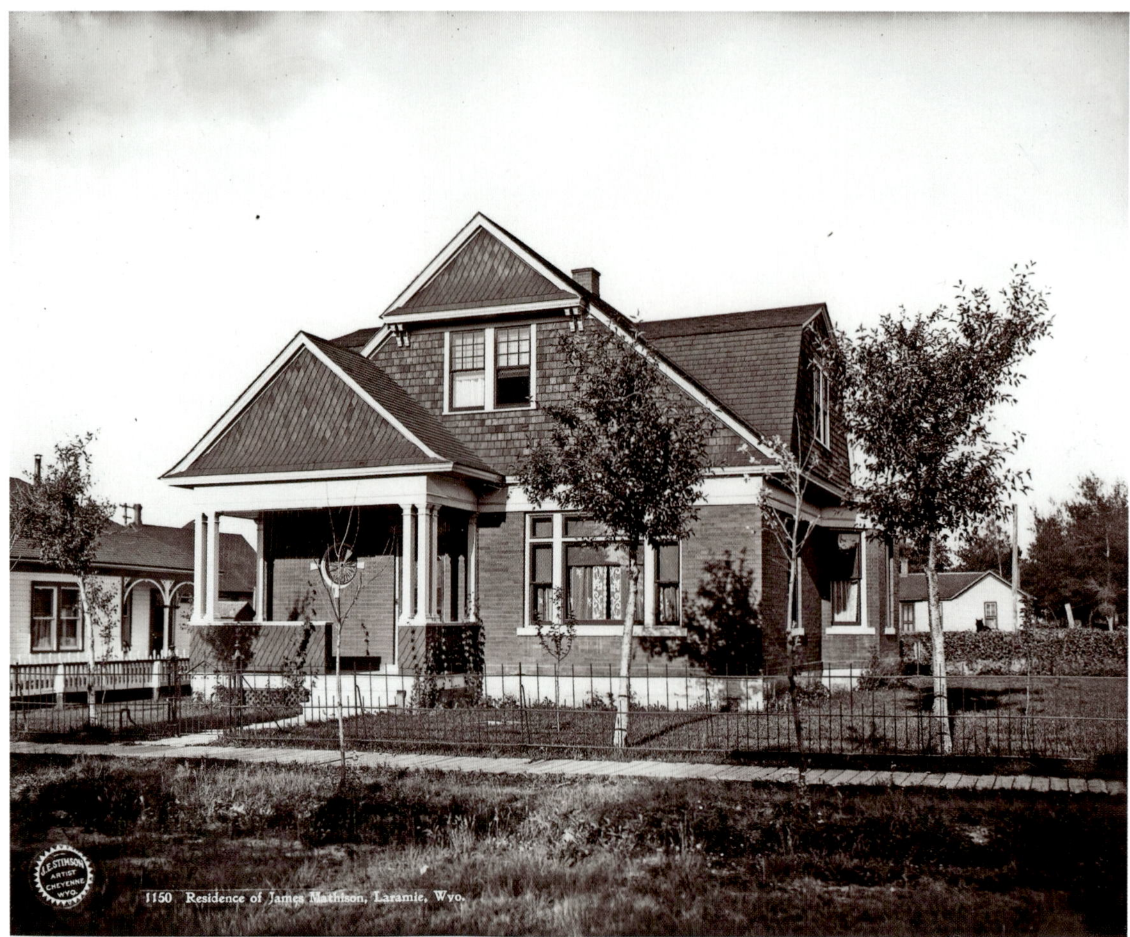

20. #1150

Residence of James Mathison, Laramie, 1905, 1987, 2007
GPS COORDINATES: 41 18.546N, 105 35.397W

Stimson's final photograph in Laramie included here is also a special place. A typical "house portrait," this picture was made in the late afternoon, evidenced by the soft light and long shadows. When I originally decided to include this photograph in 1987, I thought it would be no problem to locate the house in Laramie's older neighborhoods because I could easily identify its round porch window. When I was unable to find it, I turned to an old Laramie phonebook from 1905, looked up James Mathison, got his address as 419 South Sixth Street, and found the house. Only then did I discover that the round porch window had been covered by a screened-in porch, though a new round window had been created above it to maintain the house's style. When I was taking the rephotograph, the owner of the house, after learning what I was doing, produced a small painting he had found in the attic signed J. Mathison, 1906. Through more research, I learned that James Mathison was vice president of a local newspaper and a cousin of Stimson's wife, Anna.

After reshooting the scene in 2007, I soon discovered through research conducted through the Wyoming Newspaper Project that the Stimsons often traveled to Laramie to visit the Mathisons, and vice versa. My color photograph also shows that this home has been well cared for. I especially enjoy the pink, blue, and white color scheme, but I miss that little round window.

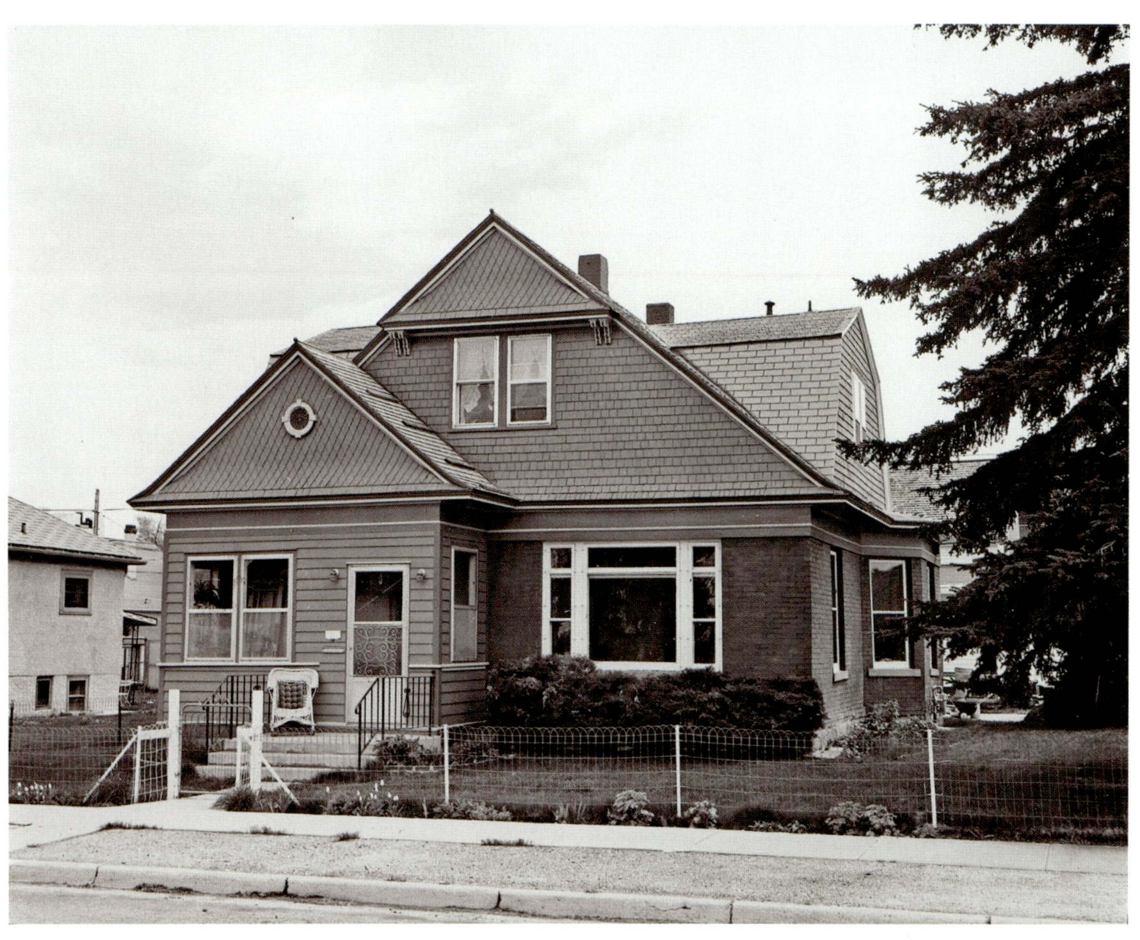

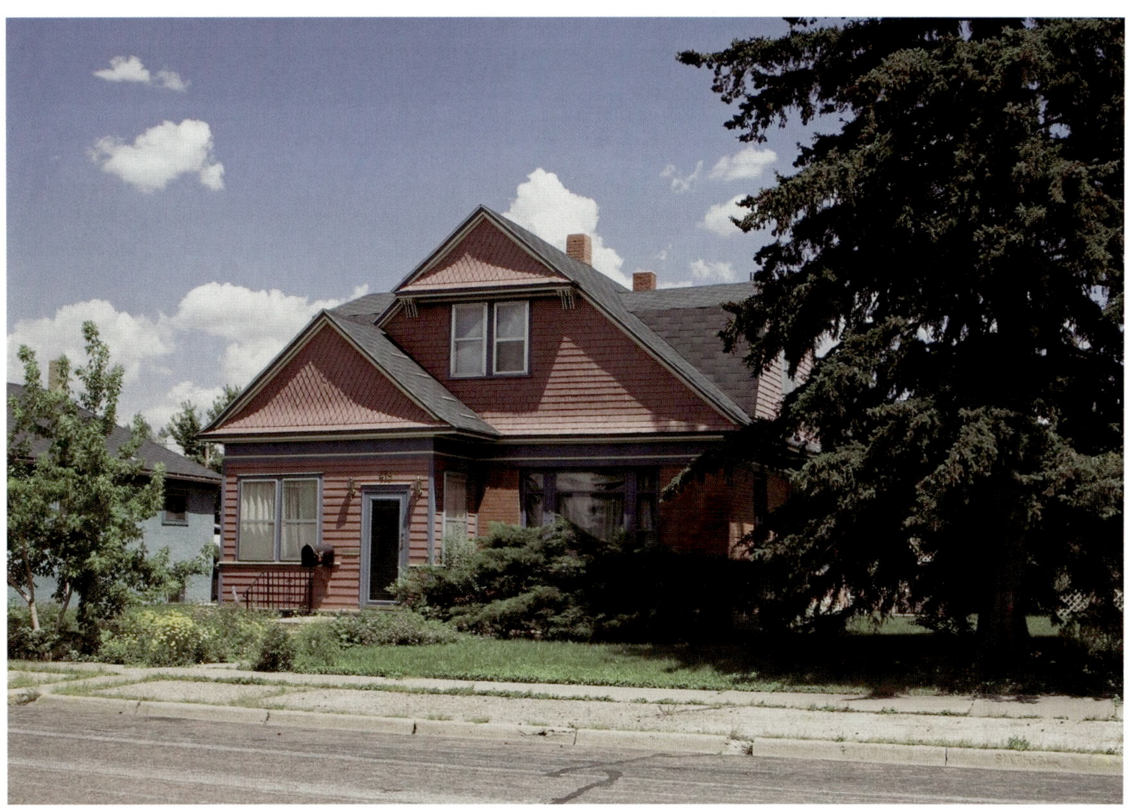

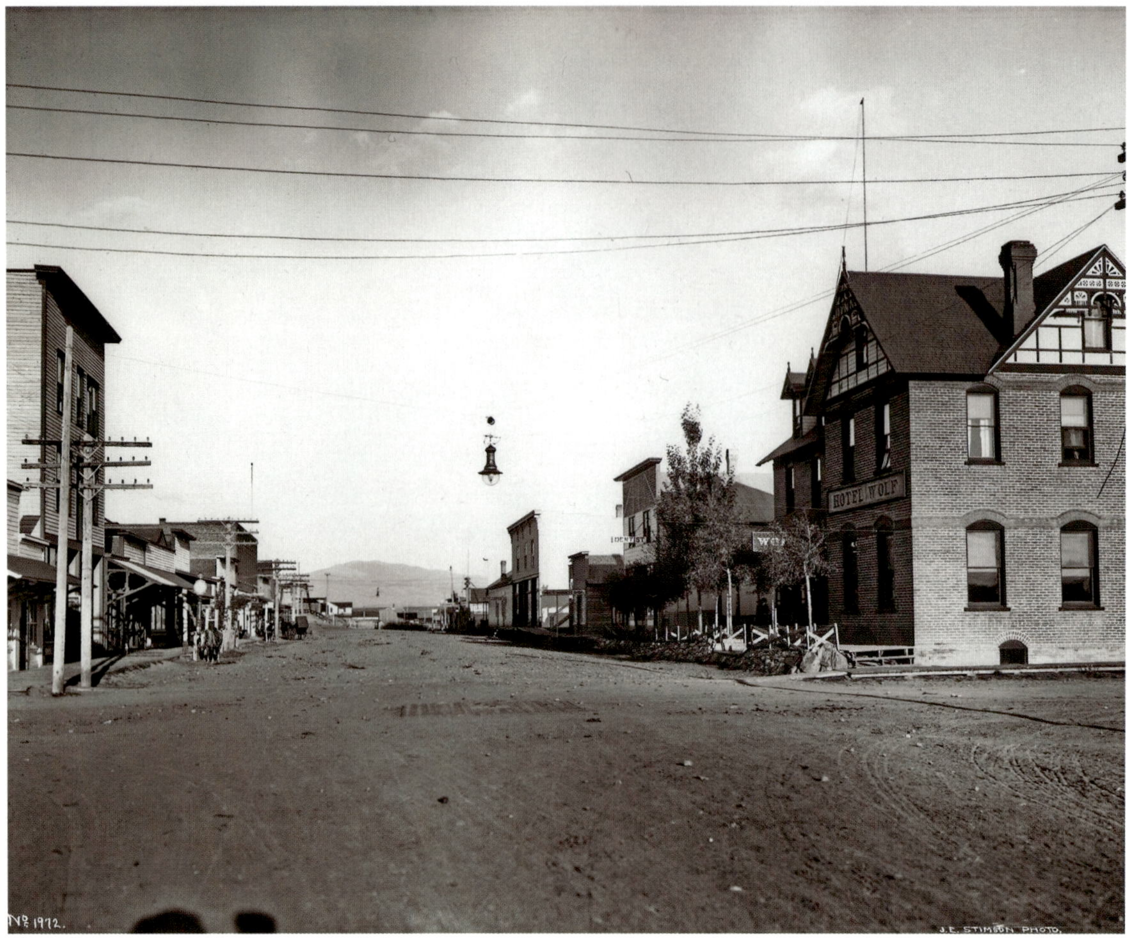

21. #1972

Street Scene, Saratoga, 1907, 1987, 2007
GPS COORDINATES: 41 27.289N, 106 48.478W

Stimson visited the small Wyoming community of Saratoga in 1907 as the Saratoga and Encampment Railway was being constructed from the Union Pacific line at Walcott south to the hot springs town of Saratoga to the copper mining town of Encampment. His view of Bridge Street looks east toward the crossing of the North Platte River. At right is the Hotel Wolf, constructed in 1894 and still operating as a small inn and restaurant. The second tall building past the hotel on the right is Shively Hardware, in business since 1925 in a structure built in 1888. In fact, despite the perseverance of many buildings still visible a century after Stimson made his photograph, these are the only two buildings on Bridge Street placed on the National Register of Historic Places. In such cases, rephotography projects such as this can be invaluable visual documents for identifying historic structures for preservation.

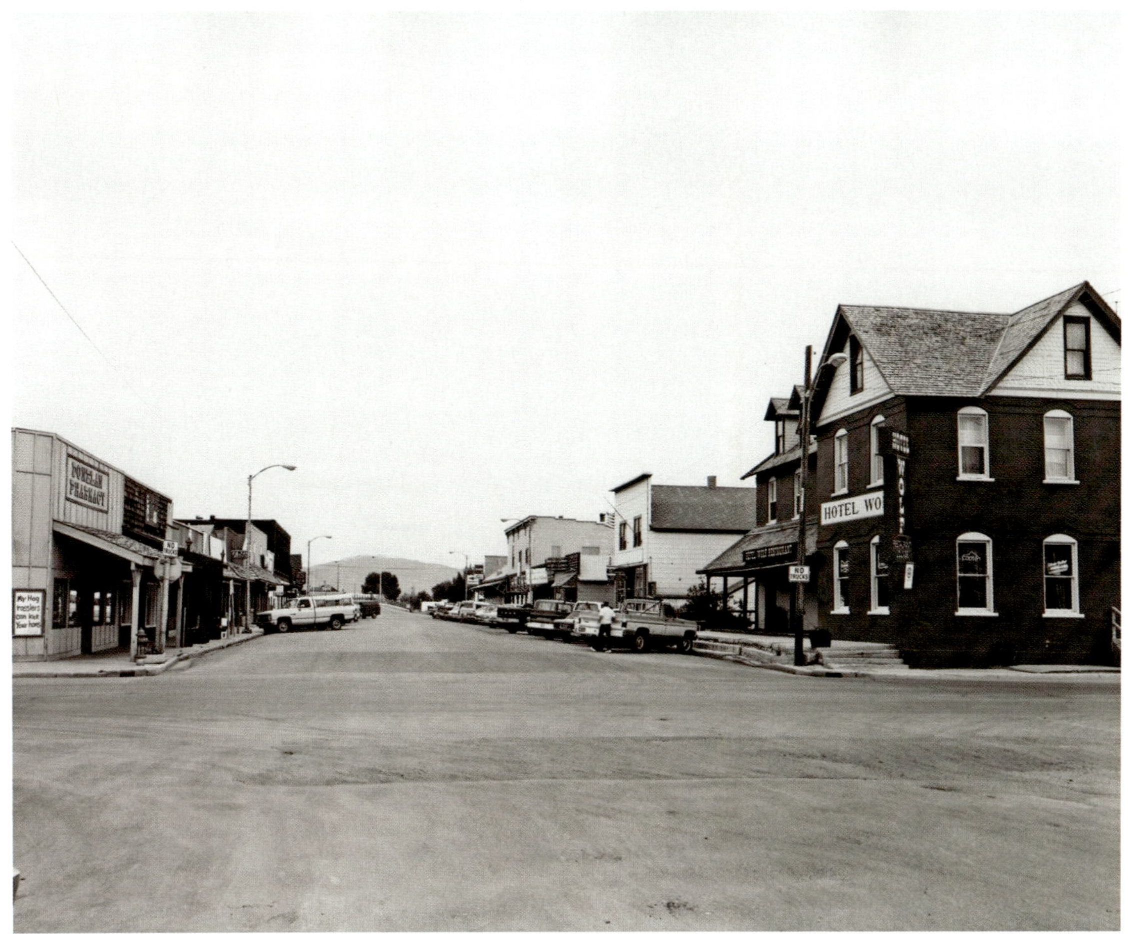

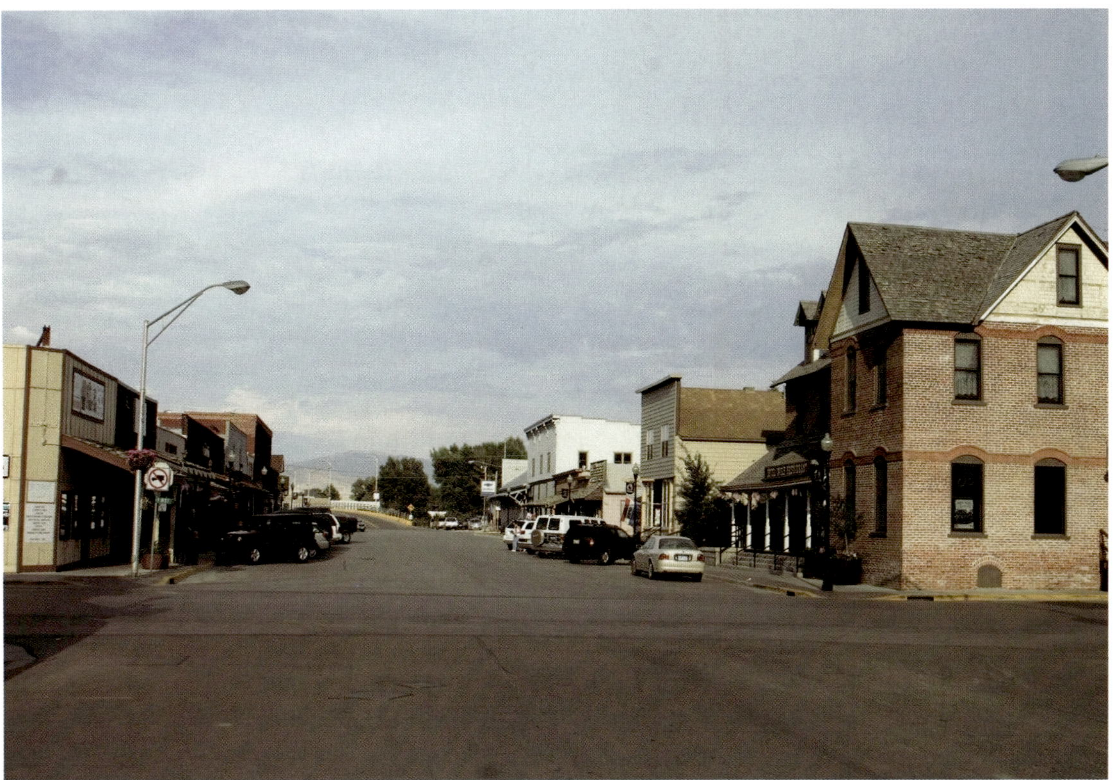

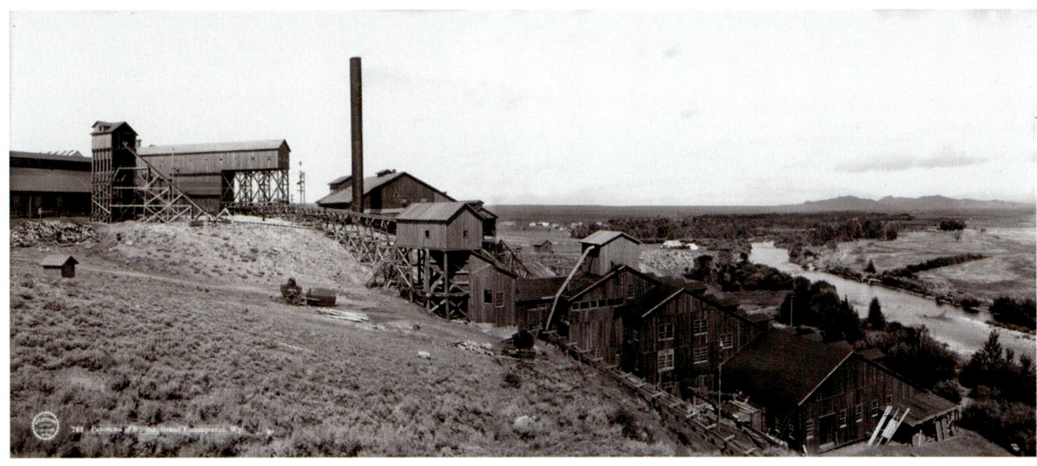

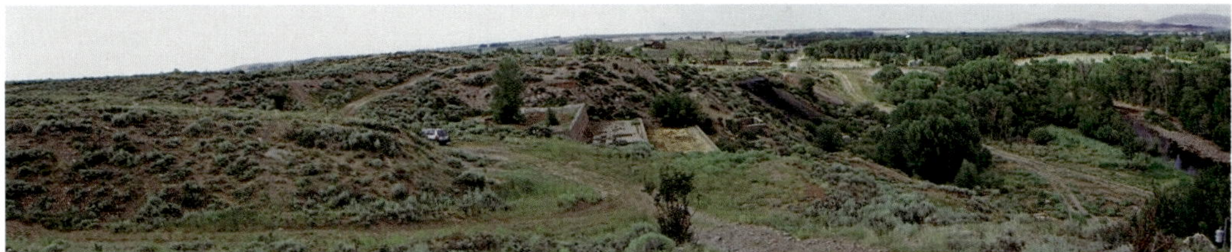

22. #765

Panorama of Smelter, Grand Encampment, 1903, 2007
GPS COORDINATES: 41 12.500N, 106 46.794W

In 1897, Ed Haggerty discovered a rich vein of copper ore high in the Sierra Madre Range west of Encampment. He named his claim for his partners, and the mining camps of Dillon, Copperton, Rambler, and Battle soon sprang up in the area. In 1902, the partners combined with eastern capital to build the Boston and Wyoming Smelter in Encampment and then constructed a sixteen-mile-long aerial tramway to haul ore from their mines down the mountains to the smelter. The plant processed up to 500 tons of copper ore each day. Its success boded well for the future, and the Saratoga and Encampment Railway organized in 1905 to connect the smelter with the Union Pacific mainline at Walcott. The boom did not last, however. After reorganizing the smelter in 1903 as the Penn-Wyoming Copper Company, the simple fact remained: the rich copper veins were playing out. Severe weather in the mountains made mining difficult, and in 1906 and 1907, fires destroyed much of the building seen here. After rebuilding, high production costs combined with falling copper prices to force the company into bankruptcy. In 1913, a Denver company salvaged the entire property.

Stimson's 1903 panorama of the Encampment smelter is a wonderful example of the kinds of promotional images he made for the 1904 St. Louis World's Fair. Another industrial portrait, Stimson used two glass plates to make a straight-on panorama of the massive structure. Selecting a high vantage point, he also hinted at the whole smelting process by showing the entire building. Looking down and across the Encampment River, the view further suggests the power of engineering over the environment. The slight double imaging along the edge of the two plates is evidence of the parallax problem the photographer often experienced in trying to shoot panoramas.

As part of my 1987 rephotography project, I re-shot part of this scene, but not the entire panorama, and included it in *Wyoming Time and Again*. Returning in 2007 with Lauren and my dog Nellie, I carefully composed the panorama by taking multiple shots left to right and then stitching them together in Photoshop. The final view, seen here, looked pretty much the same as it had twenty years earlier, with only tailings hills and a few foundations remaining from the massive structure. My Subaru Forester is partially hidden by a hillside but suggests the image's scale nonetheless.

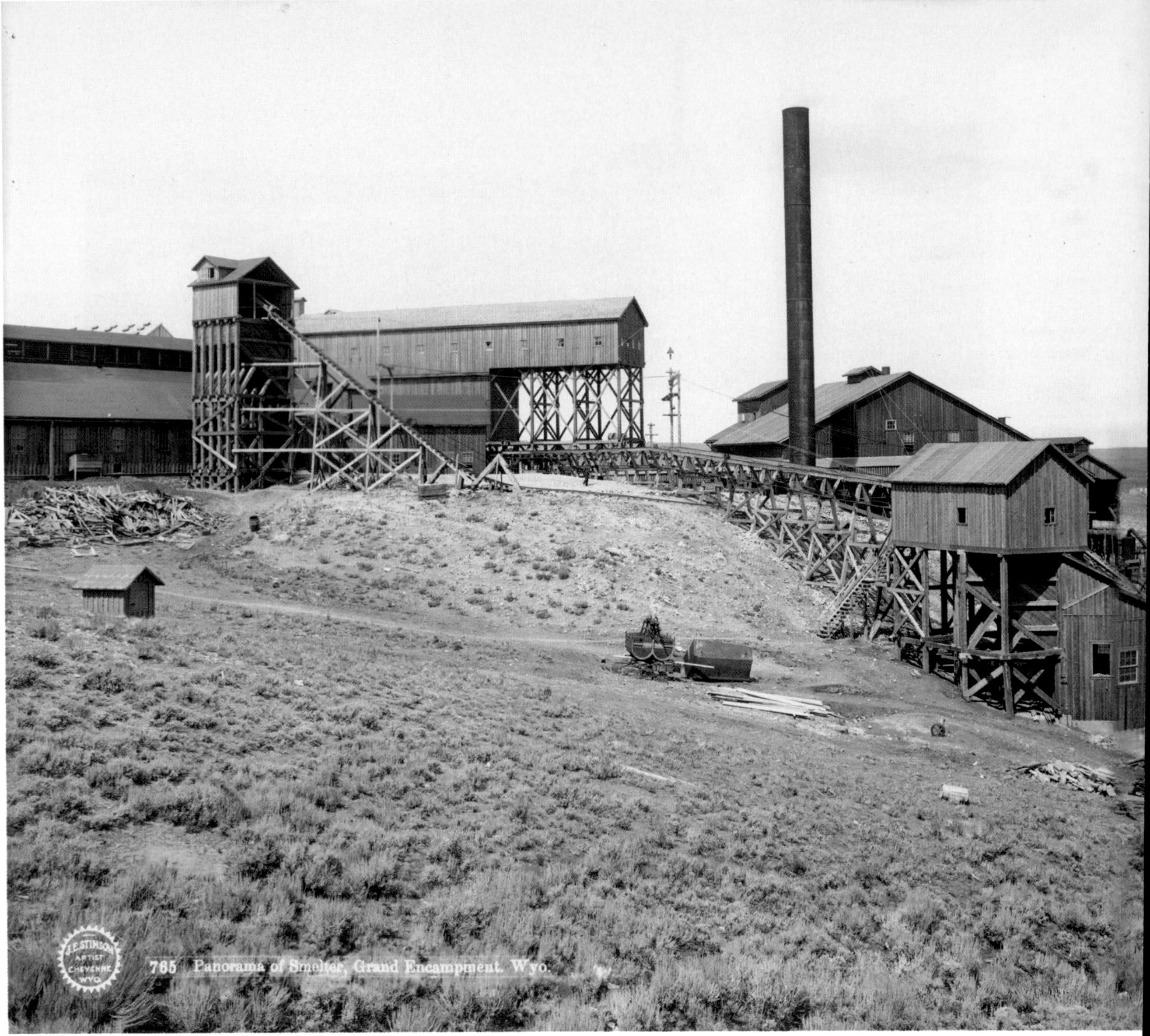

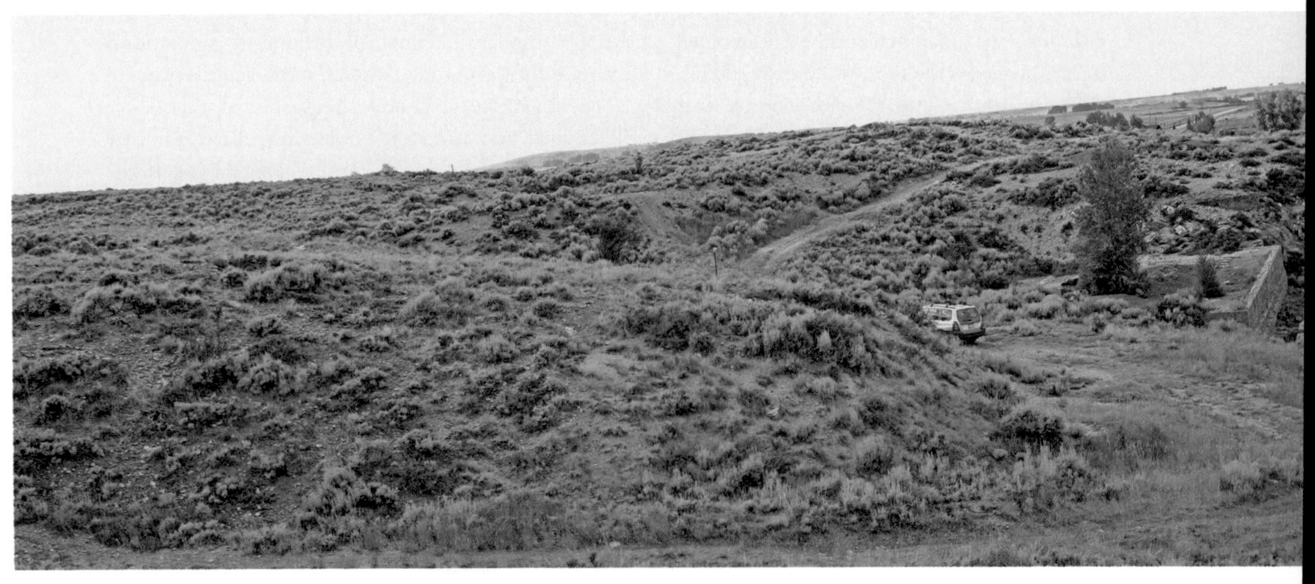
785   Panorama of Smelter, Grand Encampment, Wyo.

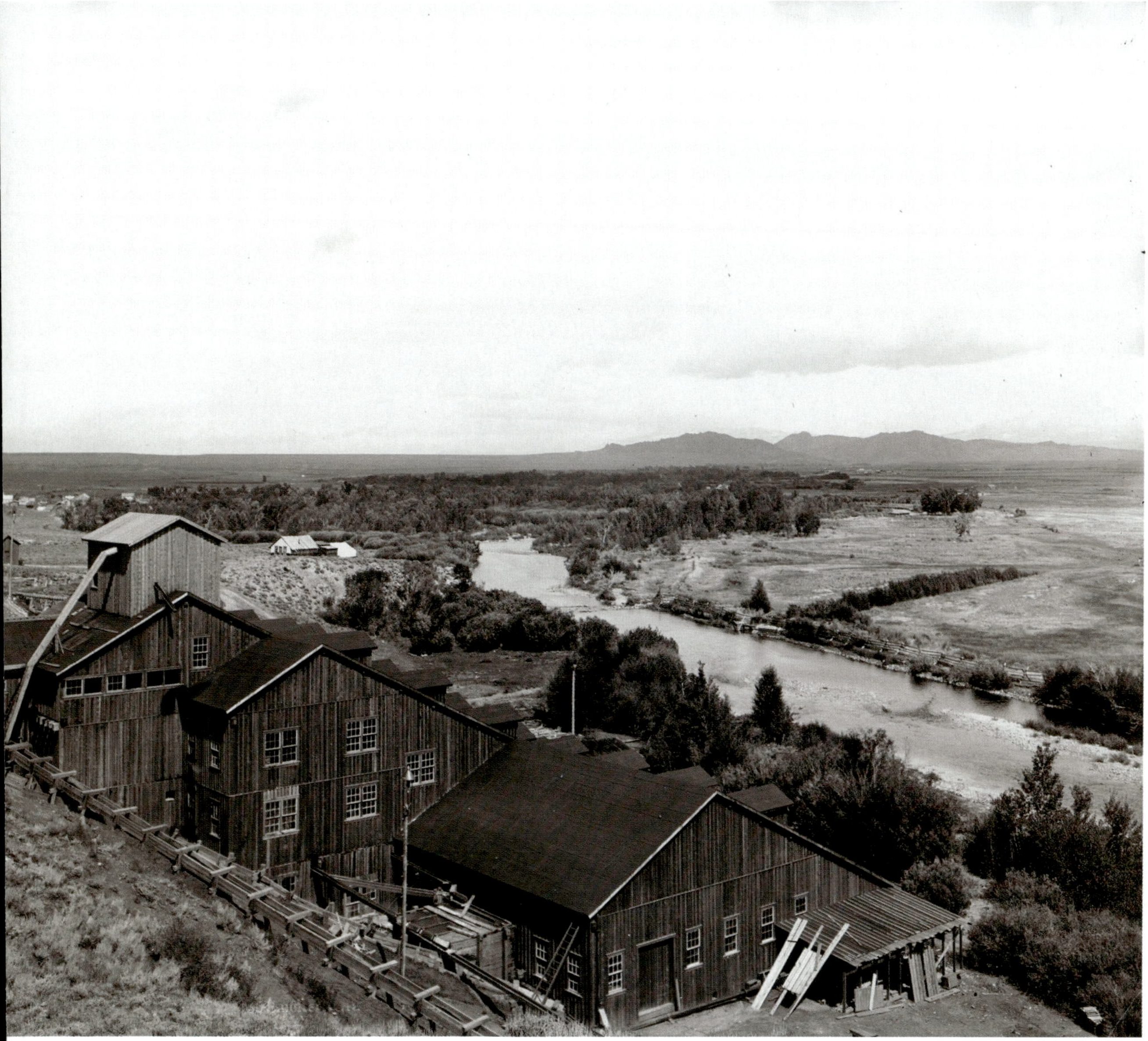

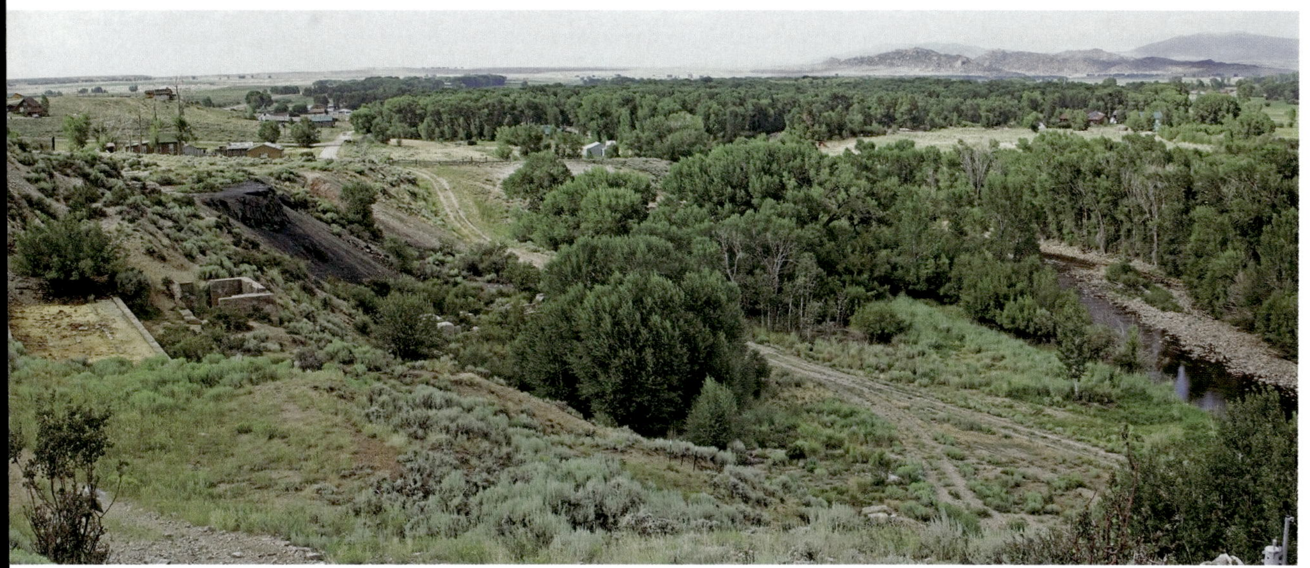

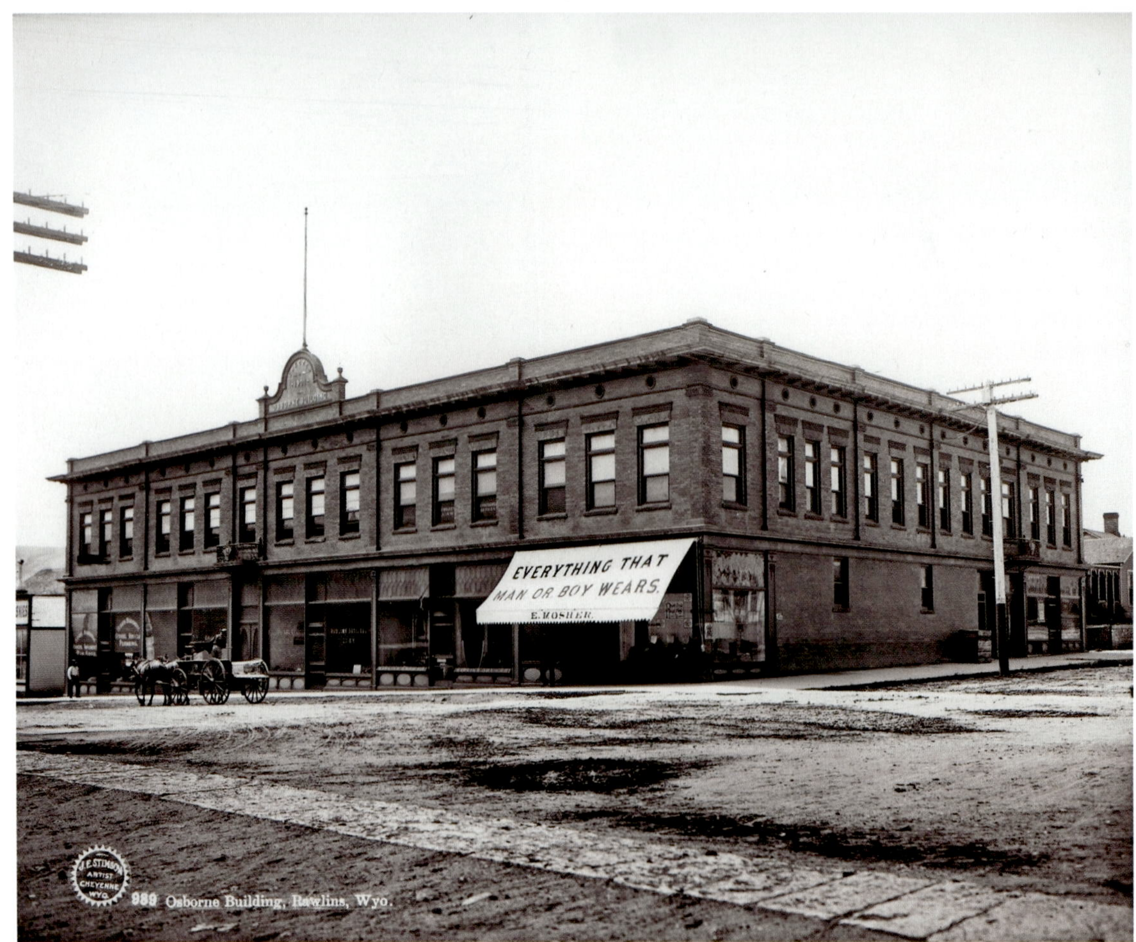

23. #989

Osborne Building, Rawlins, 1903, 1987, 2007
GPS COORDINATES: 41 47.263N, 107 14.4057W

Troops protecting the surveyors of the transcontinental railroad first discovered Rawlins Springs in 1867. After the railroad was constructed, the town of Rawlins was established at the site. It incorporated in 1886 and became the seat of Carbon County. This commercial block in downtown Rawlins was constructed in 1901 and named for prominent doctor John E. Osborne, who served as governor of Wyoming from 1892 to 1895. Stimson photographed the building as part of his 1903 state survey. Like many of his building portraits, this view shows a straight-on view of the corner so that both street sides of the building are visible. The awning over the clothing store window at right reads "Everything That Man or Boy Wears."

My two rephotographs, made in 1987 and 2007, show the effects of the Rawlins Downtown Development Authority, established in 1991, and its Main Street Program, started fifteen years later, on preserving and revitalizing the community's downtown. My first view, then, depicts the downtown at the end of its first century. A little remodeling had been done on the building, with a faux shingle roof added to the corner store and stucco to the storefront at left. Clearly, though, the pressure caused by Interstate 80 and the movement of the transportation artery away from the tracks was affecting the traditional downtown.

My 2007 view made two decades later clearly shows the positive effects of the Main Street Program. Begun in Rawlins the previous year, this community effort is part of a national program of the National Trust for Historic Preservation that focuses on revitalizing downtown economic districts. Although the faux shingle roof remains on the corner, three storefronts have been restored at left, building details have been repainted, period streetlights have been installed, and trees have been planted along the sidewalks. The effect is that the entire scene seems brighter.

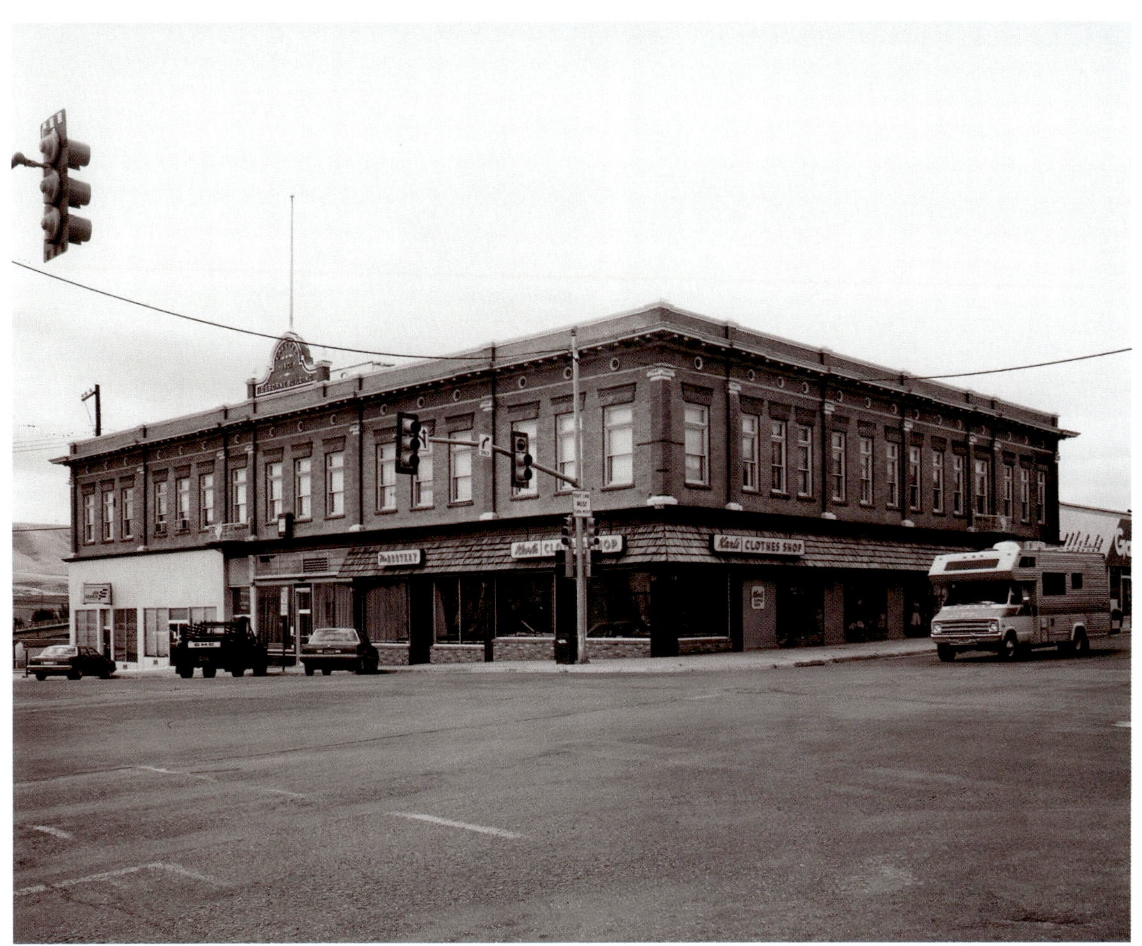

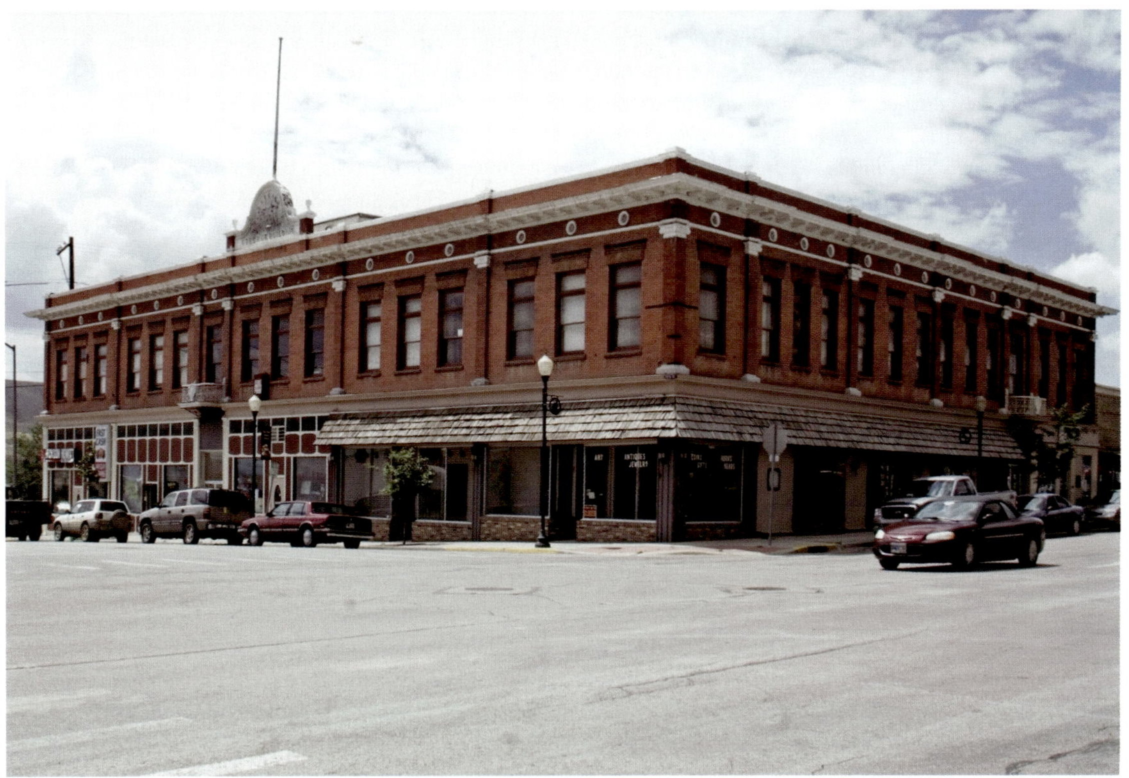

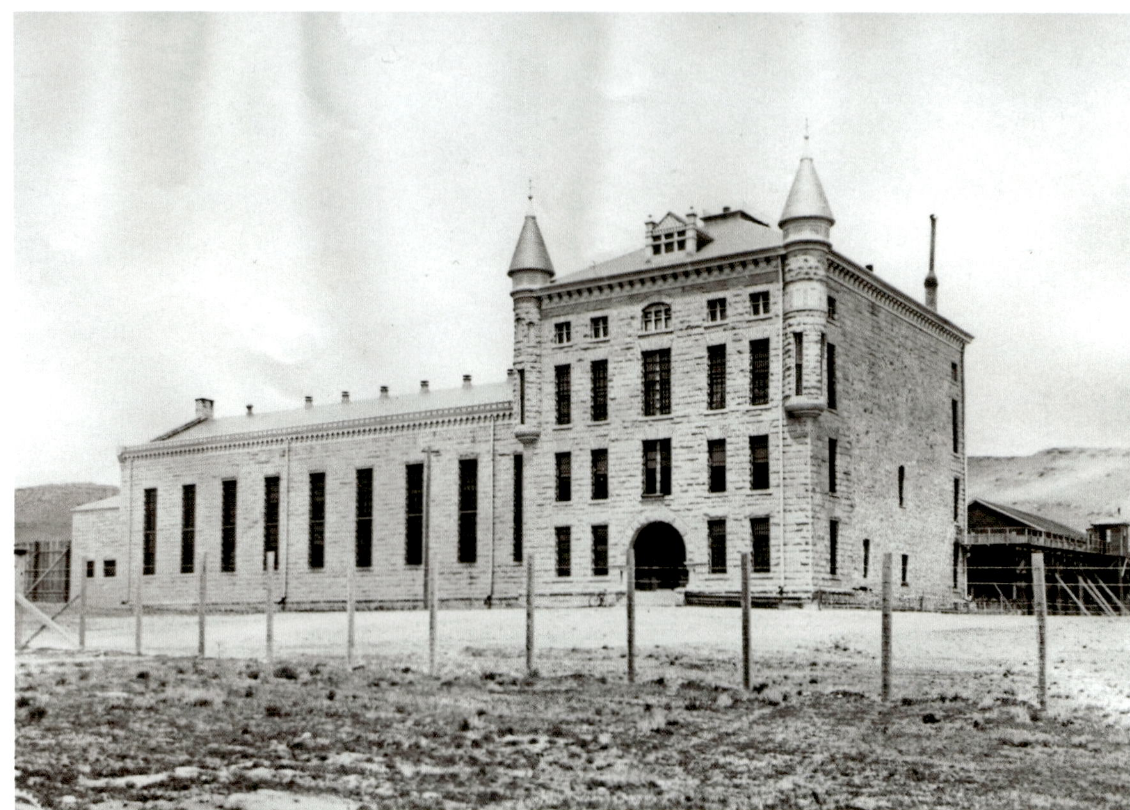

24. #992

State Penitentiary, Rawlins, 1903, 1987, 2007
GPS COORDINATES: 41 47.54733N, 107 14.506W

Rawlins has also protected and promoted the old Wyoming State Penitentiary, now dubbed the Wyoming Frontier Prison, as a historic site and, ironically, a tourist site as well. Situated on the north end of the Rawlins business district, the prison's cornerstone was laid in 1888, but funding and bad weather delayed its completion until 1901.

When Stimson photographed the prison in 1903, it boasted just 104 cells, a broom factory that used prison labor, no electricity or running water, and inadequate heating. He again used an architectural portrait style of composition. He is looking to the northwest, getting both the main southern wall and the eastern wall in his shot. A rudimentary fence is visible in the foreground. Not surprisingly, no one is visible in the photograph. While some may think it odd for a promotional photographer such as Stimson to capture a building that housed state lawbreakers, it does suggest that Wyoming was a progressive state and one under the rule of law, an especially important idea for a frontier state.

By the time I rephotographed it in 1987, the prison had been closed for six years and its inmates moved to a modern penitentiary south of town. My view showed that more buildings had been added and the grounds improved over time.

In the two decades between my two photographs, much occurred to turn the site into a tourist destination. During the year I first rephotographed it, the abandoned site served as the setting for a low-budget movie called *Prison*, which supposedly damaged much of the grounds seen in my photo. This destruction apparently led locals to start thinking about ways to preserve the property. In 1988, a joint power board with city, county, and civic leaders assumed ownership of the site, renamed it the Wyoming Frontier Prison, and established it as a museum. Three years later, a nonprofit group called Friends of the Old Pen organized to preserve and promote the site.

By the time I revisited in 2007, the grounds had been improved and the old prison turned into a tourist site featuring guided tours, a gift and bookstore that carried bumper stickers that read "I did time in Rawlins," a newsletter, and a Christmas bazaar. Like the Osborne Building, the Wyoming Frontier Prison has become a model for Rawlins of historic preservation and economic re-development.

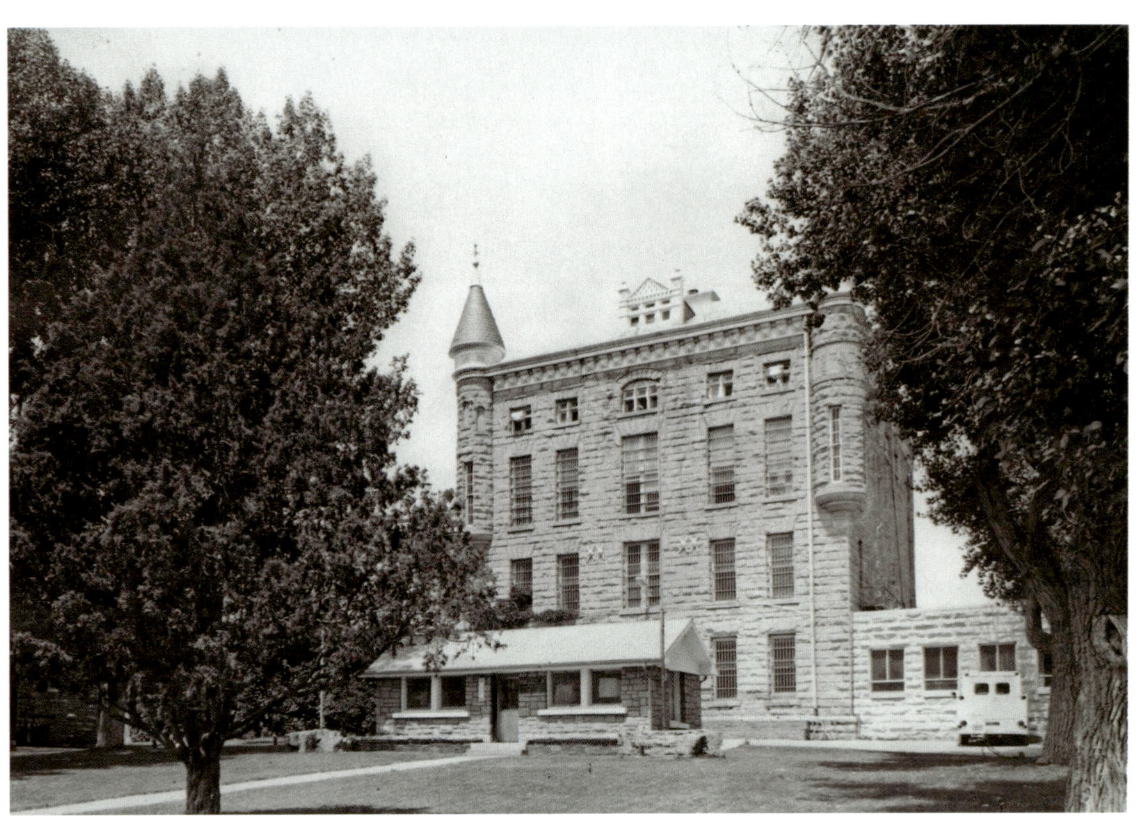

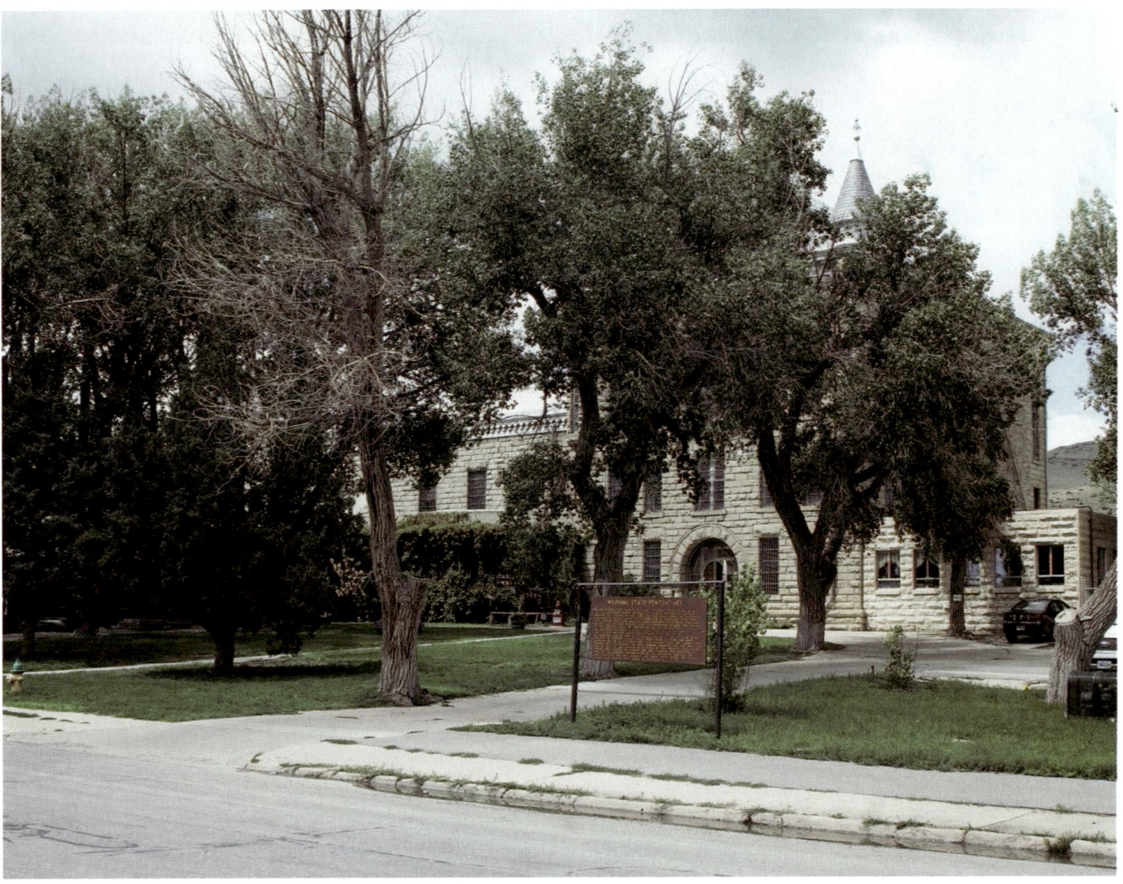

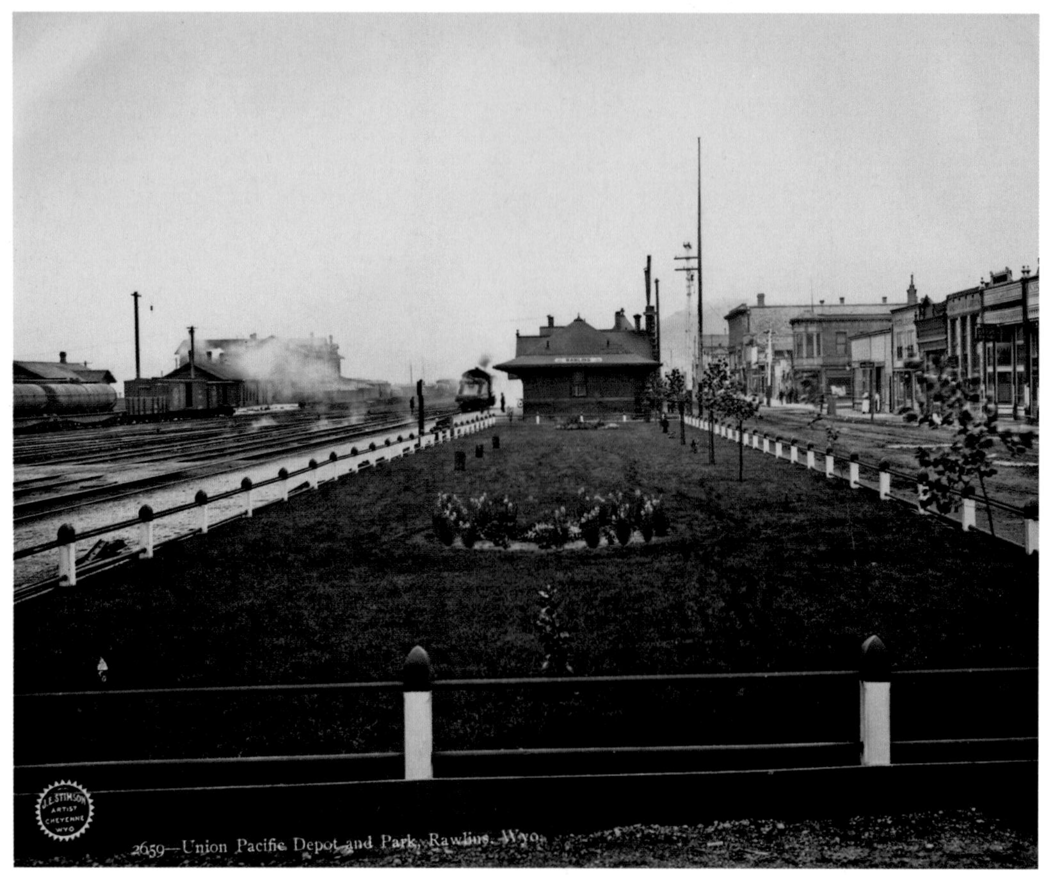
J.E. STIMSON
ARTIST
CHEYENNE
WYO.
2659—Union Pacific Depot and Park, Rawlins, Wyo.

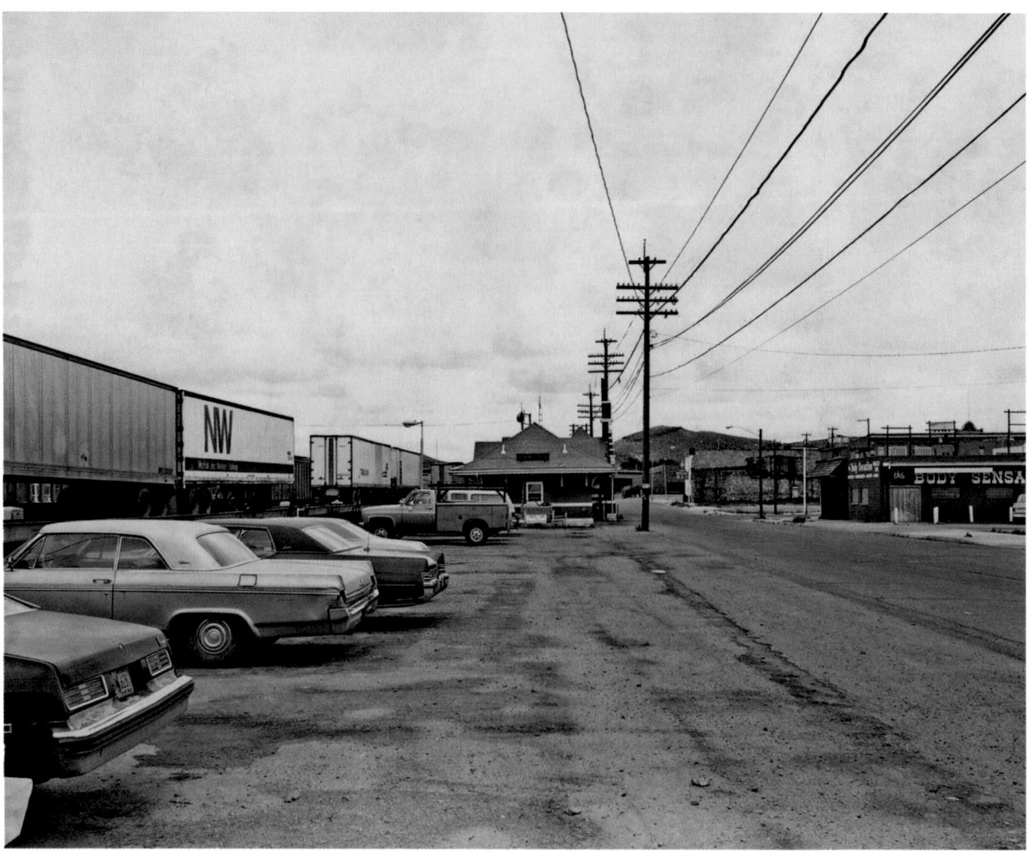
NW
BODY SENSA

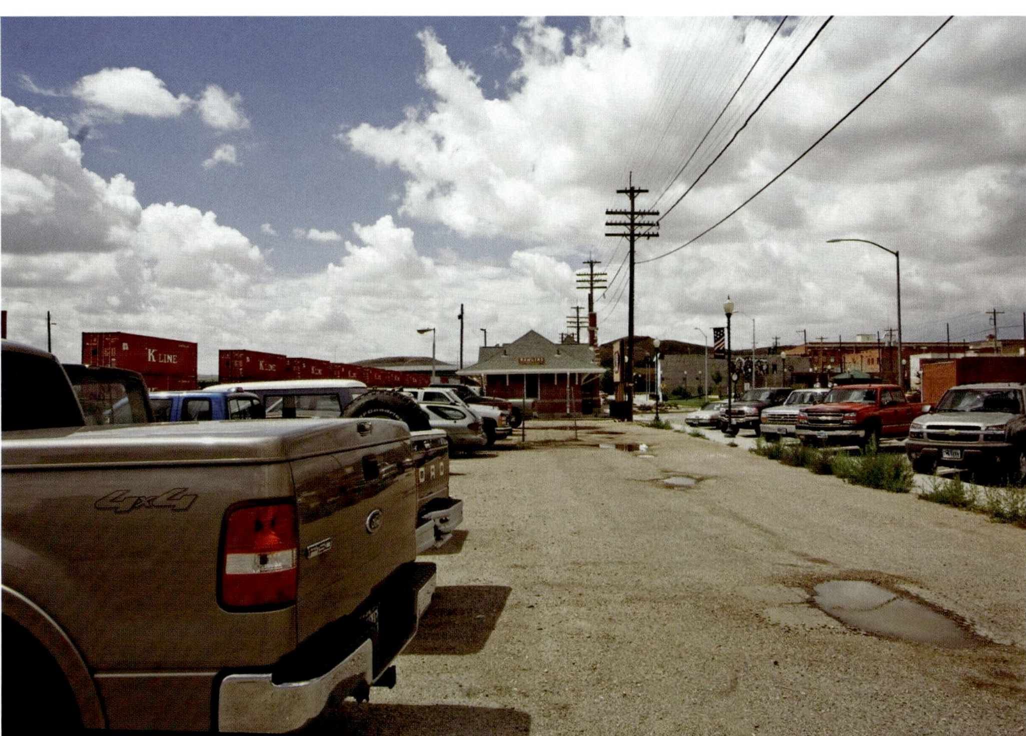

25. #2659

Union Pacific Depot and Park, Rawlins, 1909, 1987, 2007
GPS COORDINATES: 41 47.22683N, 107 14.25033W

The effects of the Main Street Program on the Rawlins Union Pacific Depot and Park are far less notable. Completed in 1901 and photographed by Stimson in 1909, the depot once served as the gateway to Rawlins. For his promotional image, Stimson chose a vantage point looking west to include the park's green grass, flowers, and trees, plus the depot and the adjacent bustling Front Street.

When I rephotographed the depot in 1987, passenger rail service had ended, the depot park had long been removed, and the adjacent downtown seemed seedy. Many buildings had been demolished, while the Body Sensations Health Spa sat across the street. A parking lot for railroad workers had replaced the park.

When I rephotographed the site in 2007, the Rawlins Main Street Program had begun making inroads into the depot area. The UP had donated the building to the city, which used it for small meetings. Although more buildings across the street had been razed and the UP parking lot remained, old-fashioned streetlights and planters had been installed, and a small park occupied the newly emptied lots.

Just as Main Street Programs help preserve what is local, changes appearing on the tracks are just as important. In Stimson's 1909 view, boxcars, flat cars, and tankers sit on tracks as a local steam engine and slope-back tender steam to the right. These are local-origin cars, connecting Rawlins producers with the national market by way of the Union Pacific. In my view almost eight decades later, a subtle change has occurred as we see not locals but a train filled with semi-trailers waiting on the tracks. Designed to be shipped on flat cars and then unloaded and pulled behind trucks, these trailers—along with the diminished depot and downtown—hint at the rise of the highway, the automobile, and the infusion of the national market into the local one.

Twenty years later a similar train passes through carrying inter-modal containers, a standardized shipping global compartment that can be moved from ship to rail to truck without ever being unloaded. Bearing the name K-Line, these trains originate in Asia, move across the Pacific Rim, then throughout the United States, bringing the homogenized world market everywhere.

Such is the power of rephotography. Three photographs, taken over the course of a century, reveal important change at work in Wyoming through both local and global forces.

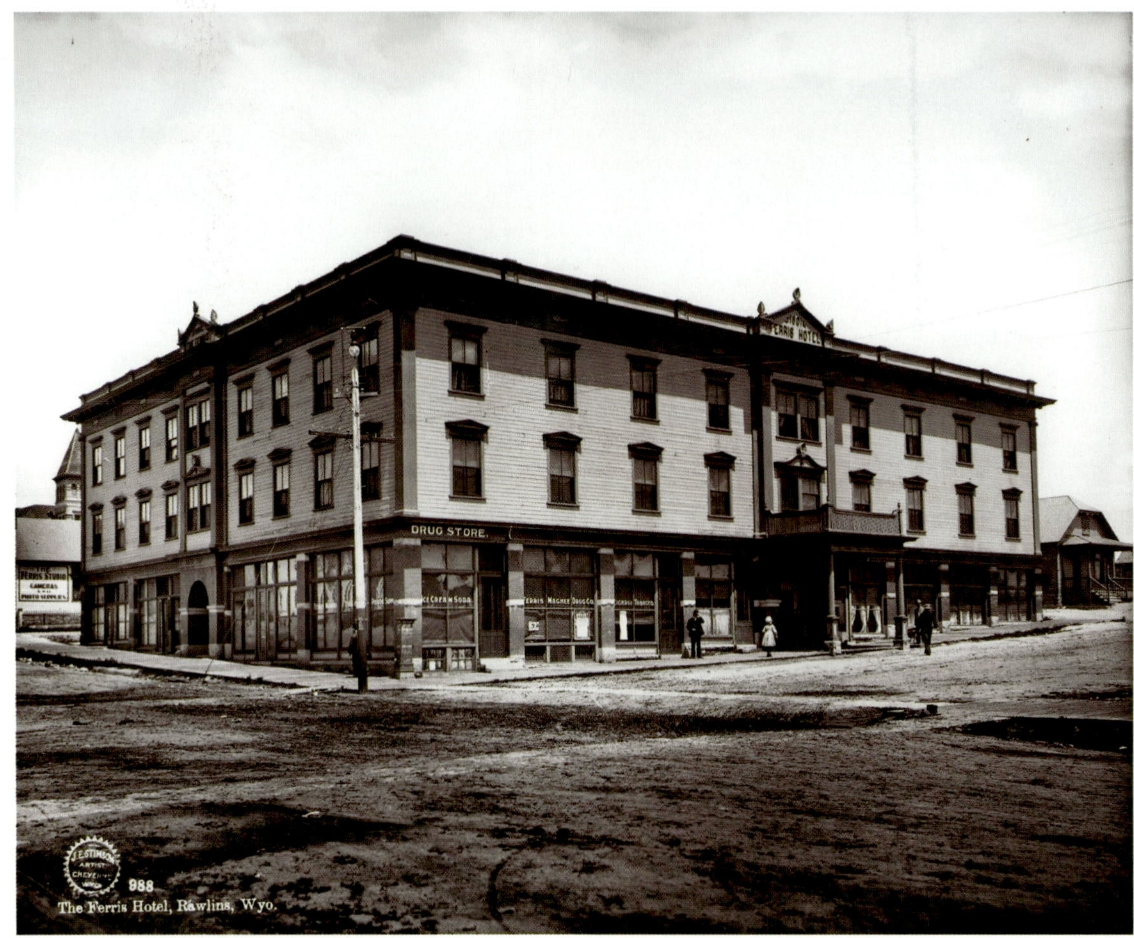

26. #988

The Ferris Hotel (site), Rawlins, 1903, 1987, 2007
GPS COORDINATES: 41 47.32267N, 107 14.363W

The Ferris Hotel, named for copper boomer George Ferris, has to be considered the biggest loss for the Rawlins Main Street Program and the State of Wyoming's historic preservation movement. Completed in 1902, the Ferris first served as a railroad hotel and featured elaborate woodwork and several small shops. Thomas Molesworth, an American furniture designer who operated out of Cody and popularized the "Cowboy Furniture style" featuring hides and horns, designed the hotel interior.

As with many of his business portraits shot during his 1903 state survey, Stimson photographed the hotel at a diagonal view to show both the south and west walls and their businesses. Close inspection reveals a man tipping his bowler to a passing lady plus a couple of other onlookers. To the left of the hotel, a small white building boasts a sign that reads "The Ferris Studio: Cameras and Photo Supplies."

When I rephotographed the Ferris in 1987, it had undergone a substantial remodel, and in 1983 it closed its doors. What remained of the hotel clearly hinted at the forces of modernization and the automobile. For example, the ornate wood siding, windows, roof line, and several of the ground-floor shops had been covered in stucco, an effect that "streamlined" the building and made it look "modern." On its roof, large neon signs had been erected, probably to attract visitors from the distant interstate. Most of the remaining shops were boarded up; the only ones open were a bar and a barbershop.

In 2007, having already seen the effects of the Rawlins Main Street Program on the Osborne Building and the depot area, I was shocked to discover that the Ferris Hotel had been demolished several years earlier. Nothing remained. The details are still not clear to me, but apparently sometime in the first decade of the twenty-first century, the City of Rawlins decided that the Ferris was too worn down and too costly to remodel and simply tore it down. As can be seen in my 2007 rephotograph, an empty lot now occupies the space. For a community clearly invested in preserving its past, perhaps this loss will lead to further preservation elsewhere.

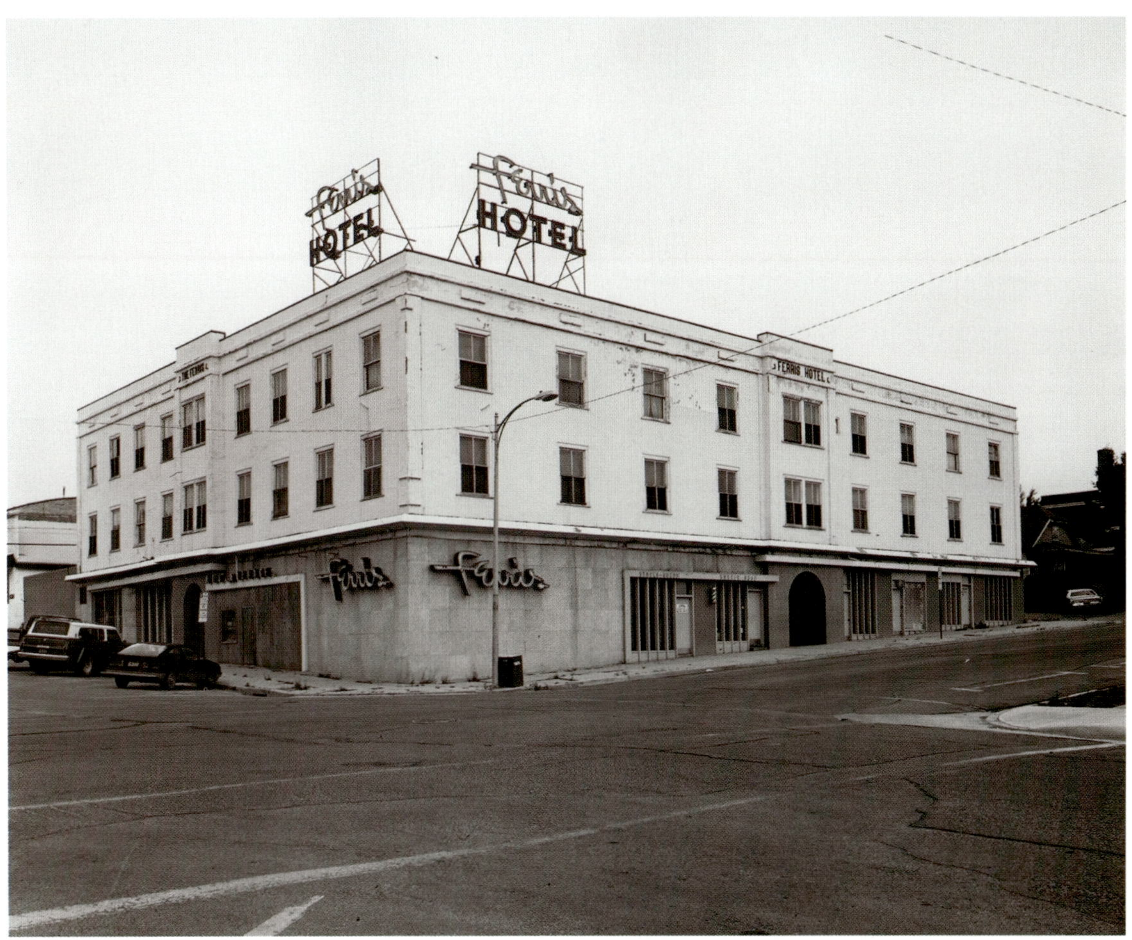
Ferris
HOTEL
Ferris
HOTEL
FERRIS HOTEL
Ferris
Ferris

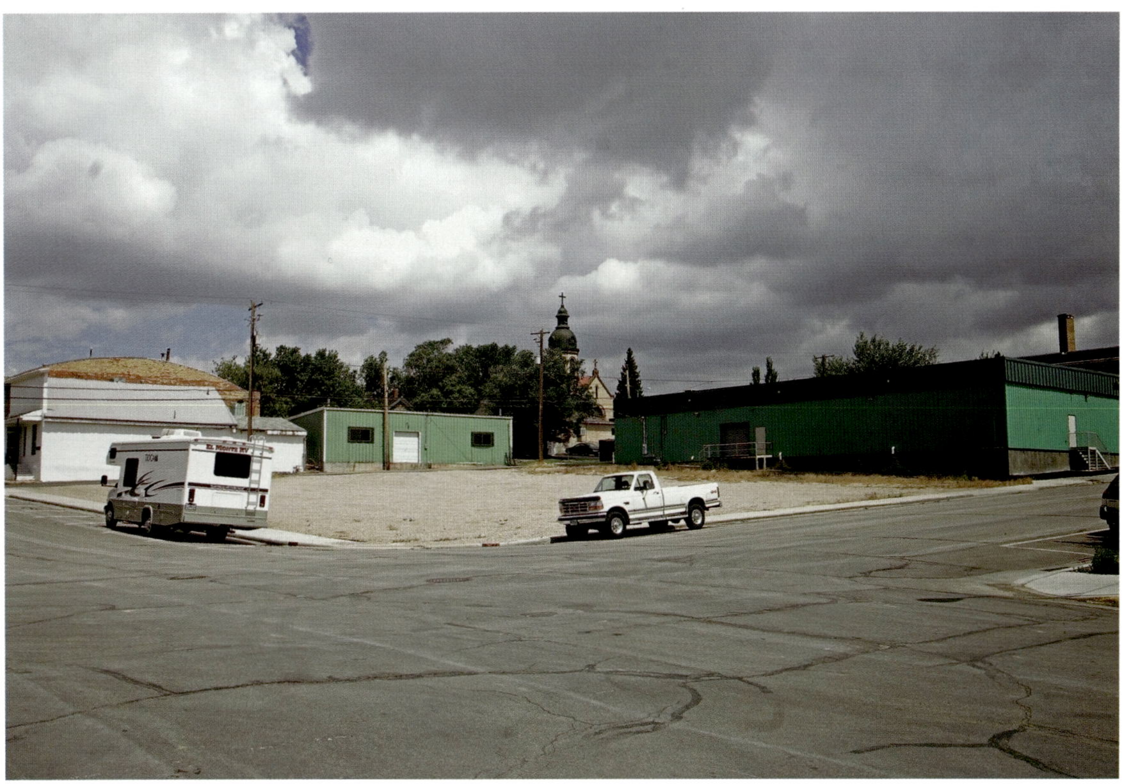

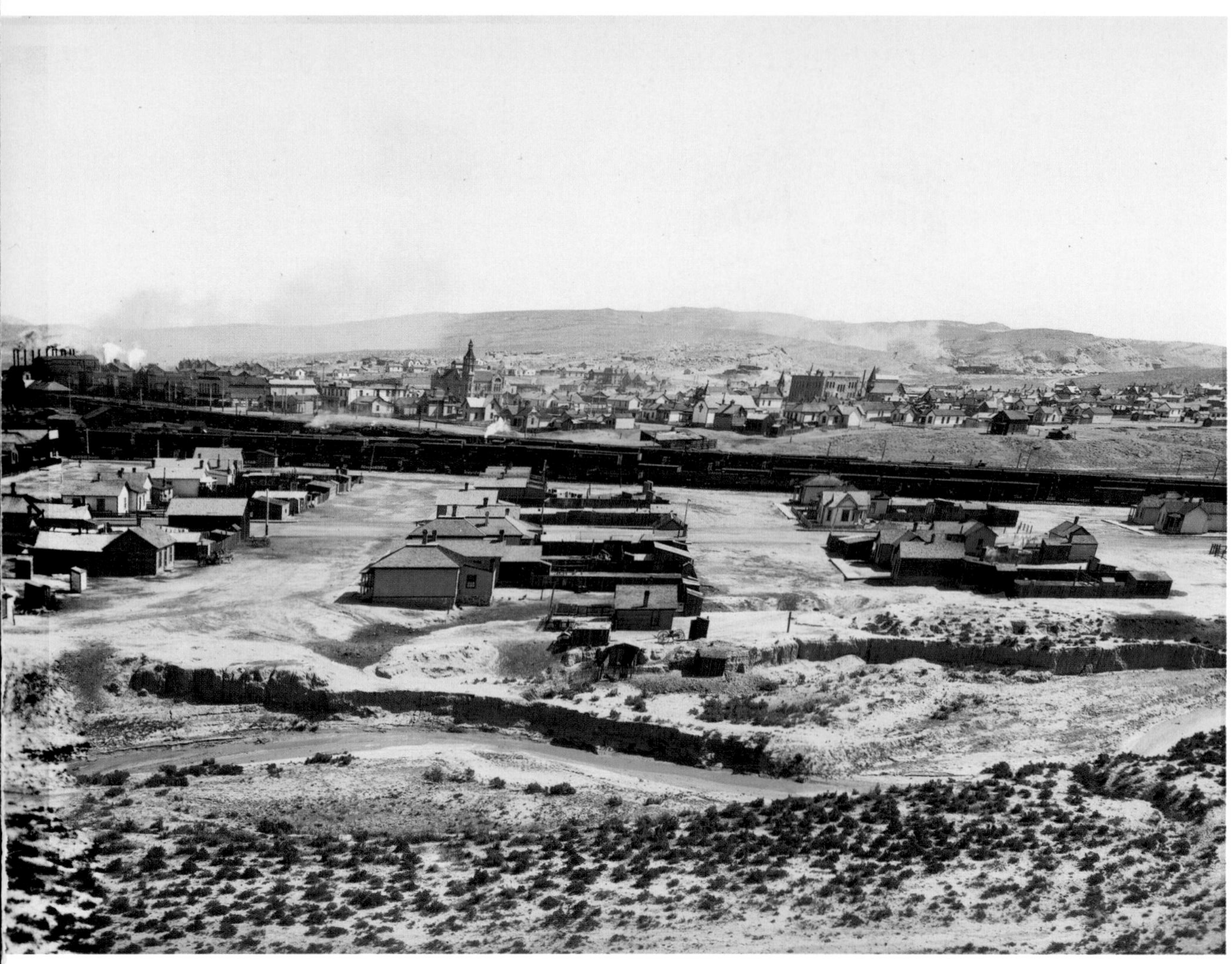

When Stimson photographed the town in 1903, its population was about 4,300. His vantage point is on the southeast side of a hill west of the town, an area referred to today as College Hill because of the presence of Western Wyoming College nearby. Like most of Stimson's panoramas, this one has parallax problems but is nevertheless a wonderful visual document showing the sagebrush-covered landscape, the town's grid, the railroad, the smokestacks of the mines, and, at center, the stone tower of the Rock Springs City Hall.

By the time I rephotographed Rock Springs in 1987, all of the UP mines within the town itself had closed, though the city had boomed in the 1970s as the economic center for the bustling oil, natural gas, and trona industries. Between 1970 and 1980 its population had grown by a whopping 66 percent, to almost 20,000. In my view, taken from a backyard on Hilltop Drive overlooking Roosevelt Elementary School, the coal stacks are gone but the number of trees stands out. as do meandering Dewar Drive at right and the downtown overpass, center. Just to the right of the overpass, the Rock Springs City Hall can still be seen.

The trees again stand out in my 2008 rephotograph. Dewar Drive, the overpass, and the tower of city hall, now the Rock Springs Historical Museum, can also be found.

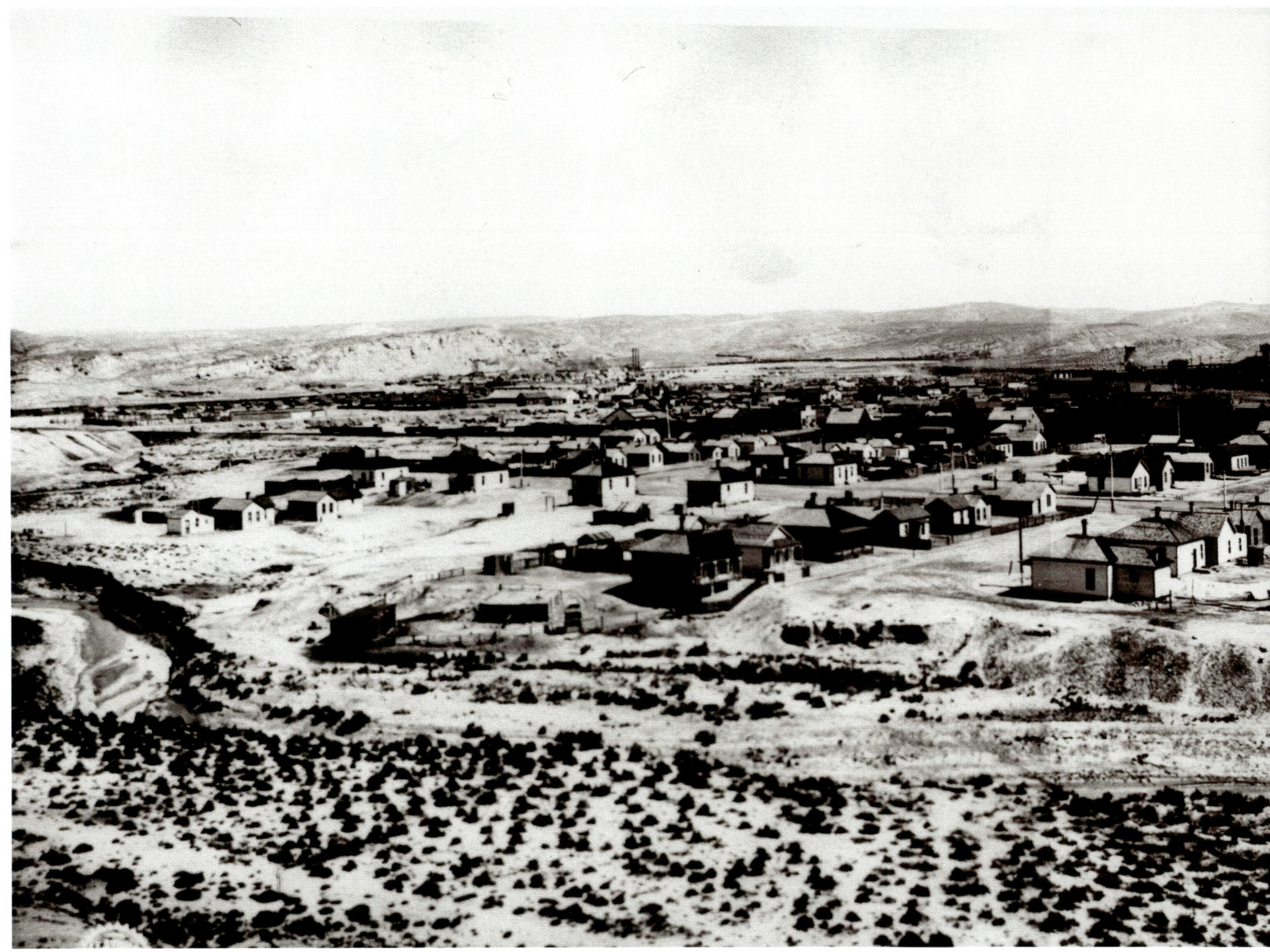

One of several bird's-eye panoramas Stimson made during his 1903 survey, this view of Rock Springs looks east over Bitter Creek toward the Union Pacific tracks, the coal mines, and the downtown district. Originally the site of a Pony Express Station, the modern town of Rock Springs was founded by the railroad in 1868 to exploit nearby coal deposits. To pacify labor, the UP imported workers of many nationalities, including Chinese strikebreakers. In 1885 the town experienced one of the worst race riots in the history of the American West when white coal miners killed twenty-eight Chinese miners, burned seventy-five homes, and drove the remaining Chinese out of town in what came to be called the Rock Springs Massacre. Following this, the Union Pacific turned to southern and eastern Europeans, eventually employing more than forty ethnic groups in the mines.

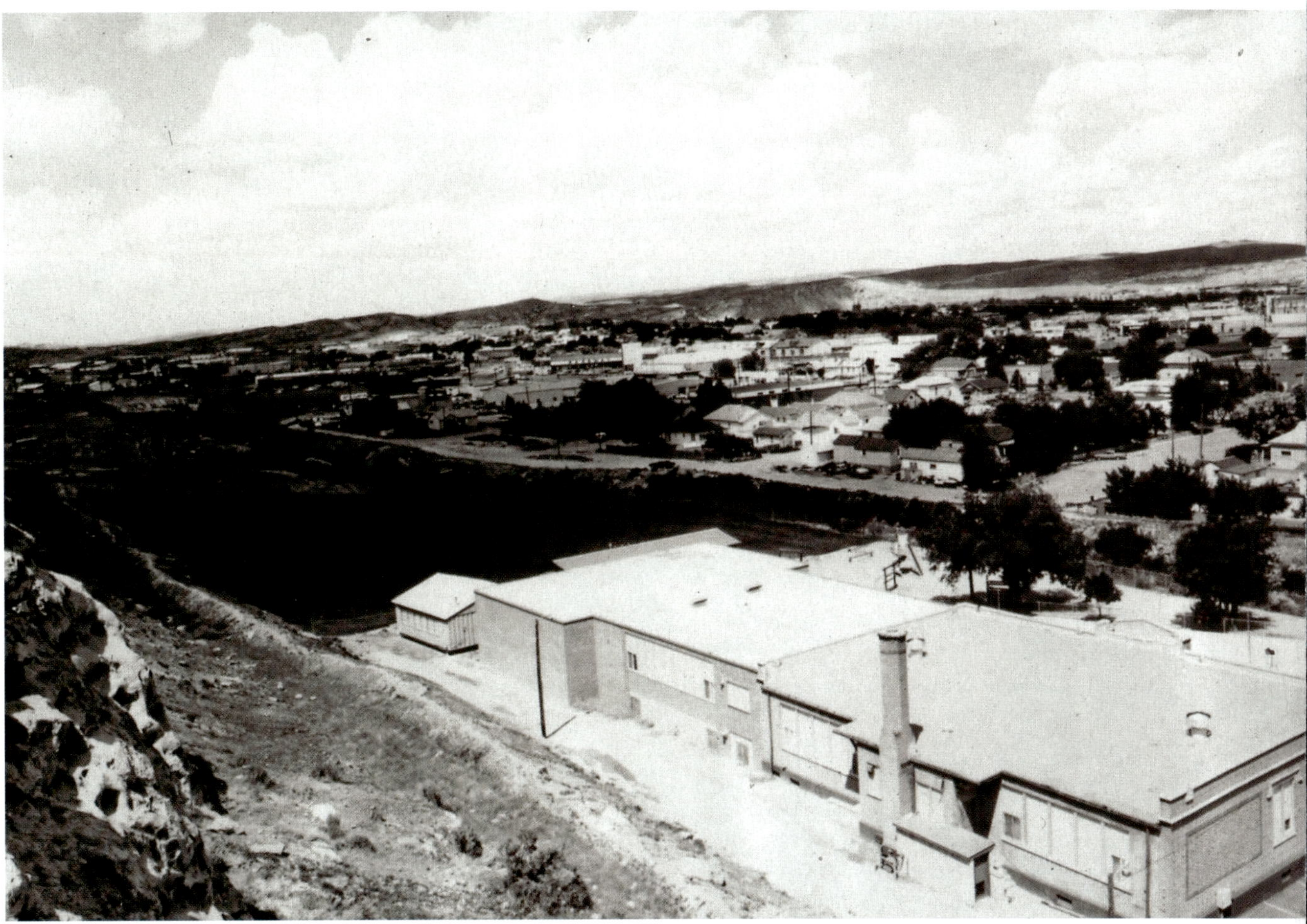

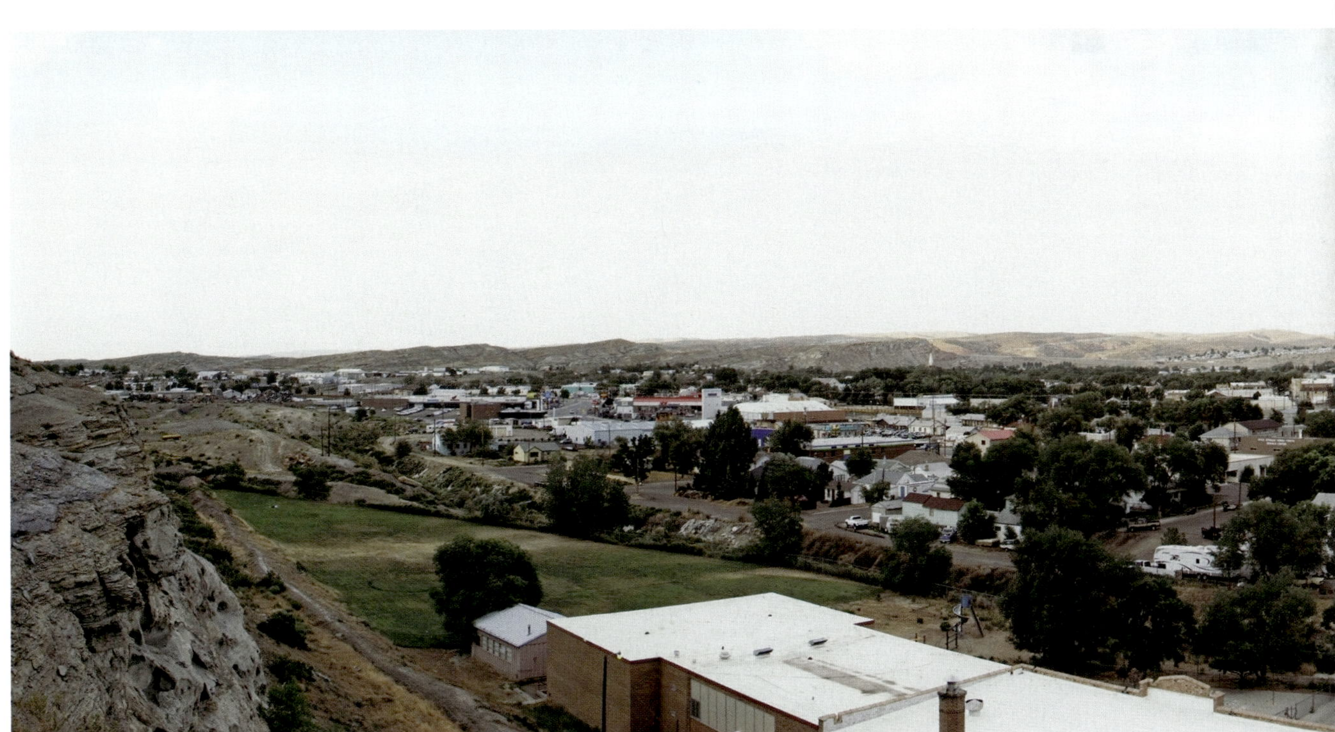

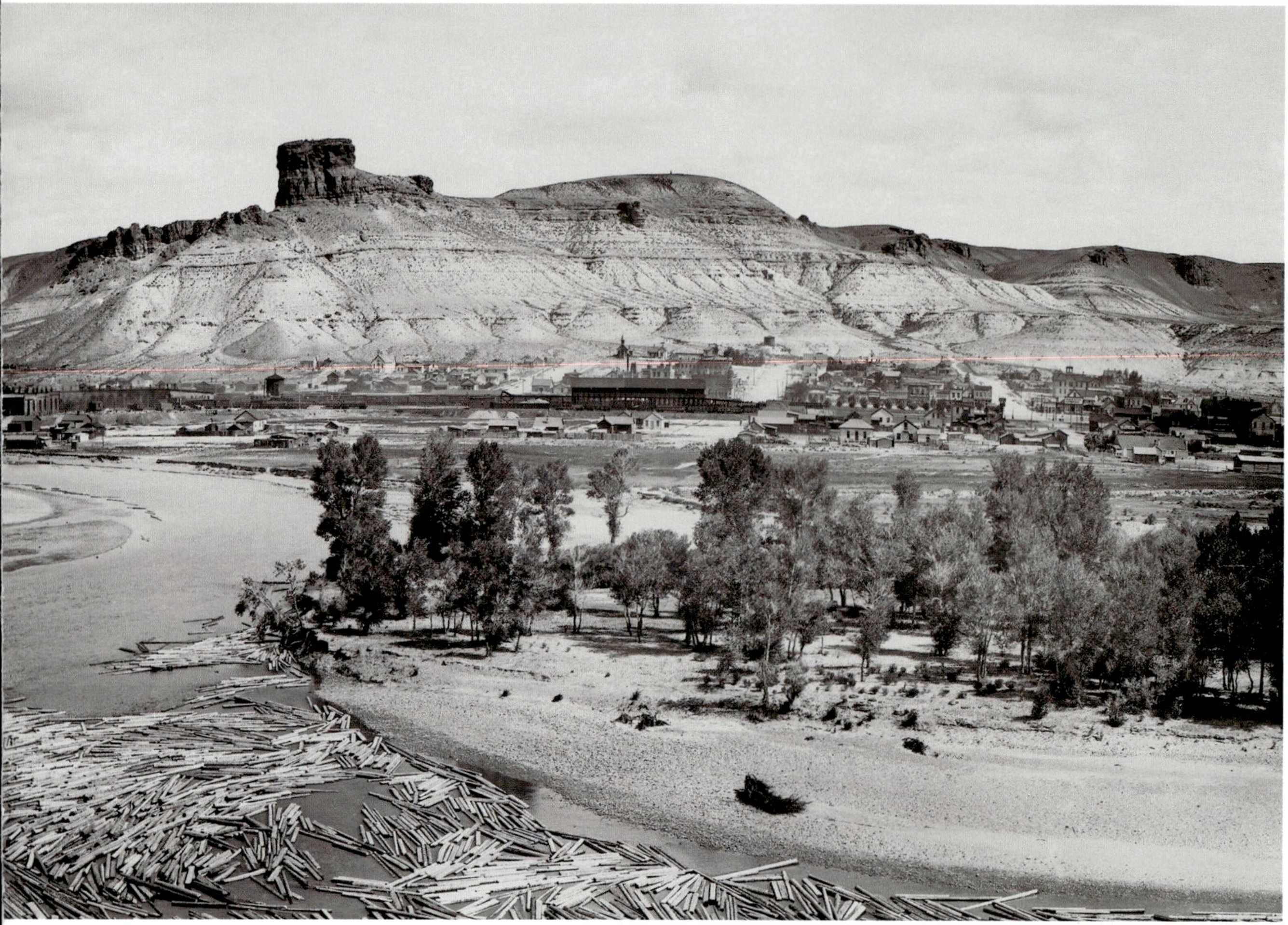

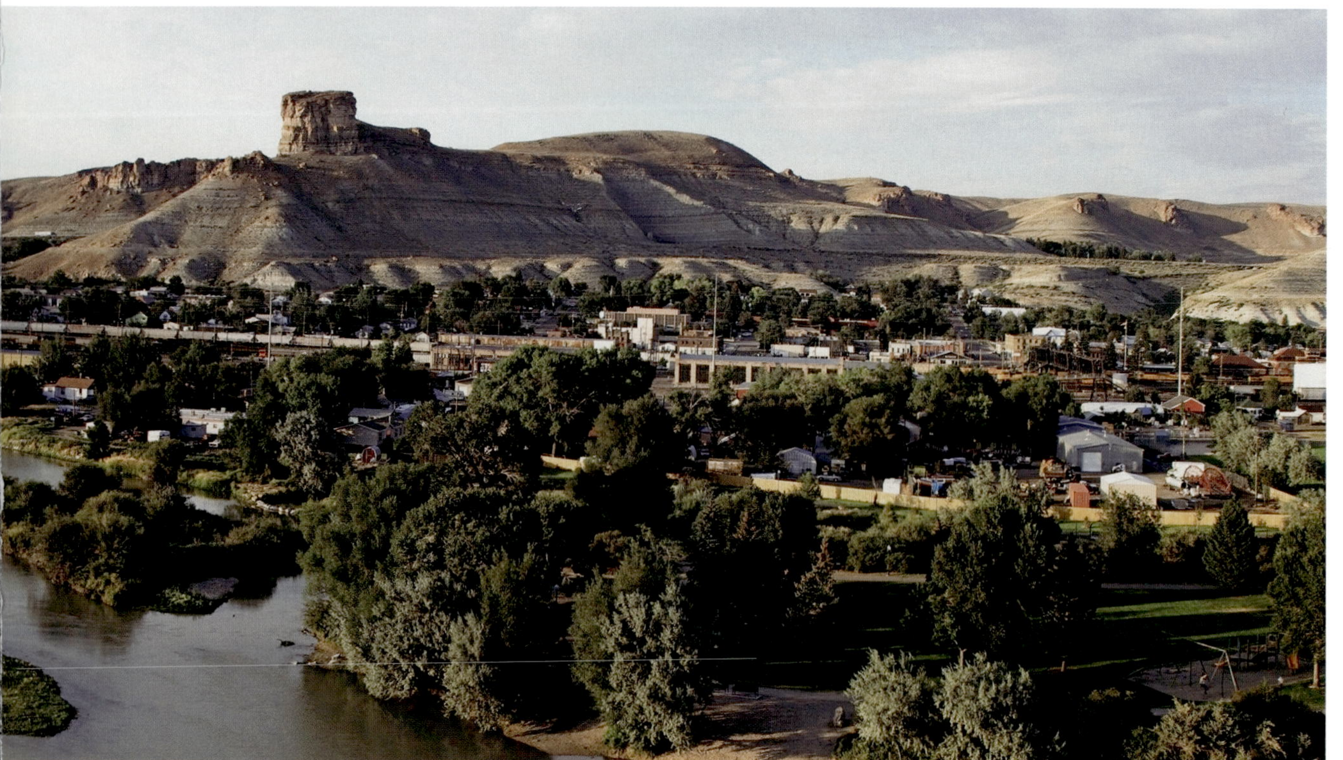

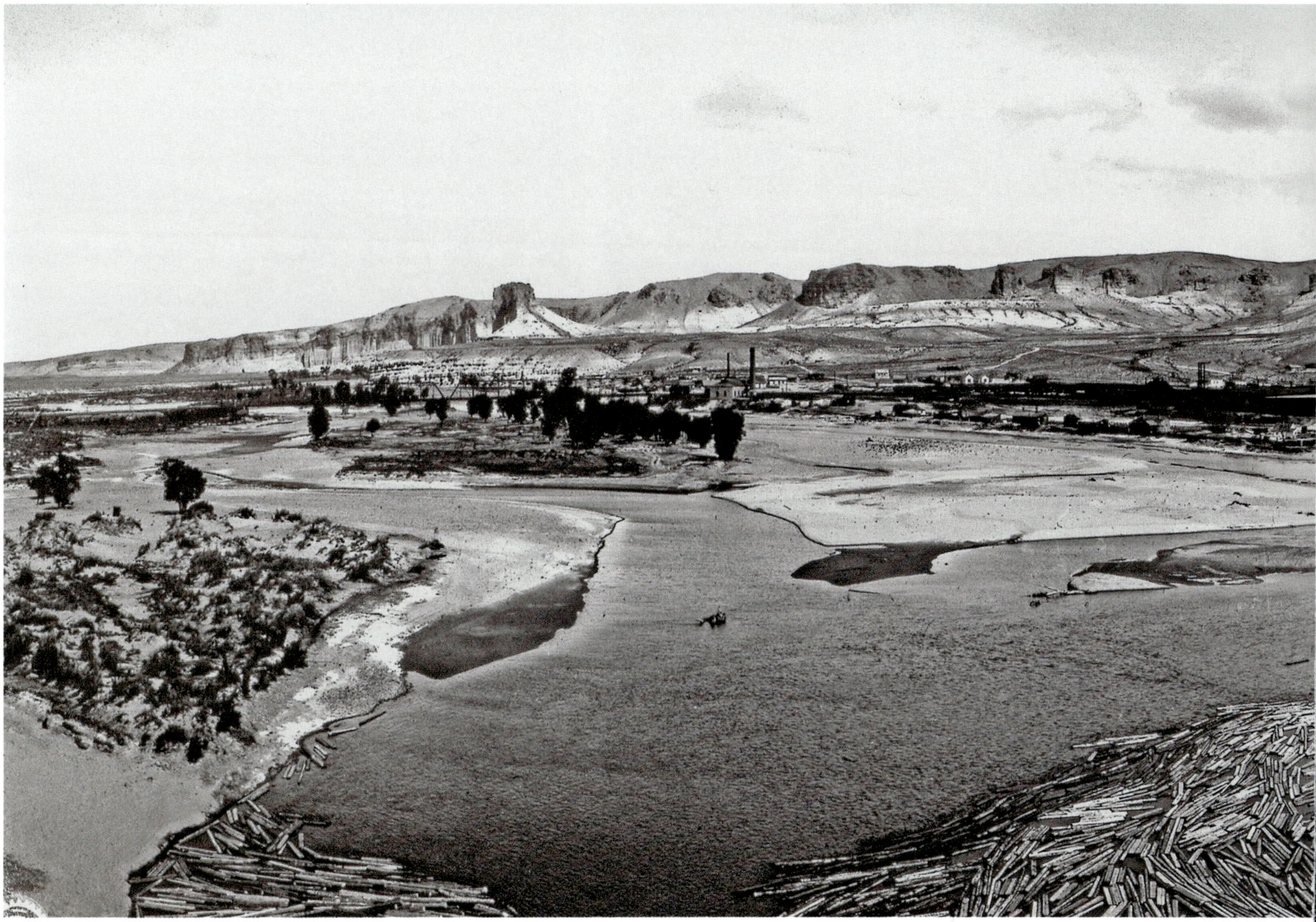

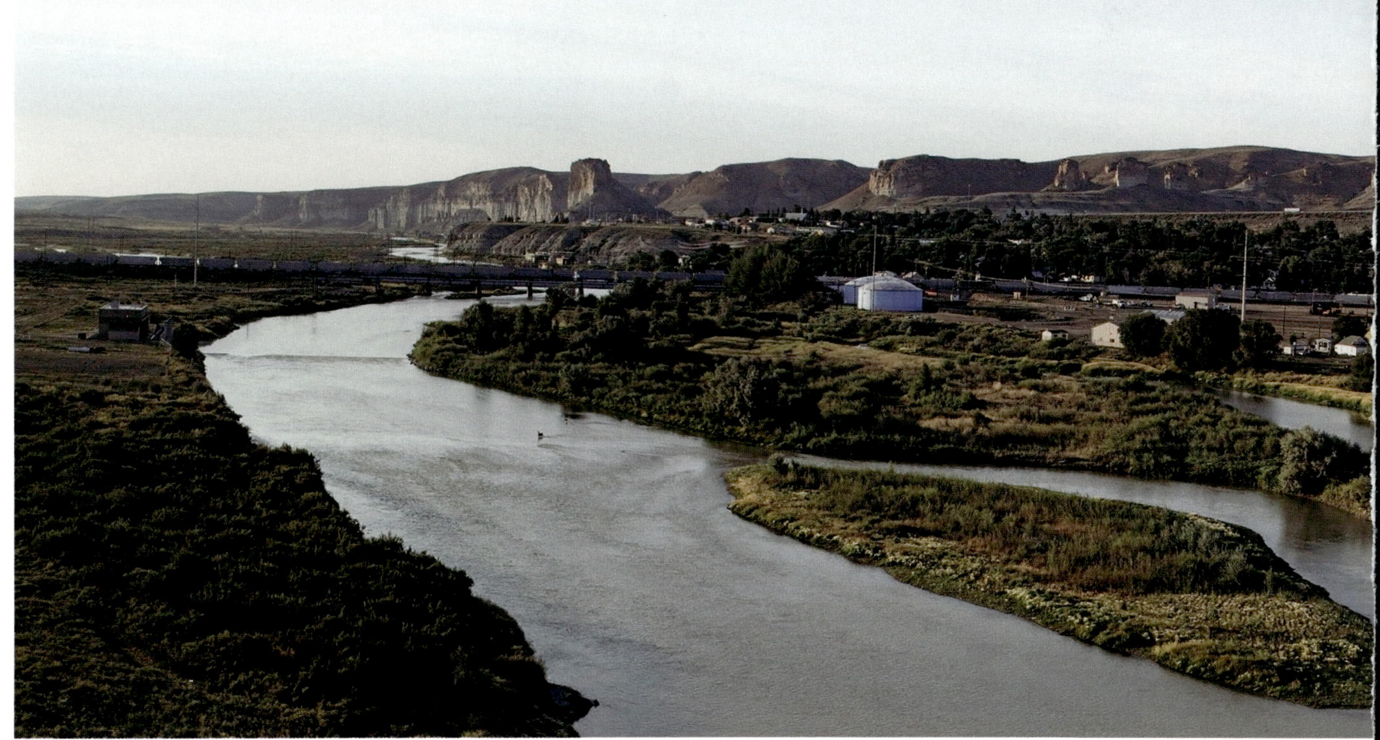

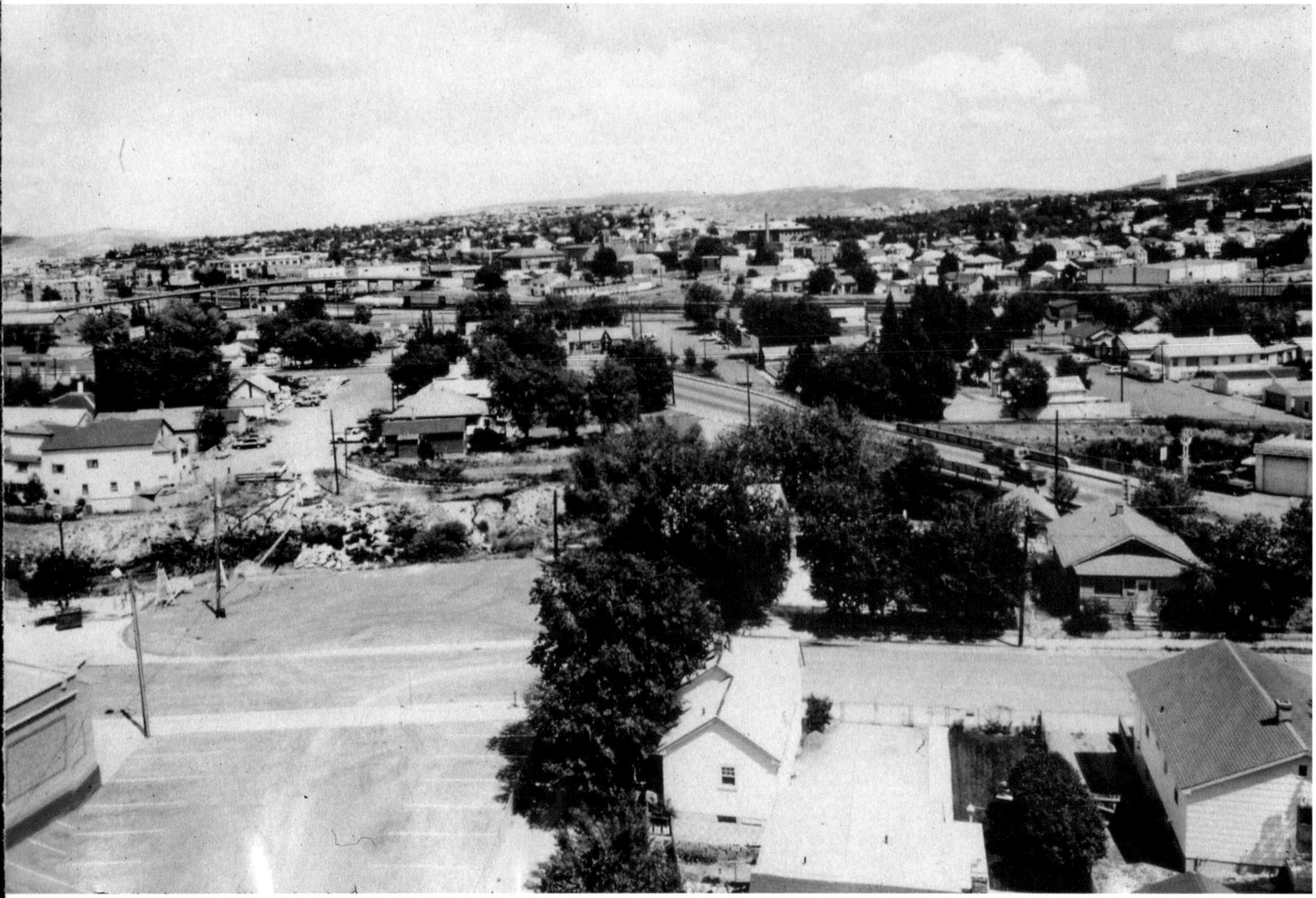

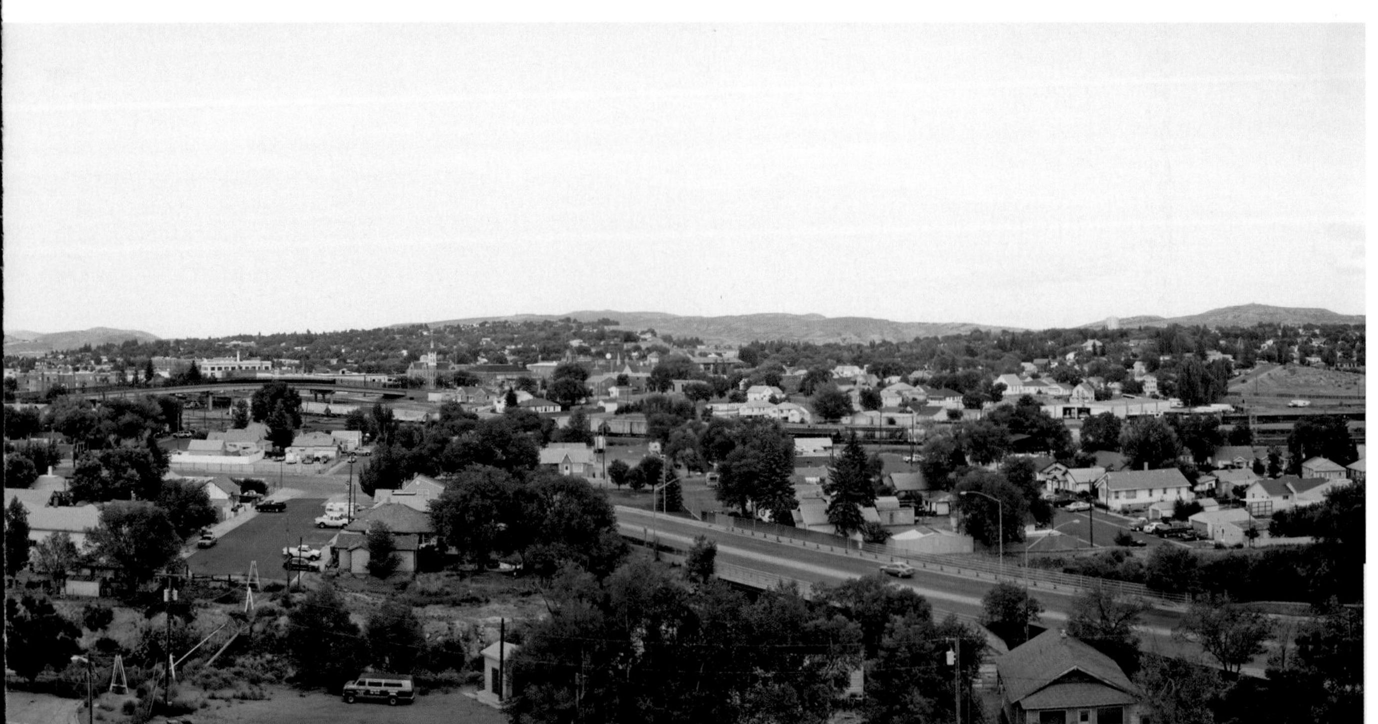

Panorama of Green River, 1903, 2007
GPS COORDINATES: 41 31.339N, 109 28.387W

Because of the presence of the Green River and its nearby buttes, Stimson's 1903 view of the town of Green River has to be one of his most beautiful panoramas. Like other southern Wyoming towns, Green River began life in the 1860s with nearby Pony Express and Overland Stage Stations and then became a formal town in 1868 with the building of the Union Pacific Railroad. In 1869, explorer John Wesley Powell took the train here and launched his boats from Expedition Island, foreground, to explore the Green and Colorado Rivers.

Stimson's view, looking north toward Castle Rock, shows a tie boom stretched across the river. Trees were cut in the foothills of the Upper Green, fashioned into ties, and then floated down the river, 300,000 strong, in spring drives, where they were collected and treated and shipped out on the railroad. In his 8 × 10 glass plates, Stimson collected a great deal of visual data. Zooming in on this scene reveals the railroad bridge across the river, the UP roundhouse, the Sweet Water Brewery (#29 below), and the phone-booth–sized elevated gate tower— the vantage point for image #30, also discussed later.

My 2007 digital photograph, taken in the golden light of early evening, reveals similar data. A close look shows the many trees creating a canopy over the town, Expedition Island's small beach, trucks traversing Interstate 80 at the base of Castle Rock, the trees and grass of Green River Cemetery on the right, the pedestrian bridge across the tracks (my vantage point for #30 below), the Palisades upstream bathed in warm light, and a lone deer wading into the Green River just above the small island at center.

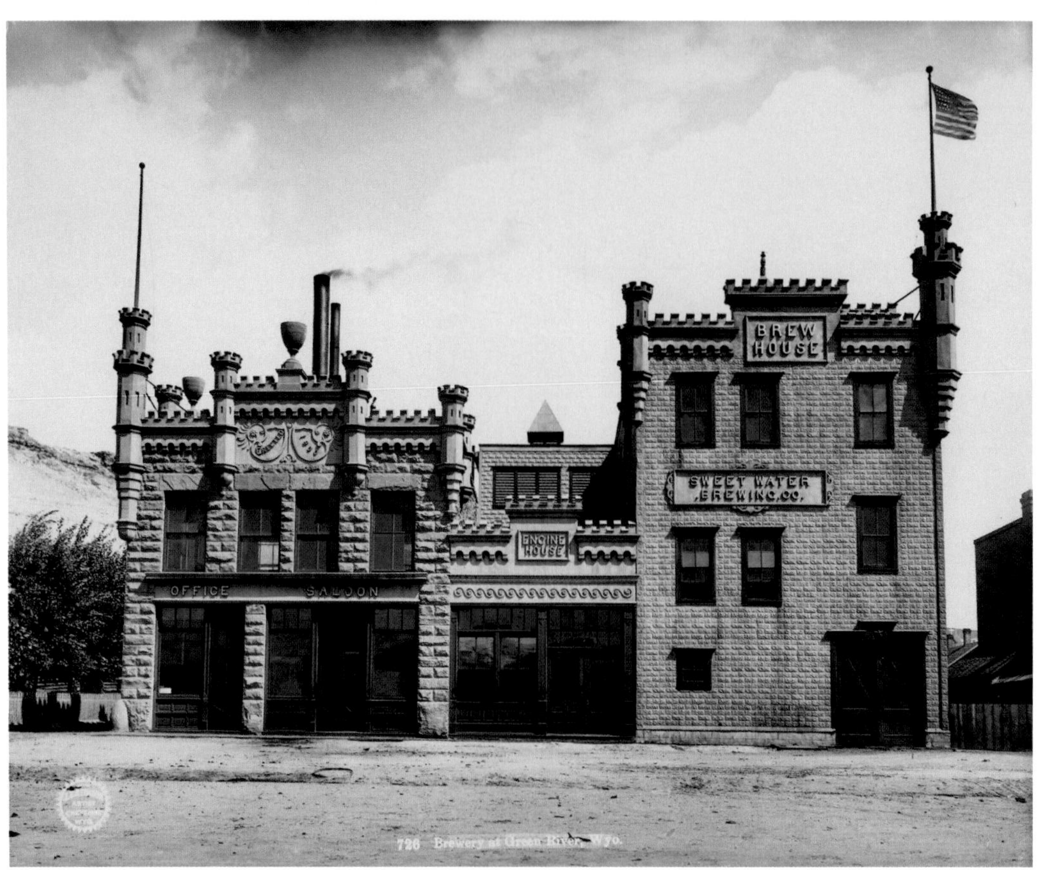
BREW HOUSE
SWEET WATER BREWING CO.
ENGINE HOUSE
OFFICE   SALOON
726   Brewery at Green River, Wyo.

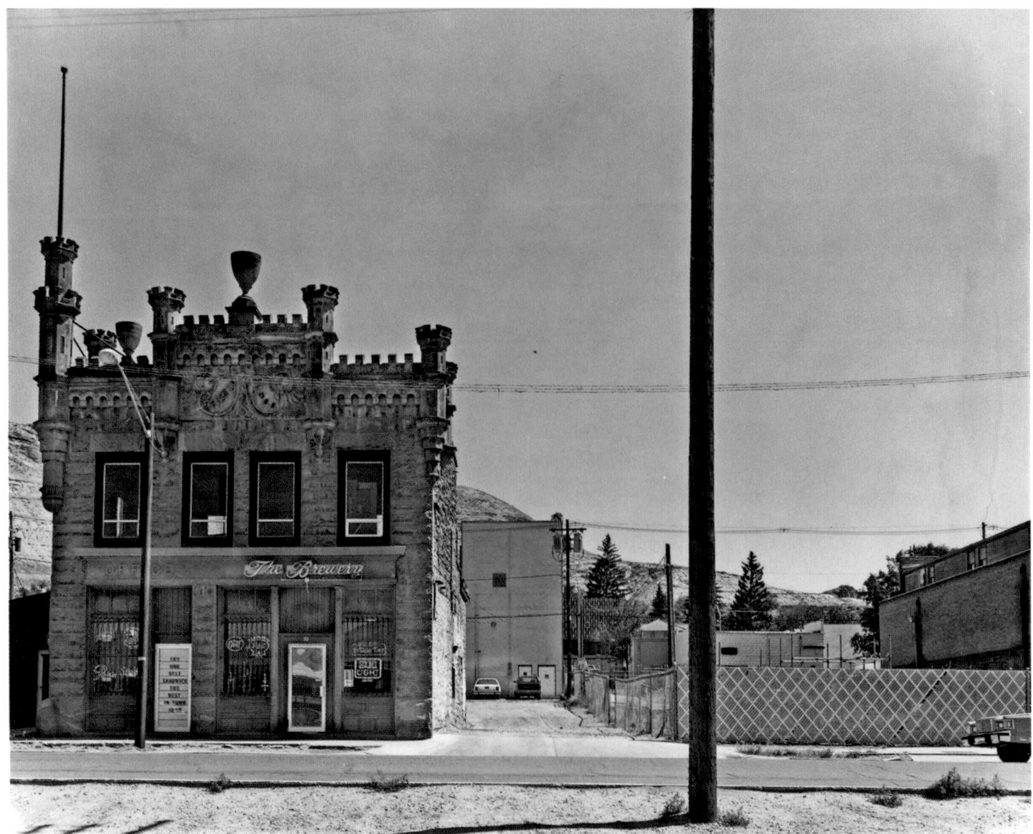
The Brewery

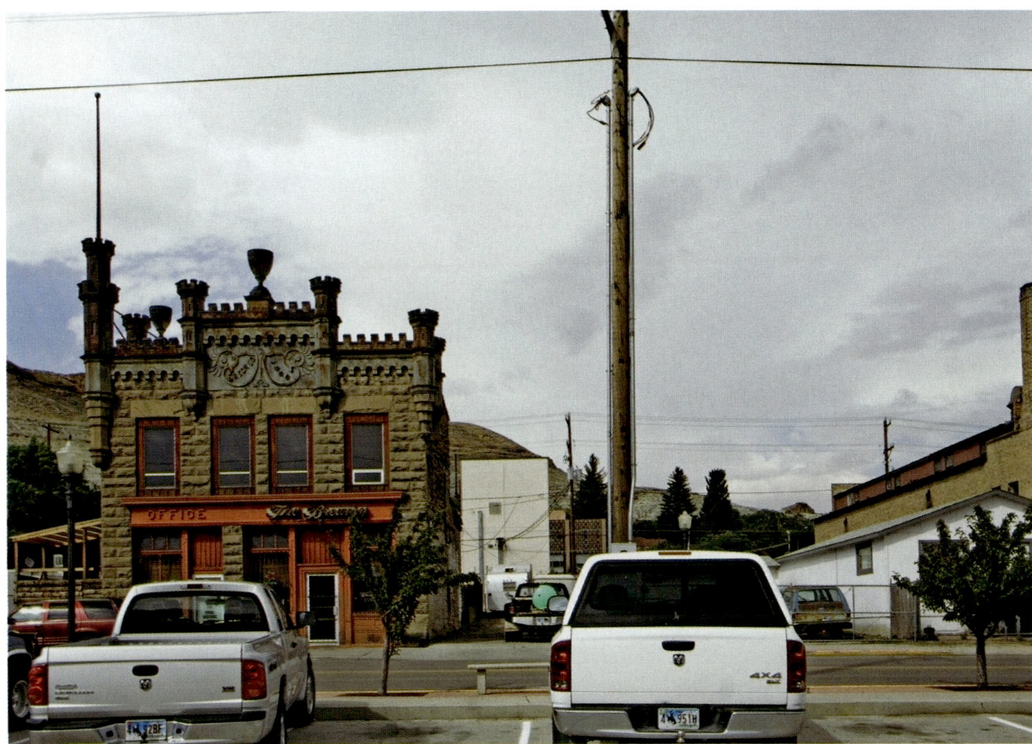

29. #726

Brewery, Green River, 1903, 1987, 2007
GPS COORDINATES: 41 31.72N, 109 28.1363W

Like many nineteenth-century western communities, Green River boasted its own brewery. Unlike many, however, the Sweet Water Brewing Company had its own architectural marvel that resembled a Bavarian castle complete with rough cut stones, towers, merlons, crenels, large stone urns resembling beer cups, and a carved stone beer barrel on the side. Constructed in 1900 for brew master Hugo Gaensslen, the Sweet Water Brewing Company produced "the Pioneer Wyoming Brew," which, like Stimson's photographs, won medals at the 1904 St. Louis World's Fair and the 1905 Lewis and Clark Exposition in Portland.

Stimson's 1903 image, expertly taken in morning light to capture the textured facade, is a straight-on portrait of the company. Detailed carved signs reveal the BREW HOUSE, ENGINE HOUSE, SALOON, and OFFICE. An American flag flies on a pole at right.

In the decades after Stimson's photograph, the Sweet Water Brewing Company experienced hard times. During Prohibition it produced various citrus crushes, a nonalcoholic beer known as Wyoming Beverage, and a lemon-lime–flavored drink called Green River. Local moonshining, though, kept these products from becoming popular, and the business failed. Gaensslen died in 1931, and the entire operation closed before Franklin Delano Roosevelt ended Prohibition in 1933. It reopened for a short time in 1936 but then closed permanently.

My 1987 image, not so expertly exposed midmorning, leaves the front facade in shadow. Nevertheless, it is obvious that only one-third of the original building remains, with the brew house and engine house demolished. Only through the technology of Photoshop have I been able to lighten the shadows to reveal some detail on the remaining building. Still, those details hint at significant changes.

In *Wyoming Time and Again*, I lamented the loss of the local beer to the homogenized marketing of national beers such as Olympia and Bud Light advertised in the remaining saloon, then called, ironically, "the Brewery."

By 2007 my rephotography skills had improved, and I captured this shot in the proper light, revealing a new wood trim on the remaining building. But I also noticed that, over the last two decades, locally produced craft beers had begun to enter the market. Although no such brews are made in Green River, it might be possible to go into the Brewery and grab a Coal Porter or Red Desert Ale made by the Bitter Creek Brewing Company from nearby Rock Springs.

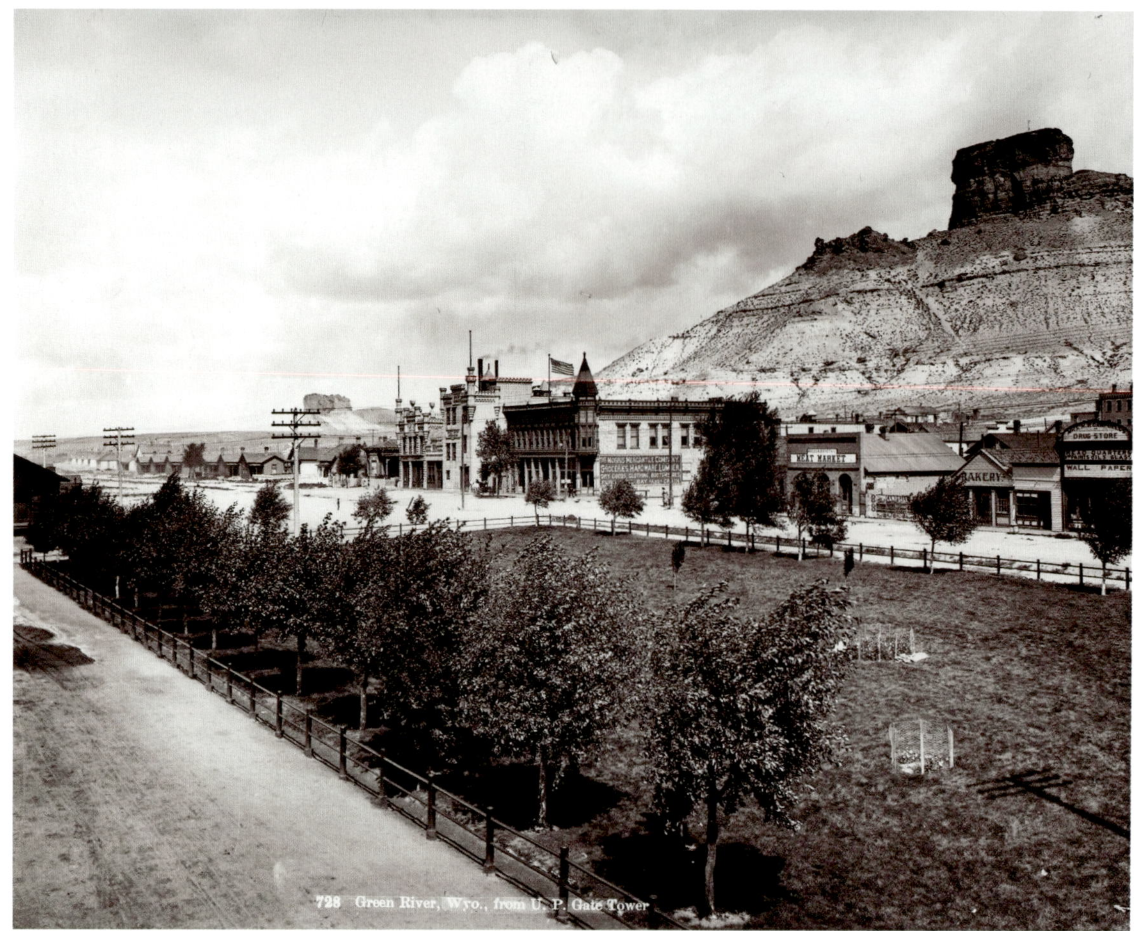

30. #728

Green River Depot Park from UP Gate Tower (footbridge), Green River, 1903, 1987, 2007
GPS COORDINATES: 41 31.6345N, 109 28.053167W

Stimson used the UP gate tower, seen in the panorama of Green River, to elevate his camera and look down on the city's depot park. This tower, about the size of a small room, was occupied by a man who watched for trains and controlled the crossing gates that allowed pedestrians and wagons to safely cross over the rails. The vantage point also allowed the photographer to shoot over the trees and see the large, grassy depot park; Railroad Street, including the Sweet Water Brewery; and Castle Rock, rising 1,000 feet above the town. Depot parks were important in the days of passenger trains because they provided weary travelers with a green, pastoral break from the trains. They also served as symbols of the power of the railroad to impose its will onto the landscape by offering the only green grass and trees for miles. Indeed, stories report that the UP supposedly resorted to importing soil to its Wyoming depots to give the grass a chance to survive. But by having Castle Rock above the park, the overall effect is to balance nature's power, as expressed by the rock formation and the wind (note the flag and the trees), against the equal power of the railroad (the trees and the park).

My 1987 visit to Green River found that much had changed. Neither the gate tower nor the railroad crossing still existed. Instead, a very old pedestrian bridge was present in about the same space and served as my vantage point. Likewise, the scene before me had changed. With no more passenger travel, the depot park and adjacent businesses were either long gone or in disrepair.

Twenty years later, I saw a bit of hope. While nearby businesses still seem neglected, a new row of trees, albeit perhaps a little too orderly, provide a visual break between town and trains.

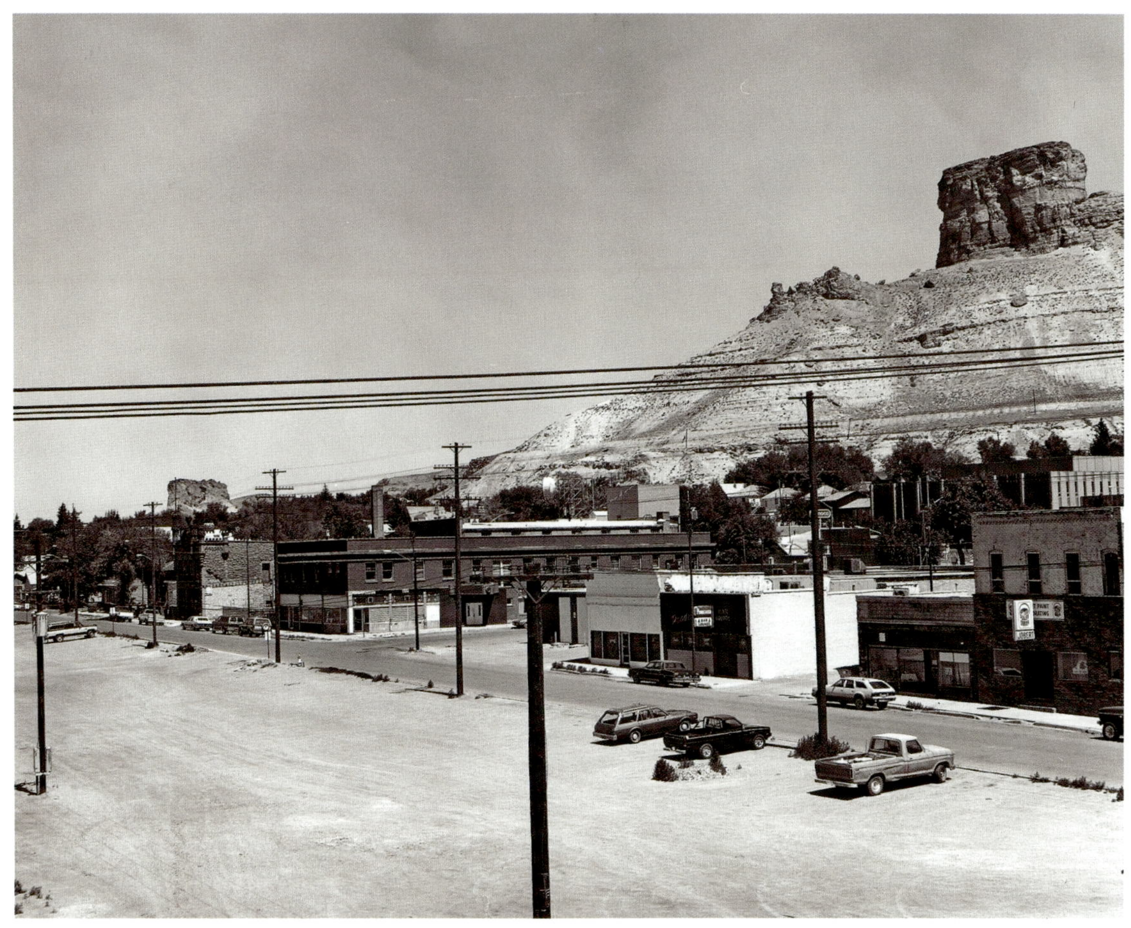

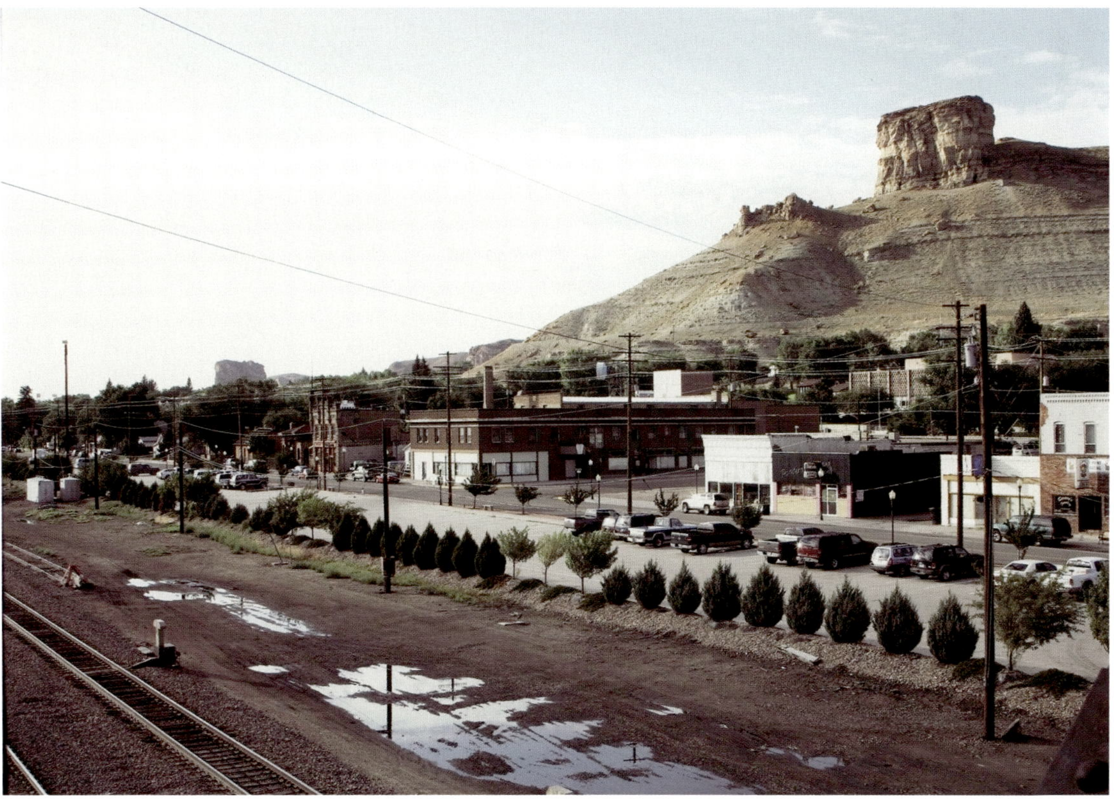

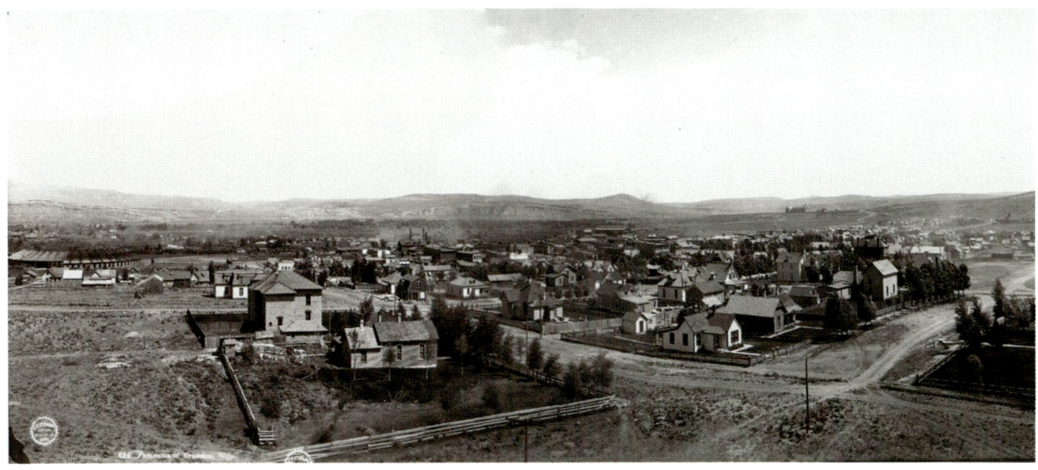

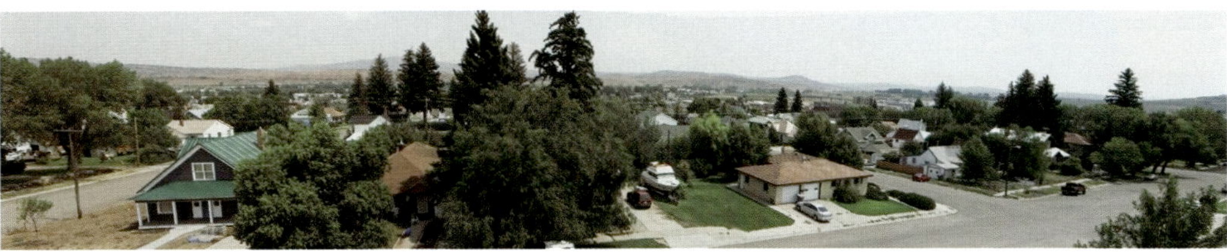

31. #685, 686, 686a

Panorama of Evanston, 1903, 2007
GPS COORDINATES: 41 16.031833N, 110 58.28933W

Established by the Union Pacific in 1869, Evanston is the last major UP town heading west through Wyoming. Once home to a large Chinese population, especially after the 1885 Rock Springs Massacre, the town boasted one of only three Chinese folk temples—so-called joss houses—in the United States. Evanston's economy revolved around the Union Pacific; its place as the seat of Uinta County; nearby farms, ranches, and dairies; and the fact that the town received the last handout from the territorial government (Cheyenne had the capitol, Laramie the university, and Rawlins the state prison) with the 1887 creation of the Wyoming State Insane Asylum, now called the Wyoming State Hospital.

This Stimson panorama was probably taken atop a school. Like all of his multiple-sheet views, this one has parallax problems. Nevertheless, it is a remarkable visual document that promotes Wyoming's communities, industry, and government. In the foreground, the imposition of the grid and its neat, orderly houses and lawns suggest the power to overcome nature. Moving back and examining the image left to right, one can see Evanston's business side, including the Union Pacific roundhouse and shops at left; the original two-story dark-colored UP depot, as well as the newer brick depot to its right, at center; behind the depots a flour mill; to the right the downtown, with the large four-story Blyth and Fargo Building; above that, on the far horizon, the Wyoming State Insane Asylum.

My 2007 photograph also suffers from parallax problems. Indeed, just getting this shot was a problem. I fairly quickly identified the vantage point as on top of a new school still under construction. The workers allowed me, at my own personal risk, to climb up a ladder inside the building—while carrying camera gear—to get to the roof. Once up there, I had to climb more ladders to get to the front of the building. To do all this, I had to leave my tripod behind and hand-hold my panorama, thus the visual problems. Nevertheless, my image also shows the orderly neighborhoods, the ubiquitous tree growth, and, if you look carefully, the Blyth and Fargo store, the railroad overpass, and, on the far horizon at right, the many trees of the Wyoming State Hospital.

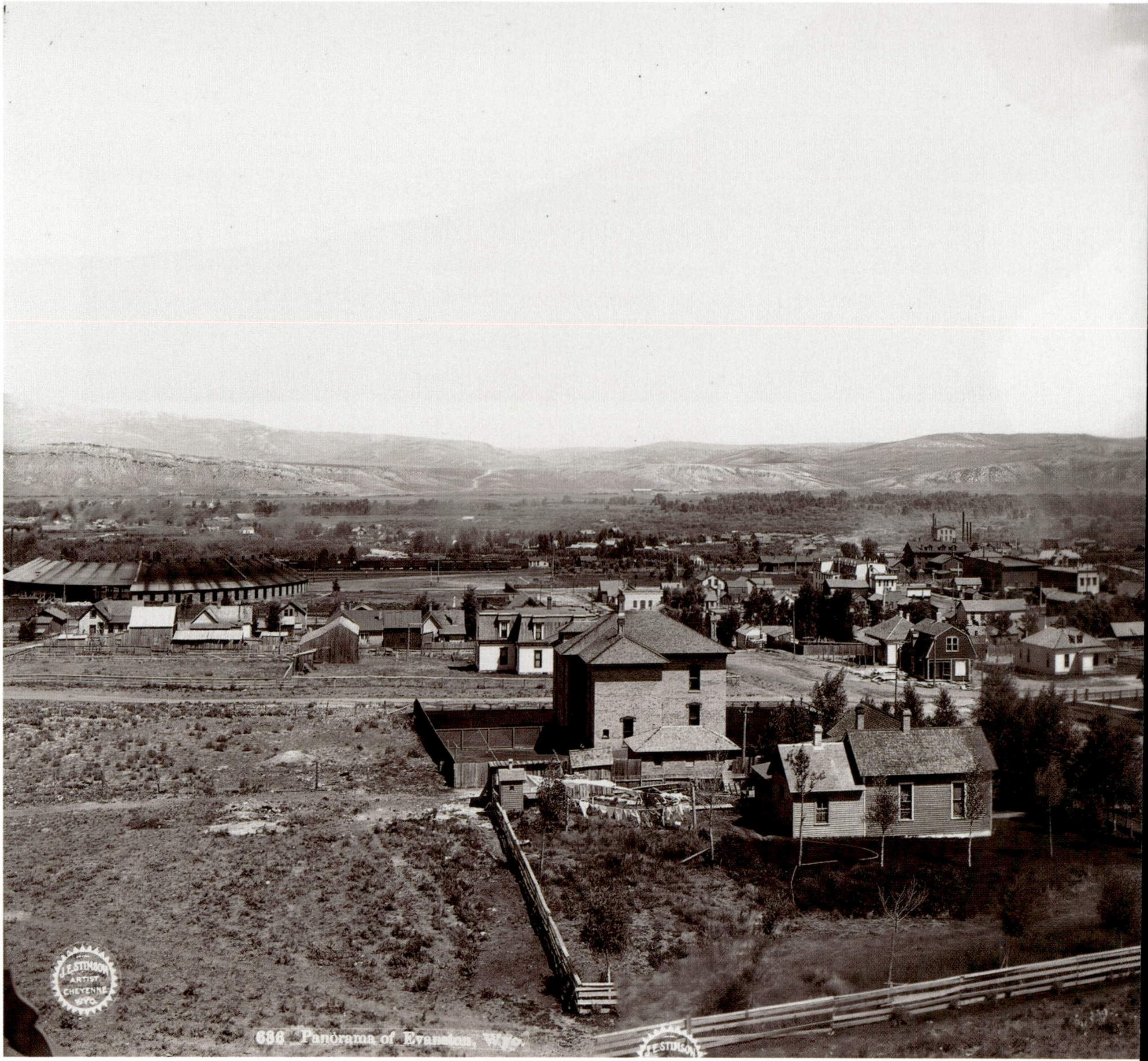

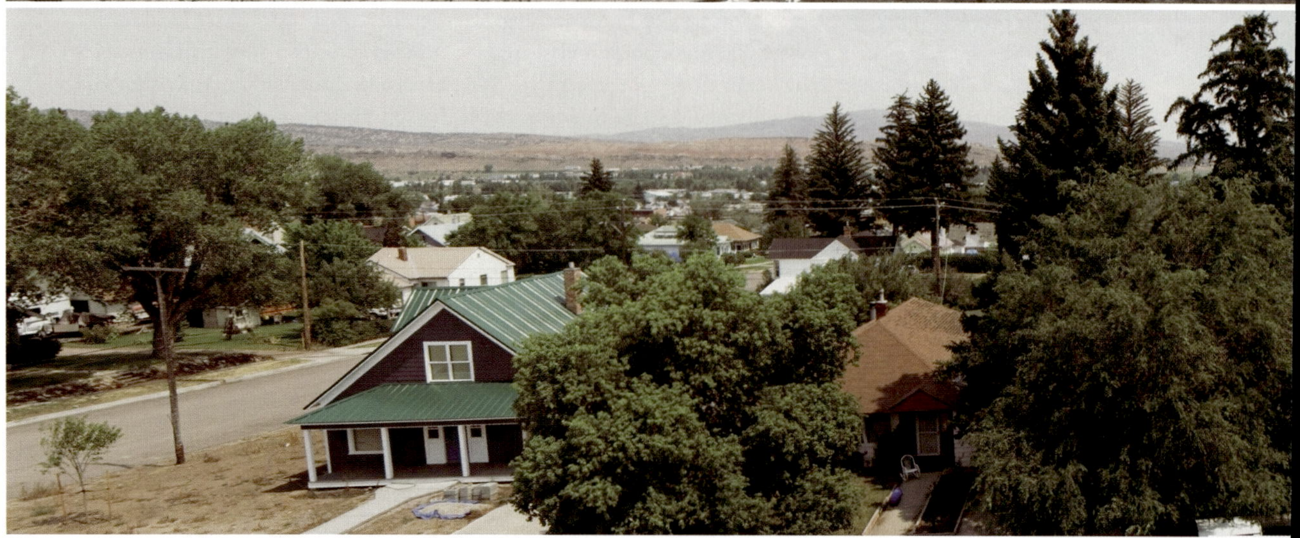

636   Panorama of Evanston, Wyo.

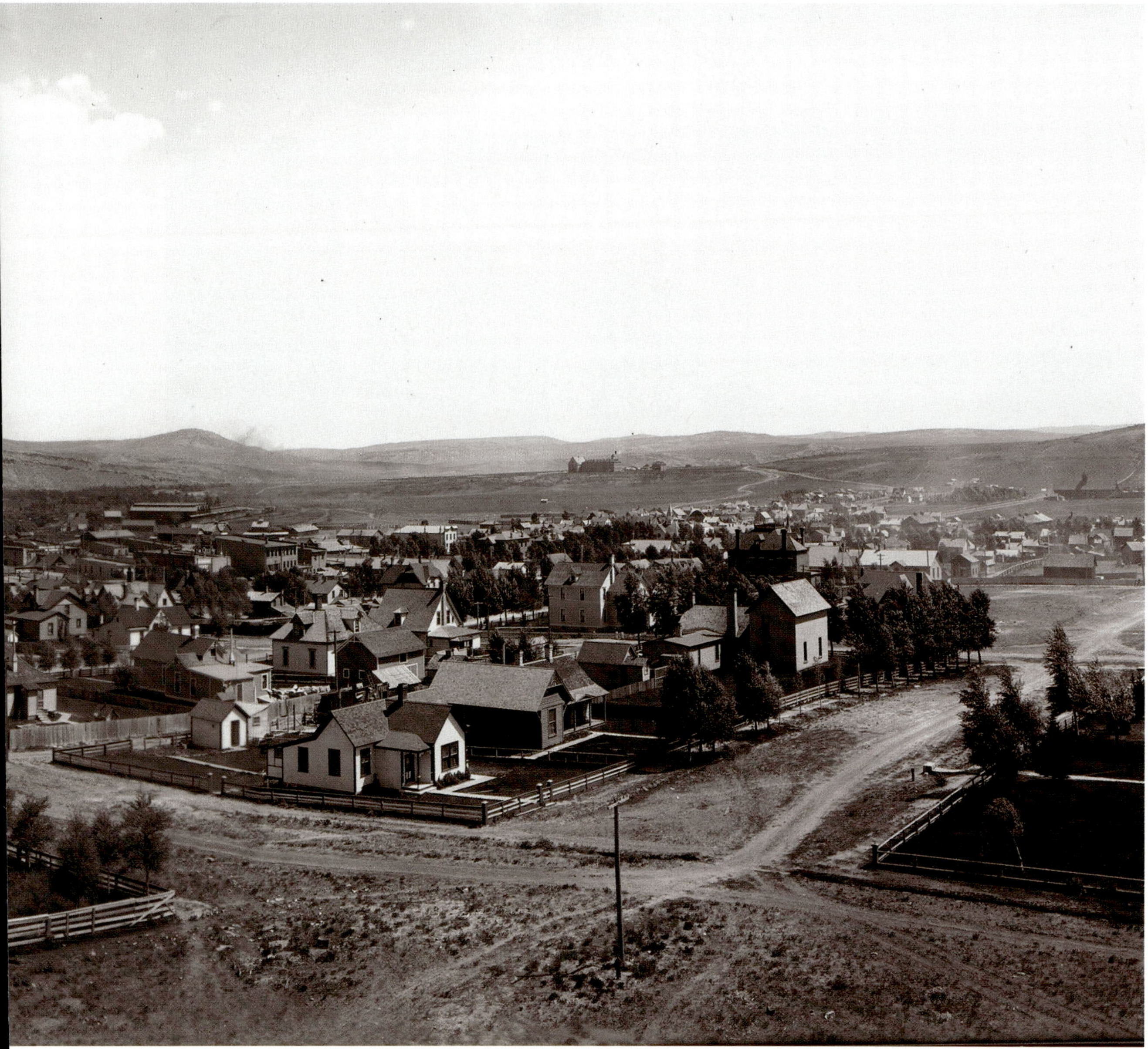

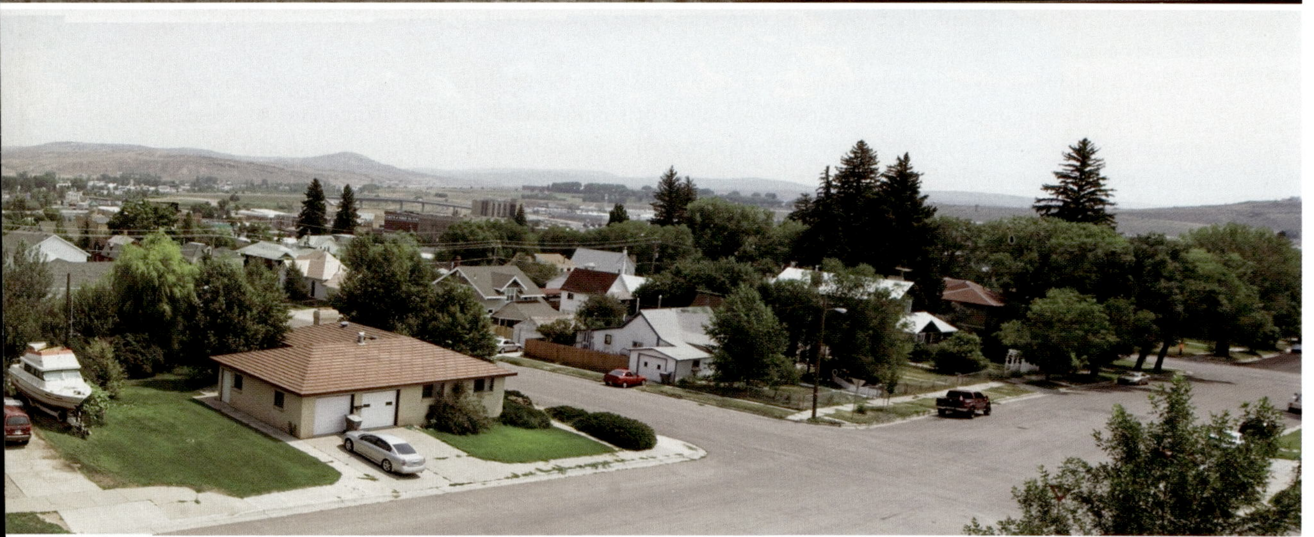

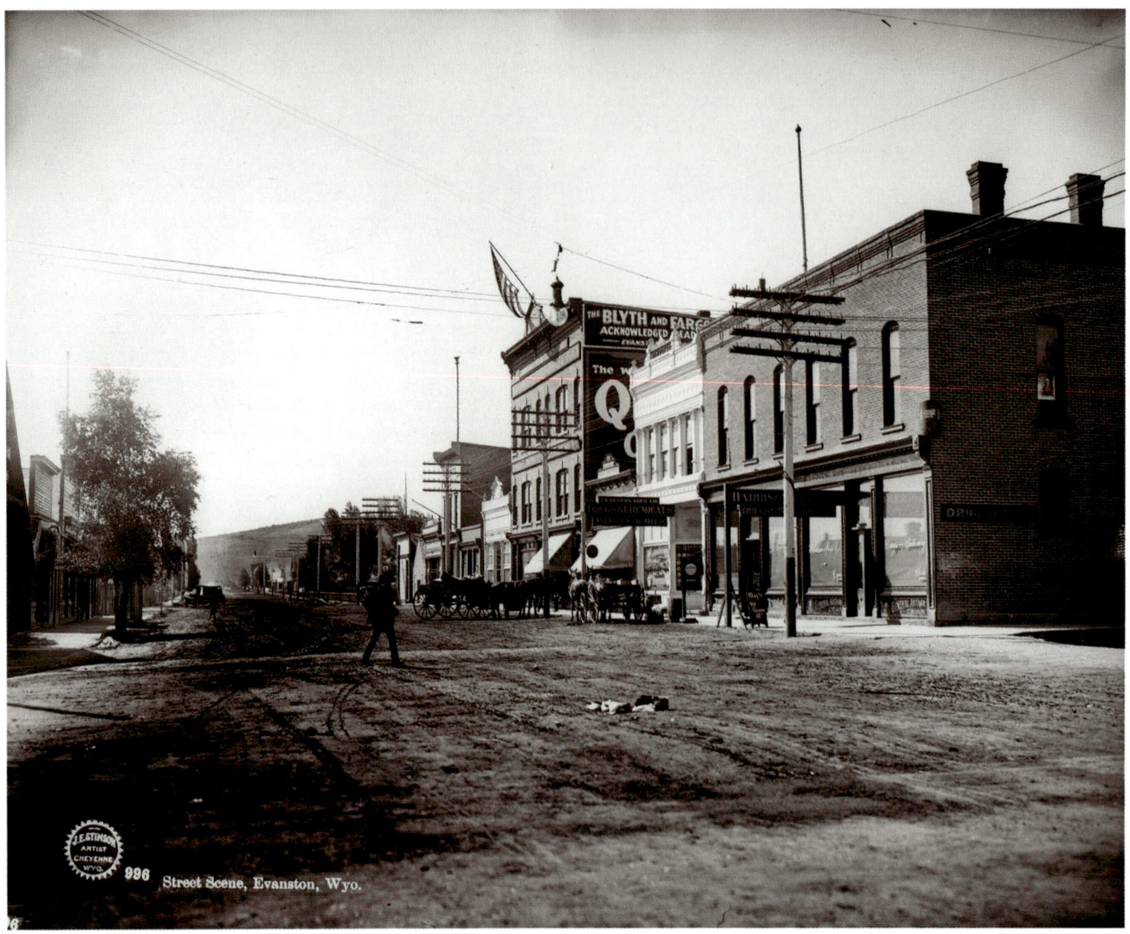

32. #996

Street Scene, Evanston, 1903, 1987, 2007
GPS COORDINATES: 41 16.074N, 110 57.949W

This Stimson view looks down Main Street from the corner on Tenth Street and depicts a typical street scene that promoted Wyoming for the Union Pacific and at the St. Louis World's Fair. Taken in late morning, the photograph includes a streetlight, telephone or power poles, and several businesses, including the four-story Blyth and Fargo Building—a mercantile, hardware, and grocer. Also pictured is a drugstore with an "Ice Cream for Sale" placard out front.

Both my 1987 and 2007 rephotographs, which comprised the cover of *Wyoming Time and Again*, show—minus the drugstore on the corner—a vibrant downtown community, including the Blyth and Fargo Building, though the latter now houses an art gallery. It should come as no surprise, then, that Evanston has had an engaged Main Street Program in place since the early 1980s, when oil and gas exploration caused a population boom to threaten the traditional heart of the city. The city created a downtown historic district in 1983 and preserved more than sixty historic buildings, including most of this street, the Union Pacific Depot, and other railroad shops. Note as well the removal of electrical wires from the downtown and the new period light fixtures. When I visited Evanston in 2007, one of the highlights was getting to tour the historic roundhouse and ride the turntable.

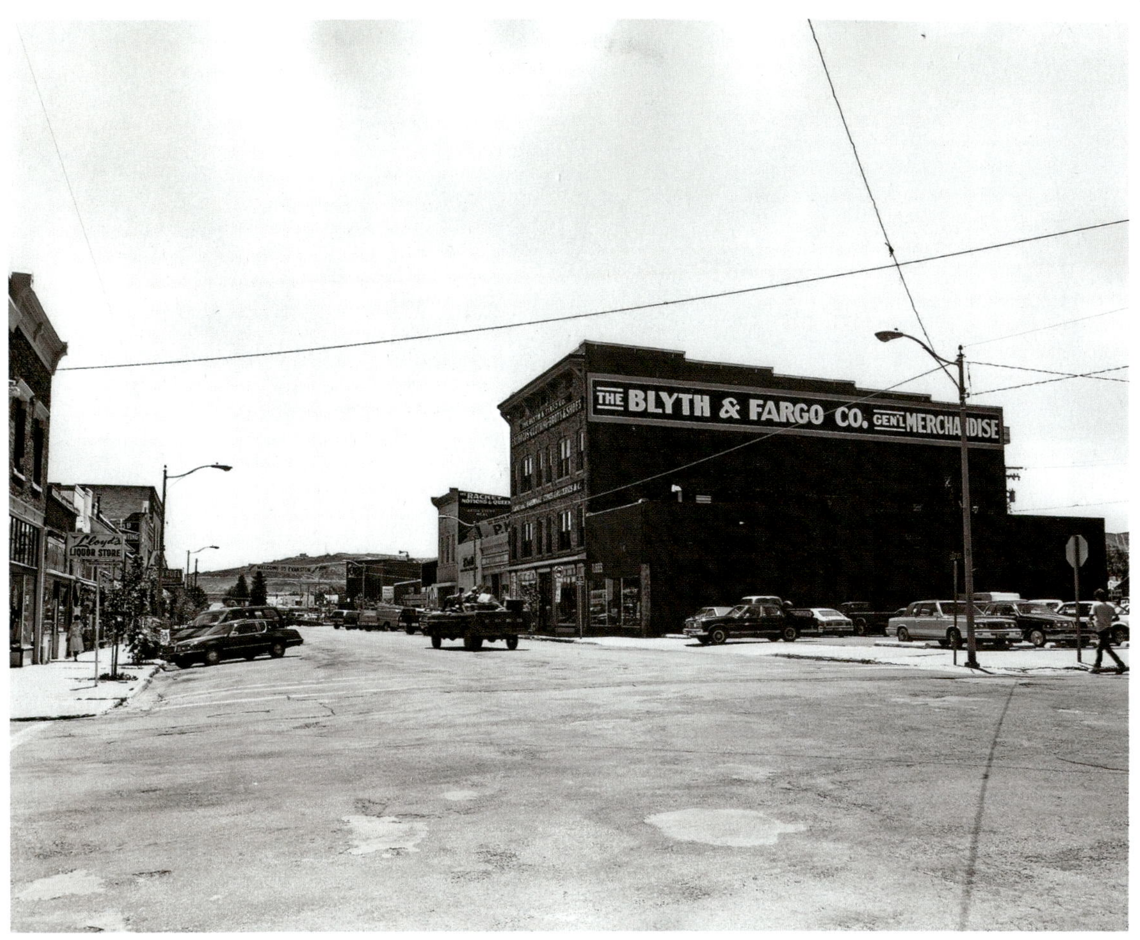
THE BLYTH & FARGO CO, GEN'L MERCHANDISE

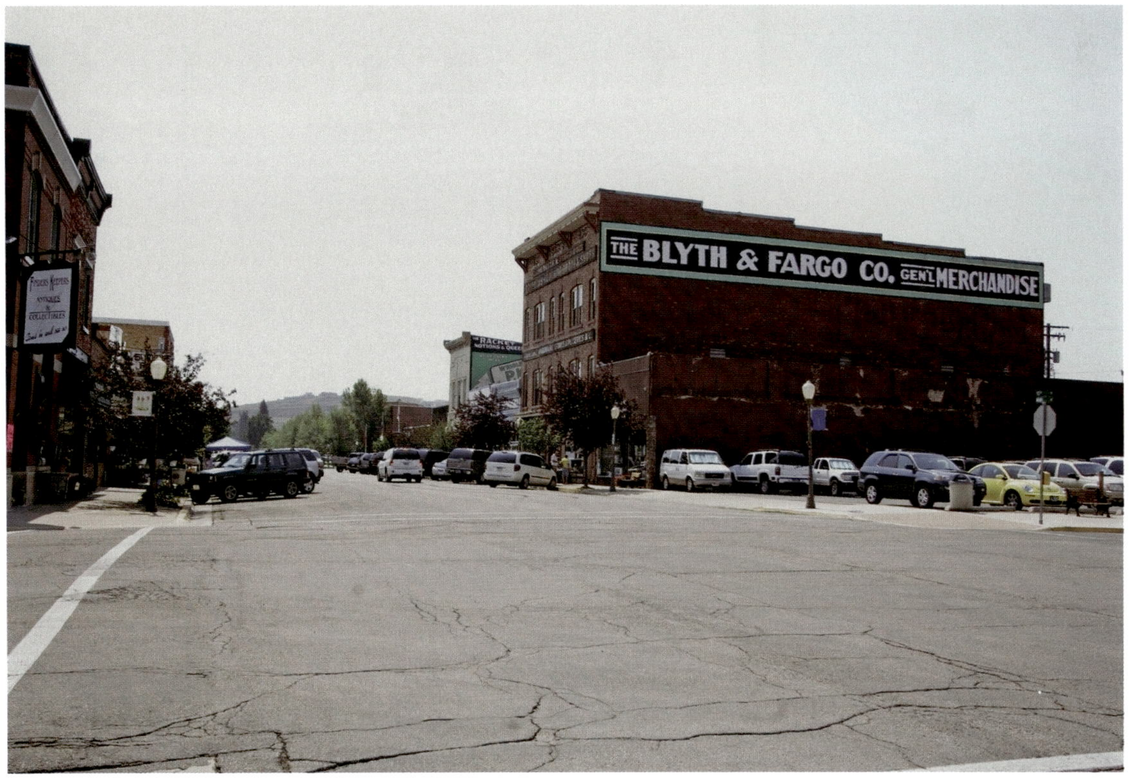
THE BLYTH & FARGO CO, GEN'L MERCHANDISE

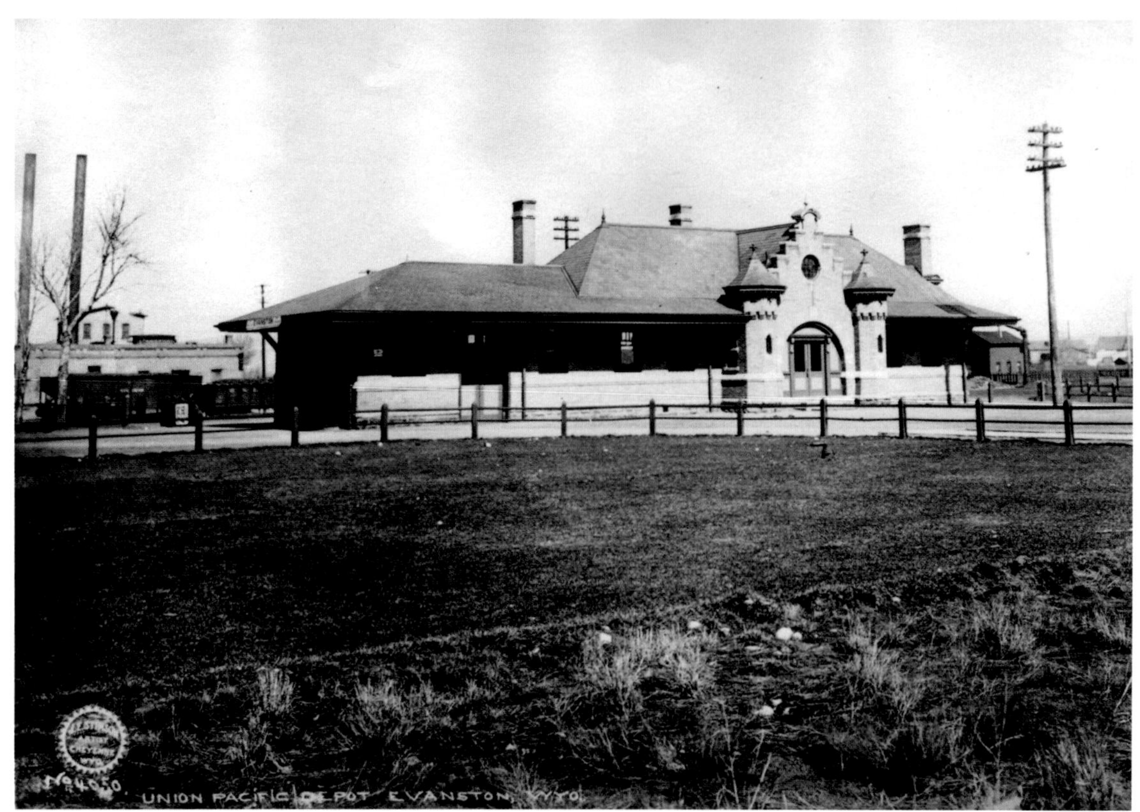
UNION PACIFIC DEPOT EVANSTON, WYO.

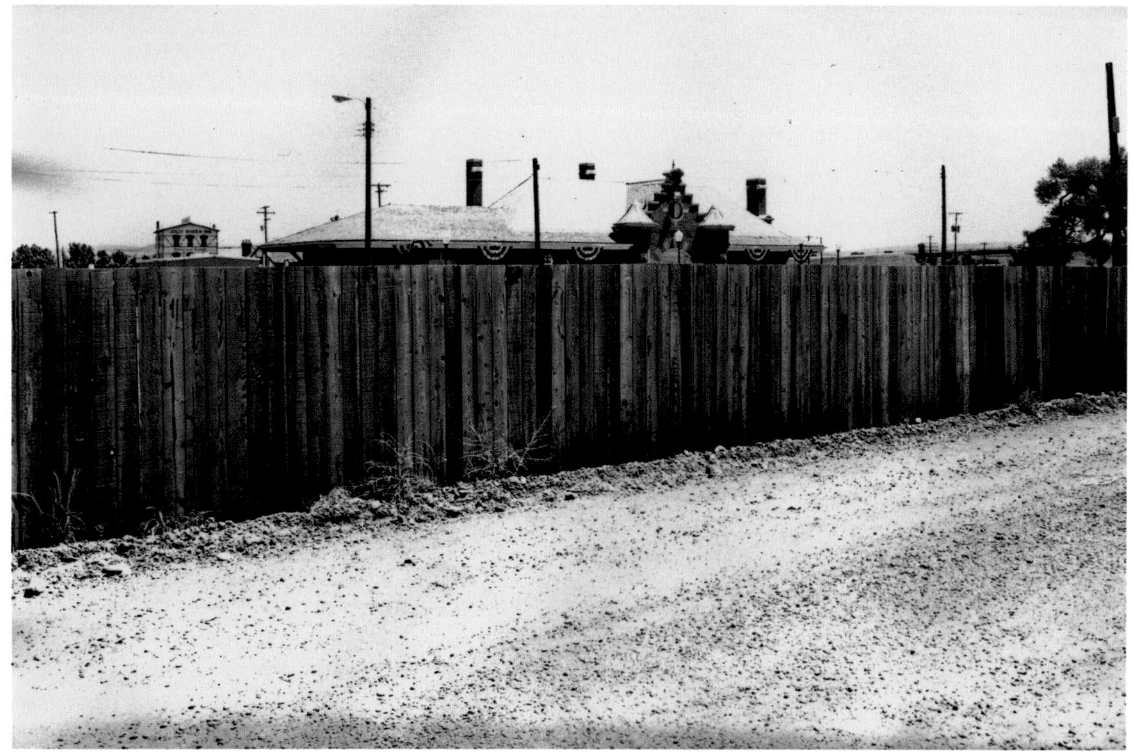

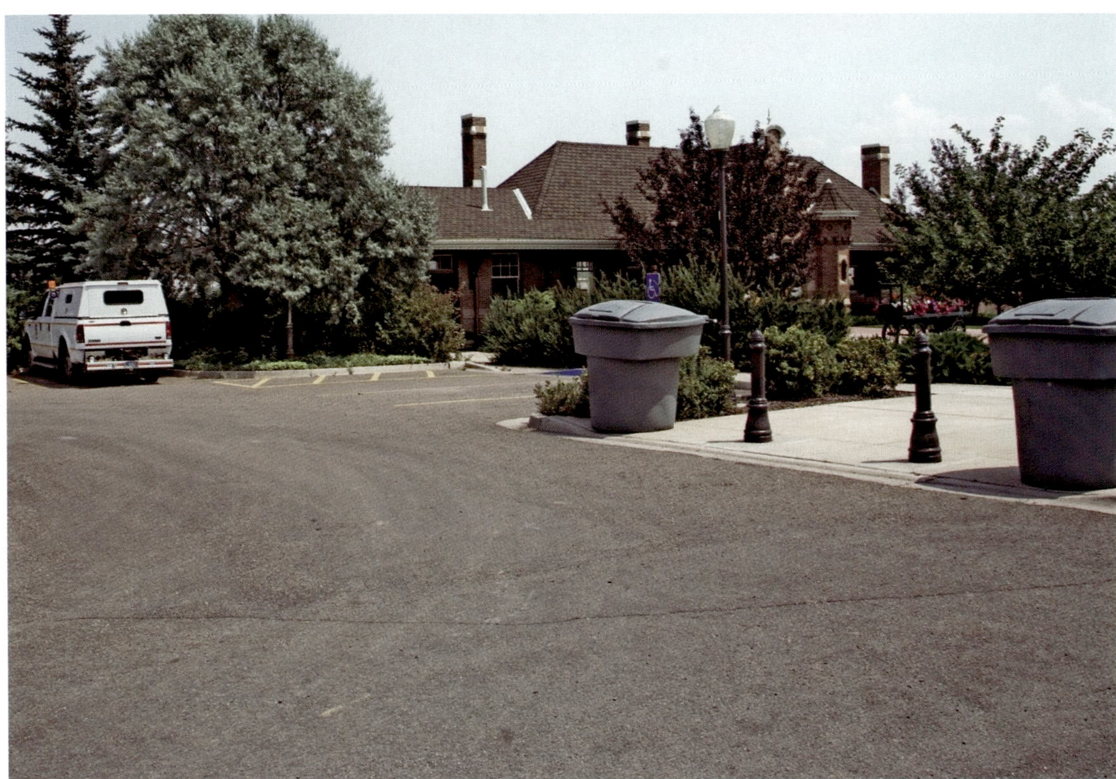

33. #4050

Union Pacific Depot, Evanston, 1908, 1987, 2007
GPS COORDINATES: 41 16.1323N, 110 57.9025W

Stimson photographed the Evanston Union Pacific Depot and its small park in 1908. An eclectic and ornamental structure, it was constructed of brick in 1900 and featured two brick towers that framed the semicircular arch entrance over double doors. This unique architecture was important, as Evanston served as either the last or the first (depending on which way they were traveling) Wyoming depot passengers saw as they crossed the state on first the UP and then Amtrak until service was discontinued in 1983.

When I rephotographed the depot in 1987, the UP no longer used it, and the city had built a six-foot-tall cedar fence around it for protection. Two years later the railroad donated the building to the city, and renovations were made the following year. Today, the depot houses special events such as weddings, meetings, and family events. My 2007 rephotograph shows, similar to Main Street, a revitalized cultural heritage treasure bursting with trees and gardens.

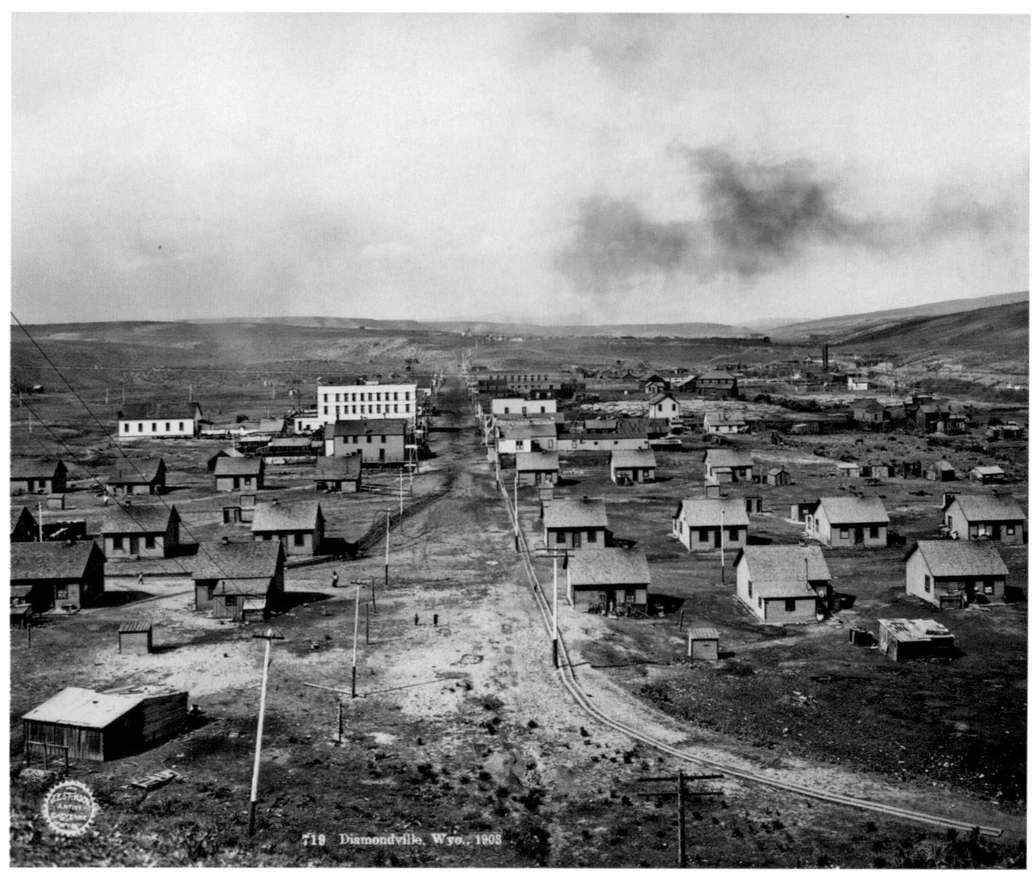
719   Diamondville, Wyo., 1905

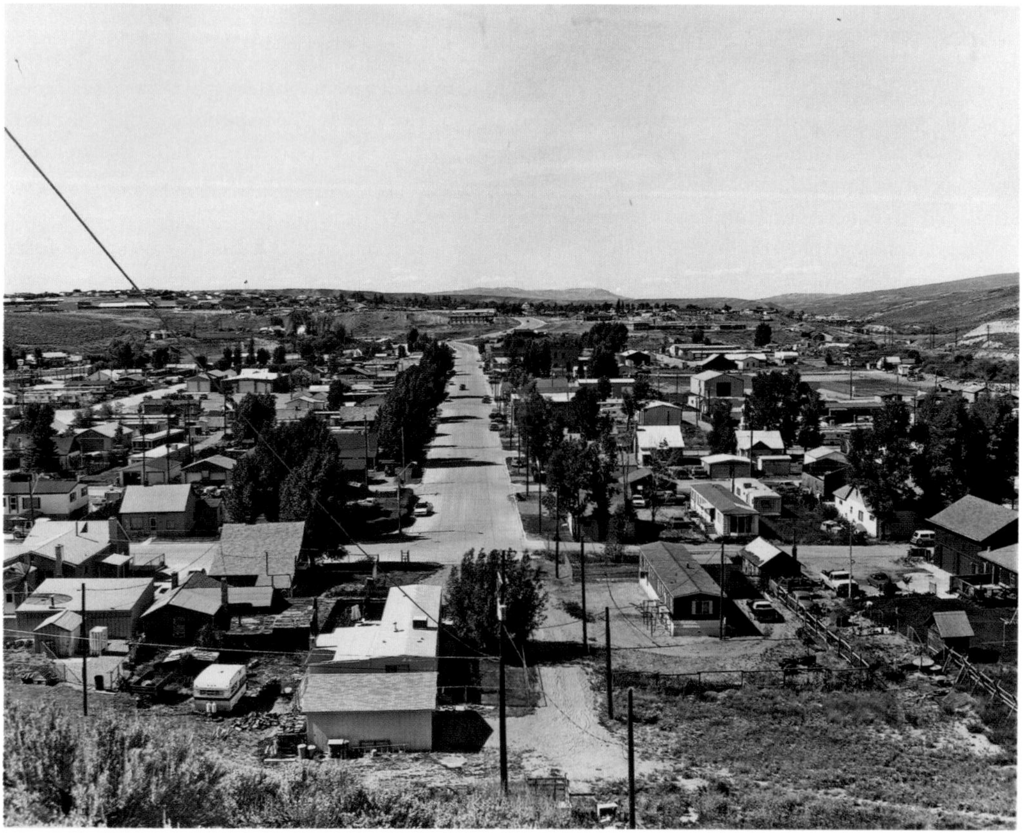

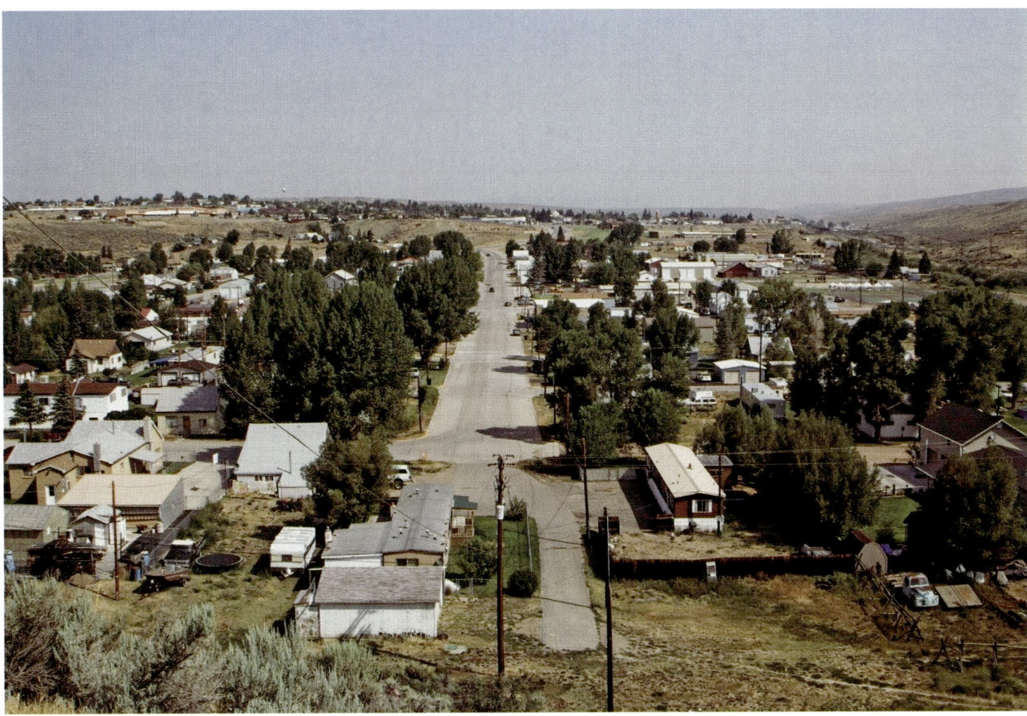

34. #719

Diamondville, 1903, 1987, 2007
GPS COORDINATES: 41 46.5307N, 110 32.20717W

Stimson photographed the small coal mining town of Diamondville from a low hill looking north over its main street, Diamondville Avenue. The Oregon Short Line, a railroad connecting the UP line at Granger, Wyoming, to Pocatello, Idaho, opened this part of the state for development in the 1880s. In 1894 the Diamond Coal and Coke Company developed the first mines and by 1900 was employing several thousand men. Like most Wyoming coal towns, the population consisted of immigrants from many southern and eastern European countries and Japan. In October 1901 a cave-in deep in one of the mines trapped and suffocated twenty-six miners. Eight months later, another cave-in at the same mine trapped and killed another twenty-two miners.

Given this violent history, it's not surprising that Stimson, wanting to promote the state during his 1903 survey, chose to photograph not the mines but the neatly organized town instead. The Mountain Trading Company, one of the area's largest mercantile outfits, is the large brick building on the right side of the street. The grade of the Oregon Short Line is at far right with the mines' smokestacks to its left. In the residential area one sees a plank sidewalk that runs the length of the town, telephone poles, and a number of residents looking up toward the photographer. The neighboring independent town of Kemmerer can be seen in the background.

By 1987, all of Diamondville's mines had closed, and the town had become a suburb of Kemmerer. Both my 1987 and 2007 rephotographs, amazingly, show many of the same features still in place more than eighty and a hundred years later, respectively, including "temporary" miners' cabins, the same power line running down the hill, the Mountain Trading Company building, and even remnants of the board sidewalk in the foreground. Modern "temporary" housing in the form of trailers dots the landscape. Kemmerer's growth can be seen across the background hills.

My mom grew up in Kemmerer, where my grandparents, Al and Frances Zakotnik, lived for more than fifty years. When I was taking this picture in July 2007, a man came out of a house behind me and we started talking. He had gone to high school with my mom and knew my grandparents very well. With a population of barely over 500,000, Wyoming has often been described as one big town with very long streets. That afternoon in Diamondville, I knew what the expression meant.

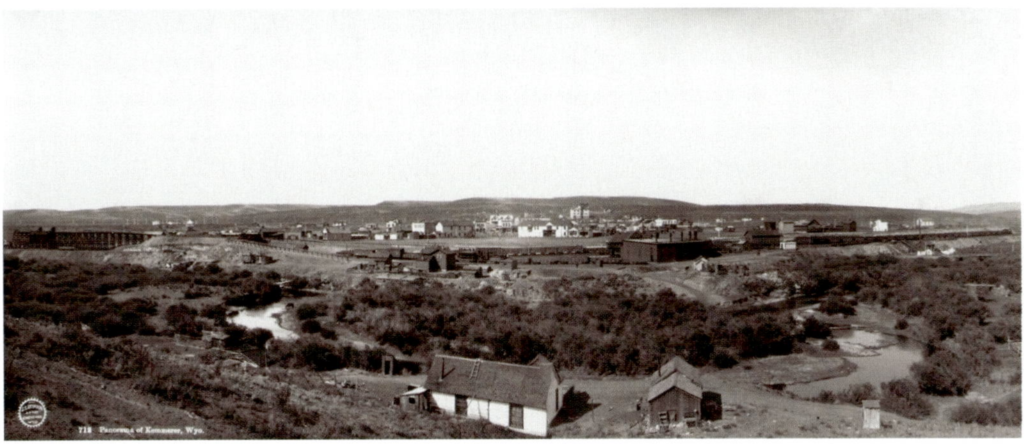

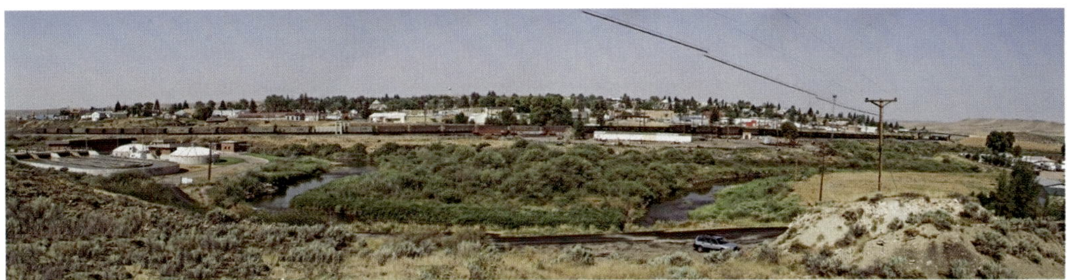

35. #712

Panorama of Kemmerer, 1903, 2007
GPS COORDINATES: 41 47.714N, 110 31.970W

As an introduction to Kemmerer, a little family history is in order. As mentioned, my mom, Joan Zakotnik (now Amundson), grew up in Kemmerer. Her mother, Frances Felician, was born in the small mining camp of Sublet, north of Kemmerer, in 1913. Her mother, my maternal great-grandmother, had moved to Sublet after losing her first husband in a mine accident in Scofield, Utah. She then met my maternal great-grandfather and moved to Sublet, where my grandmother Frances was born. In 1922, when my grandmother was just nine years old, her mother was widowed a second time when her husband (my grandmother's father) and son were killed in a mine explosion at Sublet. My grandmother was one of four surviving children. In 1930 the coal company closed Sublet, and her family moved to Kemmerer, where she met my grandfather, Albin Zakotnik, who had moved from the Iron Range of northern Minnesota to find work as a coal miner in Kemmerer during the Great Depression. Ironically, his father had been one of only four men to survive the 1924 underground flood at a mine in Milford, Minnesota. My grandparents, both children of Slovenian immigrants, married in 1939 and honeymooned at the San Francisco World's Fair. My mother was born the following year, grew up in Kemmerer, and brought our family back there regularly until my grandfather passed away in 1995 and my grandmother died a decade later.

This personal history means that I know Kemmerer. The seat of Lincoln County, Kemmerer was organized by Patrick J. Quealy as an independent town in 1897 and soon became the economic and political center of the regional coal industry. J. C. Penney started his first store there in 1902, and Stimson made this panorama of the town the following year on his trek across the state. This view, taken at the base of Oyster Ridge, looks west across the Hams Fork River, with the Oregon Short Line tracks, depot, and roundhouse to the right; a coal tipple to the left; and, up the hill, the Kemmerer business district.

My 2007 panorama still shows the Hams Fork oxbow as well as the Kemmerer water treatment plant at left, the railroad tracks, and the tremendous growth of the town up the hillside. A few remaining buildings can be discerned, but the tree growth makes closer examination difficult.

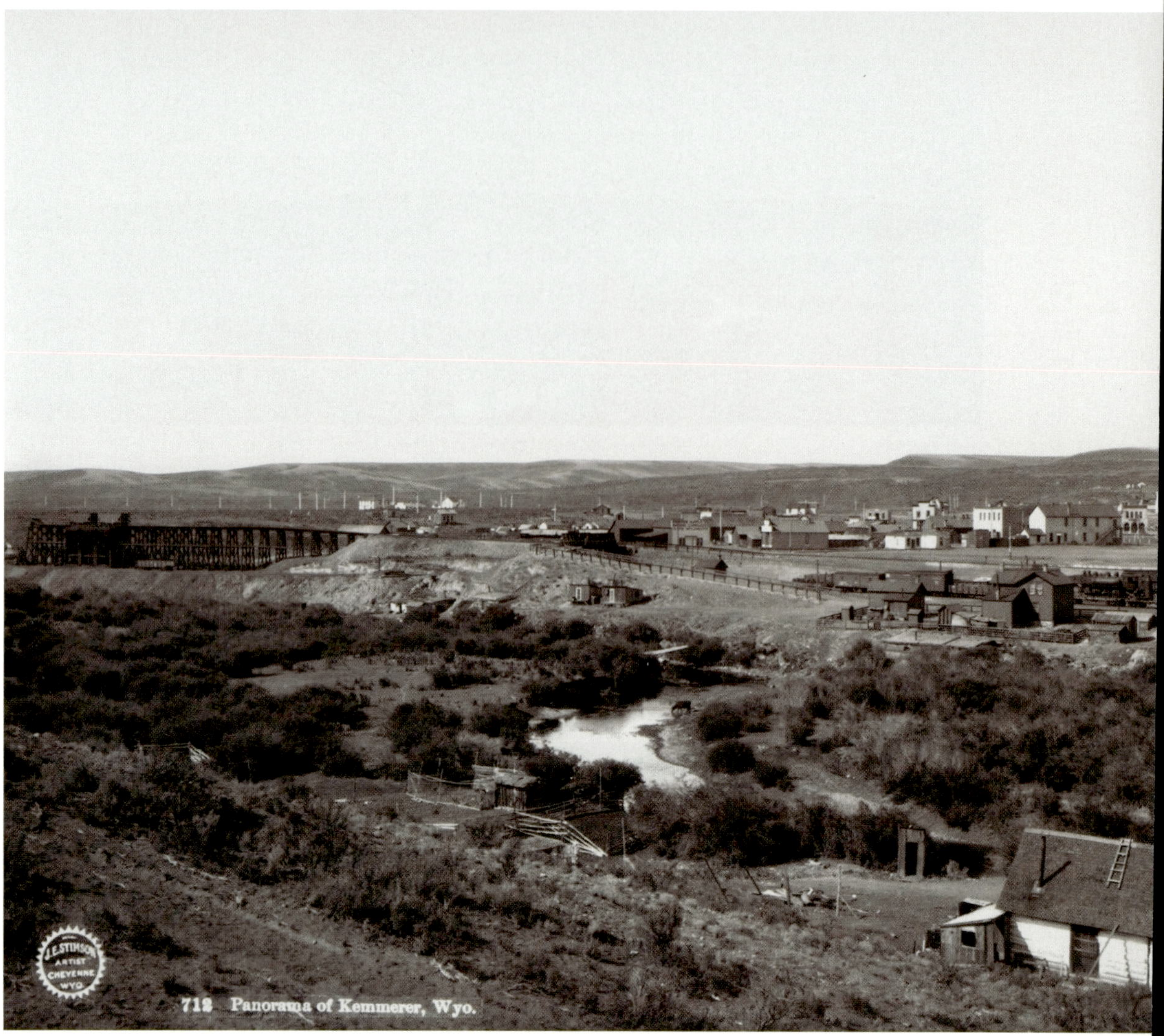

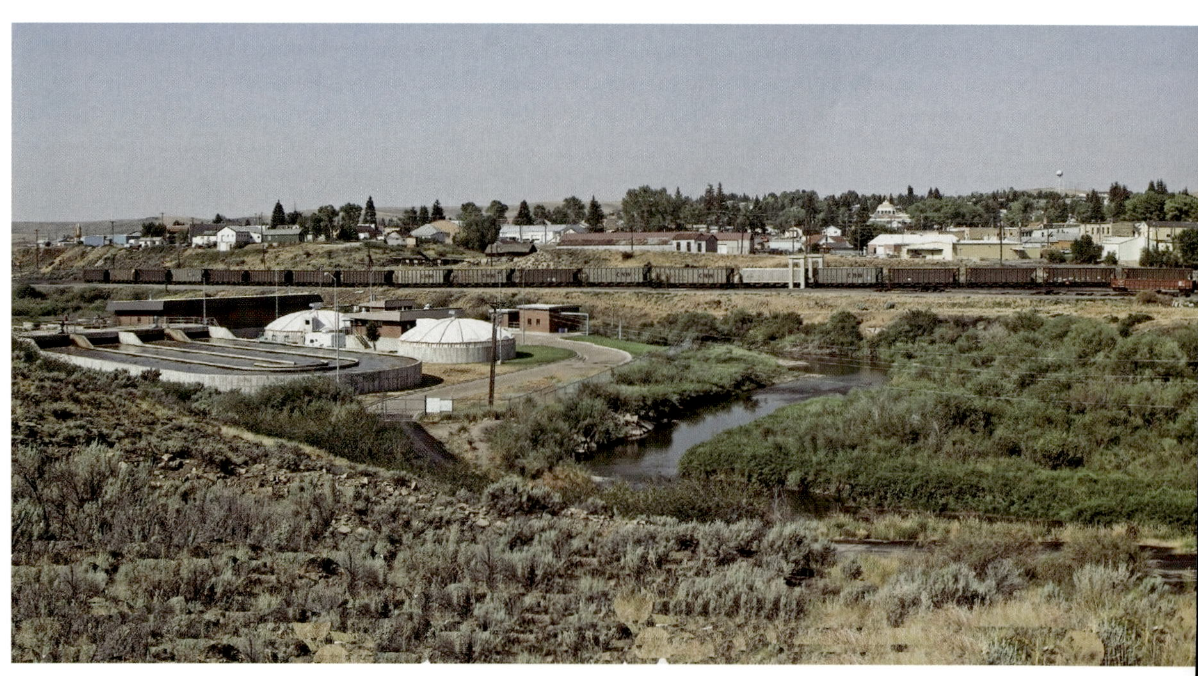
712   Panorama of Kemmerer, Wyo.

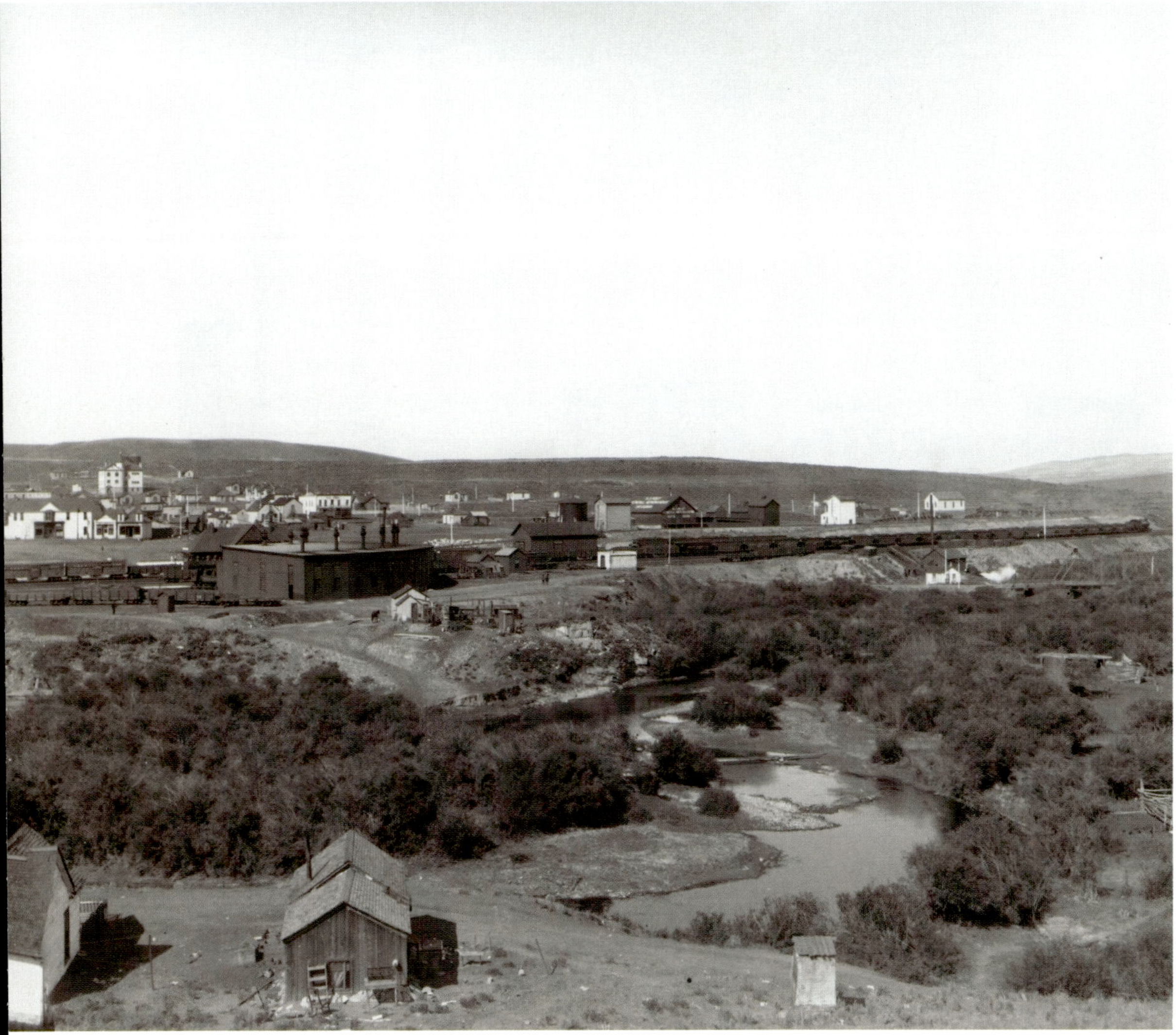

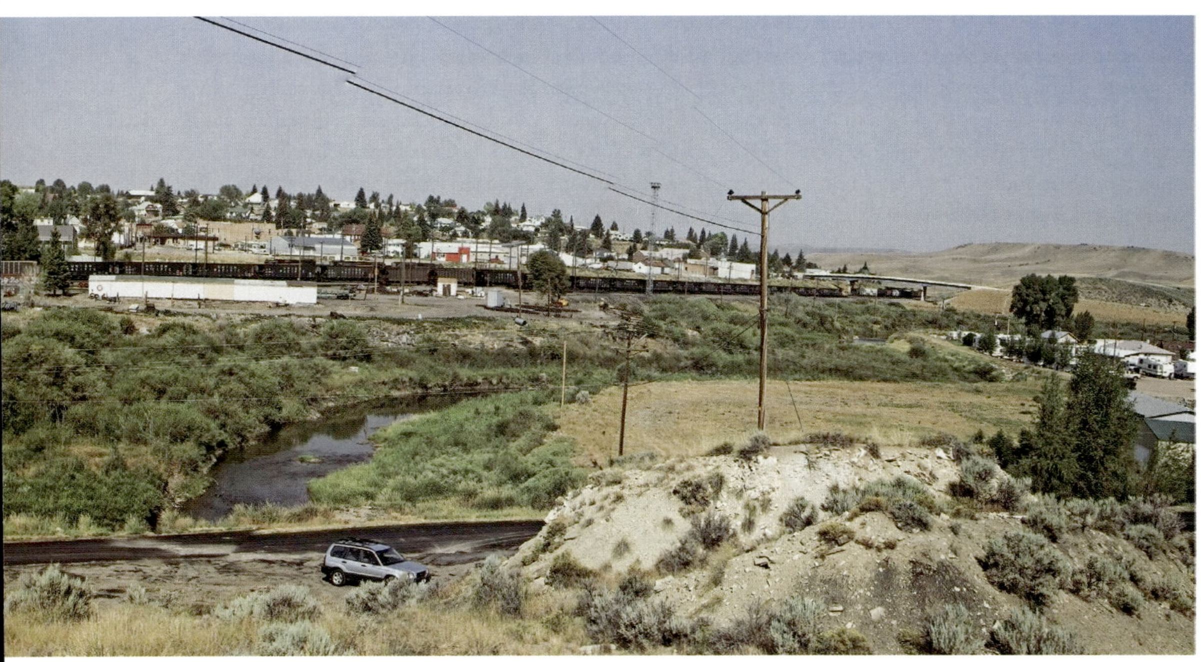

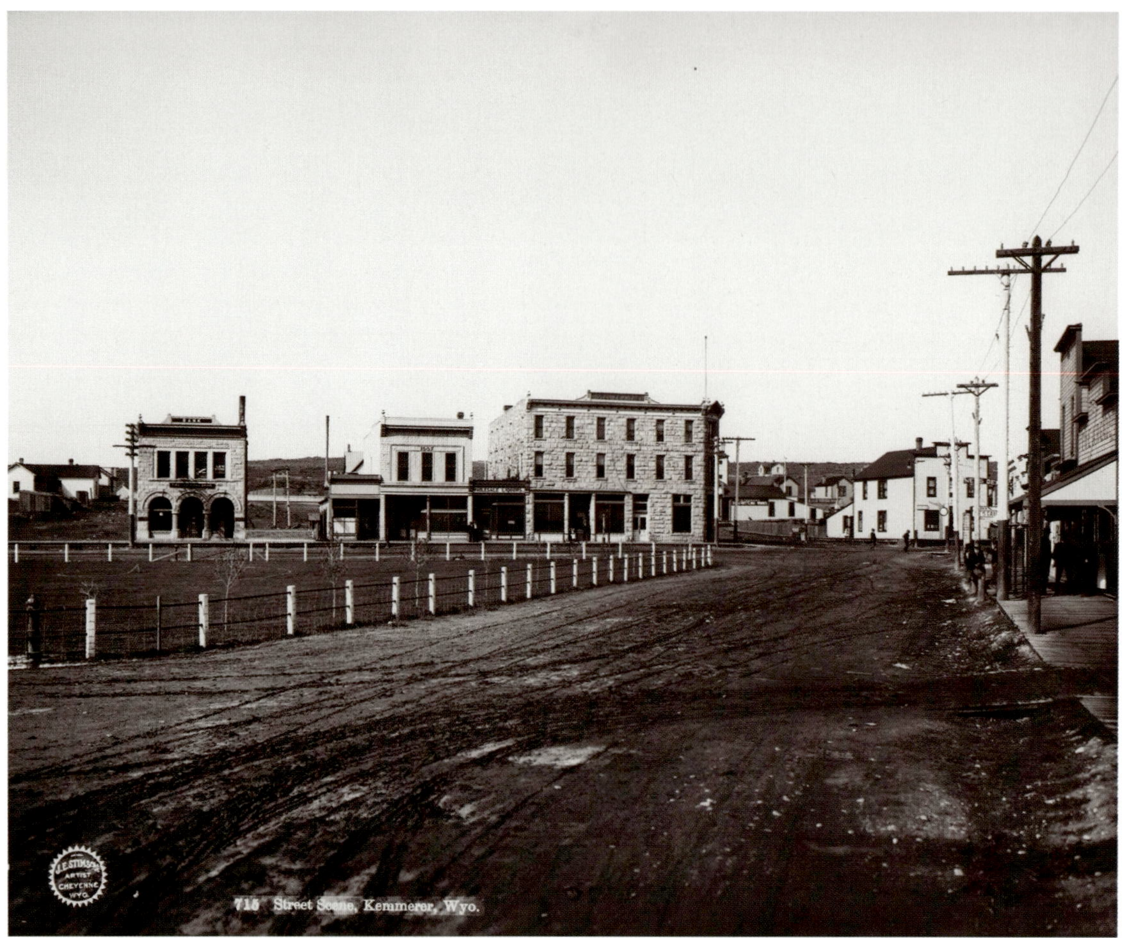

36. #715

Street Scene, Kemmerer, 1903, 1987, 2007
GPS COORDINATES: 41 47.689N, 110 32.22567W

This second Kemmerer view shows the north side of the unique three-sided business district, appropriately named the "Triangle." In fact, locals wag that their town is so small that the town square is actually a triangle! The large three-story building near the center of the photo is the Kemmerer Hotel, constructed in 1898. The building at left with three arches is the First National Bank, opened in 1900. The first J. C. Penney store, the Golden Rule, opened in 1902. Stimson is looking west in this street view across the vacant interior of the triangle, where only saplings can be seen inside the fence.

My 1987 rephotograph shows how well those saplings did. It also shows a still bustling Triangle, thanks to the continued growth of the area's coal, oil, and natural gas industries. The Kemmerer Hotel remained in place, although a close look through the trees at left reveals that the First National Bank building had been demolished.

Twenty years later the energy boom continued in Kemmerer, but its historic structures were faring less well. In 2004 the city engineer discovered that the hotel's stone walls had cracked and moved. After a valiant effort to save the hotel failed, the city demolished it later that year.

Personally, it was hard for me to visit Kemmerer in 2007. I had many memories of being with my grandparents there and walking downtown to see my grandmother at the bakery where she worked (on the right side of the 1987 photo). I still have aunts, uncles, and cousins there. But when I visited the town in 2007 as part of my whirlwind tour of the state, I made my two pictures and left quietly.

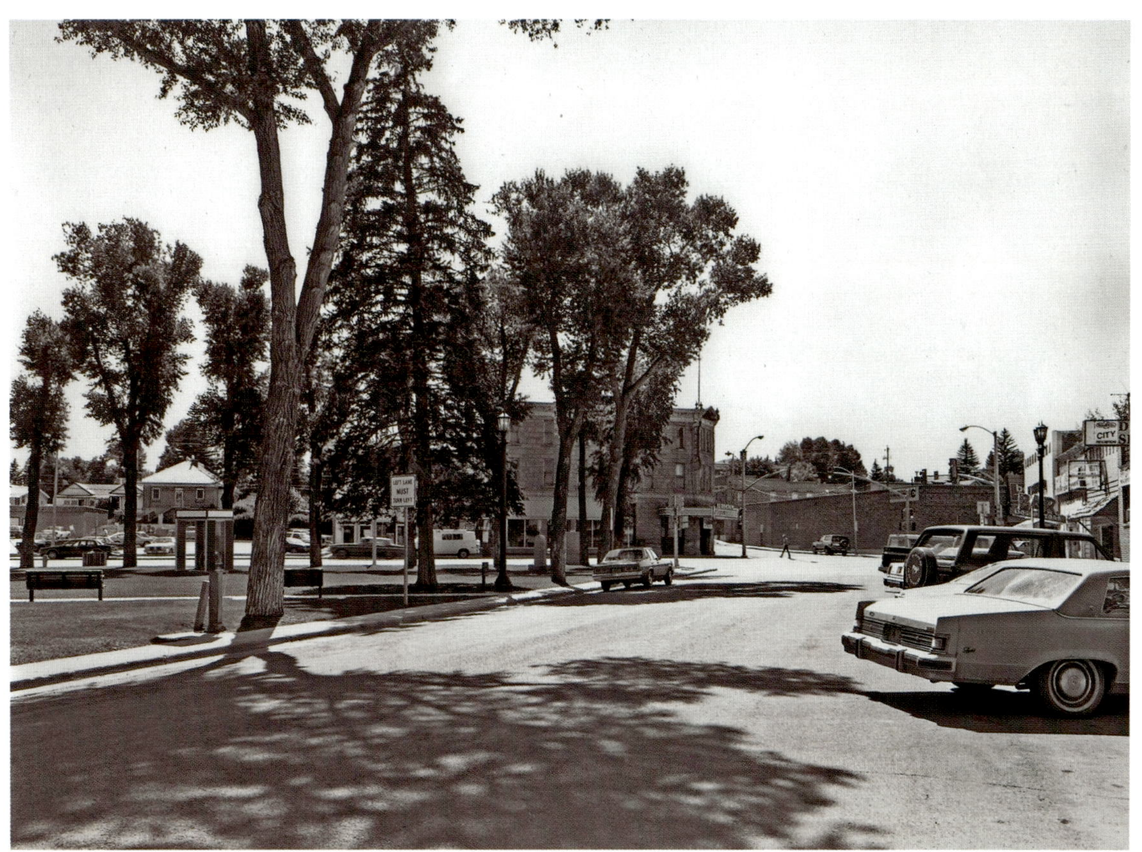

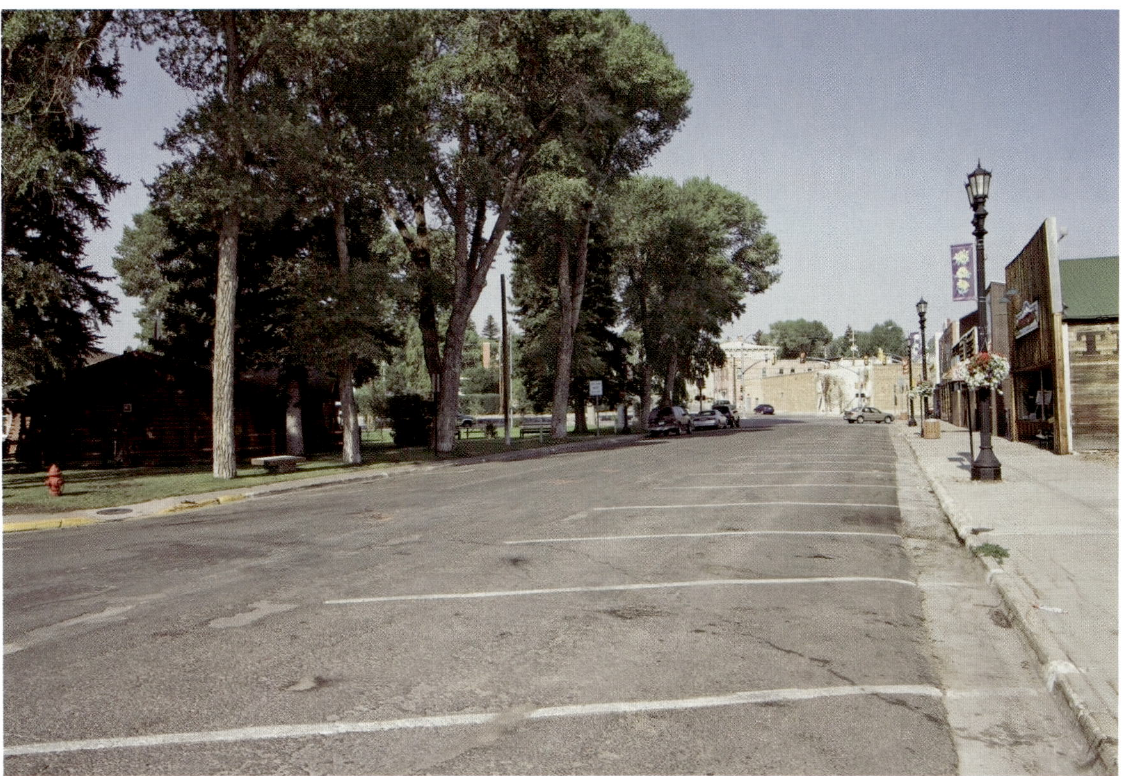

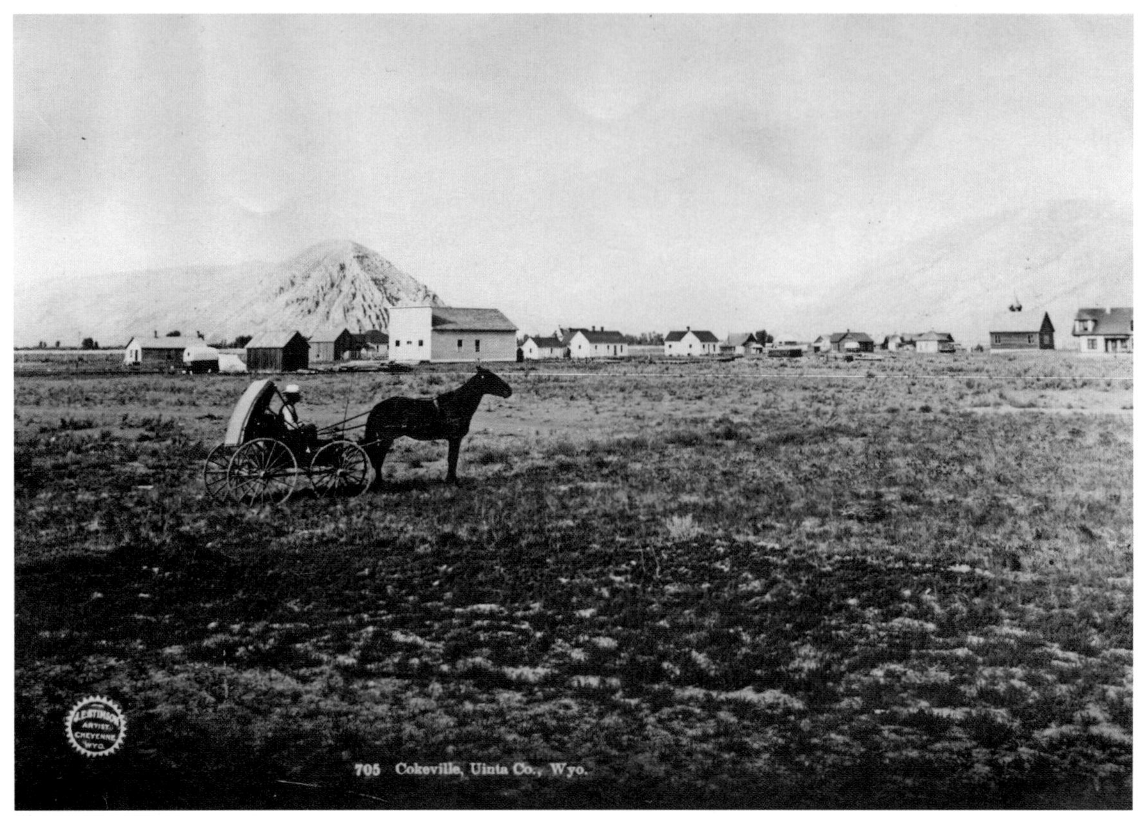
705 Cokeville, Uinta Co., Wyo.

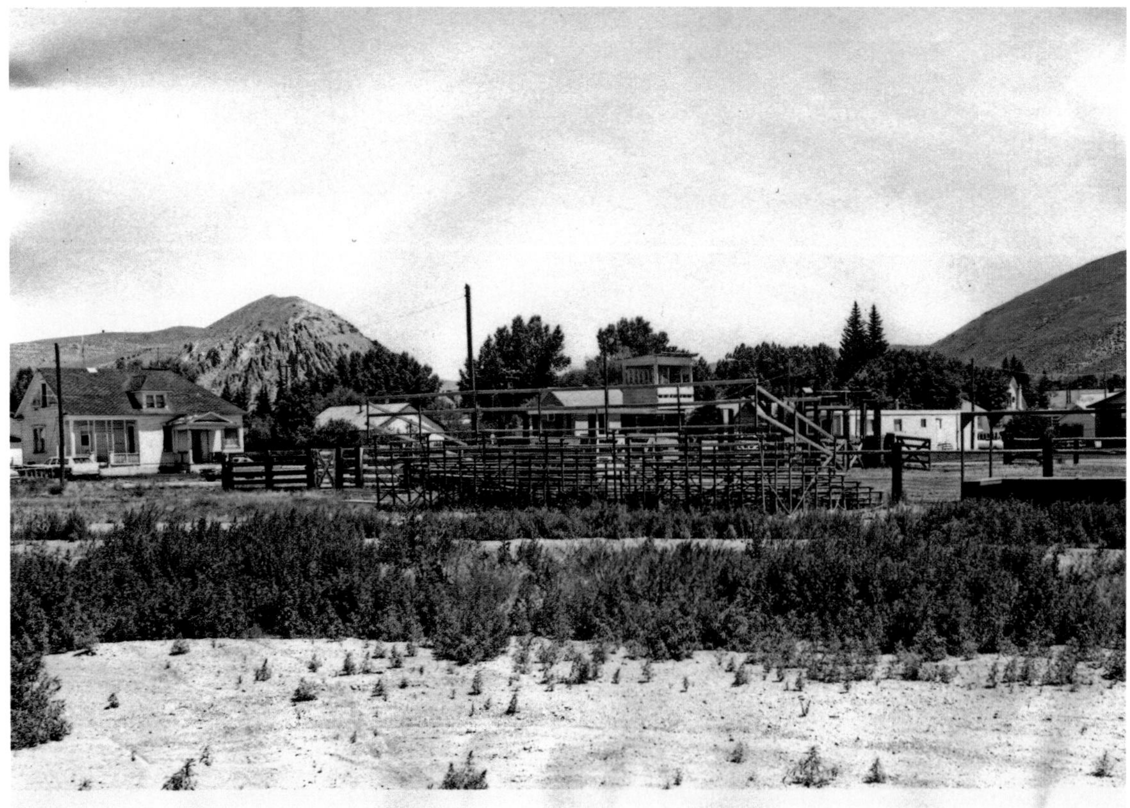

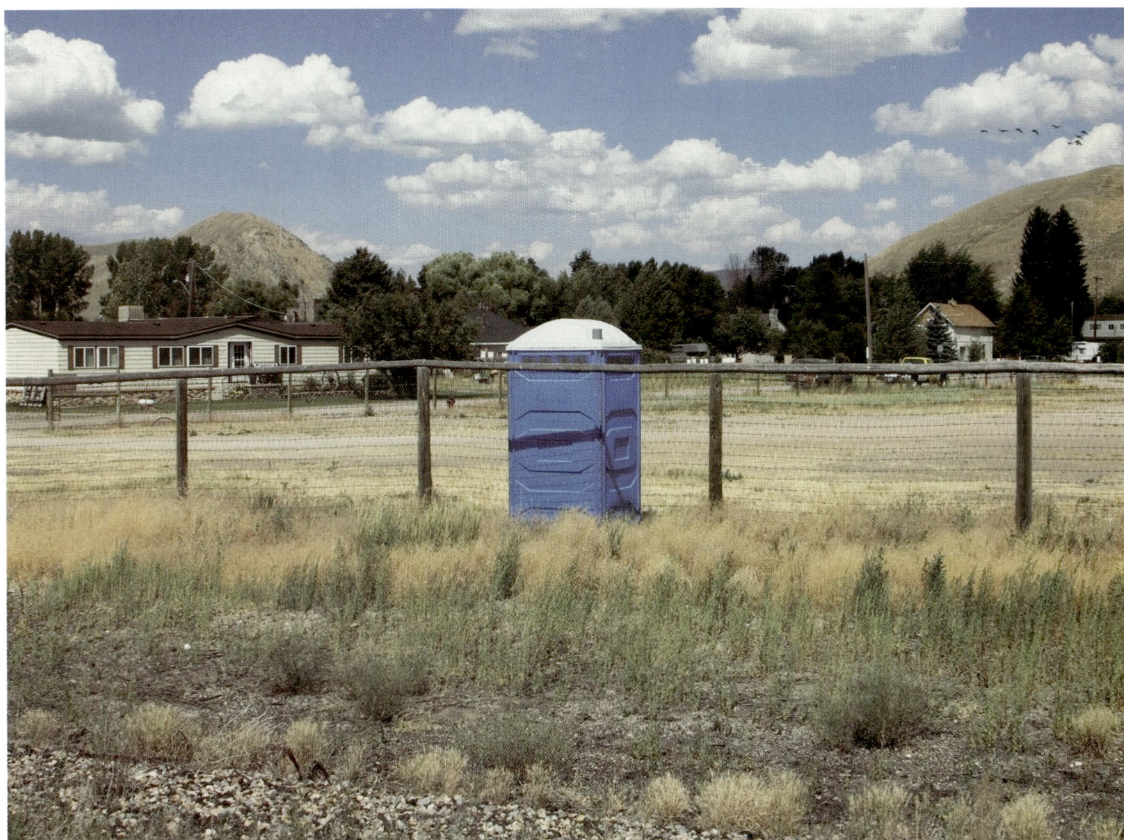

37. #705

Cokeville, Uinta Co. (now Lincoln County), 1903, 1987, 2007
GPS COORDINATES: 42 04.984N, 110 57.556W

Cokeville is the last station on the Oregon Short Line leaving Wyoming to the west and the cultural entrance to the Mormon settlement of Star Valley to the north. Shoshoni Indians lived in the area, and the first white settlers arrived in the 1870s. When the railroad came through in 1882, it platted the town and named it Cokeville for some coal mines in the area. Sheep ranching later developed there.

Stimson visited the fledgling community as part of his 1903 survey and photographed it from the railroad grade looking northeast to the formation known as Rocky Point. The year before I made my 1987 view, Cokeville made national news when the former town marshal and his wife took 167 children and adults hostage at the local elementary school. All of the hostages escaped after a bomb exploded, killing both hostage takers.

During my visits there in 1987 and again in 2007, I could make out individual buildings remaining from Stimson's image, but the tree growth blocked their view from the original vantage point near the tracks. In fact, to make my 2007 image, I had to move my camera to a location farther back because the fence around the rodeo ground and the blue portable toilet blocked the view.

The area around Fort Laramie had a nineteenth-century history tied to the old fur trading post, emigration on the Oregon Trail, open-range cattle ranching, and the Indian Wars of the 1870s. But for Stimson, who first traveled to the area in the 1890s, it had a second history that focused on the mines around Hartville and Sunrise, Wheatland's irrigated farms, cattle ranching near Chugwater, the town of Douglas, and the beginnings of tourism at the old fort.

In my first rephotography efforts in the 1980s, I photographed Fort Laramie, Hartville, Sunrise, Wheatland, Douglas, and Ayres Natural Bridge—a Converse

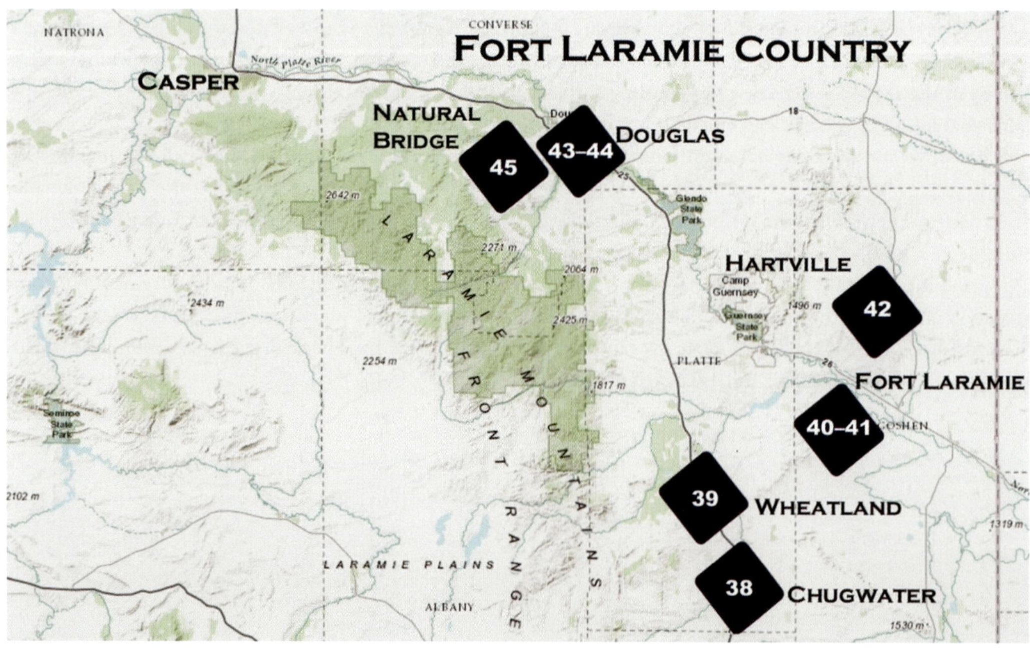

County park outside Douglas. Twenty years later I added Chugwater to the list but could not access the now closed company town of Sunrise.

Unlike most of the subsections in this group of images, Fort Laramie Country is my own description of an area that does not really have a regional identity. Today, much of this region between the Black Hills and the Union Pacific is tied to the central Wyoming city of Casper. But Stimson did not photograph the Oil City, so it remained for me to connect the dots.

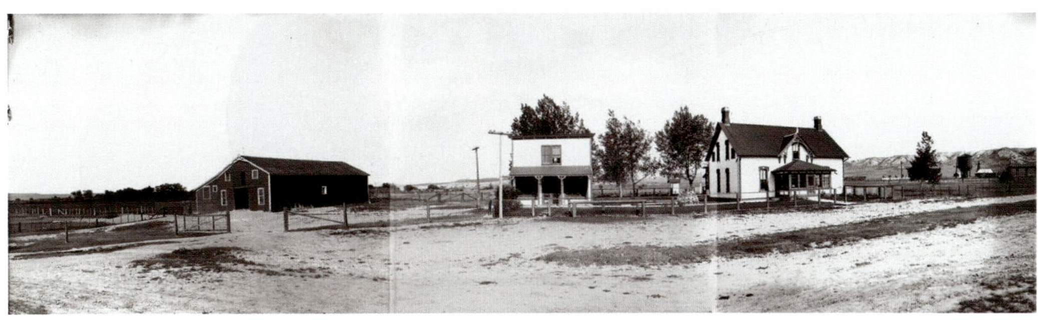

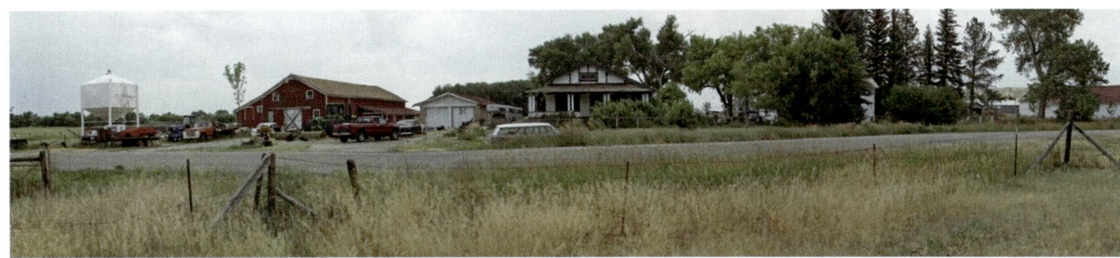

38. #408

Panorama of Al Bowie's Ranch, 1903, 2007
GPS COORDINATES: 41 45.305N, 104 49.134W

I began my second rephotography project on Stimson and Wyoming in July 2007 at this site in Chugwater. The Al Bowie Ranch was originally the 1876 homestead of Thomas Maxwell and then, most famously, the headquarters of the first large corporate cattle company, the Scottish-owned Swan Land and Cattle Company. Managed by Alexander Swan, the ranch epitomized Gilded Age open-range ranching operations. Following the publication of James S. Brisbin's 1881 *Beef Bonanza: Or, How to Get Rich on the Plains,* which explained how ranchers could use the grasses of the West's public domain for enormous profits, in 1883 Swan and his partners brought in Scottish capital to consolidate a number of ranches under one management. From Chugwater, Swan controlled more than 4.5 million acres and ran more than 100,000 head of cattle. Initial prospects were good, but the infamous winter of 1886–87 decimated plains ranching and exposed the fact that herd counts often varied widely from their book counts. Swan was estimated to have "lost" about 20 percent of the corporation's cattle and was relieved as manager. The ranch struggled on into the twentieth century. By the time of Stimson's visit during his 1903 survey of the state, ranch manager Al Bowie was operating on only 5,000 acres.

In Stimson's panorama, the original ranch house can be seen at the far right and another building and a large barn to the left. In the far distance at right, the tracks of the Burlington Railroad and its water tower can be seen.

After Stimson photographed the place, the Al Bowie Ranch lived on through World War I and barely survived the Great Depression. It began liquidating lands in 1943 and within five years had sold all its property, save for what is shown in Stimson's photo. At a special stockholders meeting in 1948, the company deeded that property, valued at only $36,000, to its last manager as thanks for his work. It sold its last cattle two years later and dissolved in 1951.

When Lauren and I visited the site in 2007, we found much of the original ranch still in place. The small false-front office building had burned in 1918, but the original 1876 ranch house, though hidden by trees, was still there, as were the front fence and the large barn, right. To ascertain our vantage point, we aligned fence posts against the backdrop of the original house.

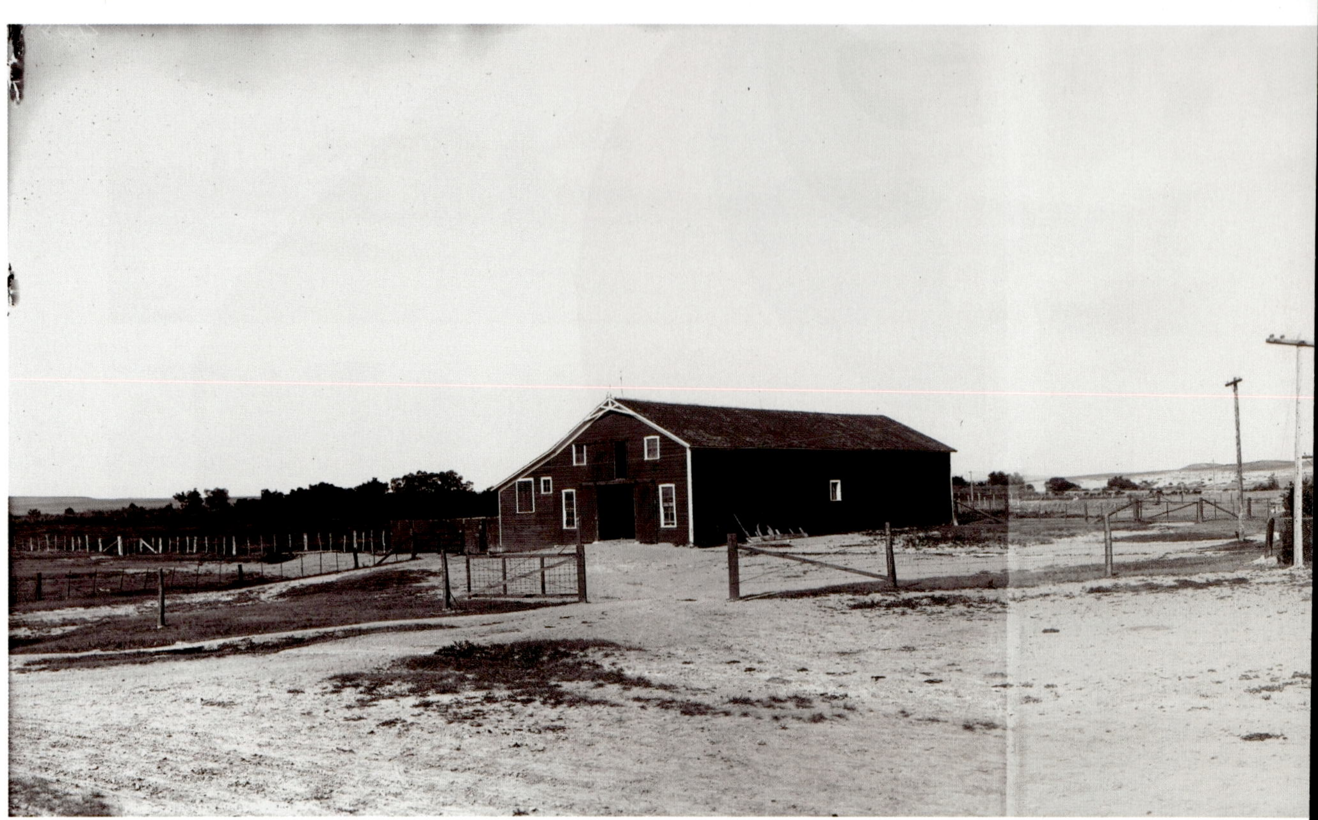

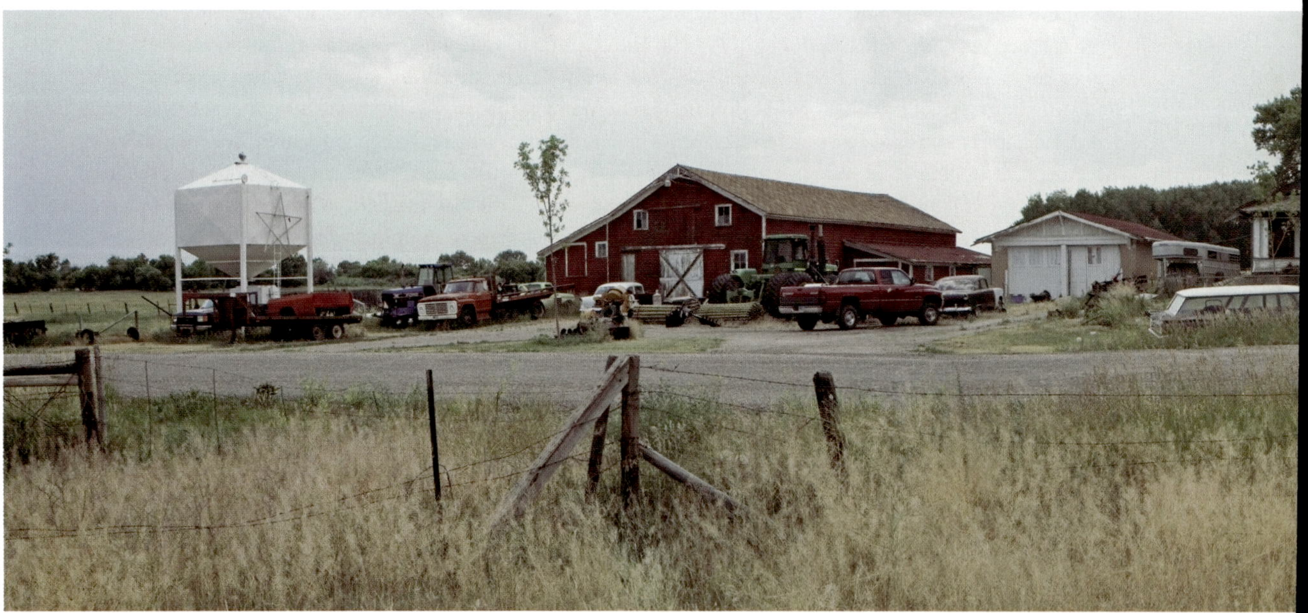

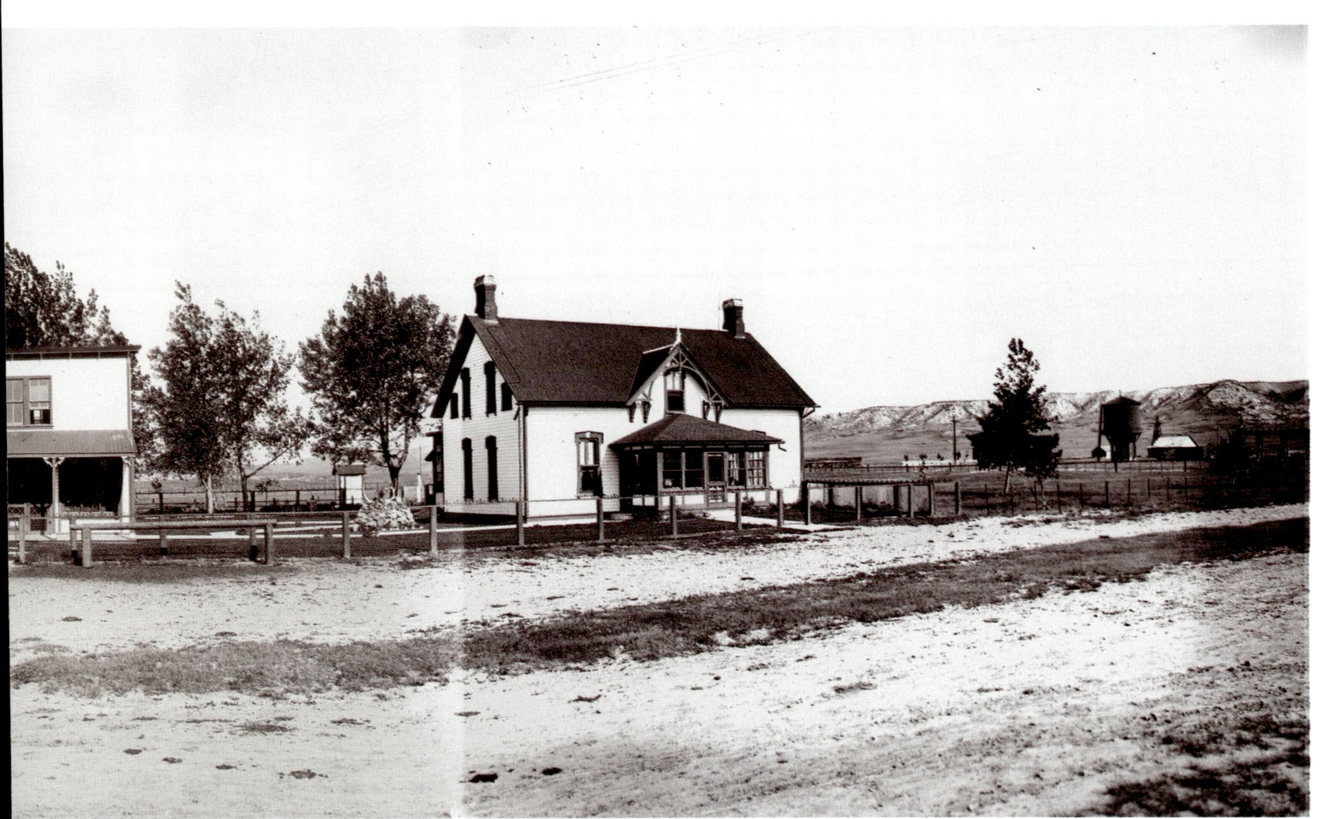

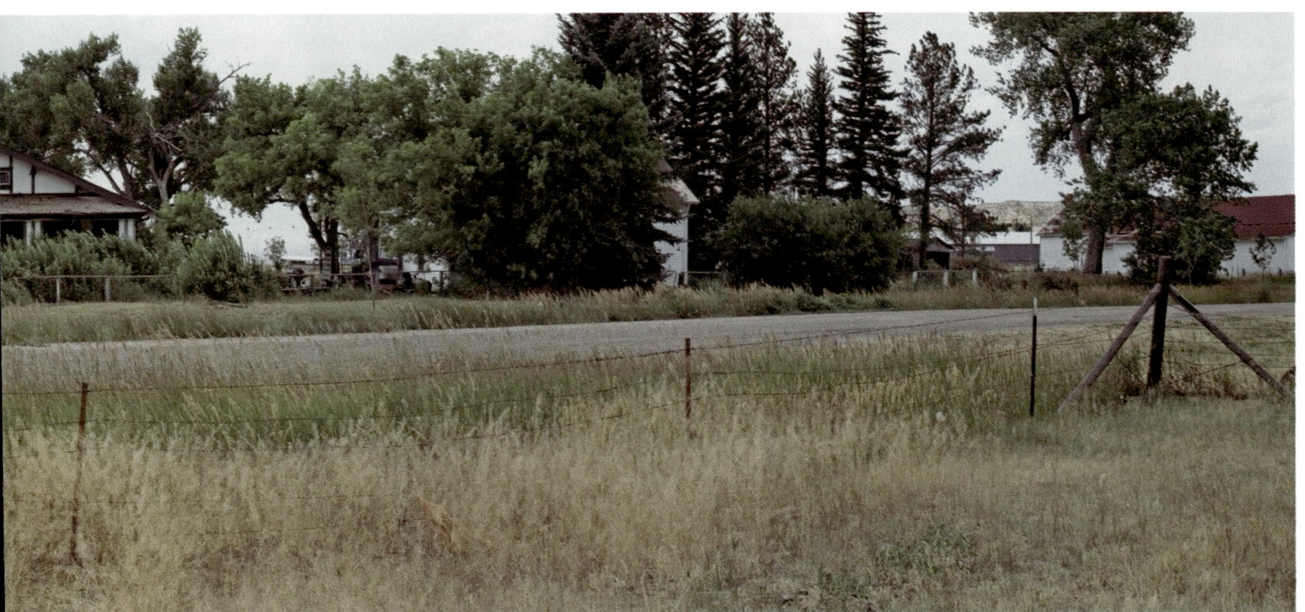

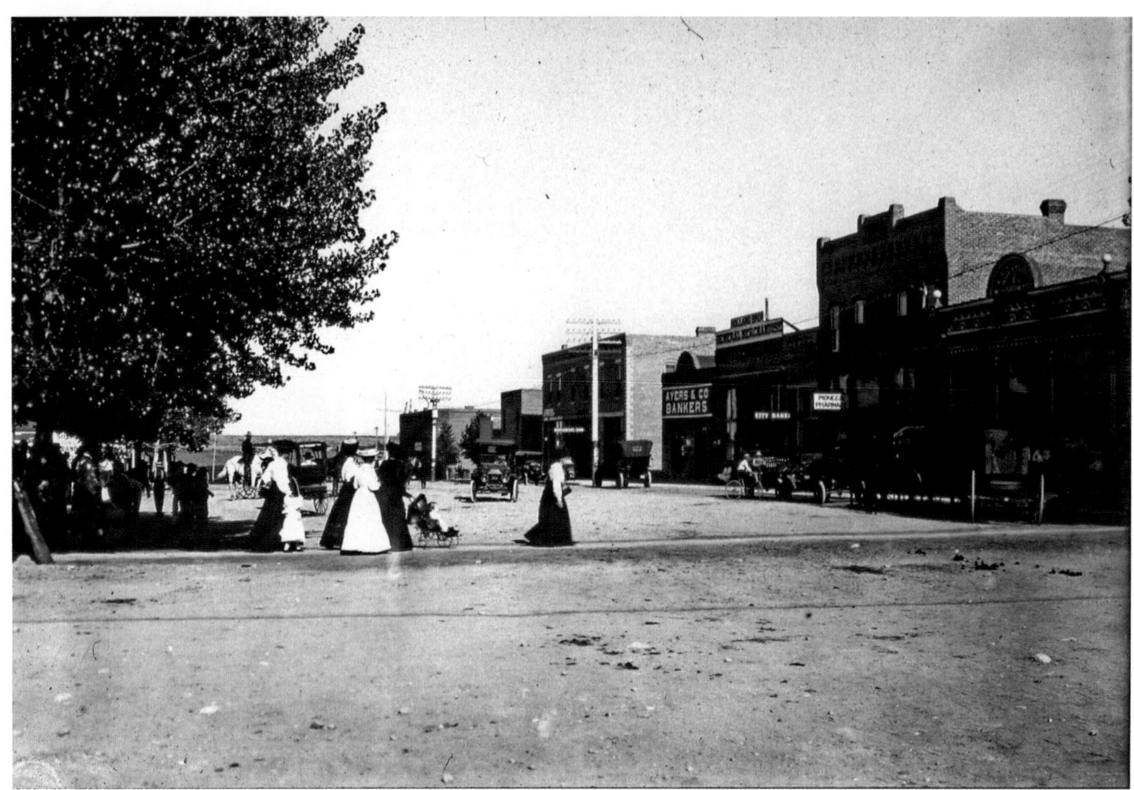

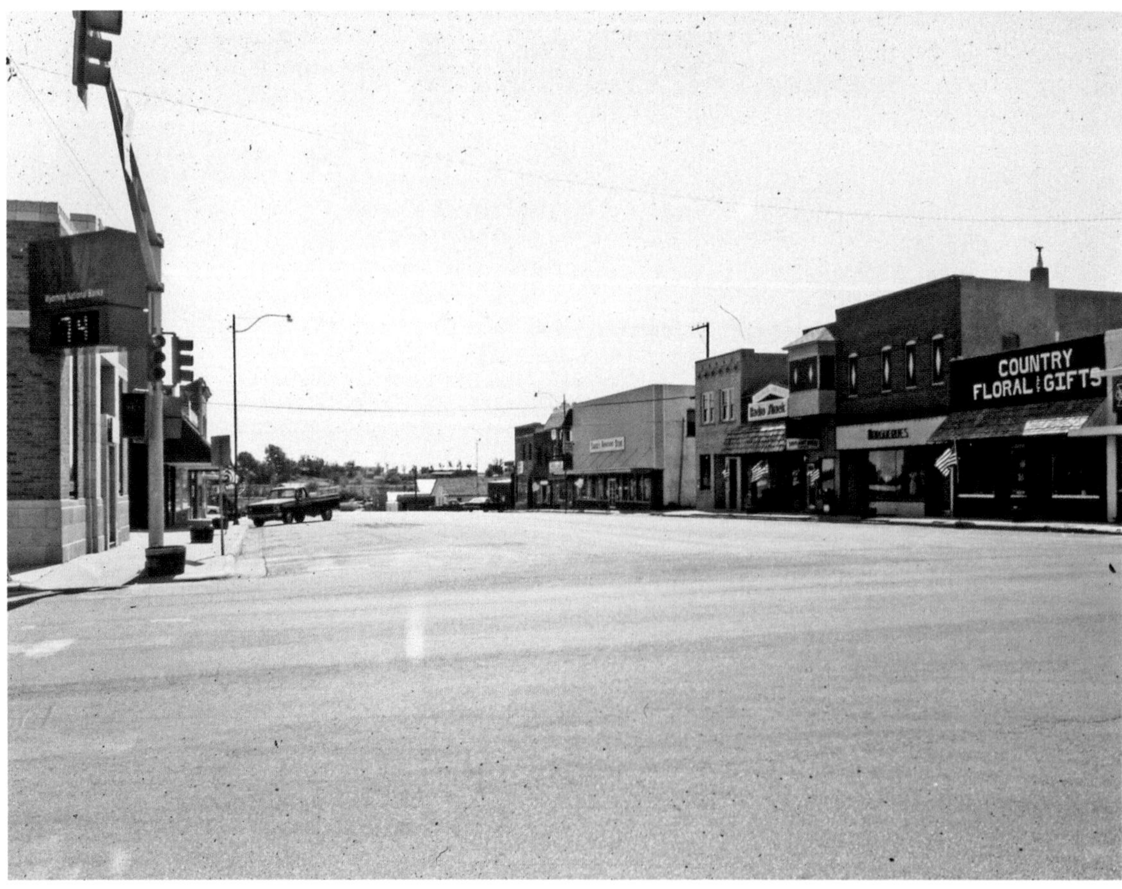

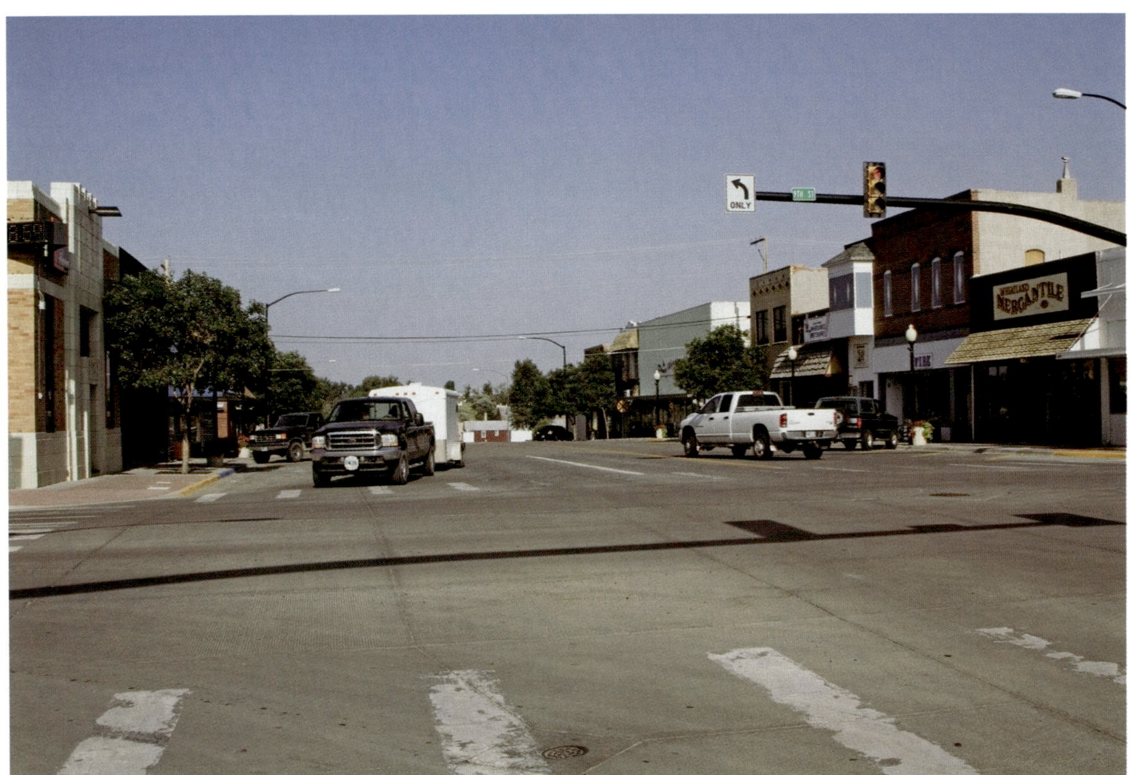

39. #2912

A Saturday Afternoon, Wheatland, 1910, 1987, 2008
GPS COORDINATES: 42 3.270167N, 104 57.208W

The small farm community of Wheatland, seventy miles north of Cheyenne, seems to have been a special place for J. E. Stimson. It was one of the first places he visited during his 1903 state survey, he invested in farmland there, and in 1912 the photographer broke his leg after running into a mud hole and being ejected from his car. The main reason for his interest, though, was probably the way irrigation was transforming desert lands into new farms, an important concept for a promotional photographer like Stimson.

The history of this irrigation system was also unique in that it was a privately funded enterprise, with no state or federal support. Organized in 1883 by large area ranchers, including Francis E. Warren and Joseph Carey, the Wyoming Improvement Company gained access to more than 50,000 acres in an area known as Wheatland Flats and built two irrigation systems to bring water to it. The company then sold farms as a way to profit from the venture. With the arrival of the Cheyenne and Northern Railroad in 1887, the area boomed. Town lots were auctioned off in 1894. By the time Stimson took this photo in 1910, the town boasted a population of about 1,000.

A fairly typical Stimson street scene, this one shows Wheatland's downtown commercial buildings, including a bank and mercantile at right, and a large group of female pedestrians at left. The large tree at left hints at the effects of irrigation, while the telephone poles and many autos on the street suggest that Wheatland was a modern place.

Although there are no trees or pedestrians in my 1987 image, the main buildings are still there, as is a traffic light. Twenty-one years later, trees had returned to the downtown, and businesses still occupied the historic buildings at right.

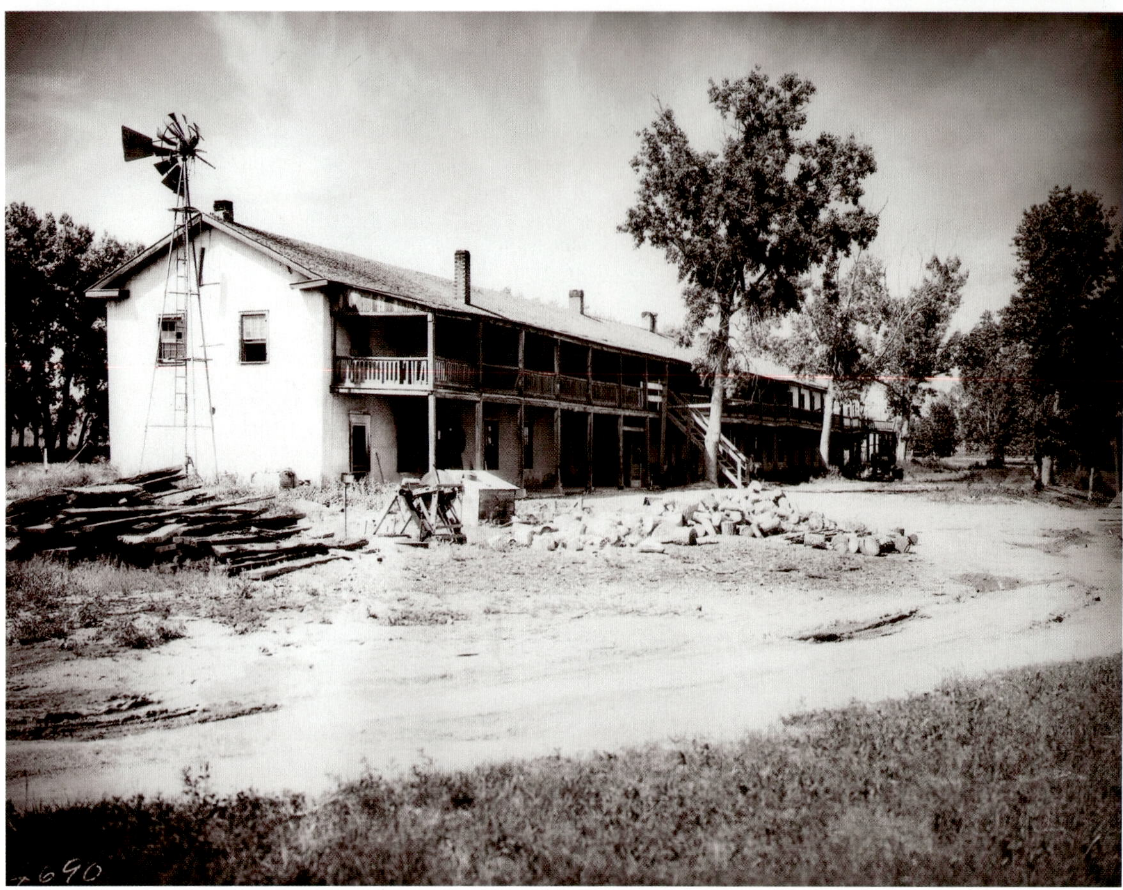

40. #4690

Old Cavalry Barracks, Fort Laramie, 1930, 1987, 2008
GPS COORDINATES: 42 12.247N, 104 33.4163W

In the early summer of 1930, as the Historic Landmark Commission of Wyoming made plans to celebrate the 100th anniversary of the first wagon train to travel the Oregon Trail to what became Fort Laramie, J. E. Stimson drove up from Cheyenne and photographed the remains of the historic old fort. Originally constructed by William Sublette as the fur trading post Fort William in 1834, in 1841 the American Fur Company purchased the stockade and renamed it Fort John. Eight years later the United States Army bought the post to help protect travelers going to Oregon and California. The post served as the site for important treaties with Plains Indians in 1851 and again in 1868 and as a staging area for the post–Civil War Indian Wars. By 1890, the post's importance had decreased to the point that the army sold its buildings to area homesteaders. They remained in private hands until re-purchased by the federal government and were designated Fort Laramie National Historic Monument in 1934.

Stimson's 1930 photographs show the aging fort as it appeared just before restoration efforts began. For example, this view of the Old Cavalry Barracks, built in 1883, shows the building in a state of disrepair after being used for a time as an automobile motel.

After the federal purchase in 1938, the barracks served as home, office, museum, and storage site for various superintendents working to preserve the fort. In the 1940s the government established an adjacent temporary parking lot for visitors. Restoration efforts began and continue to the present. In 1985, while an undergraduate history major at the University of Wyoming in Laramie, I participated in a living history week at the fort and lived in the barracks as an infantry soldier.

My 1987 rephotograph shows that, although the building clearly had been restored and the grounds landscaped, the "temporary" parking lot was still in place four decades later. In 2007, rehabilitation of the barracks was ongoing, although the parking lot had been moved. In its place, a series of pedestrian paths lead visitors around the site.

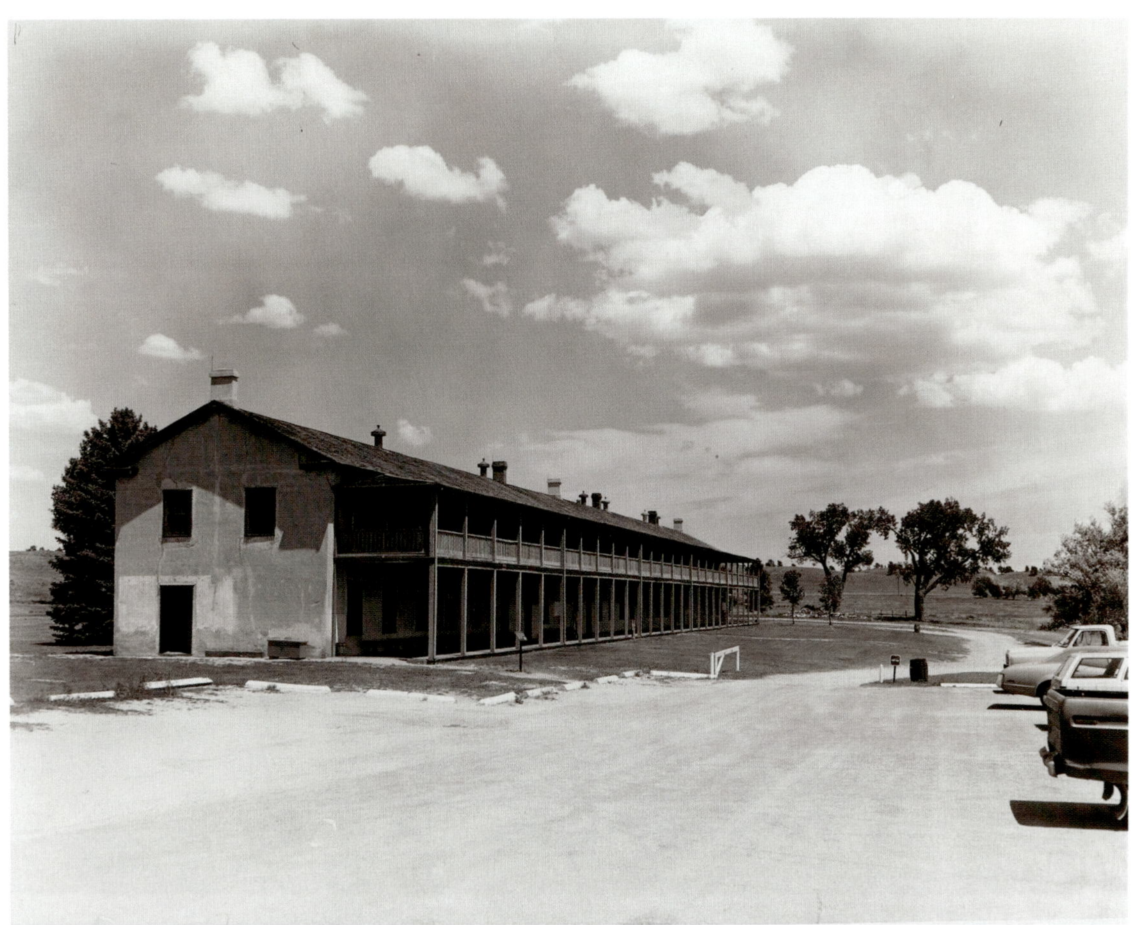

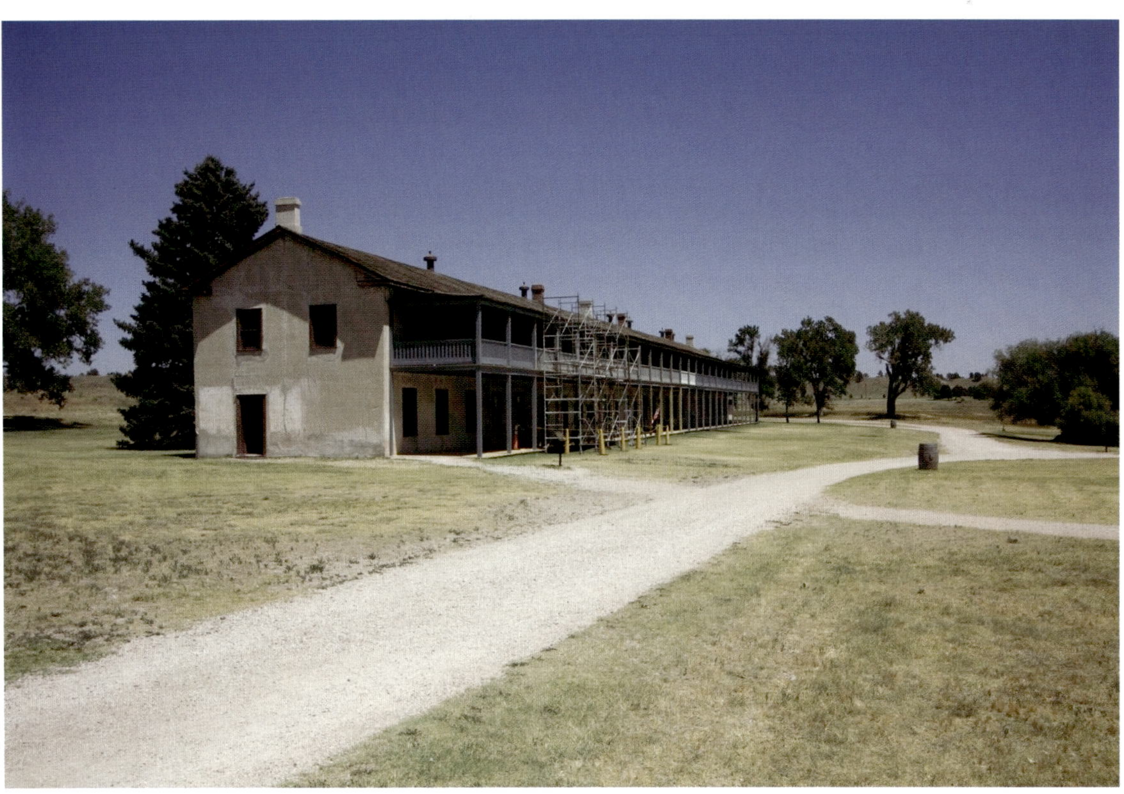

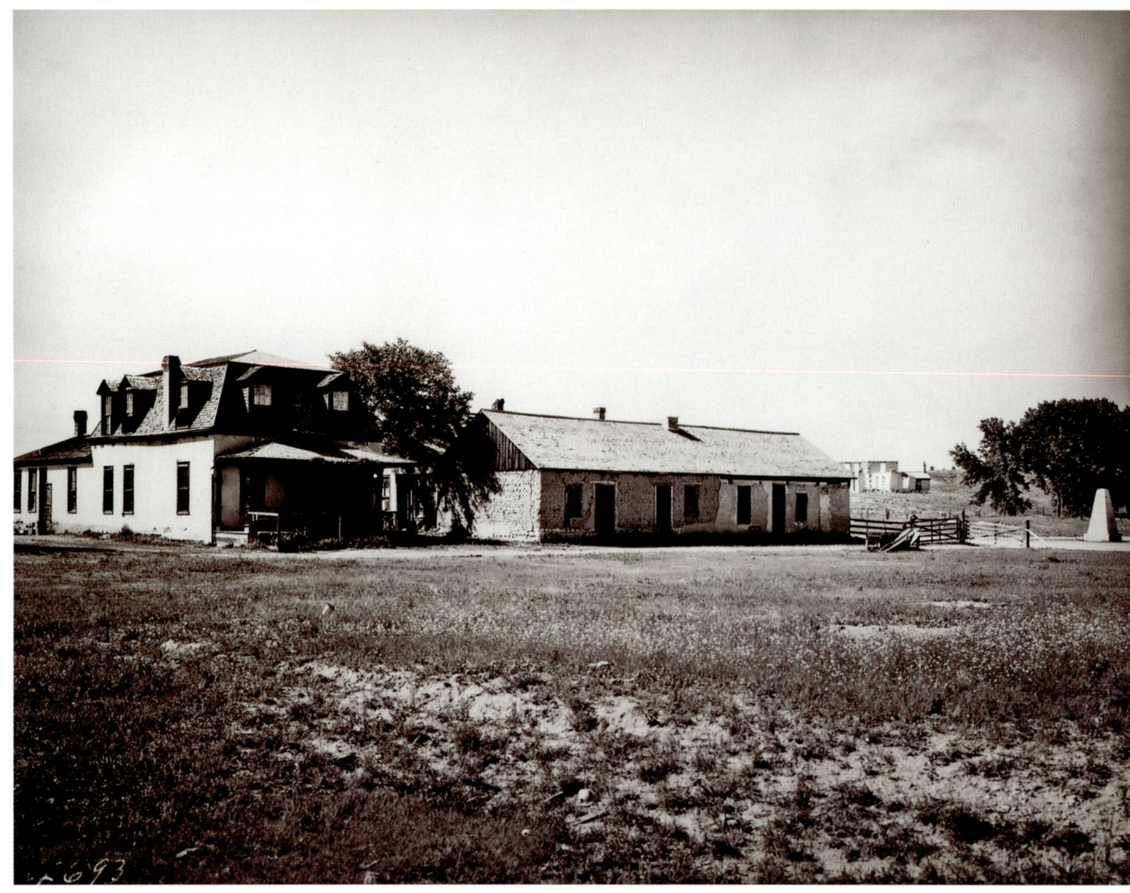

41. #4693

Old Sutler's Store, Fort Laramie, 1930, 1987, 2008
GPS COORDINATES: 42 12.167N, 104 33.460W

One of the oldest buildings in Wyoming, part of the sutler's store, at right, dates back to the 1830s. The walls are adobe, more than two feet thick. The northern half of the store, at right, was built in 1852. The sutler, a civilian post trader, sold a variety of goods. The Army Corps of Engineers built the Burt House, left, in 1885. It served as living quarters for several post families. Wyoming historian Grace Raymond Hebard and a group of concerned Wyoming historians placed the white obelisk, at the far right of the photo, in 1915 to commemorate the site of the fort on the Oregon Trail.

As with his view of the cavalry barracks, Stimson's 1930 view of these two structures is an important visual document of what they looked like toward the end of their "private" existence and their condition at the beginning of federal restoration. Also visible to the right of the sutler's store are the remains of the old post hospital.

My 1987 view shows the restored structures, revived landscaping, and, most important, several groups of visitors touring the fort. Twenty years later, more trees constitute the major difference.

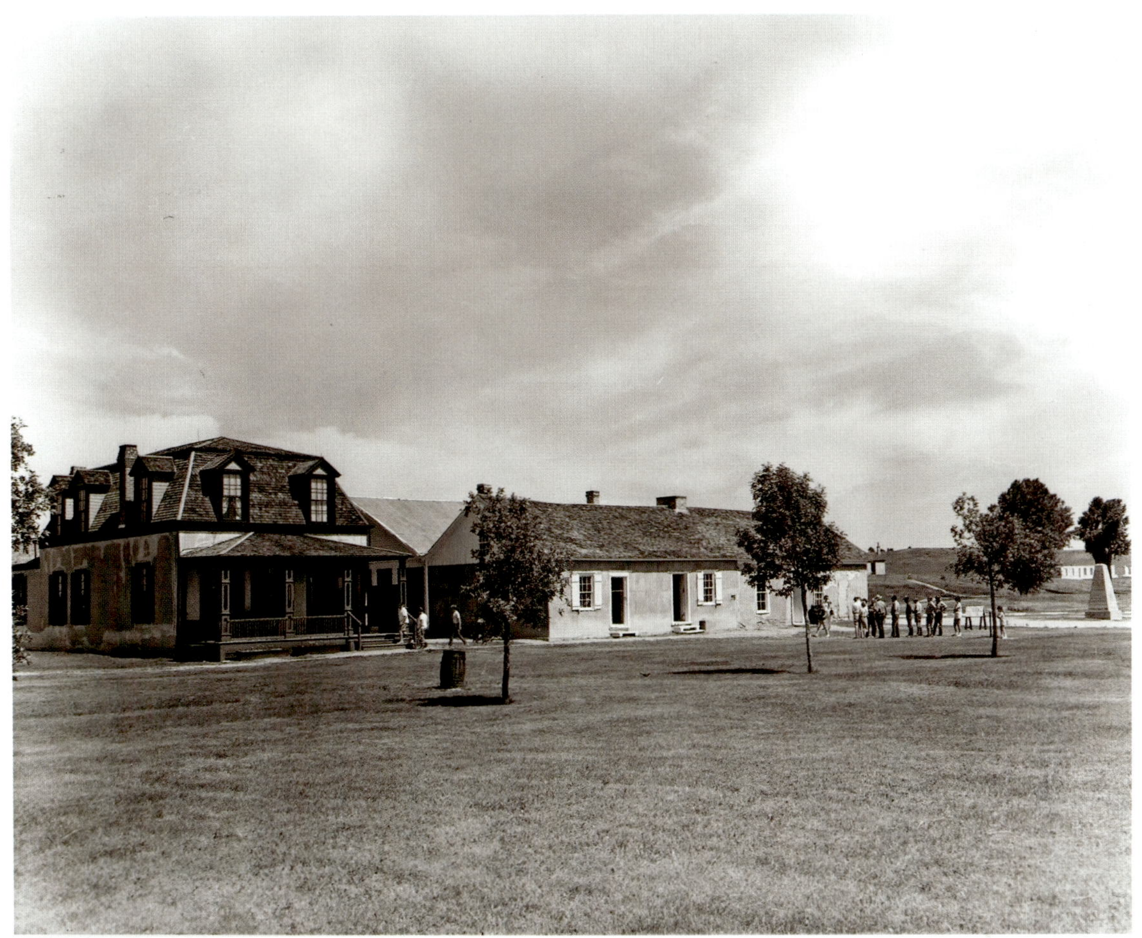

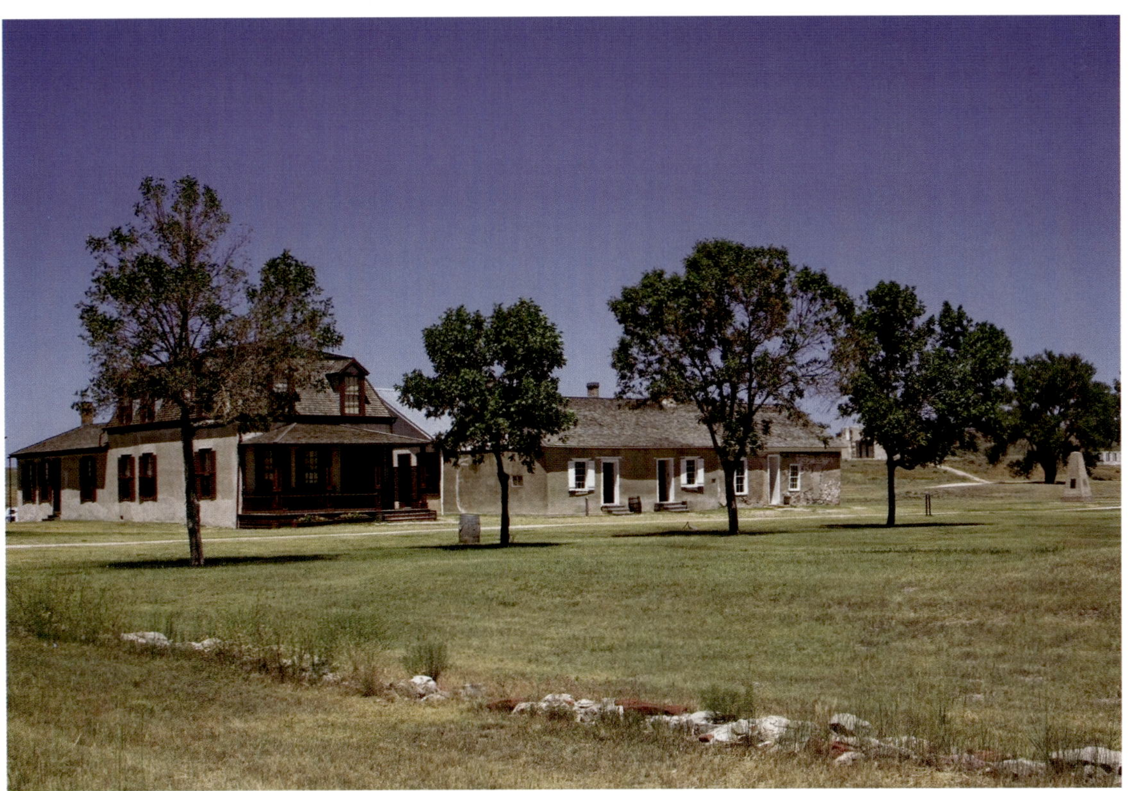

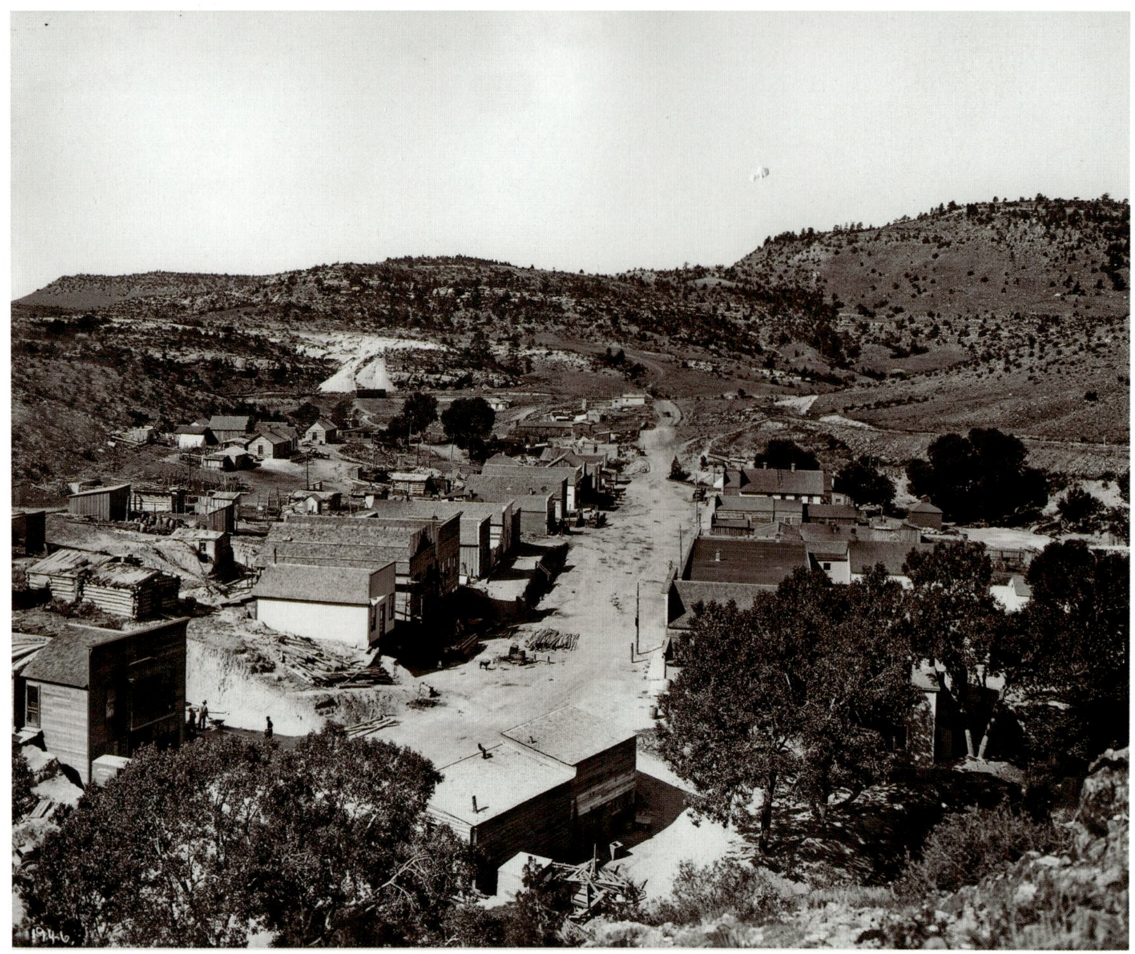

42. #1946

Hartville, 1907, 1987, 2008
GPS COORDINATES: 42 19.677N, 104 43.484W

Located five miles north of Guernsey, Hartville has been the home of iron, copper, and limestone mining. Miners moved to the area in the 1870s, and the town began around 1881. It had a reputation as a wide-open community in the early days and boomed again when the Burlington built a branch line to the nearby company town of Sunrise in 1900. In contrast to Sunrise, Hartville was always an independent town, having incorporated as a municipality shortly after the railroad came.

Another of Stimson's community bird's-eye views, this 1907 photograph looks west over the town's Main Street from a small hill. The building boom was still in progress, as evidenced by the construction work in the left foreground. The recently built railroad grade can be seen at the base of the far hill.

Through much of the twentieth century, Hartville was a drinking spot for miners from nearby Sunrise. When the latter closed in 1980, Hartville's population dropped from its 1970 high of 246 to just 78 by 1990. My 1987 photograph reflects that decline. Although many of the original buildings from Stimson's view are still there, they appear to be closed. Only a handful of cars can be seen on the street.

Twenty years later, although Hartville's population had dropped to 62, the town continued to boast that it is "Wyoming's Oldest Incorporated Community That Is Still in Existence." My 2008 rephotograph showed a few more buildings open on Main Street and a little more traffic as well.

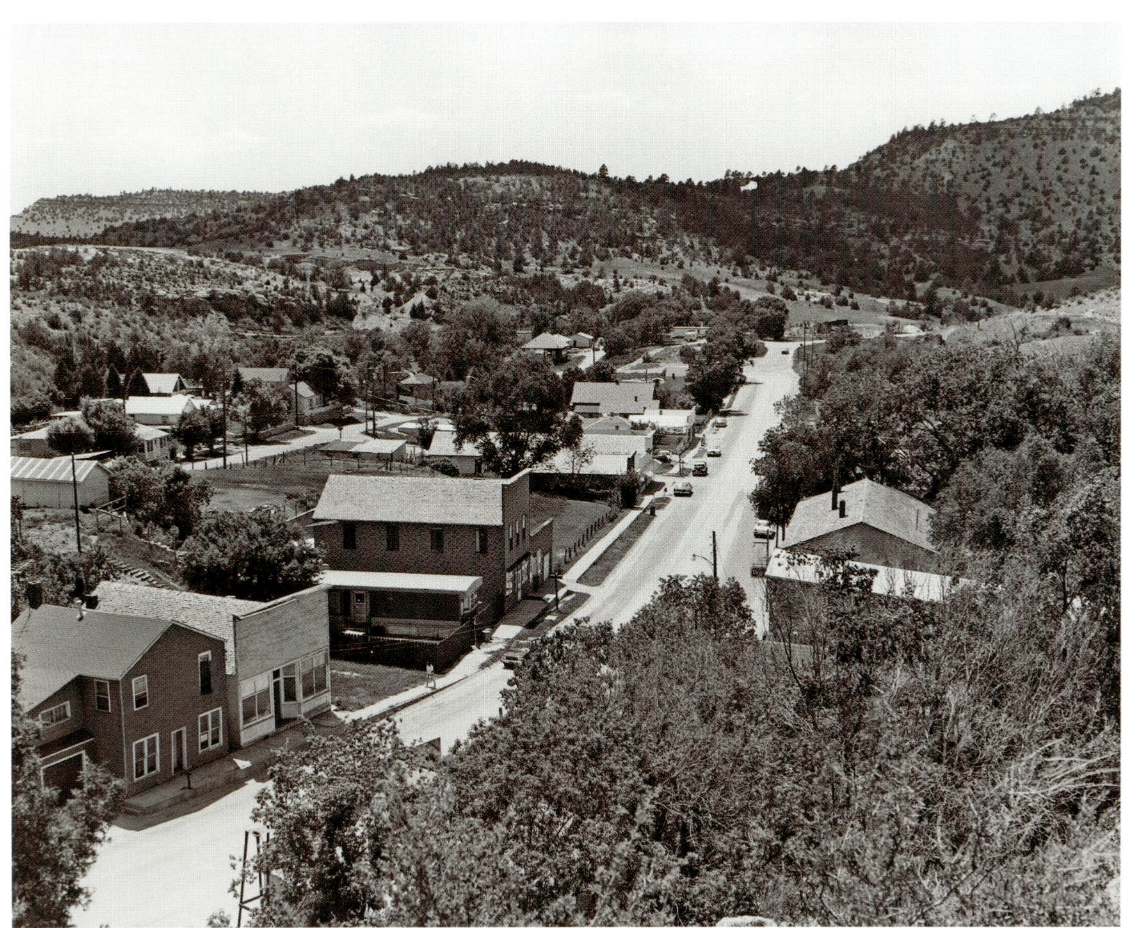

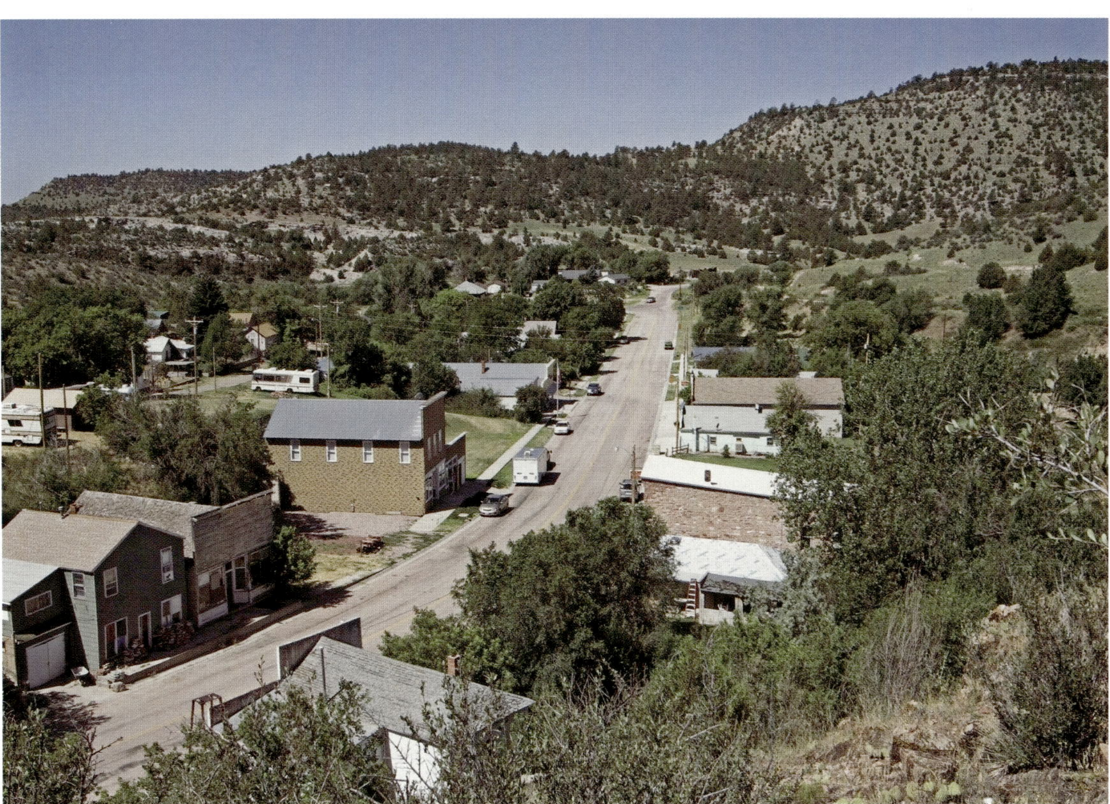

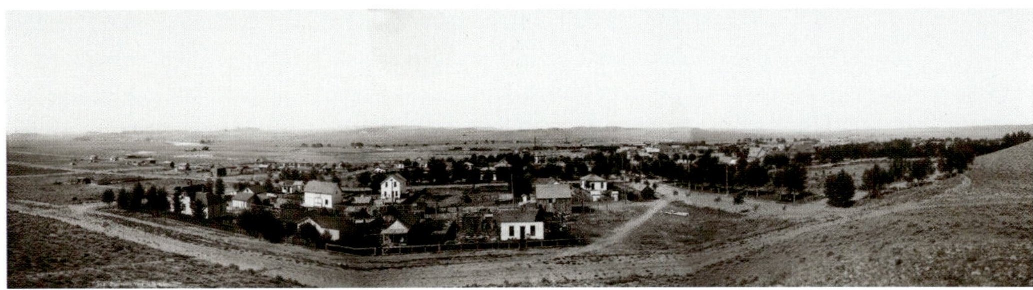

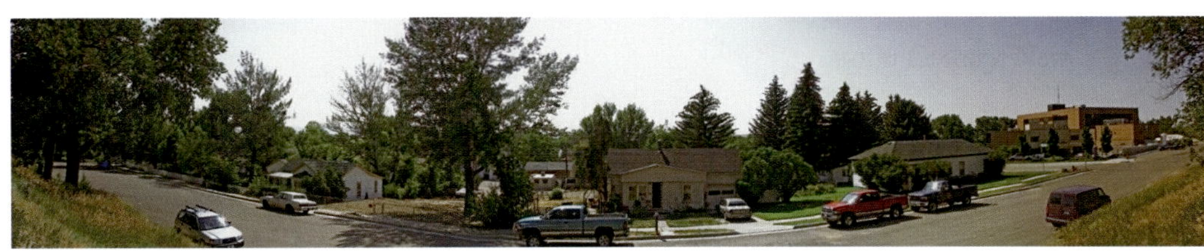

43. #813

Panorama of Douglas, 1903, 2008
GPS COORDINATES: 42 45.452N, 105 22.774W

The area around Douglas had first been settled when Fort Fetterman was constructed eleven miles to the north in 1867. When the Wyoming Central Railway built into the area in 1886, the new community of Douglas, named for Senator Stephen Douglas of Illinois, was established on the banks of the North Platte River. It became the seat of Converse County two years later and an economic hub for nearby ranches. Bill Barlow, the "Sagebrush Philosopher," edited the town's paper and gained fame as a journalist and humorist.

Stimson's panorama of Douglas was made during the photographer's 1903 survey of the state for the St. Louis World's Fair. The vantage point is on the east side of the original town plat at the base of a hill near today's Memorial Hospital of Converse County. Despite its parallax problems, Stimson's photograph is a wonderful visual record of small-town Wyoming life in the early twentieth century. Because of the elevated camera station, the photograph is peering into the residential area, providing insight into front and back yards, gardens, clotheslines, telephone poles, fences, sheds, and the like. Can you find the shed with the antlers on its roof? In the distance, the town's commercial district is visible, with the industrial corridor of the railroad beyond that.

In 1905 the Wyoming legislature made Douglas the official home of the Wyoming State Fair, and it continues in that role to this day. In an agricultural and ranching state like Wyoming, this means that most of the state's residents have been to Douglas at one time or another. During World War II, the town also had an Italian and German prisoner of war camp. Most famously, Douglas sells itself today as the "Jackalope Capital of the World" and has several statues of the mythical beast outside the town's visitor center.

My 2008 rephotograph also suffers from parallax problems, as well as the ubiquitous problem of large trees blocking my view. Nevertheless, the presence of so many big trees does suggest something about life on the plains. A careful look will find many of the same houses in the foreground. The hospital is to the right.

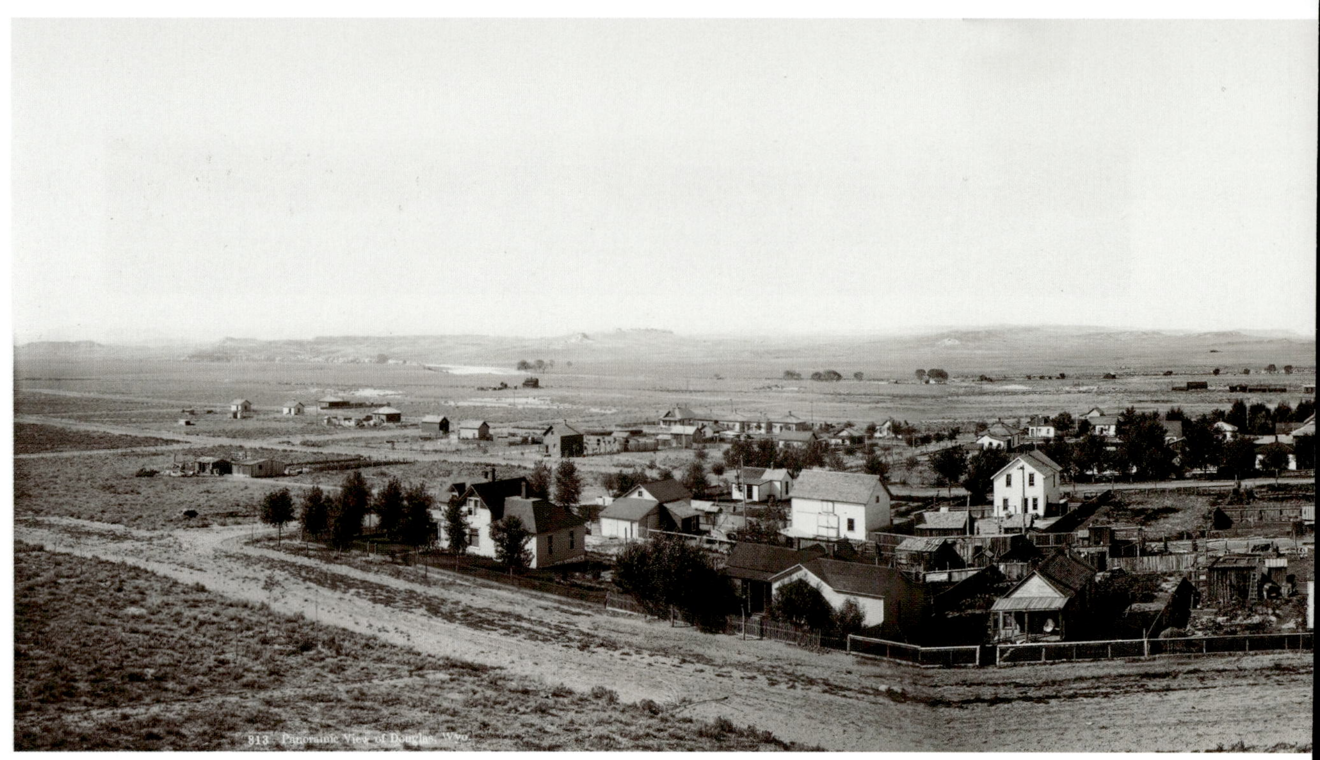
913. Panoramic View of Douglas, Wyo.

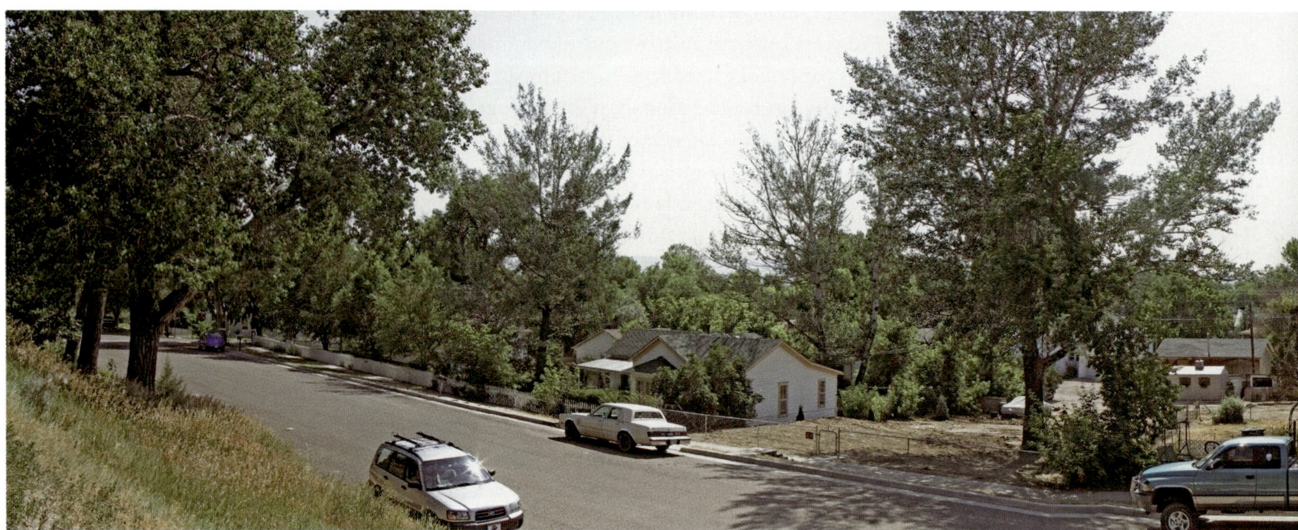

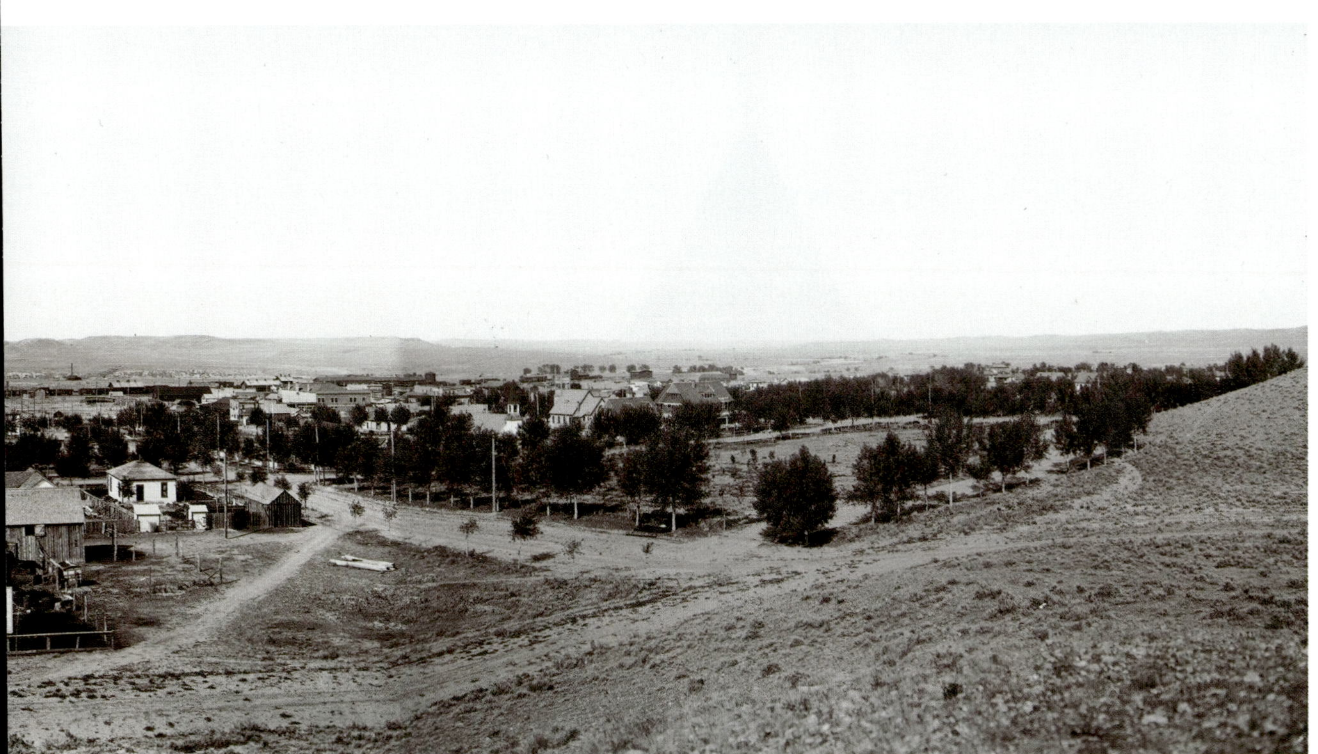

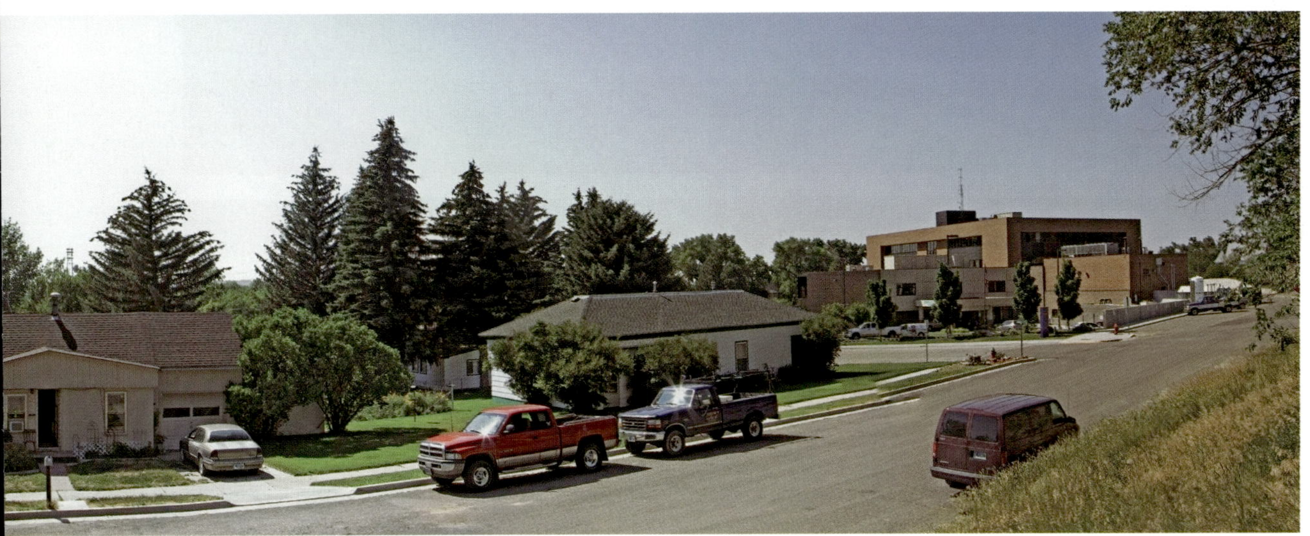

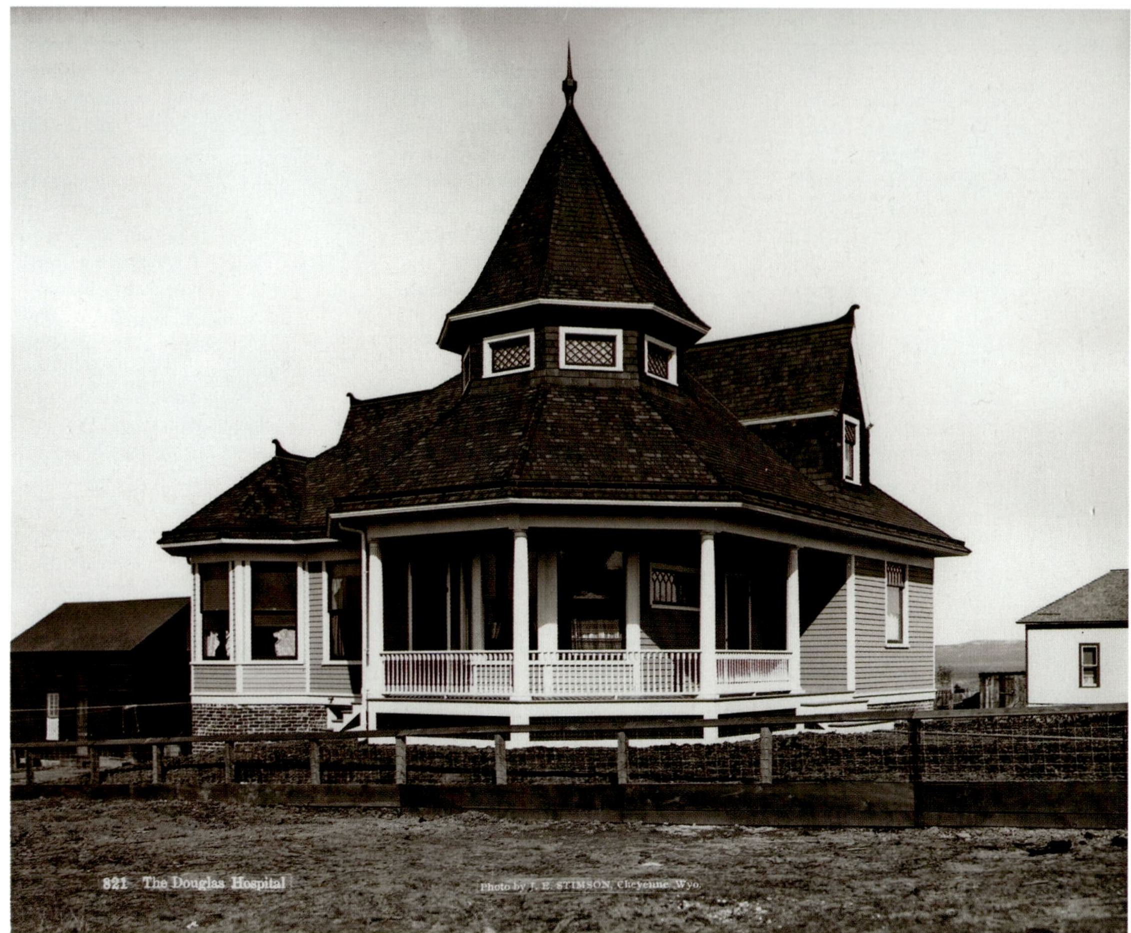

44. #821

The Douglas Hospital (now a private residence), 1903, 1987, 2008
GPS COORDINATES: 42 45.67967N, 105 22.79967W

In the previous view of Douglas, the modern Memorial Hospital of Converse County could clearly be seen on the right side of the panorama. This 1903 Stimson view shows the original Douglas Hospital, a block north of the current one. As someone promoting the state, it was important for Stimson to show that even small Wyoming towns like Douglas had their own healthcare facilities. Similar to many of his business photographs, this is a straight-on portrait taken in warm morning light. When I rephotographed the site in 1987, I learned that the building was a private residence. Twenty years later it remained a well-cared-for home. In comparing all three images, the lack of trees in Stimson's 1903 view seems the most interesting point of contrast.

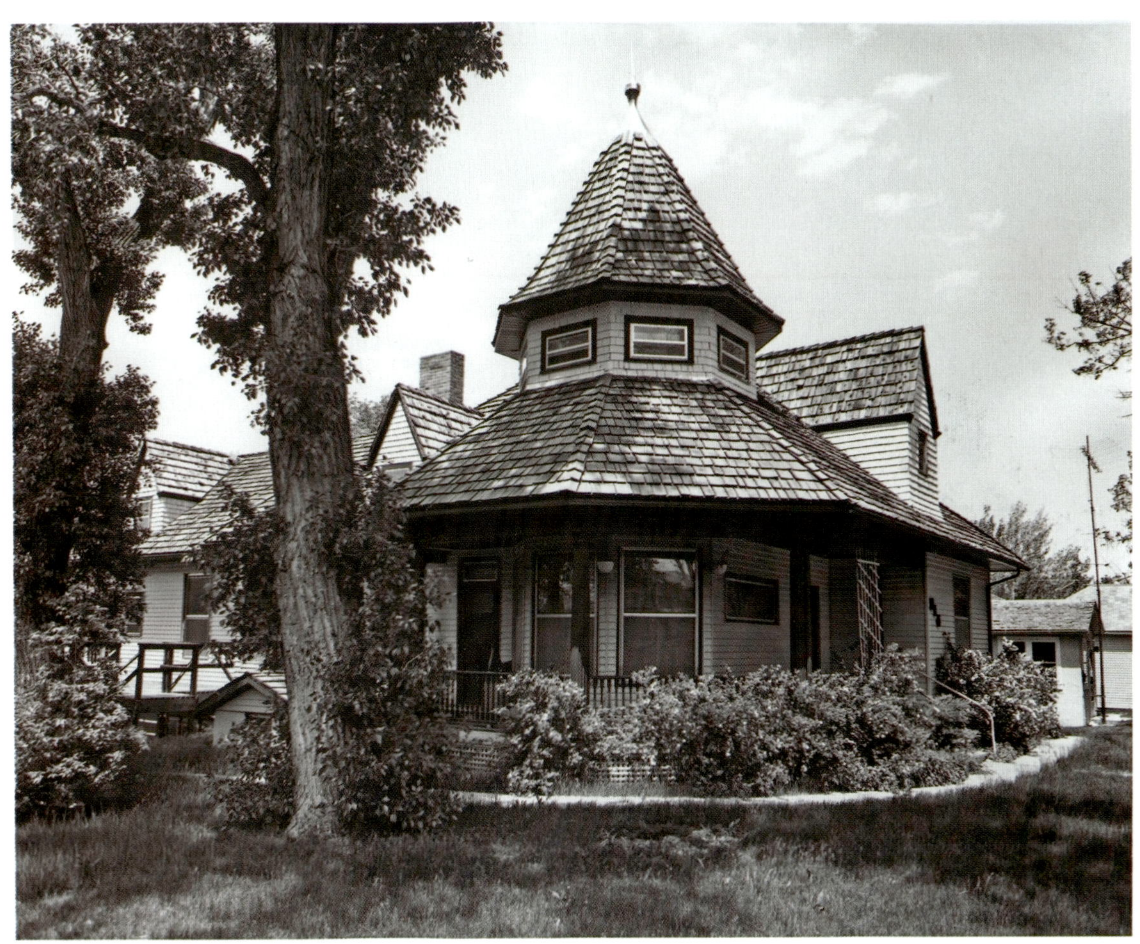

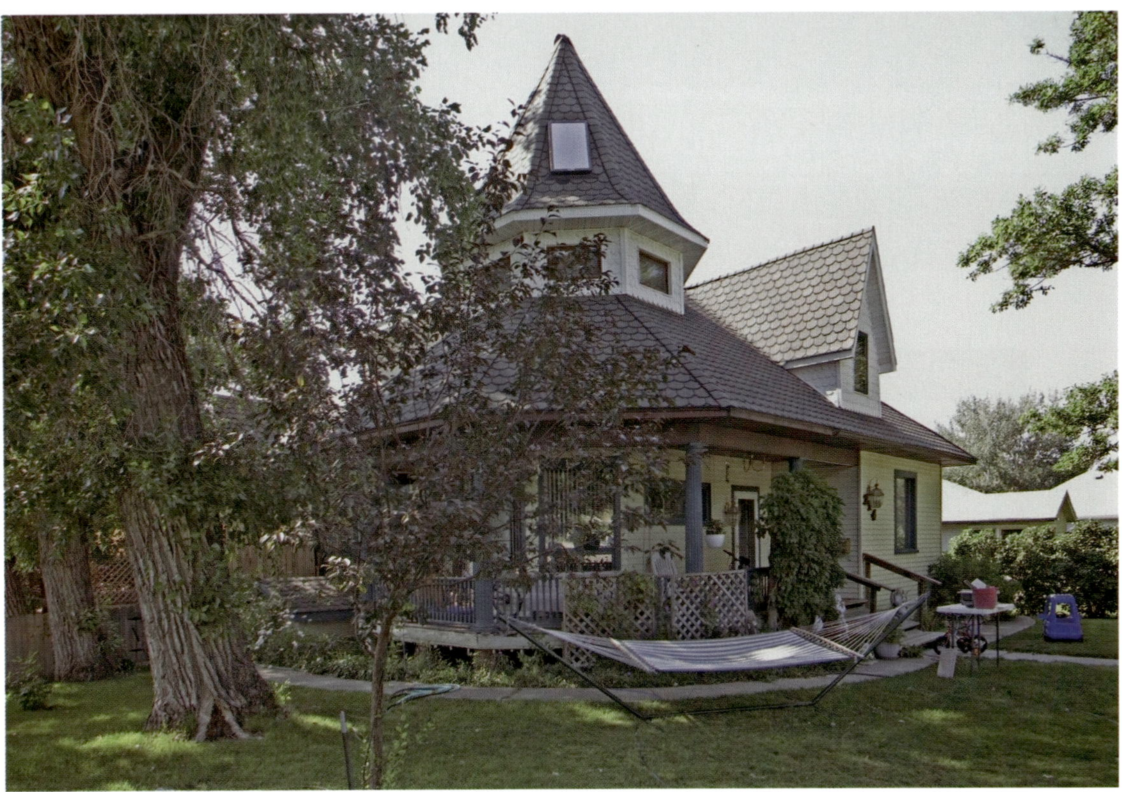

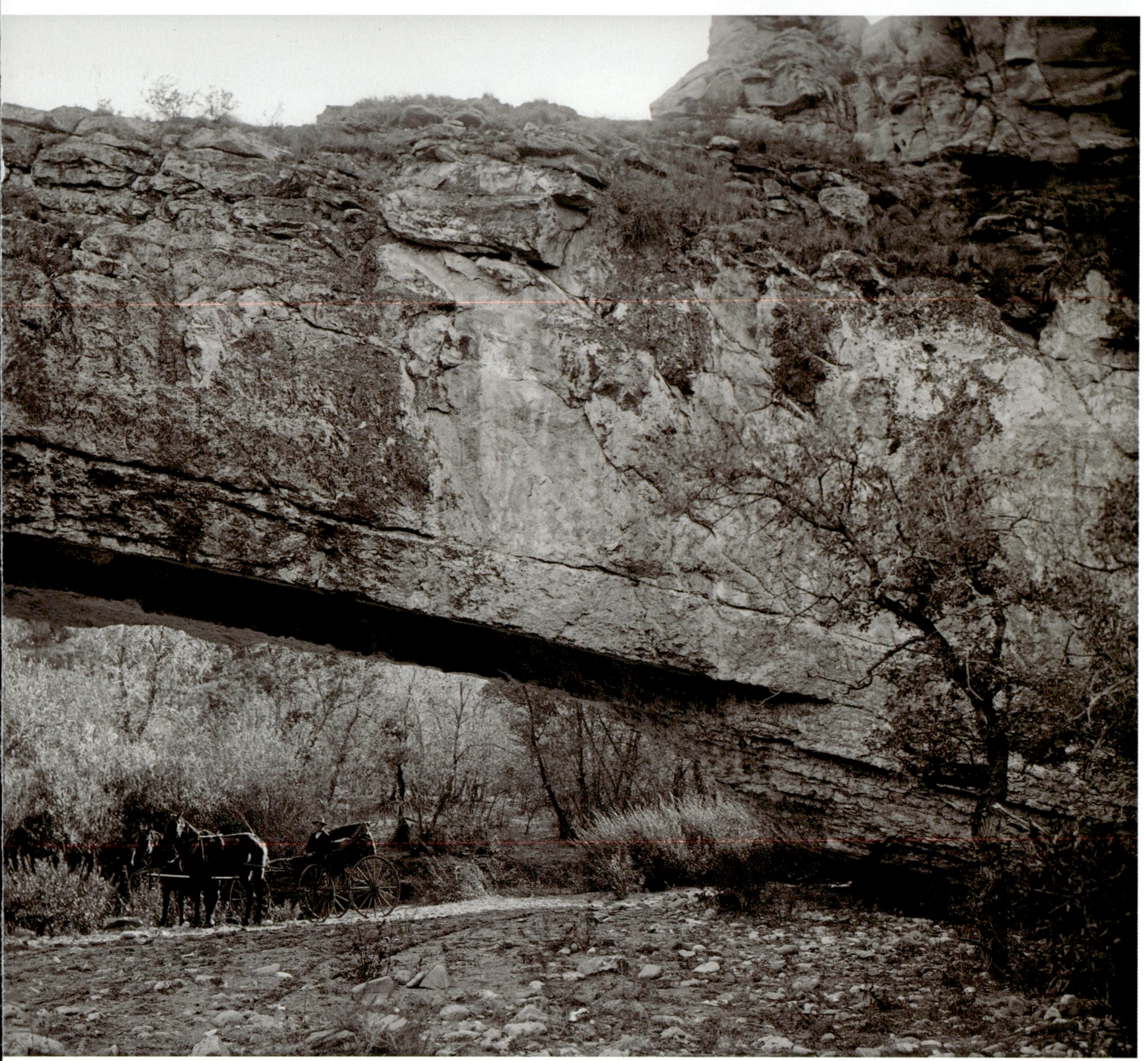

45. #814

Panoramic View of Natural Bridge, Converse Co., 1903, 2008
GPS COORDINATES: 42 44.068N, 105 36.724W

Ayres Natural Bridge spans La Prele Creek about a mile below La Prele Dam near Douglas. Composed of red sandstone, the bridge is thirty feet high and ninety feet across. Since the site is just a mile south of the Oregon Trail, emigrants going west often sidetracked to visit it. The famous pioneer photographer William Henry Jackson first photographed the bridge in 1870.

Stimson visited the area in 1903 on his photographic survey of the state for the St. Louis World's Fair. He made several compositions, but this two-sheet panorama is by far the best. A classic study of the picturesque, Stimson presents the wildness of the creek and the bridge framing his horse and buggy escort. As with his photos of

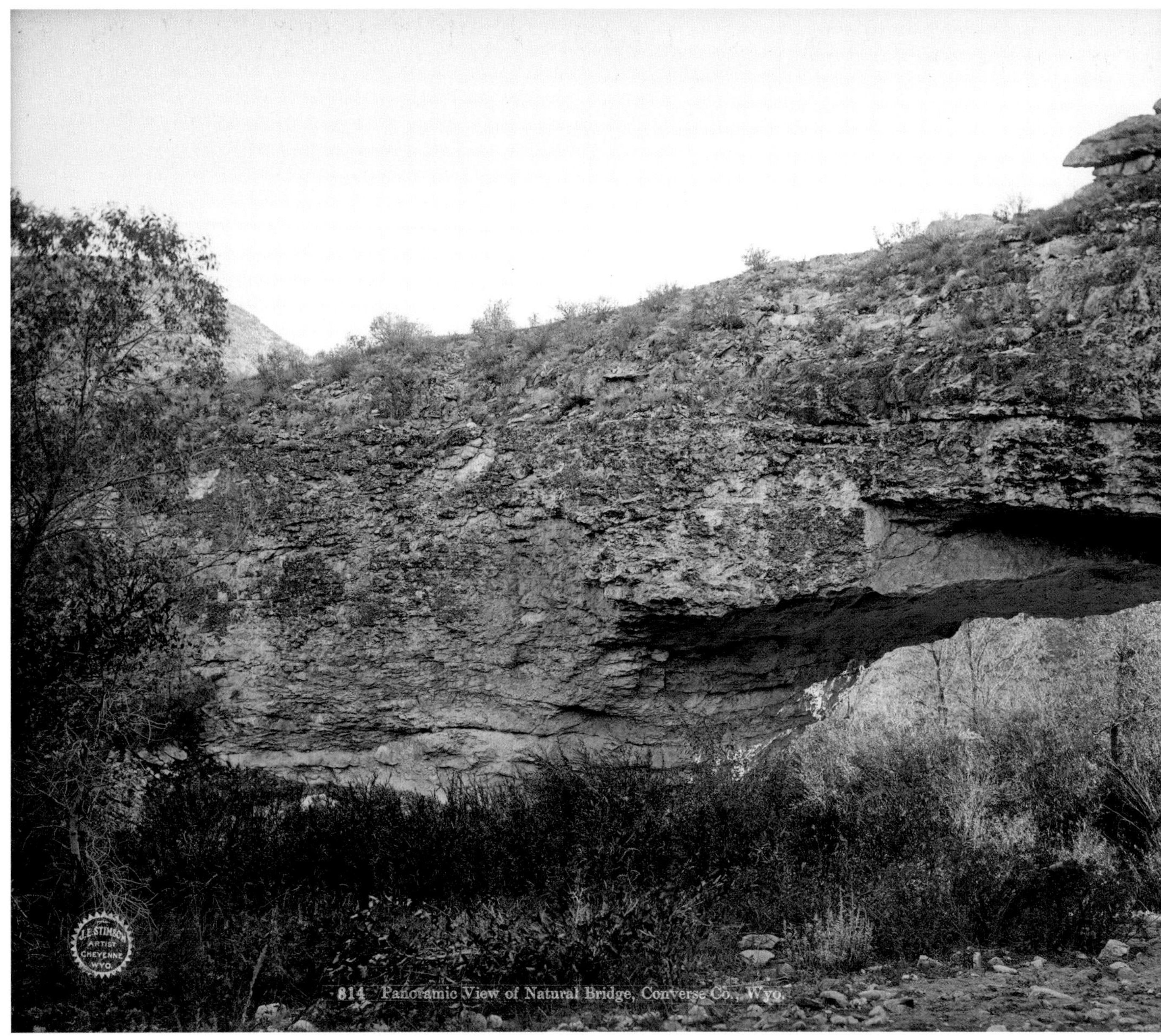

814   Panoramic View of Natural Bridge, Converse Co., Wyo.

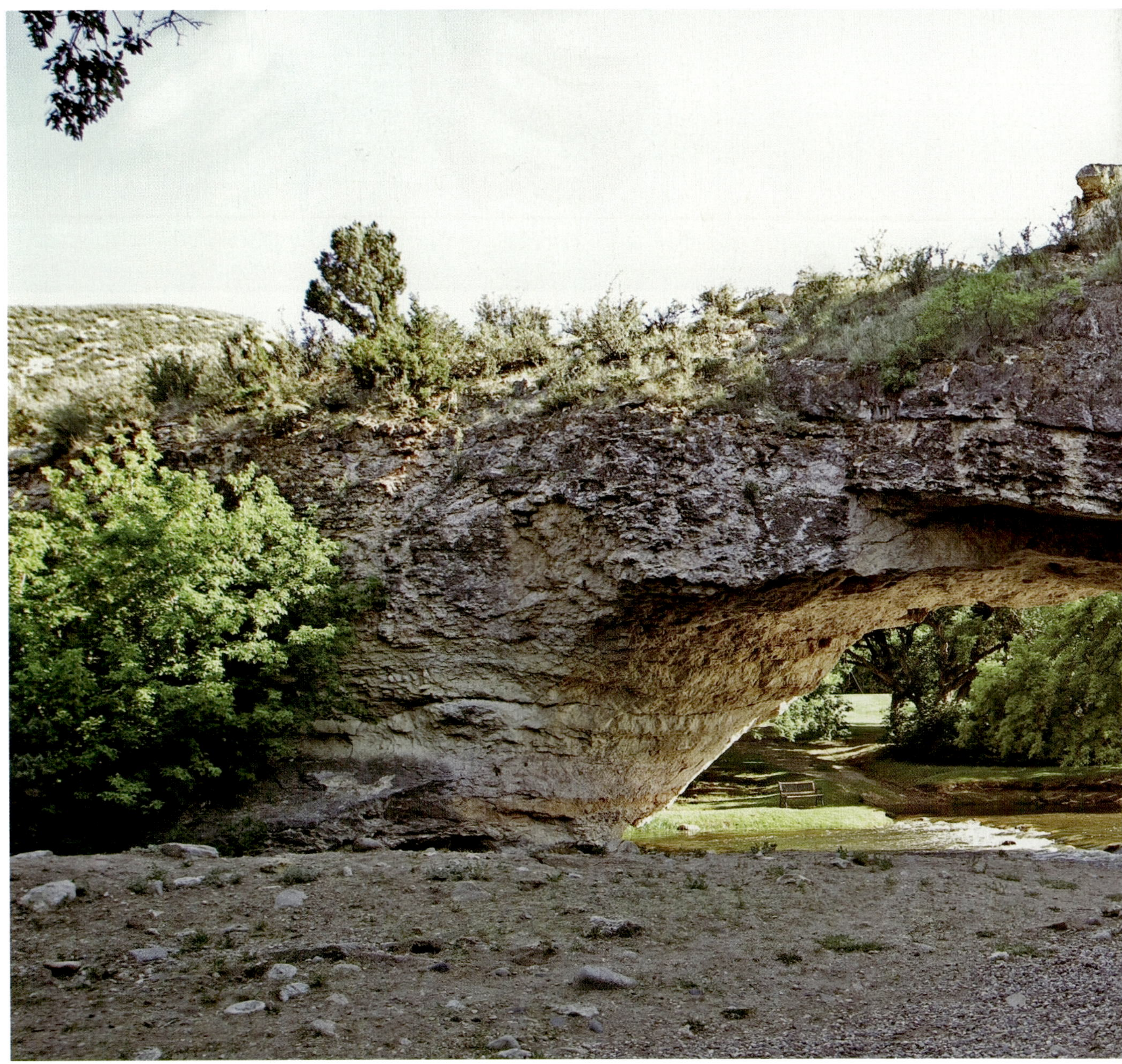

Devil's Tower, the Red Buttes near Laramie, Yellowstone, and the Tetons, Stimson's image of the Natural Bridge helped to push Wyoming's early tourism industry.

The site is now known as Ayres Natural Bridge, for early resident Alva Ayres who owned the area. In 1921 his family donated the land to Converse County to be used as a public park. Still a county park today, the site has a small campground, picnic area, and covered tables. A preserved power house from a local irrigation project is also located there. As discussed in chapter 3, the bridge's preservation as a county park makes it an unusual example of a sacred landscape in Wyoming.

My 2008 rephotograph shows the bridge looking about the same as it did a century ago. The water level in the creek is higher as a result of the controlled release from the upstream dam. To make my 2008 panoramic rephotography, I had to ask the children playing in the stream to stand still for a few moments so they would not end up on both sides of the image as I pivoted my camera.

Although most people probably associate the Black Hills with South Dakota, the western flank of their timbered mountains lies in northeastern Wyoming and includes Devil's Tower and the small towns of Sundance and Newcastle. In Stimson's day, the area was home to mostly cattle ranching and coal mining. Sundance, the seat of Crook County, had begun in 1879 as a trading post for area ranchers. In 1889 the Chicago, Burlington, and Quincy Railroad built into the area farther south to tap into the coal mining town of Cambria, and the new community of Newcastle was born. When Weston County was carved out of the southern half of Crook County, Newcastle became its seat.

Stimson visited the Black Hills of Wyoming during his 1903 survey of the state for the St. Louis World's Fair. He made both scenic landscape pictures touting

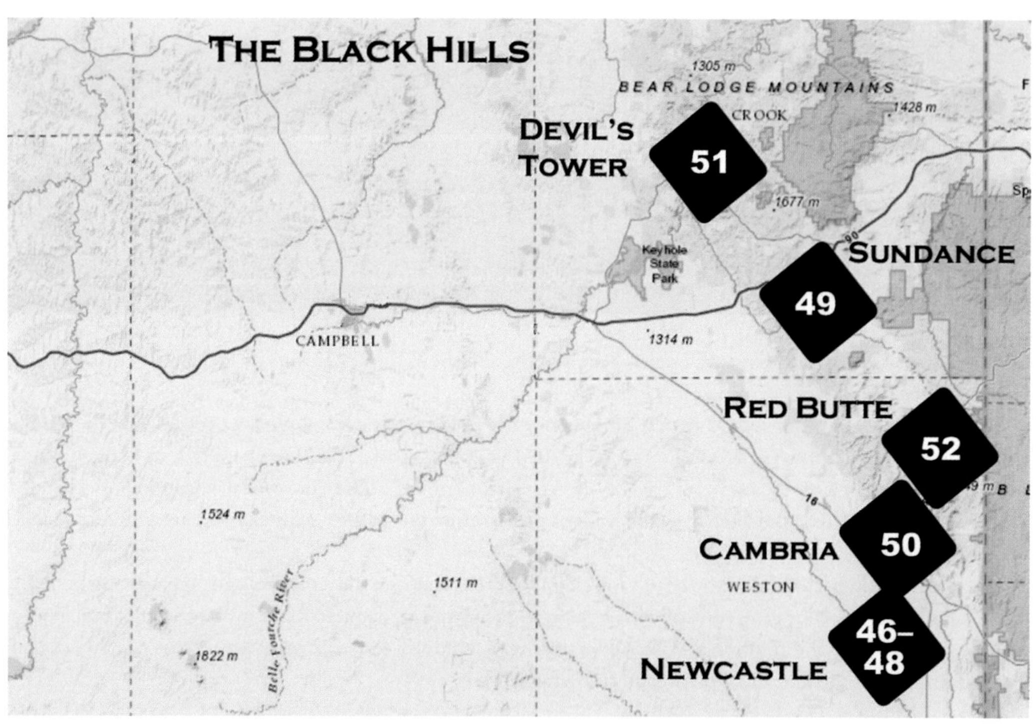

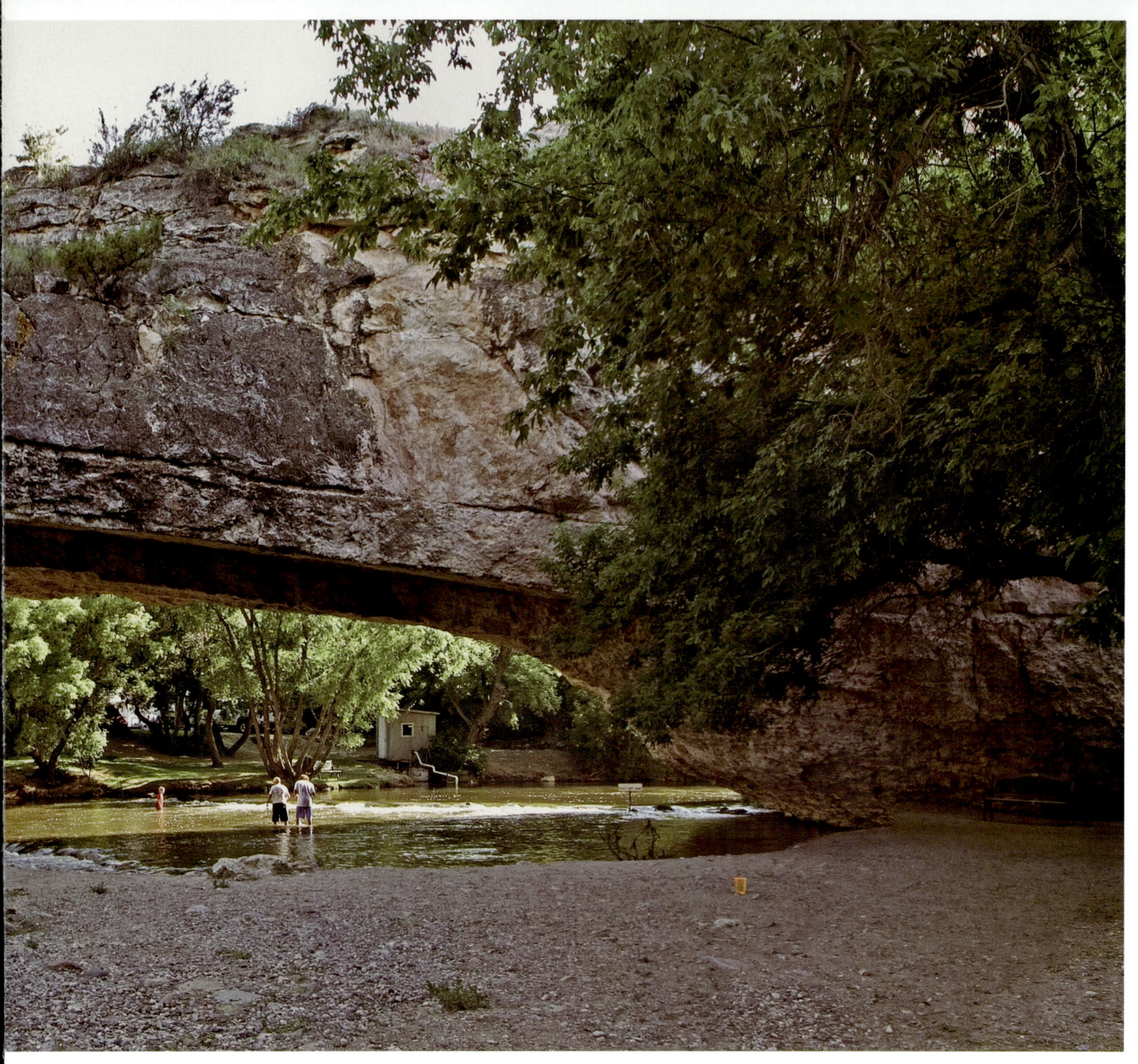

tourist possibilities, with images of Devil's Tower and the Red Butte, as well as photographs promoting the area's towns and economies. Stimson's photographs of Devil's Tower show the area three years before President Theodore Roosevelt made it the country's first national monument. His photographs of the area's three largest communities—Newcastle, Cambria, and Sundance—include both bird's-eye views and street scenes.

I rephotographed the Black Hills in 1988 and again in 2008. The most interesting site each time was Cambria because so much had changed. Access there required special permission from the landowner and a guide to get me to the site. Each time, locals went out of their way to accommodate me.

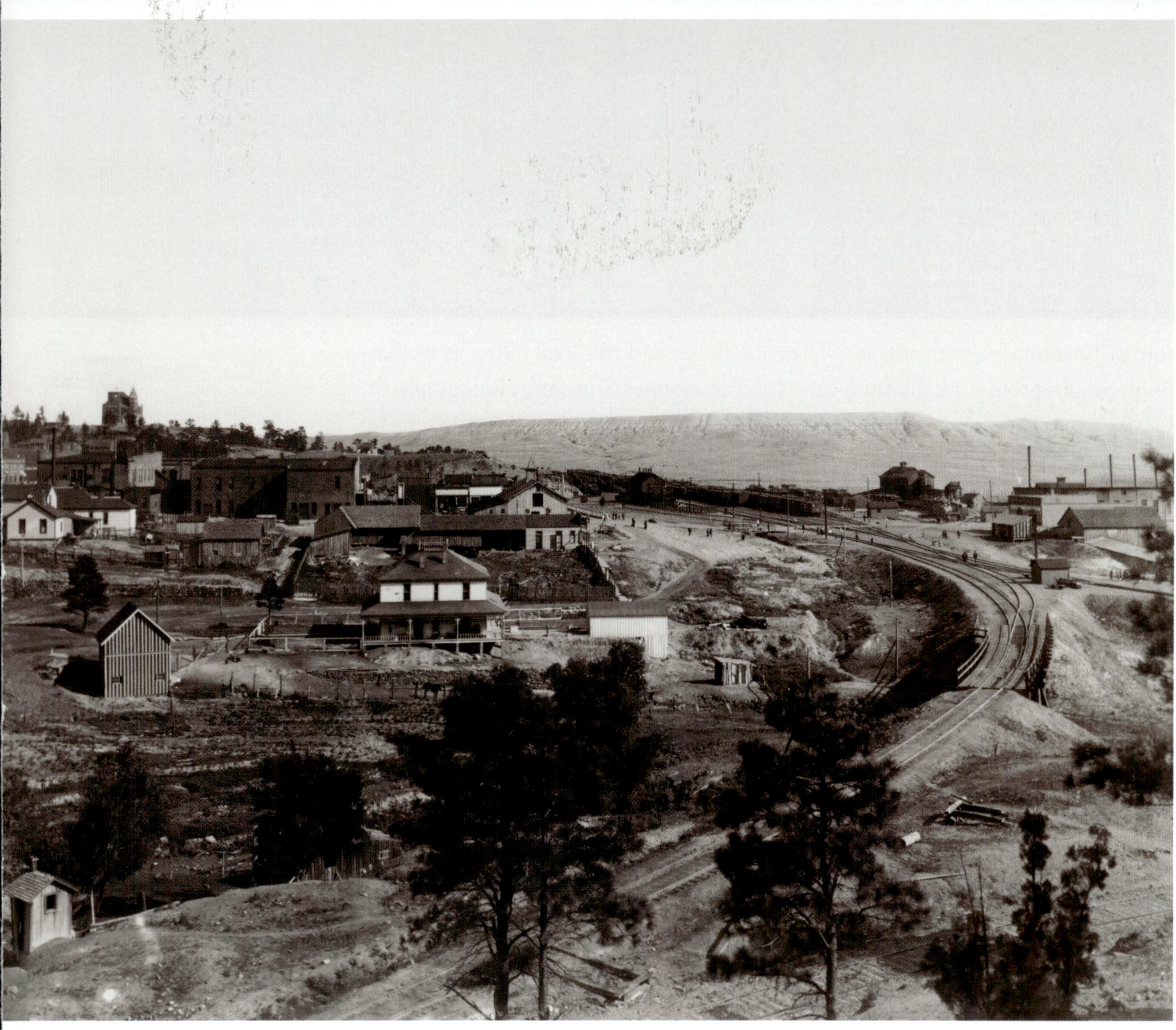

46. #436

Panoramic View of Newcastle, 1903, 2008
GPS COORDINATES: 43 51.40967N, 104 12.4295W

The Chicago, Burlington, and Quincy built Newcastle in 1889 as the line tapped into the nearby coal deposits at Cambria. As with many Wyoming towns, Newcastle's early days were rough, with nearby cowboys, miners, and railroad workers often competing to see who could be the rowdiest. Within a year of Newcastle's founding, the Wyoming legislature carved Weston County from Crook County and named Newcastle the new county seat. The town's most famous resident was Frank Mondell, onetime sheriff and longtime Wyoming congressman, serving during the periods 1895–97 and 1899–1923. By the time Stimson visited during his 1903 survey of the state to prepare images for the St. Louis World's Fair, the town had a population of about 800.

Stimson took this remarkable panorama from a hill northwest of downtown. Mondell's house sits on the hill at left and the Newcastle school on the center hill, directly opposite the vantage point. To the right, the railroad's

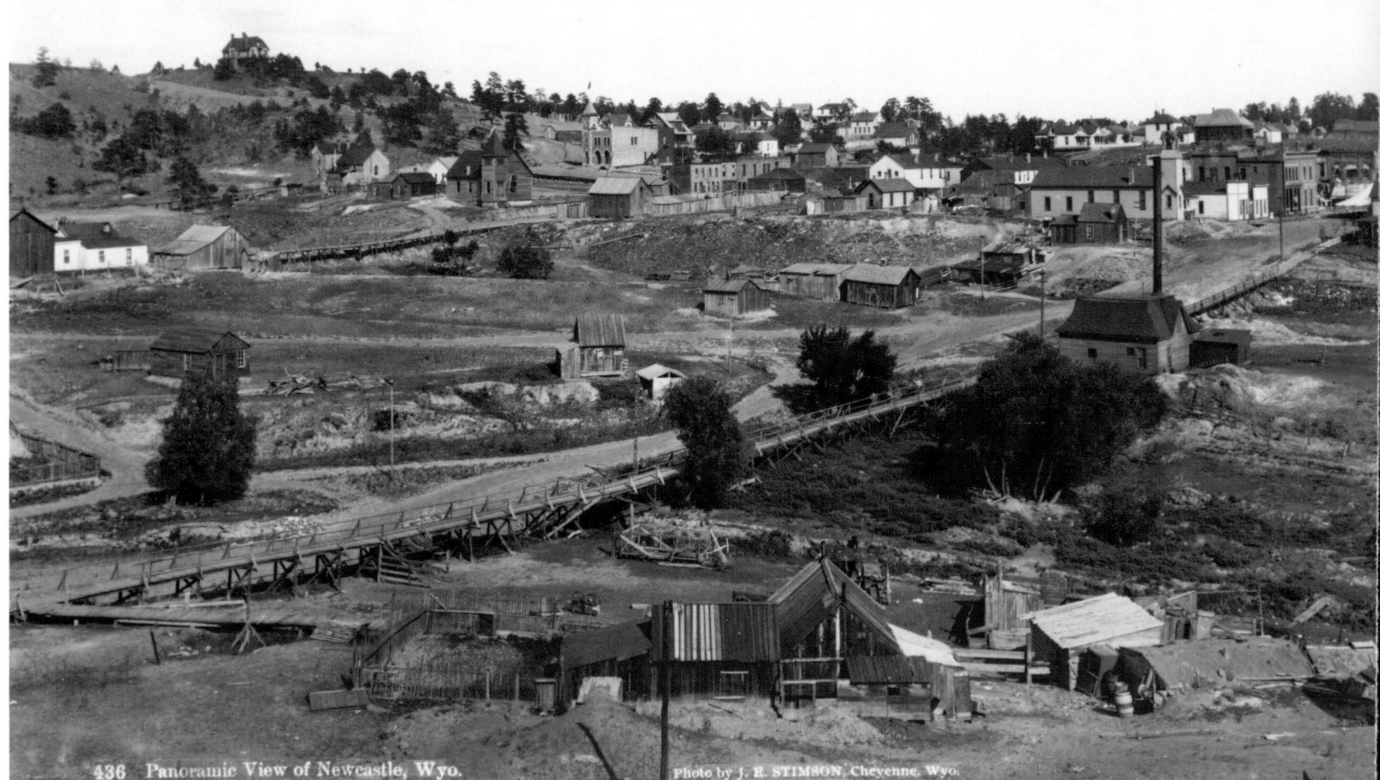

436 Panoramic View of Newcastle, Wyo.
Photo by J. E. STIMSON, Cheyenne, Wyo.

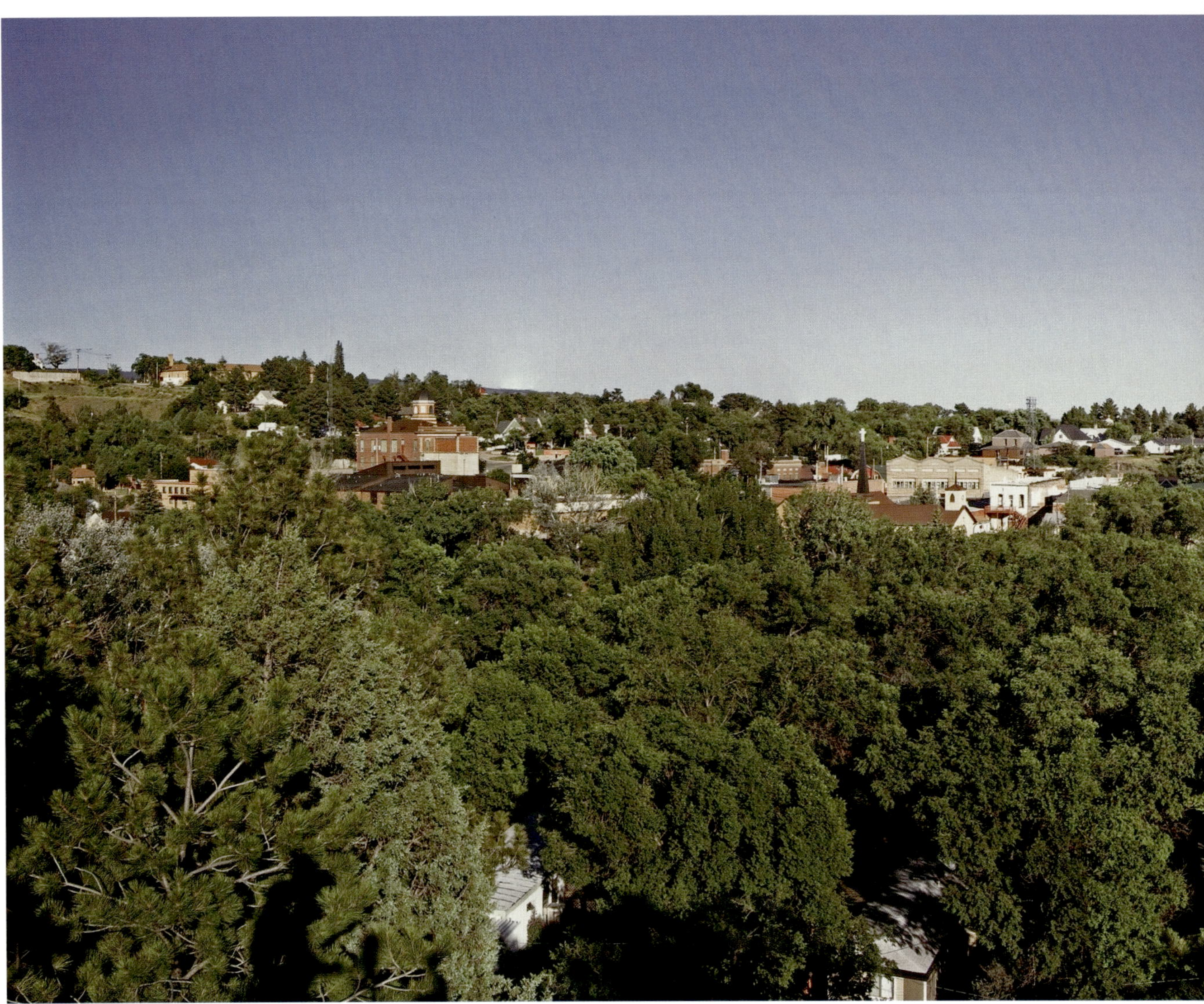

switch directs traffic off the main line toward Cambria. The commercial district lies in the center of the photograph; the backs of half its buildings are toward Stimson. The Weston County Courthouse is at the left end of the Main Street. In between these key places, the everyday life of early-twentieth-century Wyoming can be seen. Houses, churches, the depot, and an elevated sidewalk are visible.

I shot my 2008 panoramic rephotograph from the side of a hill near a large antenna northwest of downtown, just off Ackley Avenue. The most obvious change is the number of trees blocking out much of the view. Nevertheless, a close examination reveals Weston County Health Services on the far left hill and a hospital on land donated by the Mondell family. Moving left to right, the Weston County Courthouse is visible, as well as church steeples and the downtown business district. The tracks mark the railroad at right.

Like so many of his bird's-eye and panoramic images made in 1903, this one of Newcastle was designed to promote the town by including industry, government, education, and town life in one grand scene. But by doing so, Stimson captured a lot of everyday life as well. Therefore, his images, such as this panorama of Newcastle, are more than promotional photographs. They are also visual documents of the vernacular landscape and common scenes of normal everyday life.

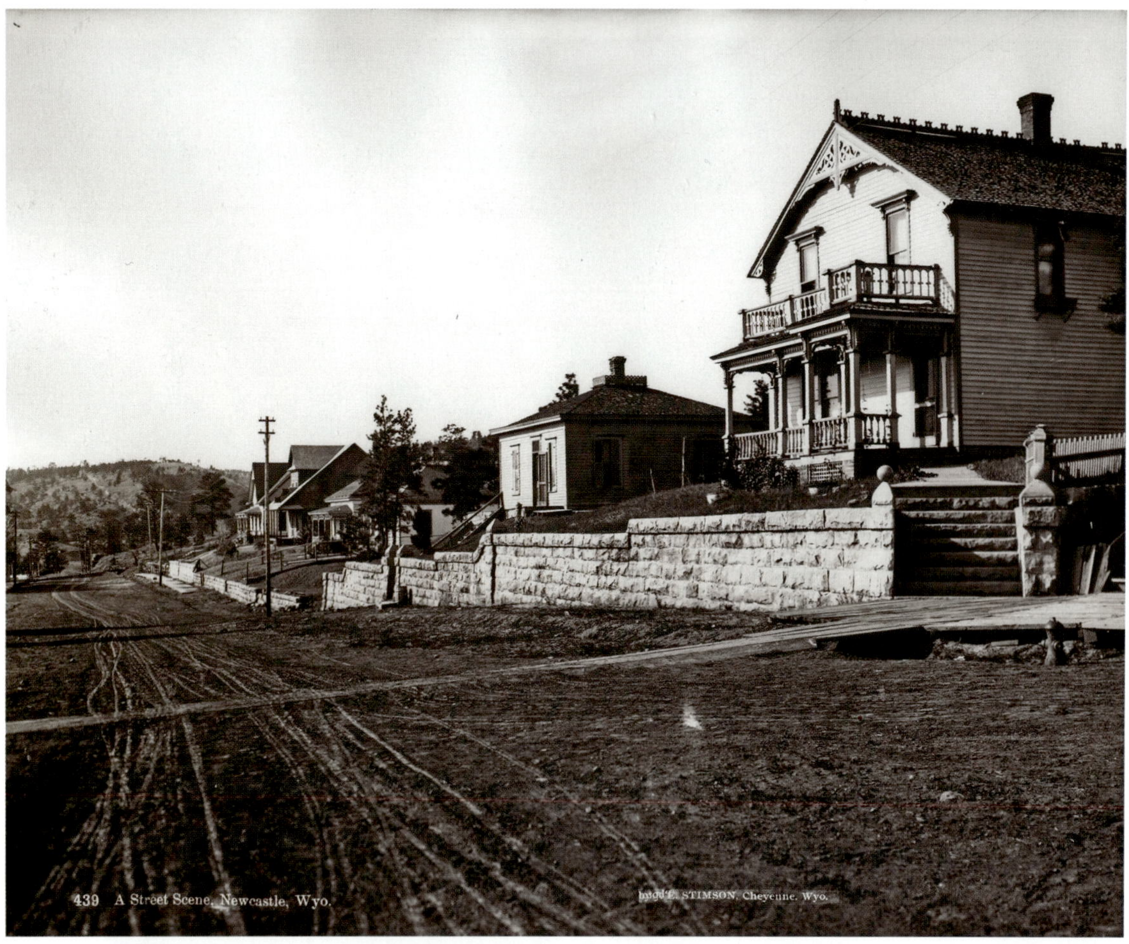

47. #439

A Street Scene in Newcastle, 1903, 1988, 2008
GPS COORDINATES: 43 51.22967N, 104 12.0373W

Residential neighborhoods were also an important focus for Stimson as he prepared images for the St. Louis World's Fair. Street scenes, houses, and hand-crafted stone walls such as this one looking north on Summit Street toward the downtown indicated stability and permanence, important factors to would-be investors. The gingerbread features on the house closest at right suggest that people in Newcastle were not only getting by but actually flourishing. By photographing from the top of the hill, Stimson also used the wall as a vanishing point, carefully leading the viewer deeper into the photograph.

Although trees block much of the view in both my 1988 and 2008 rephotographs, many of the original homes are still standing, as is the stone wall. The gingerbread house at right, sans the flourishes, is also there. Note the sign for the motels in my rephotographs, right. In 2008, Lauren and I had a delightful stay at the Pines, a refurbished 1950s motel three blocks north of Summit Street.

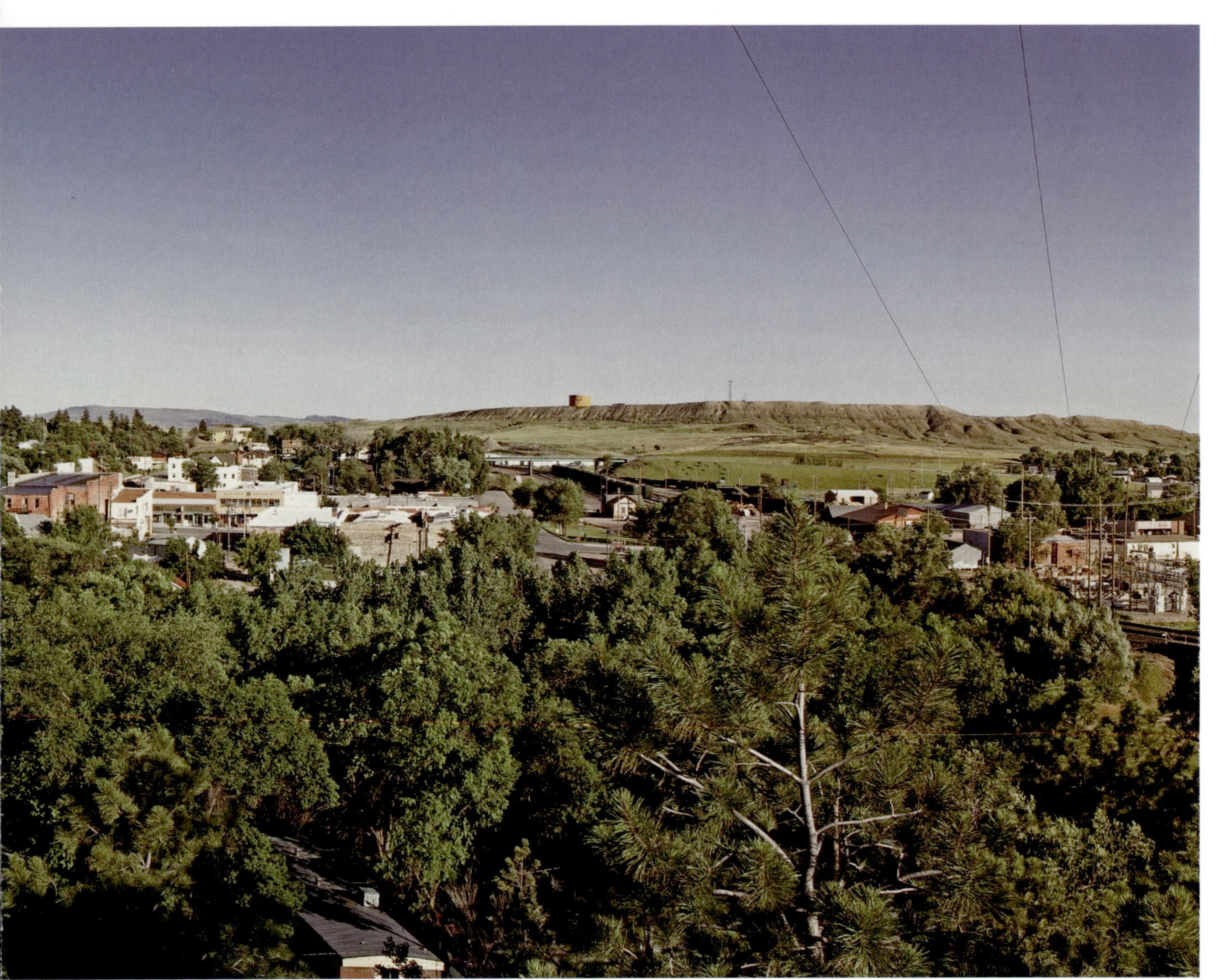

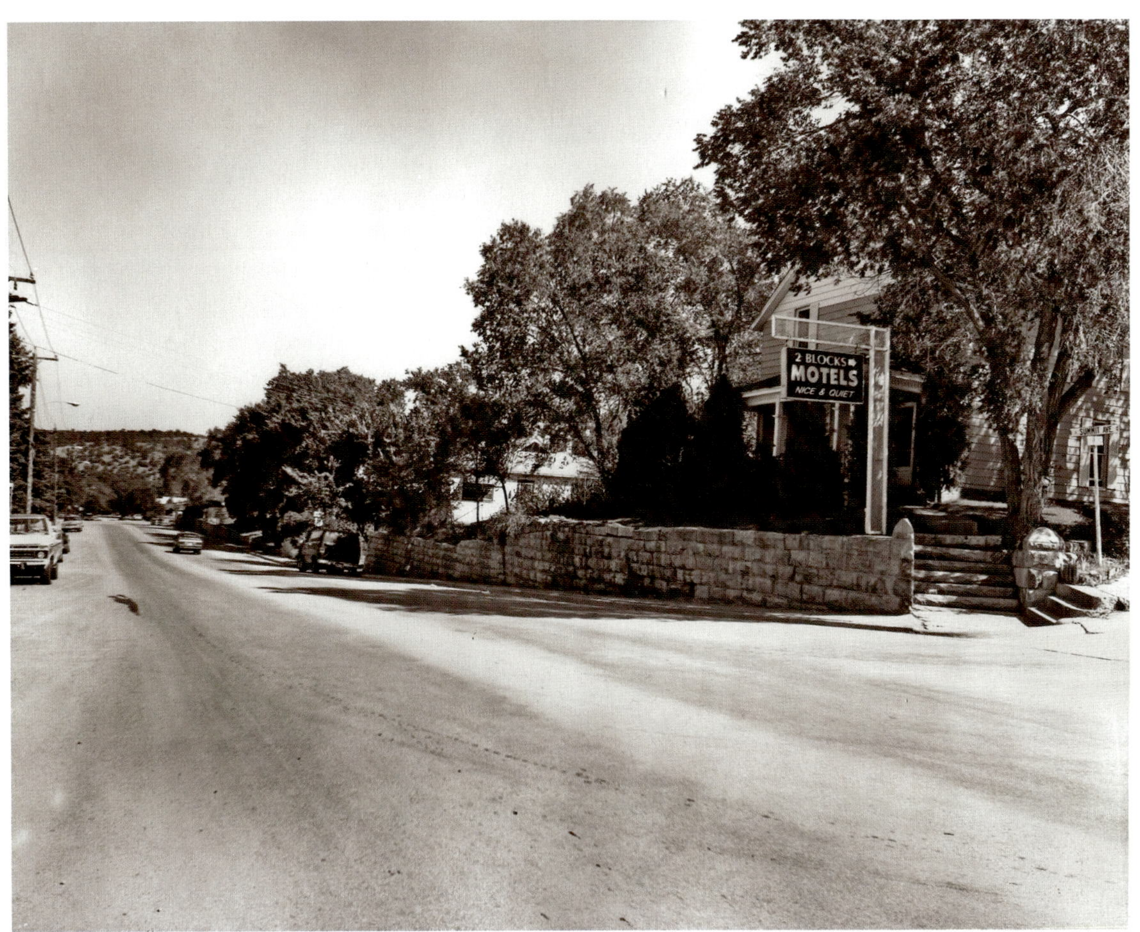
2 BLOCKS
MOTELS
NICE & QUIET

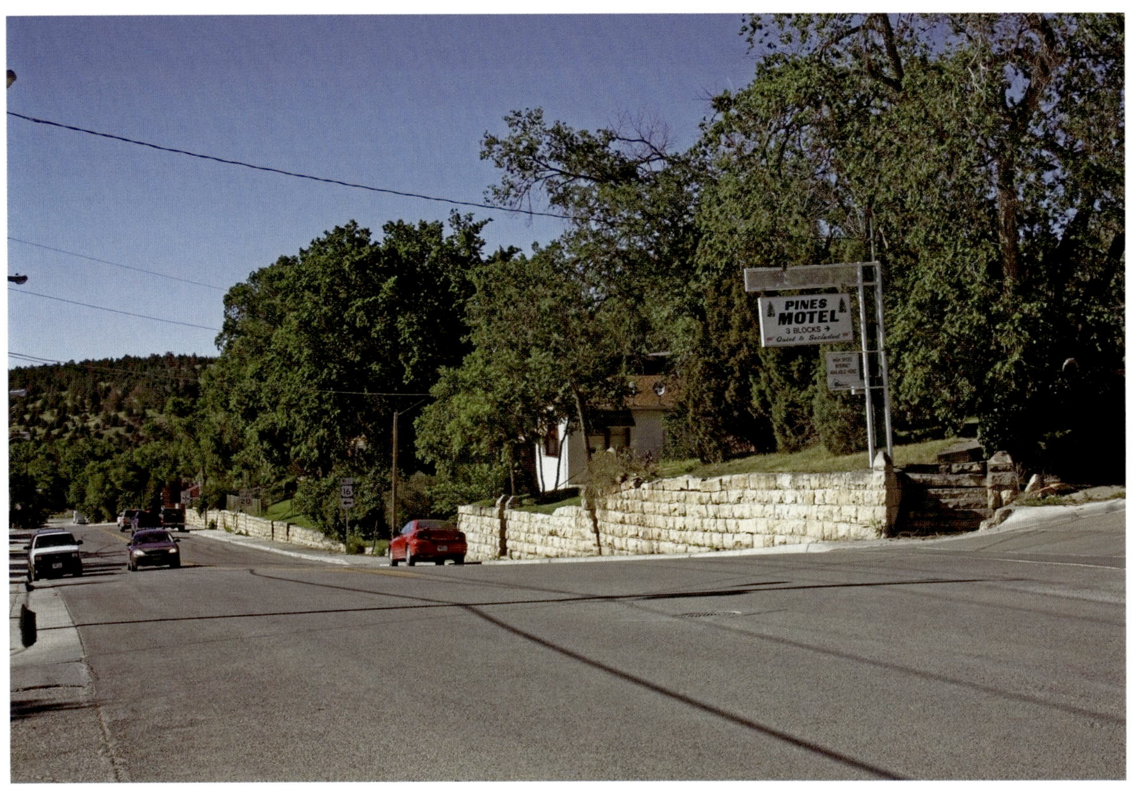
PINES
MOTEL
3 BLOCKS →
Quiet & Secluded

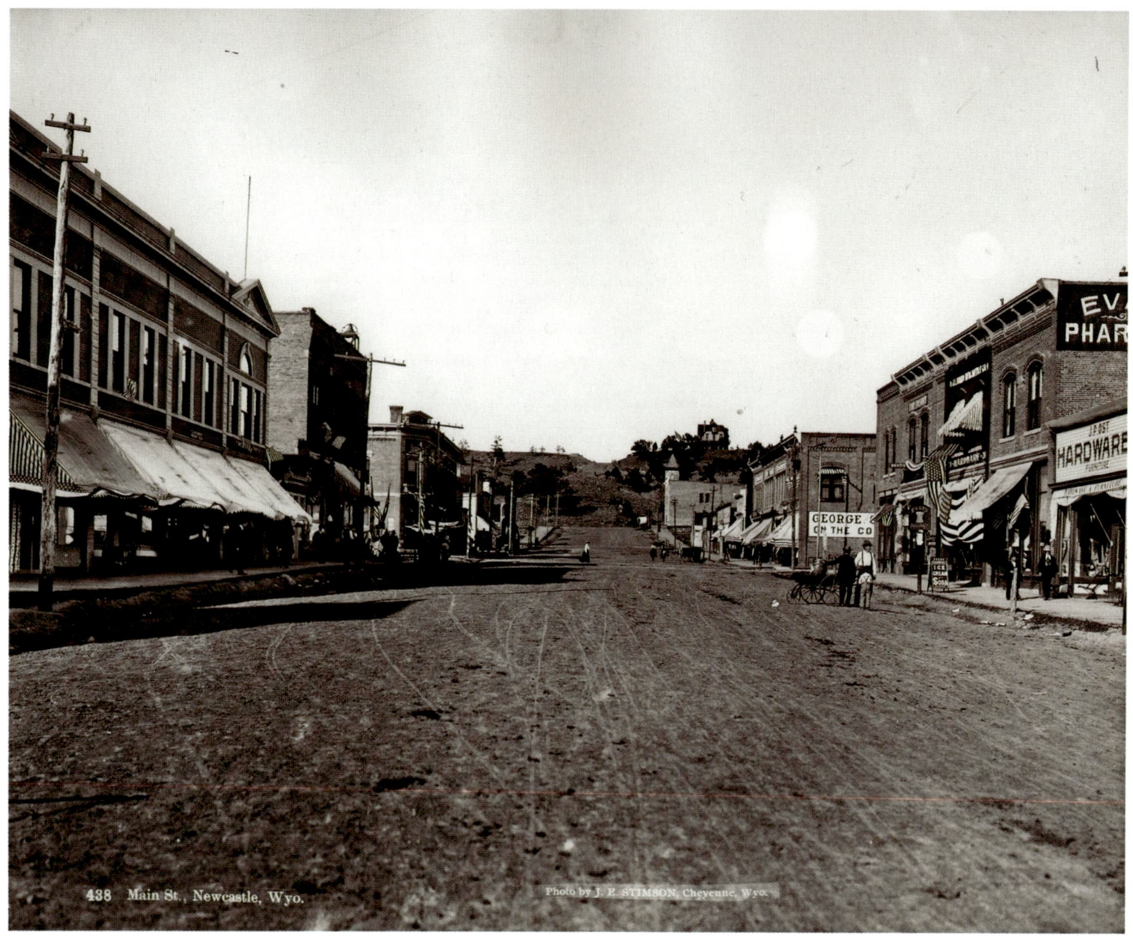

48. #438

Main Street, Newcastle, 1903, 1988, 2008
GPS COORDINATES: 43 51.259N, 104 12.3233W

This view of Newcastle looks east up Main Street toward Frank Mondell's home atop the hill. Main streets were an essential ingredient in Stimson's 1903 state survey. They not only depicted commerce, but brick buildings such as these in Newcastle suggested prosperity and permanence compared to the infamous false-front buildings often seen in the West. The telephone poles at left contributed to this progressive spirit. A hardware store can be seen, as well as another store that sold ice cream. The numerous flags and bunting at left suggest that perhaps a parade or some type of festival was about to commence.

My 1988 rephotograph shows that the Newcastle downtown remained a thriving economic center for the community. When I took this shot on a Saturday morning—with a policeman nearby to direct traffic around me—the streets were lined with cars (note the many gas guzzlers) and their passengers were patronizing the various businesses, including a Coast to Coast hardware, a café, and a men's clothing store, still housed in many of the same buildings. The Weston County Memorial Hospital can barely be discerned where Frank Mondell's home once stood.

My 2008 rephotograph was made on a much less busy day. Lacking a police escort, I darted into the street, took my photo, then darted back out. Again, many of the same buildings appear to be still standing and still housing businesses. Although Newcastle is not a member of Wyoming's Main Street Program to help re-develop and preserve downtowns, it looks a lot like those that are, with its new old-fashioned–looking streetlights, stoplights, and the careful preservation of downtown buildings.

Main Street Programs can be important factors in preserving and developing decaying, neglected, old downtowns. But so can continued use. With no mall to take business away from the downtown, Newcastle continues to use its downtown as it was intended. In so doing, the town has continually re-developed and protected its investment of more than a century ago, preserving its built environment along the way.

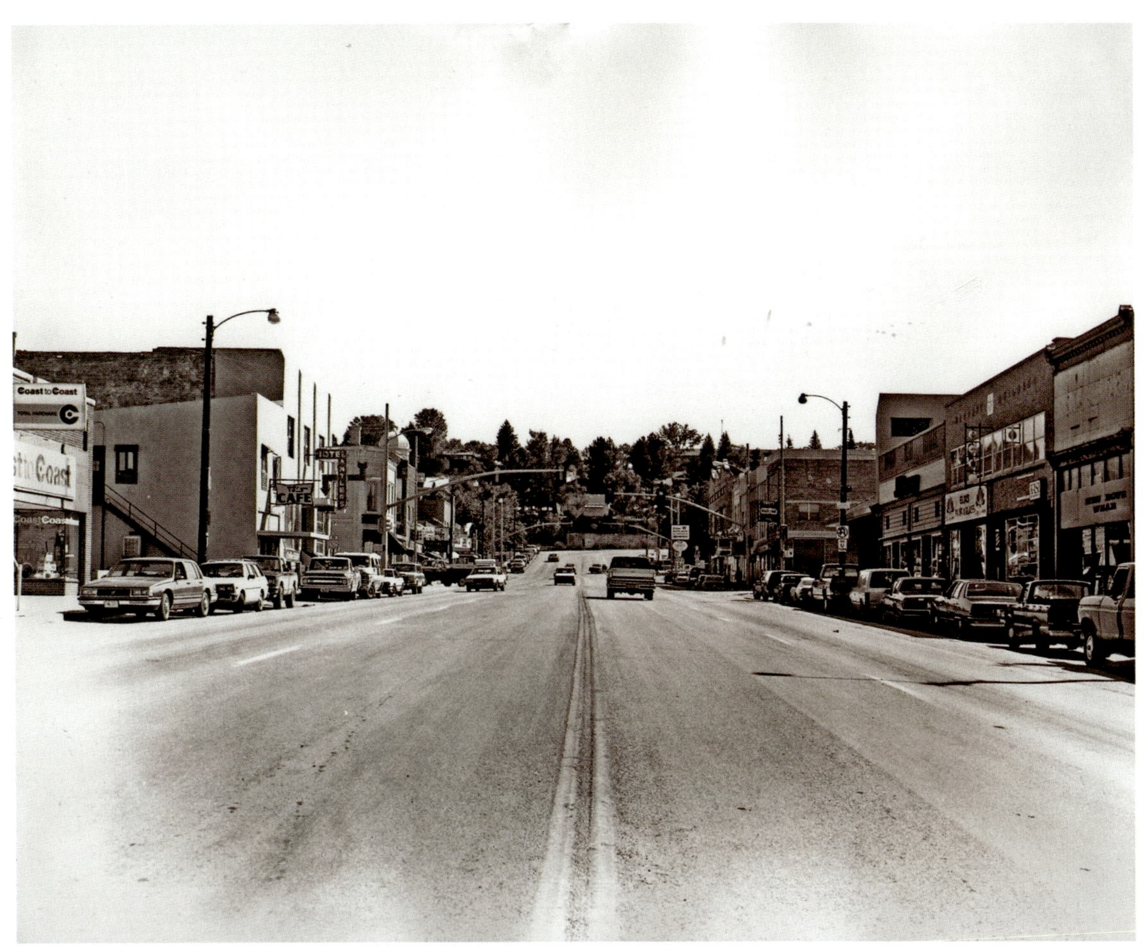

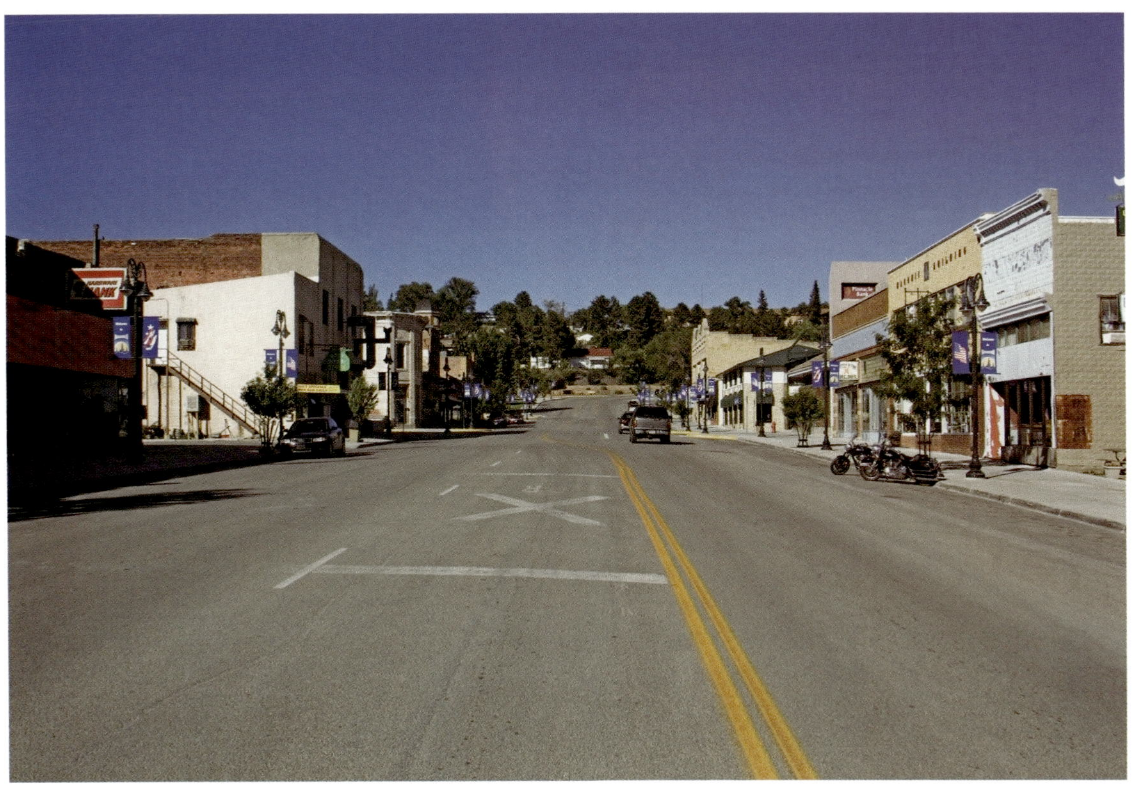

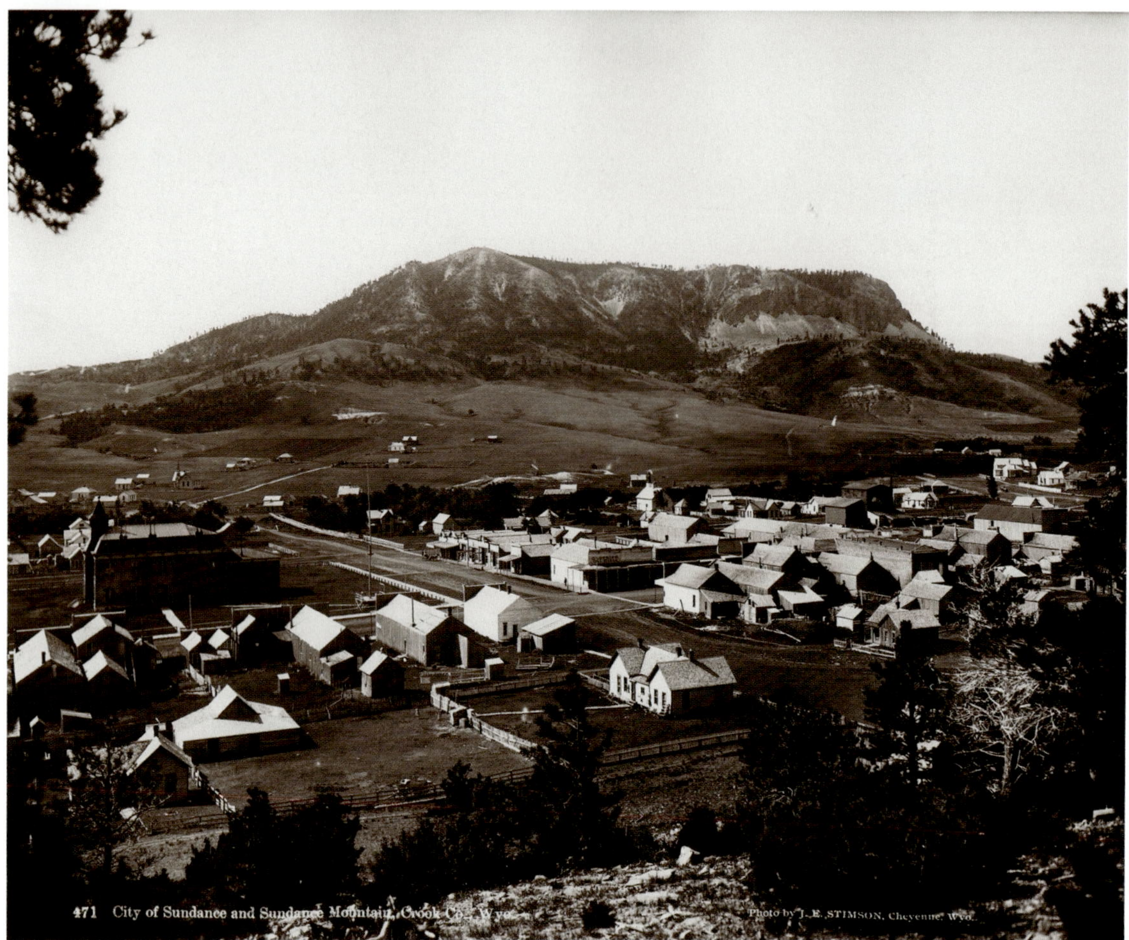

49. #471

City of Sundance and Sundance Mountain, 1903, 1988, 2008
GPS COORDINATES: 44 24.4725N, 104 22.809167W

The charming little town of Sundance sits at the base of its namesake mountain in a little valley of the Bearlodge Mountains. Established in 1879 as a trading post for area ranchers, the town is the seat of Crook County and is probably best known for convicting and jailing—until he escaped—nineteenth-century outlaw Harry Longabaugh, the Sundance Kid.

Although Stimson's 1903 photograph is another bird's-eye view, this one of Sundance is one of his best in terms of composition and lighting. Using Sundance Mountain as a backdrop, Stimson situated the town diagonally in his picture, with the pines from his vantage point framing the foreground and sides. The photo was taken in the early morning, and the warm eastern light bathes the left-hand roofs of the buildings. The Crook County Courthouse is at left and the small downtown in the middle right. In comparison to the many brick buildings visible in Stimson's view of Main Street Newcastle, this image of Sundance shows mostly wooden false fronts, with only one brick building to be seen. A few of the several hundred residents are visible on the board sidewalks.

Both my 1988 and 2008 rephotographs also captured the beautiful morning light and composition because I got out early and found the vantage point, a small hill on the north side of town. Sundance remains a small town, with over 1,000 residents. Although the courthouse was replaced in 1968, many of the homes in Stimson's picture are still standing. The downtown false fronts have been replaced by brick buildings, though it seems as though there are fewer in number. Sundance Mountain remains mostly undeveloped; in fact, the forest on the visible north slope seems fuller today than it was a century ago.

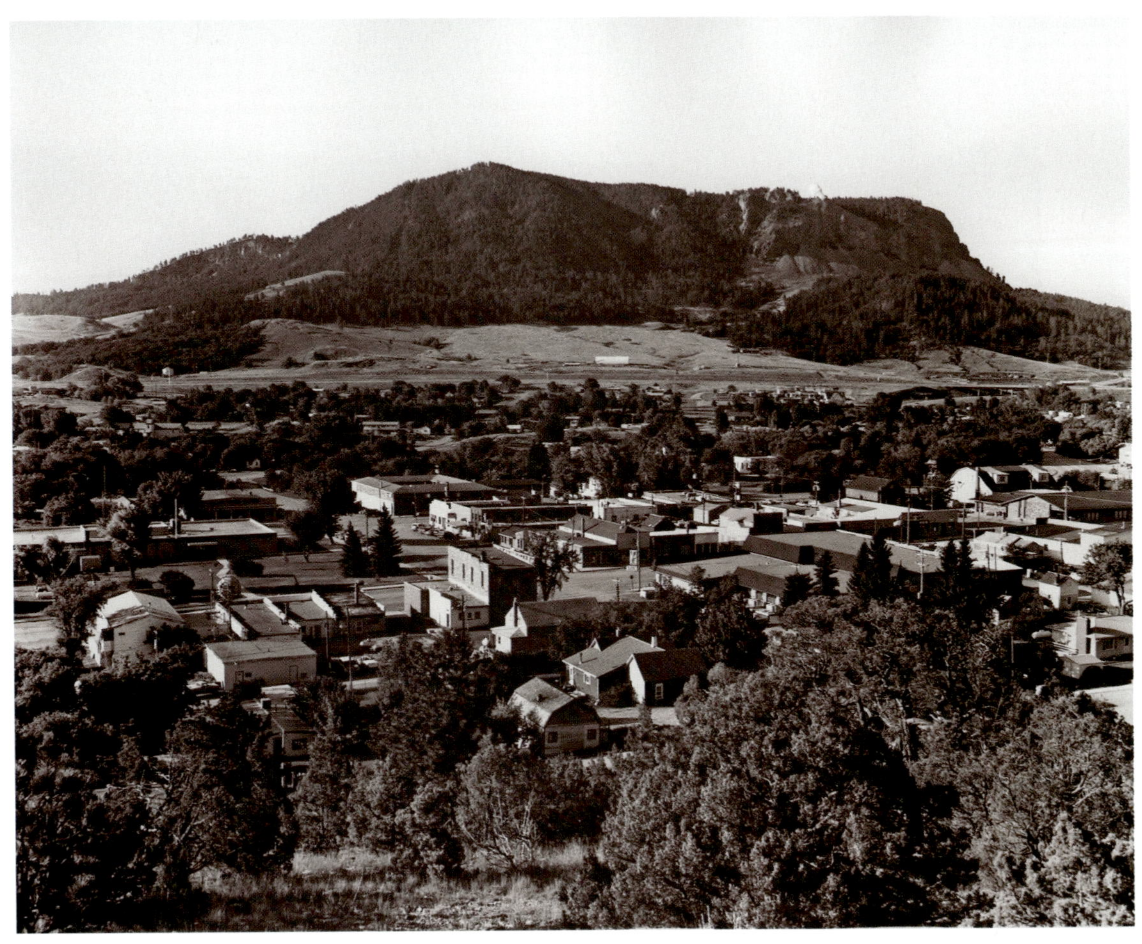

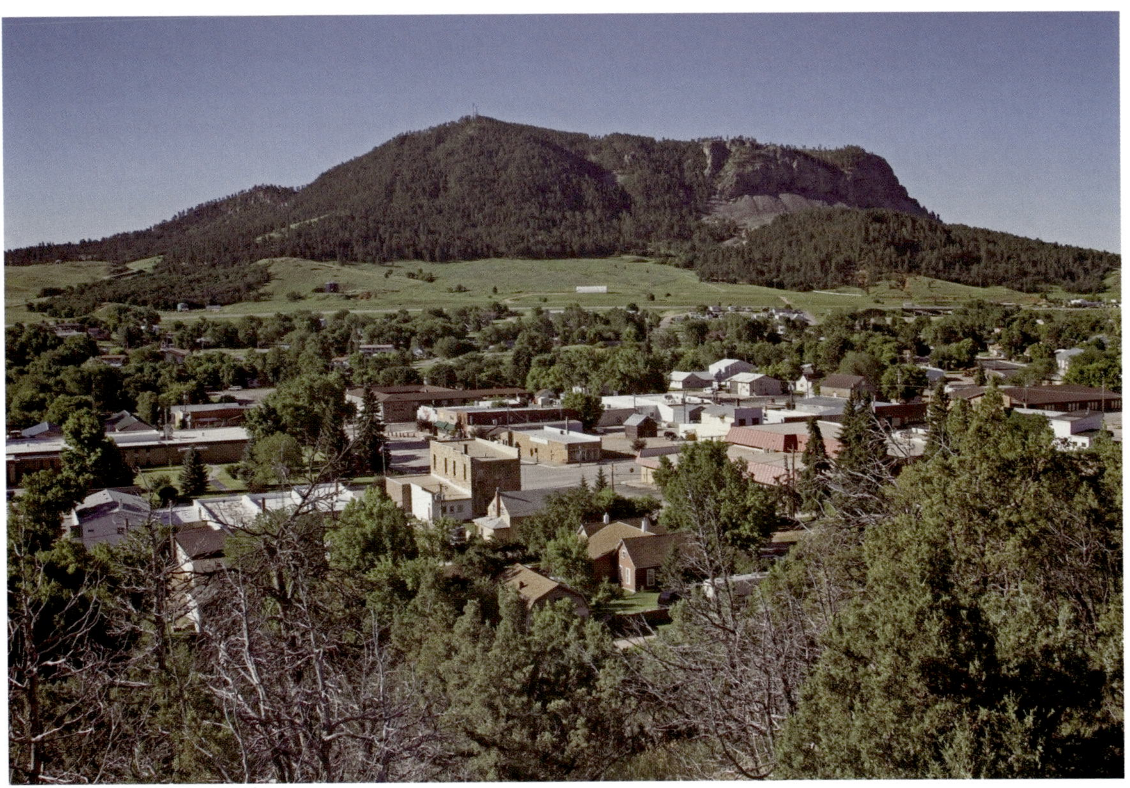

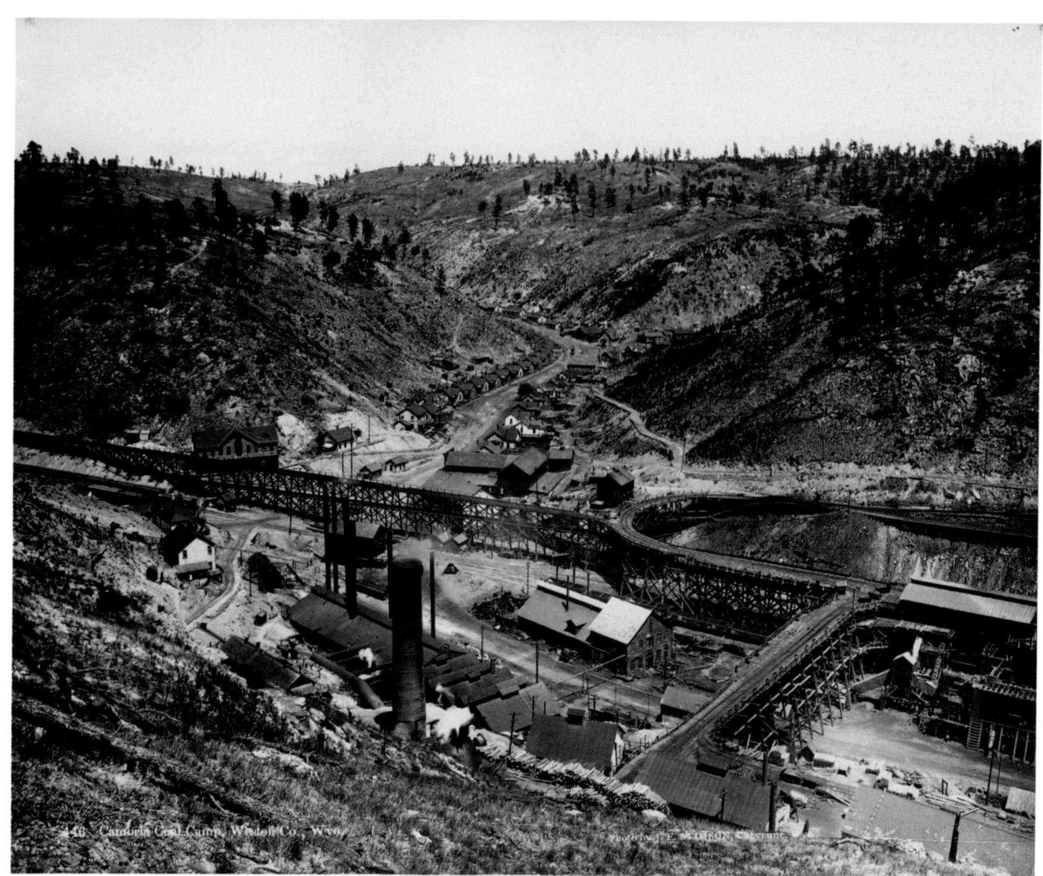
446 Cambria Coal Camp, Weston Co., Wyo.
Photo by J. E. Stimson, Cheyenne

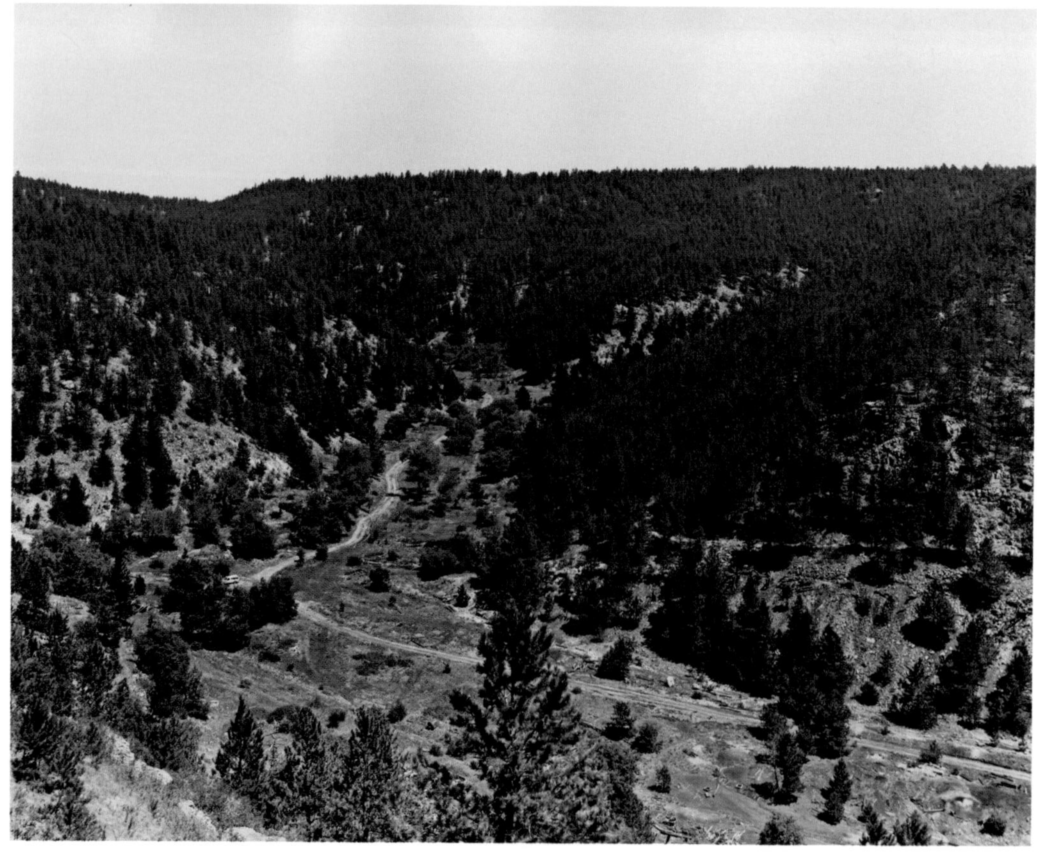

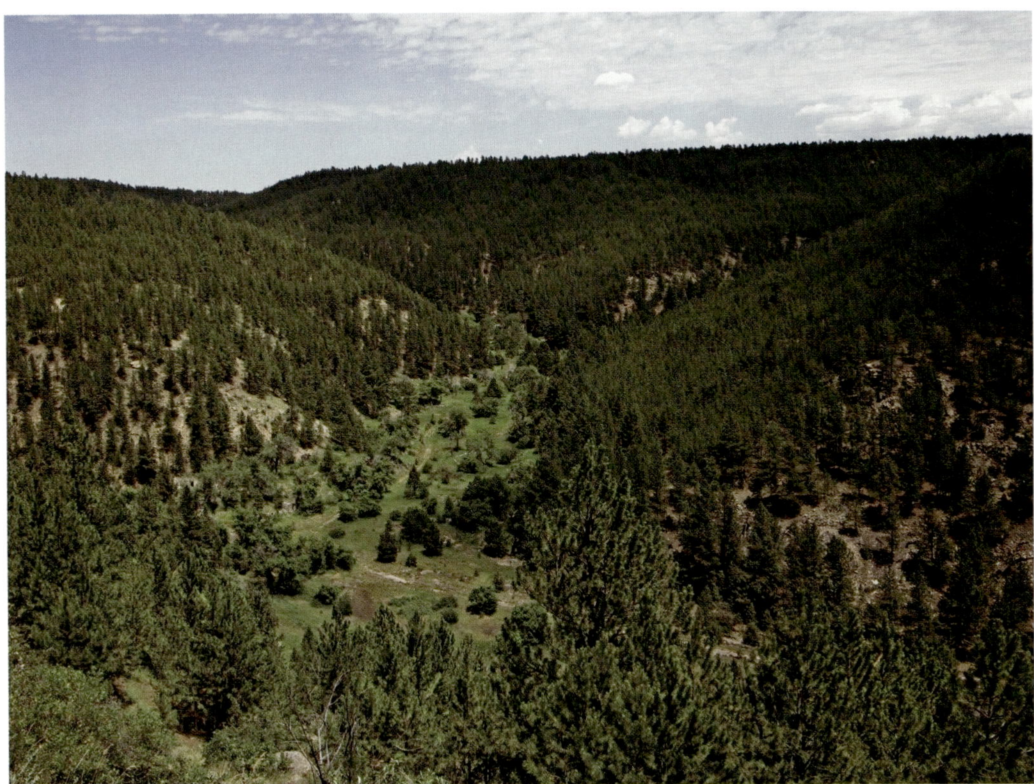

50. #446

Cambria Coal Camp, 1903, 1988, 2008
GPS COORDINATES: 43 56.297N, 104 12.637W

Cambria was a company town owned and operated by the contractors who built the Chicago, Burlington, and Quincy Railroad into the area. It was founded in 1887 when Frank Mondell discovered anthracite deposits and was reached by railroad in 1889. By 1903 the population was about 1,400. Like most company towns, Cambria was dry and had a cosmopolitan citizenry—both of which resulted from deliberate company actions intended to control labor, in the latter case by hiring workers of many nationalities who tended not to intermingle. As was also the case in many company towns, the workers were paid in company scrip redeemable only at the company store. Houses were located throughout the canyon floor and were connected to the hilltop school by long staircases that made students walk 365 steps in each direction. Cambria also boasted its own town band, three fraternal orders, a gymnasium, and several churches.

Stimson photographed Cambria during his 1903 survey and pointed his camera "up canyon" from above the Antelope Mine's enormous coal tipple. The company store is partially seen at left. The main housing district curves up the canyon, center. Note the denuded hillsides. Although they lived in a coal town, residents often burned wood, and the mine used it for timbering. As with many of his industrial photographs, this one used a bird's-eye view vantage point to capture the whole scene and make comprehensible an otherwise bewildering place.

By the spring of 1928 the coal deposits had failed, and the company closed both the mine and the town. Buildings were hauled into Newcastle or scavenged by locals. Many others vanished.

Both my 1988 and 2008 rephotographs show that little of Cambria remained. In 1988, a man I met at the wonderful local museum guided me down the road to the bottom of the canyon (note my white pickup, left), and I hiked up to Stimson's vantage point. Although the main street was visible, little else remained. The forest had grown back substantially.

In 2008, Lauren and I met the property owner who ranches the Cambria site. He led us on a wild pickup chase through forest and field along the top of the canyon almost to the cemetery. We then hiked down to the vantage point. The forest looked thicker still. As far away from the world as I felt at that moment, I'll always remember our guide telling us proudly what great cell phone coverage he had in Cambria.

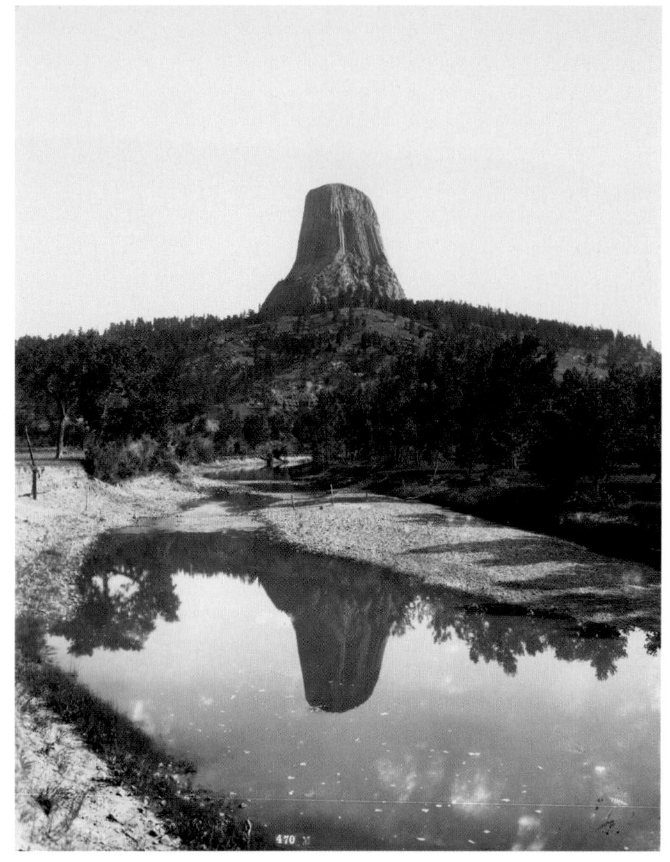

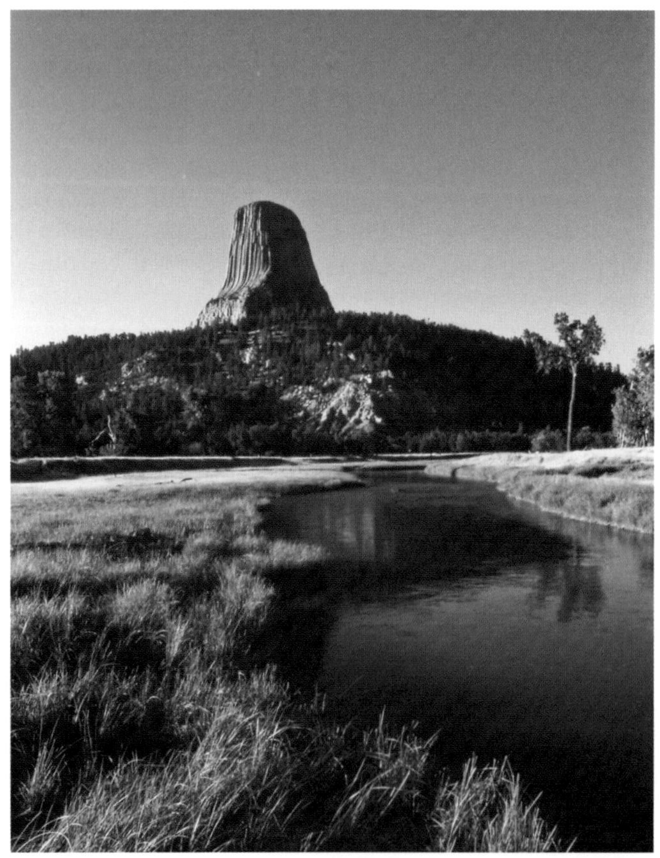

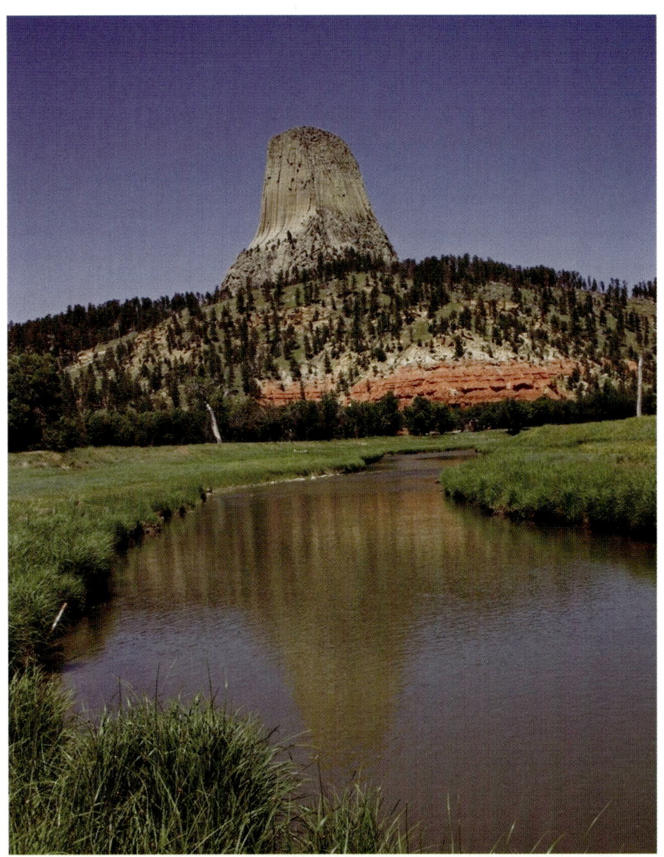

51. #470

Devil's Tower from Belle Fourche River, 1903, 1988, 2008
GPS COORDINATES: 44 34.741833N, 104 43.058833W

Although President Theodore Roosevelt, supported by Wyoming congressman and Newcastle resident Frank Mondell, made Devil's Tower the first US national monument in 1906, the 1,267-foot-high igneous intrusion has a long cultural history that made it a key place for Stimson to photograph in 1903. Plains Indian tribes—including the Arapaho, Cheyenne, Crow, Kiowa, Lakota, and Shoshone—all have cultural and geographical ties to the tower. The first American to describe it was Col. Richard Dodge in 1875. After the Sioux Wars ended in 1877, the area opened for white settlement, though the federal government took increasing actions to protect the unusual formation. When a homestead that included the tower was filed for in 1890, the General Land Office ordered that all such claims be rejected. In 1892 the president successfully set the tower aside as a temporary forest reserve, but the US Congress failed in its proposal to make the tower a national park later that same year.

While all this was happening in Washington, locals made the tower a destination for picnics and camping excursions. The most famous staged event was the 1893 Fourth of July celebration that included the first known climb to the top, by area rancher William Rogers. Two years later Rogers's wife became the first woman to ascend it.

All of this pre-monument history suggests that when J. E. Stimson visited Devil's Tower, he was not photographing some unknown formation but a place with a long cultural history. His image, taken from the south along the banks of the Belle Fourche River, frames the tower dead center, like a personal portrait. His use of the river for reflection gives the image an element of artistic composition. A rare hand-tinted version of this photograph hangs in the Cheyenne Masonic Lodge.

The period after the tower became the first national monument saw it involved in more cultural issues, including the building of tourist infrastructure and debates over sacredness that led to today's voluntary ban on climbing during the month of June to respect tribal traditions. The tower also played an iconic role in the movie *Close Encounters of the Third Kind.*

Although my two rephotographs show the tower is basically unchanged since Stimson's day, closer examination reveals that the forest in front of the tower is denser in 1988 than in 2008, probably because of prescribed burns on the monument in the early twenty-first century.

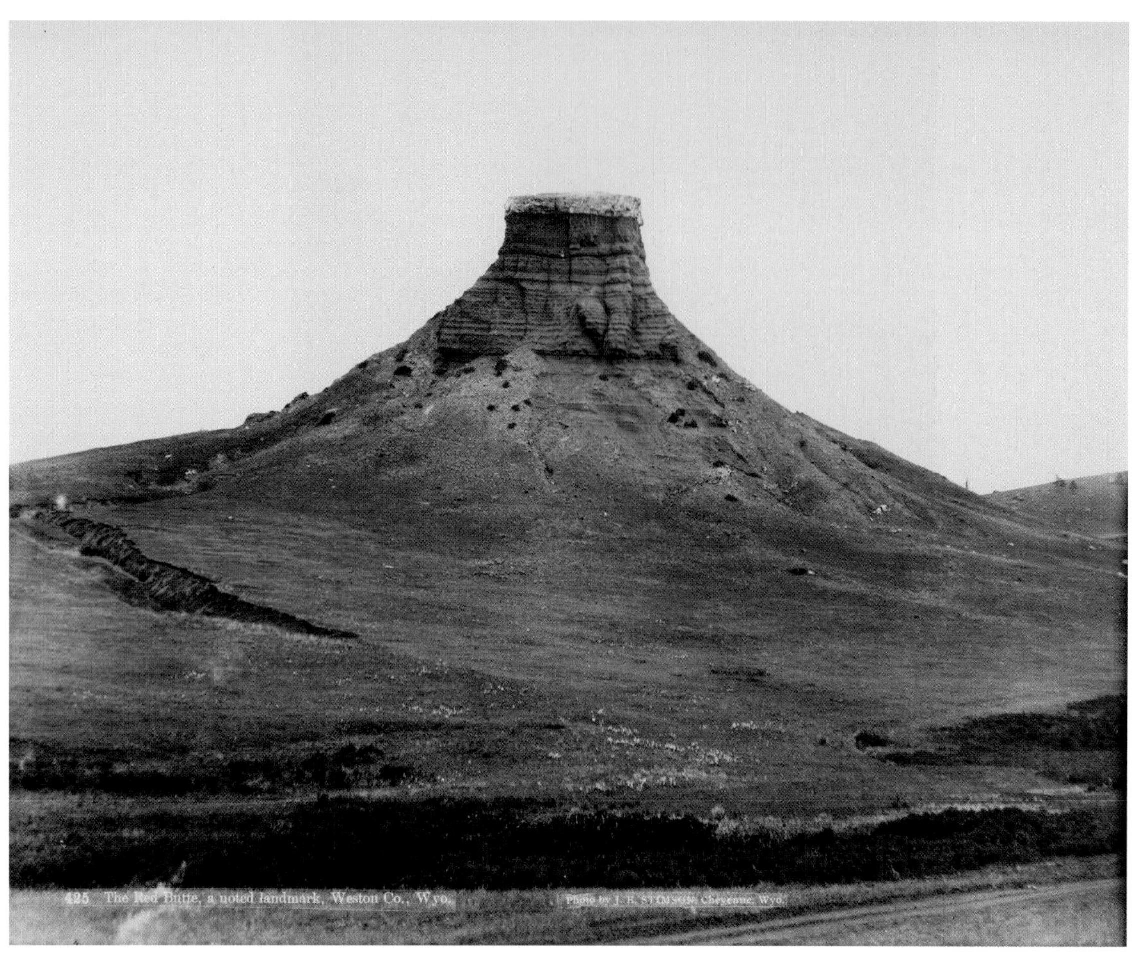

425   The Red Butte, a noted landmark, Weston Co., Wyo.
Photo by J. E. STIMSON, Cheyenne, Wyo.

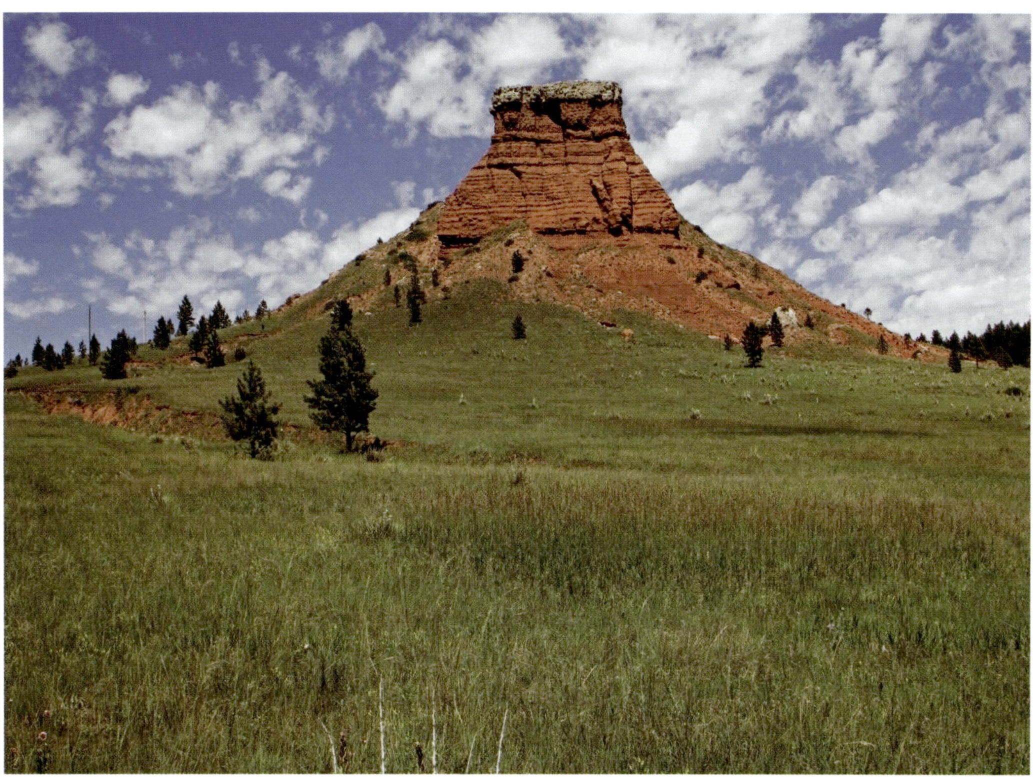

52. #425

The Red Butte, a noted landmark, Weston Co., 1903, 2008
GPS COORDINATES: 44 0.66533N, 104 10.11467W

If, as Stimson wrote on his negative, the Red Butte is indeed "a noted landmark in Weston County," I have found no evidence as to who noted it and why. Located north of Newcastle just to the east of State Highway 85 before the intersection with Highway 585 on the way to Sundance, the formation does not appear on state maps; nor does a Google search bring up anything "of note."

Stimson photographed the butte in the summer of 1903 while photographing nearby ranches in Weston County. The red shale formation with the white gypsum cap must have struck a fancy, so he decided to photograph it. He shot it looking to the northeast and framed the butte high in the center of his negative in a portrait-style format. Grass at the base of the hill appears short, perhaps from grazing, and a small eroded channel can be seen at the left base.

When looking through possible images to rephotograph, I added this view in 2008 because I thought it might be fun to find, and if it actually was "a noted landmark," there might be an interesting story as well. Lauren and I found it easily on our drive to Sundance and immediately photographed it. To do so, I wandered away from the current highway perhaps no more than a quarter of a mile. My view shows the hill basically intact, with the same eroded channel at left, a few more trees, and perhaps longer grass. My rephotograph is actually quite stunning, with the green grass and a few pines leading up to the red hill set against a clear blue sky punctuated with bright white clouds.

Red Butte appears to be part of Wyoming's profane landscape, discussed at length in chapter 3. Never protected by any government body, the butte has remained pretty much the same over the decades because of its isolation.

The area just east of the Big Horn Mountains, especially Sheridan and its hinterlands, was also one of J. E. Stimson's prime locations. Recall that pictures of the area brought to him by Elwood Mead in 1894 were one of the reasons Stimson began to turn from portrait to scenic photography. The Cheyenne artist first traveled to the Big Horns in 1895. Although his initial attempts were mostly overexposed, the area was imprinted on him as a place to return. He came back in 1899 and photographed Sheridan and Dome Lake. In 1903, during his survey of the state for the St. Louis World's Fair, Stimson photographed the area's main towns of Buffalo and Sheridan but also captured the nearby ranches and mining towns of Big Horn, Beckton, Ranchester, Fort Mackenzie, and Dietz. He was back in 1908, 1909, and 1910, photographing the mining town of Kleenburn and the Dome Lake resort.

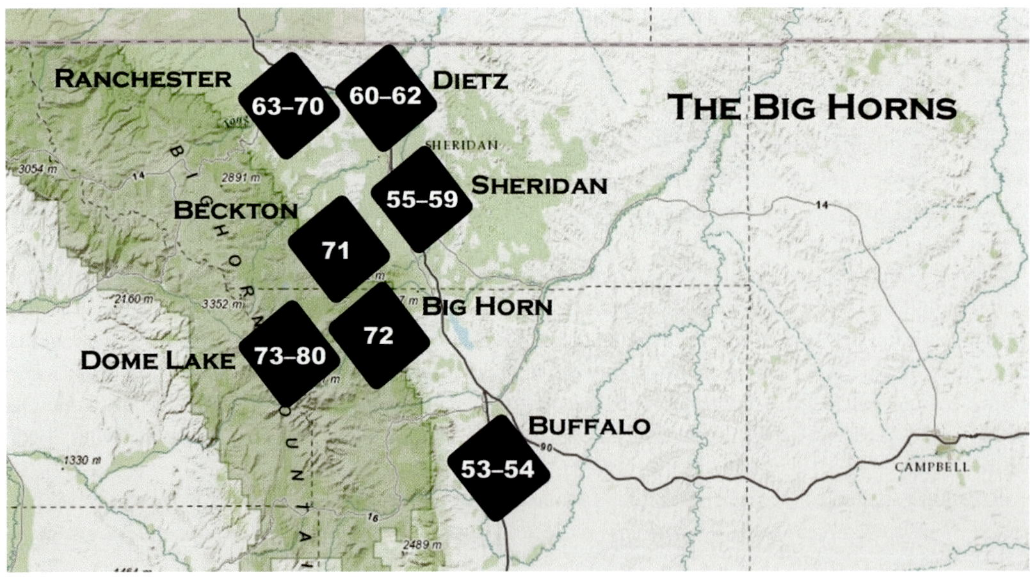

During the first few decades of the twentieth century, Sheridan served as the business and transportation hub of the mining, ranching, and resort industries. It had its own inter-urban rail line running north to the small Tongue River Valley mining camps. The town also served as a jumping-off place for wealthy easterners and Europeans coming to enjoy the growing number of dude ranches to the west and on top of the mountains.

I have long been fascinated by Sheridan and its hinterlands. My first foray into the area during my 1988 rephotography project got me interested in Dome Lake, Dietz, and the other small mining towns north of Sheridan. I eventually did my master's thesis on the polo-playing town of Big Horn. This time around, as discussed in chapter 5, the Hardin Ranch in Ranchester proved most fascinating.

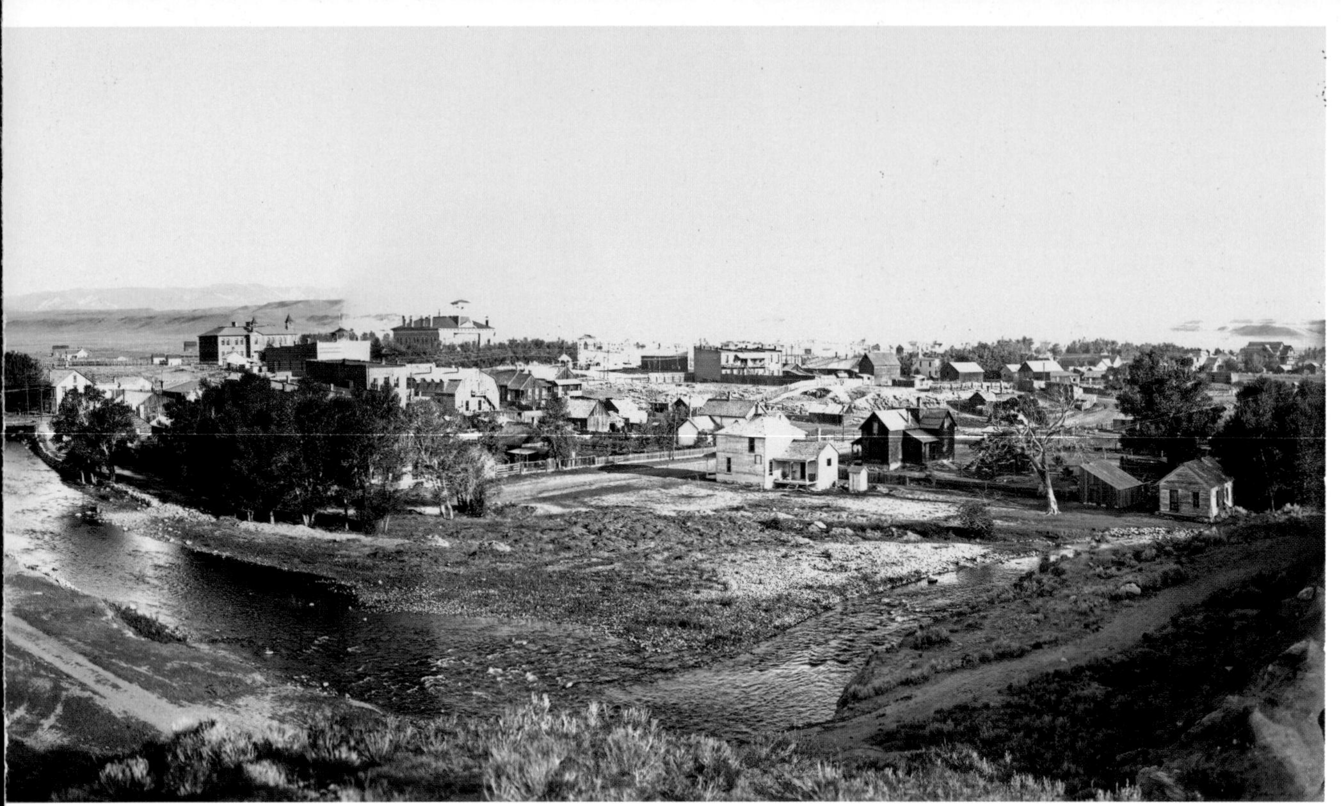

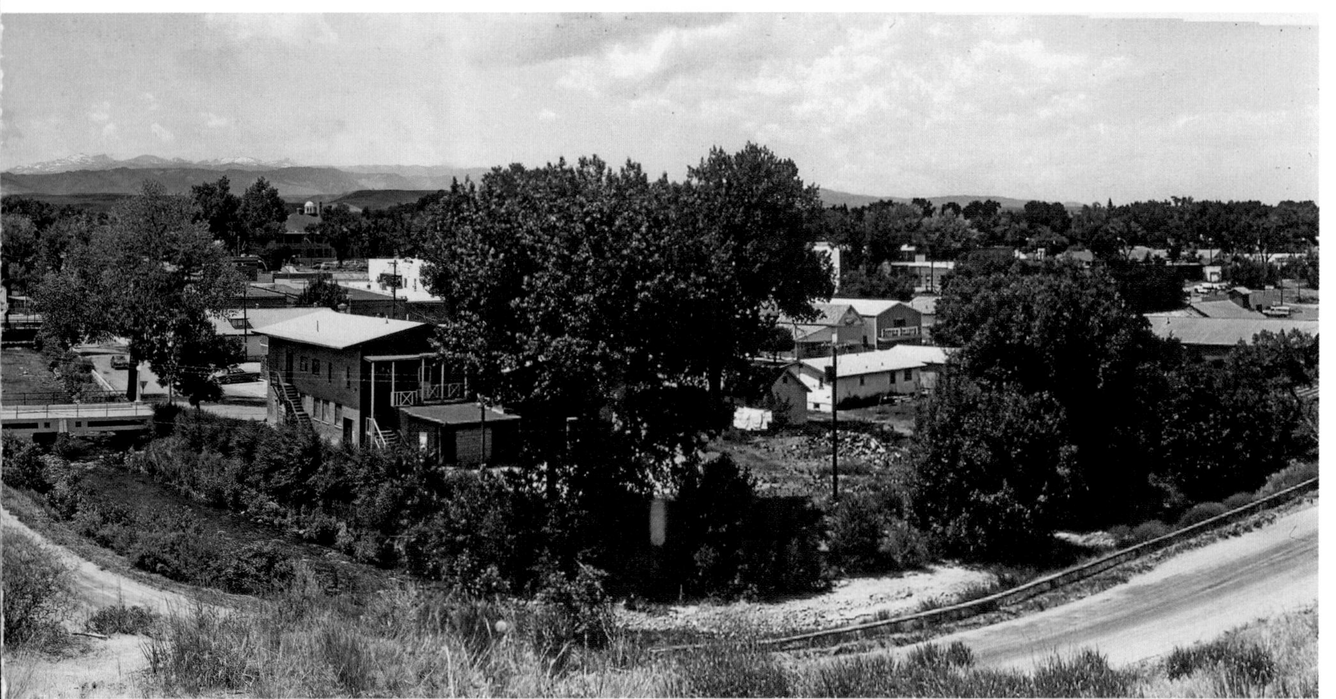

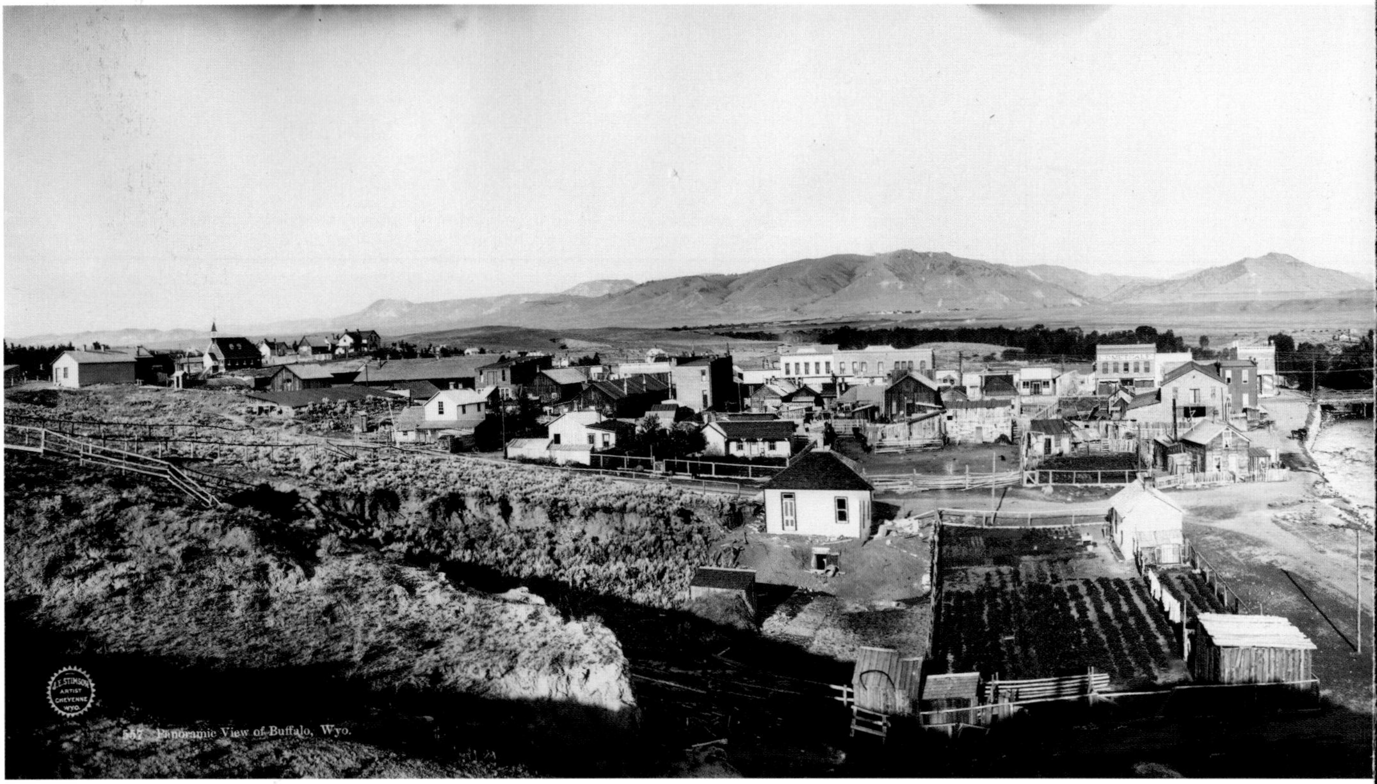

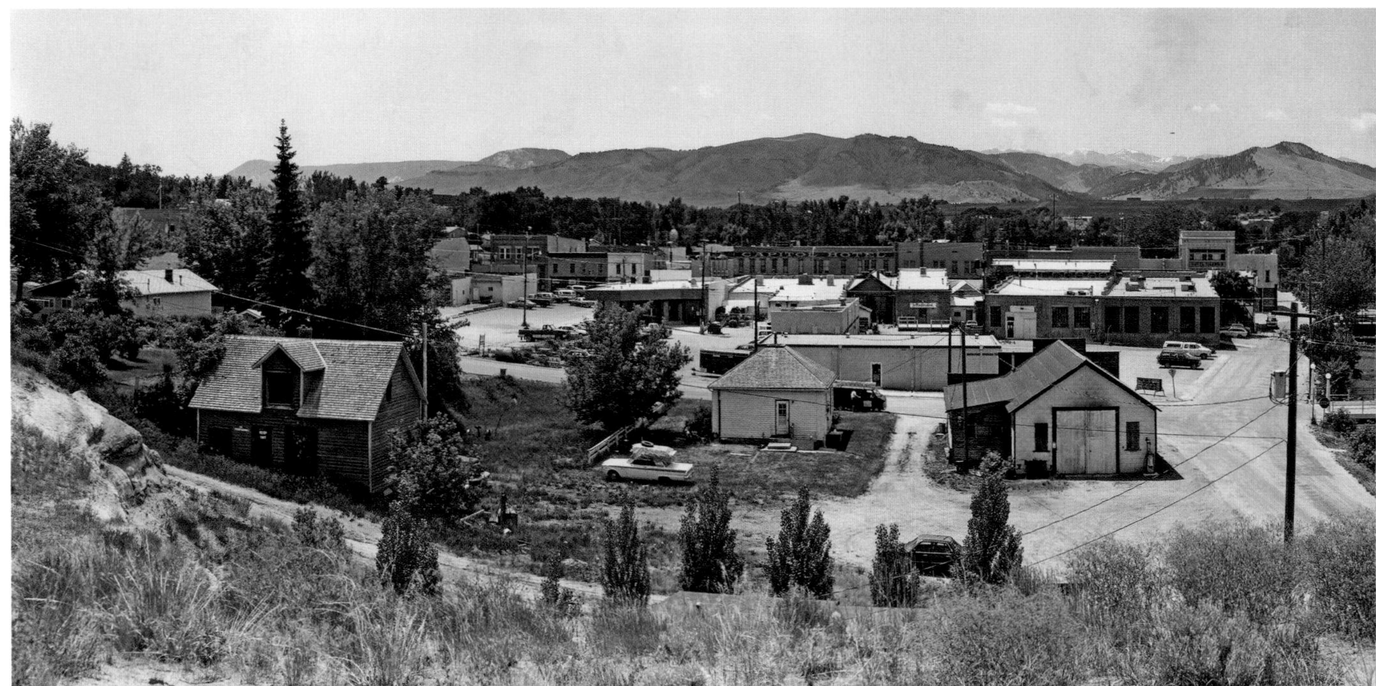
J. E. STIMSON
ARTIST
CHEYENNE
WYO.
557   Panoramic View of Buffalo, Wyo.

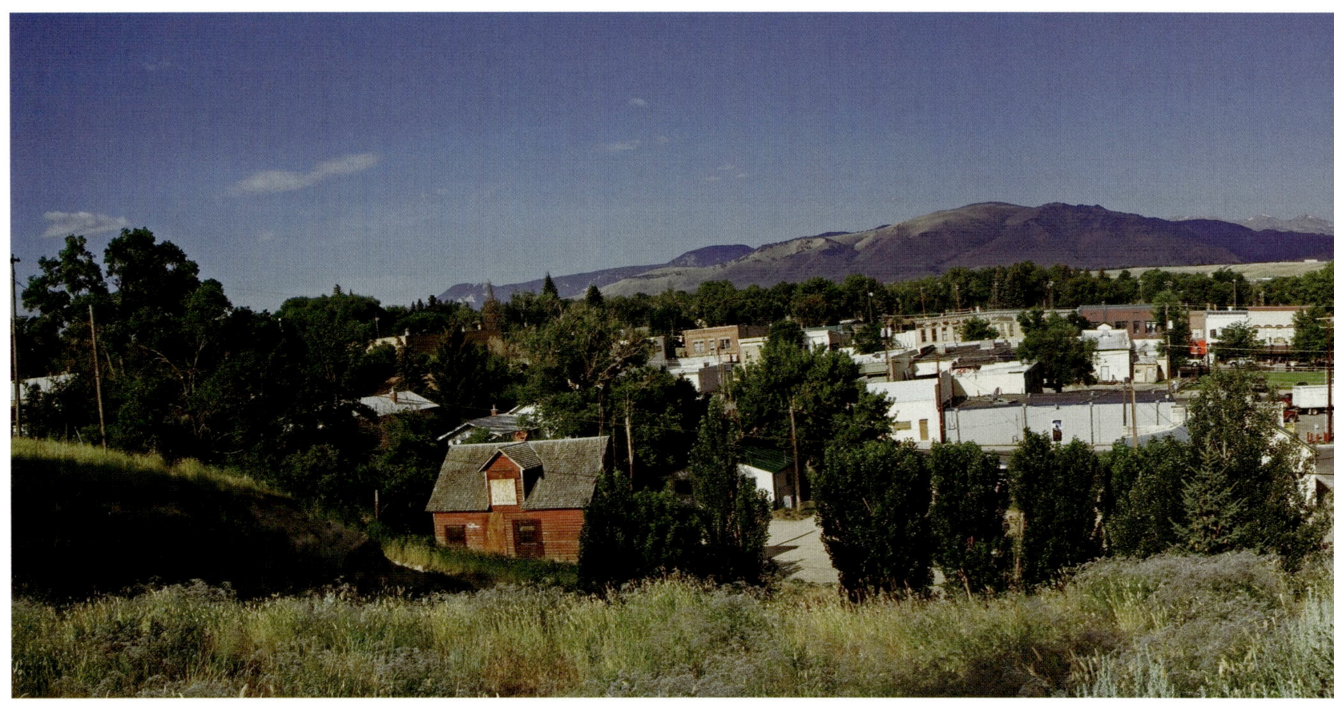

53. #557

Panorama of Buffalo, 1903, 1988, 2007
GPS COORDINATES: 44 20.808N, 106 41.772W

The Sioux Wars during the 1870s cleared the Powder River country in northern Wyoming for settlement. In 1879 the town of Buffalo, named for the city in New York, was established near Fort McKinney on Clear Creek. Two years later it became the seat of Johnson County. As both big ranchers and small farmers settled the area, disputes over the rightful use of the range developed. In the infamous 1892 Johnson County War, powerful stockmen in the Wyoming Stock Growers Association hired a posse made up mostly of Texans to root out the homesteaders. When this band of "Regulators" holed up south of Buffalo, the town's citizenry sprang to action and marched down to fight them. Federal intervention saved the hired hands. When Johnson County refused to pay for their jail time, the Texans were set free.

Stimson's 1903 panorama of the town was made a decade later while the photographer was on his whirlwind survey of the state for the St. Louis World's Fair. The *Buffalo Voice* reported on the photographer's doings about town in a story titled "A Busy Day for Mr. Stimson." The vantage point is a small hill just east of Main Street, where Clear Creek bends to the north. Stimson's common parallax problem is visible on the far mountains, where the plates don't quite match up. Nevertheless, the view of the Big Horns in the morning light is spectacular. Like many of his town promotional shots, this one used a bird's-eye view to show potential customers the commercial district. Some of these features, moving right to left, are the Johnson County Courthouse at right on the hill, the school next to it, and the original Occidental Hotel next to the creek. In the foreground, the gardens and yards are wonderful visual documents of early-twentieth-century Wyoming life.

My 1988 panorama is one of the few successful multiple-print panoramas I made that year. The greater sensitivity of my film brings out the distant Big Horns even better than Stimson's shot. The creek, yards, and downtown are quite similar to his original photo. The roof of the new Occidental can be seen to the right of the creek. As in most Wyoming towns, the growth of trees blocks more detail.

My 2007 rephotograph shows even more tree growth, although many of the original Main Street buildings can still be seen. The morning of my shot, a young deer was standing nearby.

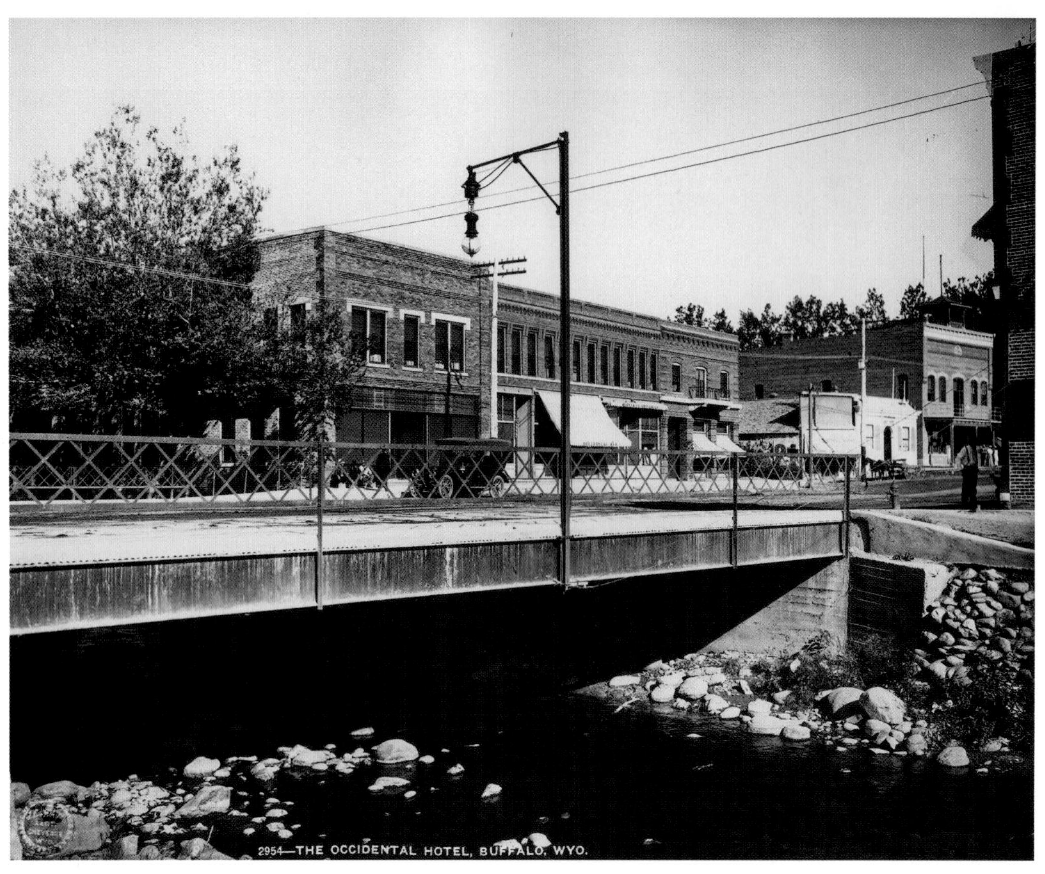

2954—THE OCCIDENTAL HOTEL, BUFFALO, WYO.

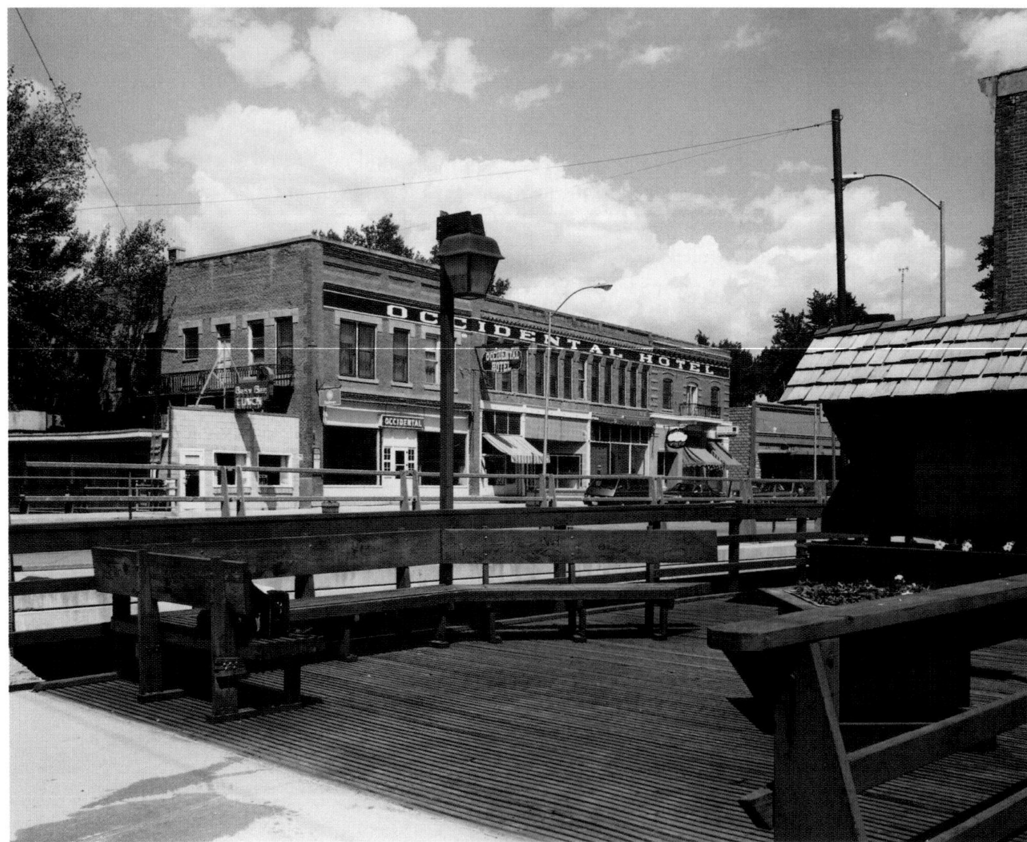

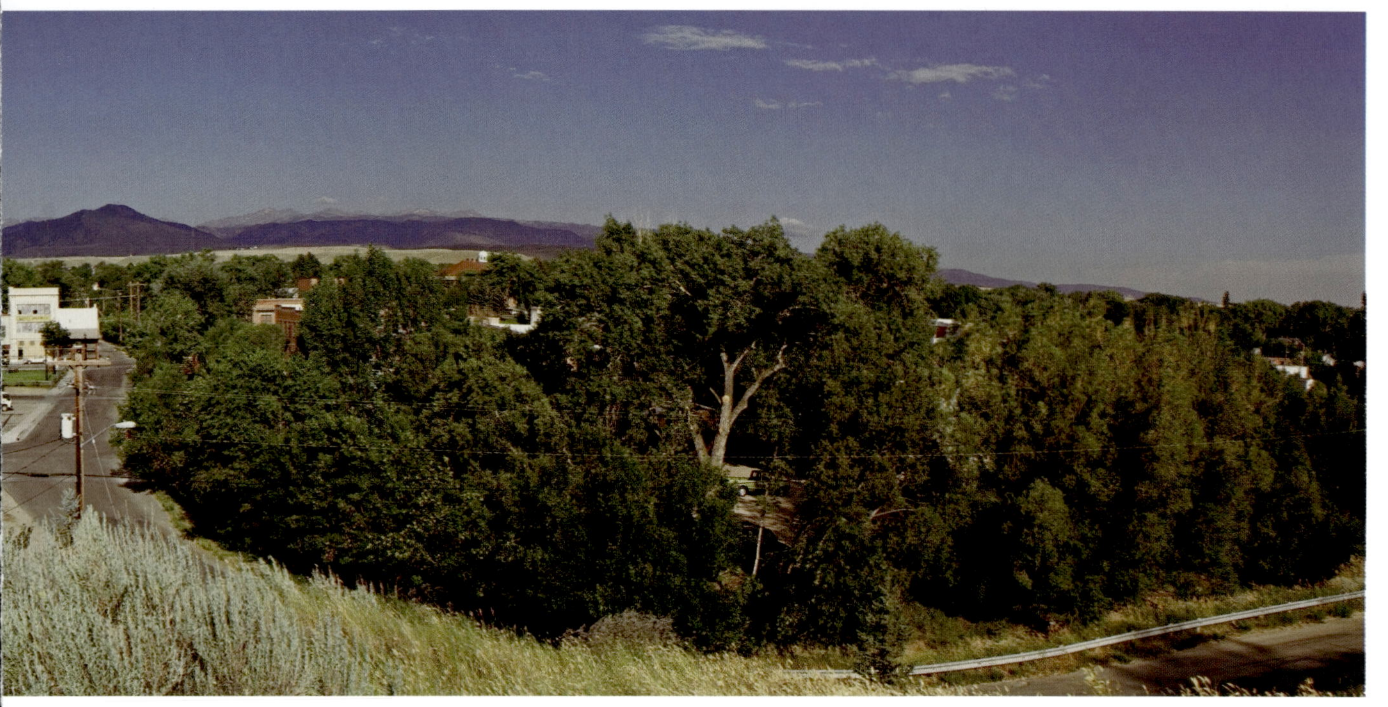

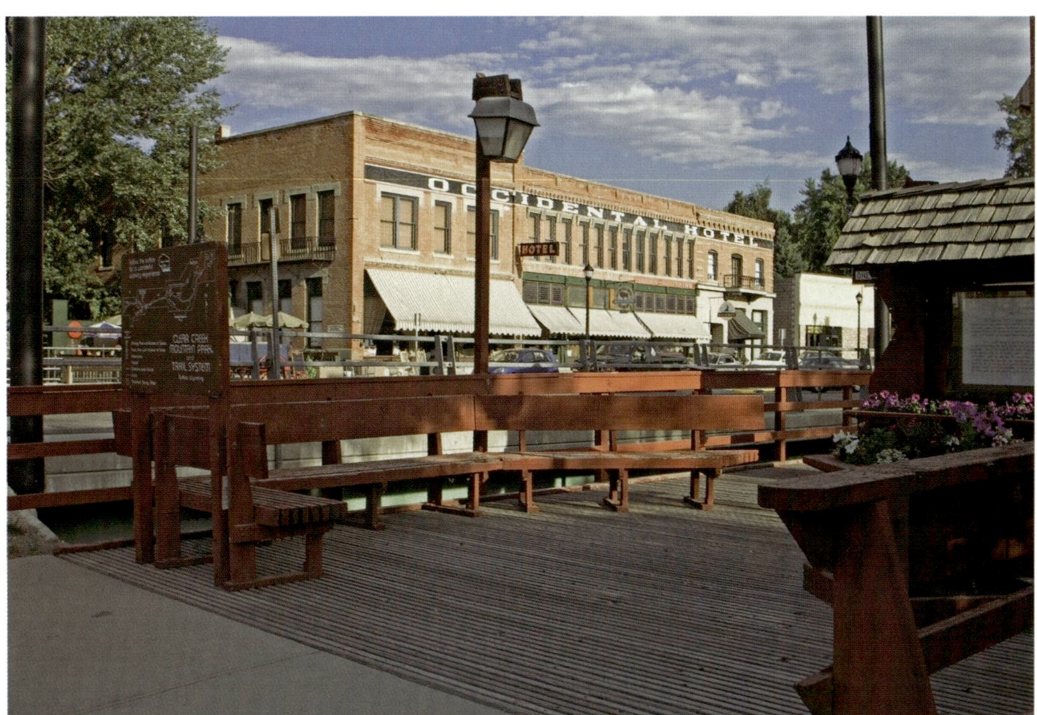

54. #2954

The Occidental Hotel, Buffalo, 1910, 1988, 2007
GPS COORDINATES: 44 20.80183N, 106 41.91683W

The original Occidental Hotel, "where the Virginian got his man," was constructed in 1880. The first section of the current brick version was completed in 1903. In the early twentieth century the Occidental became *the* hotel in Buffalo, and many famous people stayed there, including Owen Wister and Theodore Roosevelt.

Stimson's 1910 photograph was taken across the Clear Creek bridge looking northwest. A car is parked out front of the hotel, and several men are sitting on the front steps. The view shows the Main Street bridge, with its streetlight, as well as several other buildings—a typical business portrait. Stimson captured the hotel from a slight angle, with the morning light illuminating the front. A close look reveals slight architectural differences in the hotel's facade that distinguish its 1903 version, at right, the 1908 wing, middle, and the 1910 wing, left.

In the decades following Stimson's photograph, the Occidental went the way of many downtown hotels. It did well enough in the 1920s, hit hard times during the Great Depression, and then picked up again during World War II. After the war, the increased number of automobiles and the growing number of motels pushed the Occidental toward closing. By the 1980s, the few rooms operating were rented out to retirees. In 1986, the hotel closed.

My 1988 rephotograph depicts an unusual phenomenon. Although the historic sign, the hectic Busy Bee Lunch Counter—in business since 1927—and the benches in the foreground suggested a downtown resurgence, the Occidental, despite its several signs, remained closed.

During most of the next decade the Occidental fell into disrepair and by 1997 was slated for demolition. The Busy Bee closed as well. But as has happened with many historic buildings facing the wrecking ball, the threat of demolition brought resurrection when Dawn and John Wexco bought the hotel for $180,000 and began a ten-year, $1.6 million restoration project to bring the hotel back to its glory days. By the time of my 2007 rephotograph, the Occidental had come full circle and was again the shining star of downtown Buffalo. Note as well the reference to a typical twenty-first-century urban recreation program, the Clear Creek Mountain Park and Trail System map, on the kiosk in the foreground. Finally, in 2010, the Busy Bee, now made famous by Craig Johnson's *Longmire* books, reopened.

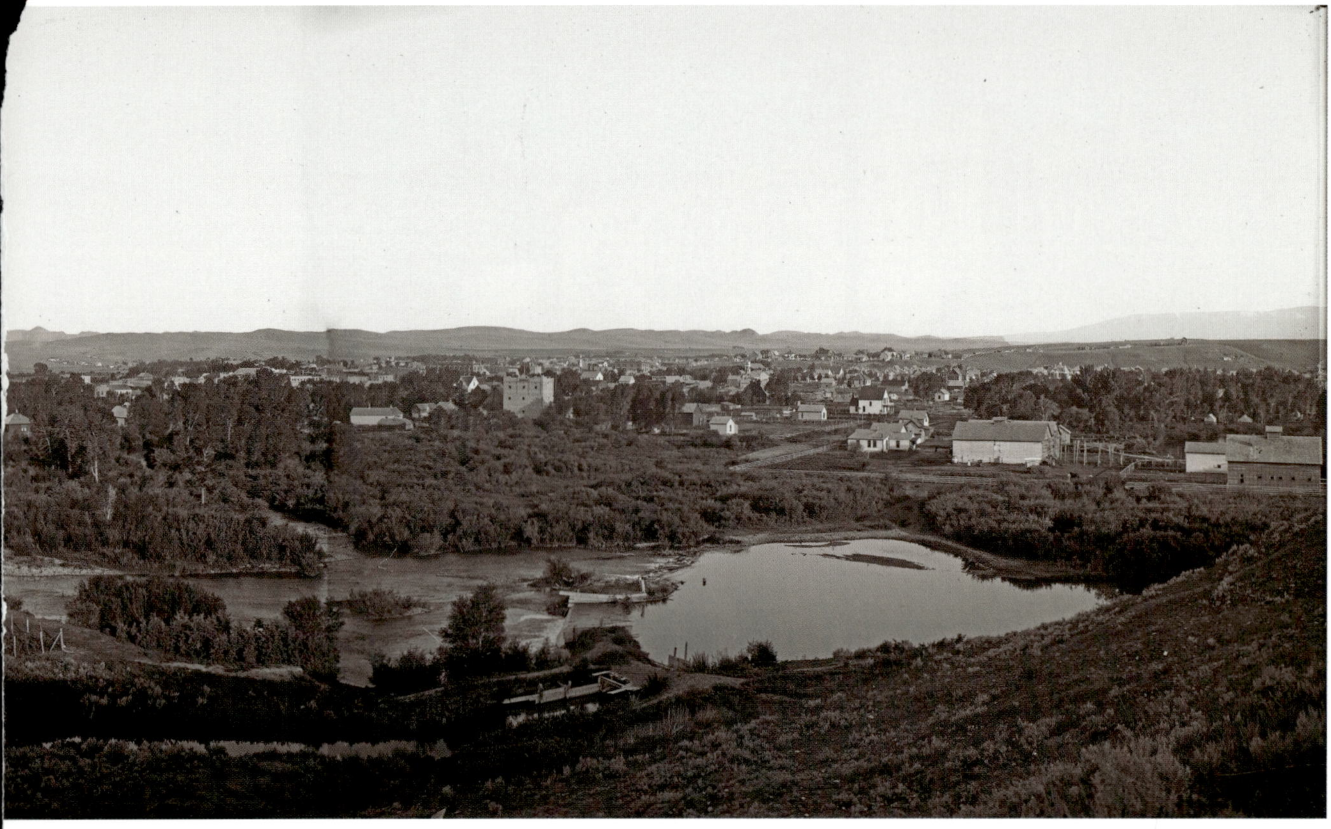

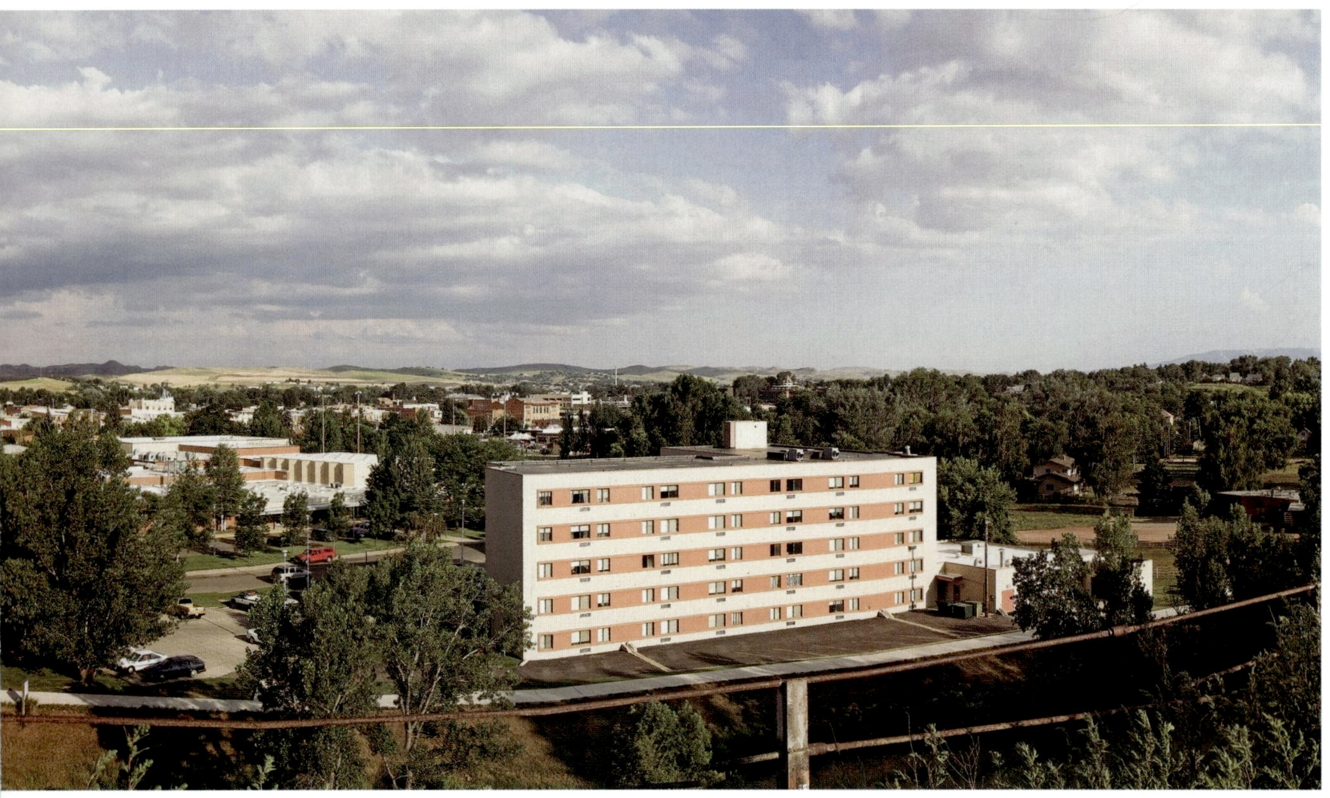

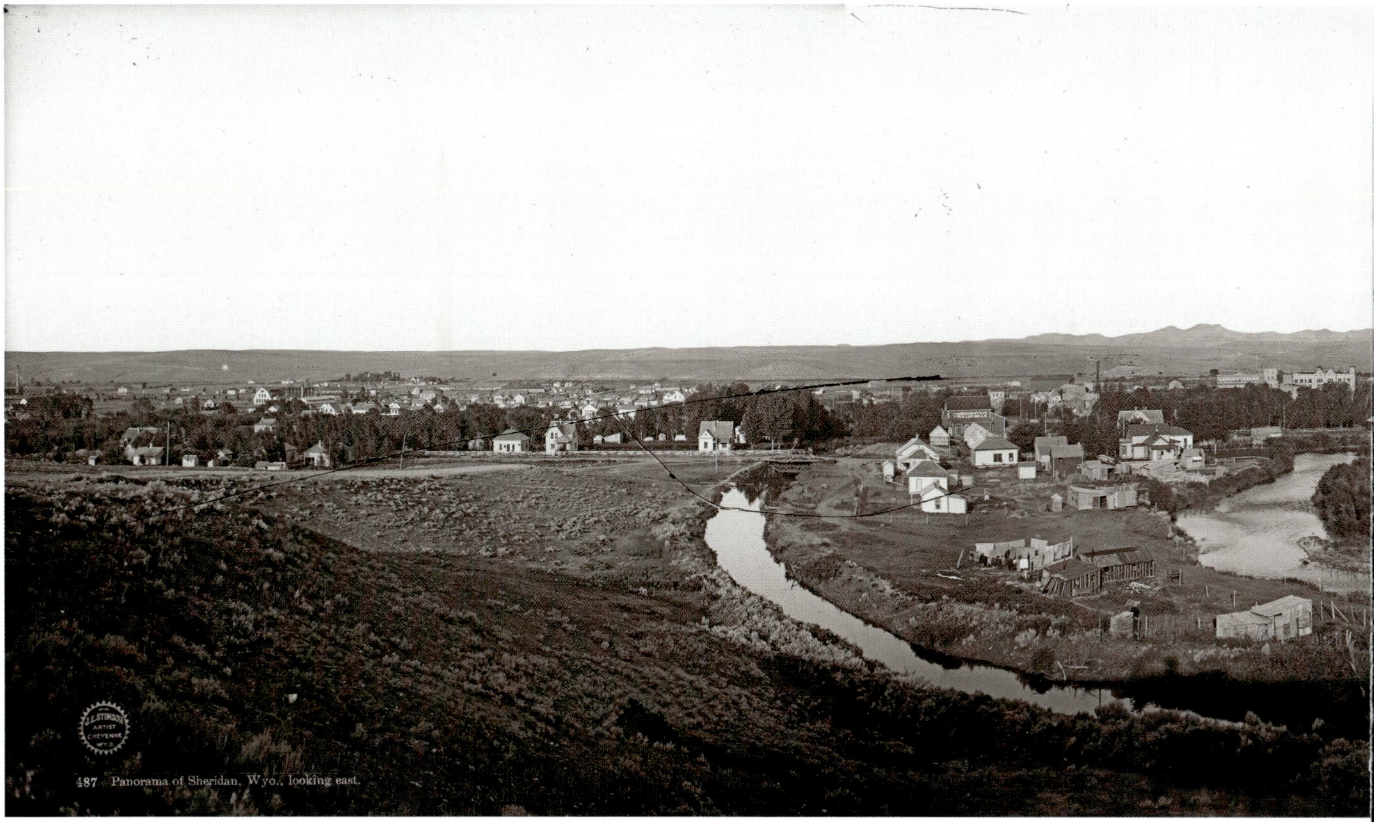

487 Panorama of Sheridan, Wyo., looking east.

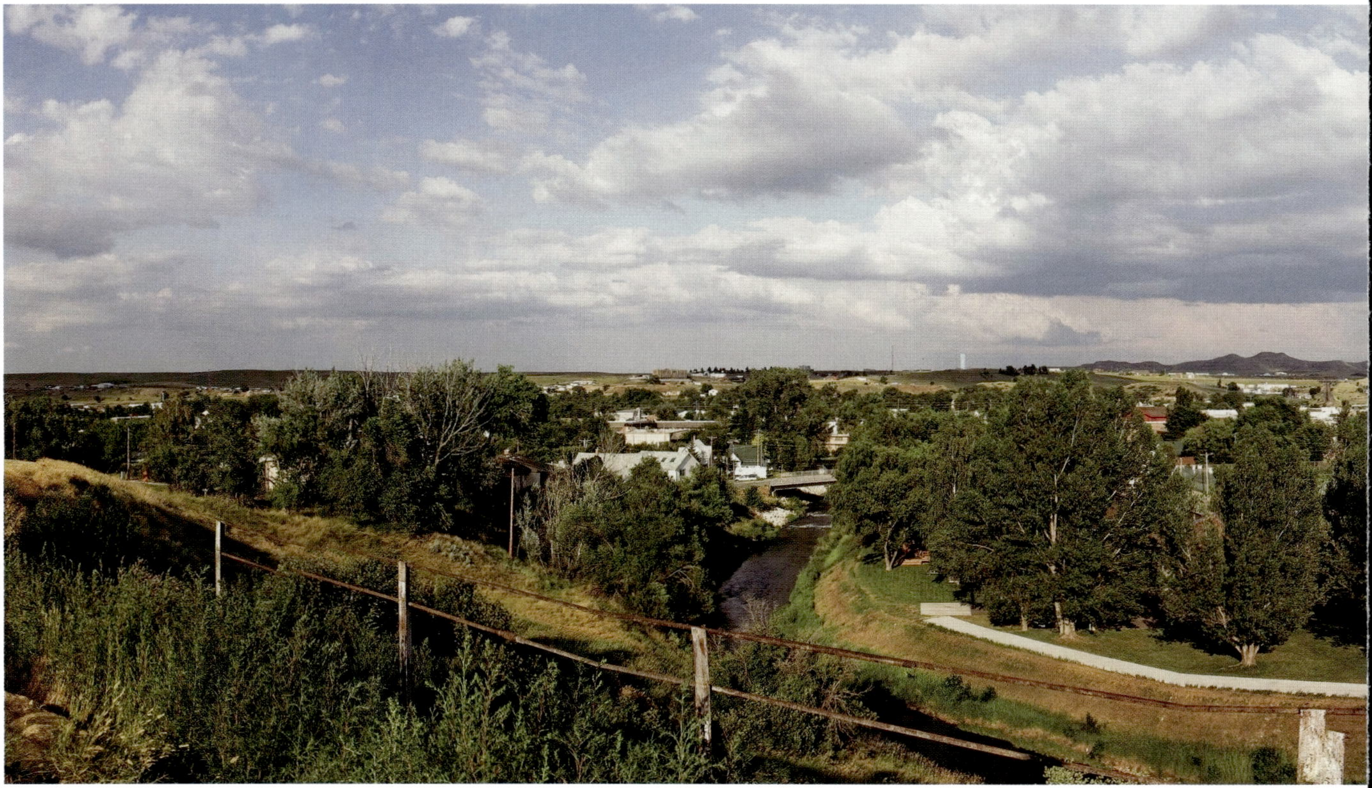

55. #487

Panorama of Sheridan, looking east, 1903, 2008
GPS COORDINATES: 44 48.176N, 106 57.740W

The town of Sheridan lies just east of the Big Horns on Big Goose Creek at an elevation of 3,743 feet, low by Wyoming standards. It was the ancestral home of the Crow people, and the region served as the staging area for the 1876 Plains Indian Wars that forced the Sioux and others onto reservations. The first settlers arrived in the late 1870s and platted Sheridan in 1882. It became the seat of Sheridan County in 1884. The 1892 arrival of the Burlington and Missouri Railroad brought tourists in and shipped cattle, horses, and coal out. When Stimson visited in 1903, the population was probably about 5,000.

Sheridan is one of my favorite Wyoming places to visit. Having spent time there conducting research for my master's degree, I became interested in both the community and its hinterlands, including the coal mining towns in the Tongue River Valley, the dude ranches along the base of the Big Horns, Dome Lake on top of the mountains, and the many old ranches in Big Horn, Beckton, Wolf, and Ranchester.

I love downtown Sheridan. Perhaps because the town does not have a mall to pull customers away, the downtown remains a long shopping hub of interesting historic buildings. Then there's Trail's End, Senator John B. Kendrick's mansion. Unfortunately, the old Ritz Sporting Goods burned down—the only place I knew where you could get a burger, a shake, and a basketball in a place that had been visited by Queen Elizabeth II.

Stimson made this panorama overlooking the bend in Big Goose Creek in the late afternoon from a site now occupied by Sheridan Junior High School. Despite the parallax problem and the cracked glass, it is an amazing photograph. Close examination reveals details in every direction, including the Sheridan Inn (left), the downtown (center)—featuring the elaborate stonework of the Helvey Hotel and Cady Opera House (which still had the third floor that burned in 1906)—and residential areas all around. Note as well the early irrigation system and the Sheridan Brewing Company (right).

I made my panoramic rephotograph on a summer evening in 2008. Despite the many trees, the irrigation canal is visible, as are the downtown and many of the same houses.

As with all of these bird's-eye–view panoramic pairs, this one of Sheridan is a fascinating visual primary source.

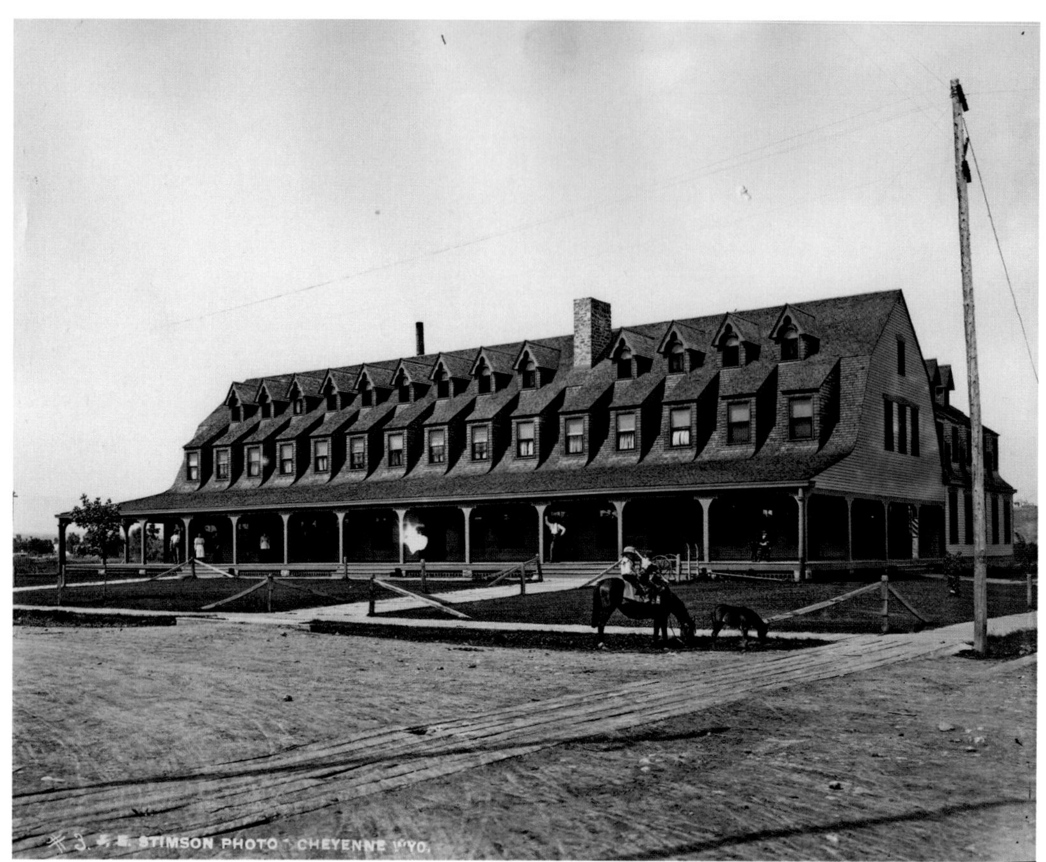

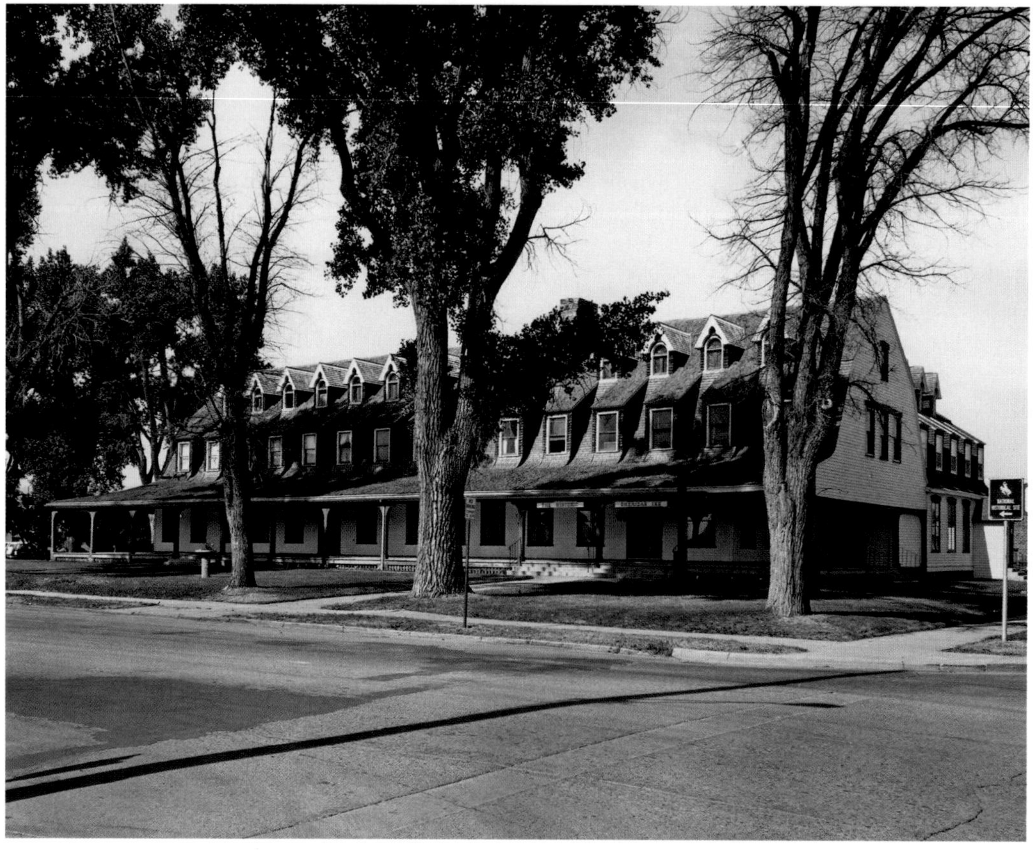

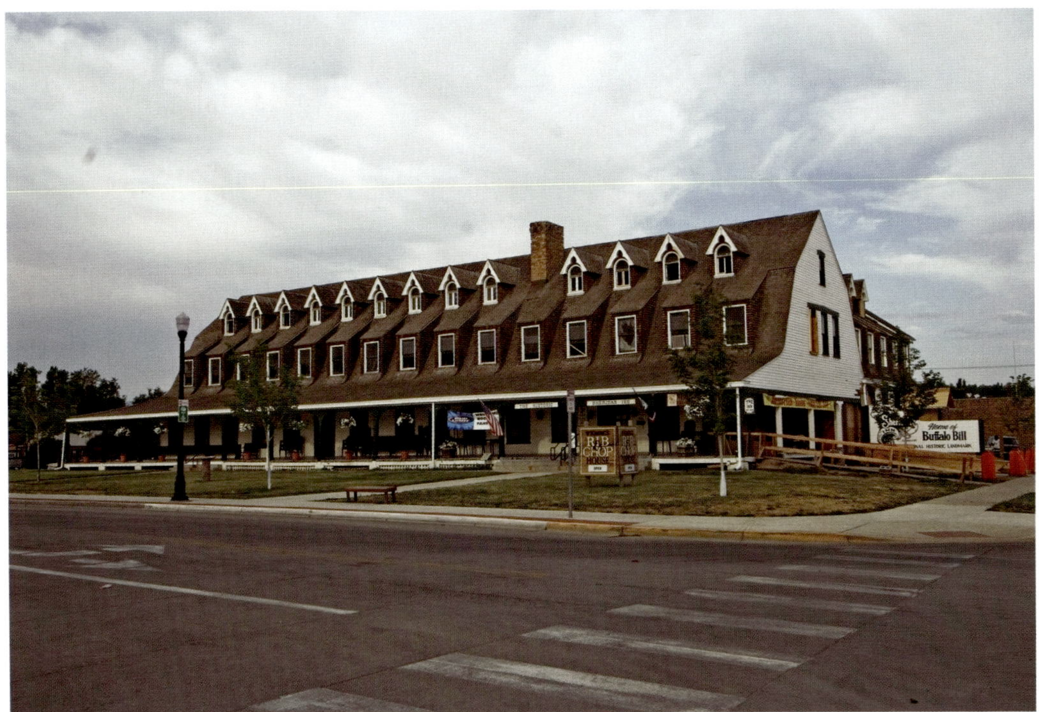

56. #5747

Sheridan Inn, Sheridan, ca. 1900, 1988, 2007
GPS COORDINATES: 44 48.4075N, 106 57.1934W

The Burlington and Missouri Railroad and the Sheridan Land Company constructed the Sheridan Inn in 1892–93 at a cost of $25,000. Thomas R. Kimball, a noted Omaha architect and designer of the Dome Lake Lodge, modeled the inn after a Scottish one he had visited. When it opened in June 1893, the inn housed the first bathtub and electric lights in Sheridan. There were sixty-two guest rooms, a dining room, a saloon, and a lobby. Between 1894 and 1896, Buffalo Bill Cody operated the inn. Like many small-town railroad hotels, the Sheridan Inn hosted celebrities and politicians, as well as tourists and hunters heading into the Big Horns. When tourists began arriving in cars, the inn faced difficulties because motels were more conveniently located. Designated a National Historic Landmark in 1964, the inn ceased operation as a hotel the following year and was condemned in 1967. That same year, the Sheridan County Historical Society held an emergency auction to try to save the building by selling off its interior furnishings. The building was saved, but barely.

Neltje Doubleday Kings, a New York heiress who had just moved to Sheridan, stepped in. Neltje bought the inn and began a twenty-year restoration effort, reopening the saloon and many of the rooms along the way. More struggles occurred in the late 1980s, though. The Sheridan Heritage Center purchased the inn in 1990 and has renovated the building into a twenty-two-room boutique hotel.

Stimson took this exterior view of the inn in 1900 as he embarked on a trip into the Big Horns. As with most of his business portraits, he captured this one in the morning light from a slight angle. Note the split rail fence and the small saplings.

In my 1988 view, trees tower over the restored building. Unfortunately, though, my view was made during a "down time" when the inn was closed.

My 2007 rephotograph shows the inn alive and doing well. A second generation of young trees is back in place, flowers hang above the deck, and a restaurant is in business. Note the ADA-compliant ramp at right and the effort to tie the inn to Buffalo Bill on the banner behind it. The future looked bright.

Unfortunately, the housing bust brought another round of economic difficulties to the Inn and by the summer of 2012, it faced immediate foreclosure. Then, in October 2013, Bob and Dana Townsend purchased the historic property and began restoration work. The first floor is currently available for banquets with the restaurant, museum and seven guest rooms set to reopen in spring 2014.

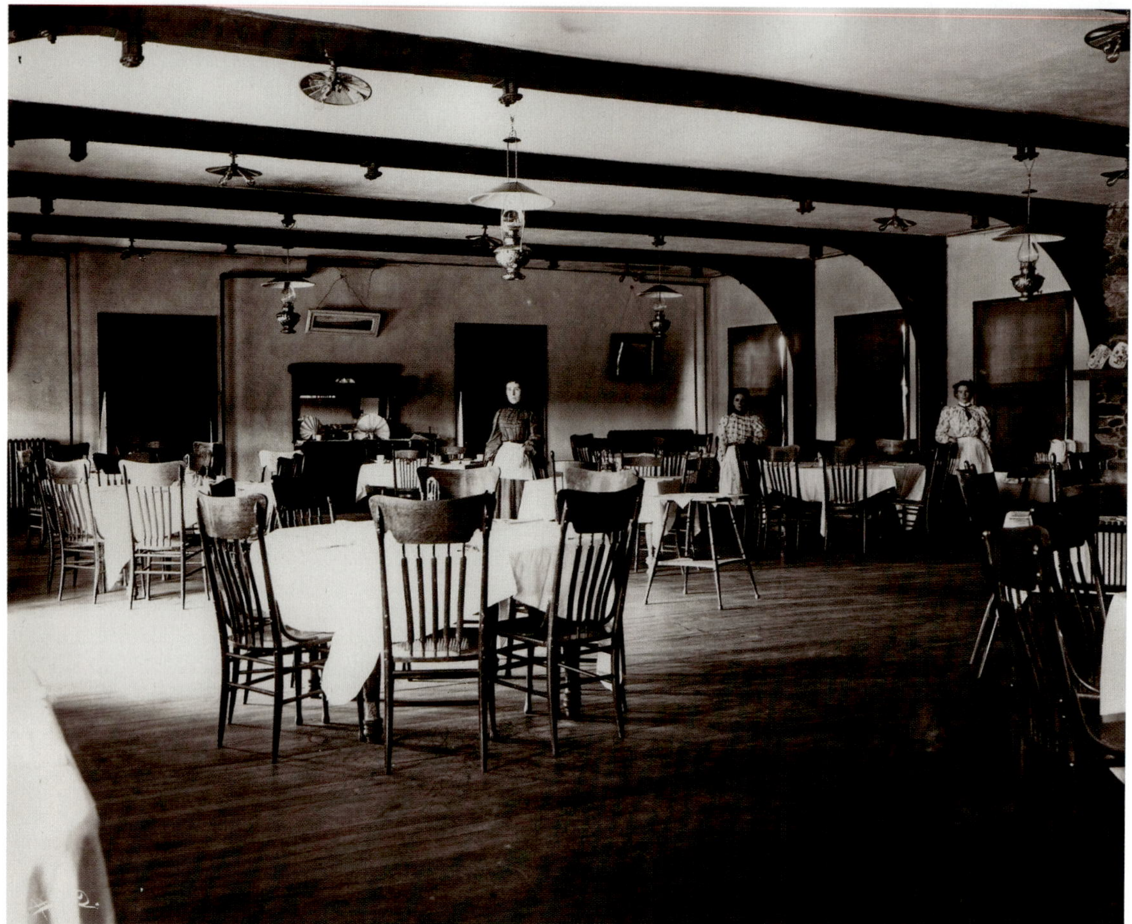

57. #E22

Sheridan Inn Dining Room, 1899, 1988, 2007
GPS COORDINATES: 44 48.379167N, 106 57.23083W

The Sheridan Inn's dining room had a seating capacity of 150. Breakfast was priced at twenty-five cents, with lunch and supper at fifty cents each. Locals could purchase meal tickets for thirty cents. The room also served as a ballroom for Sheridan and hosted many grand balls and parties. The ceiling beams and fireplace, right, were made from locally produced materials.

My 1988 rephotograph shows that the beams and fireplace survived, though a dance floor was added as well as a few period-looking lights. Almost twenty years later, the inn's continued economic ups and downs had left the dining room much as it was twenty years earlier.

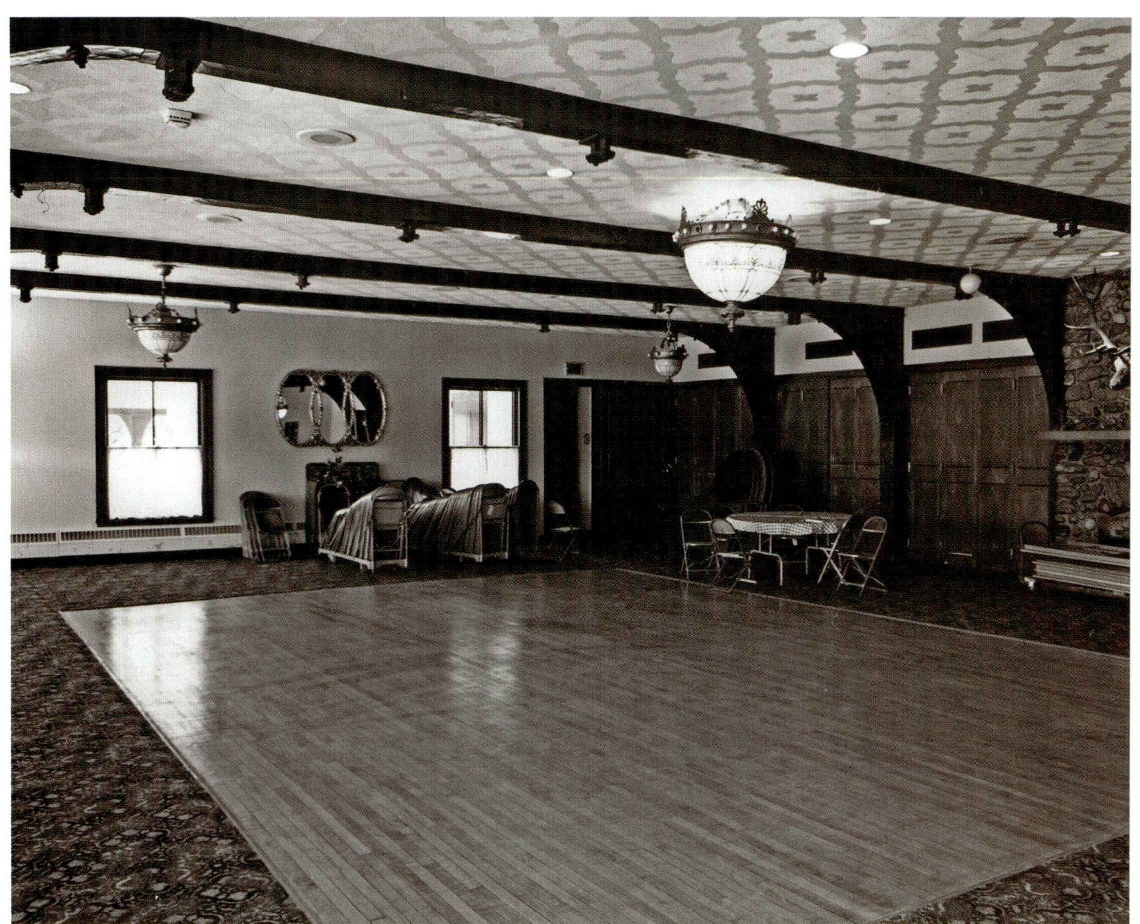

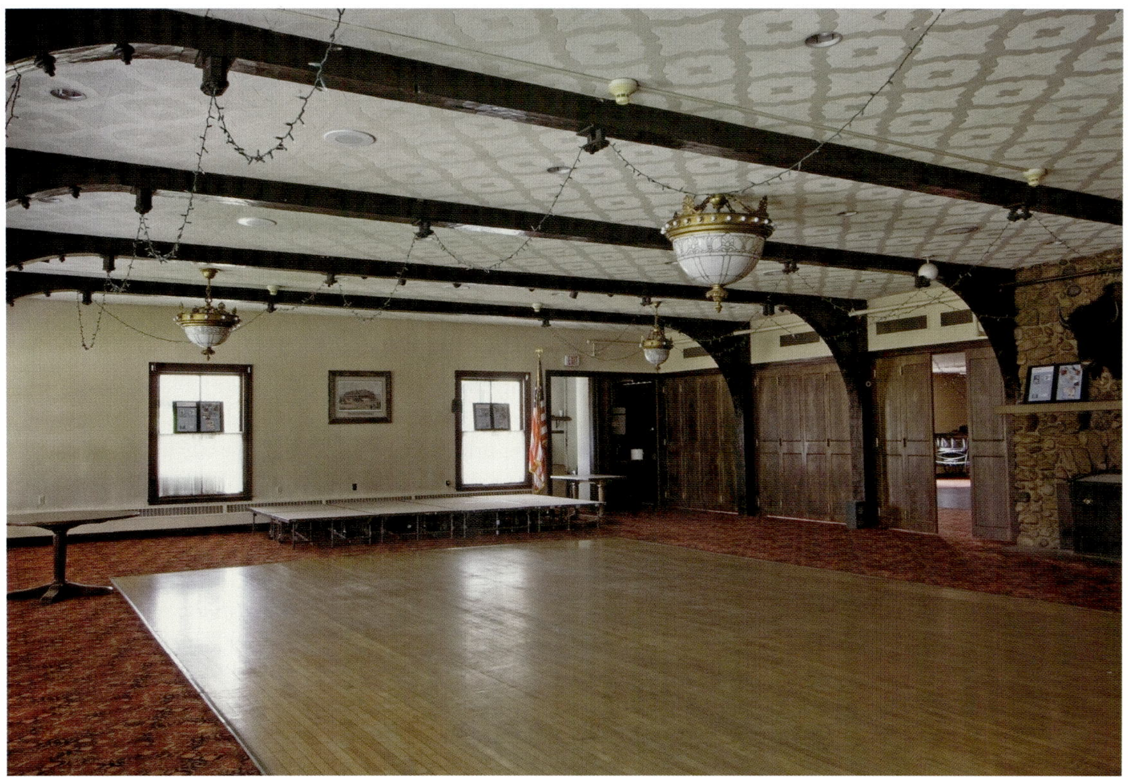

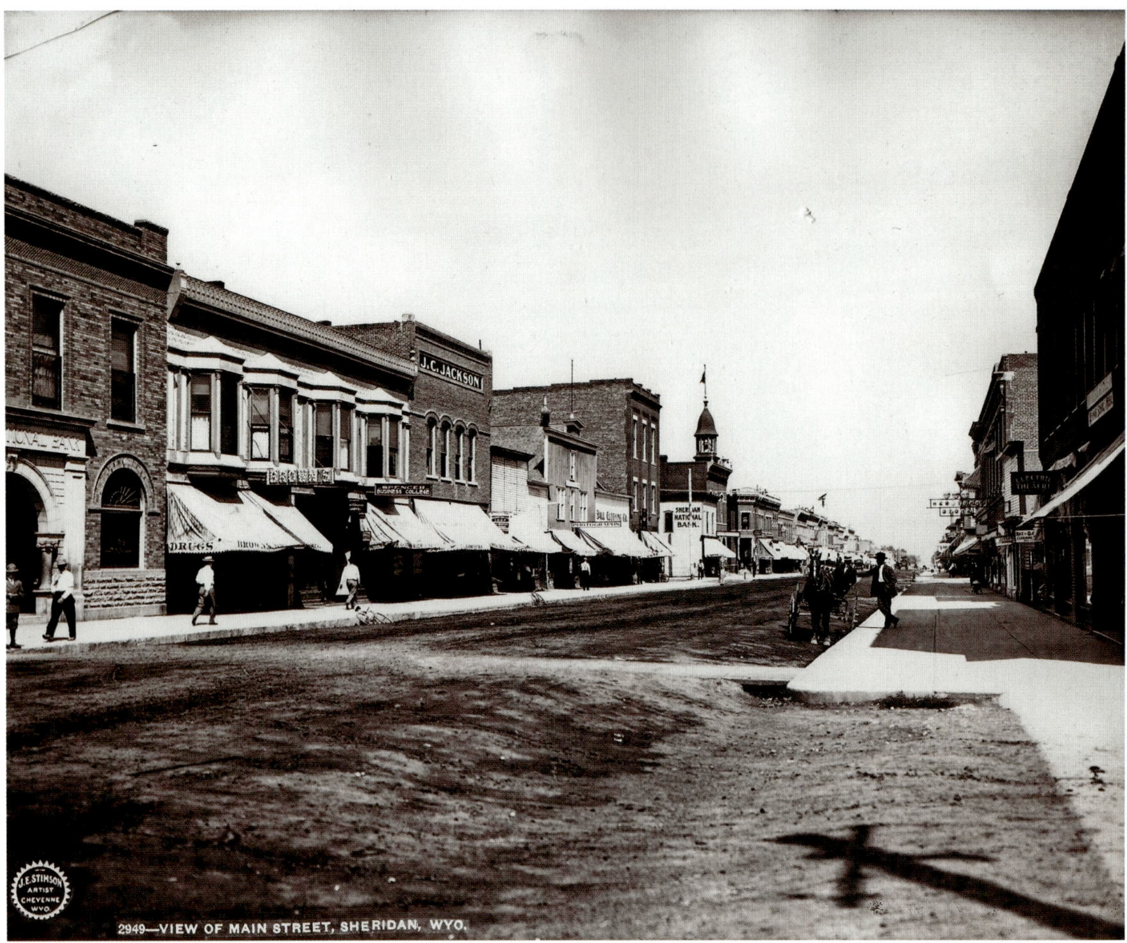

58. #2949

Sheridan Main Street, 1908, 1988, 2007
GPS COORDINATES: 44 47.833167N, 106 57.345167W

The arrival of the Burlington and Missouri Railroad in 1892, along with the ensuing development of nearby coal mines and cattle, horse, and dude ranches, started Sheridan on a twenty-year boom. The town's population quadrupled, and most of the present brick and stone buildings in downtown Sheridan were constructed.

Stimson made this shot looking north on Main Street from the intersection with Loucks Street in the warm light of morning. On the left are the city hall building with its tower and past that the Bank of Commerce building with the angled entryway. A few pedestrians are strolling down the concrete sidewalks, and a man with a horse and buggy is staring at the photographer. Not a single automobile can be seen.

A couple of years after Stimson made his photograph, the City of Sheridan installed an electric streetcar system that ran up Main Street, then connected with an inter-urban system that went all the way to Fort Mackenzie and on to the Tongue River mining camps. Increased automobile use in the 1920s doomed the line, and when the streets were repaved in the mid-1920s, the line was discontinued. Over the years, the Sheridan downtown continued to be the region's economic hub. In 1982 the Main Street Historic District was placed on the National Register of Historic Places, and today the city has an active Main Street Program.

These efforts are clearly indicated in my two rephotographs of Main Street. Although the 1988 image shows many restored buildings, the view from 2007 includes new trees, new old-fashioned–looking streetlamps, and better signage. As in Rawlins, Cheyenne, and many other Wyoming communities, the Main Street Program is helping not only to preserve historic downtown structures but also to re-develop them into viable businesses people want to visit.

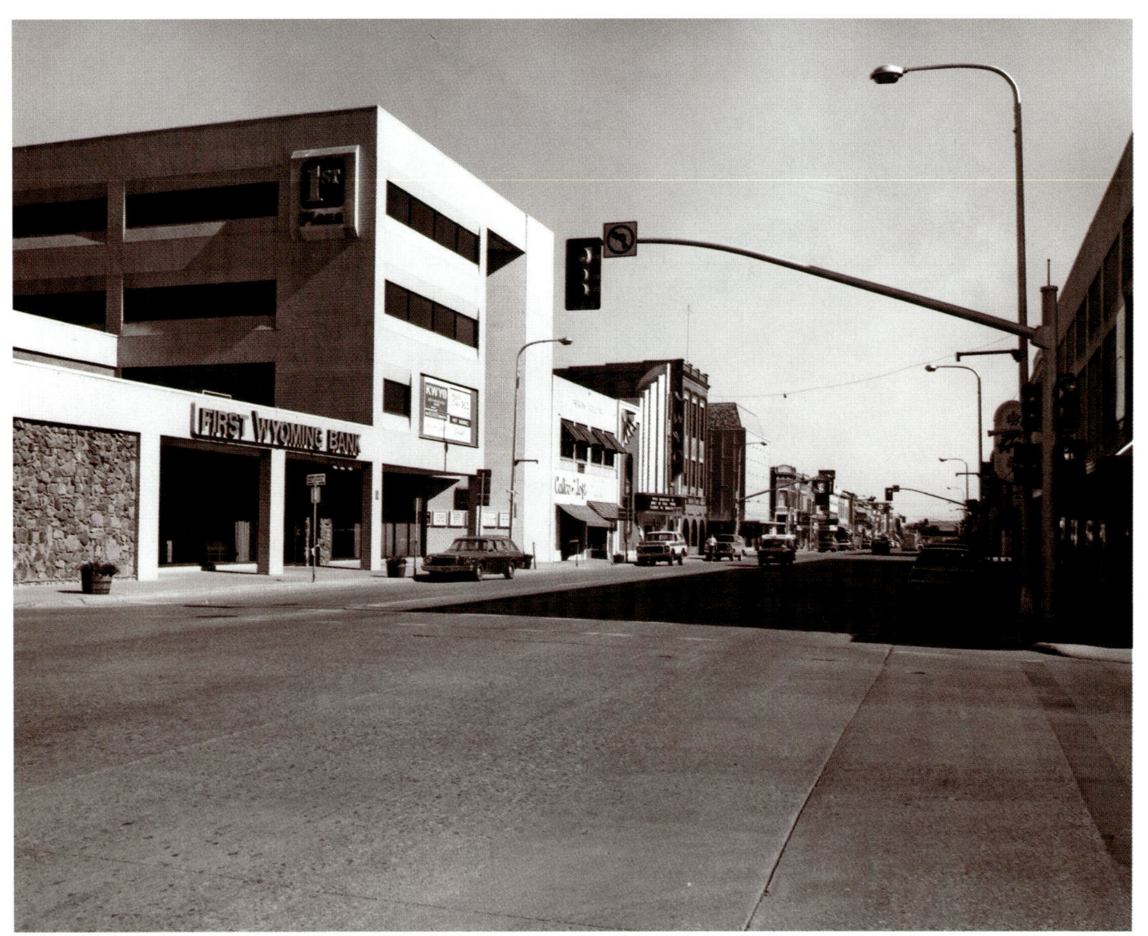
1ST
FIRST WYOMING BANK
KWYO

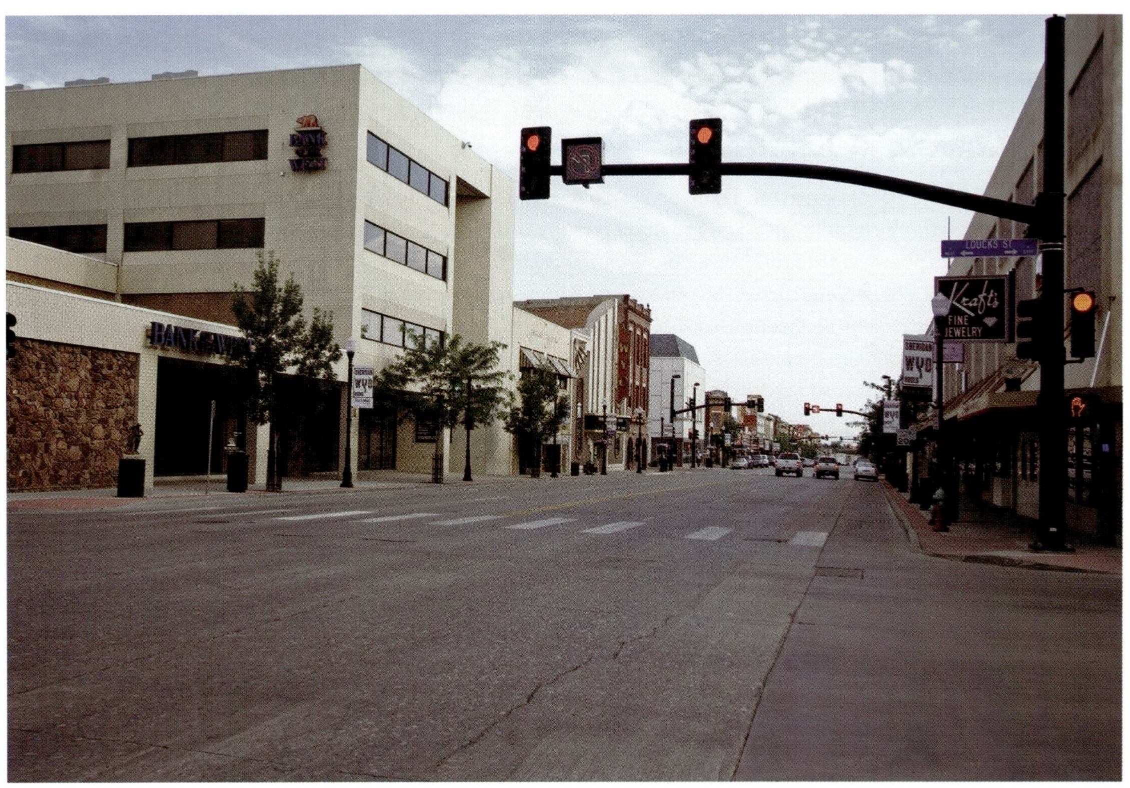
BANK of the WEST
BANK of the WEST
LOUCKS ST
Kraft's
FINE
JEWELRY
SHERIDAN
WYO
WYO

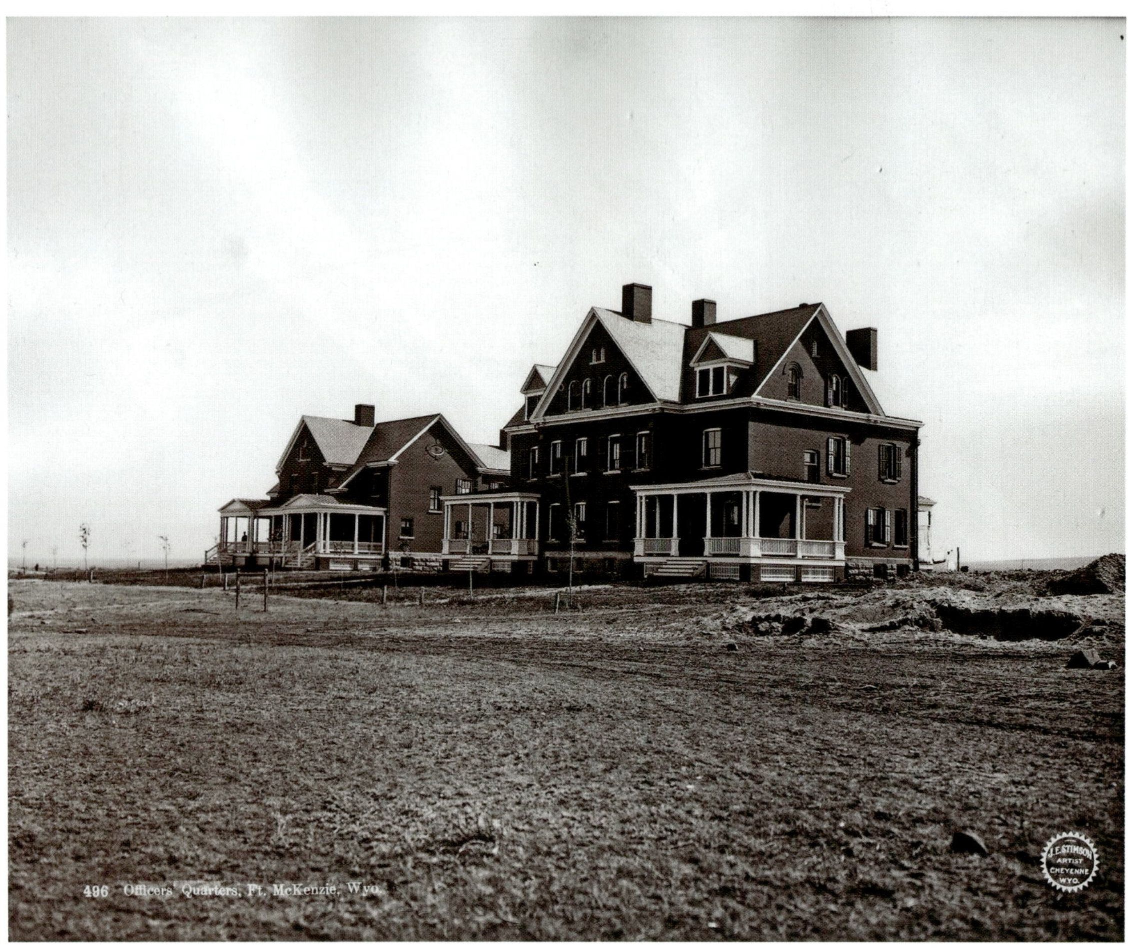

59. #496

Officers' Quarters, Fort Mackenzie, near Sheridan, 1903, 1988, 2007
GPS COORDINATES: 44 49.8867N, 106 59.516167N

The large number of Native Americans on nearby reservations led Wyoming senator Francis E. Warren to ask that a military fort be built in Sheridan, and the construction of Fort Mackenzie north of town commenced in 1899.

Stimson photographed this view of the Officers' Quarters during his 1903 survey of the state. Note the typical red brick buildings constructed the previous year in a neoclassic style. At the time, African American Buffalo Soldiers, veterans of the Spanish American War, were garrisoned there. The absence of any trees on the high prairie is also evident. Nevertheless, like those of any other business or industry, images of developing military bases such as this one showed economic growth for Wyoming and Stimson's employers. It also assured potential customers that the frontier was indeed closed.

The threat of an Indian uprising never materialized, and the army closed the base in 1918 and abandoned the grounds four years later. The government transferred the post to the US Bureau of Health that year, and the fort became a fatigue hospital for World War I veterans. In 1972, the site was listed on the National Register of Historic Places. It has remained a veterans' hospital to this day

Access on the site is tightly controlled, though I was able to make my rephotographs in 1988 and again in 2007 with no problem, as long as I made sure no patients were included in my images. The two buildings remain, although tremendous tree growth blocks much of the view, forcing me to move back from the original Stimson vantage point.

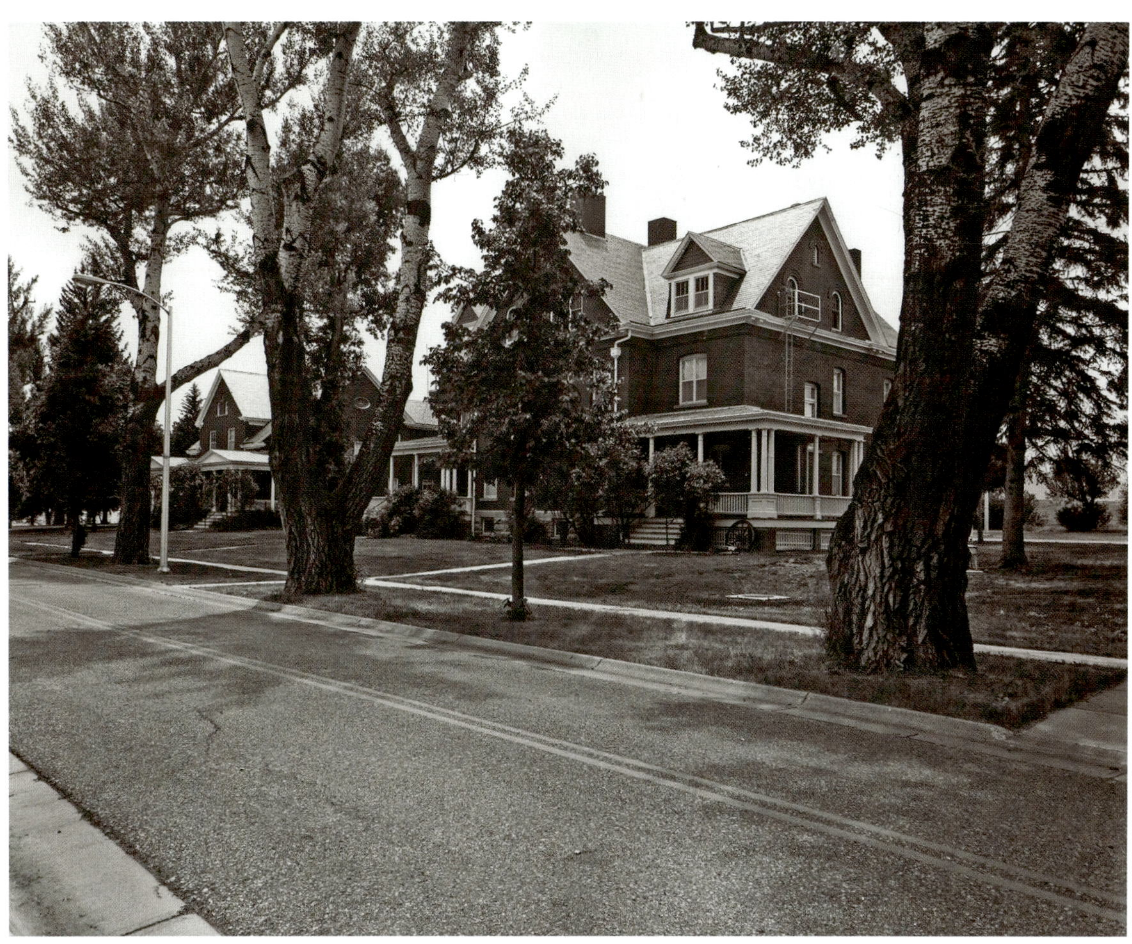

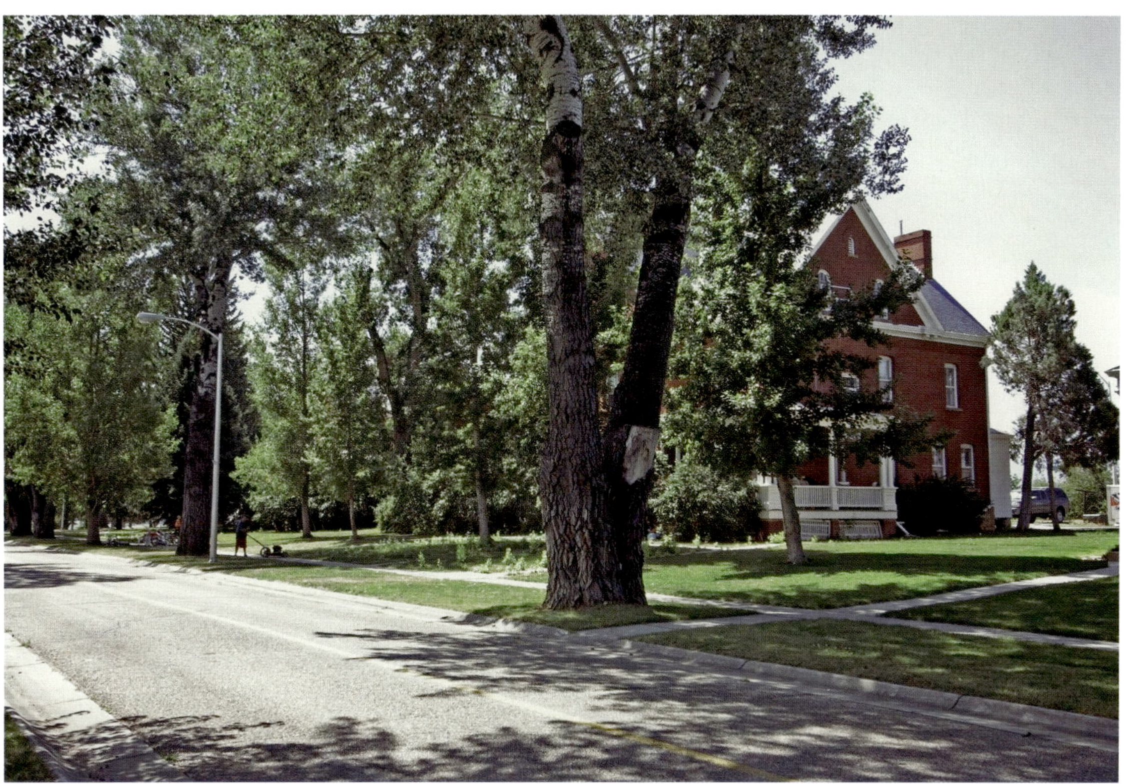

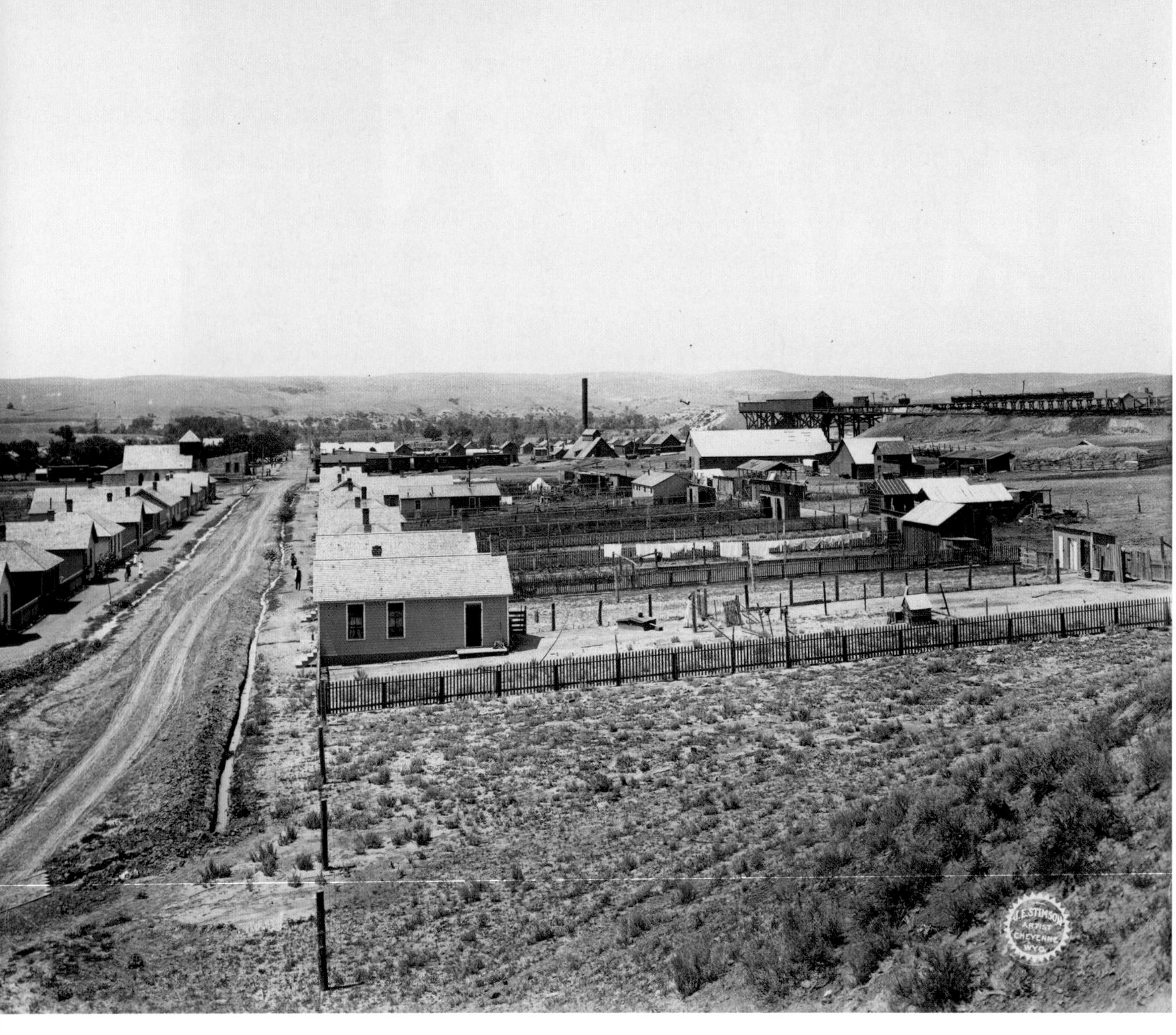

near the hospital and aligned it with the fence, shooting west straight down the main street. He set his guide's buggy left of the curve, inviting the viewer in for a closer look. What we find is an orderly camp, with tidy houses, large yards, privies way out back, and ditches on each side of the street carrying water through the town. This angle also placed the industrial section, with its smokestack and tipple, far to the back. In a world where coal camps often suggested labor violence, pollution, and mining disasters, Stimson depicted Dietz as safe, clean, and a good investment.

Decreasing coal prices drove many camps, including Dietz, out of business in the 1930s. Residents hauled many of its houses into Sheridan. By the time I visited in 1988 and again in 2007, nothing remained of the tranquil domestic scene Stimson had portrayed. The main street wound through an open field, with only traces of Dietz visible, such as the darkened earth of a slag pile, upper right. The bridge on the horizon marks State Highway 338, and the extensive fills indicate the level path of Interstate 90 in the distance. In 1988 my father's white pickup (which I totaled later that summer) is pointed out of town, seemingly asking the viewer to turn away; in 2007 my Forester points toward the town site, perhaps inviting twenty-first-century viewers back for a closer look.

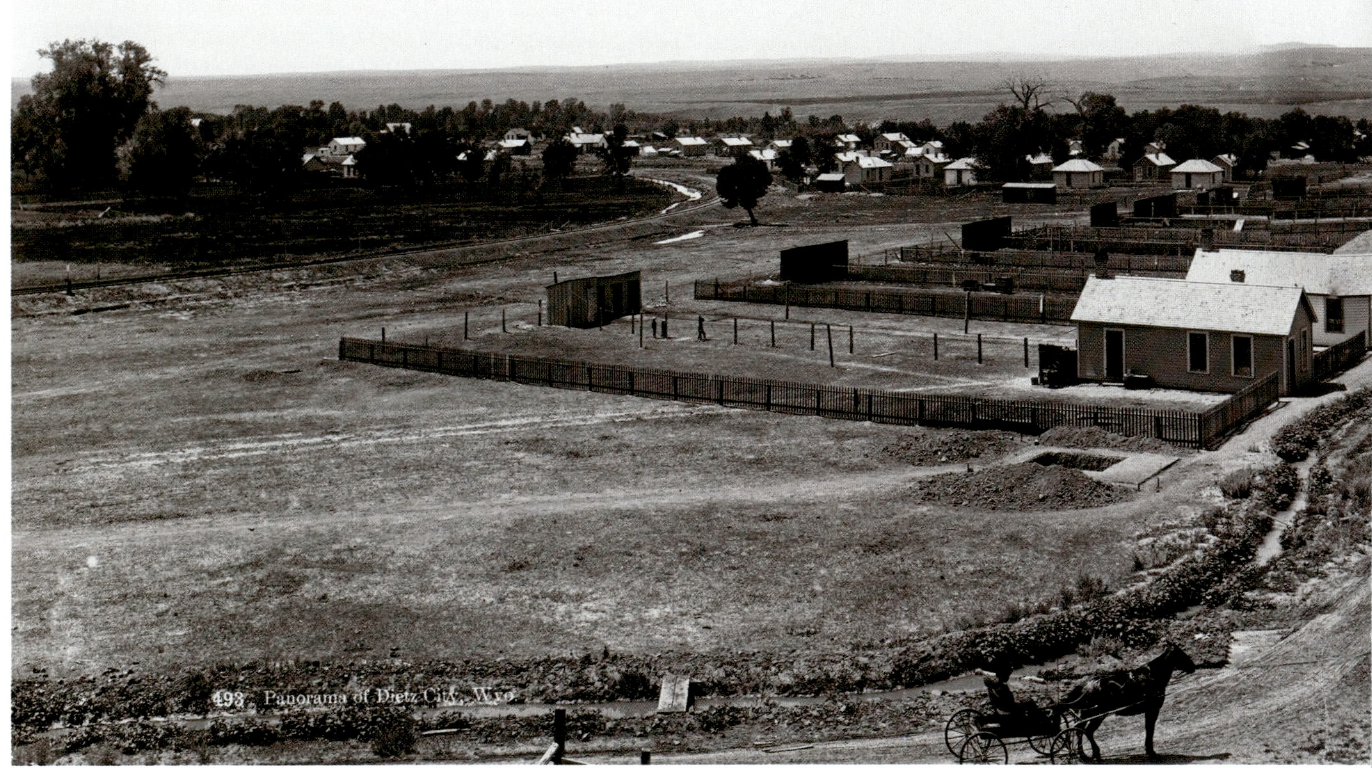

Panorama of Dietz, 1903, 1988, 2007
GPS COORDINATES: 44 52.339N, 106 58.264W

Dietz was one of several coal towns located six miles north of Sheridan in the Tongue River Valley. In fact, Dietz consisted of several camps, located near different mines and numbered to match each mine. Originally called Higby in 1894, the town's name was changed in 1901 when Charles N. Dietz—the owner of an Omaha lumberyard, president of the Sheridan Coal Company, and an original Dome Lake Club investor—purchased an interest in the mine. In 1900 the town had 400 residents and boasted Catholic and Methodist churches, two schools, a company store, two saloons, a pool hall, a union hall, a hospital, and a hotel.

In this two-part shot, one of his best panoramic bird's-eye views, Stimson made more than just another photograph promoting a Wyoming coal town. Instead, the photographer appealed to would-be investors by producing a domestic invitation to view the town's neat, orderly appearance. To do this, he positioned his camera on a hill

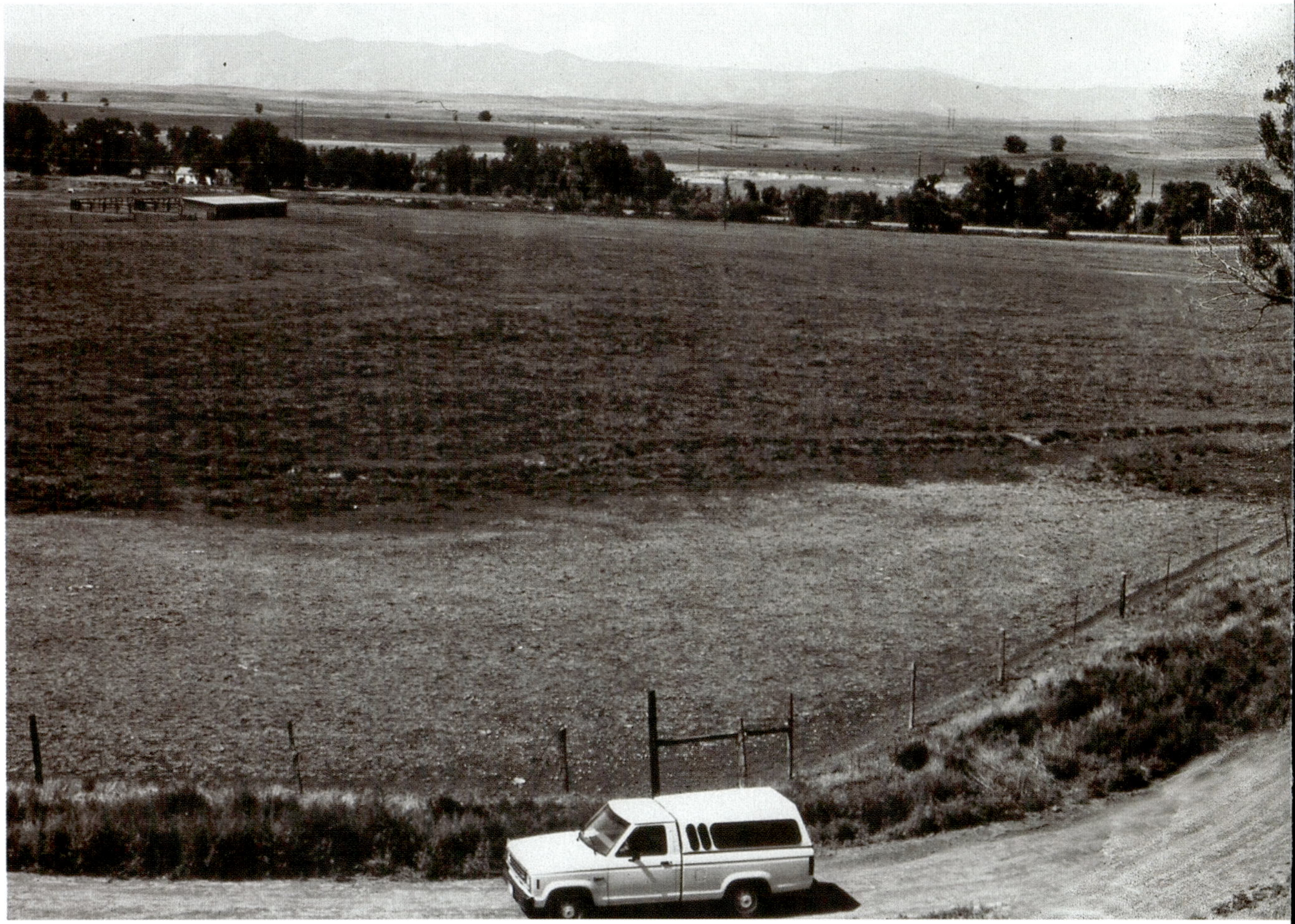

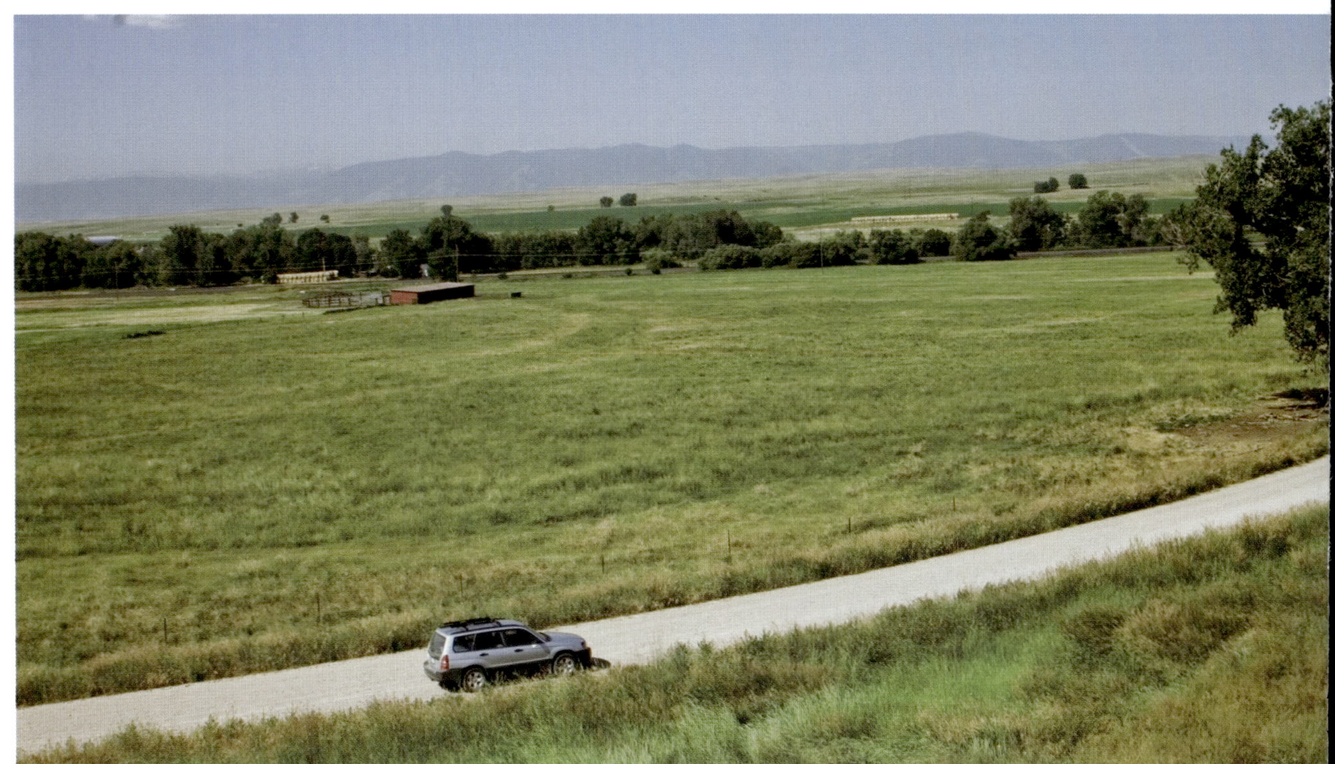

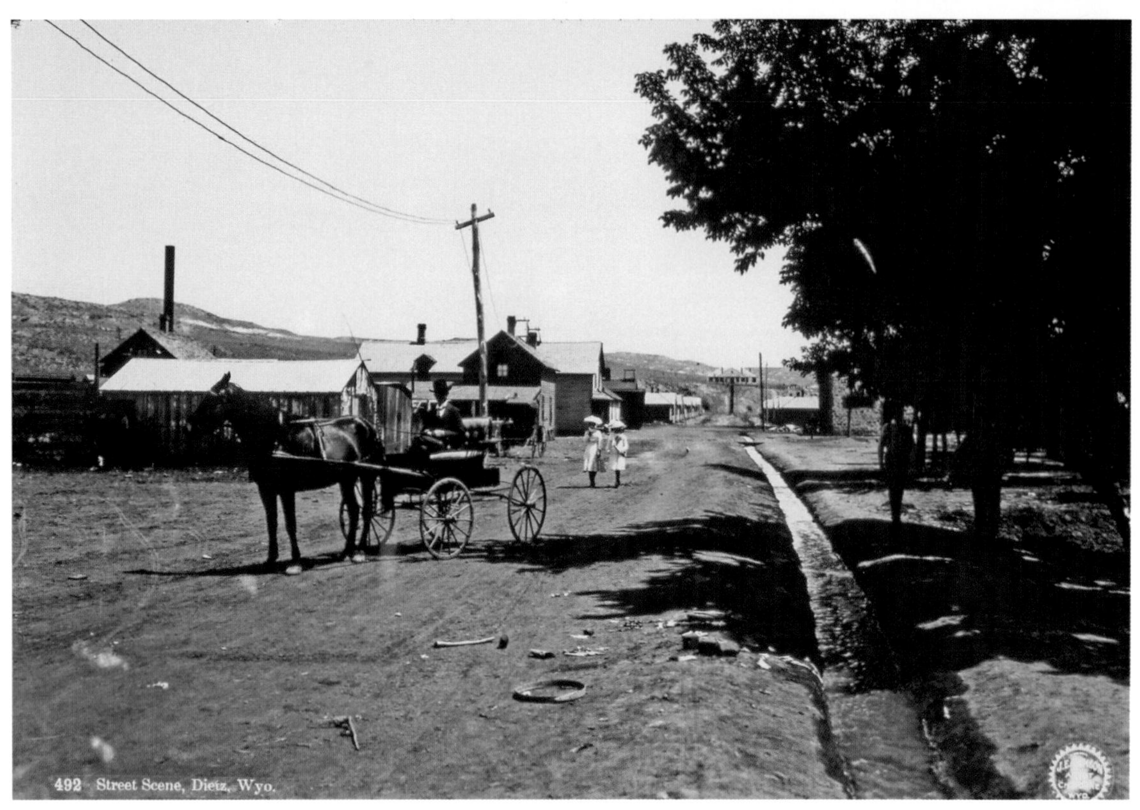
492 Street Scene, Dietz, Wyo.

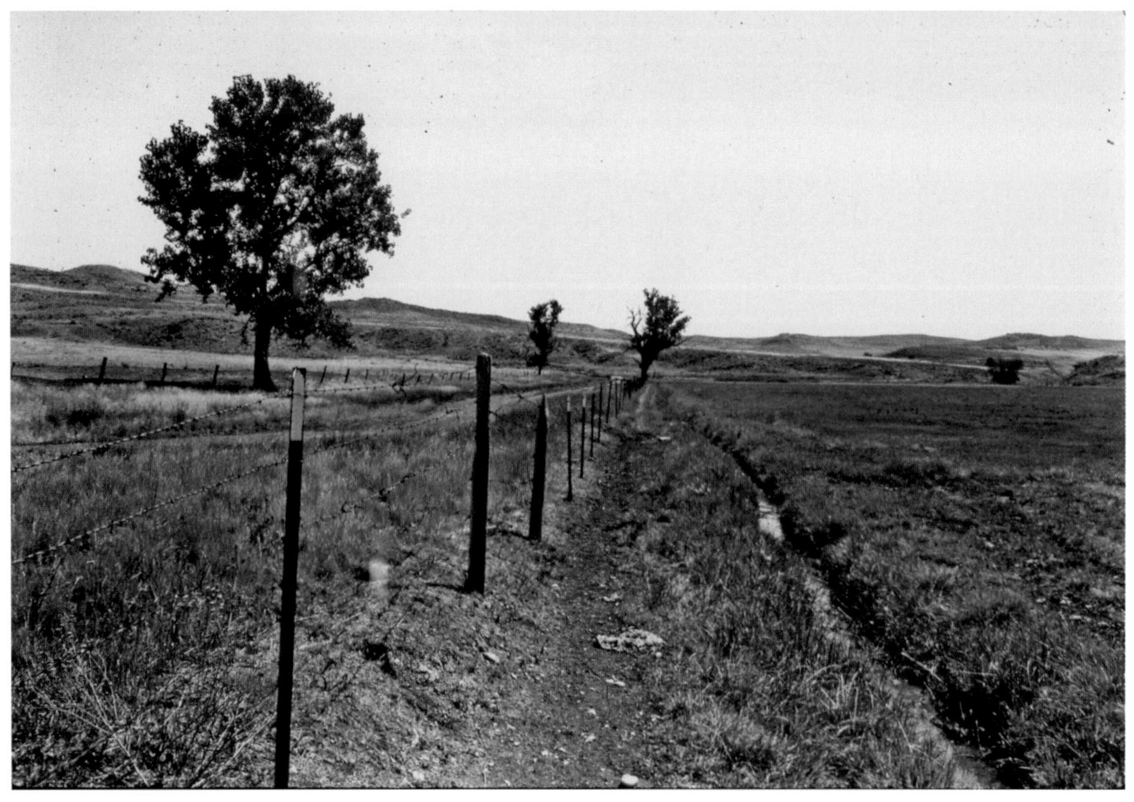

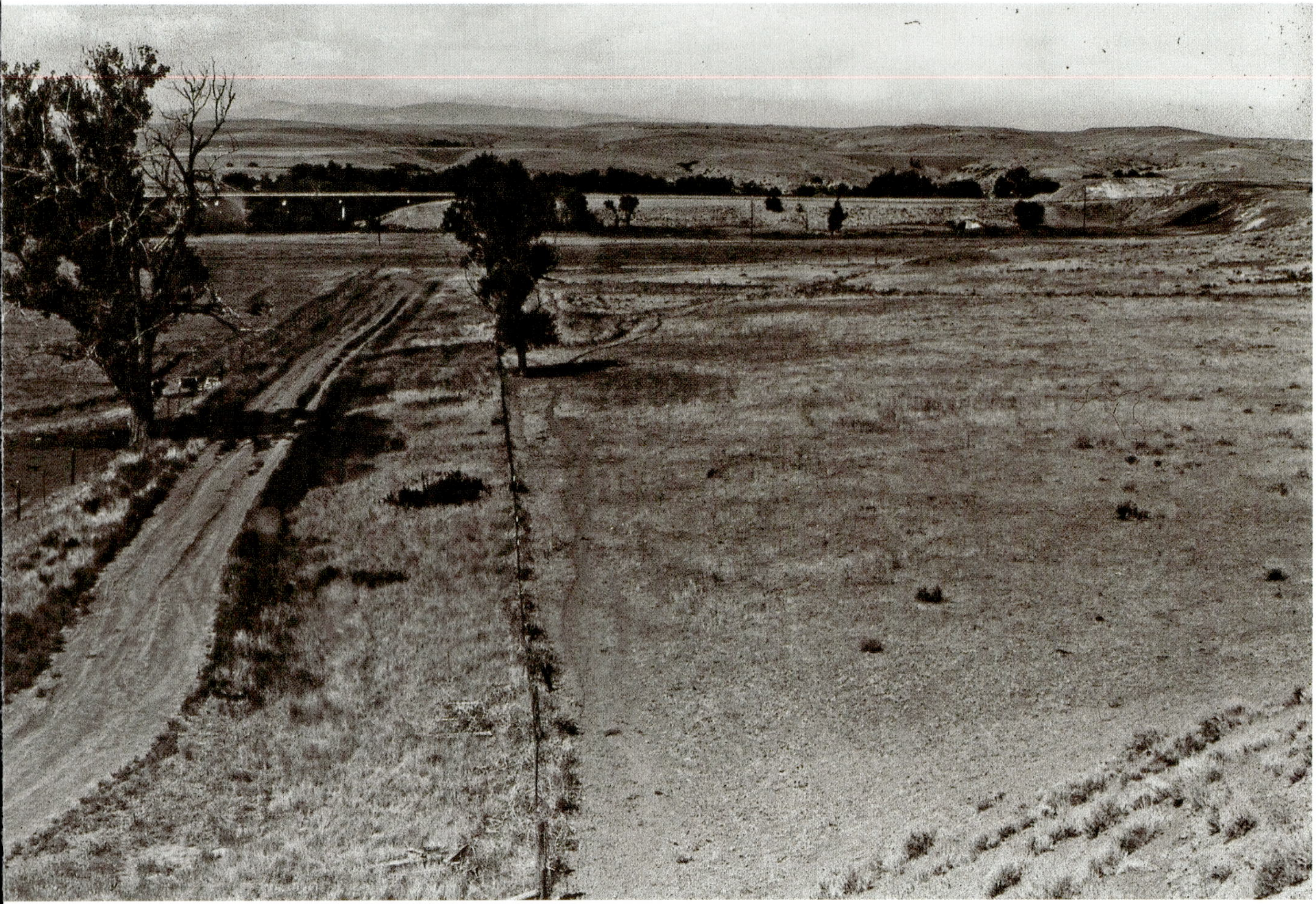

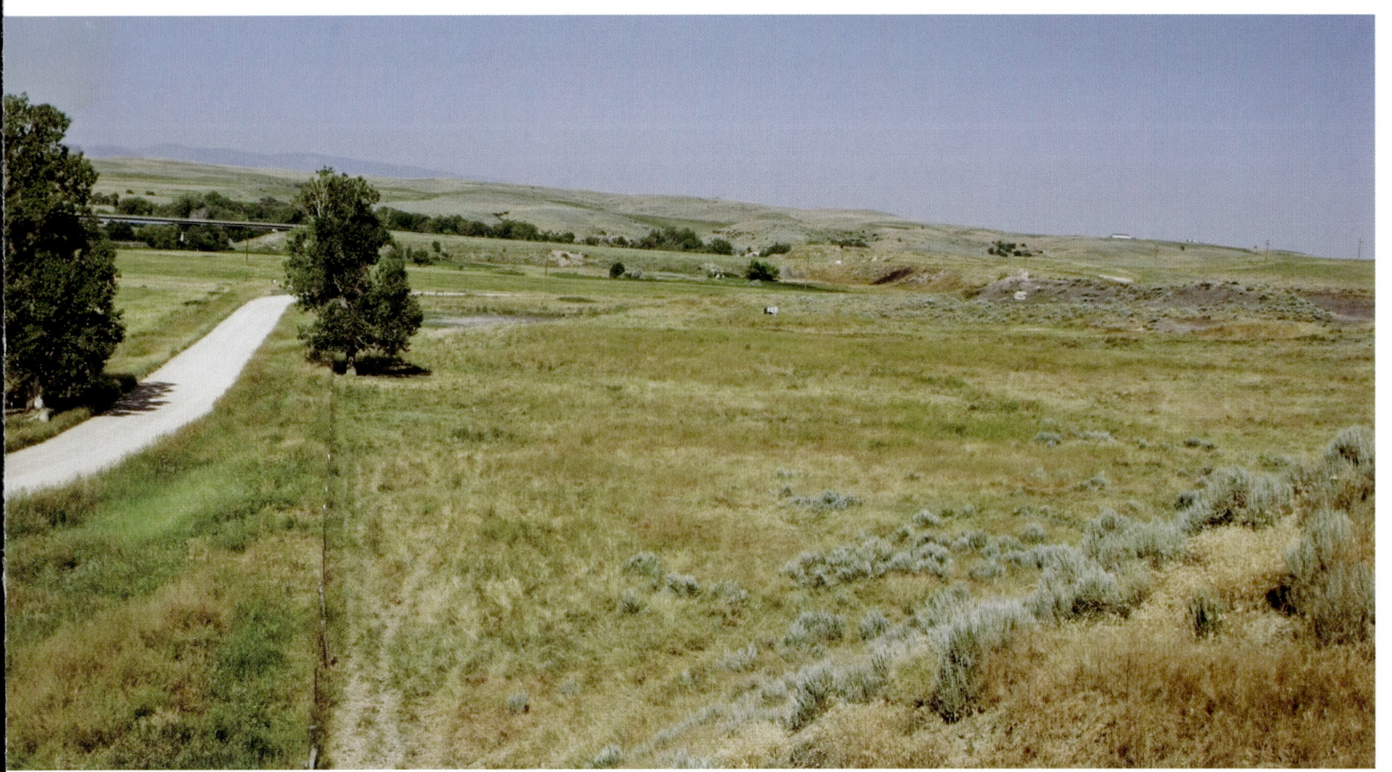

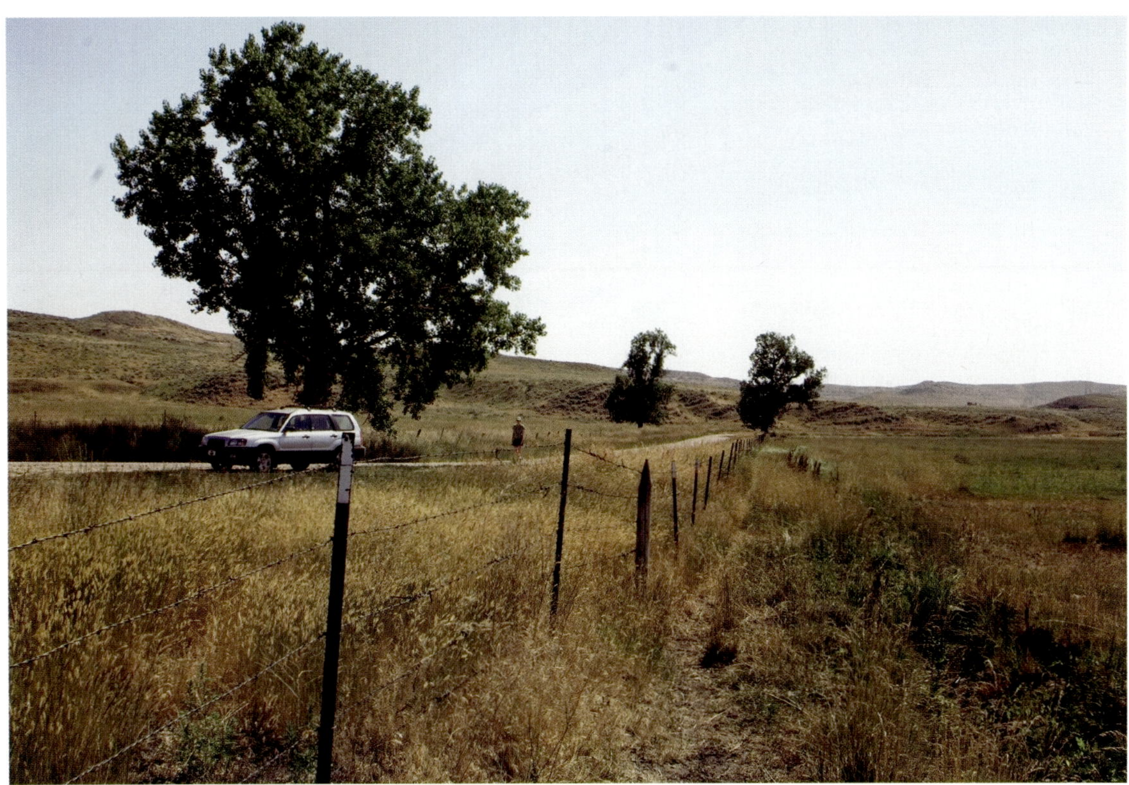

61. #492

Dietz Street Scene, 1903, 1988, 2007
GPS COORDINATES: 44 52.326N, 106 58.507W

In this second view of Dietz, Stimson stationed himself all the way to the west on the main street and is looking east toward his last vantage point next to the hospital. Another wonderful domestic composition, Stimson framed this view with the tall trees on the right and his suited guide and conveyance in the center. The telephone line, distant hills, and water ditch pull the viewer's eye deeper into the picture, where we see two ladies nicely dressed and sporting large hats. Two men can be seen in the shade at right. In the far distance, the residential area leads the viewer to steps that go up the hill to the hospital. The only semblance of industry is the smokestack, at left.

My 1988 view found little remaining in Dietz. The tall trees, the road, fence lines, and irrigation ditch suggest the former town site. In 2007 I parked my Forester near where Stimson's buggy had been and had Lauren walk down the road, but the scene looked pretty much the same as it had in 1988, though perhaps the field on the right was thicker. After taking this photo, we walked up the distant hill and found several red bricks where the hospital once stood.

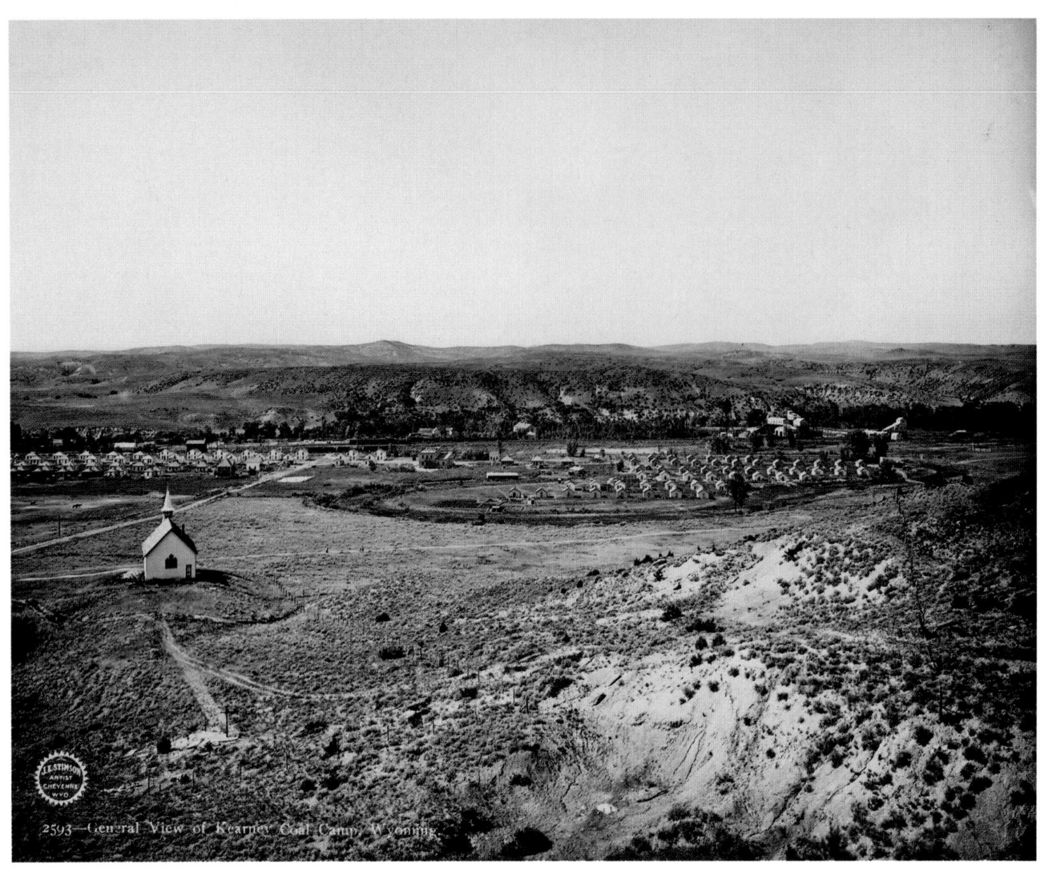
2593—General View of Kearney Coal Camp, Wyoming

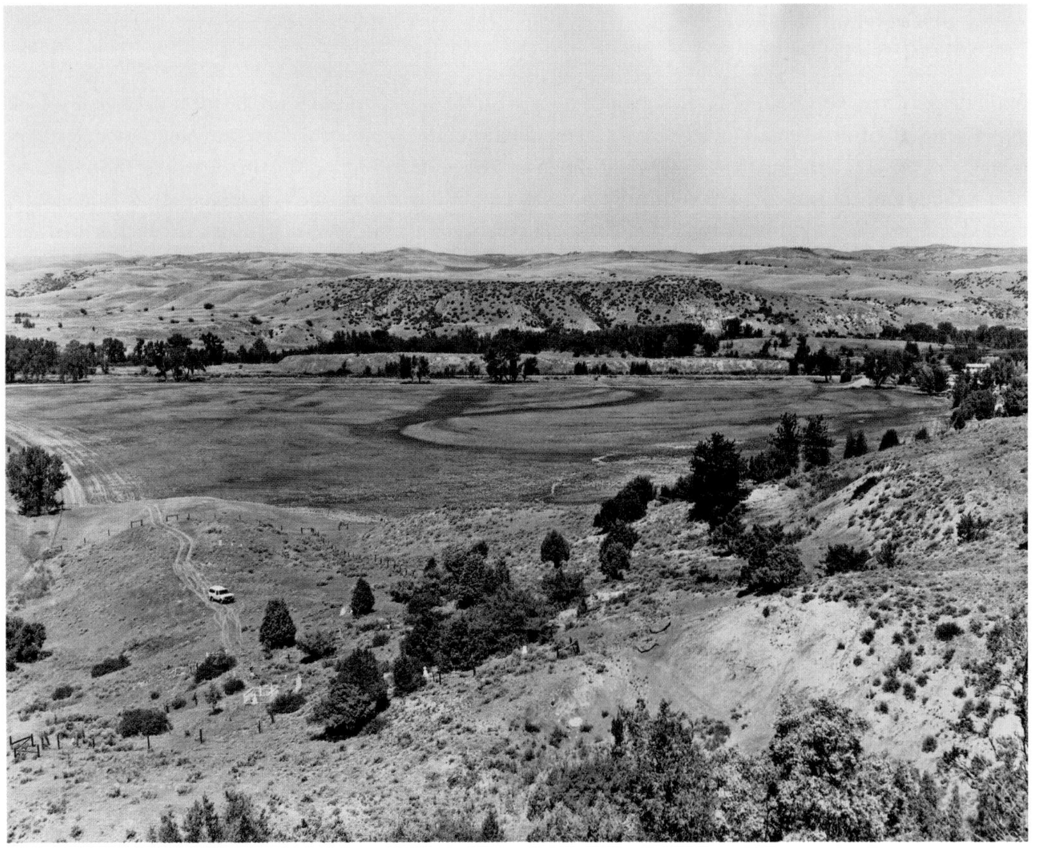

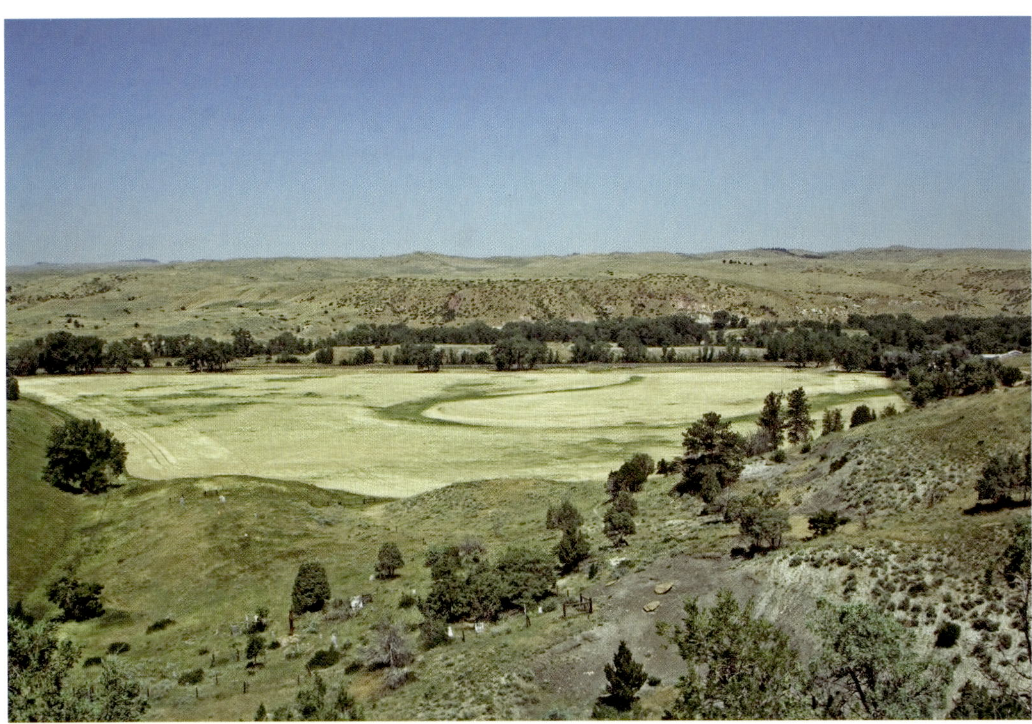

62. #2593

General View of Kearney Coal Camp (Kleenburn), 1909, 1988, 2007
GPS COORDINATES: 44 53.765N, 107 0.757W

The actual spelling of the coal camp in this view is Carney or Carneyville. Located in the Tongue River Valley north of Sheridan near Dietz, this camp was developed by William Carney of Chicago and his brother, Bernard Carney of Omaha. Their company, the Carney Coal Company, started the town in 1904. Like other area coal camps, Carney boasted an international workforce, though the largest ethnic group was the Poles.

Stimson made his photograph in a typical bird's-eye view from the southern bluff overlooking the Tongue River Valley. The large building in the foreground was the St. Thomas Catholic Church. Between it and the vantage point, close examination reveals the headstones of the Carney cemetery. Spread out through the valley below is the town of about 1,400. As in his views of nearby Dietz, the camera station chosen for this photograph projects a neat and orderly community, dominated by the Catholic Church.

Carney prospered in the decade or so after Stimson made his photograph. At the end of the World War I boom, however, labor strife erupted in the town. Eventually, the National Guard entered the northern Wyoming coalfields, followed by a roundup of suspected agitators. In 1923 the Carney Coal Company was sold to Peabody Coal and the town's name was changed to Kleenburn, to reflect the low-pollution coal mined there. As was the case in all Wyoming coal towns, the 1920s soon turned to bust. By 1933 the mine at Kleenburn ceased operating, and the town closed.

For my 1988 rephotograph, I parked my pickup near the former site of the church (which burned in 1920) and hiked to the top of the hill. Although nothing remained except the cemetery, land-use patterns can be discerned throughout the valley.

In 2007, Lauren and I parked along I-90, hopped a fence, and climbed to the top of the bluff to make my rephotograph. The fields below were fuller, and, except for the cemetery, there was even less to see. Subsequent to this photograph, in 2009 the Wyoming Department of Environmental Quality began a $395,000 cleanup of part of the Carney site, so future rephotographers will likely have even less to see.

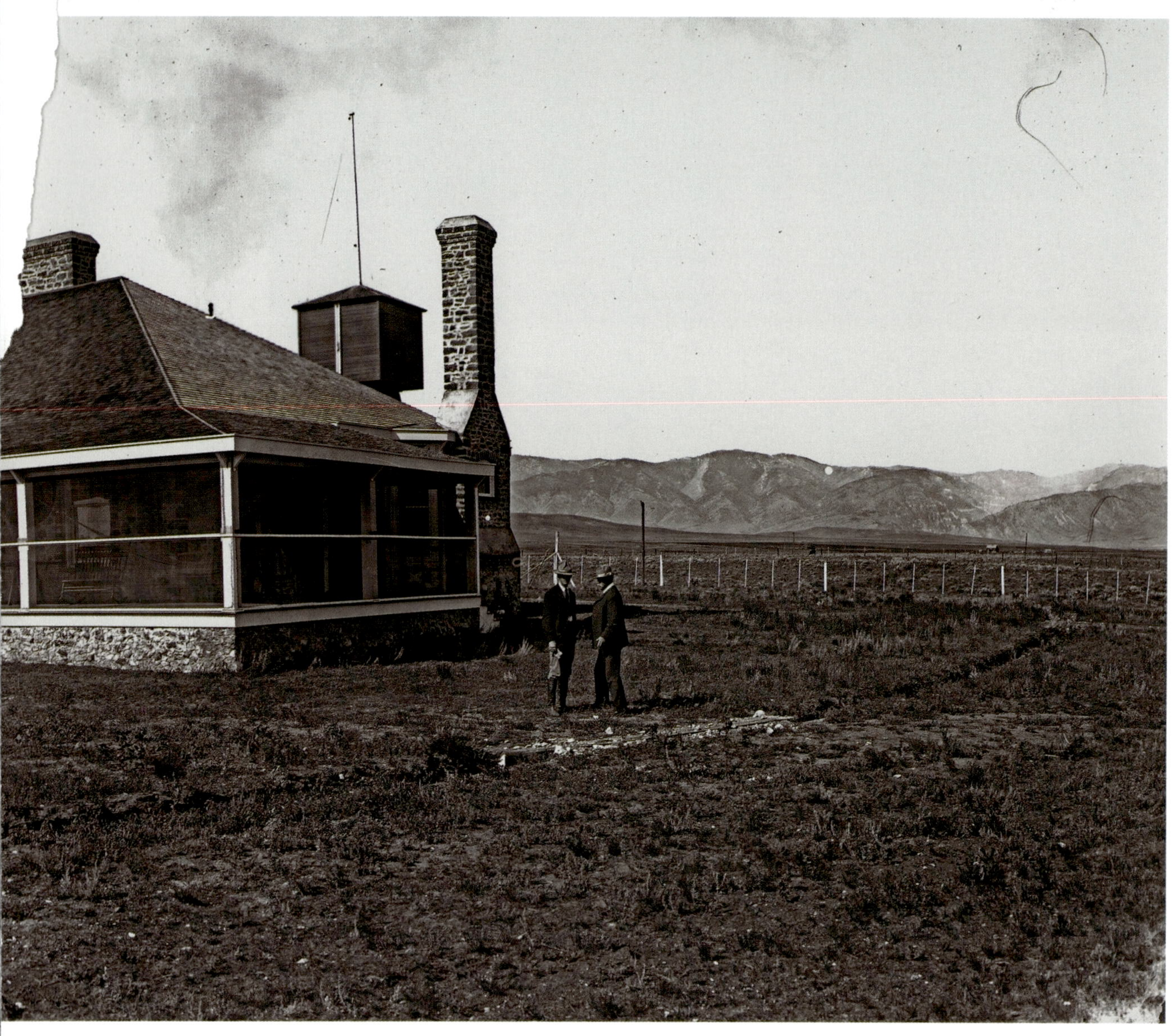

63. #537

Panorama of the Hardin Ranch, Sheridan Co., 1903, 2007
GPS COORDINATES: 44 53.5N, 107 10.558W

As discussed at length in chapter 5, these views of the Hardin Ranch outside Ranchester and my rephotographs reflect Stimson's purposes when he was photographing, as well as larger cultural ideas of the modern and postmodern. Recall that Stimson had been commissioned by the Union Pacific and the State of Wyoming to survey the state—a very modern exercise—and capture images of its best features to promote for the railroad and at the St. Louis World's Fair. This commodification of the landscape—turning images into capital—was also a very modern exercise. Because my rephotographs document those images today not from new, original vantage points

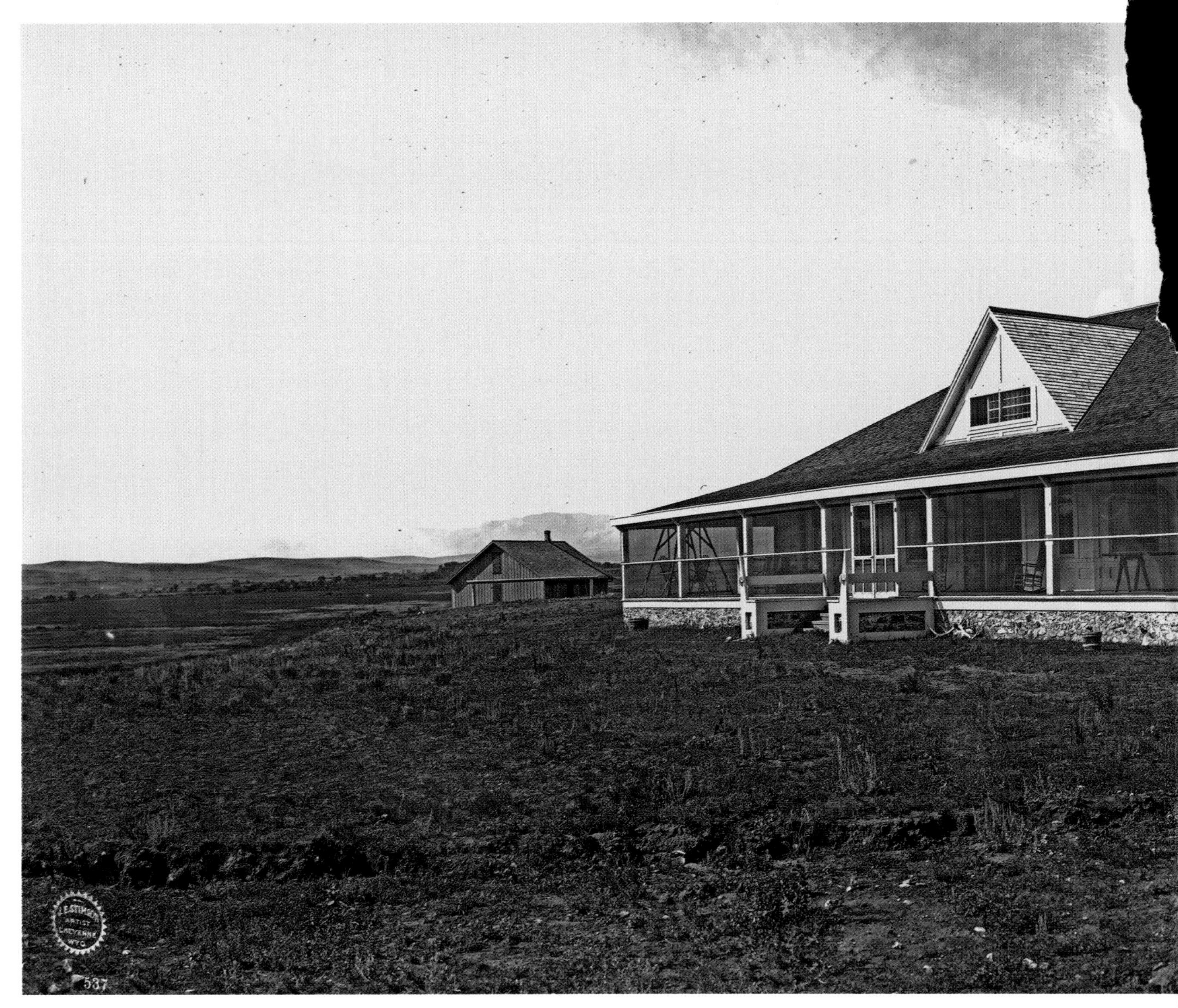
J.E. STIMSON
ARTIST
CHEYENNE
WYO.
537

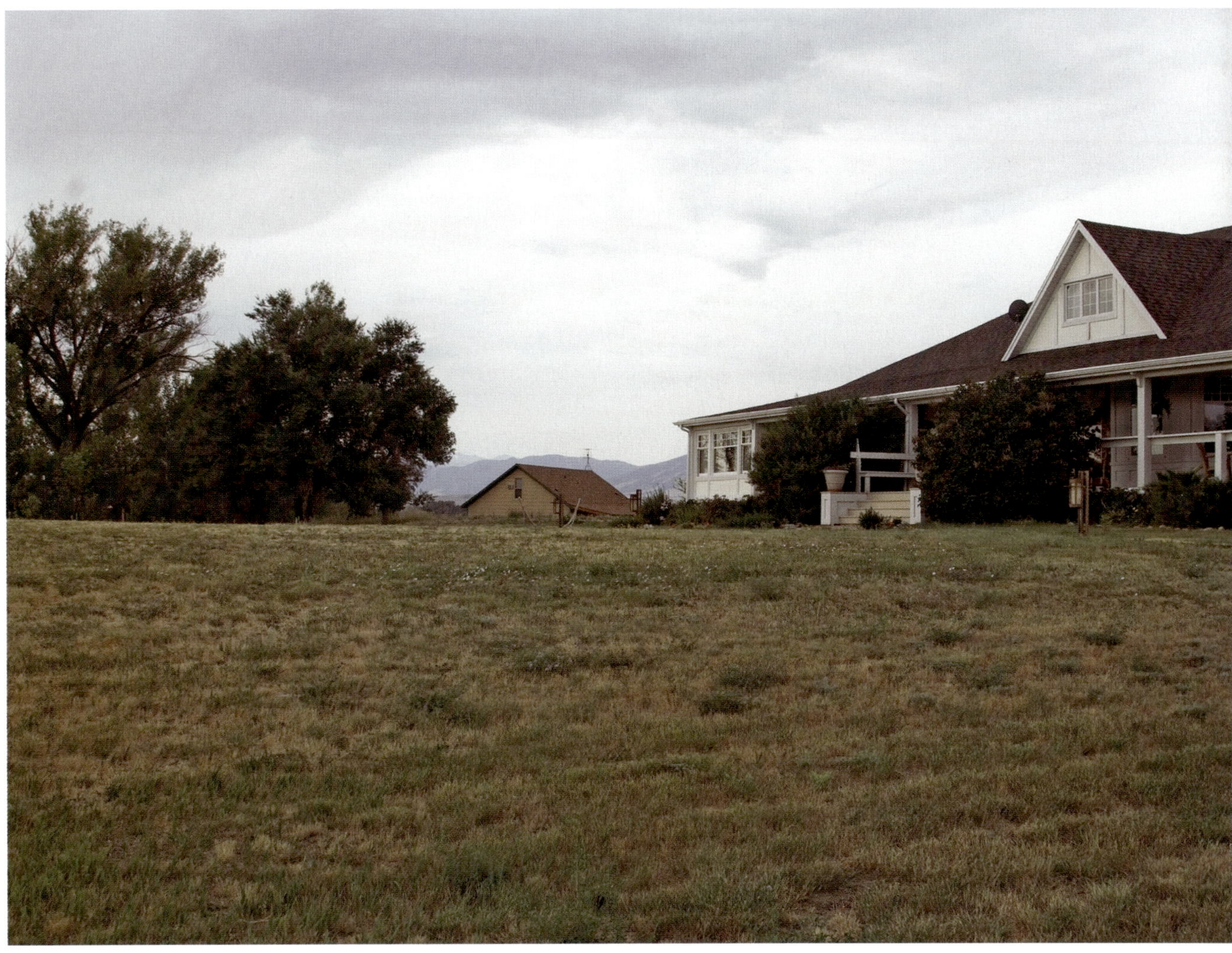

but instead from Stimson's camera stations of old, they reflect back on the modern to see what has become of it and are therefore postmodern.

In 1903 Stimson produced two panoramas—very unusual format choices—of the exterior of the Hardin Ranch. This view looks southwest toward the Big Horns and utilizes the typical portrait style of a building, viewing it from a corner so as to see two sides of the structure. In this view two men, presumably Samuel Hardin and his stepson, are at right. The house with its screened-in front porch sits atop a small hill, completely devoid of any trees or bushes. Fences, a water tower, and another structure are visible in the back, while an irrigation ditch crosses in the foreground. The ranch house strikes a grand pose from this low angle.

My 2007 rephotograph shows a few changes to the porch, a new garage at right, some added bushes and trees, but basically the same house Stimson photographed 104 years earlier.

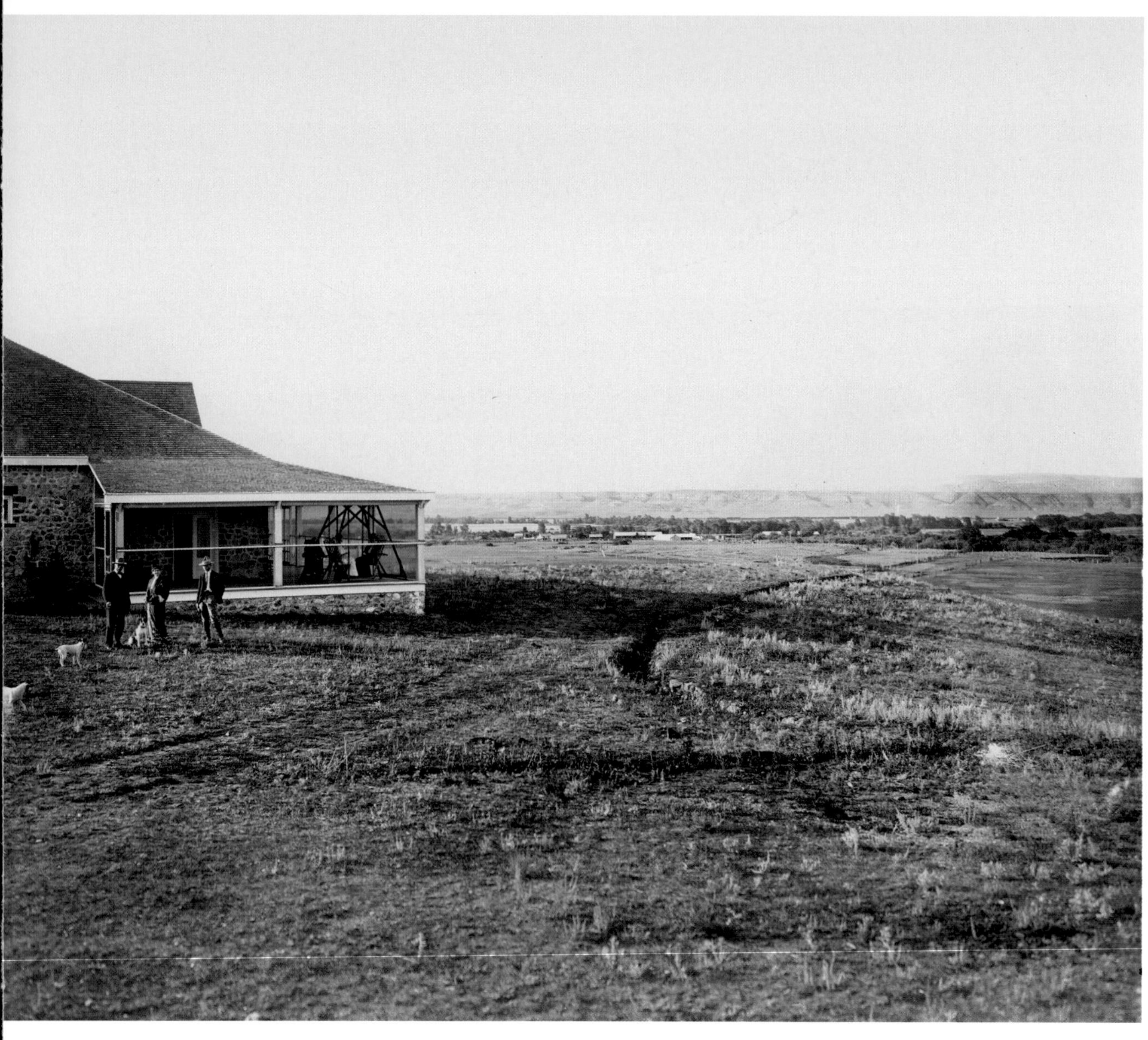

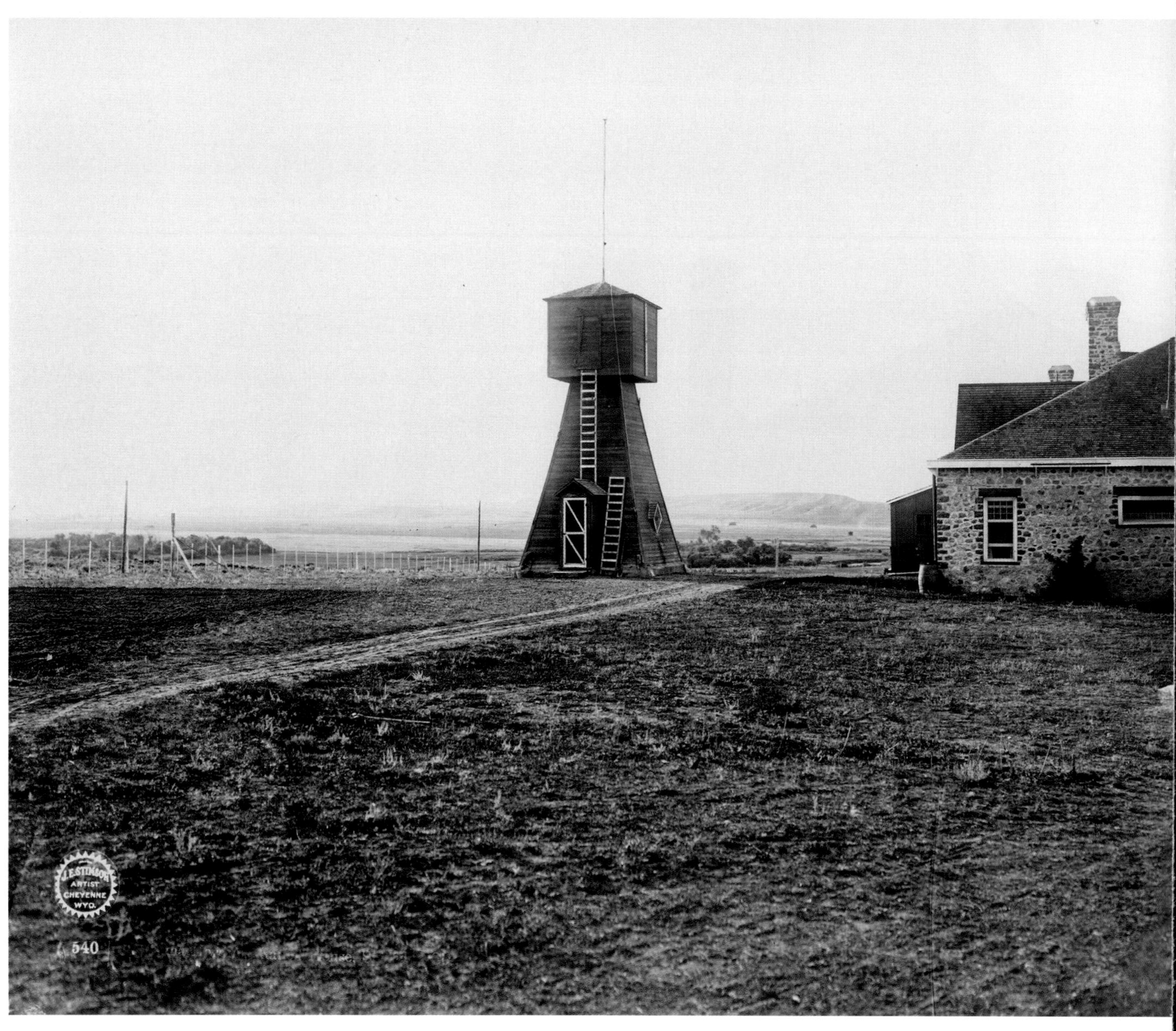

J. E. STIMSON
ARTIST
CHEYENNE
WYO.
540

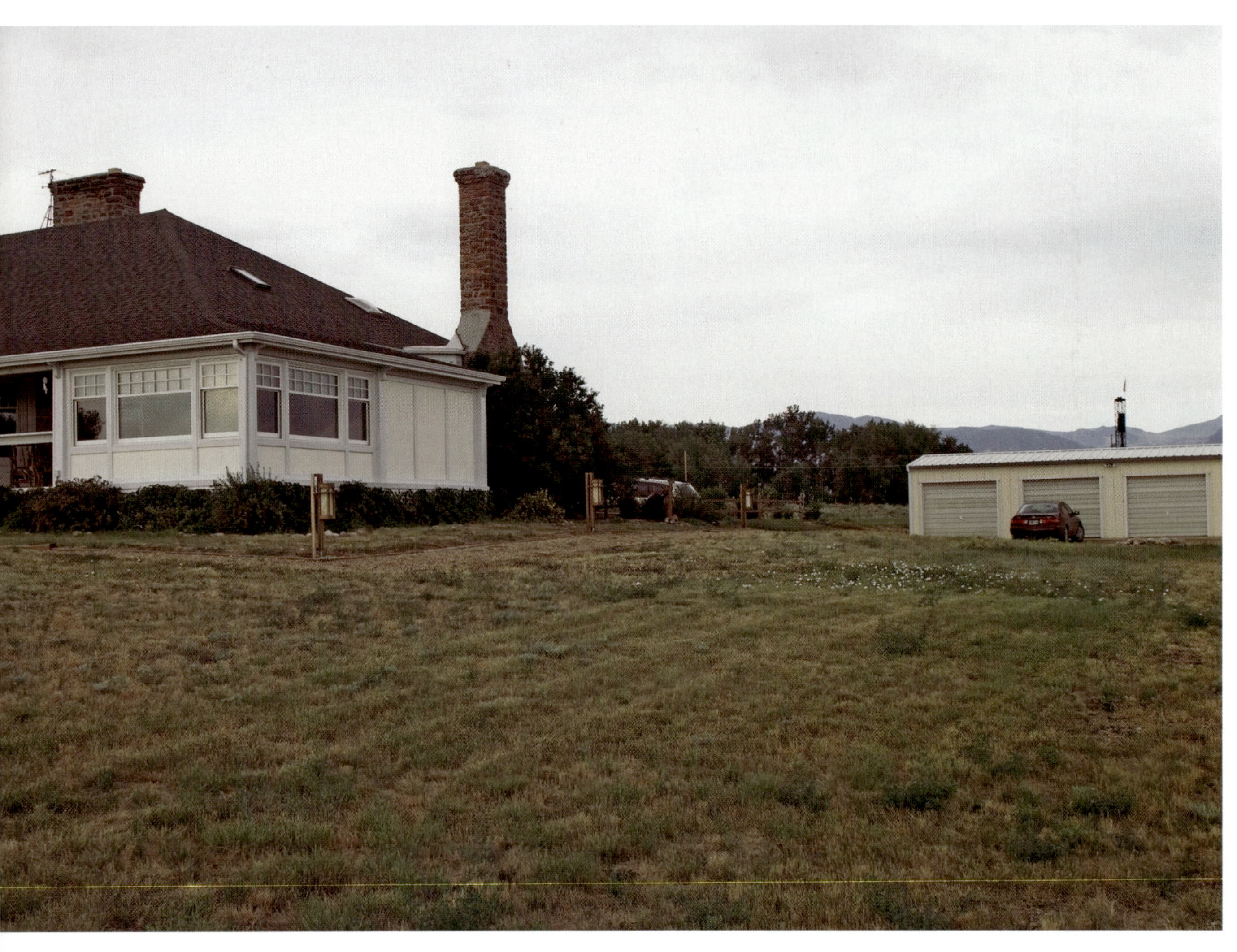

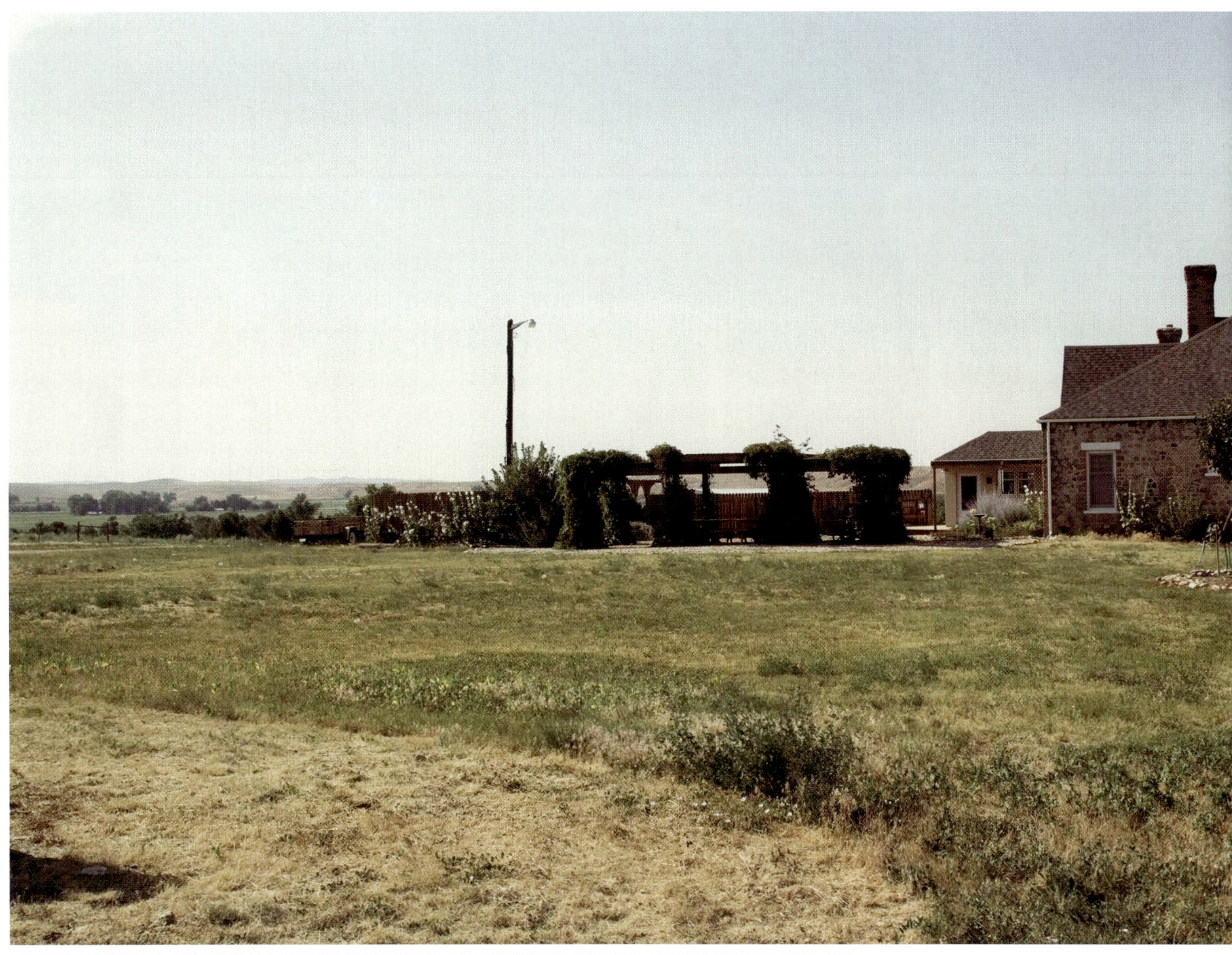

64. #540

Panorama of Hardin Ranch, Looking North, 1903, 2007
GPS COORDINATES: 44 53.45167N, 107 10.5823W

For this second exterior panorama, Stimson has swung his camera to the south side of the building and is now looking at the other side of the home, to the north. The large water tower is clearly visible. A rain barrel can be seen at a downspout, as well as several bushes along the wall. In front of the house, three people—presumably Samuel Hardin, his wife, and his stepson—are visible, as are three dogs. On the screened-in porch, several people occupy what appears to be a large swing. Telephone/power poles can be seen in the distance. At right, in the far distance, lies the Tongue River Valley.

In my 2007 rephotograph, more trees, a television antenna atop the roof, a small addition in the back, and the garage are visible. The porch is now enclosed, but, interestingly, an outdoor swing is visible against the house just to the left of the bush, center.

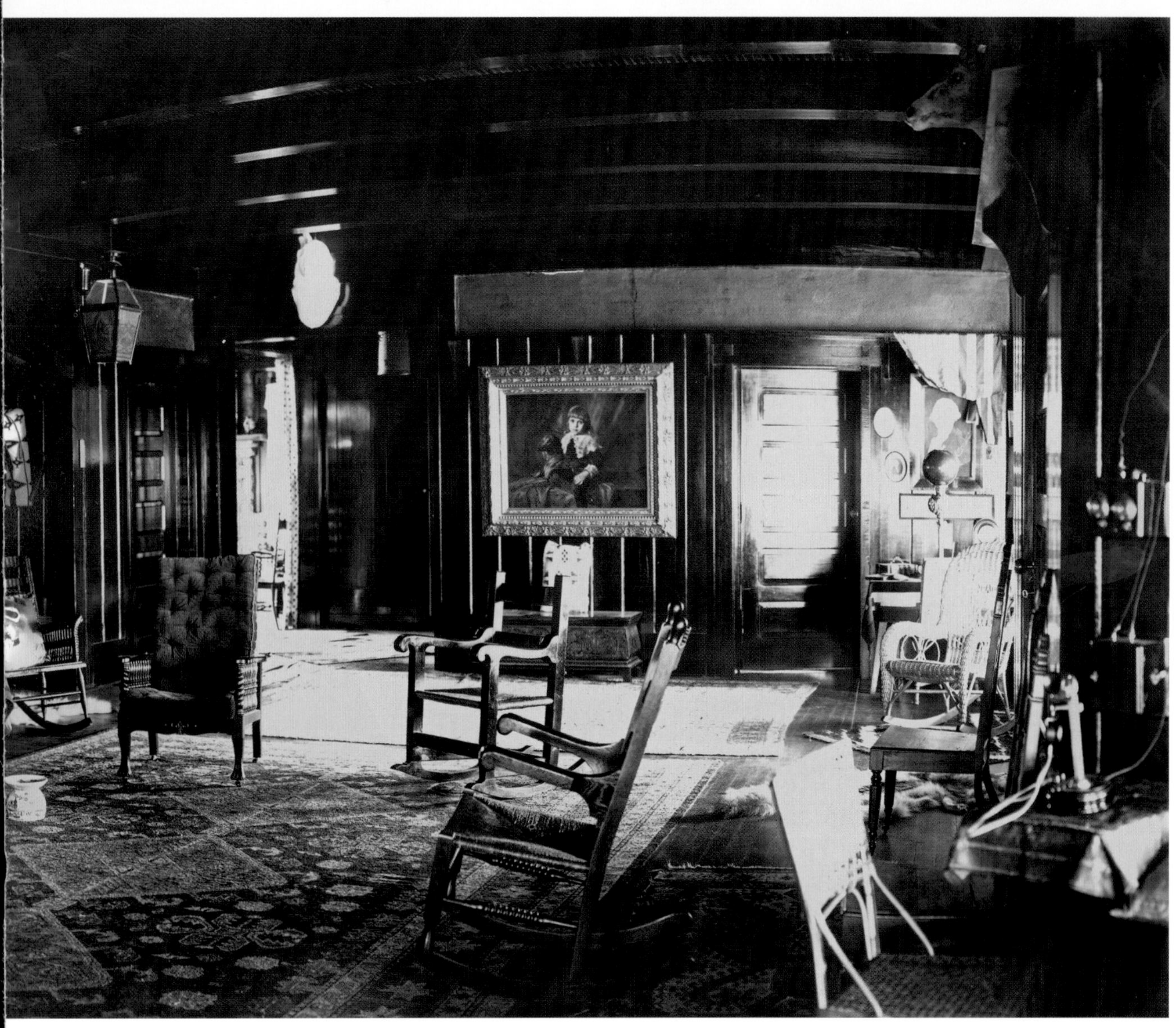

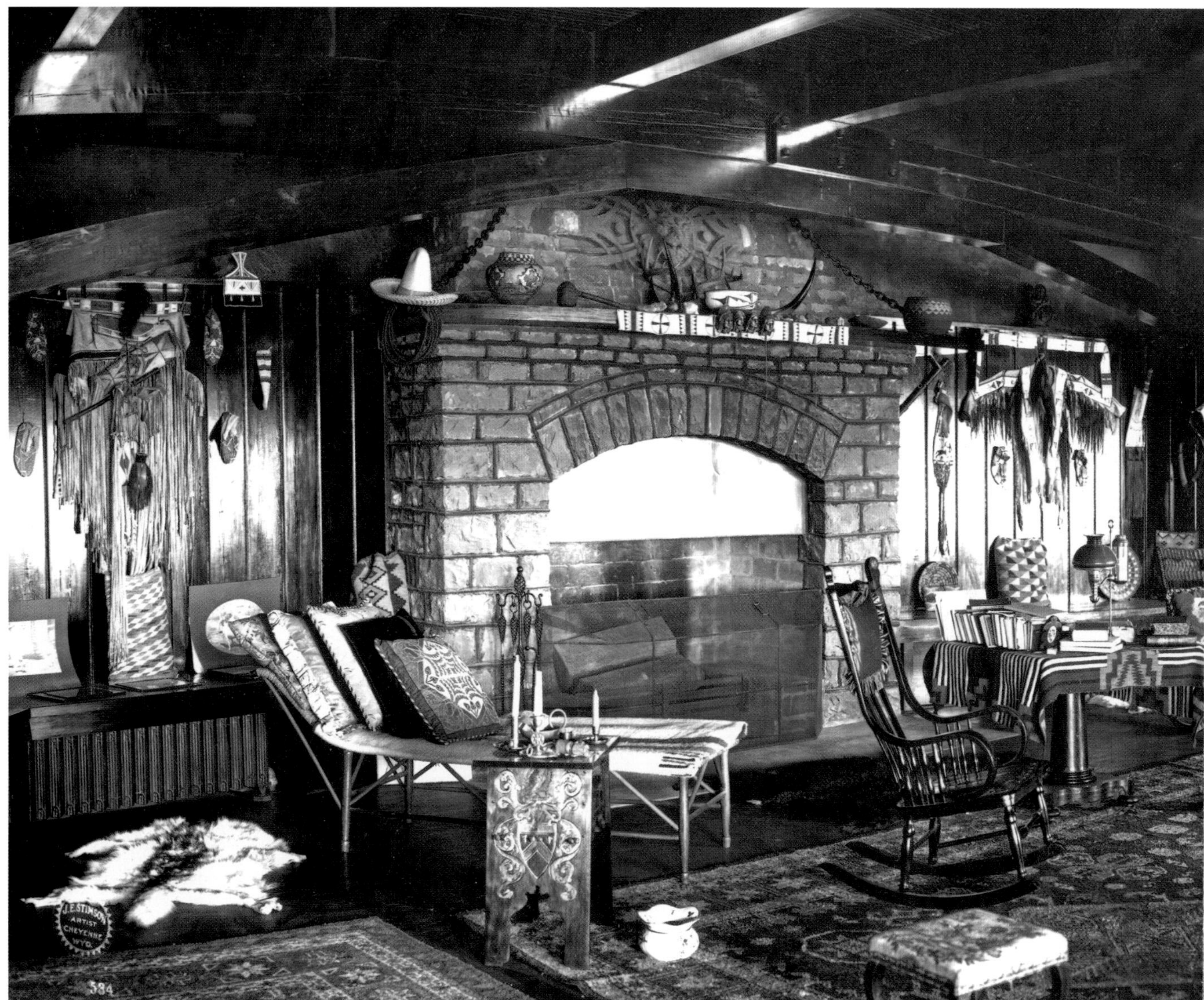
J.E. STIMSON
ARTIST
CHEYENNE
WYO.
384

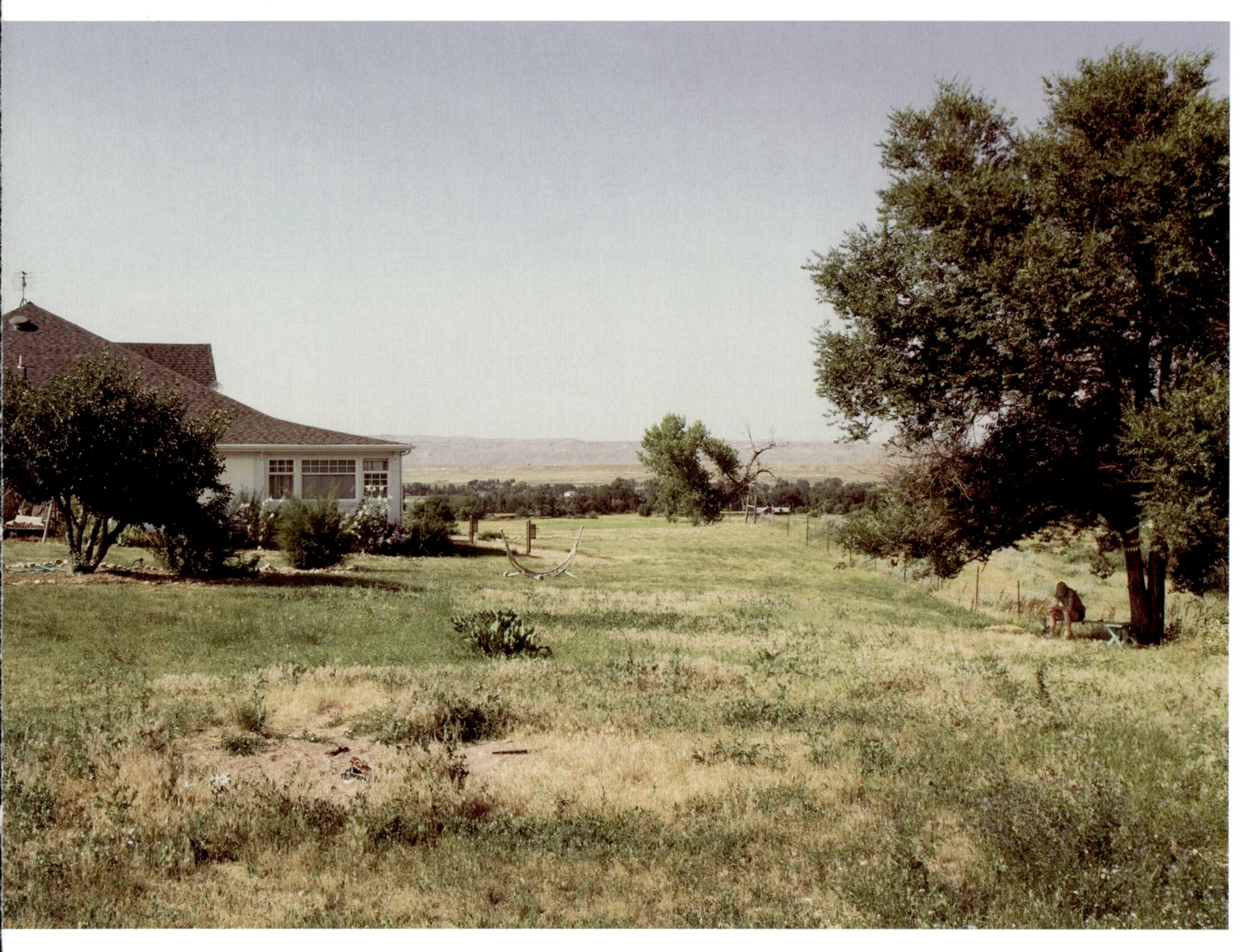

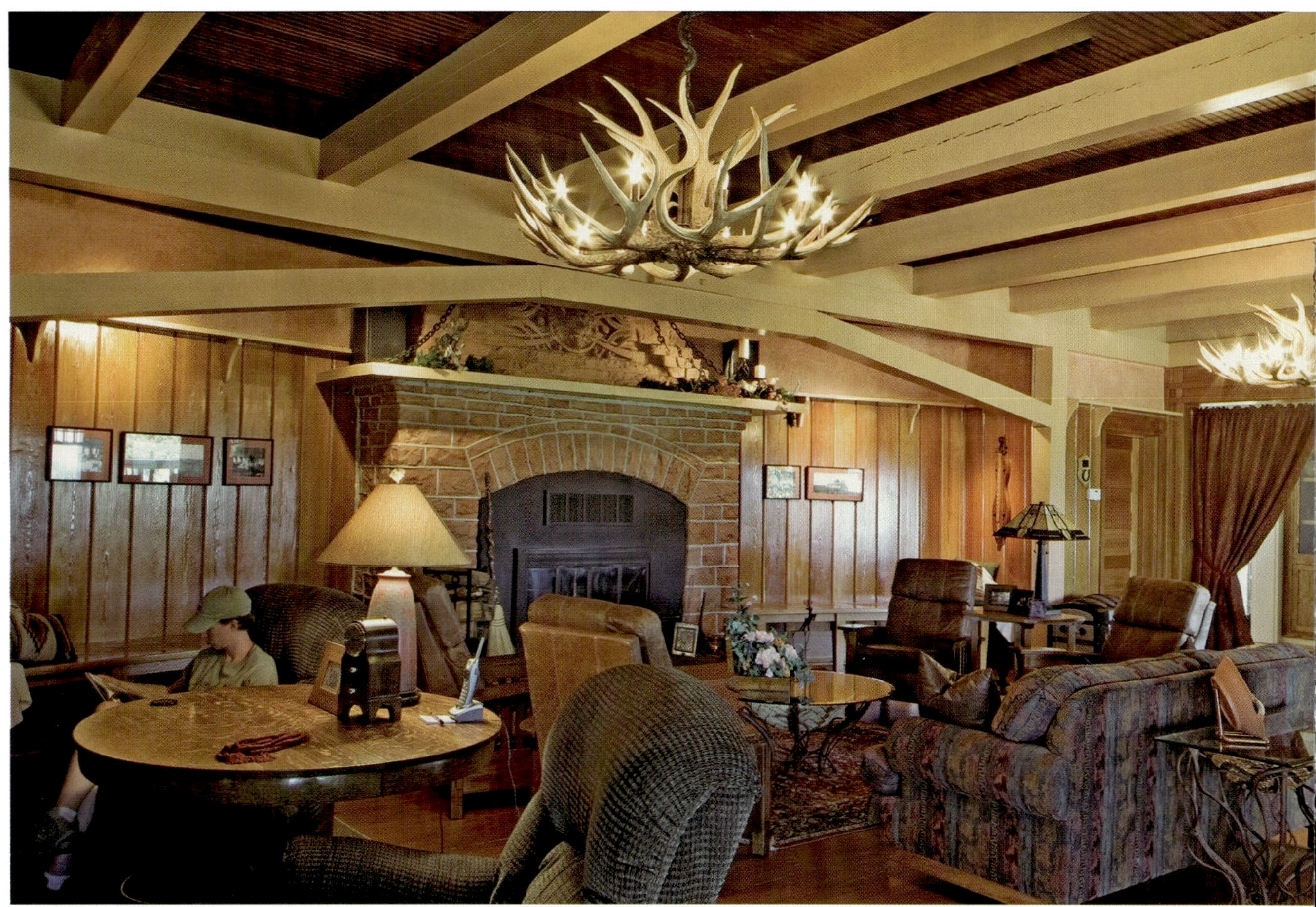

65. #534 and #534a

Interior Panorama, Hardin Residence, Sheridan Co., 1903, 2007
GPS COORDINATES: 44 53.481833N, 107 10.590833W

As discussed at length in chapter 5, this very rare interior panorama of the Hardin Ranch is full of icons of modernism, while my rephotograph panorama follows suit with the postmodern. For J. E. Stimson, who was trying to capture the best Wyoming had to offer, this interior must have been stunning. After all, he took seven more shots of it. In this view, moving left to right, we see Native American clothing displayed as ornamentation, Oriental rugs and embroidered pillows, Craftsman furniture and pottery, southwestern pottery and basketry, more Native American clothing, and another Arts and Crafts table covered with a Navajo rug and holding a pile of books. To the right, more Craftsman chairs, rugs, oil paintings, and a candlestick telephone can be seen. Each of these items could be discussed as representative of modernity. Thinking even more broadly, the openness of this great room suggests the modern rather than the closed-off little spaces of Victorian America.

My 2007 rephotograph similarly hints at the postmodern. Again, moving left to right across the room we find Craftsman-style tables and chairs, a sofa, and reproduction Tiffany lighting, all of which reflects back on modernity. Moving back toward the fireplace, we find antler chandeliers—reflections of the Old West—and, aside the fireplace, the clearest examples of the postmodern: modern prints of Stimson's sioginal photographs of this house. As I discovered that day, these images were used as visual templates to recreate the home as a postmodern visual simulacrum of the original. Finally, to the right are more Craftsman-inspired chairs and tables and a bookcase with period-looking lighting. Just as Stimson must have been fascinated by what he found, I, too, was enthralled by this beautiful postmodern interior.

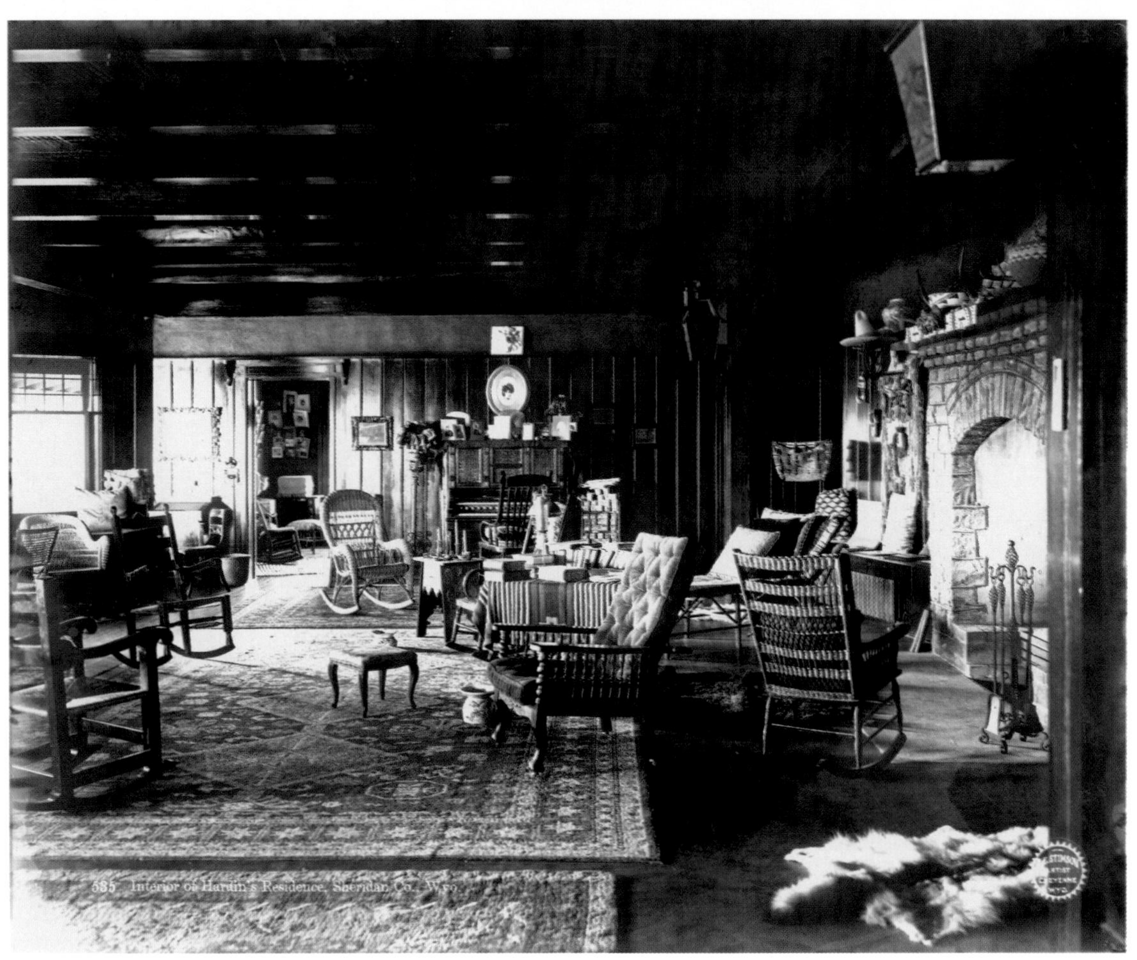
585   Interior of Hardin's Residence, Sheridan Co., Wyo.

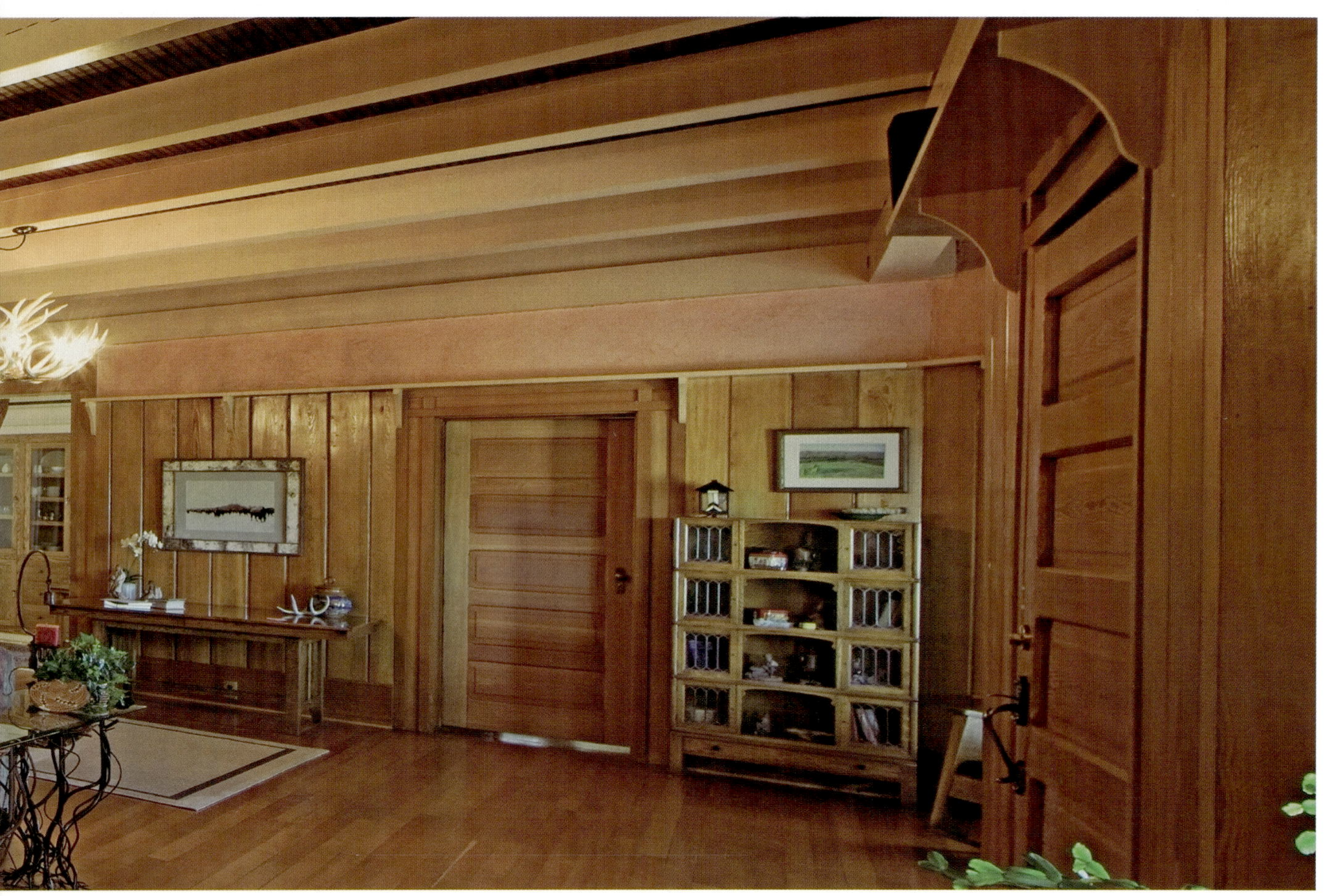

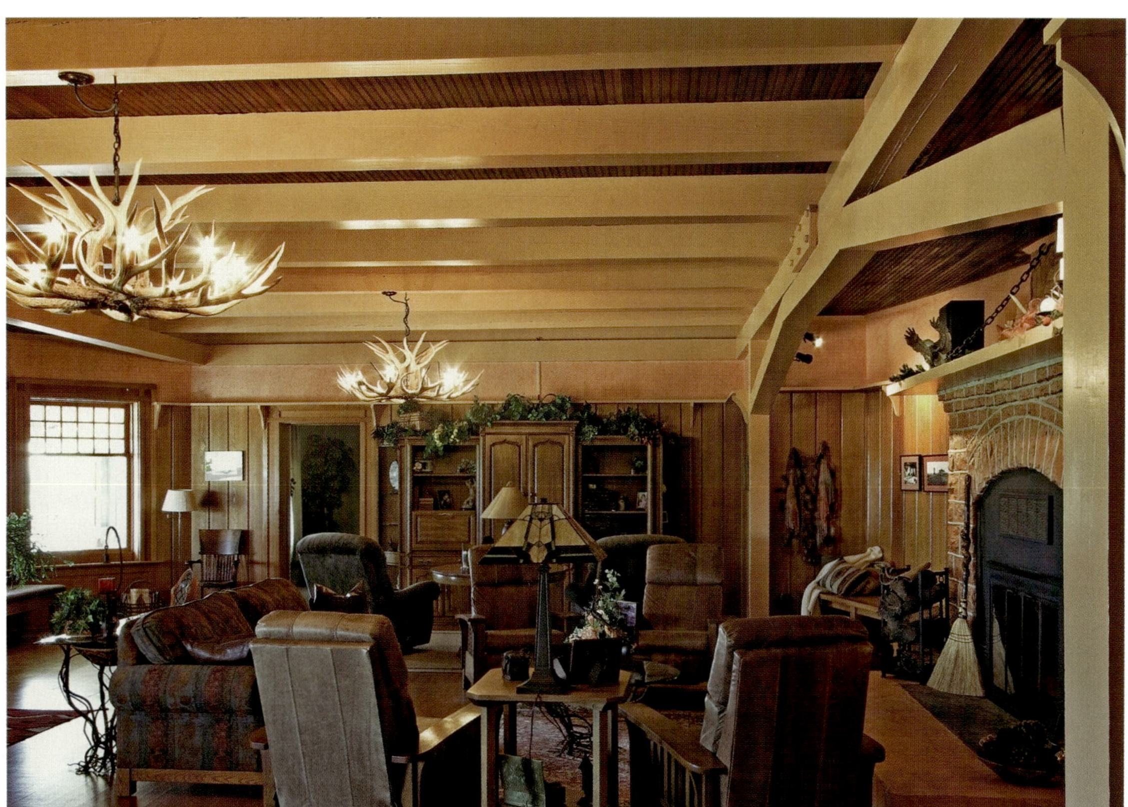

66. #535

Interior of Hardin Residence, Sheridan Co. (looking south), 1903, 2007
GPS COORDINATES: 44 53.481833N, 107 10.590833W

For this view of the Hardin Ranch interior, Stimson moved his camera across the room and turned back, looking south, with the fireplace to the right and the front door to the left. In addition to the items viewed in the previous photograph, the modern great room affords a view of more Craftsman rocking chairs, an Arts and Crafts fireplace set, pottery cuspidors, wicker chairs, a chaise-style lounge, and, on the back wall, an Aeolian player organ with a large selection of paper reels to its left. This organ, which could be played by pumping the pedals and striking the keys, could also play "recorded" music that had been inscribed into the paper reels and then played back through the organ like a player piano when someone pumped the pedals. Above the organ is what appears to be a group of portraits, no doubt of family members. Beyond the organ, an open door reveals another sitting area and more family photographs.

In my 2007 rephotograph, the Craftsman-style chairs, table, and lighting are more visible. In the back, where the organ stood, a large shelf unit and, to its left, Arts and Crafts–style textiles and pillows are visible. In the adjacent room is a large indoor tree.

As stated earlier, the current owners of the Hardin Ranch have done a beautiful job of restoring and refurbishing this gorgeous home. Just as Hardin's efforts reflected his modern era, this remodel represents a postmodern one.

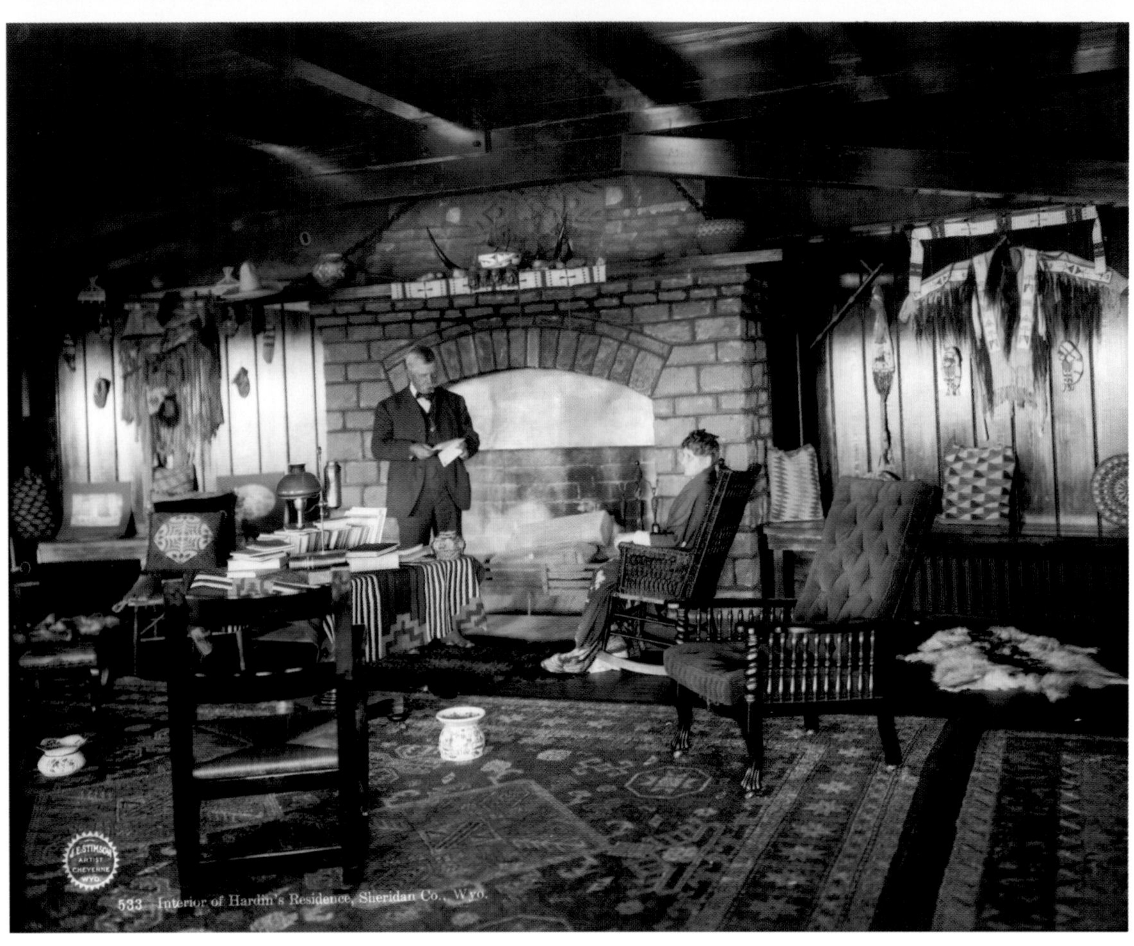
533 Interior of Hardin's Residence, Sheridan Co., Wyo.

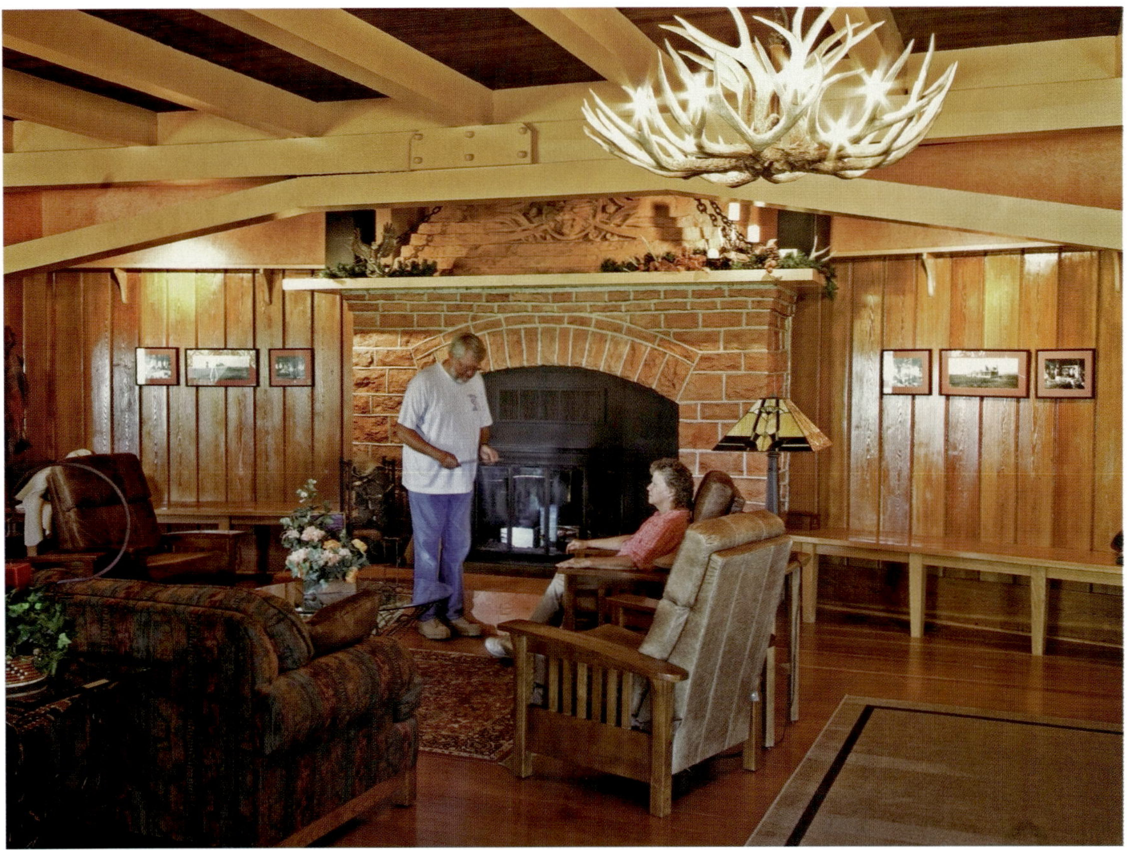

67. #533

Interior of Hardin's Residence (couple at fireplace), 1903, 2007
GPS COORDINATES: 44 53.481833N, 107 10.590833W

In his view, Stimson posed Samuel Hardin and his wife, Jessie, in front of the great room's fireplace, with its intricately carved stone above the mantle. Surrounding them are symbols of modernity, including the Oriental rugs on the floor, the Craftsman chairs, and embroidered pillows. Moreover, the use of Native American handiwork as artwork suggests the modern cultural idea of primitivism. That is, in a world increasingly driven by machines, handmade goods—including the southwestern pots and basketry near the fireplace, the Navajo rug on the book table, and the Lakota tunic and moccasins on the wall—serve as primitive reminders of America's increasingly modern conquest of the West.

My 2007 view also exhibits many symbols of the postmodern West. As Rebecca Solnit explains in *Yosemite in Time*, the act of seeking out a previous modern photographer's vantage point and then purposely duplicating that shot is a "spectacularly postmodern exercise" because it reflects back on how the modern view held up over time. Solnit further argues that rephotography has moved from modern recorder of the world around us to postmodern shaper as historic preservationists use rephotographs of the modern to recreate its look today.

This is exactly what is going on in my rephotograph. By posing the current owners of the Old Stone Inn in similar stances as Samuel and Jessie Hardin, I unknowingly replicated the modern view. More important, instead of the Indian tunics, pottery, and basketry—tropes of the modern conquest of the West—the current owners have placed framed modern prints of Stimson images of the home, which served as templates in its restoration. Combined with the neo-Craftsman furniture and the antler chandelier, these images do not create a new look but instead replicate an earlier, modern era. As such, they are perfect examples of the postmodern—trophies to the conquest of the modern West.

As someone hired to photograph the best of Wyoming, J. E. Stimson must have been dumbfounded by his discovery of this quintessentially modern ranch house in the middle of nowhere in Wyoming. He did, after all, make ten views of this one house. In repeating these shots, I felt much the same.

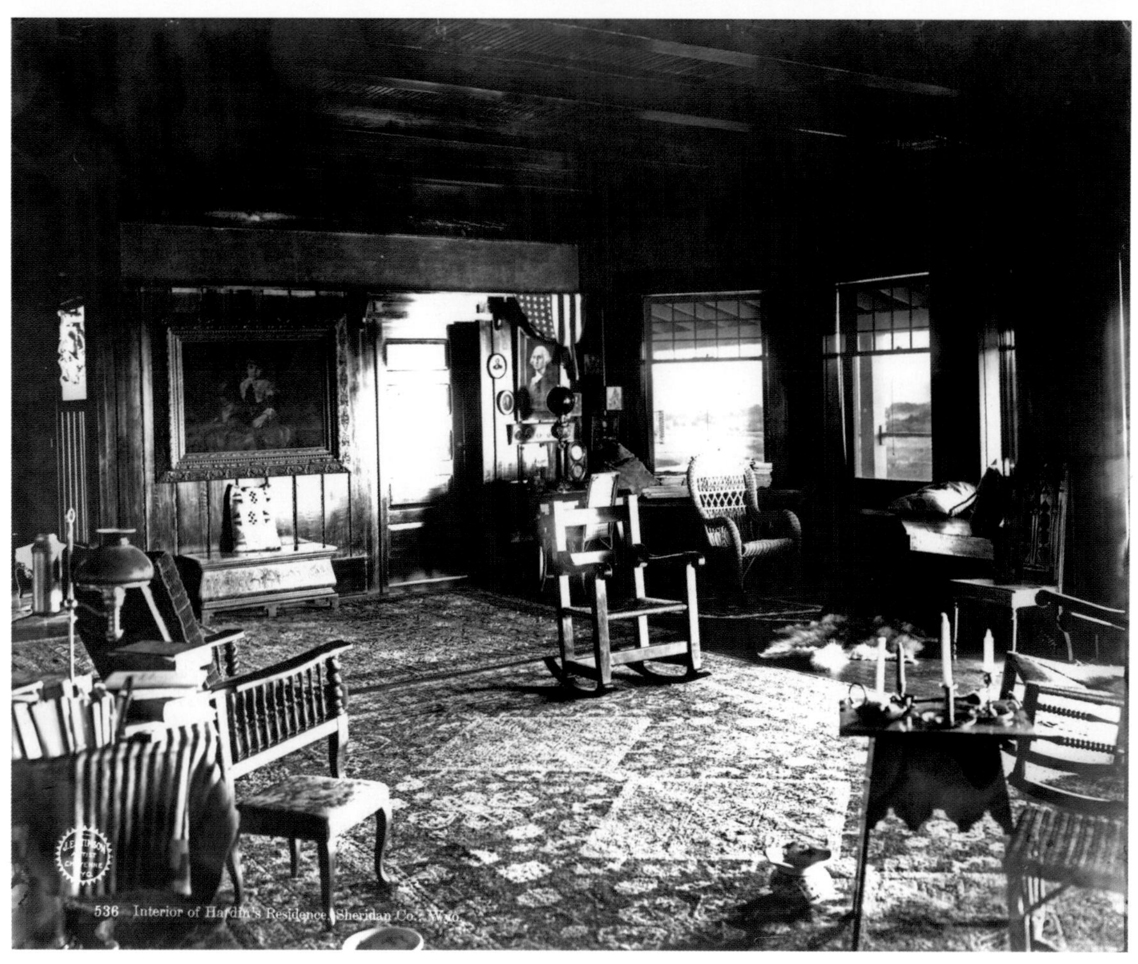
536 Interior of Hardin's Residence, Sheridan Co., Wyo.

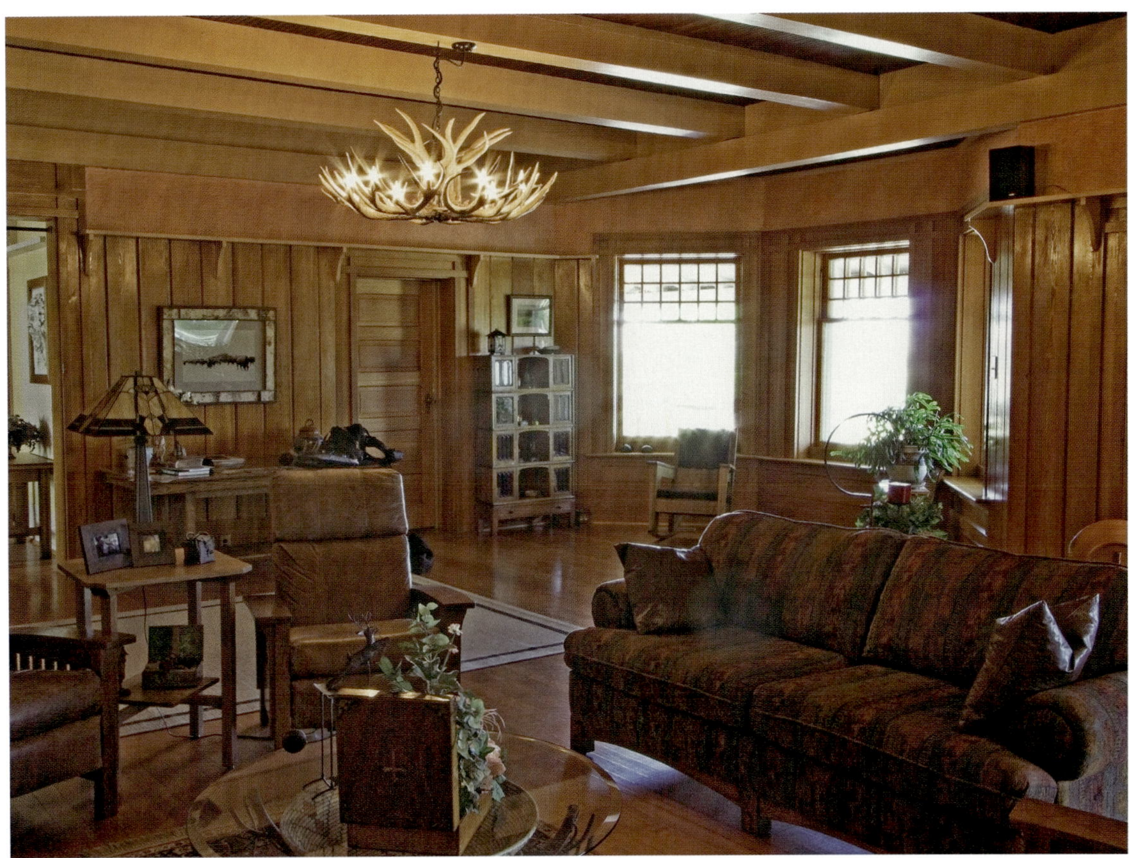

68. #536

Interior of Hardin Residence (looking NE), 1903, 2007
GPS COORDINATES: 44 53.481833N, 107 10.590833W

Rounding out the interior views, Stimson moved to the south side of the fireplace and pointed his camera northeast toward the front porch. Morning light floods into the room, illuminating the Oriental rugs, Craftsman chairs, the large oil painting of a boy and his dog, and, new to this view, a corner dedicated to American history. On the small desk are a large lamp and weather station; above that, an American flag is draped over a familiar portrait of George Washington, while smaller images of Abraham Lincoln and Thomas Jefferson are visible to the left.

My 2007 rephotograph illuminates a Craftsman-style rocker, small curio case, and an Arts and Crafts–style table, over which hangs a painting of cattle or buffalo.

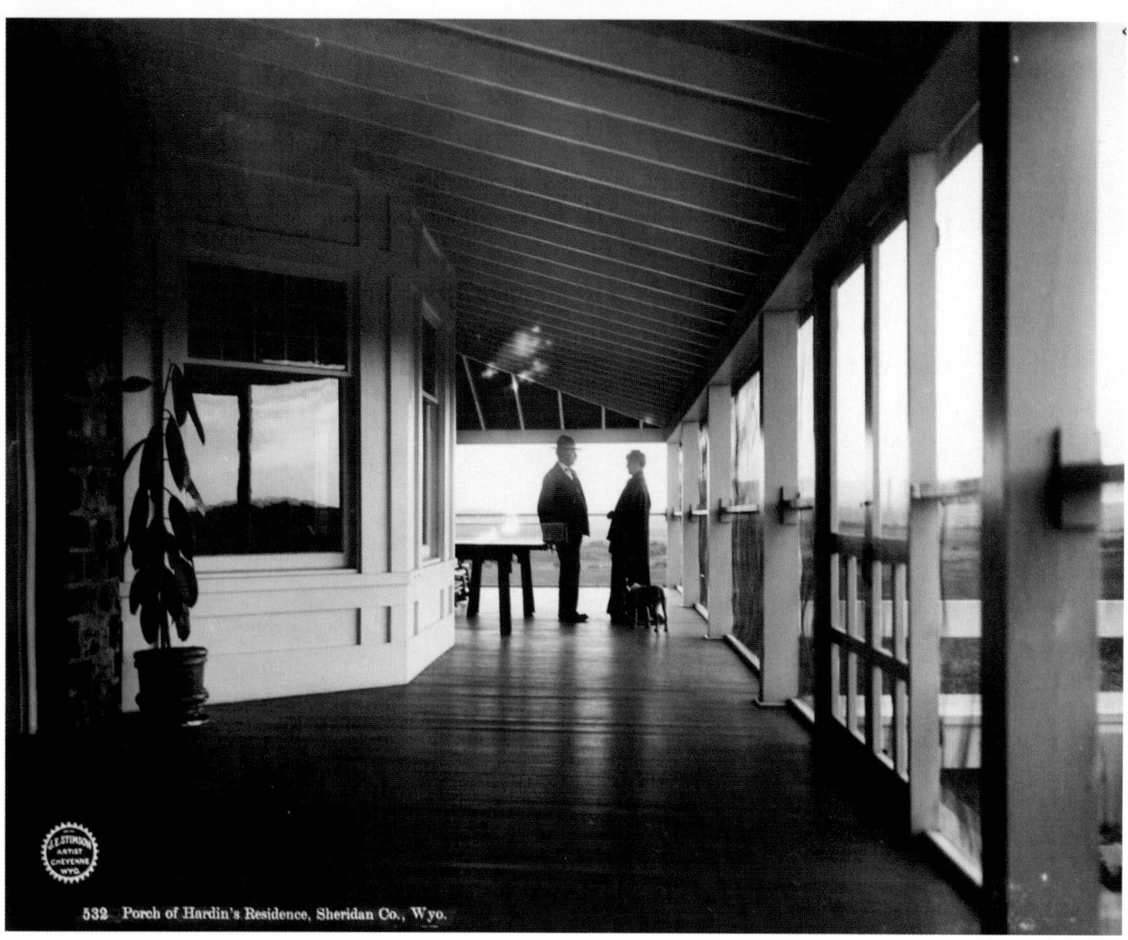

532   Porch of Hardin's Residence, Sheridan Co., Wyo.

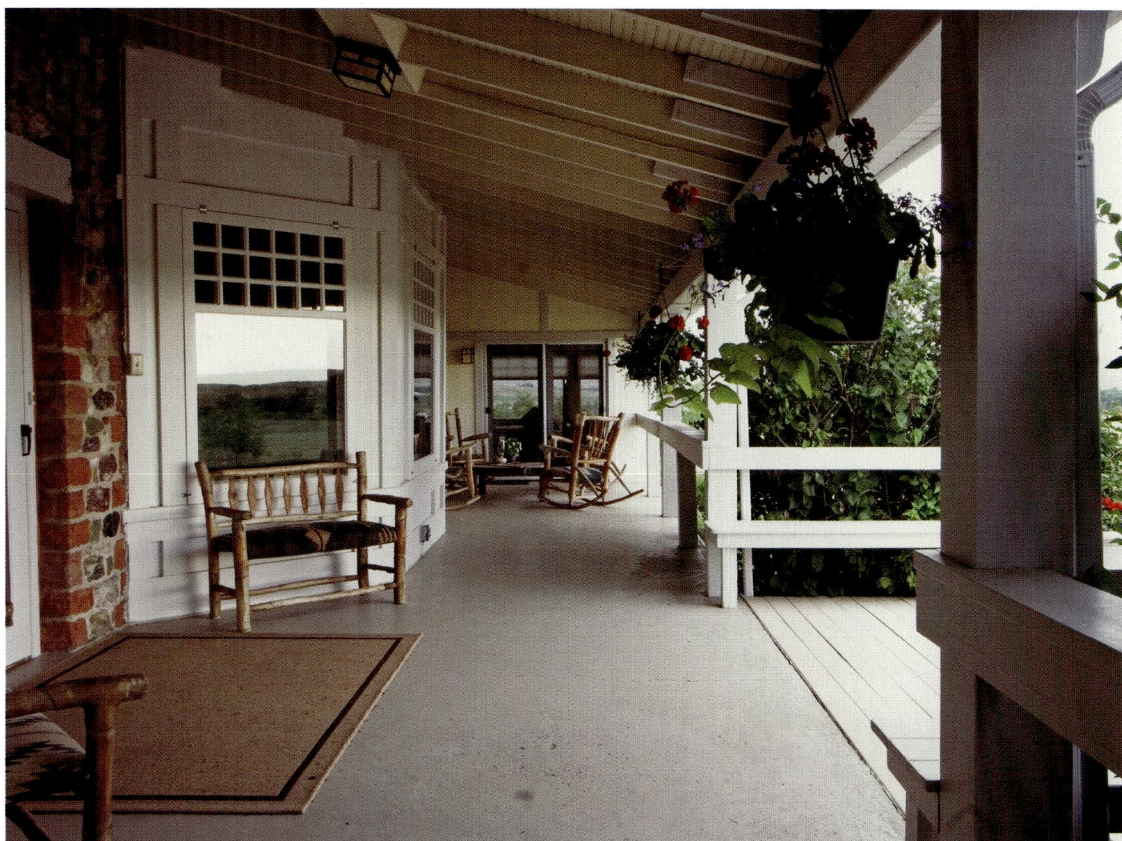

69. #532

Porch of Hardin's Residence, Sheridan Co., 1903, 2007
GPS COORDINATES: 44 53.481833N, 107 10.590833W

In what appears to be a simple view looking north on the enclosed front porch, Stimson has used the tight walls and reduced light emanating from the screens to focus our attention on what appear to be Mr. and Mrs. Hardin and one of their dogs standing near a table. What looks like a potted rubber tree stands near the front door.

As in every other view of this house, my 2007 rephotograph picks up postmodern symbols, including the Craftsman-style porch lights and log pole–style furniture with Navajo-style seats. A simple porch rug and hanging potted plants add to the charm. Even the front windows, partitioned into three rows of six panes each, hint at the originals, which had three rows of five panes each.

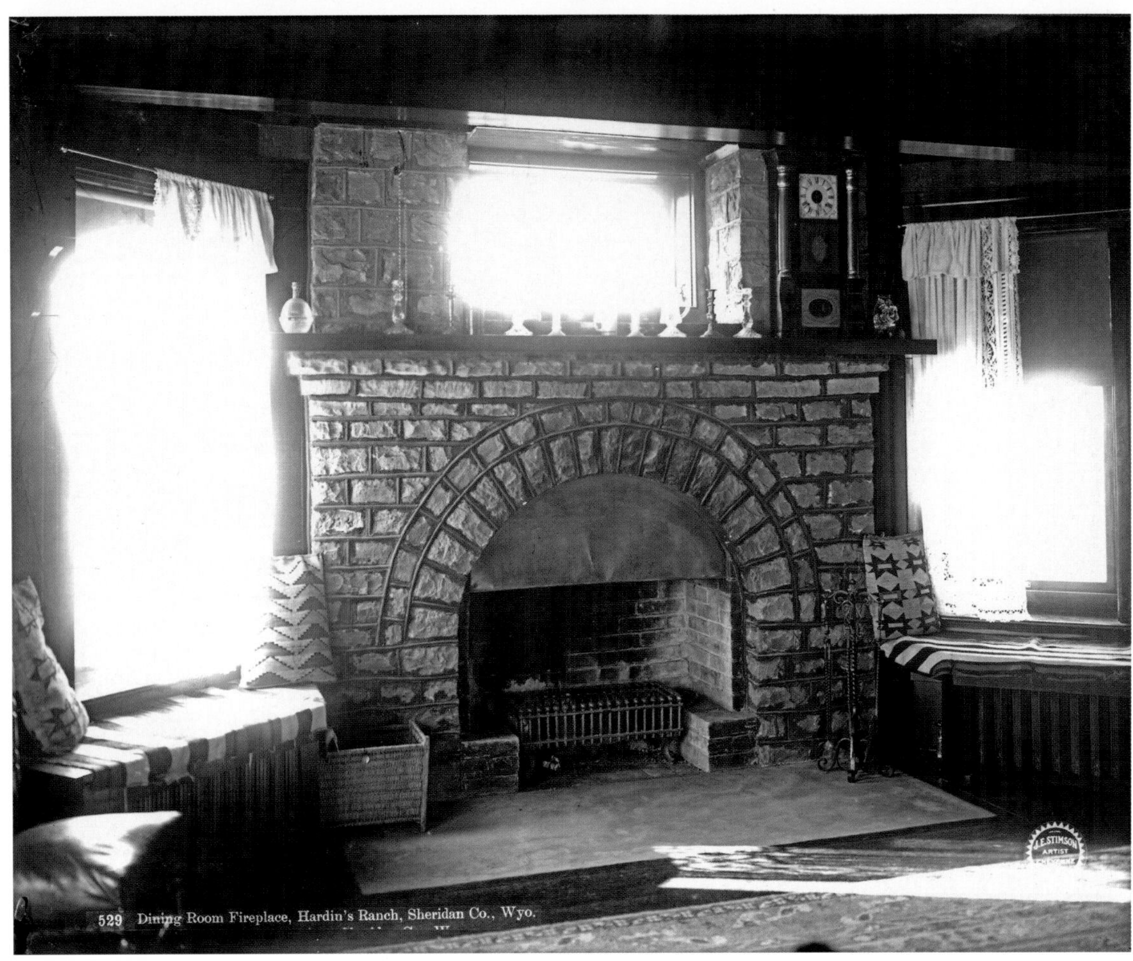

529   Dining Room Fireplace, Hardin's Ranch, Sheridan Co., Wyo.

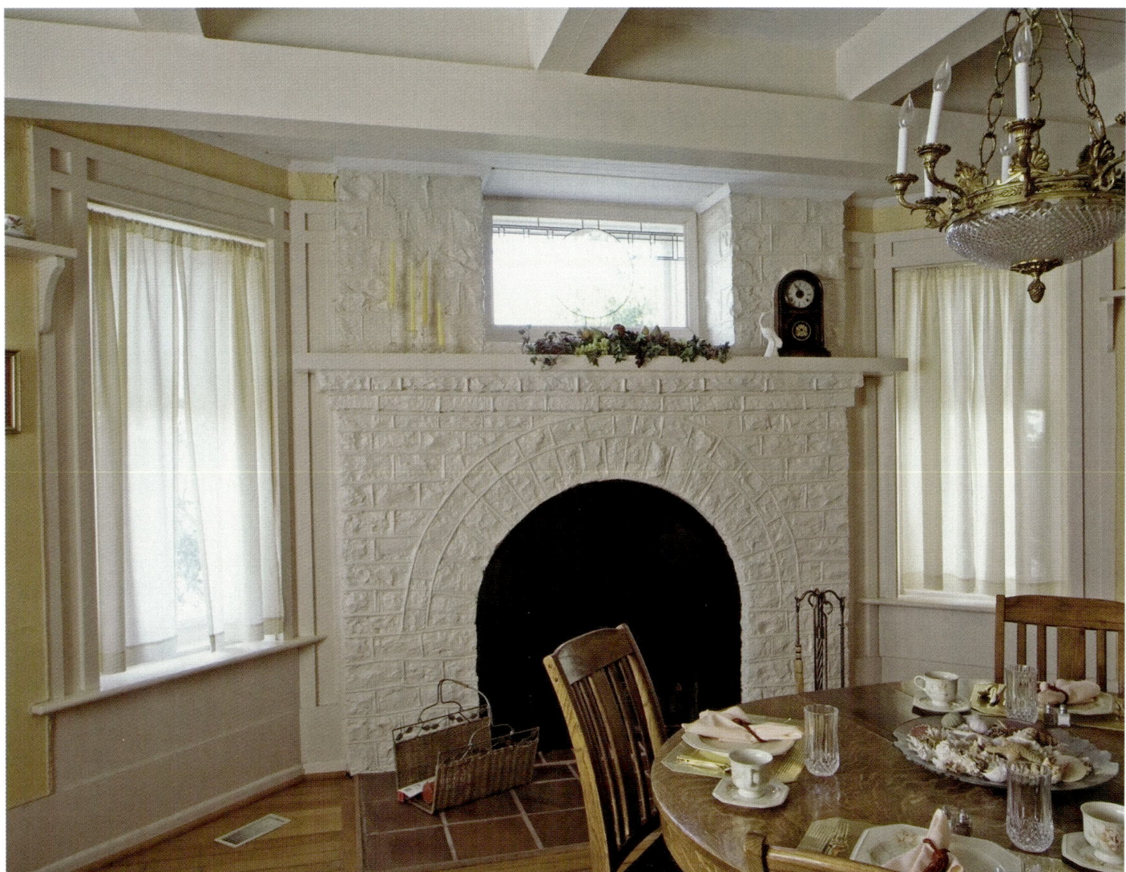

70. #529

Dining Room Fireplace, Hardin's Residence, 1903, 2007
GPS COORDINATES: 44 53.481833N, 107 10.590833W

The final pair of images of the Hardin Ranch interior moves out of the great room into a small dining room on the northwest side of the home. Stimson placed his camera at the room entrance, capturing the ornate stone fireplace bathed in late afternoon sun. That light, coming in from the West, confirms that the photographer had worked at the house all day. In addition, he captured a beautiful mantle clock and an assortment of candleholders and ornate glass nearby. In the inglenook beside the fireplace, another Craftsman fireplace set, a wicker basket, and two benches covered in Navajo textiles complete the image of modern domesticity. The only thing missing, ironically, is a dining room table.

In my 2007 rephotograph, a beautiful oak dining table sits ready for a meal. The fireplace across the room has been painted white and its inglenook benches removed. An Arts and Crafts–style fireplace set is hidden behind the table, with an aspen-inspired log holder to the left. On the mantle, in the same place as the original, is a small clock; next to it are a glass bird figurine and some candles. Above the fireplace, a leaded window completes the postmodern image of domesticity.

It cannot be overstated that the current owners of the Hardin Ranch, in their renovation of it as the Old Stone Inn, have done a wonderful job of restoring the beauty of the original home. But in replicating this gorgeous modern ranch home, they have followed postmodern trends and created a beautiful postmodern version. By rephotographing it from Stimson's modern vantage points rather than my own original ones, I have similarly presented postmodern views of the house. Fascinating!

71. #525

Panoramic View of Forbes Ranch, Sheridan Co., 1903, 2007
GPS COORDINATES: 44 44.64N, 107 8.17W

The Forbes Ranch is in Beckton, west of Sheridan on Big Goose Creek. George T. Beck, a friend of Buffalo Bill Cody and later one of the founders of the town of Cody, founded Beckton around 1880. He built a large Victorian house, seen at right. In the 1890s Beck sold out to Waldo and W. Cameron Forbes, Bostonians from the famous Forbes family, who had come to Wyoming as tourists and decided to stay and raise Clydesdale horses. Cameron had played football at Harvard and coached the Crimson for two years.

Stimson made his three-part panorama as part of his 1903 survey of Wyoming for the 1904 St. Louis World's Fair. It is a promotional photograph created to show the state's best offerings. In this remarkable view, Stimson is looking down from a water tower onto the ranch, its livestock, and large barns. The original Beck home can be seen at the far right and the large, new Forbes home on the distant hill. In the foreground, ranch hands are displaying their horses for Stimson as one of the Forbes brothers looks on.

W. Cameron Forbes served as governor general of the Philippines from 1908 to 1913 and ambassador to Japan from 1930 to 1932. In the 1930s he returned to Wyoming and built a large polo pony breeding ranch, one of five such operations near Sheridan at the time.

When Lauren and I visited Beckton in 2007, we knocked on the door of the old Beck home and met Cam Forbes, a descendent of the original brothers. He showed us around and explained that his family raises Red Angus cattle. He pointed me toward Stimson's vantage point, and we set out to rephotograph it. The only problem was the elevation. After figuring out that Stimson had been positioned on top of something, one of the ranch hands who was helping us locate the vantage point offered us a ten-foot ladder. I crawled up the ladder and hand-shot the panorama as a small herd of Red Angus cattle looked on eagerly.

My 2007 panorama clearly shows the historic barns, the original Beck home, the new outbuildings, and changes in the basic layout of the original ranch. The Forbes home in the background is gone.

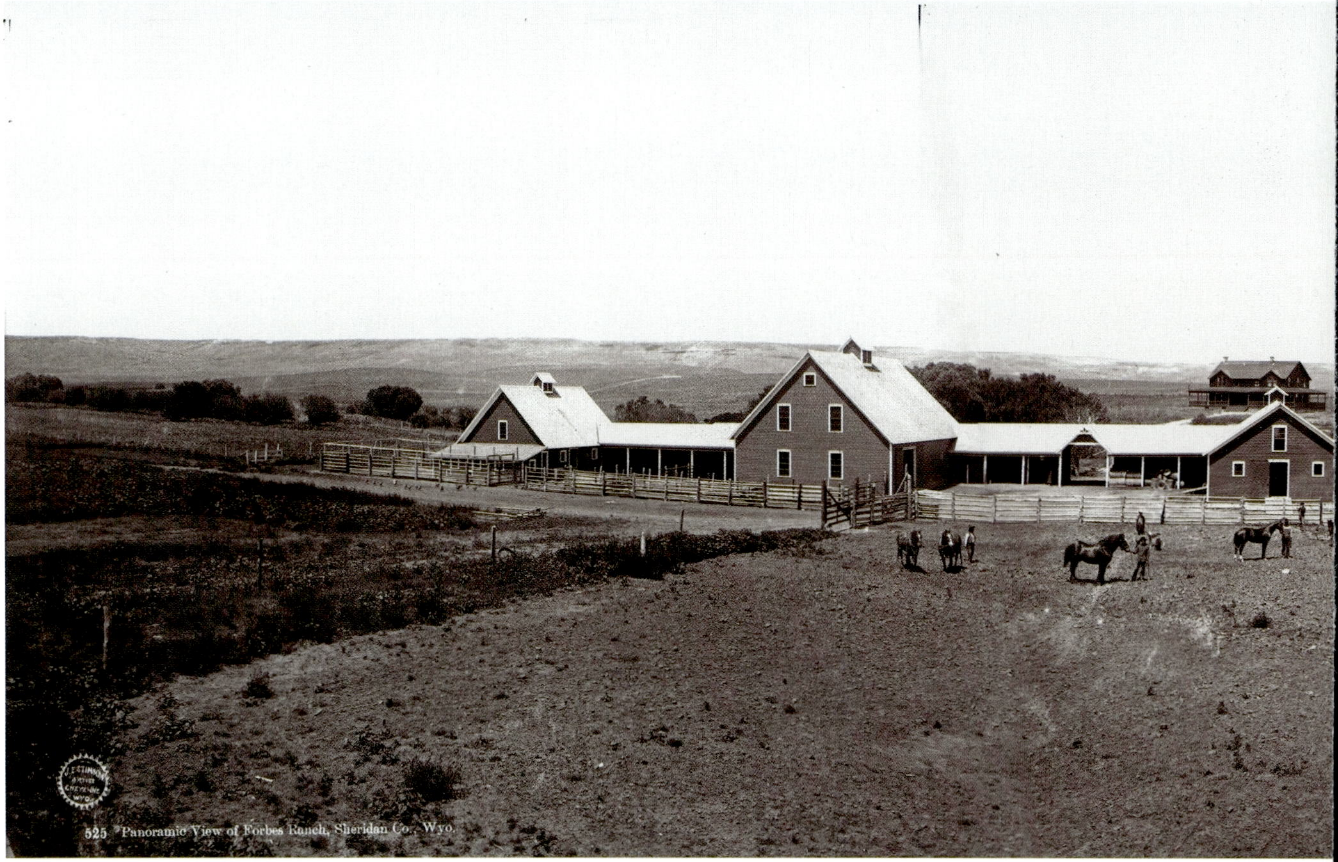

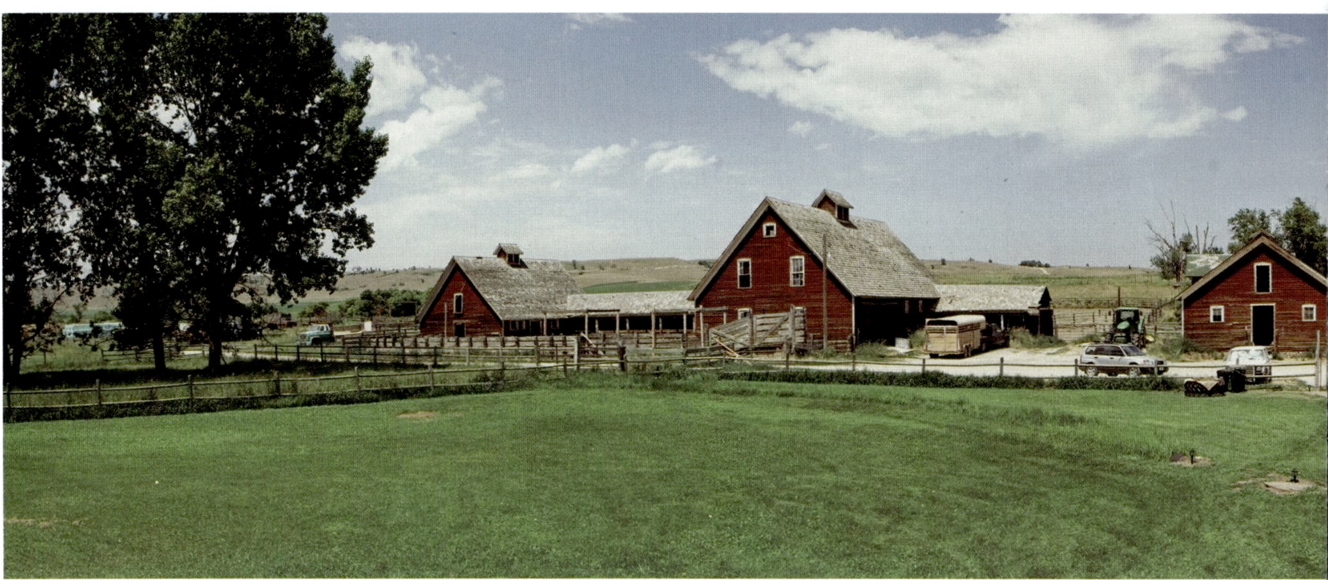
525 Panoramic View of Forbes Ranch, Sheridan Co., Wyo.

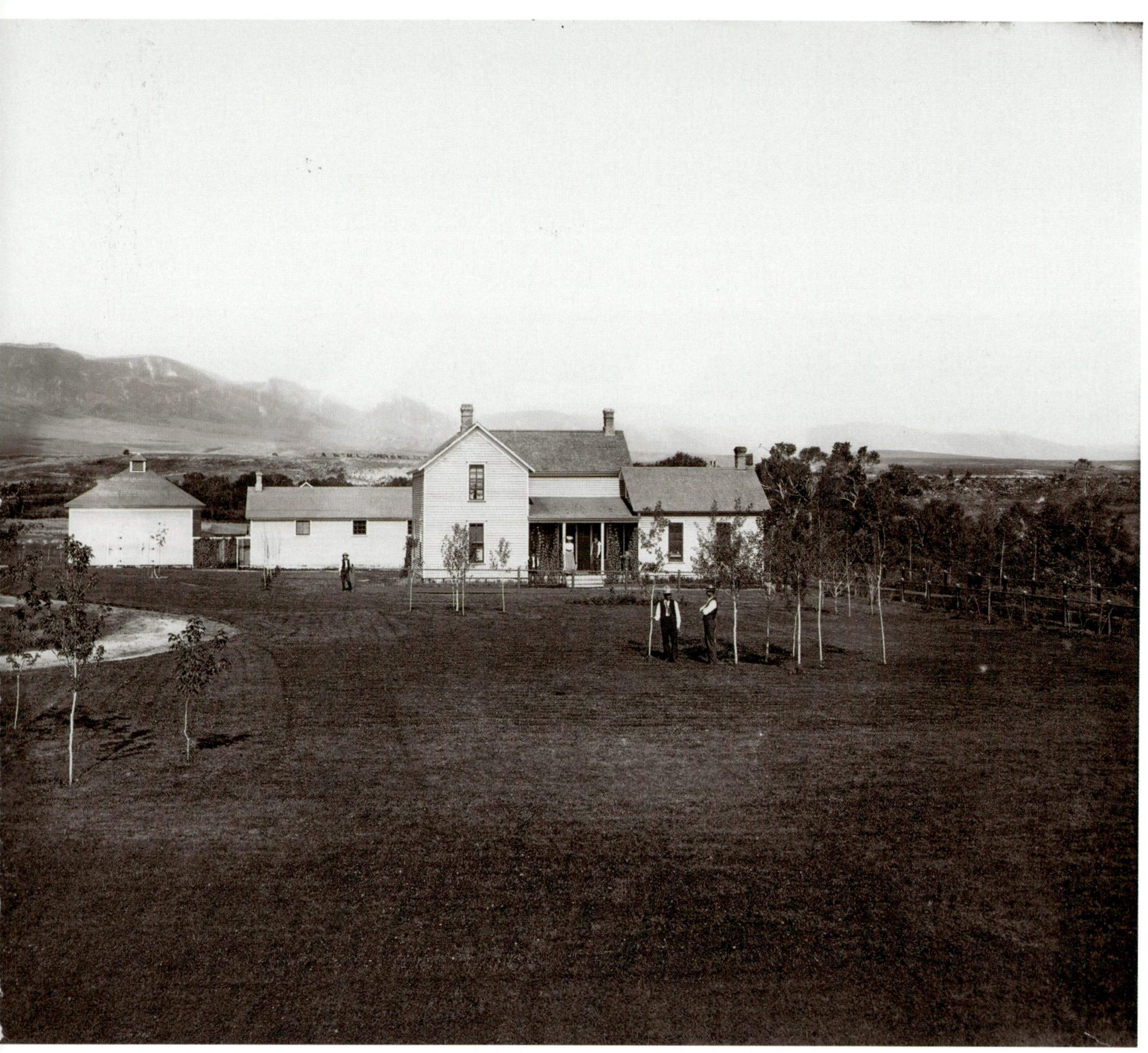

72. #483

Panorama [of] Moncreiffe Ranch, Big Horn, 1903, 2007
GPS COORDINATES: 44 38.72N, 107 0.45899N

I have long been fascinated by the small, polo-playing community of Big Horn, southwest of Sheridan. The Moncreiffe Ranch, now the Bradford Brinton Memorial, was owned by William and Malcolm Moncreiffe, the youngest sons of the Baron of Moncreiffe of Scotland. They had migrated to northern Wyoming in 1893 and established the Quarter Circle A Ranch on Little Goose Creek near Big Horn. They were drawn by the mild climate and the prospect of raising polo ponies. They built the house on the left together, then William volunteered to fight in the Spanish American War. After his return, the brothers teamed with neighbor and fellow Brit, Oliver Henry Wallop—the younger son of the Earl of Portsmouth—and started a business buying western horses to sell to the British Cavalry for use in the South African Boer Wars. Between 1899 and 1903, the partners shipped 20,000 horses from Sheridan. They also purchased horses for playing polo and built Big Horn into a polo-playing and polo pony breeding center.

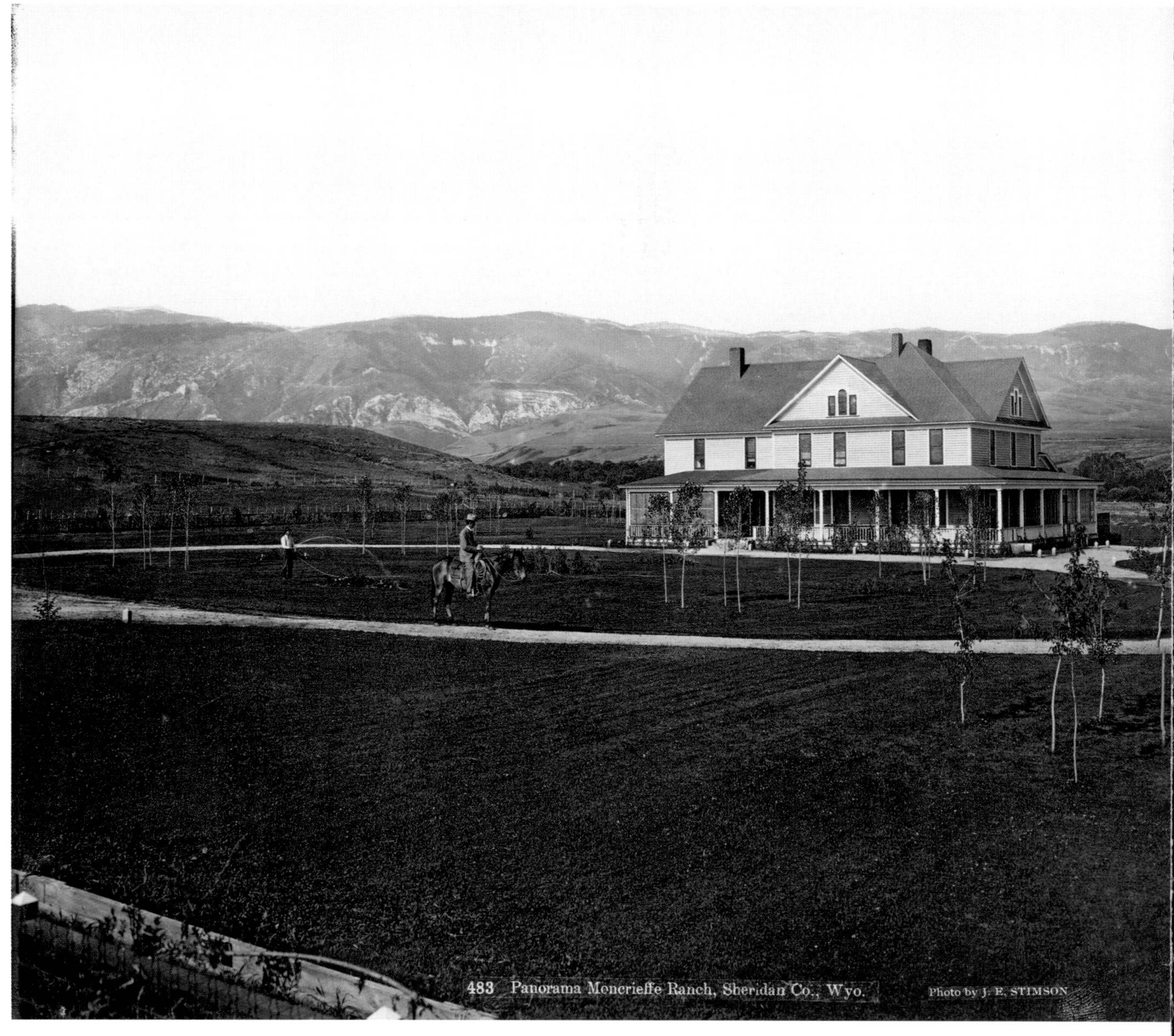

483 Panorama Moncrieffe Ranch, Sheridan Co., Wyo.   Photo by J. E. STIMSON

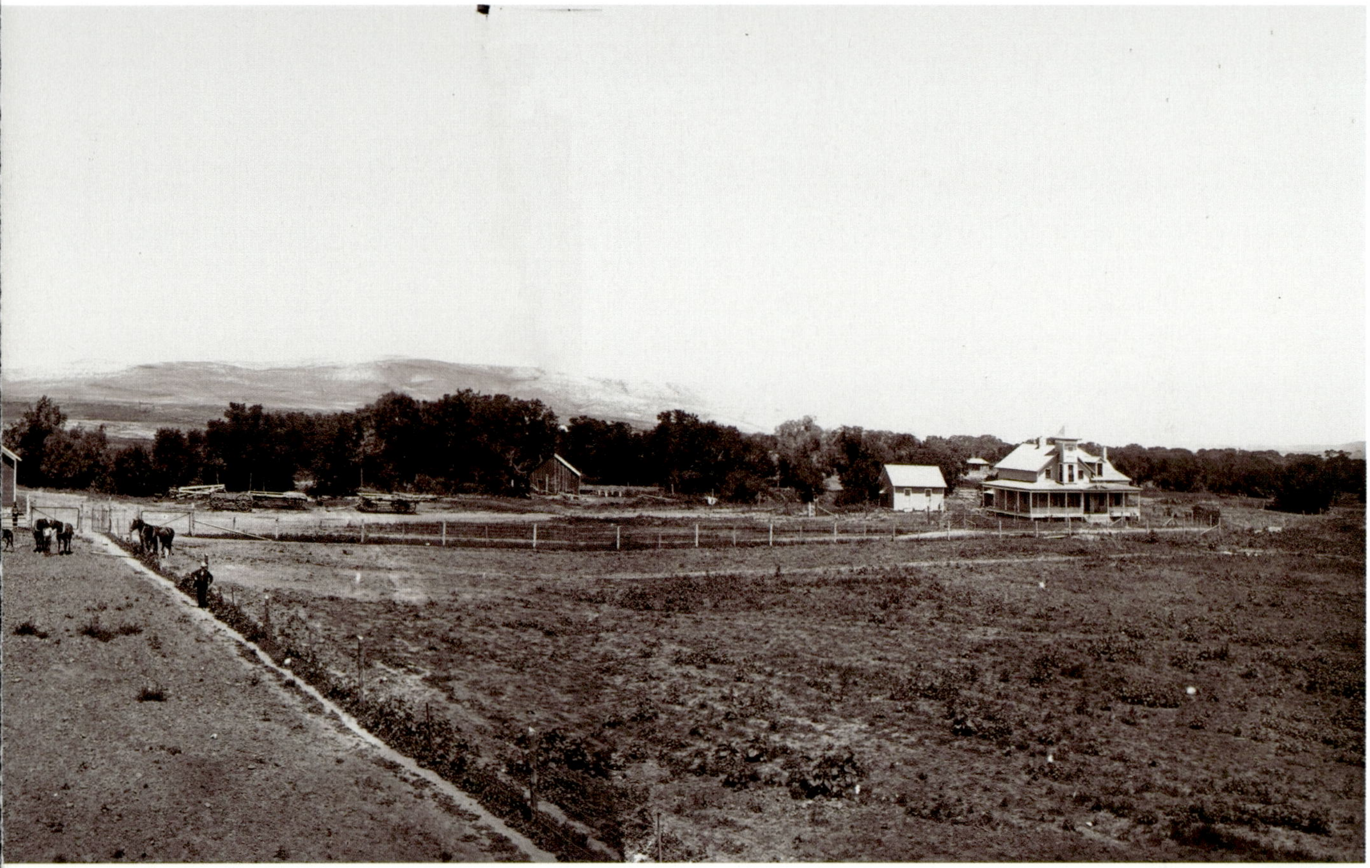

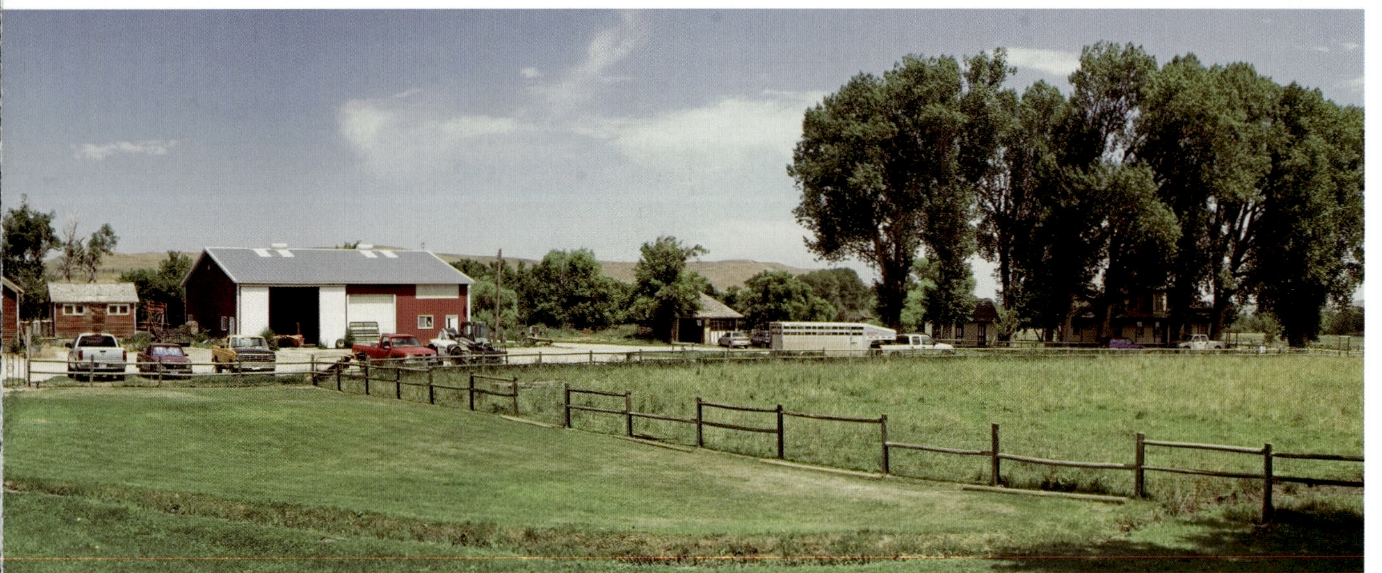

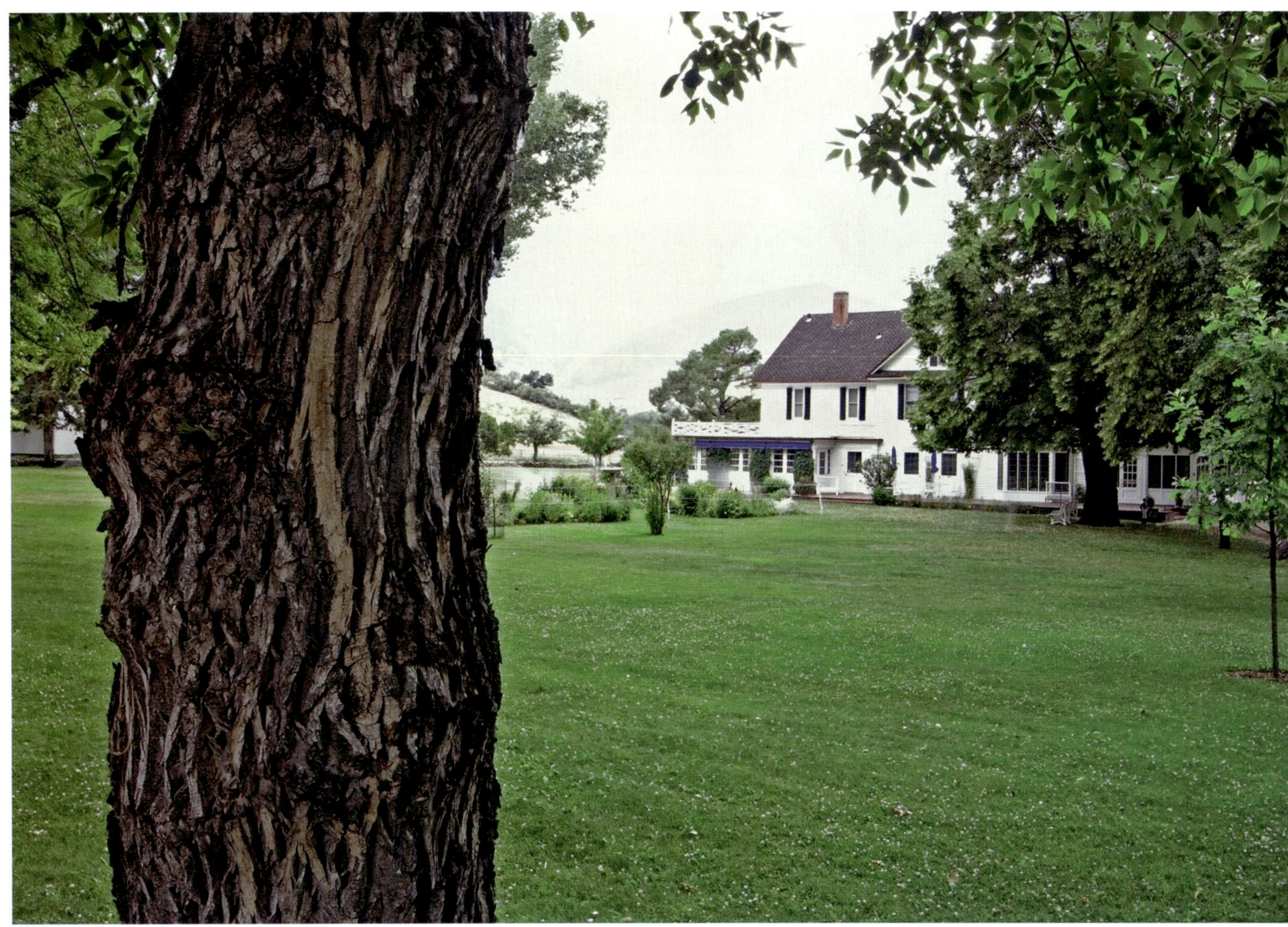

Stimson photographed this panorama in 1903 as part of his Wyoming survey for the St. Louis World's Fair. William can be seen riding on the front path before the spectacular ranch house. Note the well-cared-for grounds and the caretaker's house, right. Like the Hardin Ranch, the splendor of the Moncreiffes and their ranch must have surprised Stimson because he snapped eight different views around the ranch's exterior. Although we might see the polo-playing brothers as elites, to Stimson they were another wonderful expression of Wyoming's potential for his employers, looking to promote the railroad and the state.

In 1923 William Moncreiffe sold his ranch to Bradford Brinton, a director of the Case Threshing Machine Company, who filled the house with western paintings and sculpture. He played polo, partied, raised ponies, and had a cabin at the exclusive Dome Lake Club. After he died in 1936, his sister maintained the property until 1963, when she established the Bradford Brinton Memorial as a tribute to her brother. The house is open to the public as a museum, featuring exhibits from Brinton's collections.

Although I made other photographs of this home in 1988 and spent a few more years researching and writing about Big Horn, I did not rephotograph this panorama. My 2007 view, though, shows a well-cared-for home that remains as beautiful and unusual as it was in 1903.

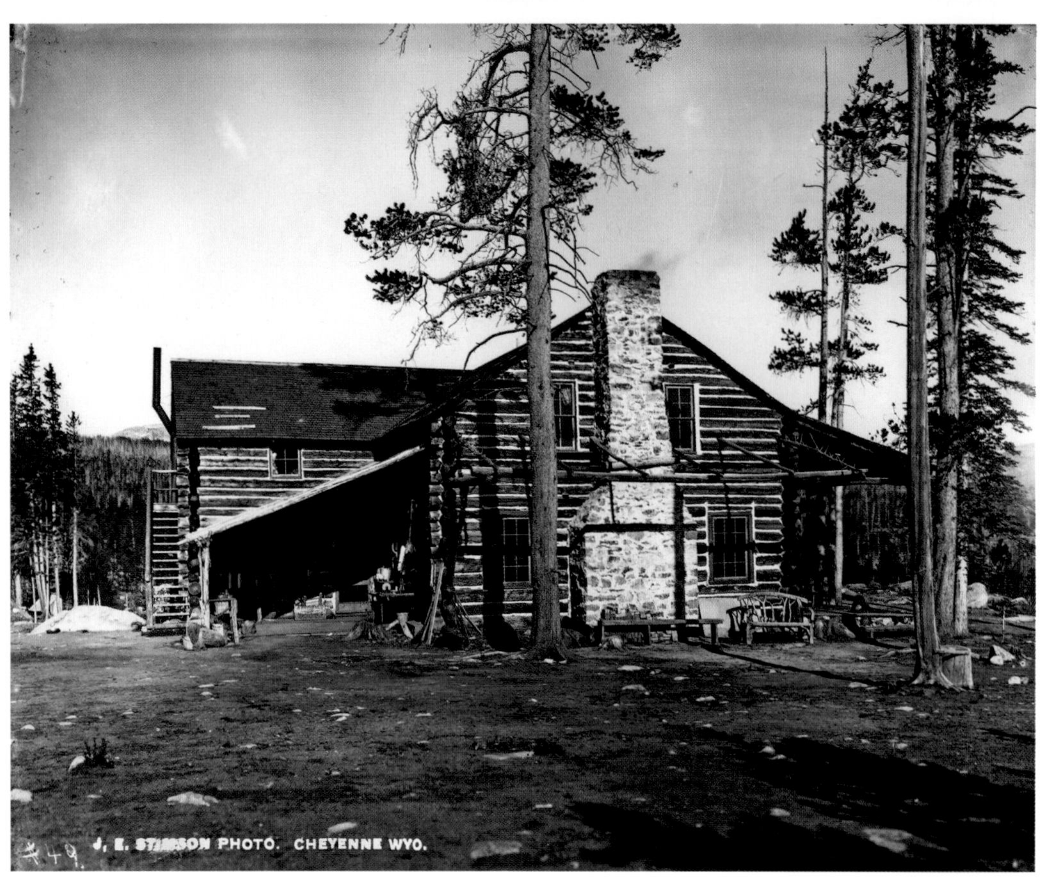
J. E. STIMSON PHOTO. CHEYENNE WYO.

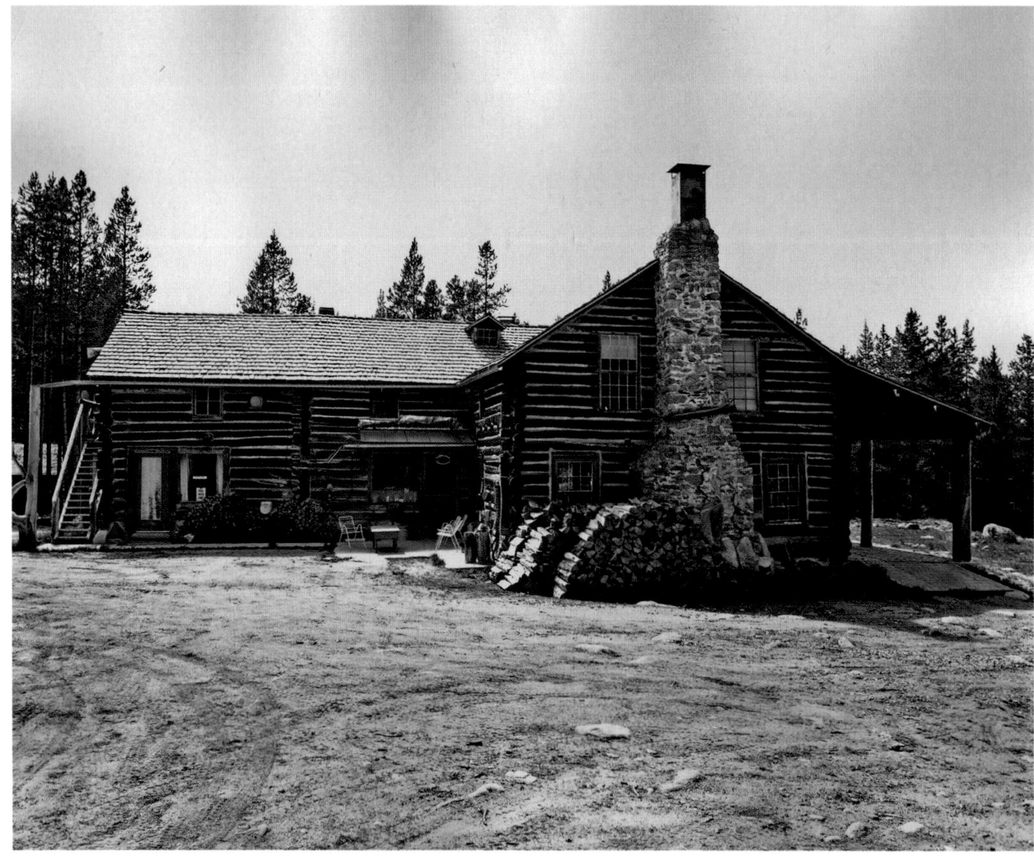

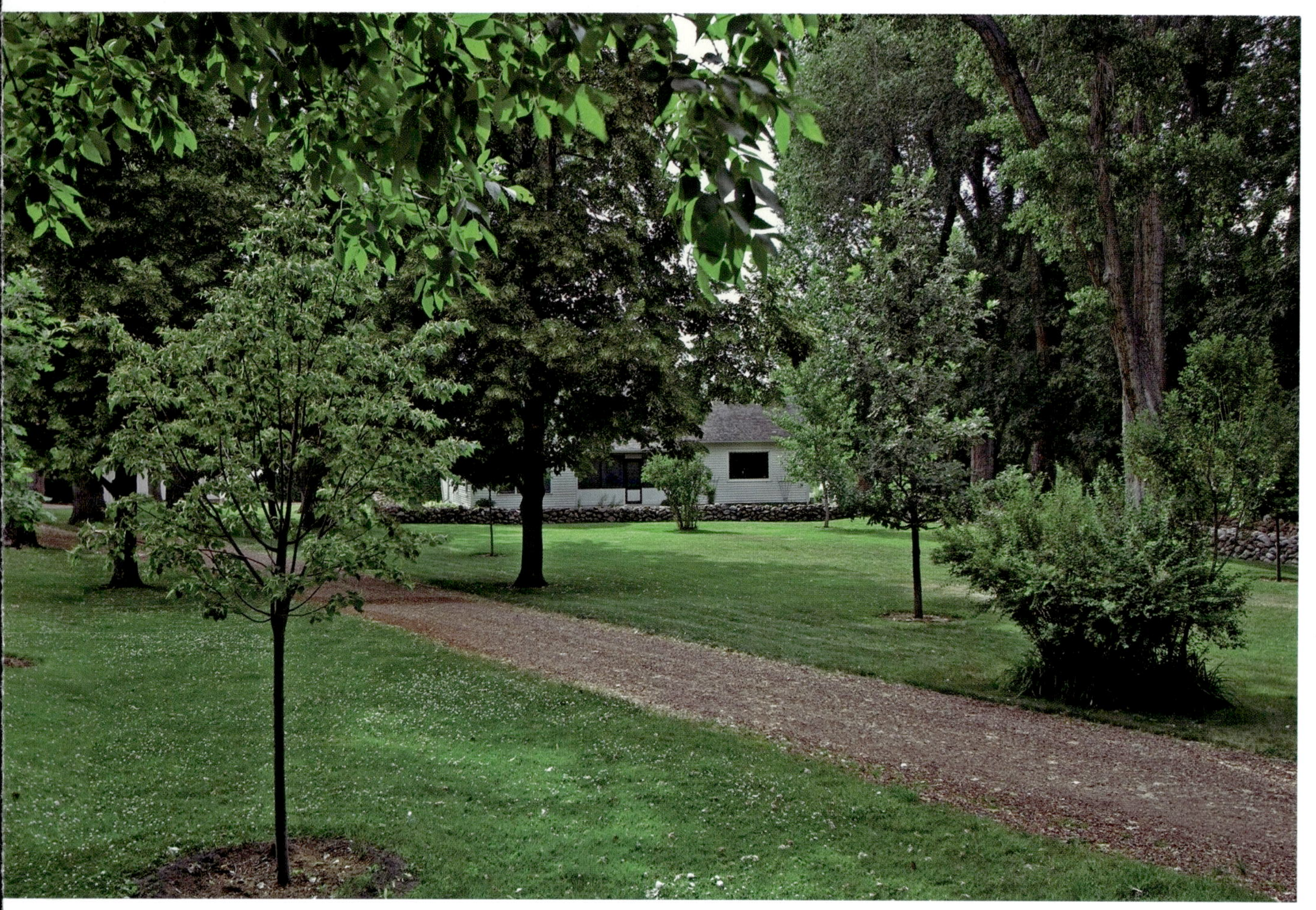

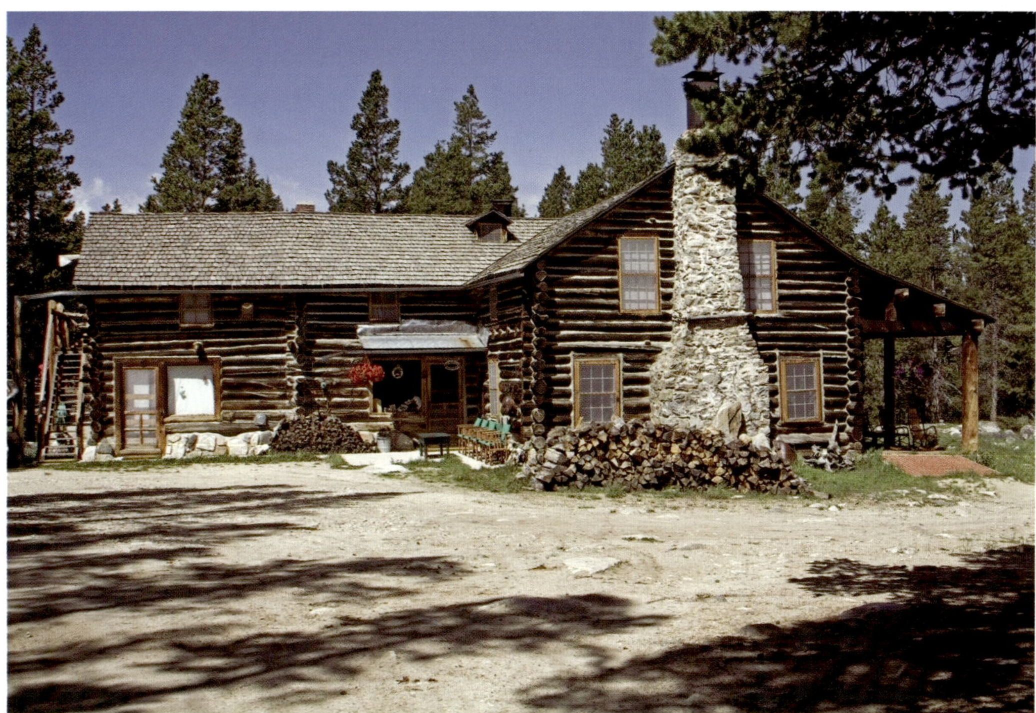

73. #E49

Club House, Dome Lake, 1895, 1988, 2008
GPS COORDINATES: 44 34.5985N, 107 17.58733W

Dome Lake is a private inholding located in the Bighorn National Forest about 40 miles southwest of Sheridan. Its history dates back to 1894, before the national forest existed, when executives of the Burlington Railroad in Omaha organized the Dome Lake Club to patent land and build a summer resort in the mountains. By 1897, members had acquired just over 1,000 acres, hired Omaha architect Thomas R. Kimball to design "cottages," and stocked the lake with more than 160,000 trout. That same year, the federal government set aside all of the surrounding lands as Bighorn National Forest. By World War I, the resort had grown into a small summer community with African American servants, a private telephone system, electrical plants, and ice houses. Since that time, Dome Lake has remained an exclusive getaway.

Given his ties to the railroad, Omaha, fishing, and promotional photography, it is not surprising that J. E. Stimson visited Dome Lake several times. In 1895 he photographed the completed clubhouse, seen here from the east. He returned in 1899 and again ten years later. His views record the condition of both the national forest and the club's properties at their beginnings.

I visited Dome Lake in 1988 and again in 2008. In 1988 I had to contact the club's caretaker by shortwave radio and travel with a friend from Sheridan to Big Horn, up Red Grade Road, past local dude ranches to the club's locked gate. When the caretaker failed to arrive, we hiked the last couple of miles in and found a mountain oasis. (We later learned that some club members helicopter in to the lake.) We saw elk, ten moose, and deer. I rephotographed a dozen sites, including this view of the clubhouse (note the many original features, plus rear expansion), now owned by Tim Travis, a Denver businessman. He took an interest in my project, posed for a photo, treated me to dinner, showed me around, and later purchased copies of my photographs and *Wyoming Time and Again* for all club members

Twenty years later, Lauren and I contacted Travis in Denver and made plans to meet him at his cabin that summer. When we arrived at the lake, I was again treated to lunch, allowed to rephotograph a dozen sites, and once again made to feel at home. It truly is a spectacular place.

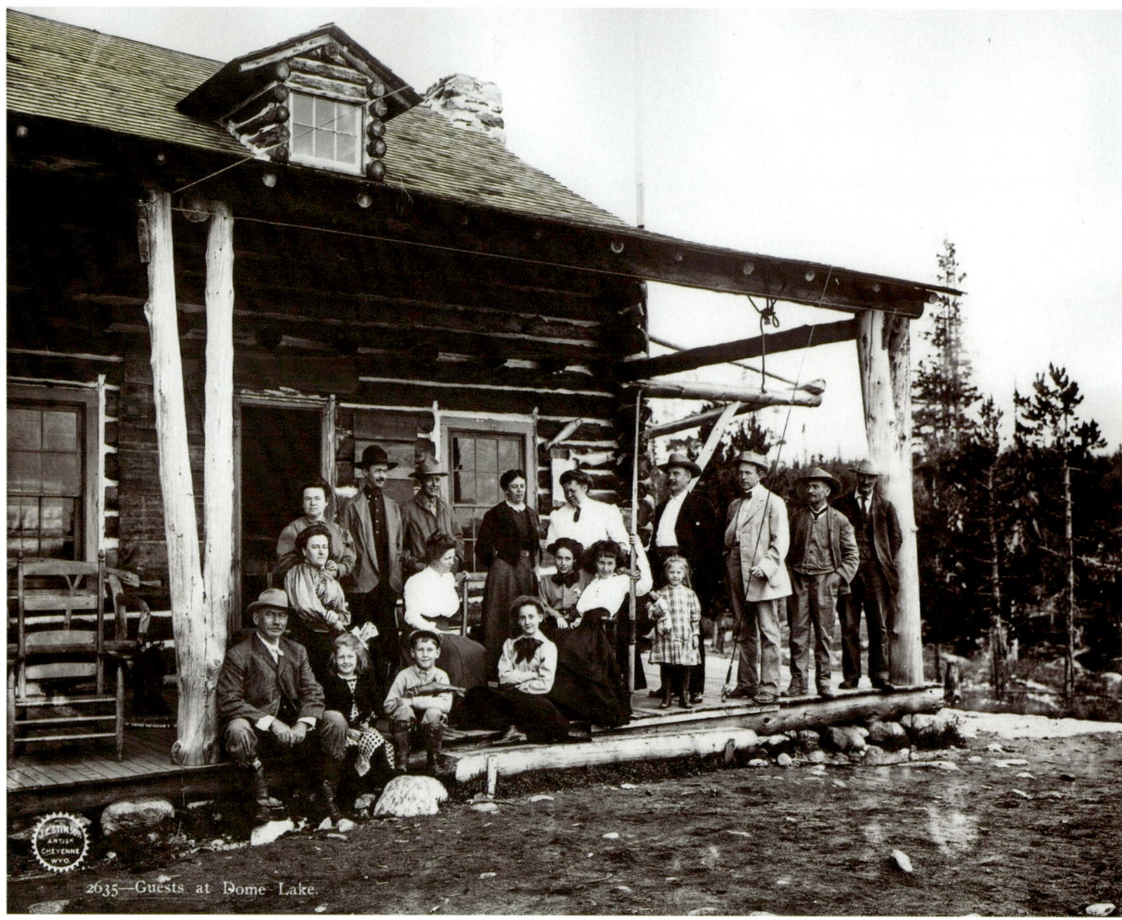

74. #2635

Guests at Dome Lake, 1909, 1988, 2008
GPS COORDINATES: 44 34.60733N, 107 17.598833W

This is one of my favorite rephotographs. Stimson made his view in 1909, looking southwest toward the clubhouse porch. Guests at the club had been assembled to pose for the photograph. Note the very long fishing pole, the boy holding a stuffed fish, and the split support posts.

When I first rephotographed Dome Lake in 1988, the clubhouse had been converted into Denver businessman Tim Travis's private lodge. He took great interest in my project, assembled his guests, and posed them on the same porch. Note the new roof, dormer, and support beams. Travis is standing third from right.

When Lauren and I planned to revisit Dome Lake in 2008, we contacted Travis (who was then president of the Dome Lake Club) in Denver to be sure our visit would occur when he was there in July. He met us at his cabin and again showed us around the lake. He was excited to duplicate this scene once again and gathered his friends on the porch; he is second from right in the cowboy hat. Note the fishing pole and the woman holding a stuffed fish.

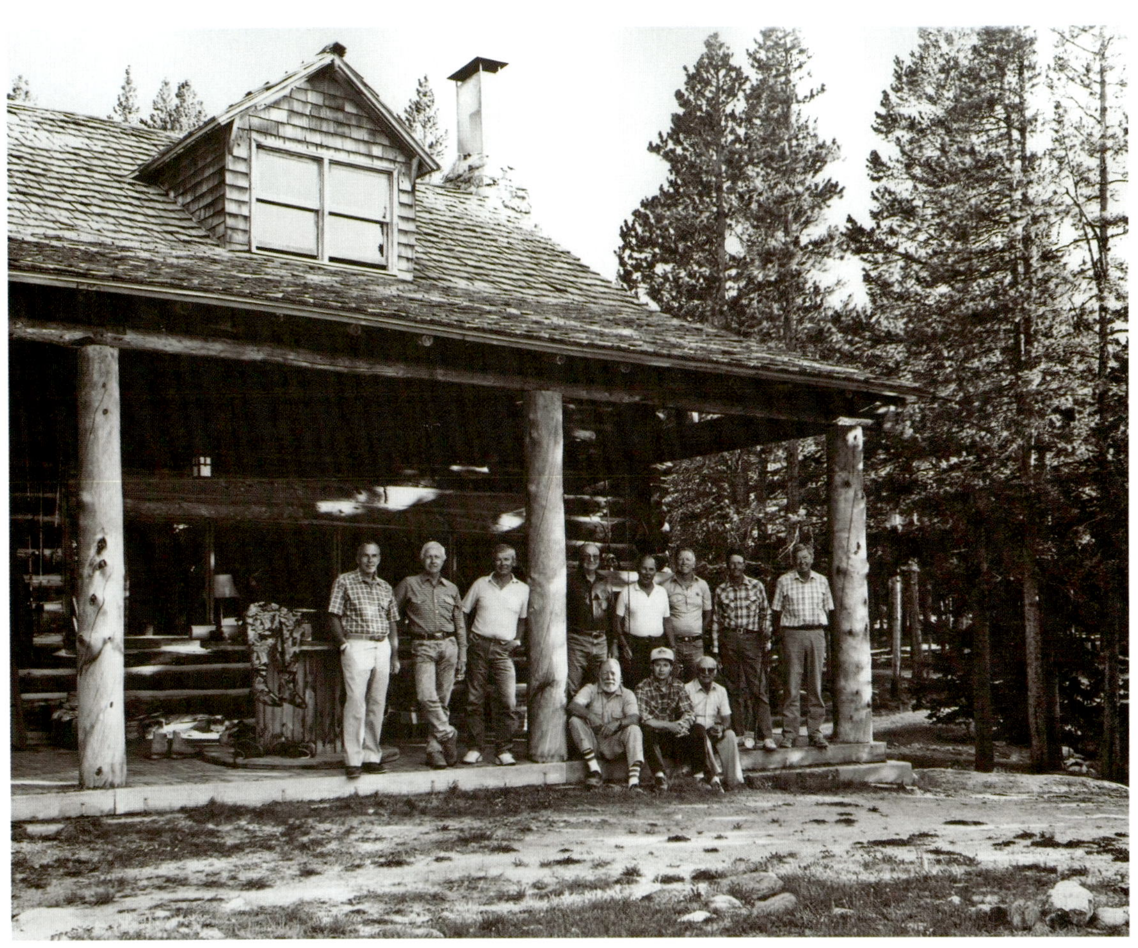

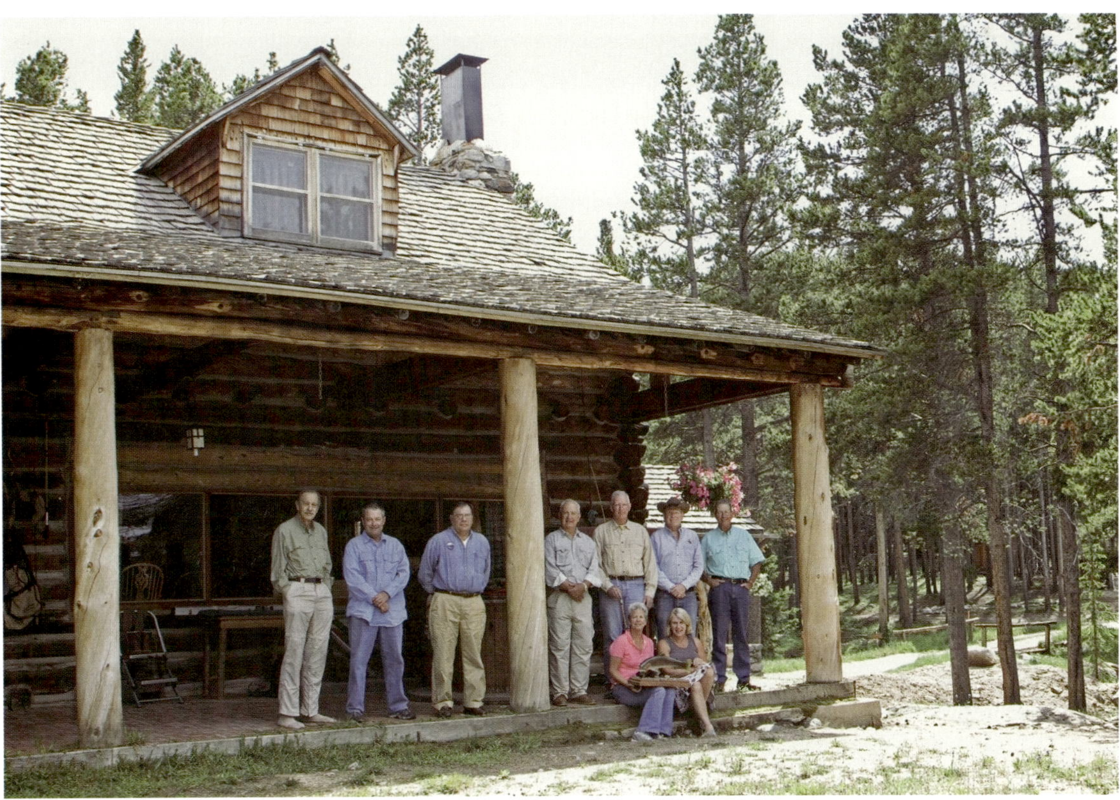

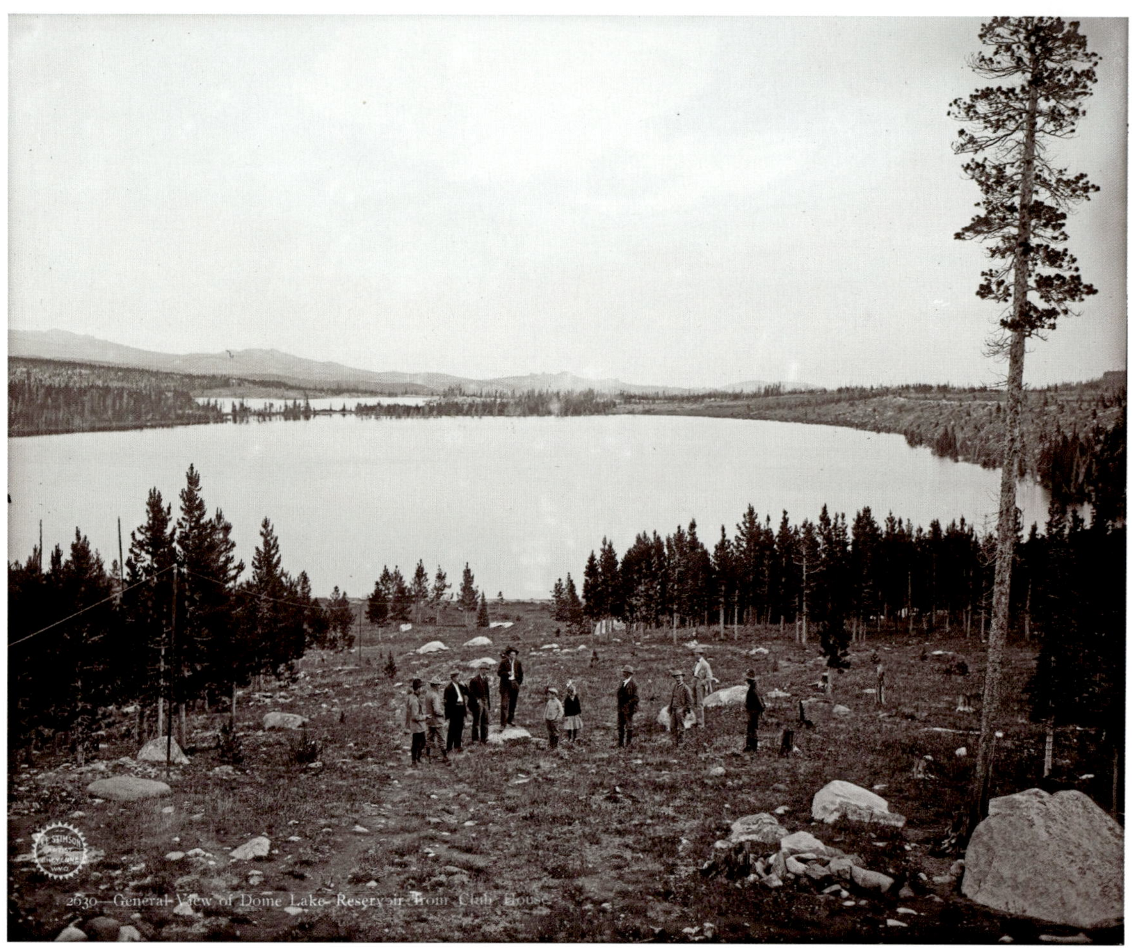

75. #2630

General View of Dome Lake Reservoir from Club House, 1909, 1988, 2008
GPS COORDINATES: 44 34.607N, 107 17.6033W

When US Army engineer and western historian Hiram Martin Chittenden visited Dome Lake in 1897, he noted in his diary that many trees had been burned during the 1870s Sioux wars and speculated that, although the lake had been turned into a "summer resort," it would "never be a success as it lacks the essential elements of attractive mountain scenery" (*A Western Epic*, p. 55). He thought the lake was "surpassed by thousands of mountain lakes . . . the timber all burned off its mountains . . . and the means of access simply abominable." Perhaps the access problem paid off for the club because the timber has rebounded and the mountain scenery is now excellent.

In his view, Stimson turned his camera around and photographed what all the guests in the previous picture were seeing: the view of Dome Lake from the clubhouse. Note that everyone from the previous photo, except the adult women, hiked down the hill to be in this photograph. A close look also reveals the open view, the telephone line strung down to the boathouse, and the burned-off forest. In the far distance, Dome Lake Reservoir can be seen.

Although none of the guests from my 1988 rephotograph joined me for this view of the lake, the big rock to the right is there. It is still an interesting picture because of the tremendous growth of the forest toward the lake and beyond. In fact, one can barely get a glimpse of Dome Lake through the trees, and Dome Lake Reservoir can't be seen at all. The rough road, center, was put in to access the boathouse.

On my return to Dome Lake in 2008, a few of the guests posed for me, including Tim Travis, second from left. More important, though, was the view, which I was told had been opened by basically clear-cutting the forest between the lodge and the lake. It certainly enhanced the view of both Dome Lake and Dome Lake Reservoir, but the method reminded me that the locale remains private.

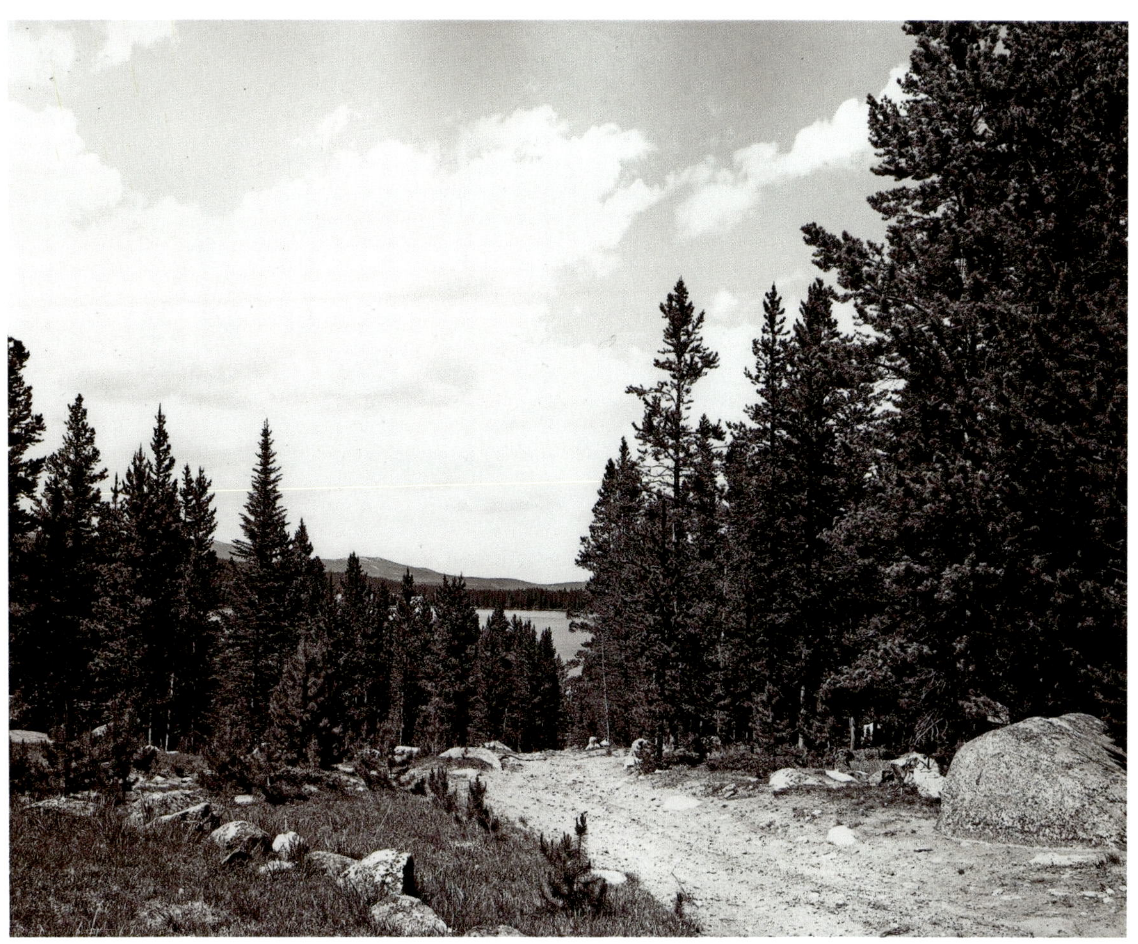

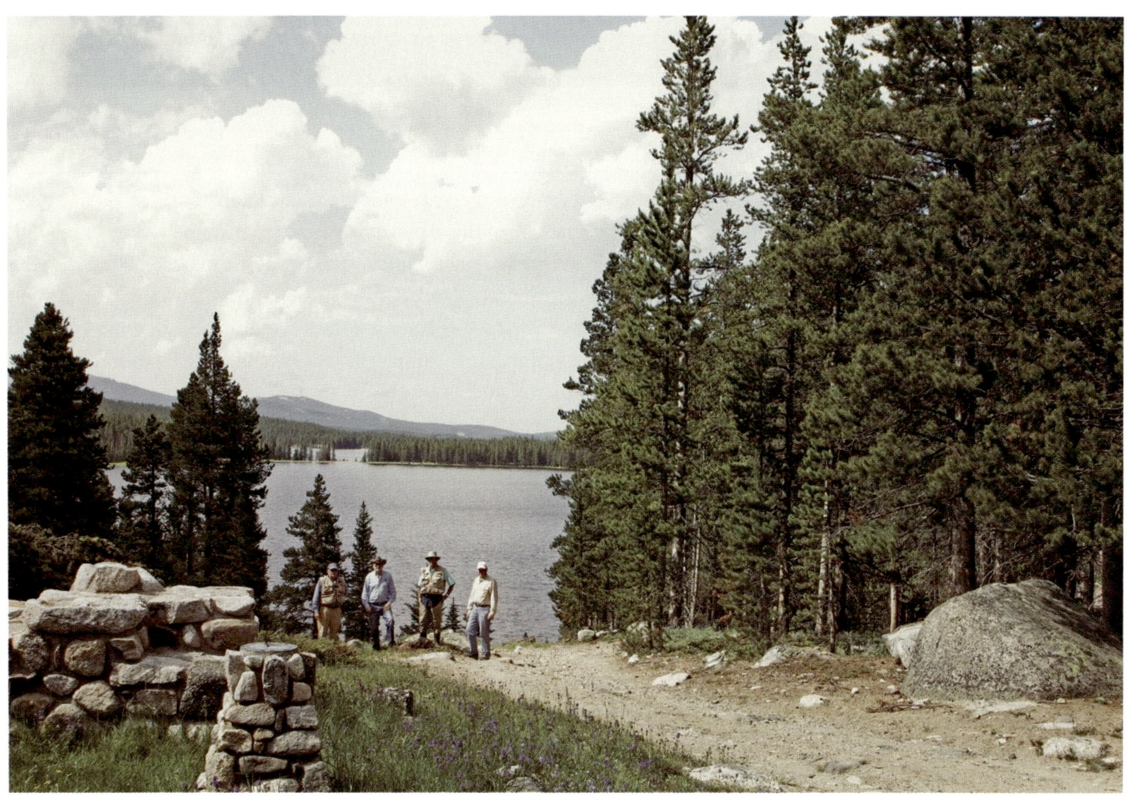

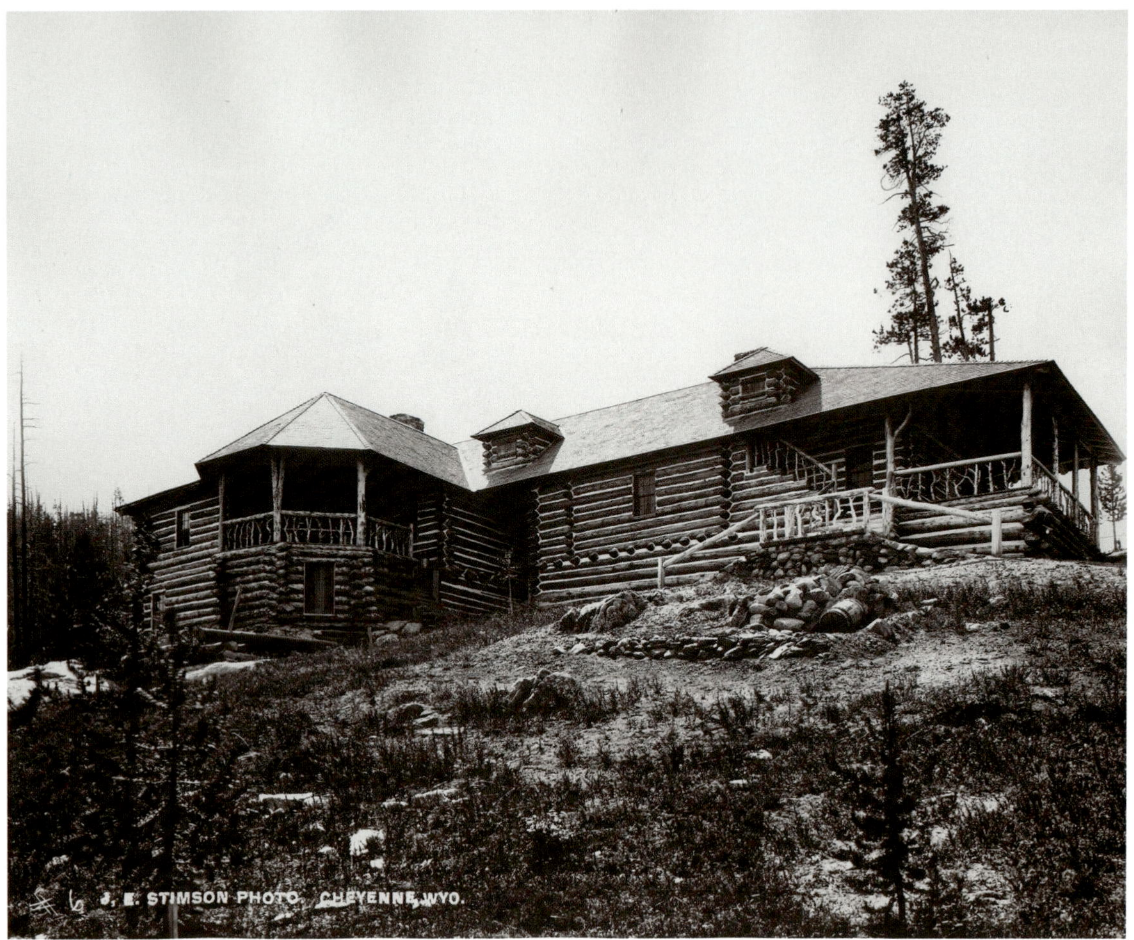

76. #E6

Holdredge's Cabin, 1899, 1988, 2008
GPS COORDINATES: 44 34.675N, 107 17.587W

The Holdredge named in this 1899 Stimson view was George W. Holdredge, an Omaha businessman, general manager of the Burlington Railroad in the West, and one of the original four organizers of the Dome Lake Club. The cabin is actually a duplex of two cabins joined by a breezeway just to the right of the large bay porch. The left-hand cabin was owned by Holdredge and the right-hand cabin by Thomas R. Kimball, an original investor in the club and a prominent Omaha architect. Kimball designed the nearby Sheridan Inn and, at Dome Lake, the layout of the cabins as well as most of the original buildings. The duplex is located downhill from, and just east of, the clubhouse, or Travis Cabin, and also overlooks Dome Lake.

My 1988 view shows that, as in the previous photograph, pines had rebounded along the lake and were beginning to block the lake view from the cabin. Twenty years later the forest had thickened, and the cabin could barely be seen from Stimson's original vantage point.

As Lauren and I were rephotographing this scene in 2008, we could hear people talking. We found the cabin's owners feeding squirrels and resting on the porch. Although the view from Stimson's camera station was no longer great, the lake view from the cabin certainly was. We learned that several of the folks were from my hometown: Loveland, Colorado! As in our experience with Tim Travis, Lauren and I were shown the utmost hospitality. They looked at our pictures and loaned us a jeep for the bumpy ride out to the spillway at Dome Lake Reservoir.

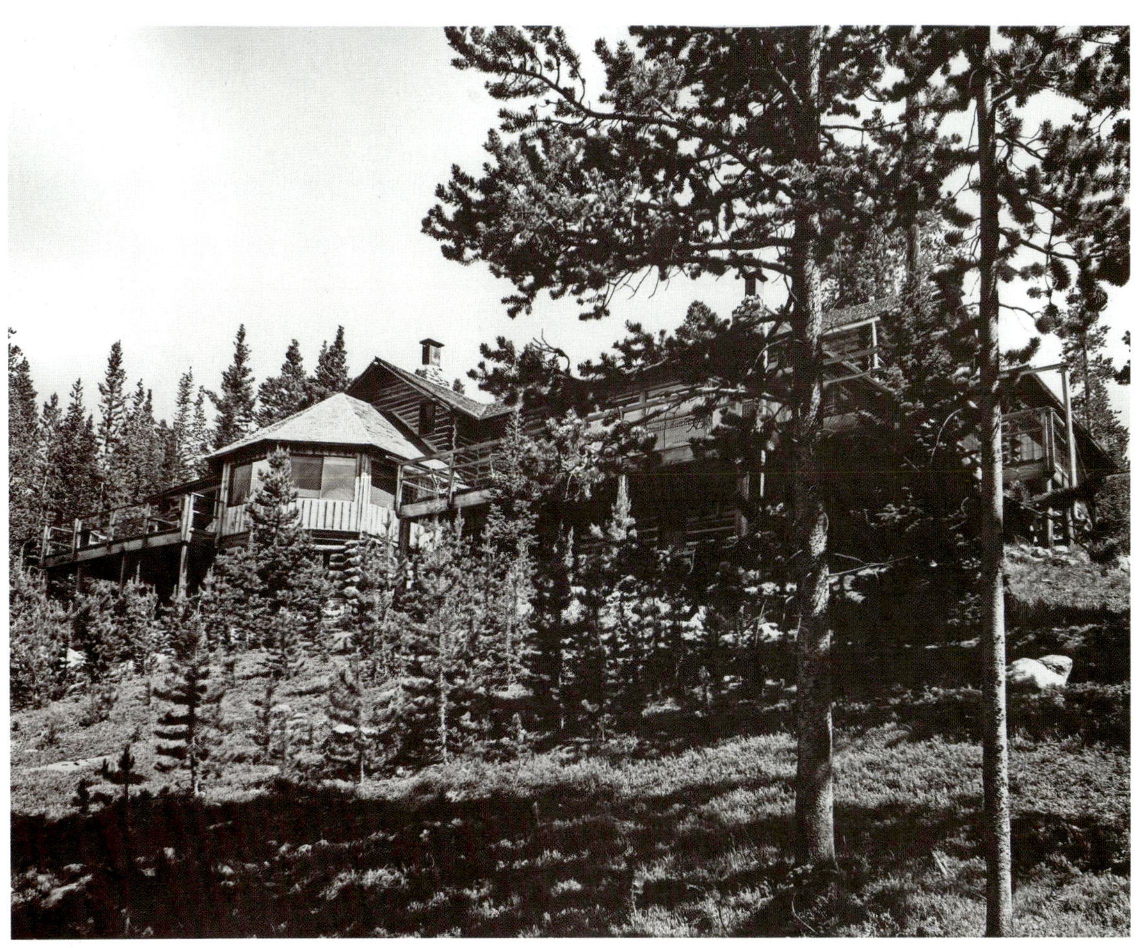

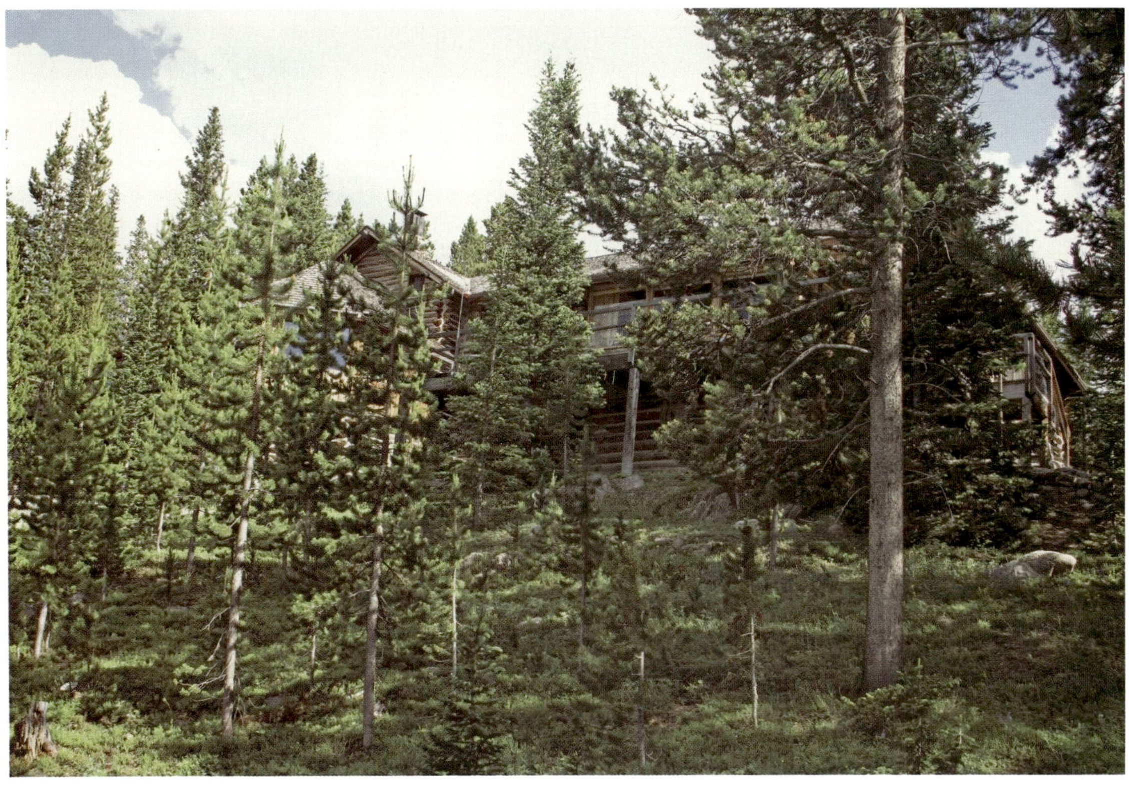

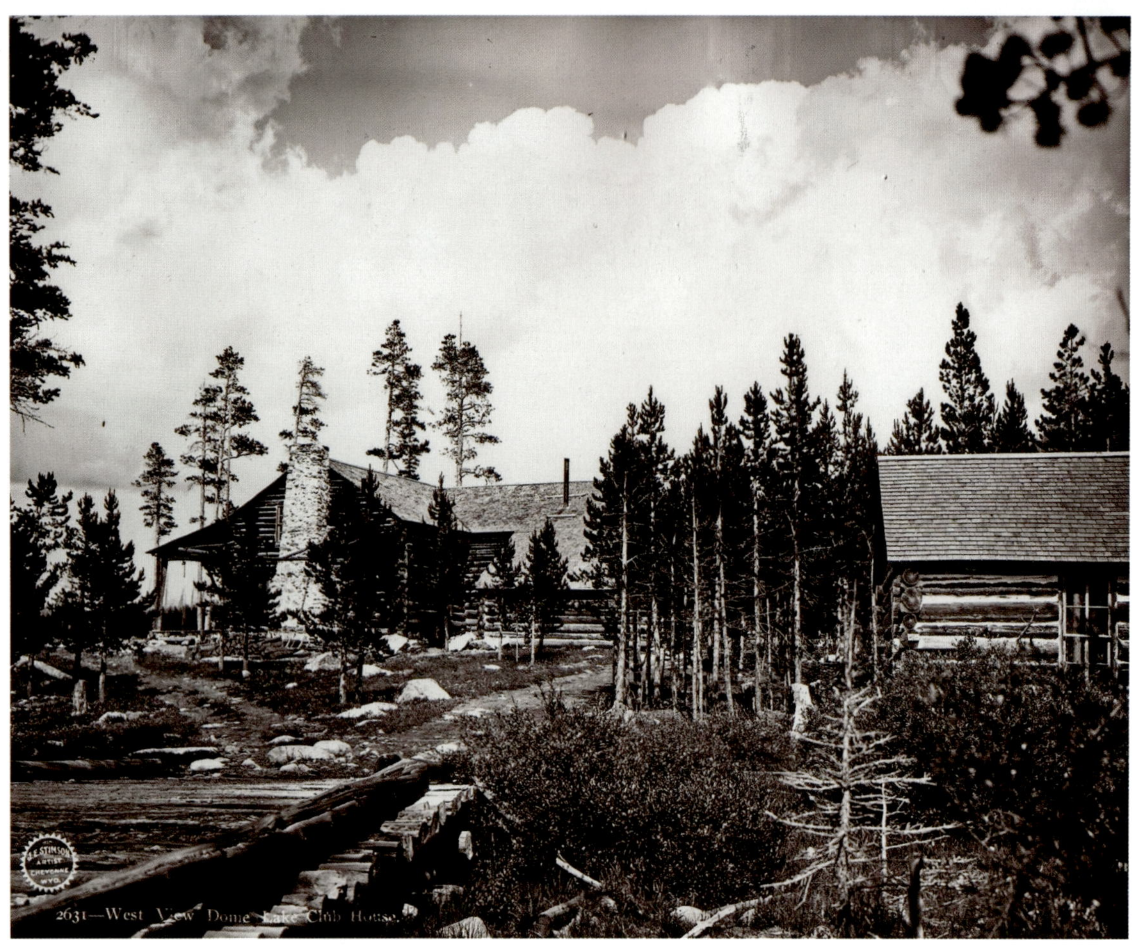

77. #2631

West View[,] Dome Lake Club House (Travis Cabin), 1909, 1988, 2008
GPS COORDINATES: 44 34.580N, 107 17.625W

This 1909 Stimson view was made just west of the clubhouse and shows a glimpse of the greater layout, as expressed by the road and small bridge, designed by Omaha architect Thomas R. Kimball. The small cabin at right is also significant because it was one of the first built at the lake, by lumbermen to live in as they constructed the clubhouse. My two rephotographs, made in 1988 and 2008, show that this landscape remains not only intact but, except for the denser forest, virtually the same.

In 1999 club president Tim Travis and member Don Carney commissioned a history of the Dome Lake Club. It was written by Colorado historian Kevin E. Rucker and is titled *Where Time Stands Still: The History of the Dome Lake Club*. Looking at views like this one, I understand his point.

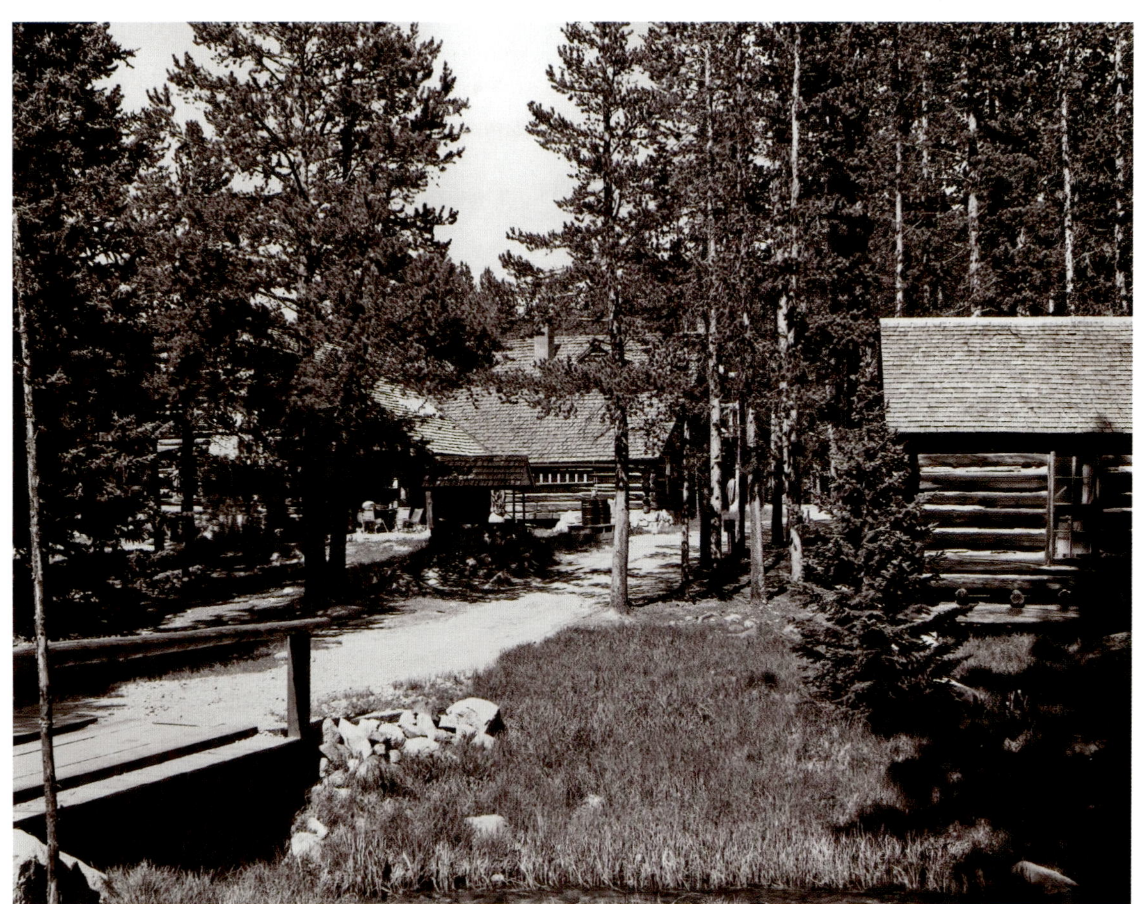

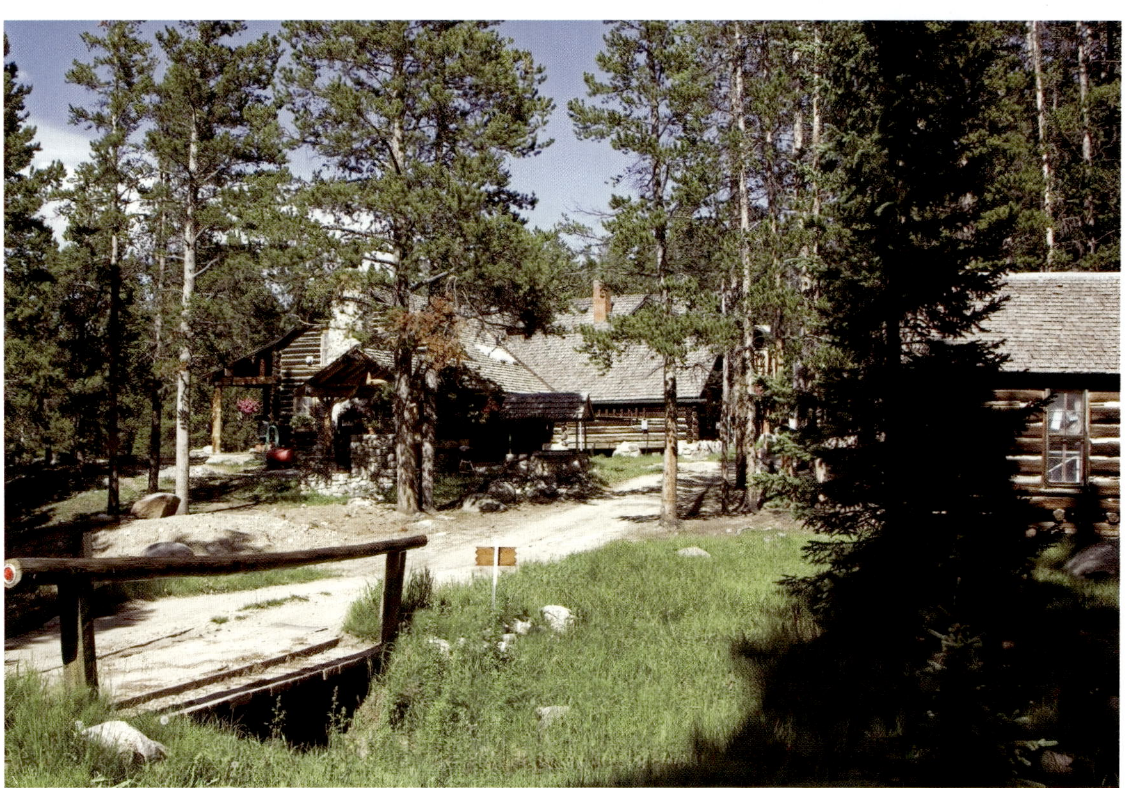

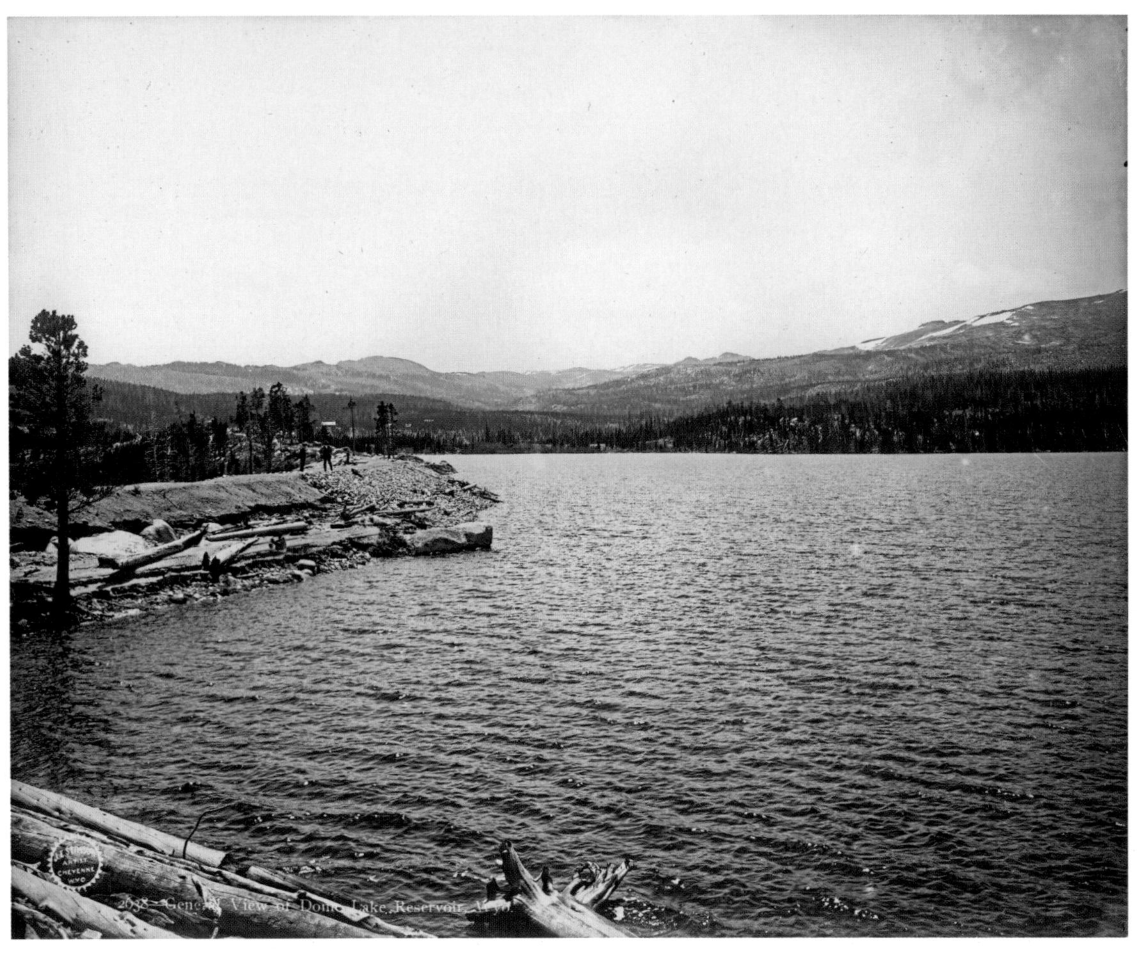
2638—General View of Dome Lake Reservoir, Wyo.

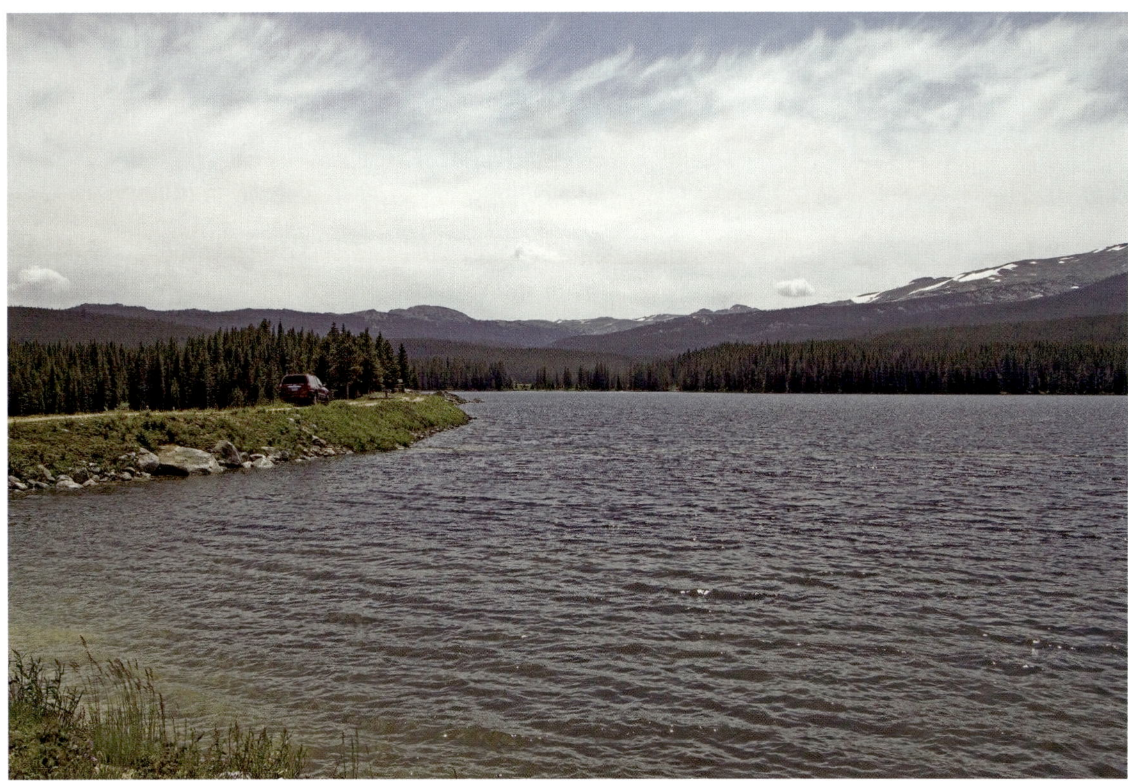

78. #2638

General View of Dome Lake Reservoir, 1909, 2008
GPS COORDINATES: 44 35.565N, 107 17.863167W

The next three sets of images were accessed using our borrowed jeep and were made on the dam of Dome Lake Reservoir. They look back to the south and the many cabins, west to Black Tooth Mountain (which Stimson called Elk Tooth Mountain) and the high peaks of the Big Horns, and east from the Dome Lake Reservoir spillway to Dome Rock.

In Stimson's 1909 view, several men can be seen on the dam at left. In the distance, the shiny roofs of several cabins are glimmering in the sunlight; beyond them are the high peaks of the Big Horns. Most striking, though, is the surrounding forest, which appears very much like Chittenden's 1897 description: "all burned off its mountains."

In my 2008 rephotograph, the borrowed jeep can be seen parked on the dam, but the cabins across the lake are nowhere to be seen because of the tremendous growth of the surrounding forest. Snowfields on the distant peaks of the Big Horn Mountains align almost perfectly.

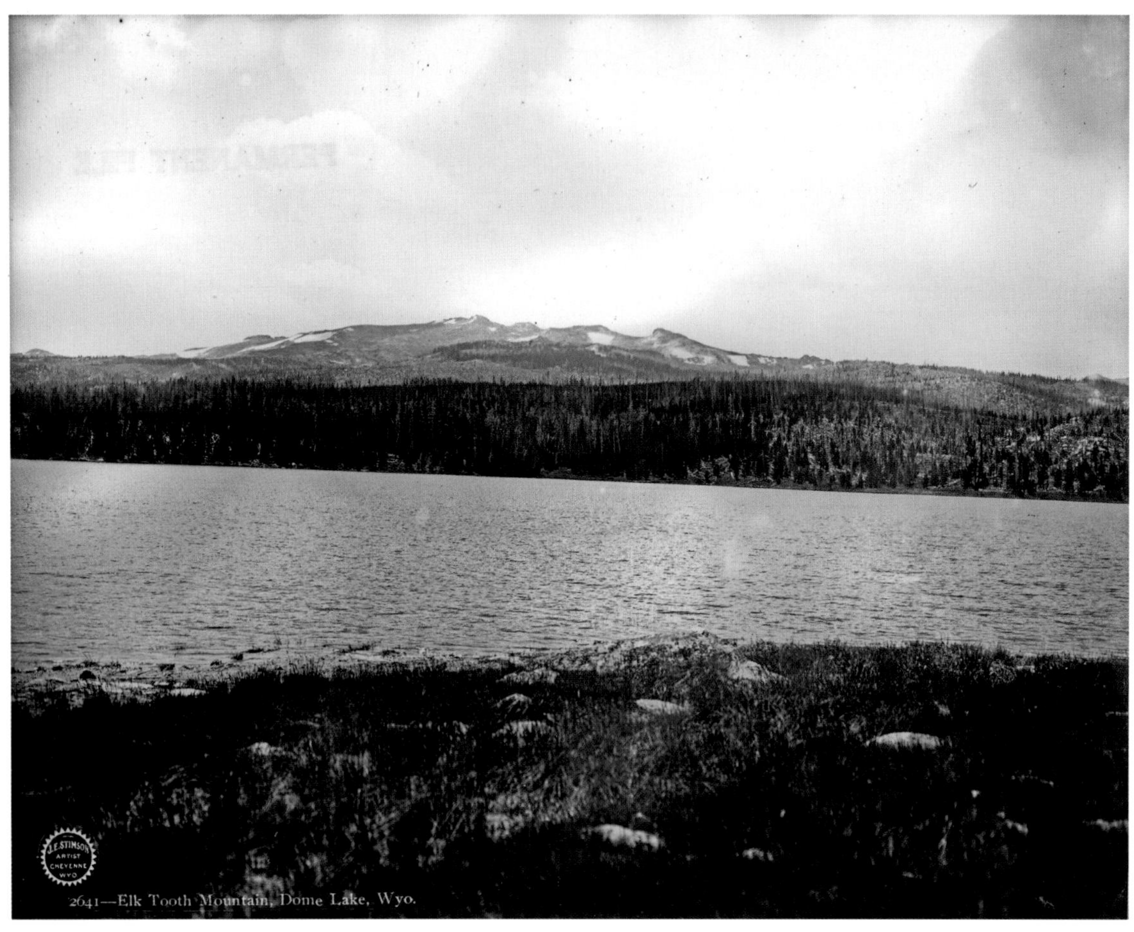

J. E. STIMSON
ARTIST
CHEYENNE
WYO.
2641—Elk Tooth Mountain, Dome Lake, Wyo.

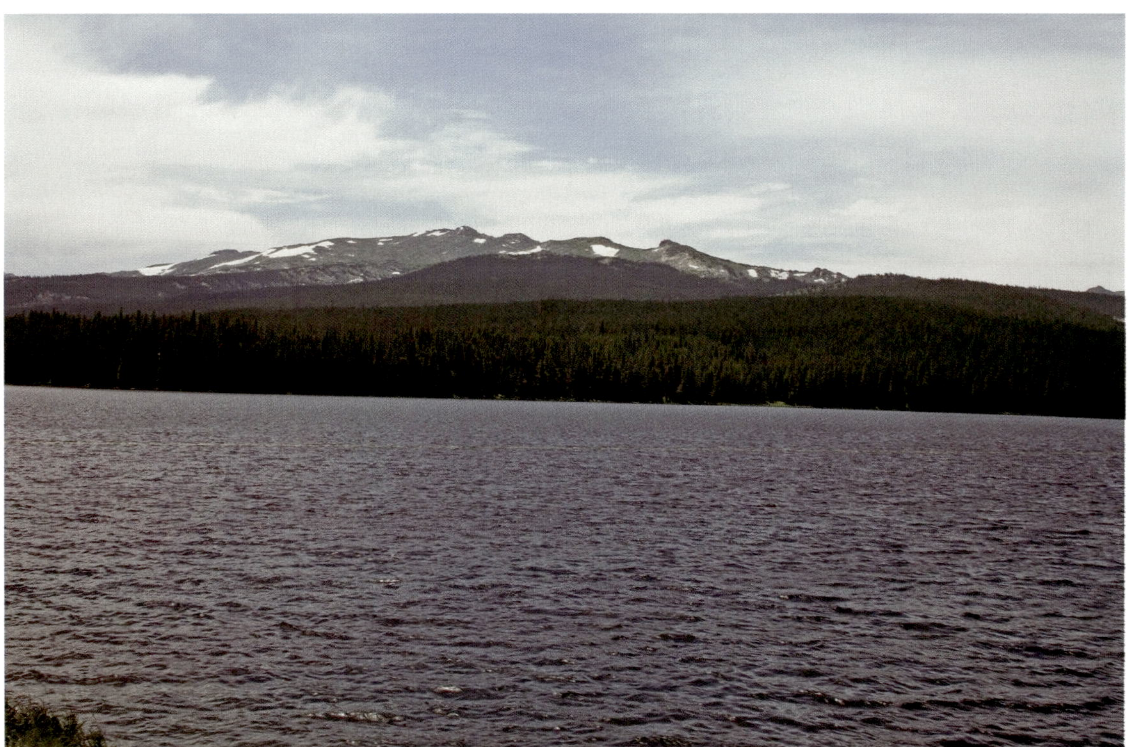

79. #2641

Elk Tooth Mountain, Dome Lake, Wyo., 1909, 2008
GPS COORDINATES: 44 35.493N, 107 17.816W

To take this photograph of Black Tooth Mountain (which Stimson labeled Elk Tooth Mountain), Stimson moved his camera near the spot where the jeep was parked in the previous photograph and turned his viewfinder west to the high peaks of the Big Horn Mountains. As in the previous views, the dense forest cover and similar-looking snowfields highlight my 2008 view.

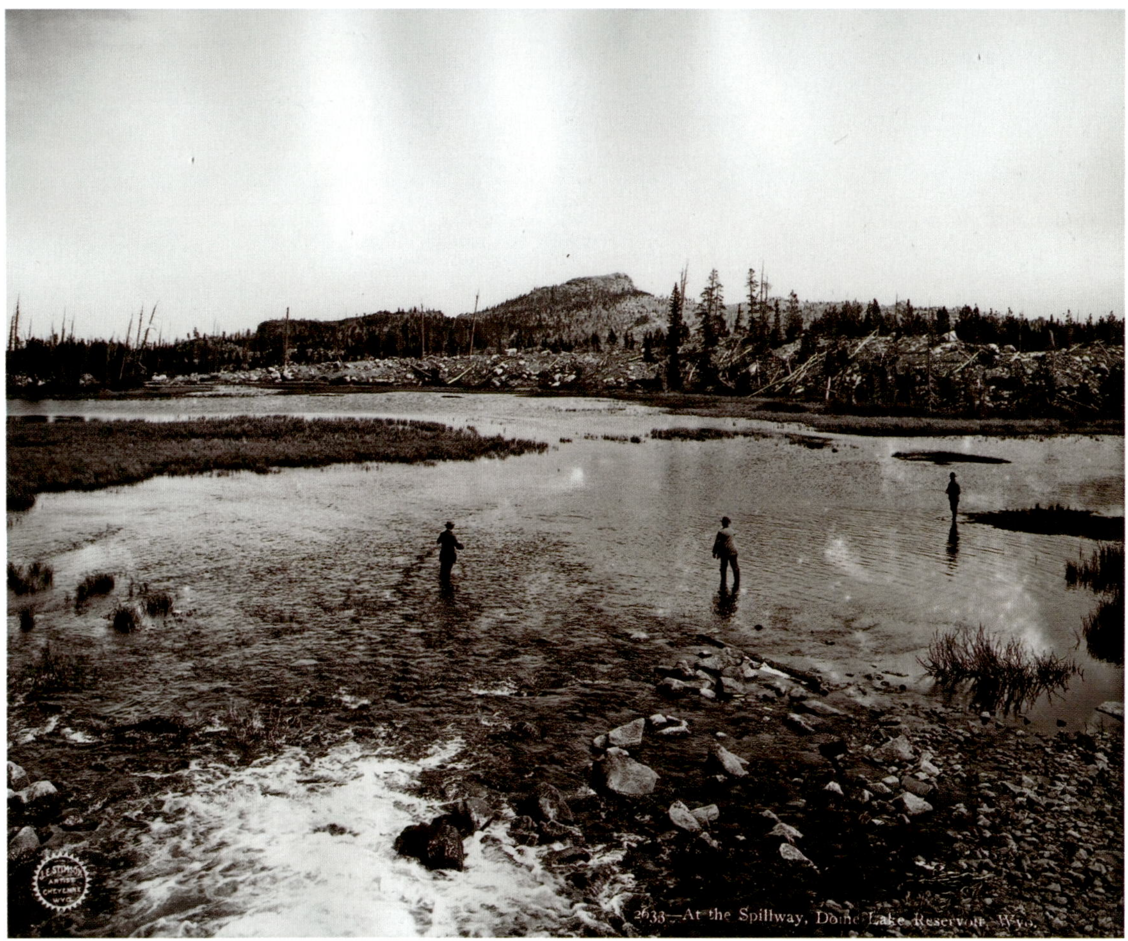

80. #2633

At the Spillway, Dome Lake Reservoir, 1909, 1988, 2008
GPS COORDINATES: 44 35.493833N, 107 17.817167W

To take the final photograph of Dome Lake included here, Stimson turned his camera 180 degrees at the spillway of Dome Lake Reservoir and captured this view of three men fishing in the released waters. In what is perhaps the most artistically composed and picturesque photograph of his many views at Dome Lake, Stimson contrasted the powerful forces of nature, as shown by the gushing water below and the burned-over forest beyond, with the image of genteel civilization, as expressed by the three gentlemen fishing in wool suits.

In my rephotographs, made in 1988 and 2008, no fisherman plied the released waters. Instead, I found a full lake and, beyond that, a completely recovered forest.

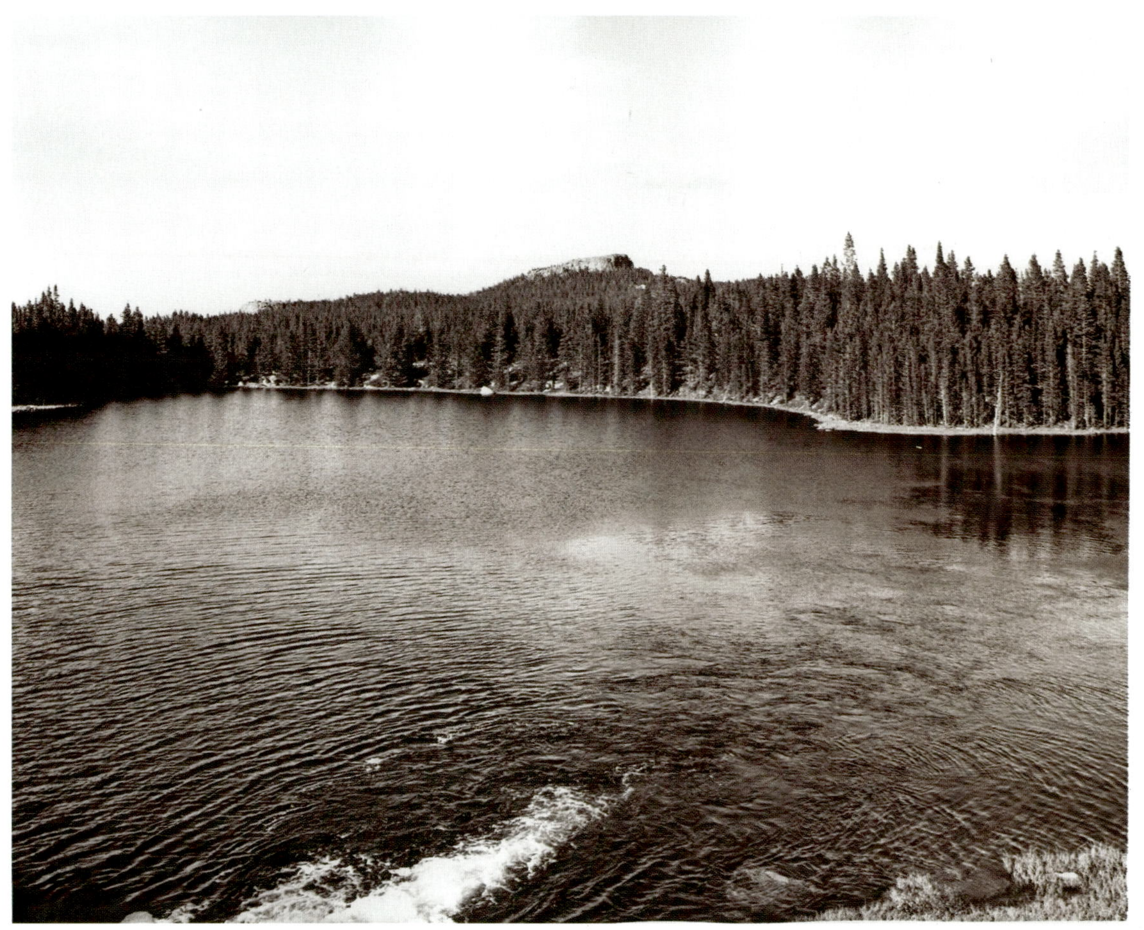

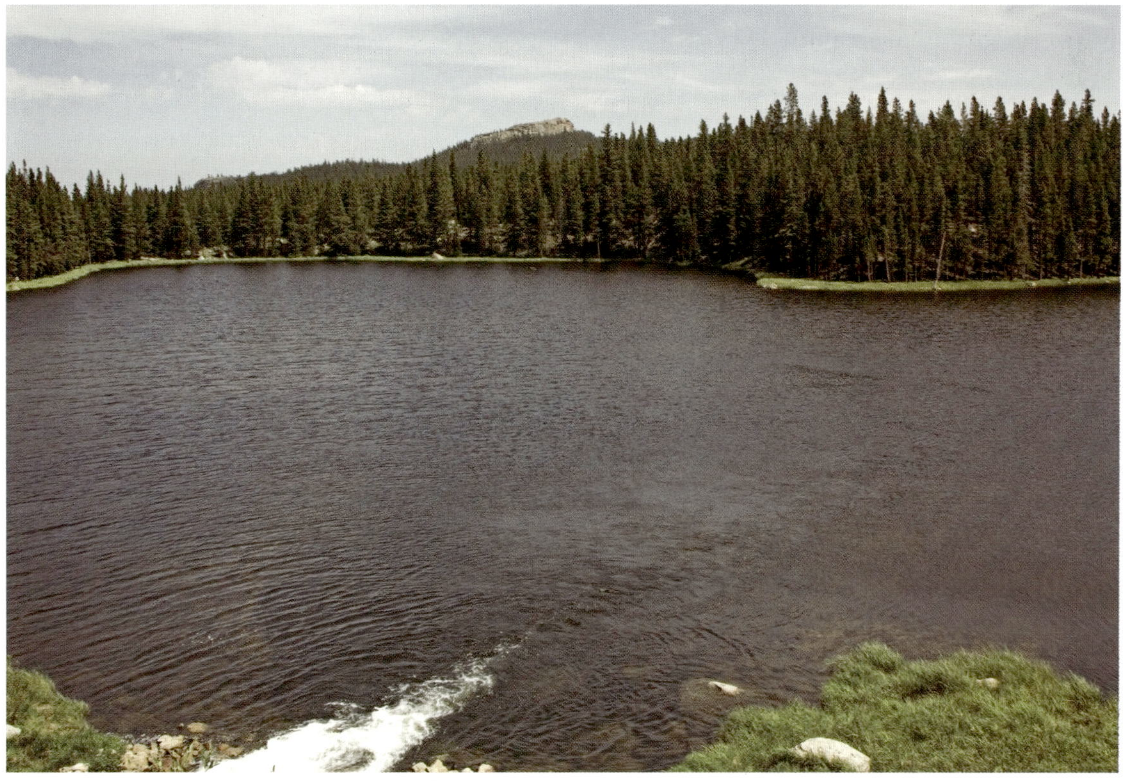

The South Pass is one of the few natural breaks in the Rocky Mountains. For thousands of years, Native Americans had used the pass. In the nineteenth century, fur trappers and, later, migrants going to Oregon, California, and Utah passed through. Gold was discovered in the area in 1868, and a small boom ensued. This first rush led to the founding of the towns South Pass City and Atlantic City. Down the hill, the site of Lander began as a small military post named Camp Augur. Although the gold boom did not last and both South Pass City and Atlantic City quickly lost population, prospectors continued to work the area. Several mines, including the Carissa above South Pass City, ebbed and flowed with activity. Lander grew as a trading and ranching community. In 1884 the state created Fremont County and named Lander the seat. In 1906 the Chicago and North Western connected the town with Casper.

Stimson photographed South Pass City, the Carissa Mine, and Atlantic City as part of his 1903 survey of the state for the St. Louis World's Fair. He returned and photographed Lander in 1910, showing the effects of the railroad on the community.

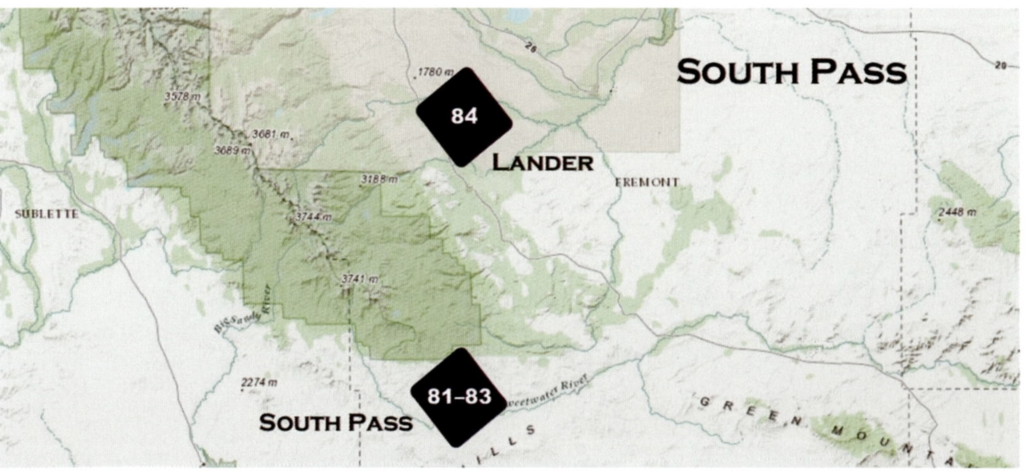

I rephotographed South Pass City and Atlantic City in 1987 as part of my first rephotography project. I accessed both places from the west side of South Pass at a ranch owned by my aunt and uncle, Joanne and Gary Zakotnik. Joanne's grandparents had homesteaded as part of the Eden Valley Irrigation Project.

After photographing that summer, little did I know that I would be living in South Pass City a year later while completing an internship as part of my master's degree program in American studies at the University of Wyoming. While there, I lived in a small trailer with three other students and got to know South Pass City, Atlantic City, and Lander fairly well. After discovering that one of my housemates was also named Michael, the curator's young son dubbed me "Other Mike." The first Mike left several weeks later, but South Pass City that summer, with a population of less than a dozen, had one guy named Mike who was known the entire summer as "Other Mike."

Twenty-plus years later, Lauren and I visited all four sites during our second summer of rephotography in 2008. At that time, the combined population of South Pass City and Atlantic City was less than seventy-five.

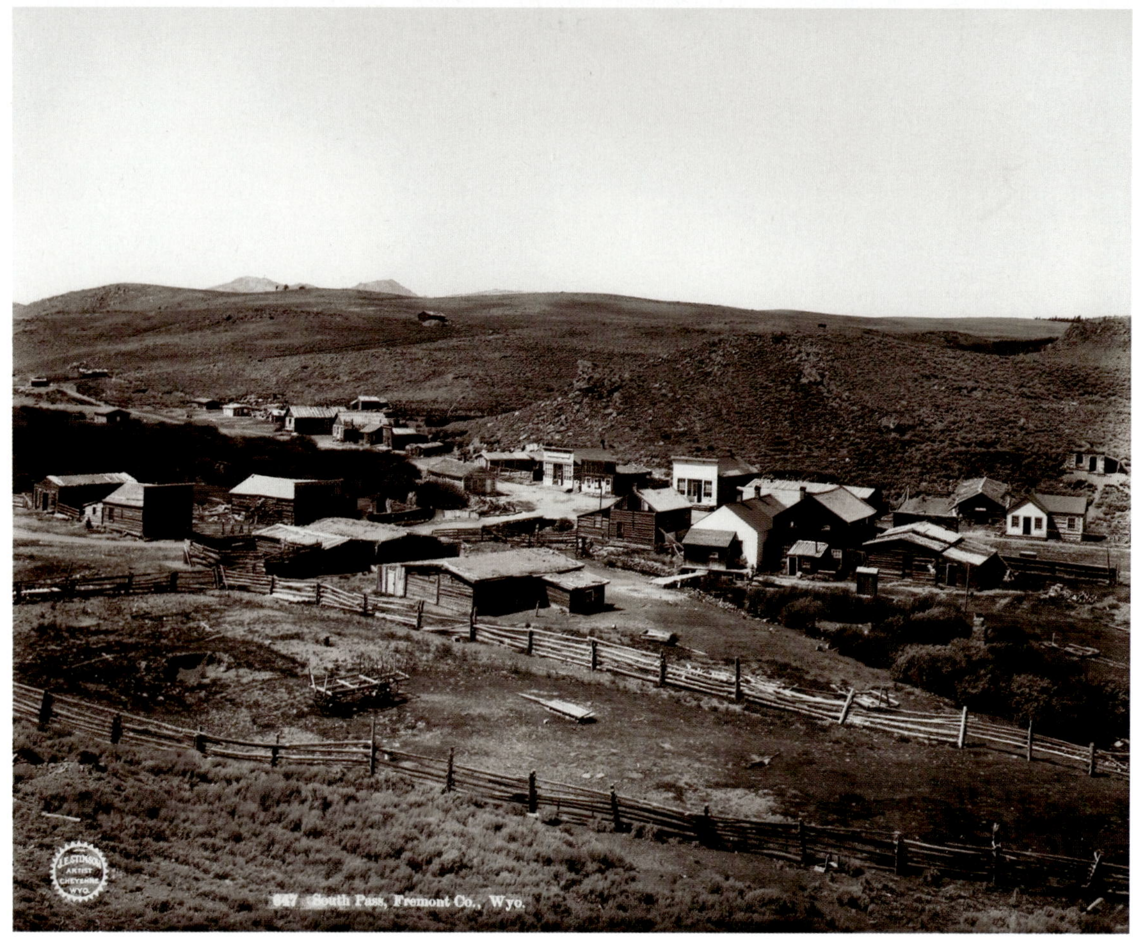

81. #647

South Pass [City], Fremont Co., 1903, 1987, 2008
GPS COORDINATES: 42 28.03133N, 108 48.0285W

South Pass City is a Wyoming State Historic Site. It first boomed in 1868 and boasted several thousand residents. William Bright, a local saloonkeeper and mine owner, represented the area in the first territorial legislature and introduced the women's suffrage bill that ordained Wyoming as the "Equality State." The following year, county commissioners appointed Esther Hobart Morris the town's justice of the peace, and she became the nation's first female judge. Bust came to the boomtown in 1872; within a decade of its founding, fewer than a hundred people called South Pass City home. Successive booms and busts hit the area in the 1880s and 1890s.

By the time Stimson visited during his 1903 survey of the state, the town clearly had seen better days. Taken from a hill to the south of town, Stimson's picture shows buildings and fences in disrepair. Not a single person, buggy, or automobile is visible on the streets. There's no laundry hanging on lines. Hardly a promotional image, this one serves more as a memento of Wyoming's history.

More booms and busts in the 1930s and 1940s followed Stimson's visit, but the most important event for the community occurred in 1967 when the State of Wyoming took over its upkeep as a State Historic Site. As evidenced in my 1987 image, much of the town had been restored and made available to the public; note, for example, the parking lot at left.

My 2008 rephotograph shows that the town remained much as it looked two decades earlier. Site managers moved the visitor parking lot out of the historic town site and added a buckboard wagon to the field at right. As with the Hardin Ranch images discussed in chapter 5, the restoration of South Pass City to look as it had around the time Stimson made his images hints at the characteristics of the modern and postmodern in Wyoming and raises questions about how preserving the past can also lead to the "end of history" at these "restored" places.

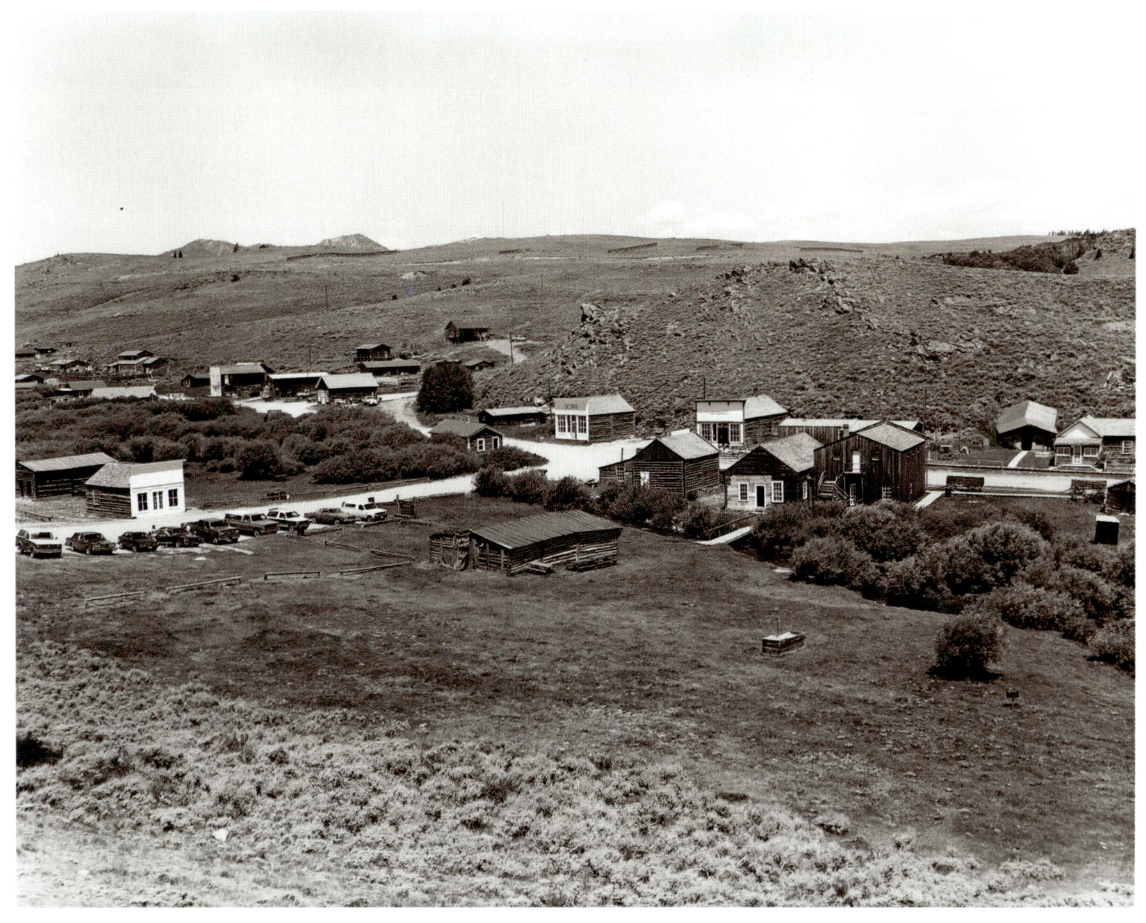

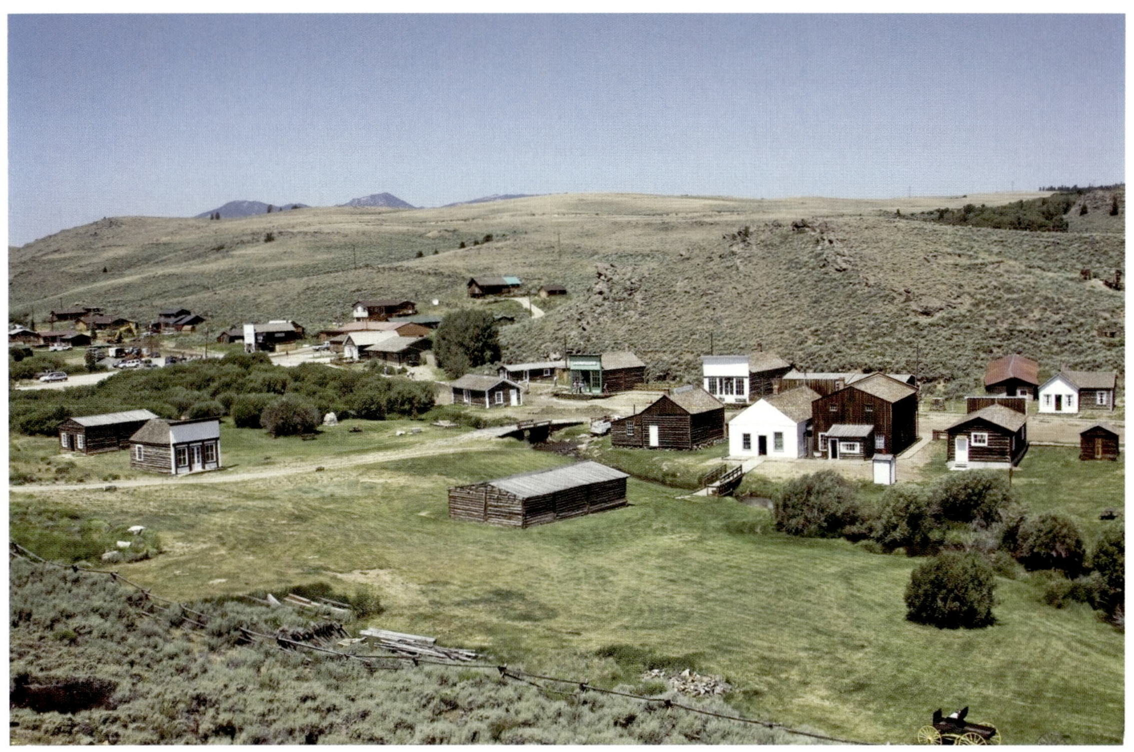

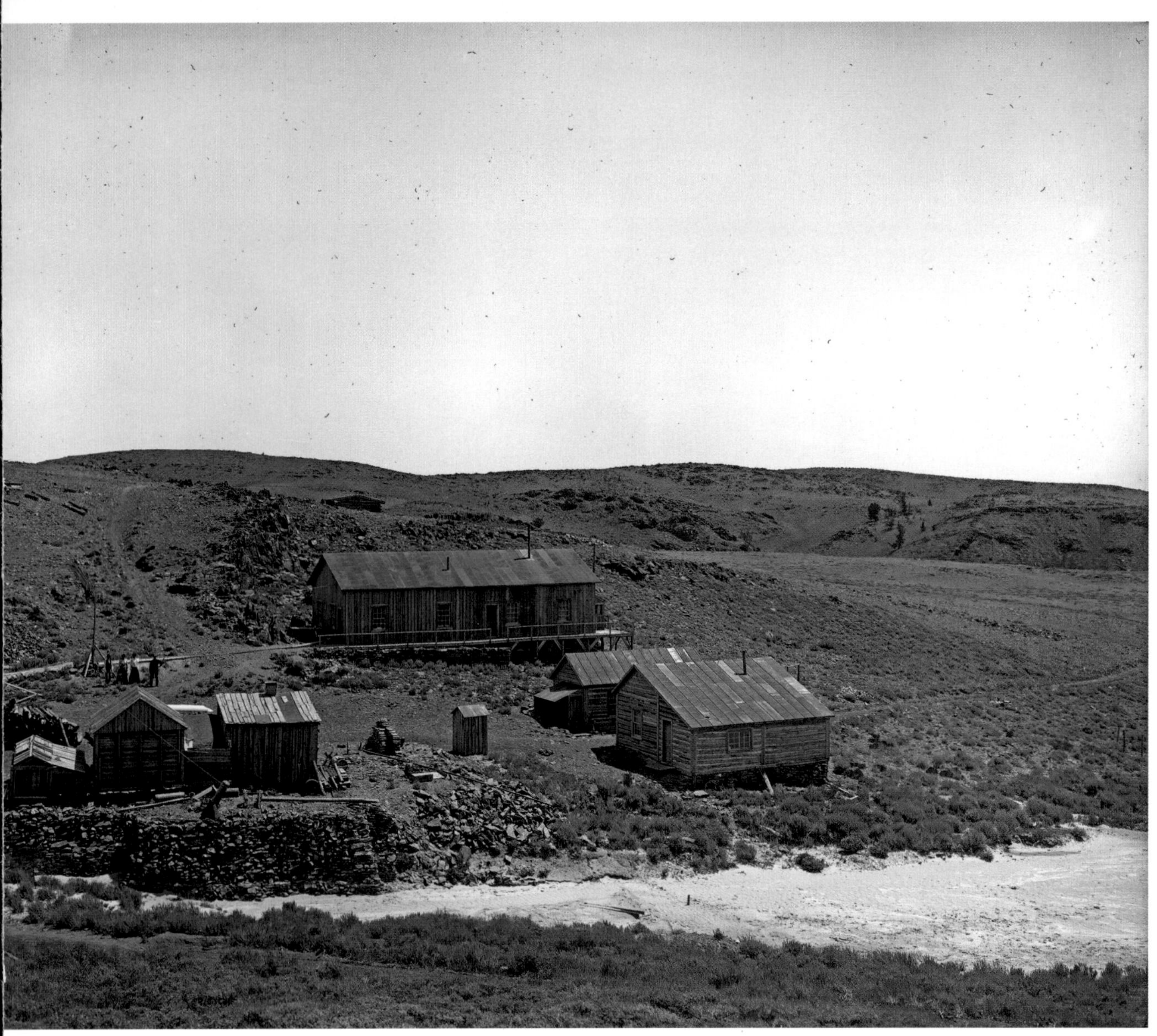

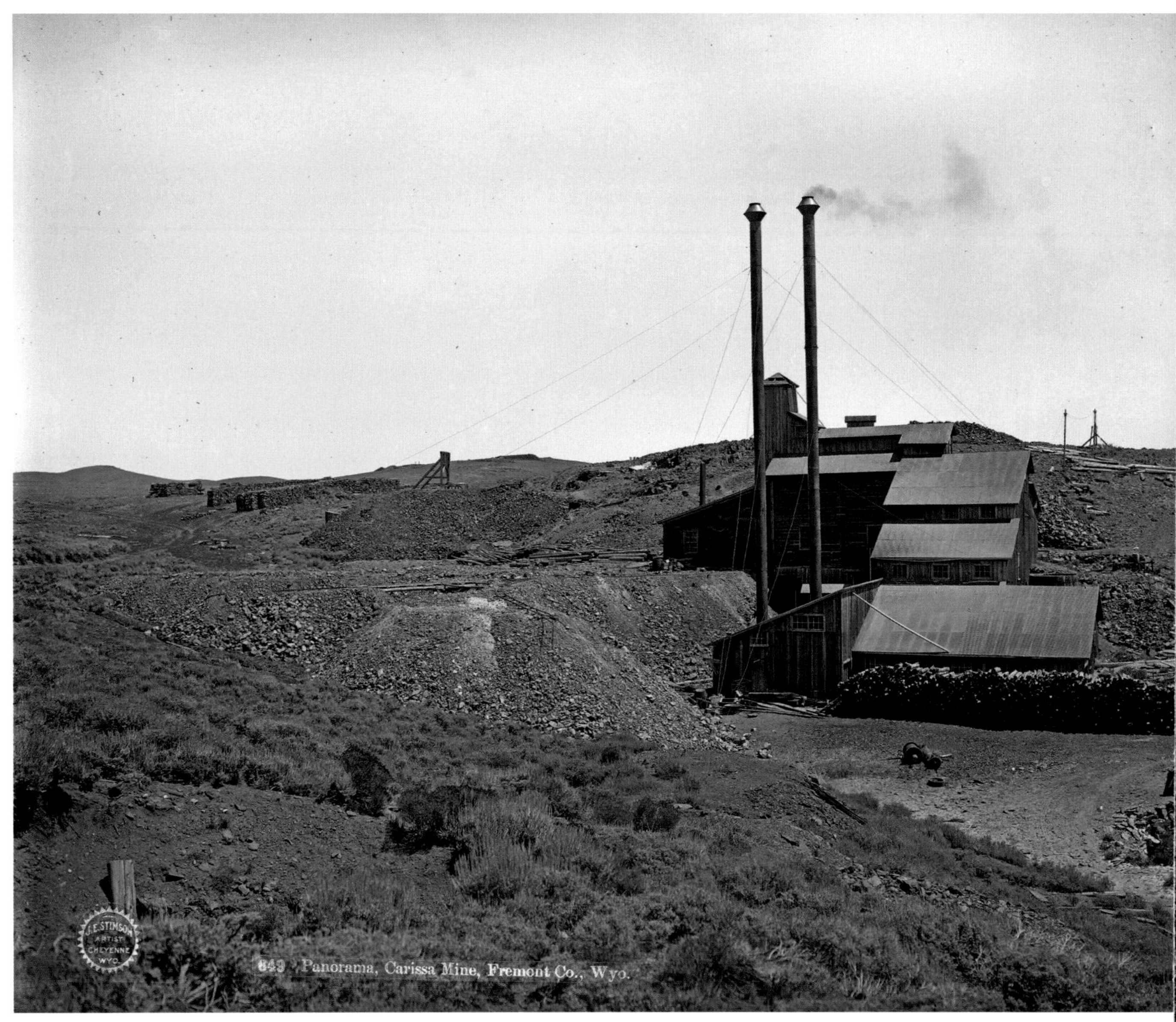

649   Panorama, Carissa Mine, Fremont Co., Wyo.

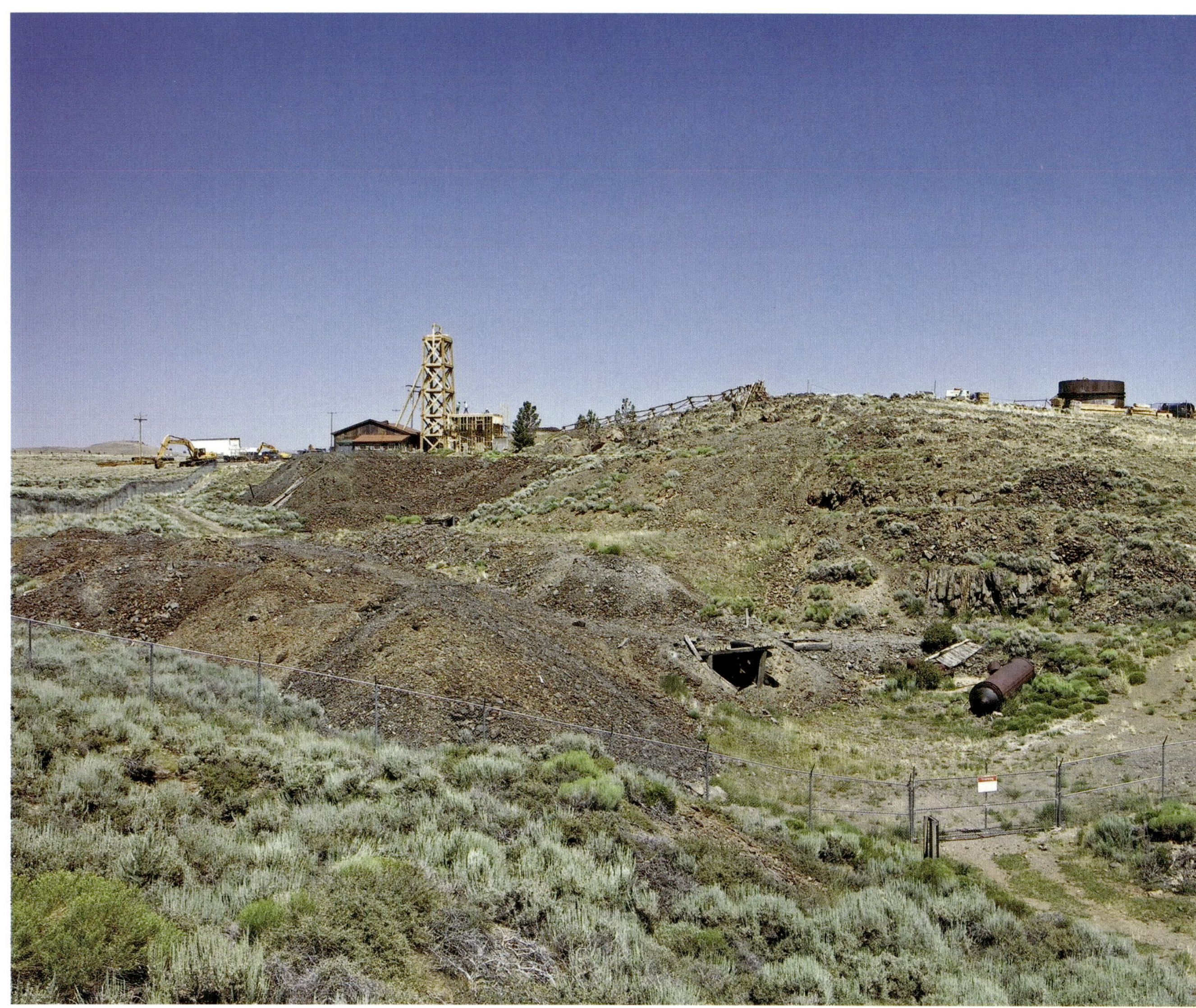

82. #649

Panorama, Carissa Mine and Mill, South Pass City, 1903, 2008
GPS COORDINATES: 42 28.448N, 108 47.806W

The Carissa Gold Mine just north of South Pass City operated in fits and starts as a working mine but was nevertheless the economic engine for the community. Beginning in 1868, it employed locals as miners, mill workers, hoist operators, and timber contractors. The mine produced more than 180,000 ounces of gold before closing in the 1890s. In 1901, Federal Gold Mining reopened the operation and extended the shaft to 300 feet using more modern equipment and techniques.

When Stimson visited the site during his 1903 St. Louis World's Fair survey, the Carissa was humming with optimism. As in many of his promotional images, Stimson used his two-sheet panorama to show clean grounds, repaired buildings, a ready stack of wood, and smoke coming from the tall stacks. To the right, two women and two men look on.

Unfortunately, this optimism faded, and the Carissa closed again in 1906. It reopened in the Roaring Twenties and the large mill house, seen in my 2008 rephotograph, was brought over from Atlantic City. The Great

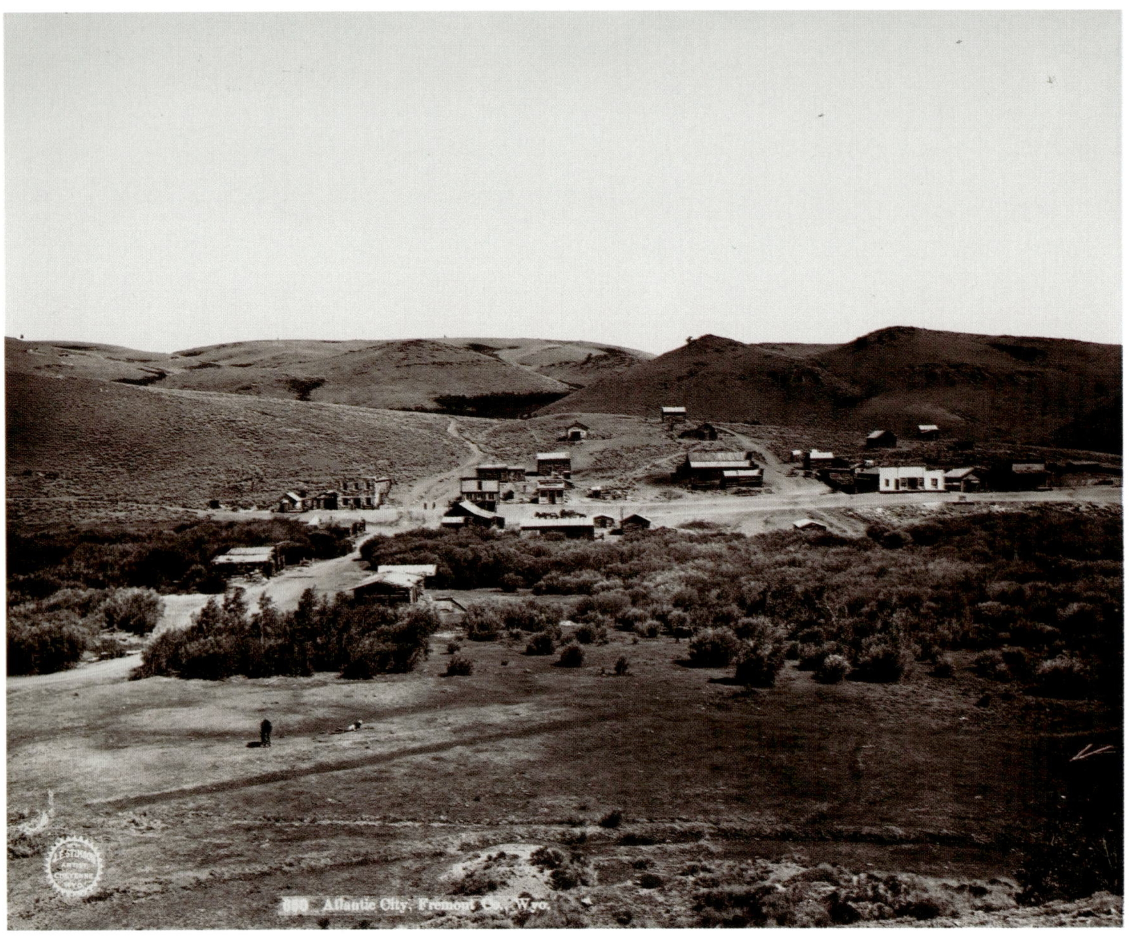

83. #650

Atlantic City, Fremont Co., 1903, 1987, 2008
GPS COORDINATES: 42 29.636N, 108 43.921W

Miners from nearby South Pass City founded Atlantic City in 1868 and named it because the new community is on the east side of South Pass. During its heyday in the 1870s, the town had a population of more than 2,000 and boasted an opera house and Wyoming's first brewery. The Atlantic City Mercantile, the white building facing front at right, opened is 1893 and is still in operation. Like many of Stimson's town images made in the summer of 1903, this photograph takes the broad view as a sort of bird's-eye image taken from the small hills to the south. In the twentieth century, the town struggled on as a vacation spot for a few families. Unlike its neighbor, South Pass City, which is preserved as a State Historic Site, Atlantic City has remained an independent community.

When US Steel operated an iron mine nearby from the 1960s to 1983, the community grew slightly. My 1987 rephotograph shows a few more streets, power lines, and denser willows along the creek. The Atlantic City Mercantile, then a bar and restaurant, was still in operation, at right. My rephotograph made more than twenty years later found a large new garage in the foreground but essentially the same town that's always been there. The population was listed as thirty-nine. The Mercantile still makes a great hamburger and remains the center of the town.

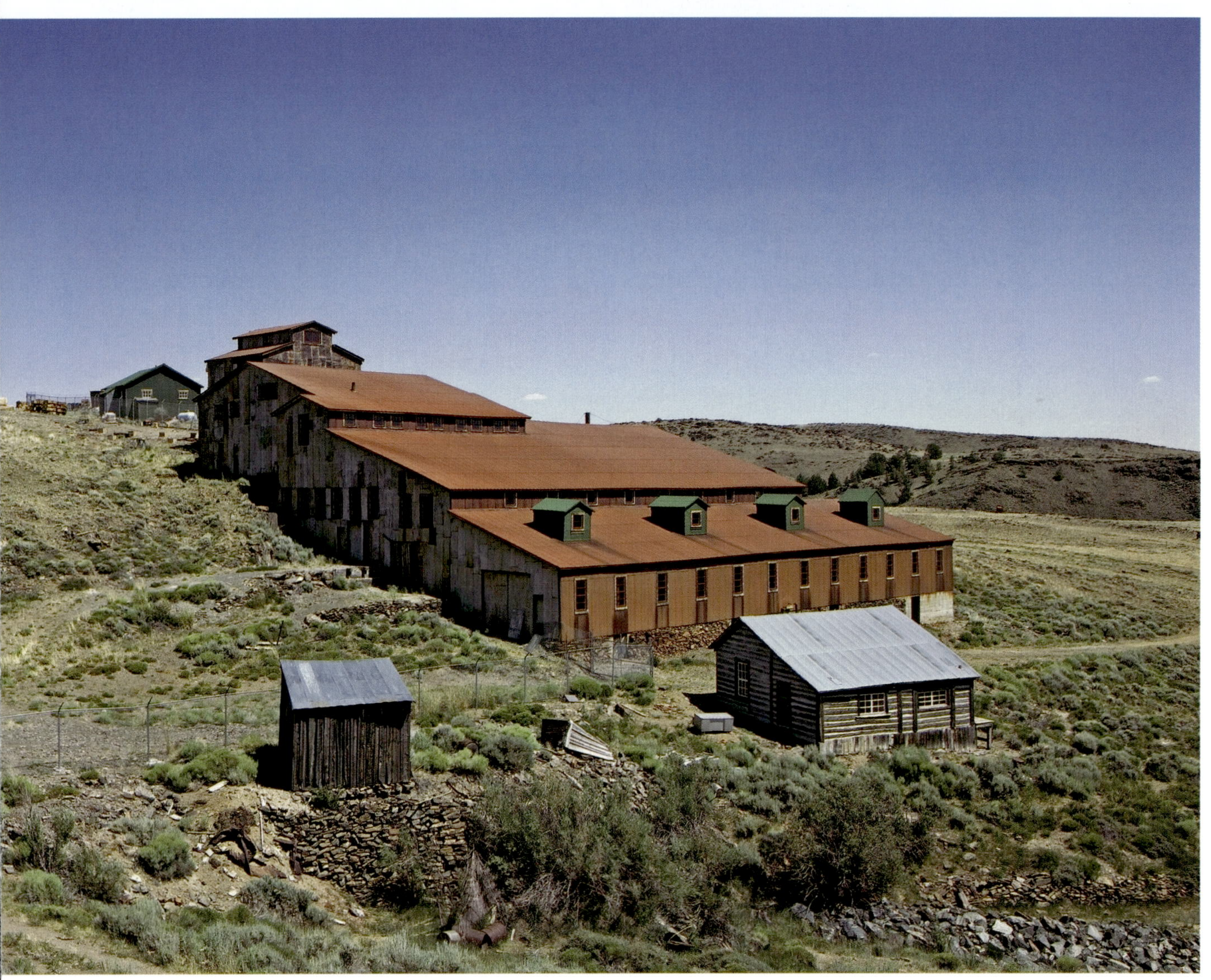

Depression caused the mine to close again, and World War II mining policies kept it closed. The Carissa operated for a few years after the war before ceasing operations in 1949. A final production run produced just over 400 ounces in 1954. In the 1980s, high gold prices temporarily raised interest in reopening the mine.

In 2003, the State of Wyoming purchased the mine and mill, and a new era as a historical site began. Starting that year, the Abandoned Mine Lands (AML) Division of the Wyoming Department of Environmental Quality began mitigating the area for tourism. It removed more than 250 tons of hazardous tailings, stabilized structures, and sealed open shafts. In addition, AML worked with State Parks and Cultural Resources to rebuild the historic head frame and trestle of the 1920s' operation.

My 2008 rephotograph shows this process in operation. At right, the 1929 mill is shuttered but intact. At center, an open adit can be seen. On the hillside at left, workers are rebuilding the head frame and trestle. A close examination of the two photographs shows that only the two buildings at right and a stone wall, center, remain from Stimson's 1903 image.

Like the Hardin Ranch near Sheridan and nearby South Pass City, the Carissa Mine and Mill will be preserved as postmodern tourist sites, historical simulations of their modern operations.

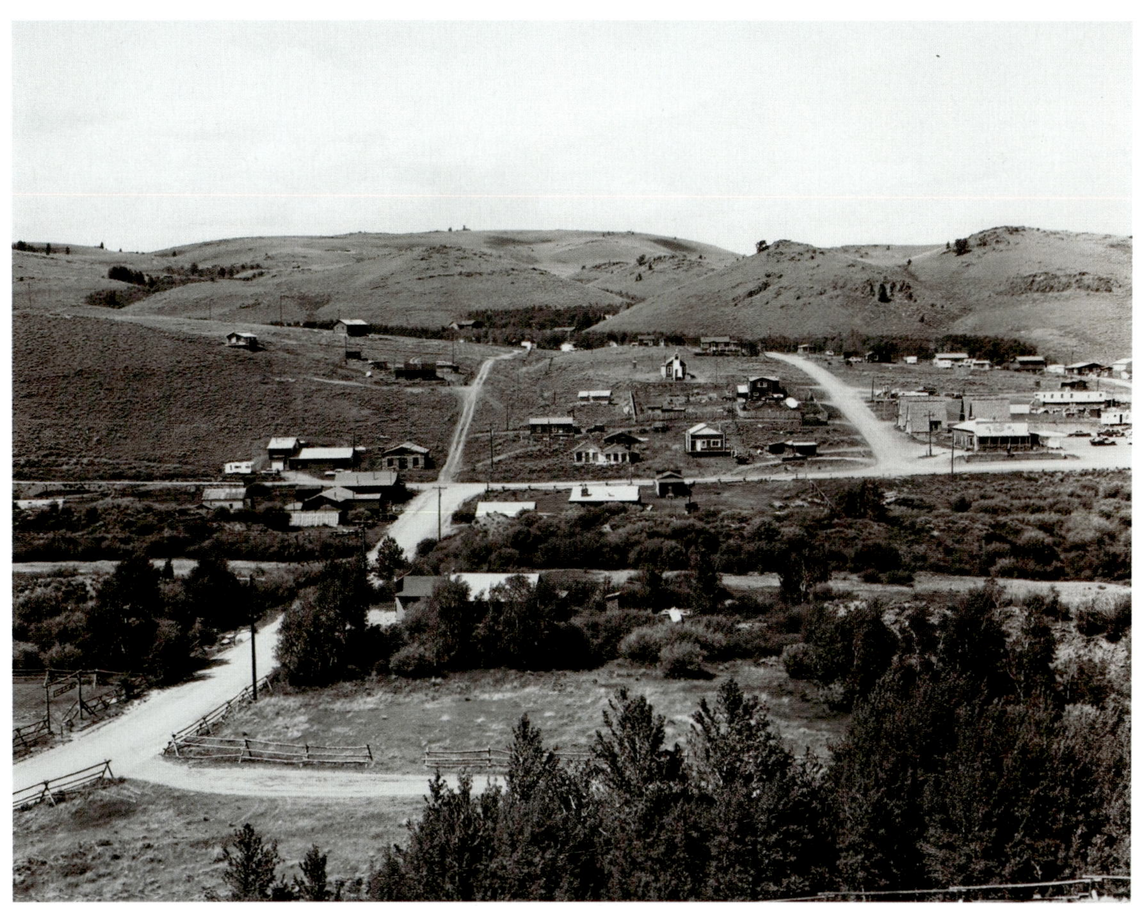

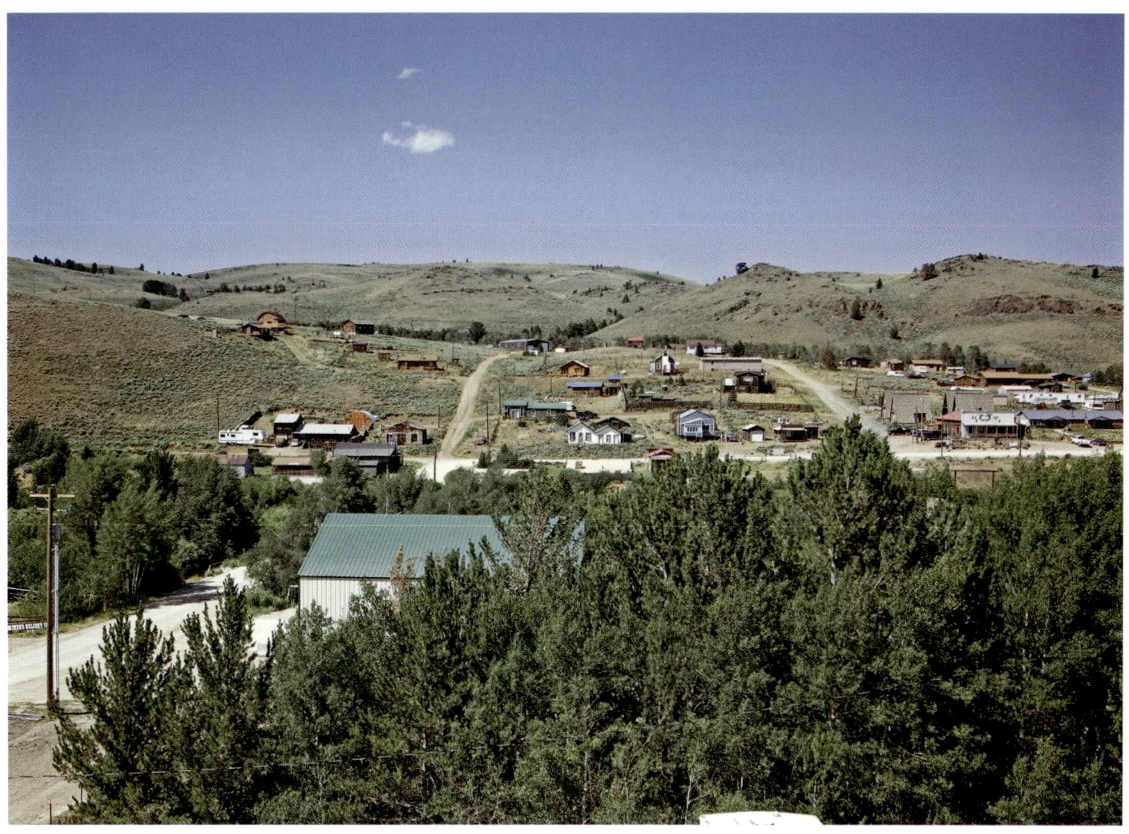

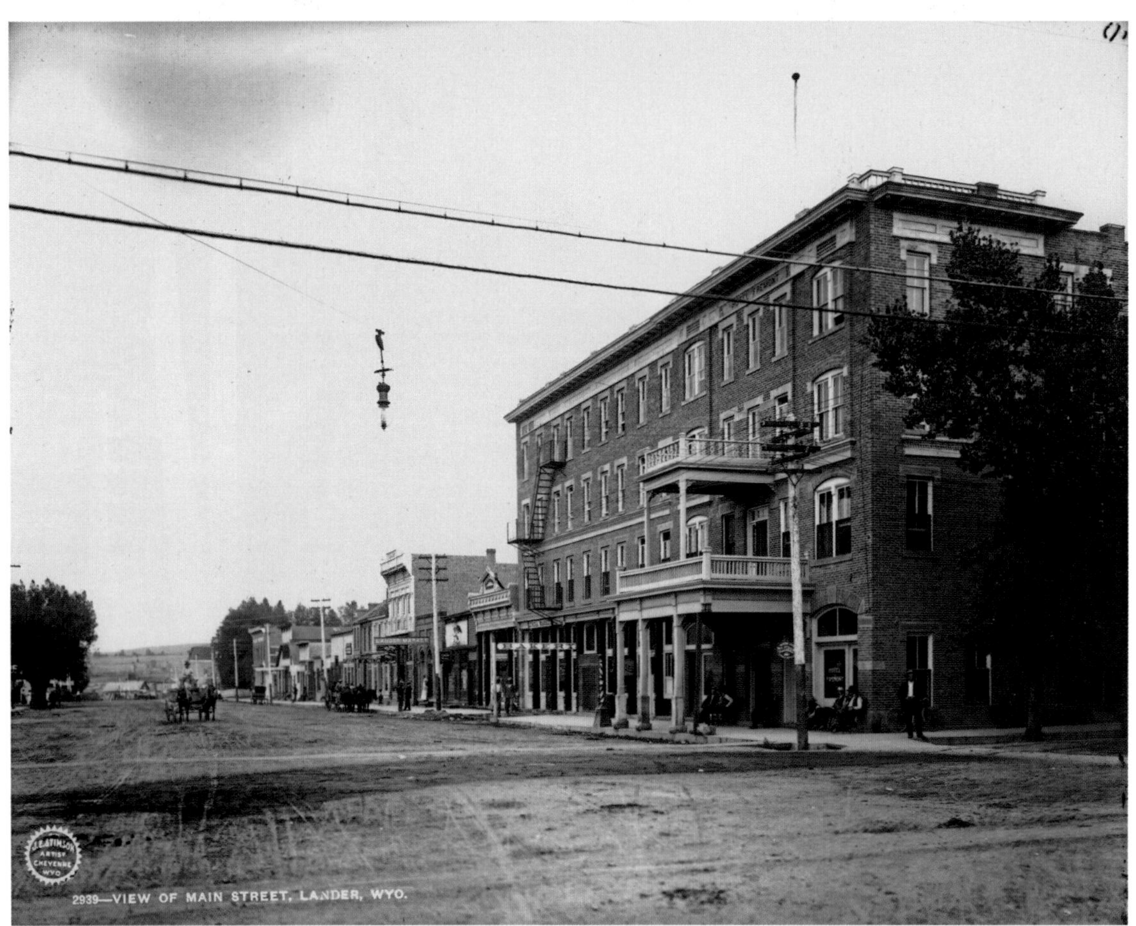
2939—VIEW OF MAIN STREET, LANDER, WYO.

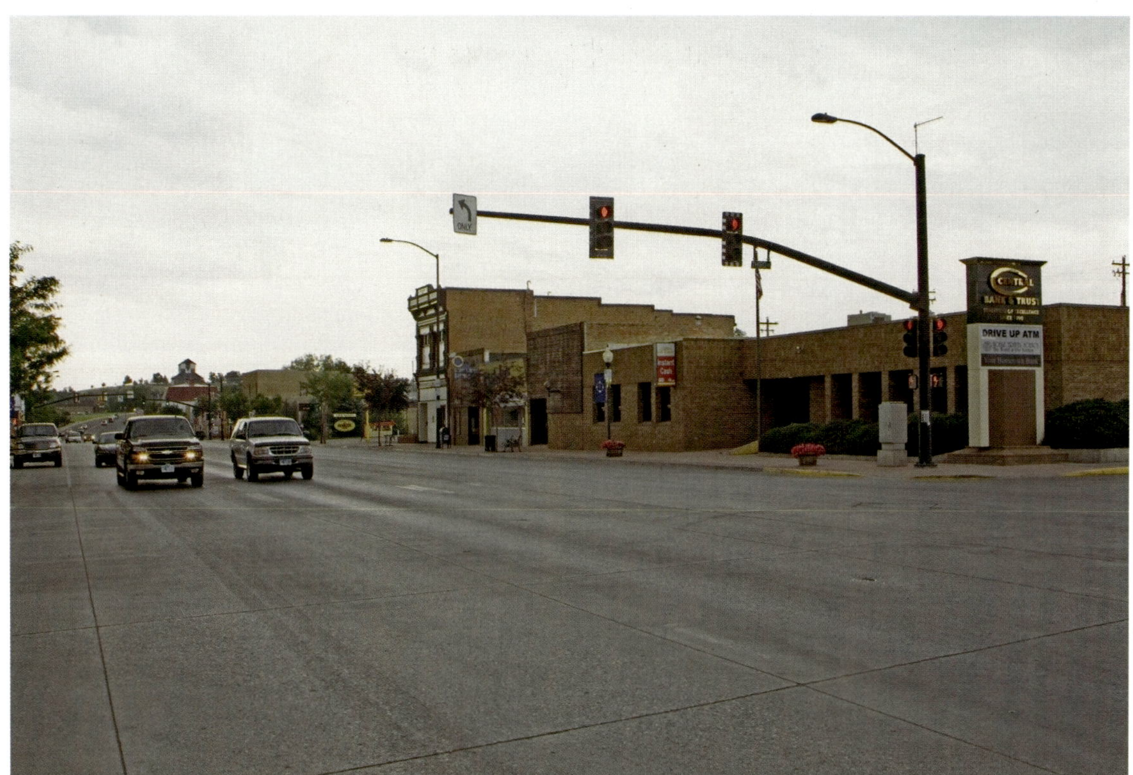

84. #2939

View of Main Street, Lander, 1910, 2008
GPS COORDINATES: 42 49.997N, 108 43.881W

Lander is one of the oldest towns in Wyoming. Its history goes back to its founding as Camp Augur, a military base established in 1869 to protect miners in South Pass, emigrants on the Oregon Trail, and Shoshone and Arapaho Indians on the nearby Wind River Indian Reservation. When Fremont County was created in 1884, Lander became the county seat. It flourished as a gateway town to the nearby reservation, South Pass mines, and Wind River Mountains. In 1906 the Chicago and North Western Railroad connected the community to Casper. From then on, the community championed the slogan "Where the rails end and the trails begin."

Stimson visited Lander in 1910 and made this shot looking east down Main Street toward the train tracks and depot. Like many of his promotional photographs, this image shows several groups of people, a large hotel, power and telephone lines, a streetlamp, and several businesses—including a bakery, a barber, and a telegraph office. In short, it is a modern scene of an up-and-coming community, the perfect sales image.

My 2008 image of Lander shows that little remains of this side of Main Street. The Fremont Hotel burned in 1971, and today the brick Central Bank and Trust occupies the site. Down the street, another two-story business retains much of its nineteenth-century charm on the second floor, but the ground story has a stucco entrance. Not a single pedestrian can be found on the street. Only a few cars negotiate what has become Highway 287.

In its own way, my rephotograph also represents a scene of progress and optimism, with the wide highway, bank, businesses, and fairly busy traffic for an early morning weekend. But not really. Instead, we miss the old hotel and the charming pedestrian Main Street. But that is one of the limits of rephotography because directly behind me, out of sight of the camera, was a busy coffee shop in a cute old historic building. Such is the nature of rephotography. The rephotographer is limited to the field of vision made by the original photographer. As such, rephotography both eliminates and illuminates change over time.

The Bighorn Basin is a plateau in north-central Wyoming that lies among the Big Horn Mountains to the east, the Absaroka Mountains to the west, and the Owl Creek and Bridger Mountains to the south. Approximately 100 miles wide, the area is drained by the Bighorn River (known as the Wind River on the Wind River Reservation), which flows north out of the region toward the Yellowstone River. Generally lower in elevation than most of Wyoming, the area is also semiarid, receiving an average of only six to ten inches of rainfall each year. The low elevation allows for longer growing seasons, but the aridity meant that no large-scale agriculture occurred until state and federal irrigation began in the late nineteenth and early twentieth century. Because of this, the basin was one of the last areas in the state to be settled.

In his 1903 survey of the state for the St. Louis World's Fair, J. E. Stimson mostly skirted the basin, photographing the western-edge communities of Meeteetse

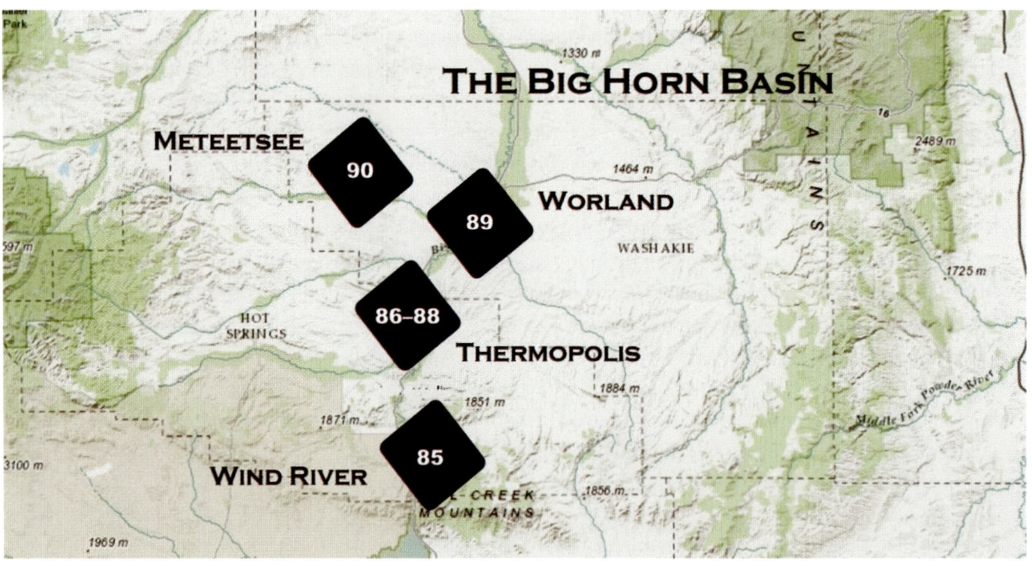

and Cody, as well as the newly opened Cody Road to Yellowstone National Park. He returned in 1906 and 1910 to promote the irrigated agriculture starting to develop around Worland and the tourist trade at the hot springs community of Thermopolis. In the 1920s, he made an auto trip to the area.

My connection to the Big Horn Basin focused on Worland because that is where my aunt and uncle, Rozanne and Doug Reachard, lived. Rozanne taught elementary school in Ten Sleep, and Doug taught high school and coached cross-country at Worland High School. In 1988 they put me up for a week as I traveled around the area taking pictures. Nineteen years later, Doug and Rozanne had since retired to a house overlooking Buffalo Bill Reservoir west of Cody. They again hosted us as I rephotographed Worland, Thermopolis, Wind River Canyon, Meeteetse, and Cody over the next two years. Doug also guided me to locales on the Cody Road included in my book *Passage to Wonderland*.

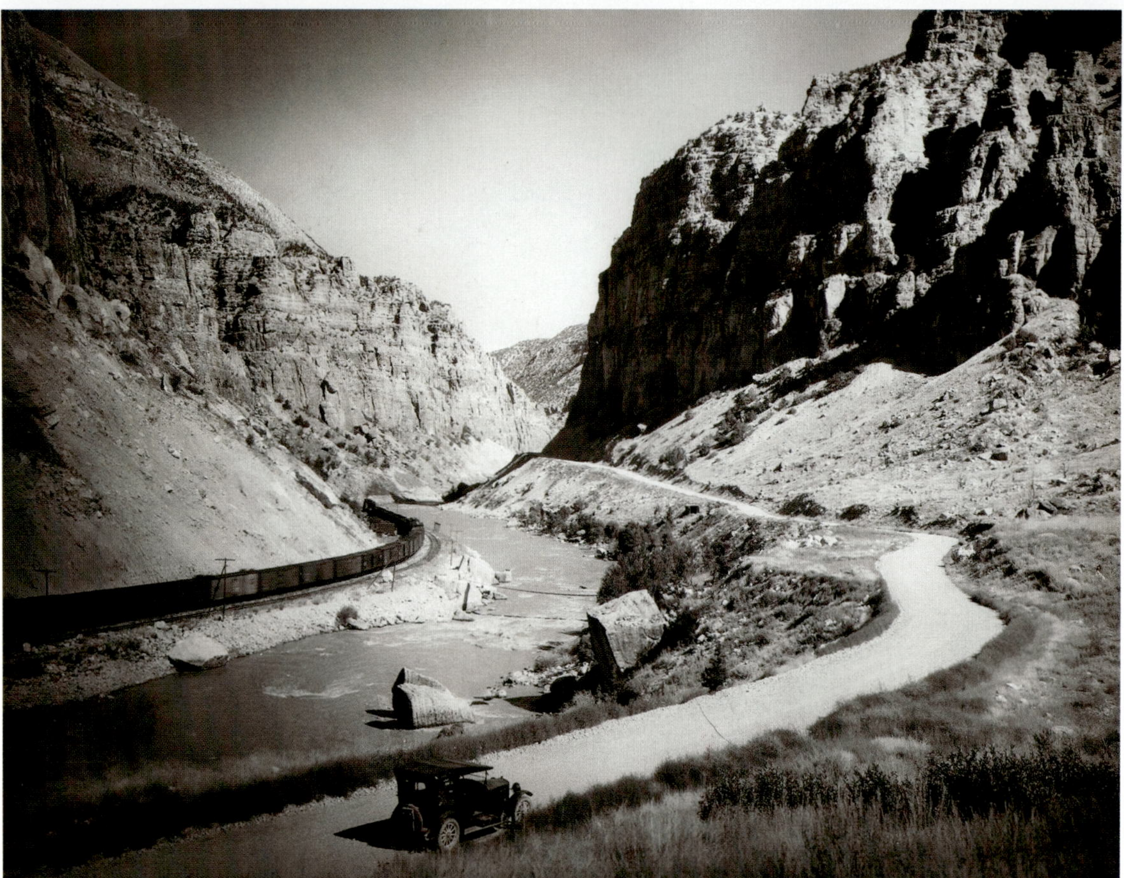

85. #5921

Wind River Canyon, ca. 1925, 1988, 2008
GPS COORDINATES: 43 31.459N, 108 10.491W

Scenic Wind River Canyon cuts through the Owl Creek Mountains. At times, it is 2,500 feet deep. It lies between the towns of Shoshone to the south and Thermopolis to the north. It also overlaps part of the Wind River Indian Reservation. Interestingly, the part of the river that flows through the canyon is called the Wind River, but after Thermopolis it is known as the Bighorn. The Burlington Railroad blasted a right-of-way through the canyon in 1913, and the parallel highway was opened in 1924.

As discussed in chapter 2, J. E. Stimson was a strong advocate of early automobile travel and a proponent of the Good Roads Movement. He made this photograph around 1925 while on an auto tour north to the Tetons. The location is about four miles south of Thermopolis and is looking north. Made more than two decades after his 1903 survey of the state for the St. Louis World's Fair, this photograph shows that the fifty-five-year-old photographer still had a good eye for composition. The canyon walls frame his view, and the s-shapes of the railroad and highway provide a vanishing-point perspective. His automobile points north, almost suggesting that the viewer follow it up the canyon.

About the time Stimson made his picture, a small concrete dam at the southern end of the canyon began silting up. After being removed in 1948, it was replaced by a large Bureau of Reclamation project called Boysen Dam that controls water releases downstream into Wind River Canyon.

My 1988 rephotograph shows the canyon basically as it was sixty years earlier. The highway has been widened and improved, and the railroad tracks remain. Interestingly, there is little tourist development in the canyon and none in this view. As noted, river water levels are now controlled by the Bureau of Reclamation. My first car, a red 1976 Ford Granada, can be seen at the extreme right side of the photo.

Twenty years later I found the canyon somewhat busier with tourists but looking about the same. My silver Forester is at the far right. Note the several motor homes and pickups pulling big speedboats north, probably going home after some fun at Boysen Reservoir.

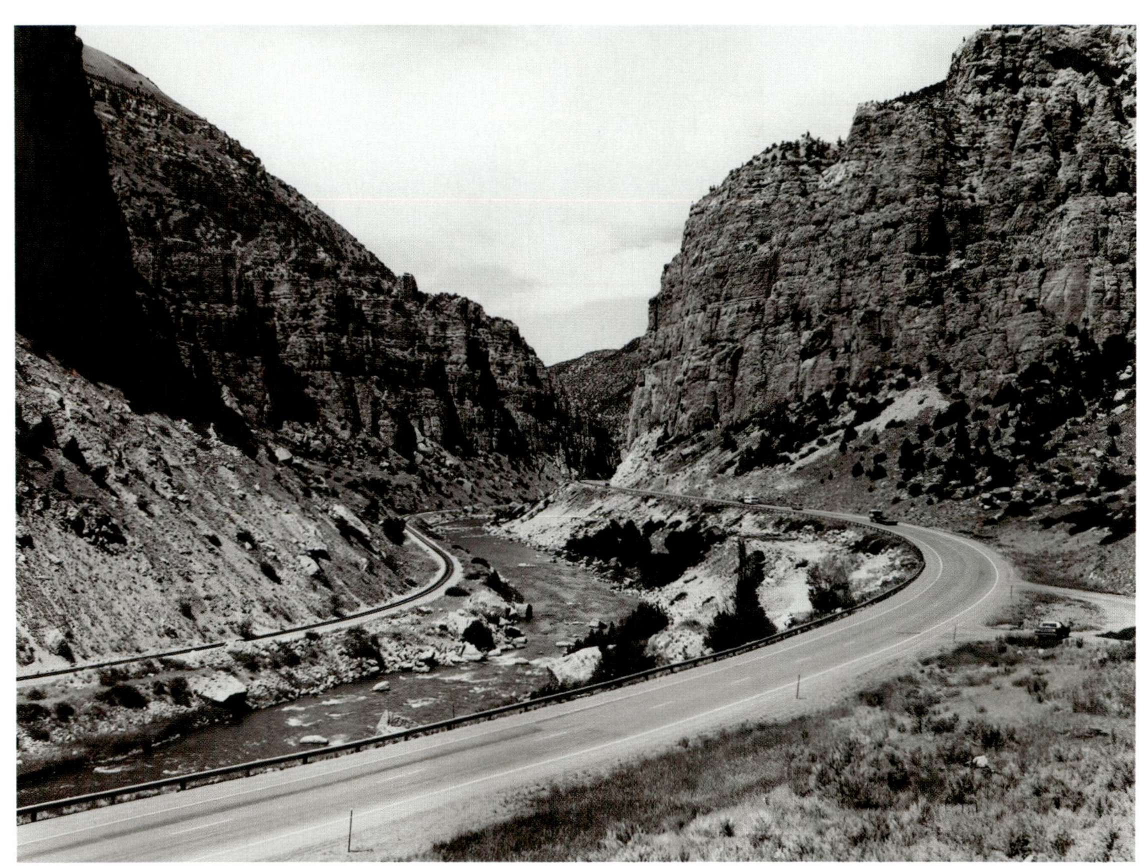

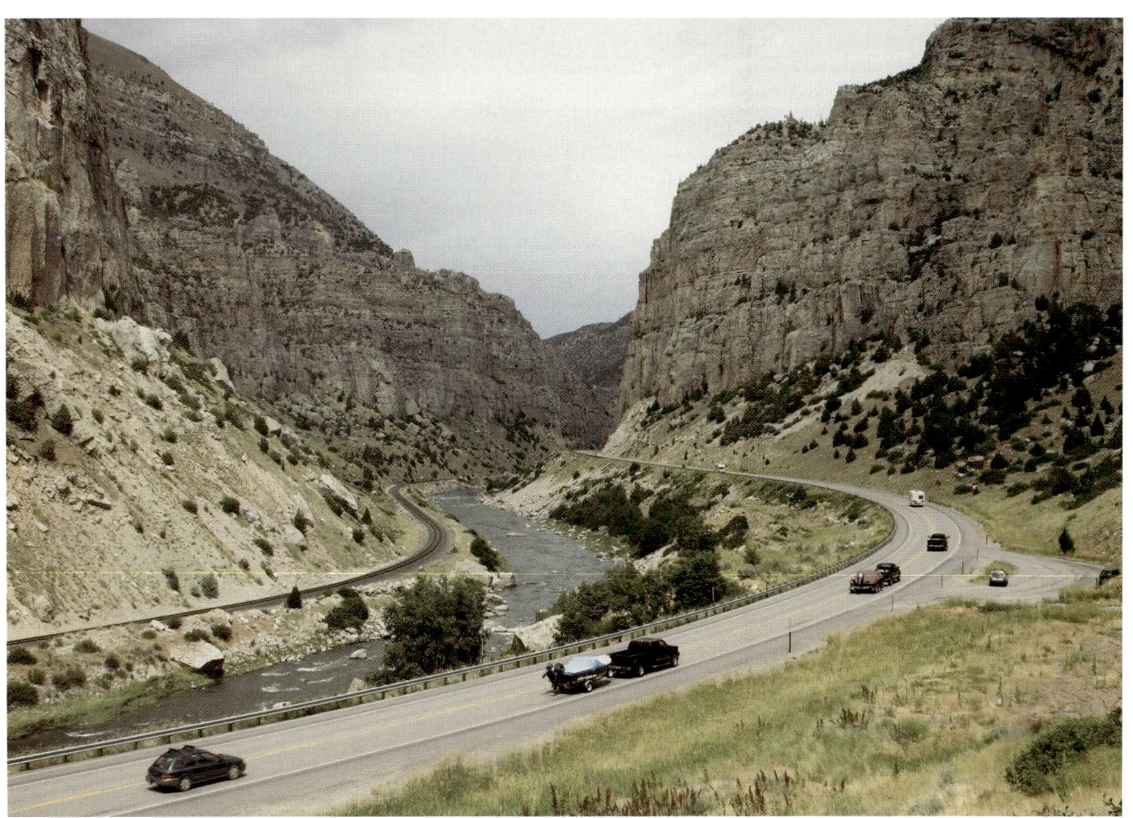

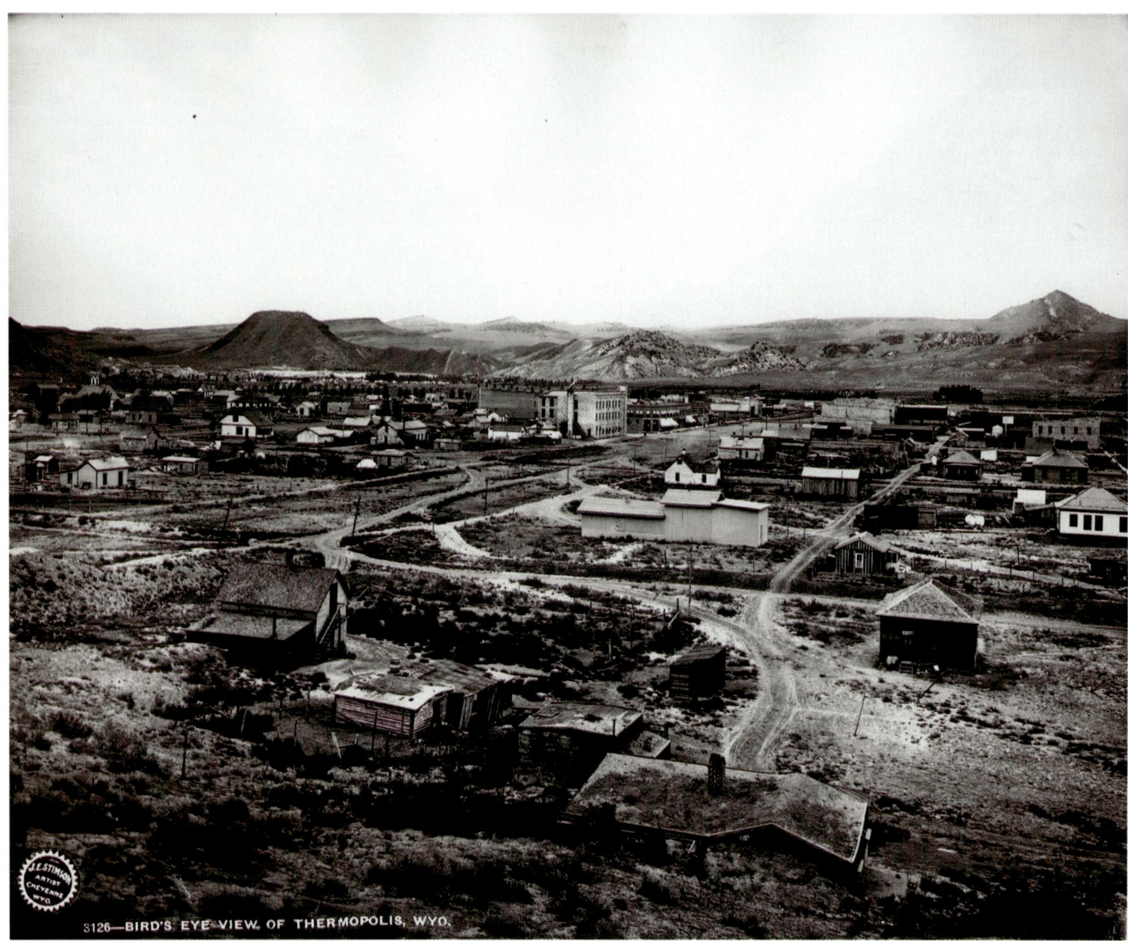

86. #3126

Bird's Eye View of Thermopolis, 1910, 1988, 2007
GPS COORDINATES: 43 38.737N, 108 13.004W

The town of Thermopolis is home to the world's largest hot spring. After a treaty with the Shoshone and Arapaho ceded this area to Wyoming from the Wind River Reservation, the hot springs became the first state park, and the town was platted in 1897. Its unusual name is derived from the Latin word *thermae* (hot bath or spring) and the Greek word *polis* (city). A special pageant, "Gift of the Waters," is enacted annually in the town. According to the terms of the treaty, access to the springs must always be free.

When Stimson visited in 1910, the population was about 1,500. He took this photograph from a small hill just west of the downtown. Like many of his city views, this one looks down on the community from a bird's-eye vantage point. Most noticeable in the view is the imposition of the regimented grid on the landscape. The wide street at left is Broadway; following it into the picture leads one to the downtown. The Emery Hotel, discussed later, can be easily located. The flattop hill, left, marks the location of the hot spring.

Three years after Stimson made his photograph, the Wyoming legislature created Hot Springs County and named Thermopolis its seat. Over the years, the tourist industry developed as people came to take in the waters and the numerous bathhouses and sanitariums. The State Bath House has always been free.

When I visited Thermopolis in 1988 and again in 2007, the town's population was just over 3,000, and its chief economy was still tourism. As in many rephotographs, the numerous trees present now block much of the view. Still, close examination of each view shows the downtown commercial block is still there, as are a number of houses.

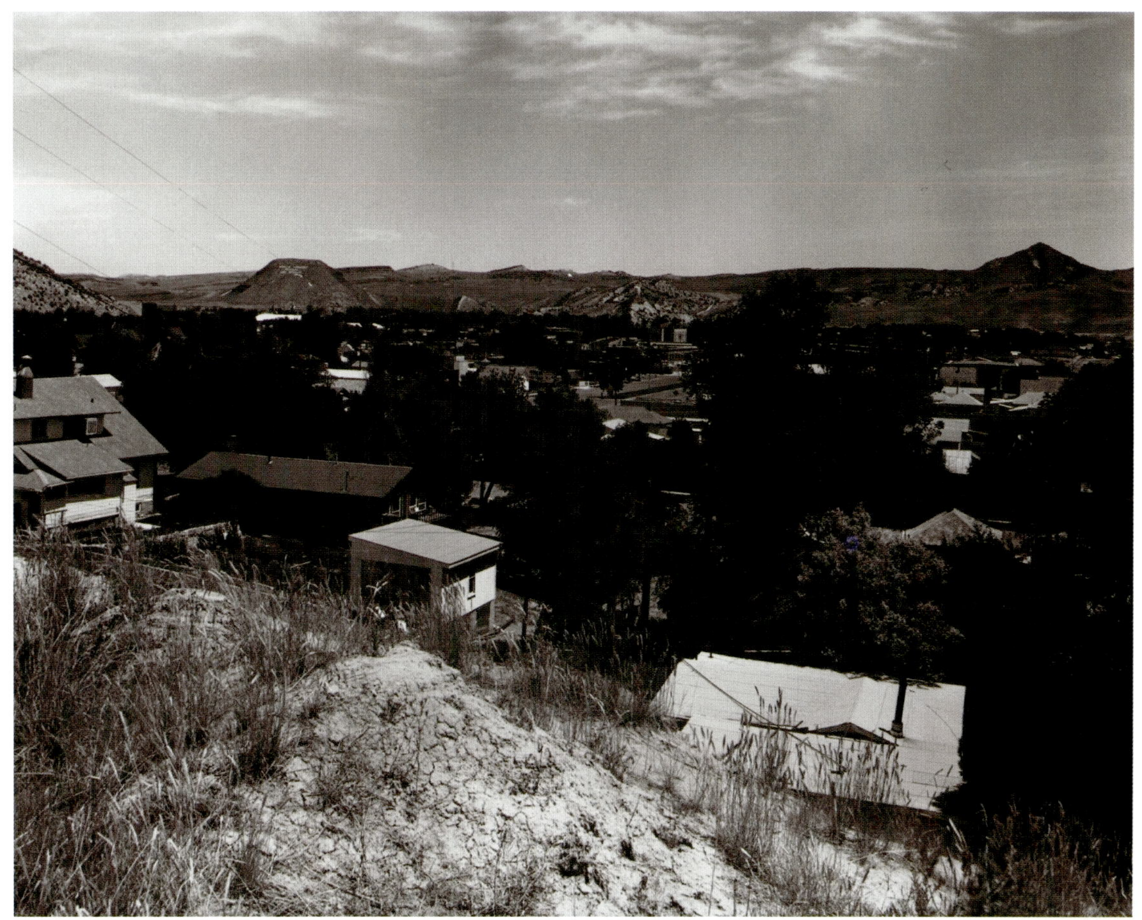

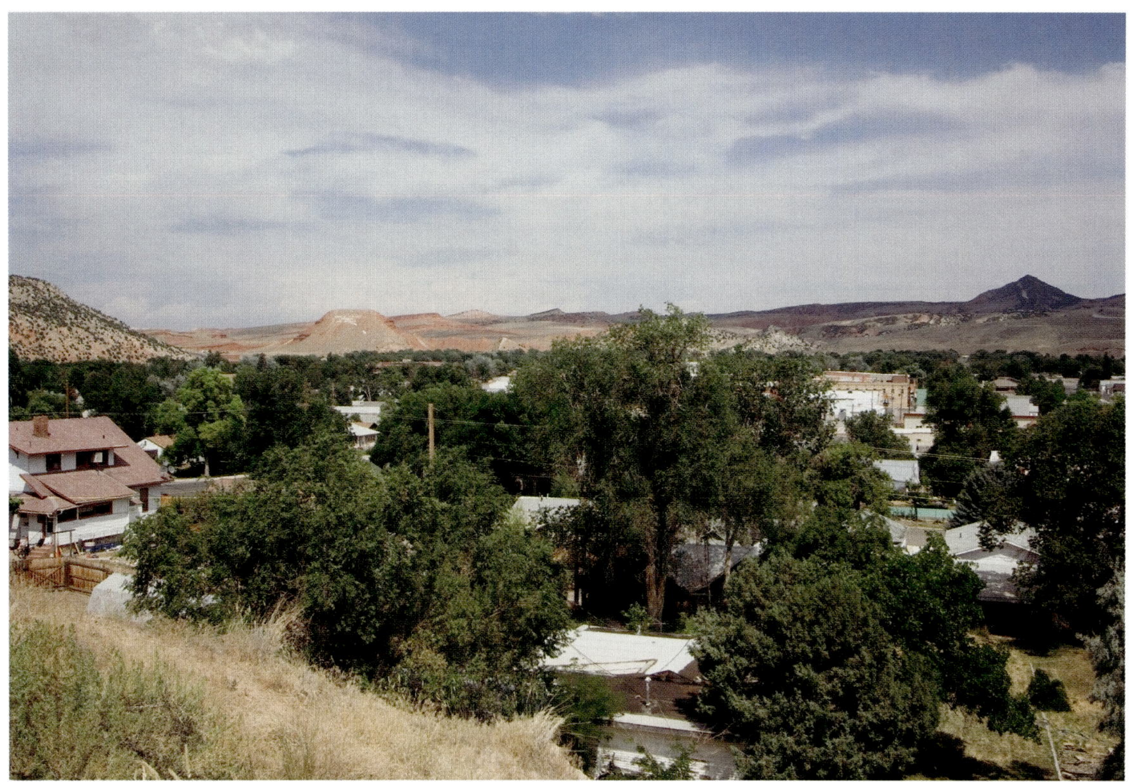

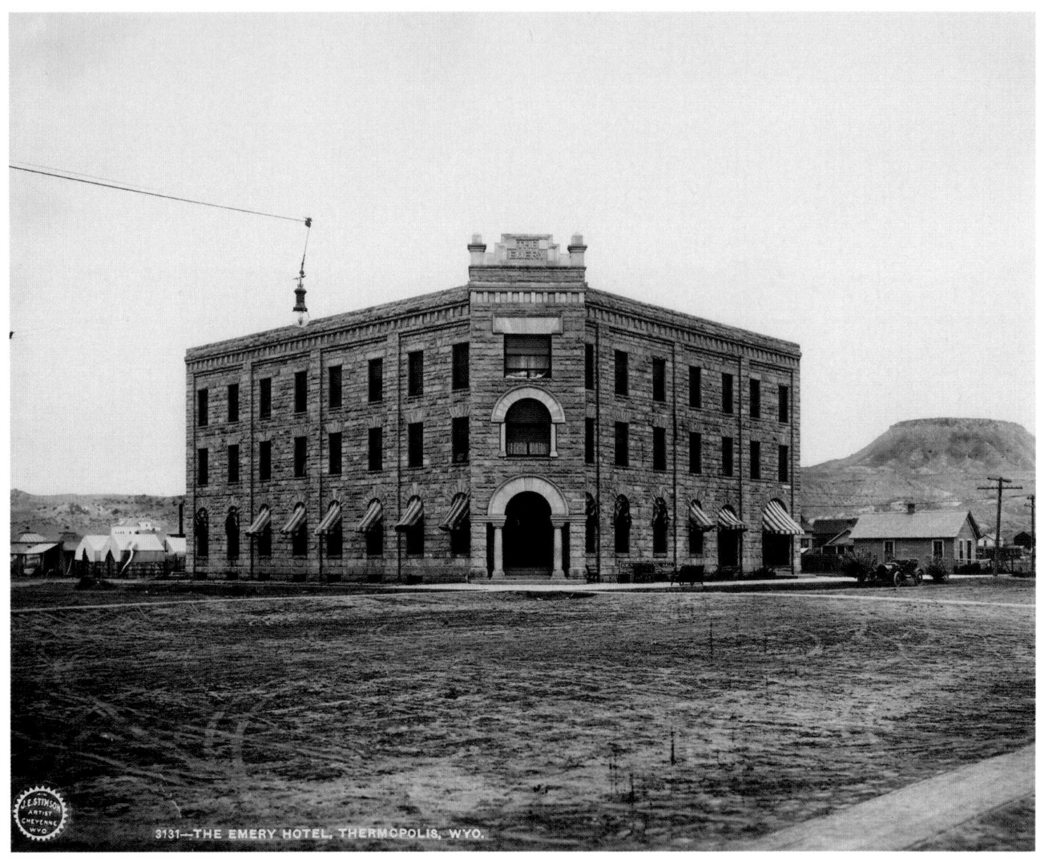
THE EMERY
3131—THE EMERY HOTEL, THERMOPOLIS, WYO.
J.E. STIMSON
ARTIST
CHEYENNE
WYO.

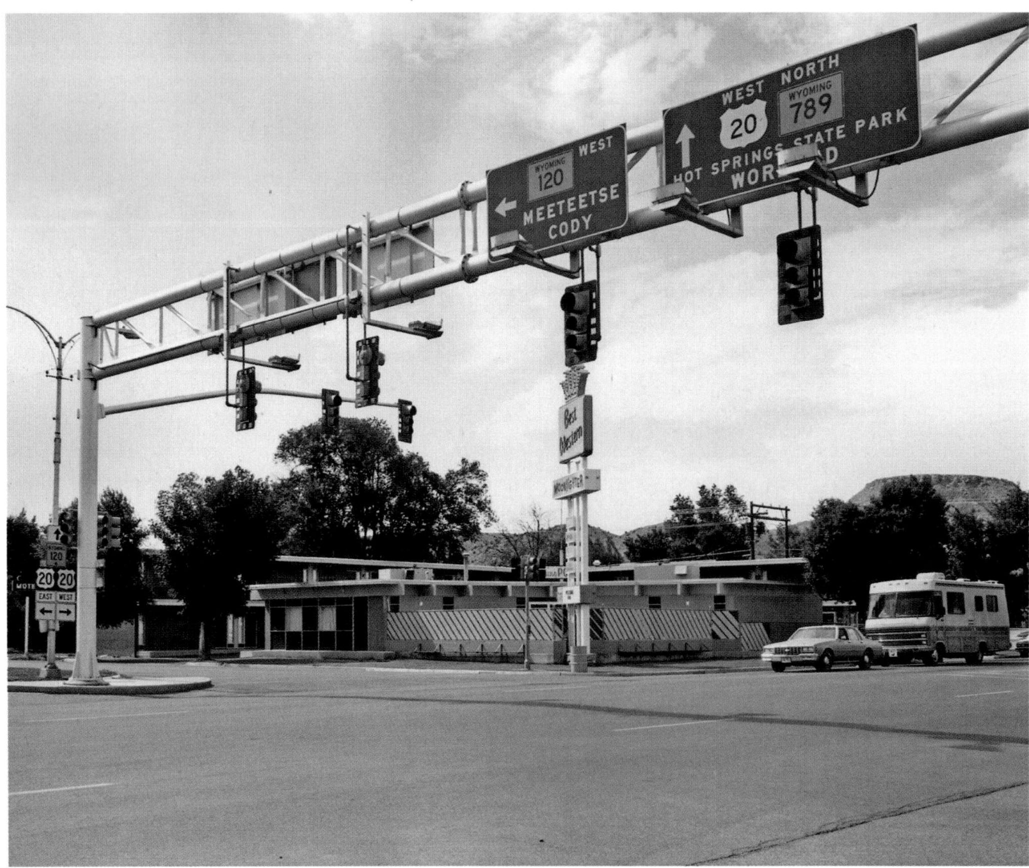
WEST NORTH
WEST
WYOMING
20
WYOMING
789
120
HOT SPRINGS STATE PARK
MEETEETSE
WORLAND
CODY
20 20
EAST WEST

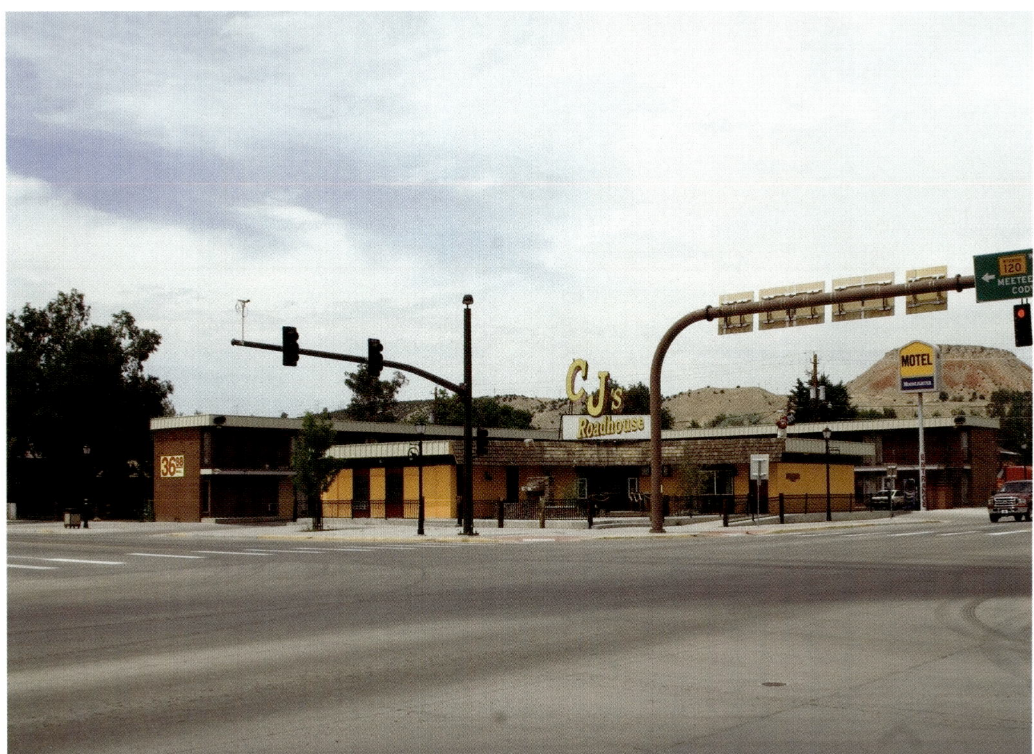

87. #3131

The Emery Hotel, Thermopolis, 1910, 1988, 2007
GPS COORDINATES: 43 38.76033N, 108 12.708833W

The Emery Hotel opened in 1906 in downtown Thermopolis. Constructed of native stone and locally cut lumber, the hotel had forty rooms, a bar, and a restaurant. Alex Halone, a local stonemason who later built the base for the Buffalo Bill statue in Cody, did the exterior stonework. A fixture on the northwest corner of the town's two busiest streets, the Emery offered tourists coming to take in the waters a beautiful place to sleep, a restaurant, a bar, a pool hall, and a bowling alley (note sign right of door).

As with most of his business portraits, Stimson photographed the Emery Hotel diagonally from across the street, providing a full view of both the south and west faces of the building. A lone streetlight hangs in front of the hotel and one automobile, possibly Stimson's, is parked alongside it. His sharp image also skillfully portrays Halone's handiwork.

The Emery remained the focal point of Thermopolis for years after Stimson made his photograph. In the 1930s, the famous cowboy Nick Knight and his wife operated the inn. But as automobile tourism began to change the face of America, in 1963 the Emery was demolished to make way for a motel. The job was so big that special equipment had to be brought in from Denver.

My 1988 rephotograph shows the Emery's replacement, the Moonlighter Motel, set at the intersection of two highways (note the signs). I lamented the loss of the historic Emery Hotel in my 1991 book *Wyoming Time and Again* and how ironic it seemed that for a town based on its hot springs, one hotel was demolished so its replacement motel could offer a heated swimming pool. My rephotograph also identified a motor home in view and wondered if that was the future of all tourism.

My 2007 rephotograph shows that the pool had been removed and CJ's Roadhouse constructed in its place. The Moonlighter was still there, though with much diminished signage.

Looking back today, I see less to lament. These three photographs clearly show the changing nature of tourism over the last century and its effects on the built environment of the city.

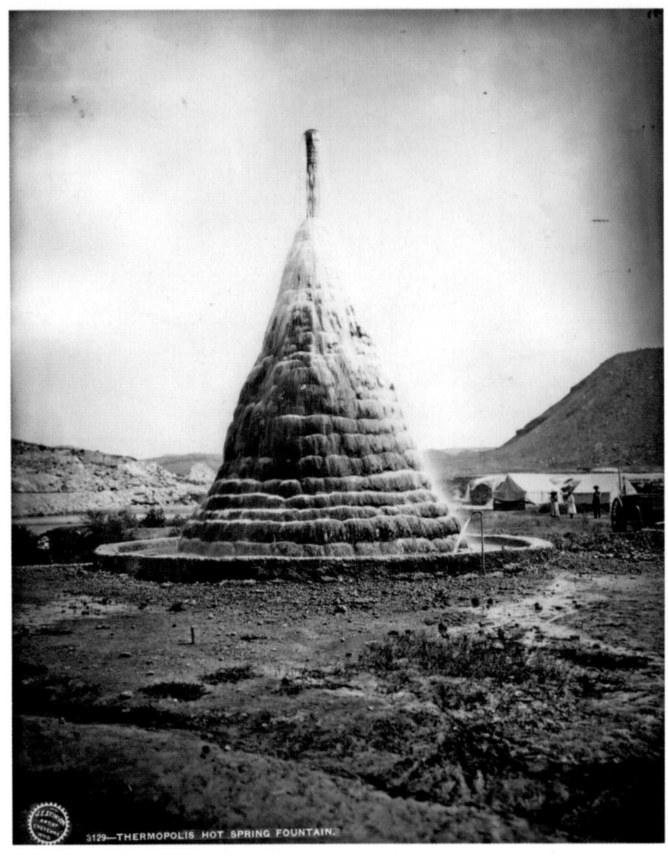
3129—THERMOPOLIS HOT SPRING FOUNTAIN.

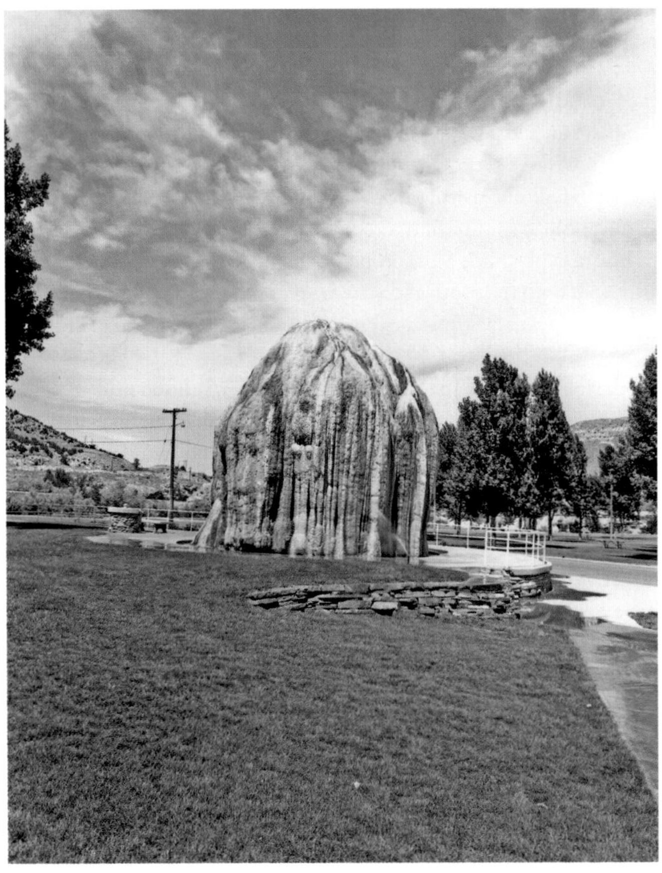

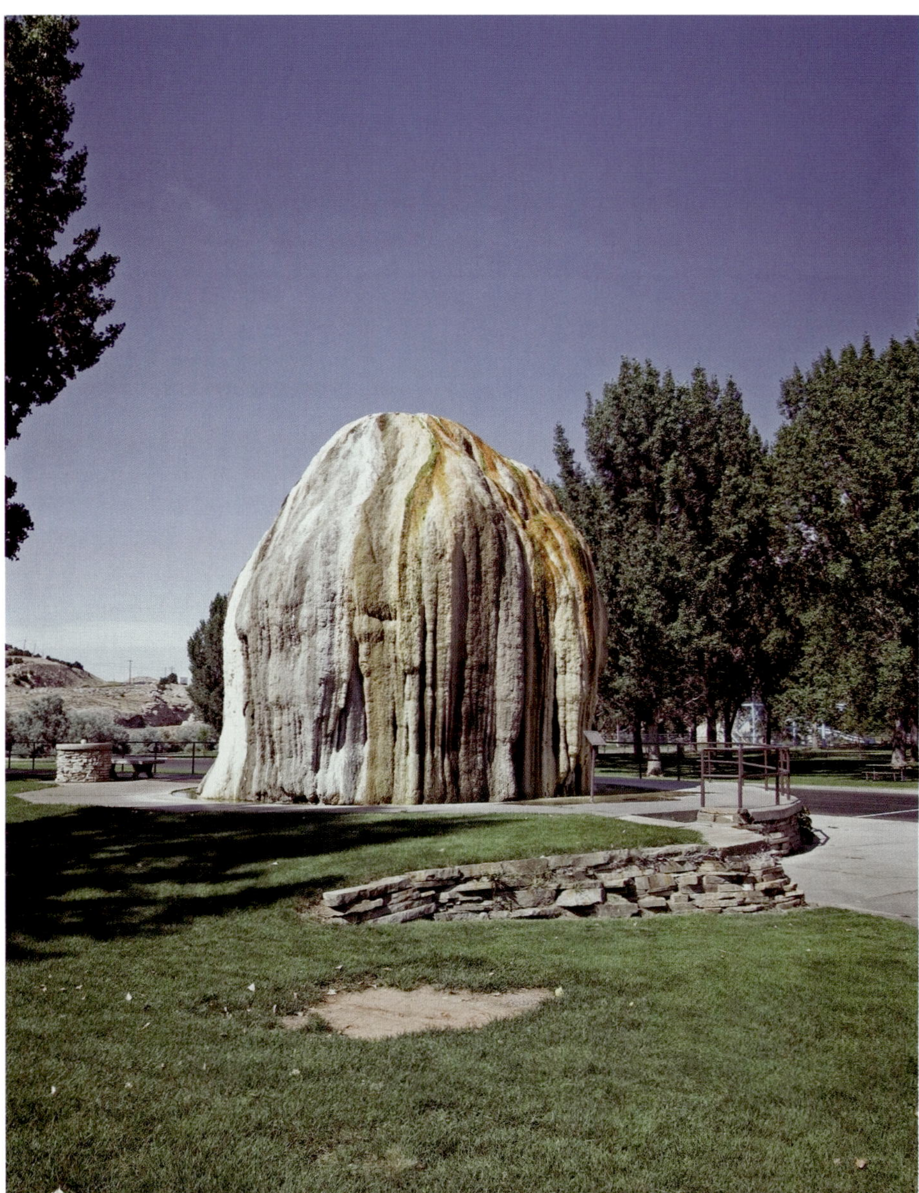

88. #3129

Thermopolis Hot Spring Fountain, 1911, 1988, 2007
GPS COORDINATES: 43 39.124N, 108 12.008W

These three views illustrate the effects of mineral water buildup over ninety-six years. As shown in Stimson's original portrait-style image, the Hot Spring Fountain is an obviously manmade cone with a pipe inserted into its middle to draw water over its top. A close look at his image also shows a number of tourists camping in the background.

When I made my rephotograph seventy-seven years later, the fountain had grown considerably in width, had changed from an obvious manmade structure to a more natural-looking object, and still had water trickling up and over it. The fountain's breadth and the background trees now covered the hill to the right. The upgraded state park grounds can clearly be seen as well.

My 2007 color image best illustrates the fountain's unusual shape and color. I had a difficult time accessing this vantage point because a small public bathroom had been built there and a large bush planted at the camera station. Lauren snapped a photo of me caught up in that bush while I was rephotographing this scene.

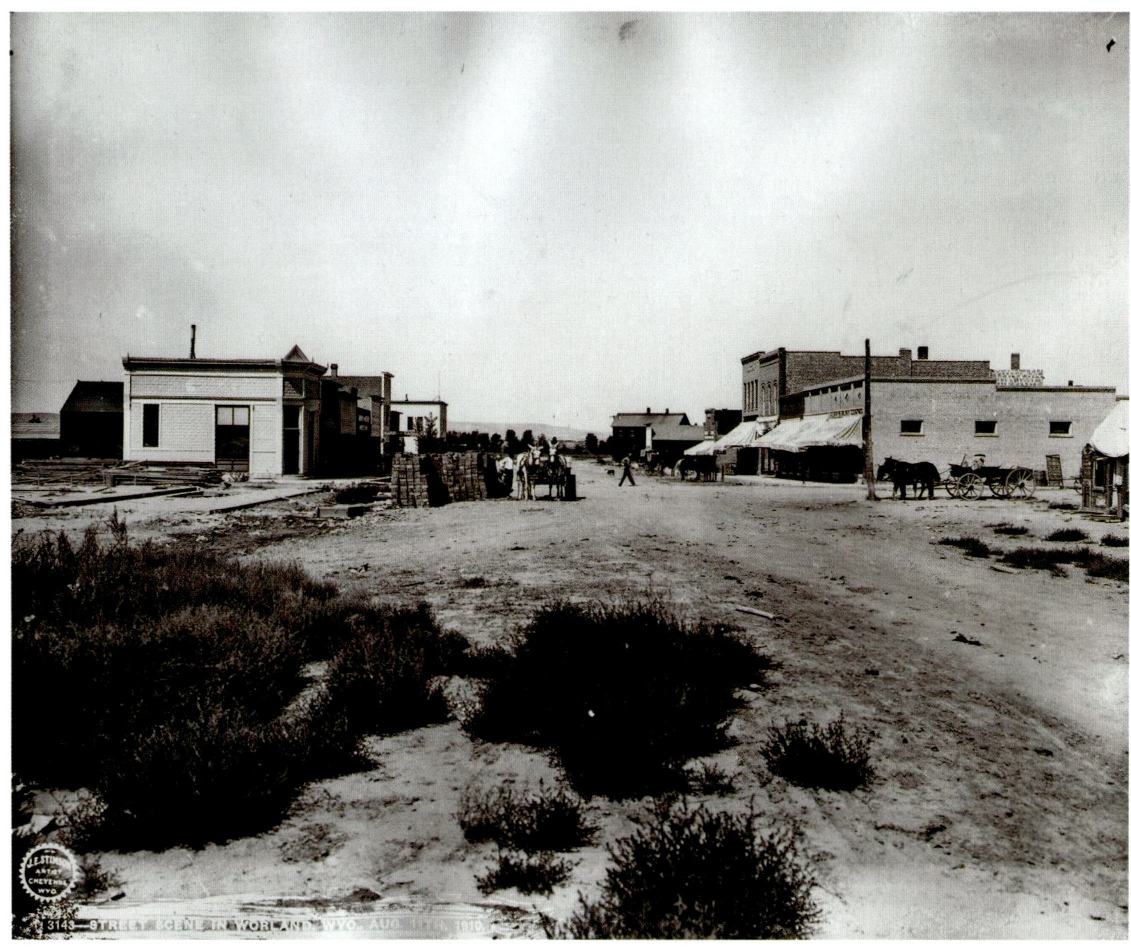

89. #3143

Worland Street Scene, 1910, 1988, 2007
GPS COORDINATES: 44 1.00933N, 107 57.57867W

Worland was named for its first settler, C. H. "Dad" Worland. By 1903, a small trading center for local farmers had sprung up around his ranch, after farmers dug several irrigation canals from the Bighorn River to bring water to their lands. In 1906 the Burlington Railroad built through, and the camp was moved to a new town site across the river. Worland became the seat of the newly created Washakie County in 1906. In 1917 Wyoming's first sugar beet processing plant was built here.

Stimson visited Worland in 1910. This powerful view looks west up Bighorn Avenue toward the railroad. By composing his image with the sagebrush in the foreground and the developing commercial district in the distance, Stimson suggests that water and the railroad can wrest civilization from the desert.

By the time I visited Worland in 1988, the town had grown into an agricultural center of the Bighorn Basin, with a population of about 6,000. In my view, the shade of a large tree provides a similar foreground to Stimson's sagebrush. On the right side of the street, several buildings remain.

When I returned nineteen years later, I found Worland much the same. The new Volkswagen Beetle and the large ATM sign mark the year. The same streetlights and signs suggest that the town, unlike Rawlins and Evanston, has not ventured into the Main Street Program of preservation and re-development.

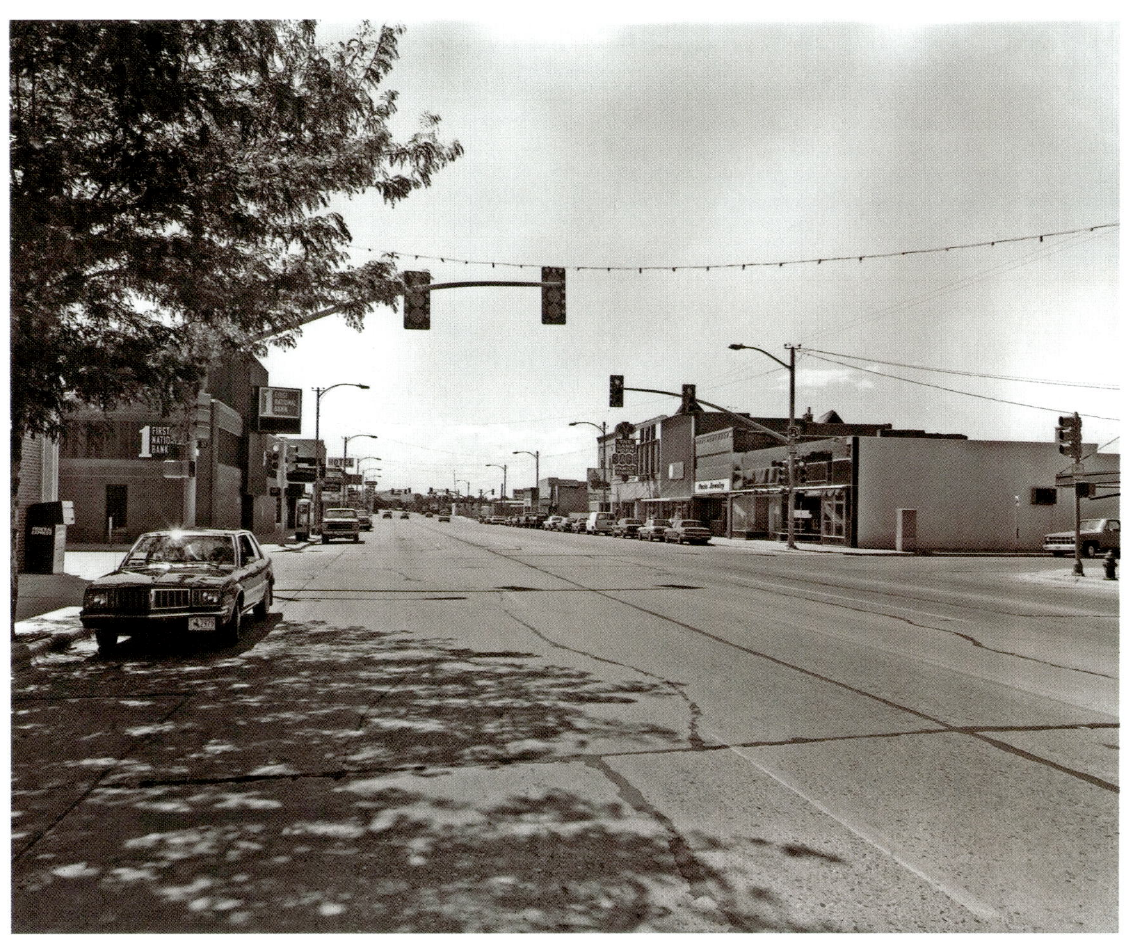

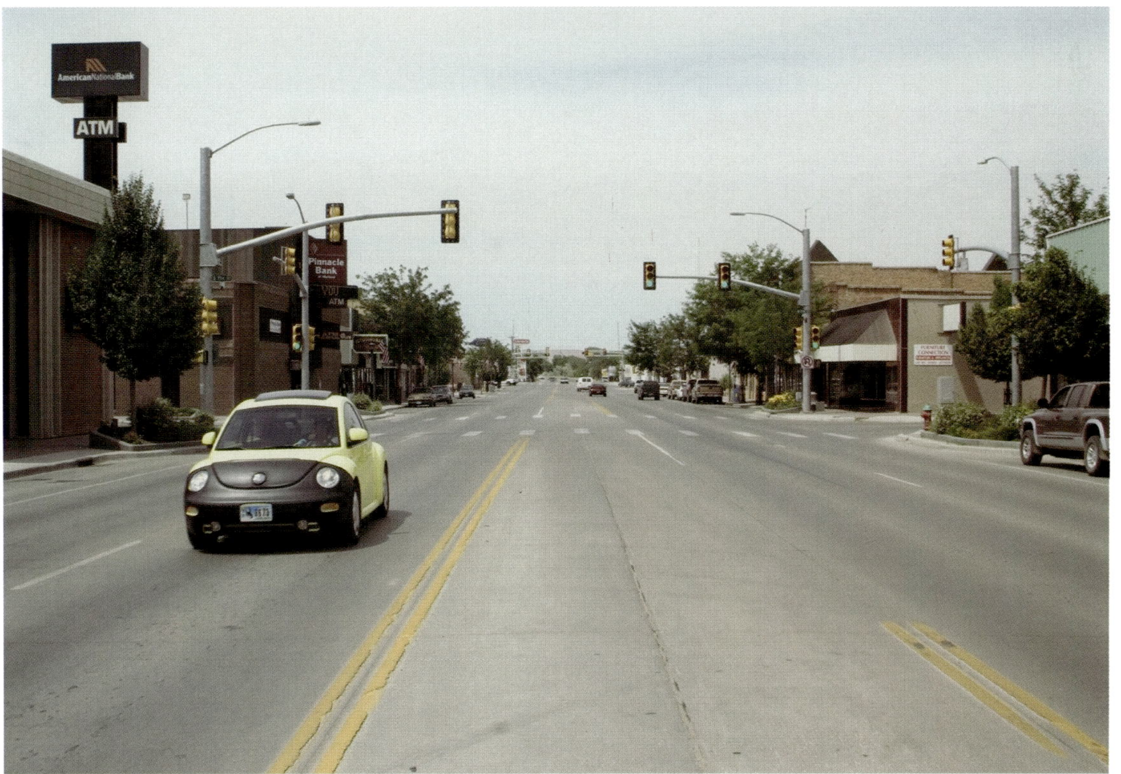

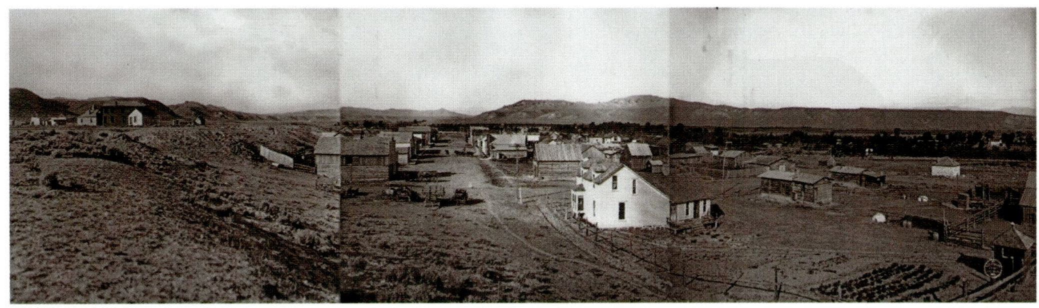

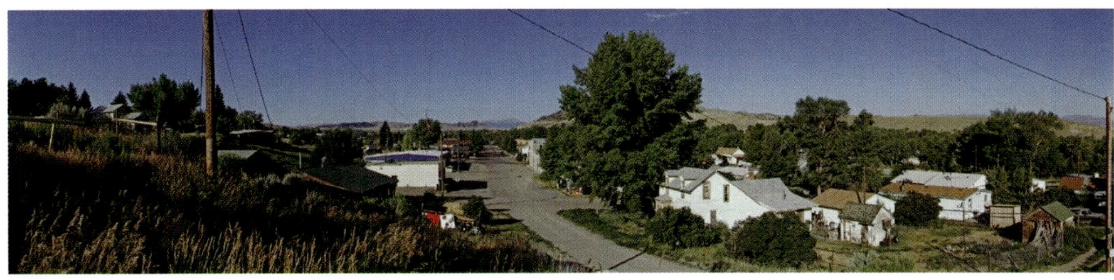

90. #645

Panorama of Meeteetse City, 1903, 2008
GPS COORDINATES: 44 09.525N, 108 52.186W

Meeteetse, about halfway between Thermopolis and Cody, is a small ranching community on the Greybull River. Its unusual name comes from the Shoshone Indian word meaning "meeting place." It began as an offshoot of the nearby Pitchfork Ranch, started by Count Otto Franc von Lichtenstein in 1878. Otto Franc, as he was known, became an area cattle baron. He died the year Stimson made his image. Meeteetse was first located on the banks of Meeteetse Creek in 1881 but moved to its present location in 1893. Most of its commercial buildings were constructed at that time.

Stimson included this panorama in his 1903 survey of the state for the St. Louis World's Fair. The original schoolhouse can be seen at left and the business district in the center. Not a bird's-eye view because the camera station is too low, the photograph looks west toward the Pitchfork Ranch and to the hills and mountains beyond, seemingly showing the town and its origins at the same time.

In the 1930s and 1940s, Pitchfork Ranch owner and photographer Charles Belden put the town on the map. After inheriting the ranch in 1922, Belden used his camera to make iconic images of cowboys at work and published them in *National Geographic* and *Dude Rancher*. An interest in airplanes led him to make sweeping aerial photographs, and another interest, this one in raising antelope, brought Belden into the business of supplying zoos. Some of his antelope even rode the *Hindenburg* to Germany.

In the 1980s Meeteetse came back into the news as the last stand of the elusive black-footed ferret, discovered nearby in 1981. Indeed, while I was playing hoops at the University of Wyoming, biologists started a captive breeding program and named one Fennis ferret, after my teammate and *Sports Illustrated* cover boy Fennis Dembo.

I visited Meeteetse in 1988 but only took the middle photograph from Stimson's three-part panorama. The limitations of large-format photography were too difficult for me at the time. Nineteen years later, with a lot more experience plus a digital camera and Photoshop at my disposal, I rephotographed the entire panorama. As with most Wyoming places, the trees today block much of the scene. Nevertheless, the view west, from the same white house at right, looks much the same 105 years later.

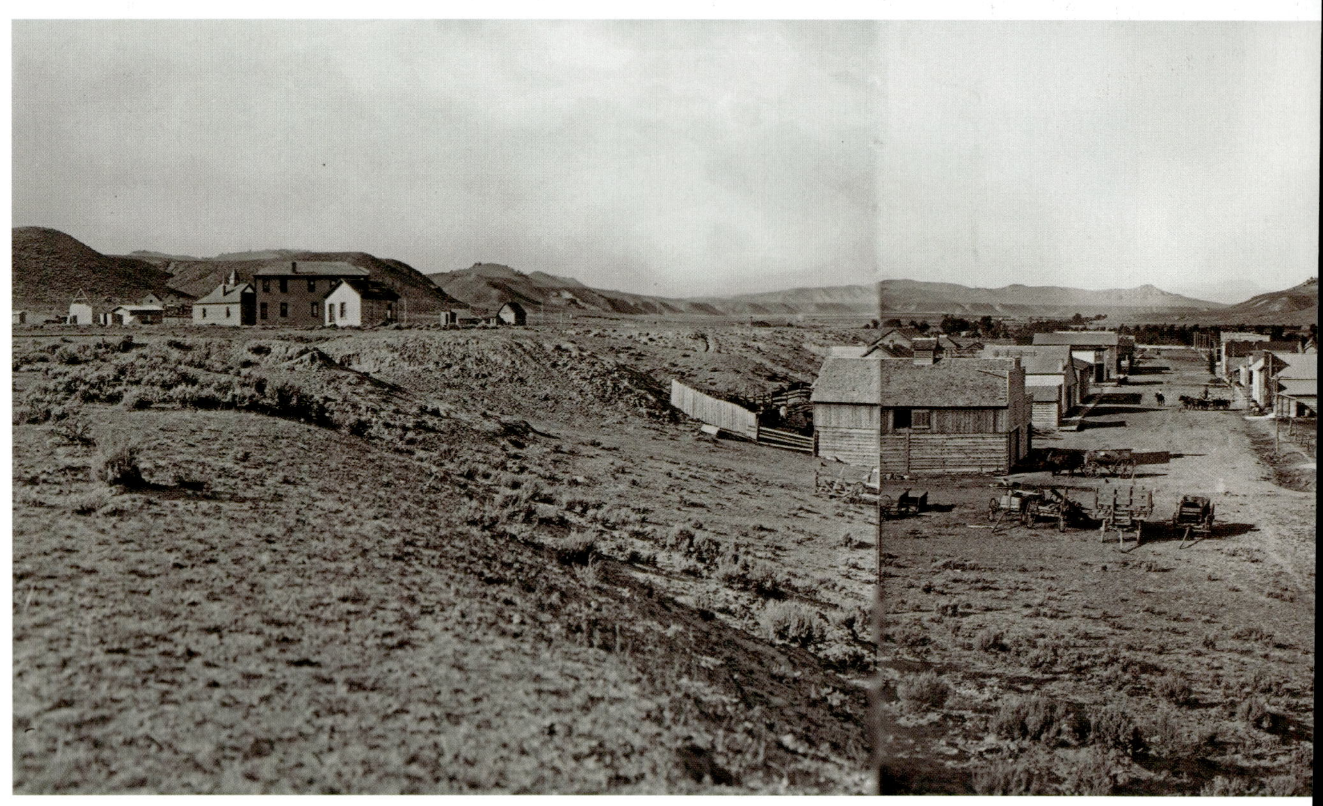

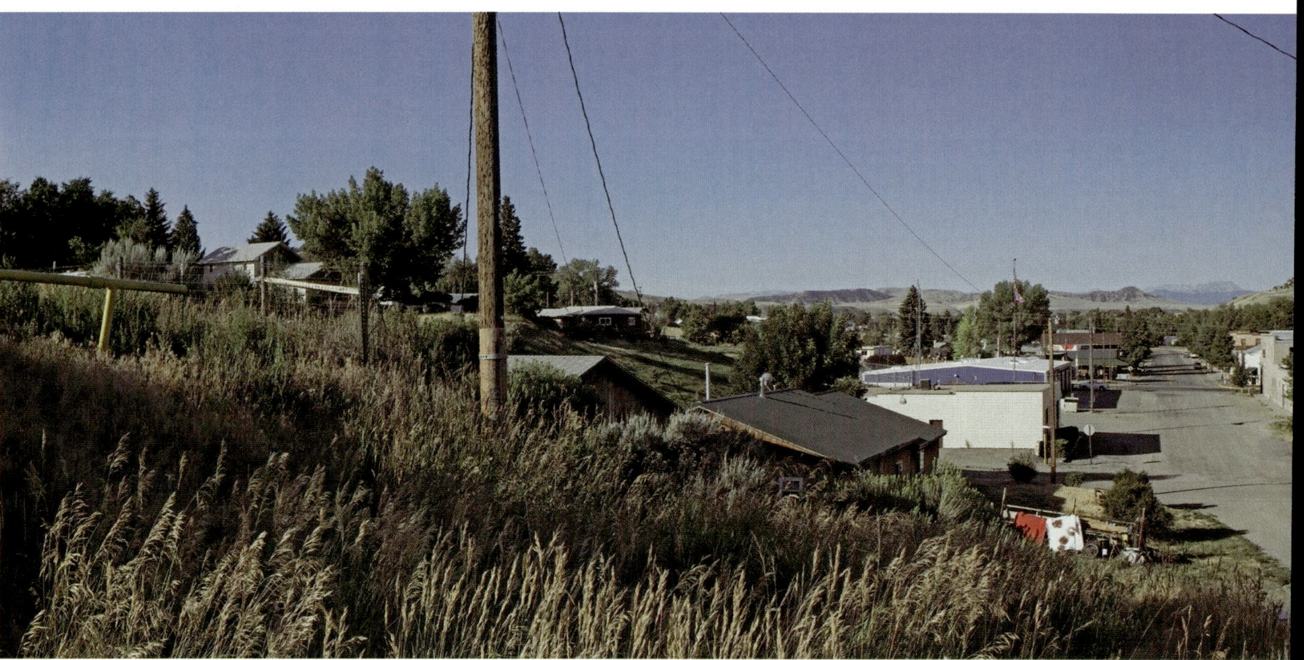

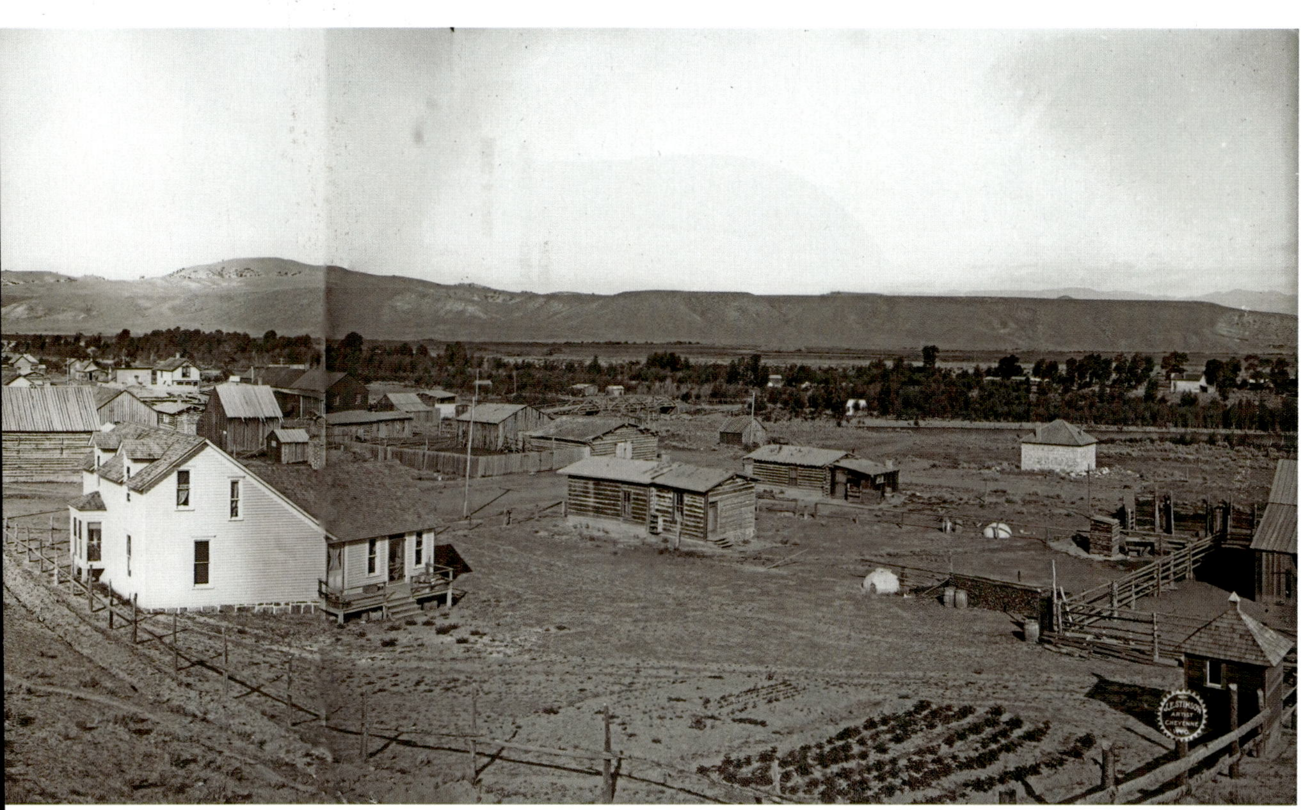

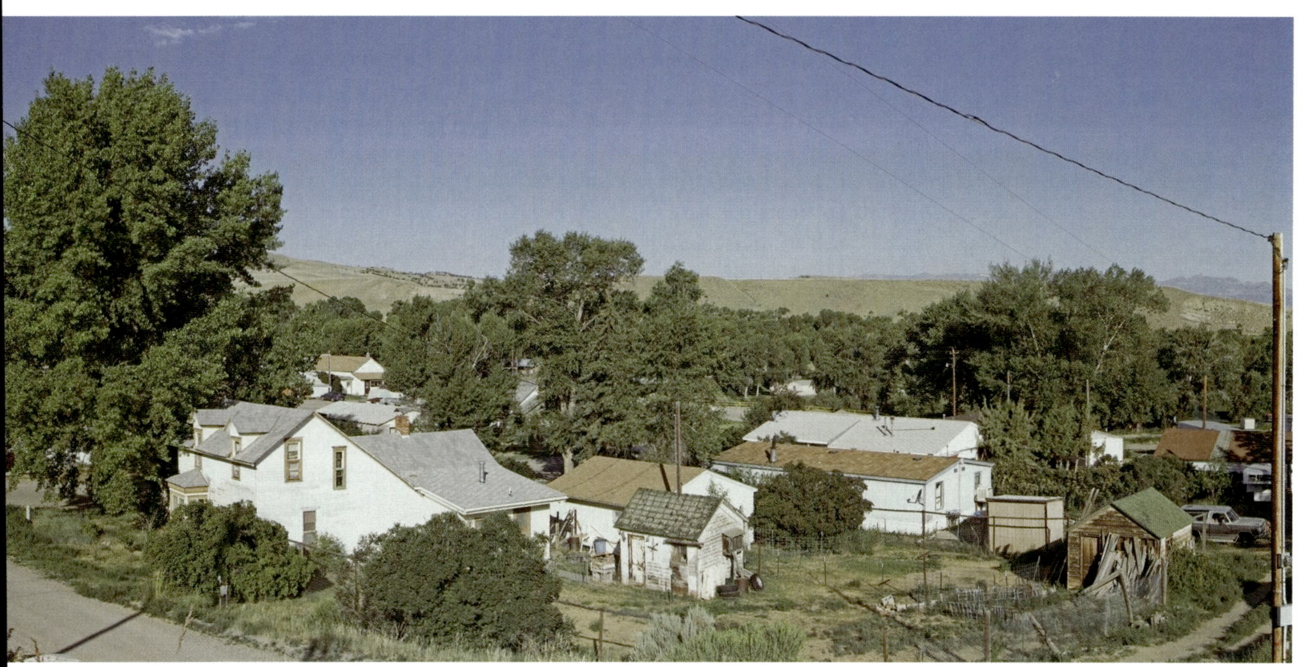

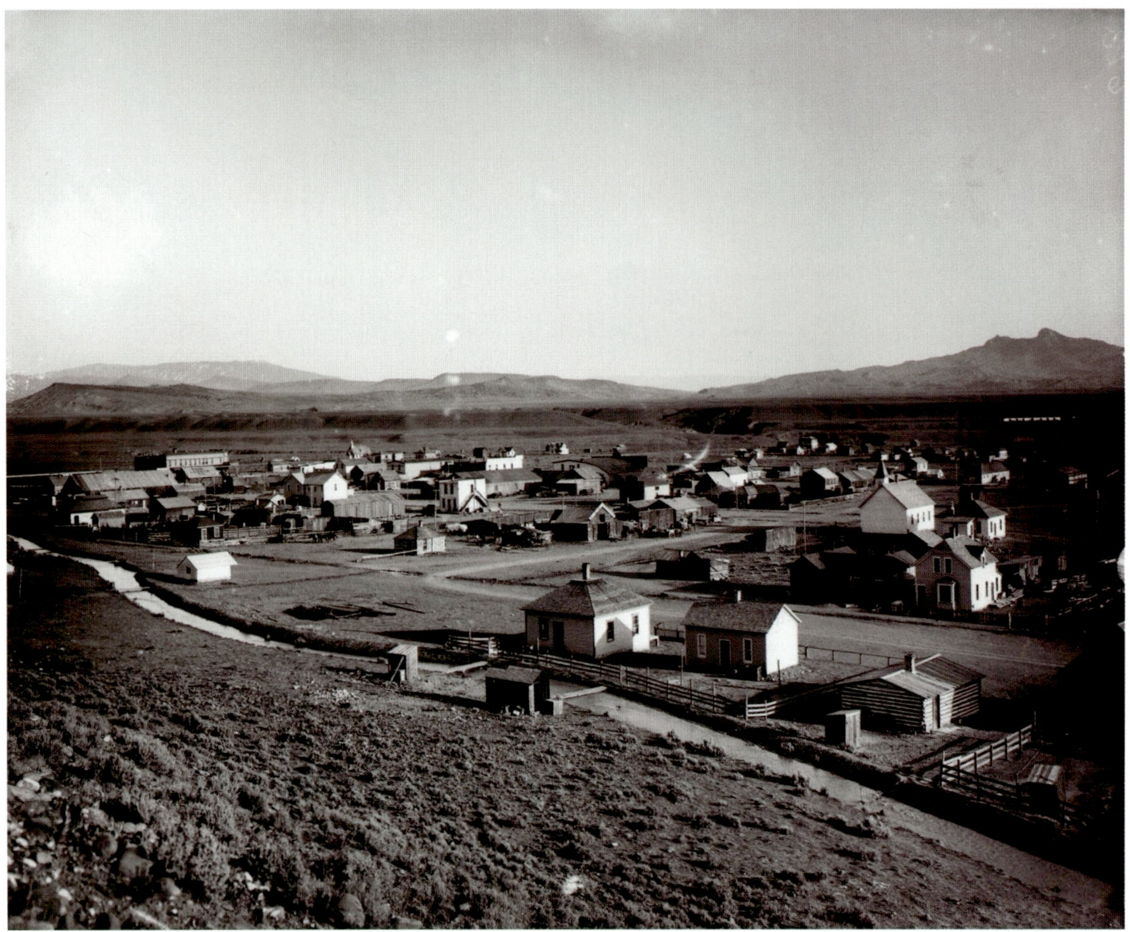

91. #613

Bird's Eye View of Cody, 1903, 1988, 2007
GPS COORDINATES: 44 31.373N, 109 03.523W

The road to Yellowstone begins in Cody, and this view is a classic Stimson shot. As with many of his town photographs, Stimson composed this one from a nearby hill to give the viewer a bird's-eye view of the town. The vantage point is the north side of Cody's upper bench below the current community building. The photo is looking to the northwest, with Heart Mountain on the right horizon, the Shoshone River in the center, and Rattlesnake Mountain to the left. The absence of the far distant mountains attests to the fact that Stimson's dry-plate emulsions were very sensitive to blue light, making both the hills and the sky white in his image. Stimson's shot was taken in the early morning, evidenced by the well-lit right walls and the long shadows. The lack of any tree taller than a person allows one to see into every property.

Like many of his views, the composition shows his boosterism ethos, with an irrigation ditch running diagonally from the mid-center of the image to the lower right corner, separating the sagebrush plain from the community. The town appears neat and orderly, with its commercial district clearly visible in the center of the image, Buffalo Bill's Irma Hotel at left-center, the town grid, telephone poles, and at least two churches in view. Moreover, with the ditch symbolically separating the "civilization" of the town from the "wilderness" of the sagebrush plain, Stimson is suggesting that water is the key to Wyoming's development.

As in so many of my 1980s rephotographs, the growth of trees attests to the transformation of the urban landscape. Nevertheless, a few individual houses can be spotted although the irrigation ditch is gone. In the most recent view, taken in the summer of 2007, the far horizon, with Heart Mountain and the far benches, identifies the vantage point. The trees on the right mid-horizon show the town's growth along Highway 120 toward Montana. As I wandered around the site, I could still pick out individual houses still standing, but this particular vantage point limited their appearance.

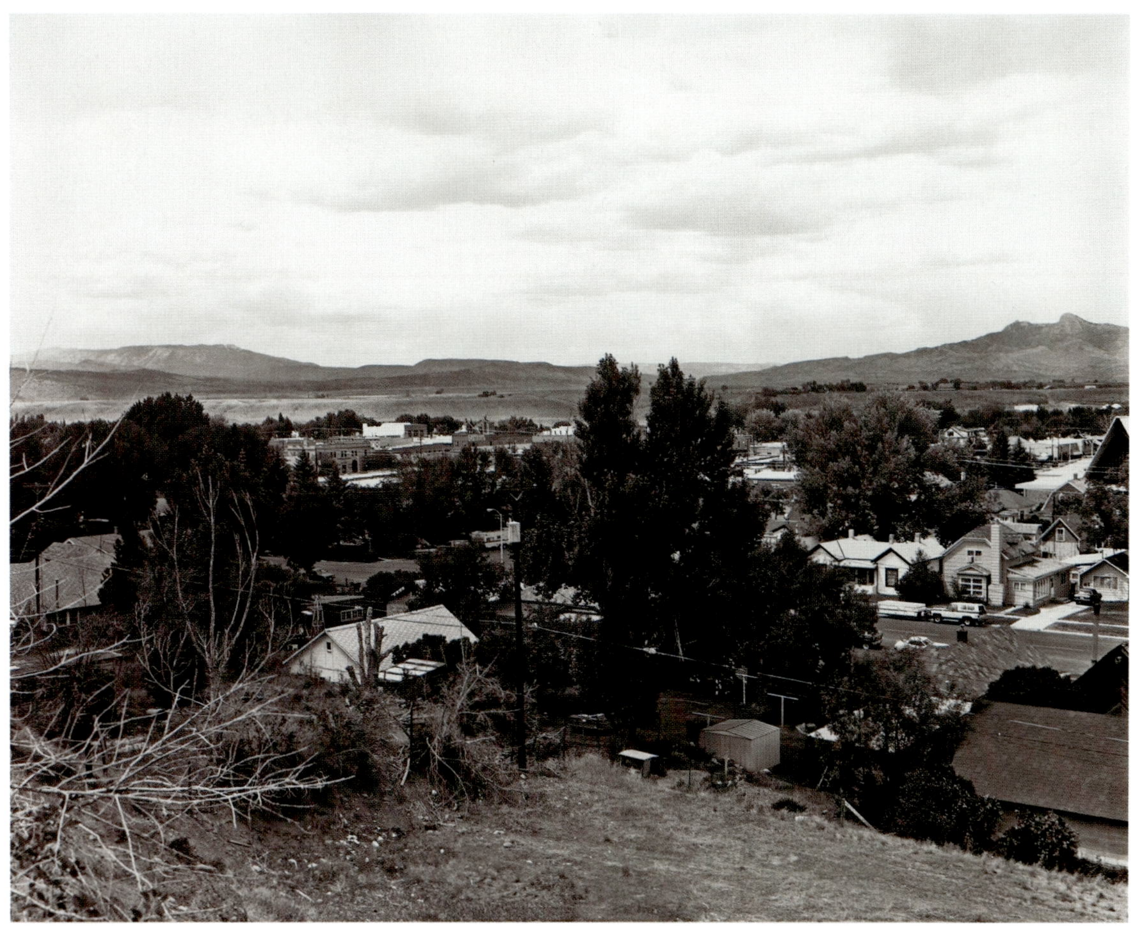

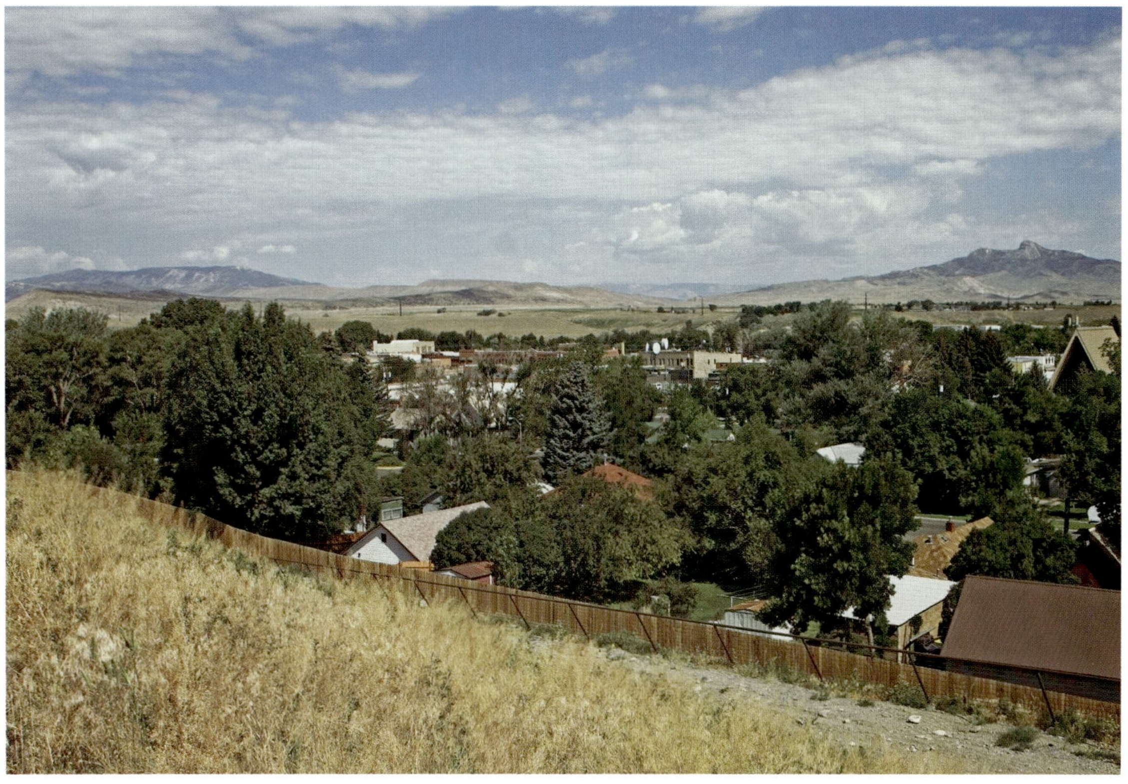

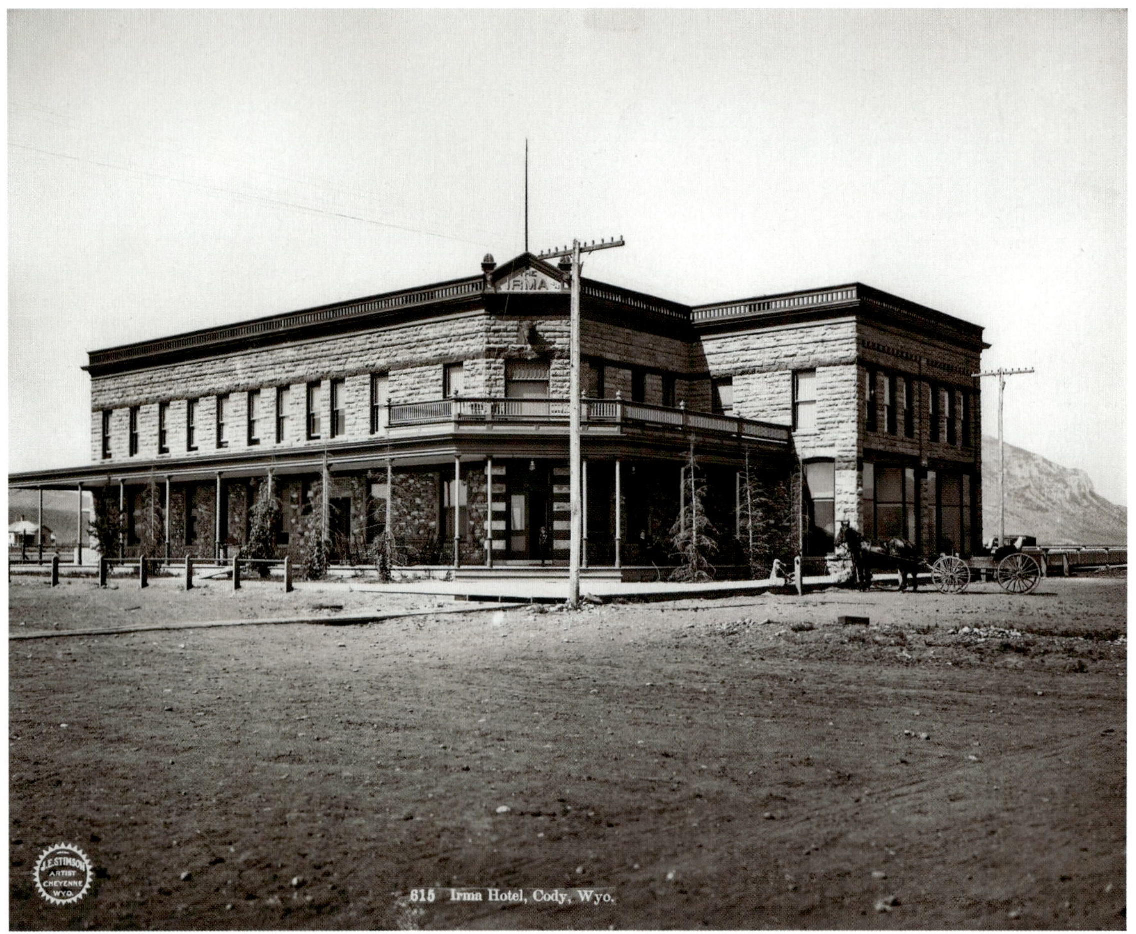

92. #615

Irma Hotel, Cody, 1903, 1988, 2007
GPS COORDINATES: 44 31.5683N, 109 03.829166W

Buffalo Bill Cody's Irma Hotel was constructed in 1902 and named for his daughter, Irma Louise Cody. The hotel, considered the finest in town, was a favorite starting point for travelers heading to Yellowstone. Within a couple of years, Cody built two more hotels along the route to the park: Wapiti Inn, thirty-eight miles from Cody, and Pahaska Tepee, just outside the park's eastern gate.

Stimson's photo was taken in the late morning, as evidenced by the well-lit eastern wall and the shadows. It is a classic building portrait, framed dead center with no other buildings in view. In Stimson's photograph, note Cedar Mountain in the distance at right and the careful composition, which includes a telephone pole as a symbol of progress but just off-center so the hotel's name and buffalo head are clearly seen.

In my 1988 view, the Irma remained the center of the Cody scene: its restaurant and Silver Saddle Lounge were always busy. By 2007, a comparison of the three images reveals that many original design elements remain, including the flagpole, name plate, buffalo head, windows, and porch. It's fun to see that automobile parking spaces have replaced the hitching posts. The many signs in the 2007 image hint at the increased competition for the tourist dollar in Cody, even at the Irma.

Although Buffalo Bill was selling the passing frontier to western fans in his Wild West shows, with his mock stagecoach attacks, cowboy paraphernalia, and fake Indian battles, the Irma was presented as a symbol of civilization for those traveling into the wilderness of Yellowstone. It's interesting that more than a century later, that role has changed to one in which the hotel serves not as the last facet of progress but as the first step into Wild West nostalgia.

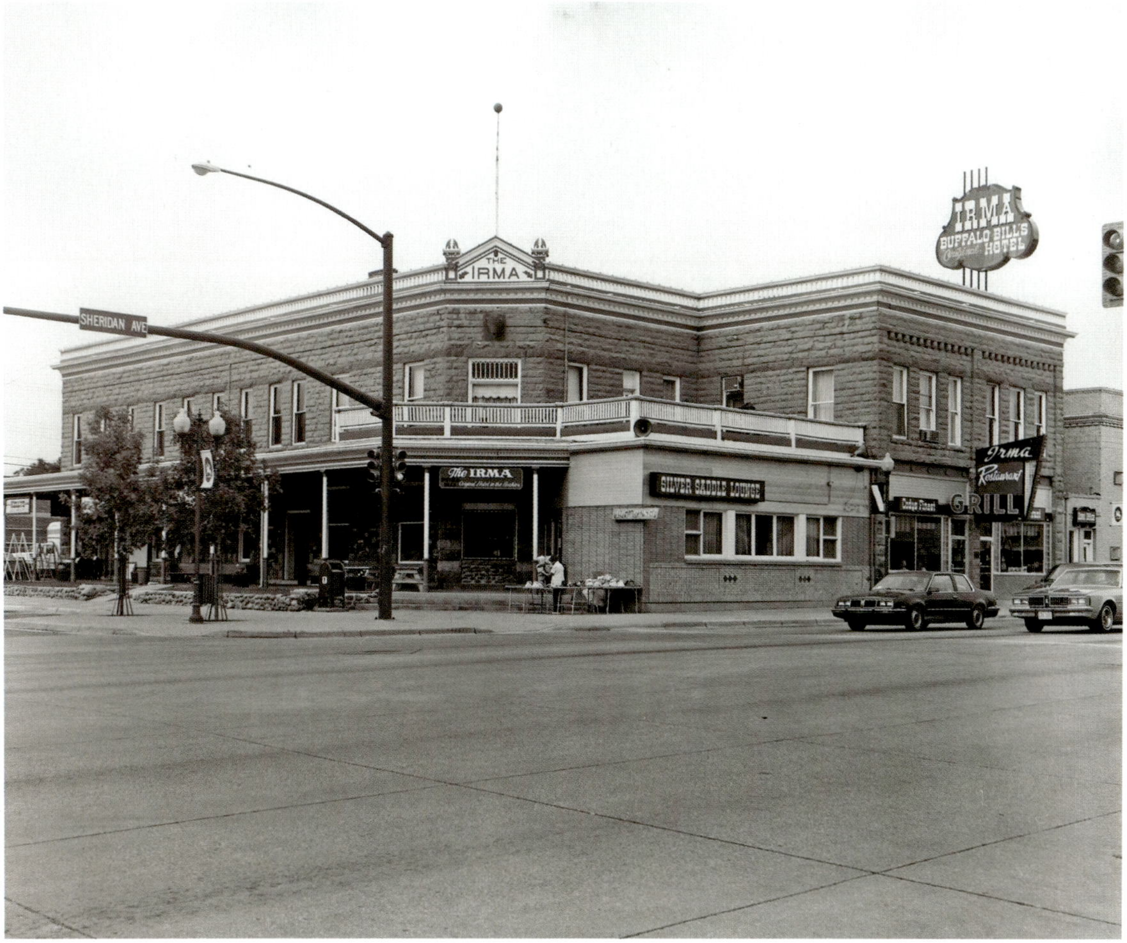

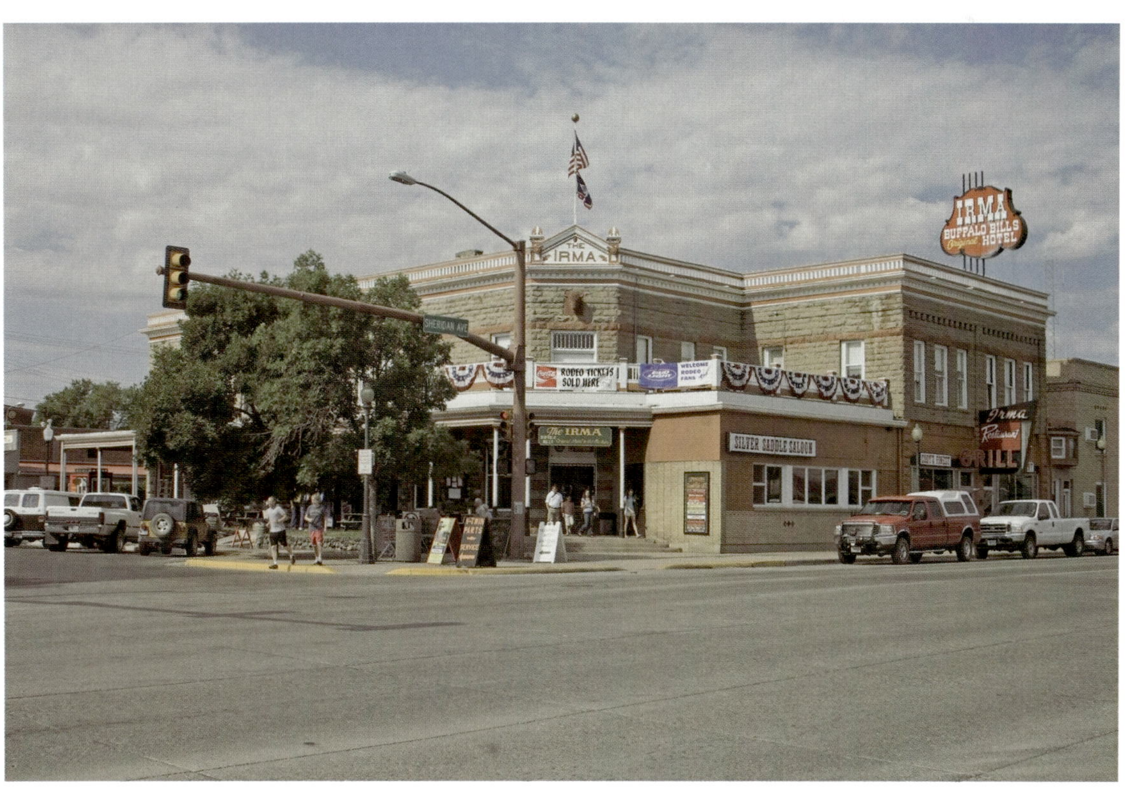
SHERIDAN AVE
THE IRMA
IRMA
BUFFALO BILL'S HOTEL
The IRMA
SILVER SADDLE LOUNGE
Irma
Restaurant
GRILL
SHERIDAN AVE
IRMA
IRMA
BUFFALO BILL'S HOTEL
THE IRMA
RODEO TICKETS
SOLD HERE
The IRMA
SILVER SADDLE SALOON
Irma
Restaurant
GRILL

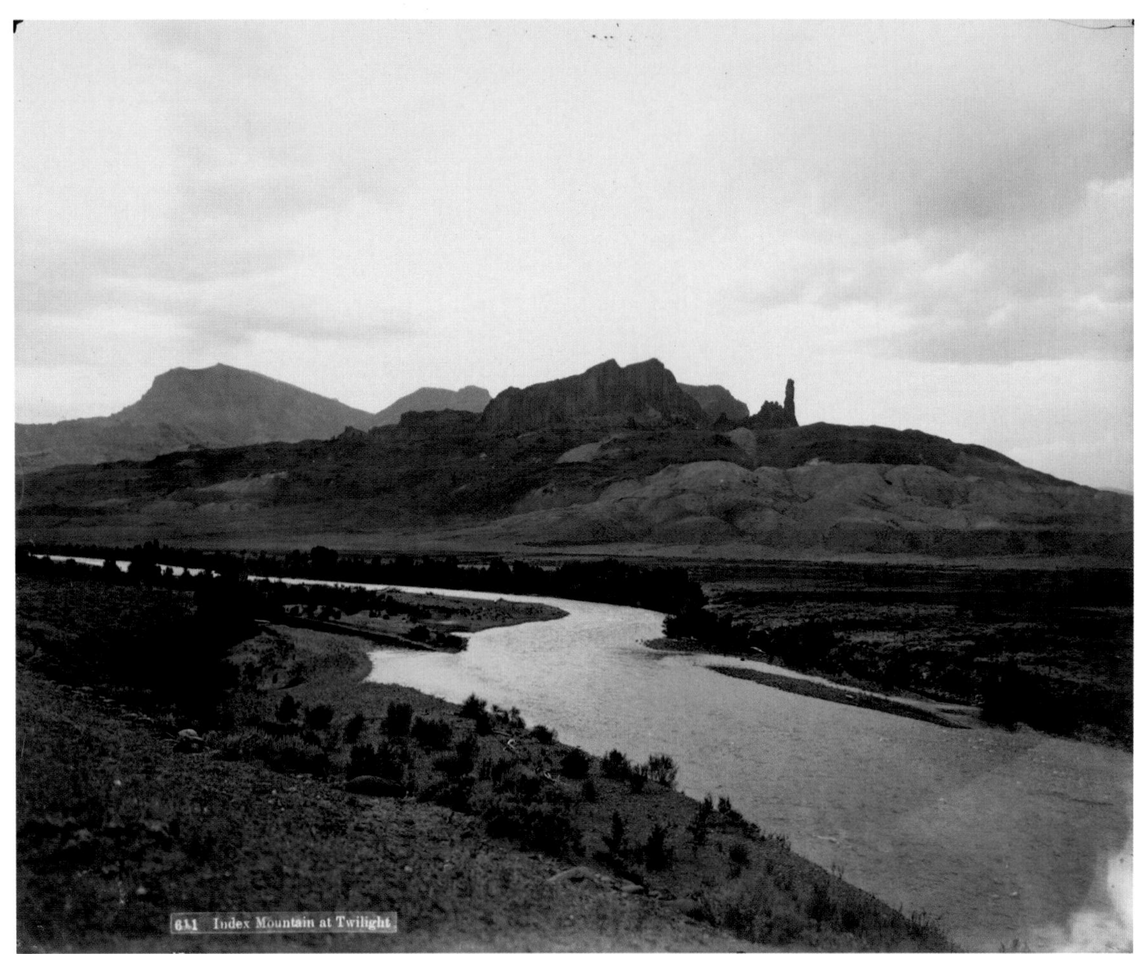
611   Index Mountain at Twilight

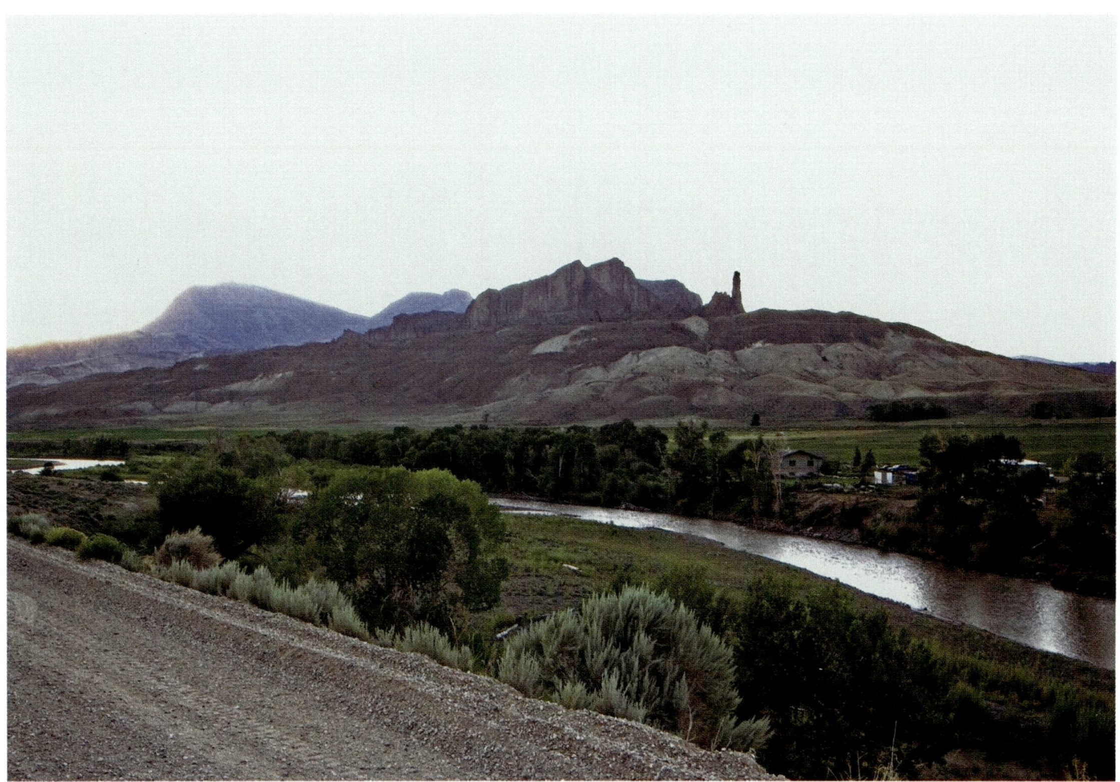

93. #611

Index Mountain at Twilight, 1903, 2008
GPS COORDINATES: 44 28.68983N, 109 21.16034W

This Stimson view is one of the few in the more than 200 images I have rephotographed that provides a clear time as to when the original photo was made. Although foliage and shadows can indicate a season and time, Stimson's title suggestion that this one was made at twilight is unique. For the actual clock time, remember that there was no daylight saving time in 1903, so twilight occurred an hour earlier for him. In July at this latitude, twilight for me would have been around 9:00 p.m. mountain daylight time.

The location of the view is along a dirt road called Stagecoach Lane, west of Buffalo Bill State Park. This road follows the original route of the Cody Road on the south side of the North Fork of the Shoshone River. Current Highway 14/16/20 runs along the north side at this point. The two roads reconnect at Wapiti.

The pair of images shows that the course of the North Fork has changed within its floodplain over the last century and that trees along the river have thickened and grown as well. Foliage on the far hills and mountains is very similar. The house along the river is new, but the silhouette of the far range would be very familiar to J. E. Stimson.

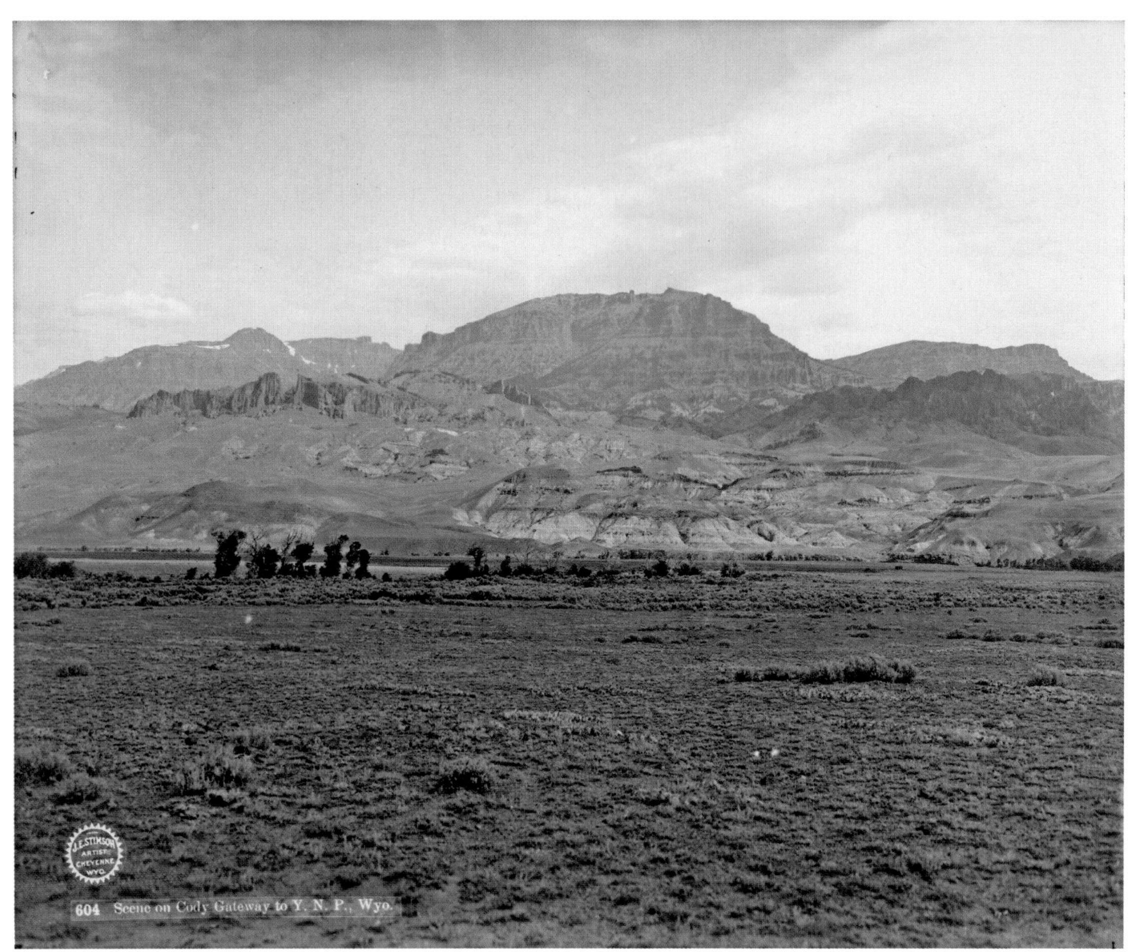
J. E. STIMSON
ARTIST
CHEYENNE
WYO.
604   Scene on Cody Gateway to Y. N. P., Wyo.

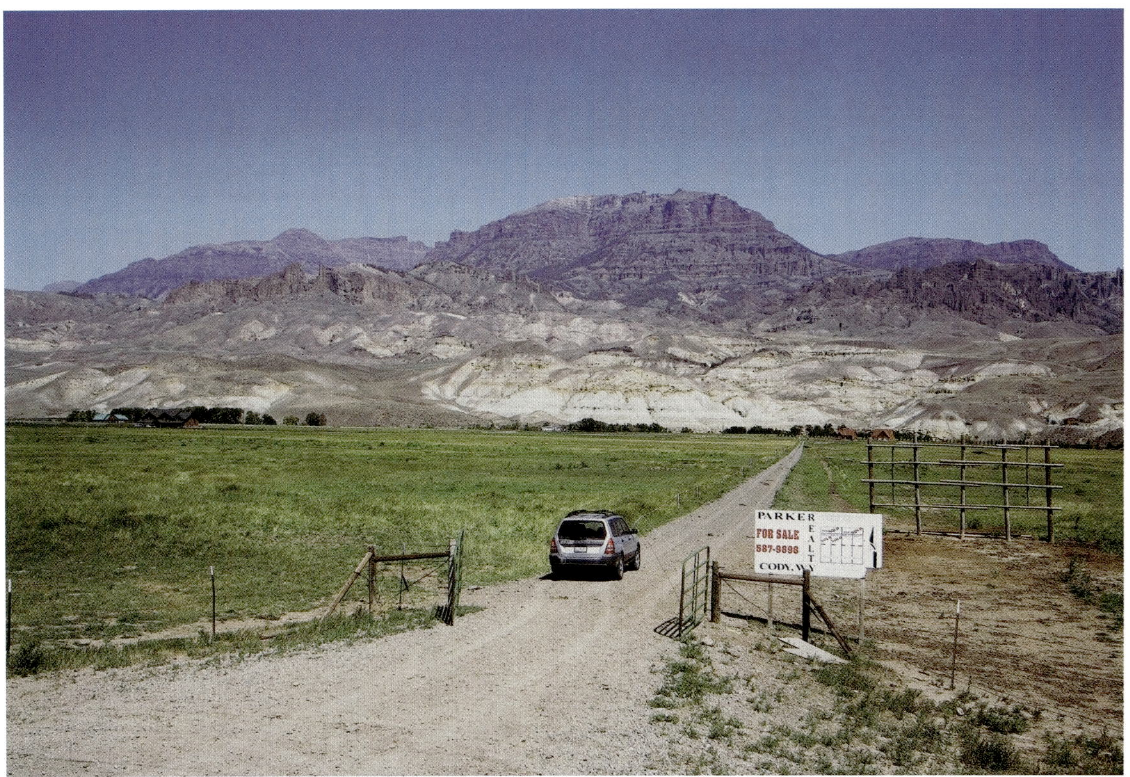

94. #604

Scene on Cody Gateway to Y.N.P., Wyo., 1903, 2008
GPS COORDINATES: 44 27.759N, 109 27.396W

This view was taken just past the small community of Wapiti, which had a direct tie to Buffalo Bill. As recent biographers illustrate, although Cody was not always an astute businessman, he was an active one, and very early on he became a promoter of the road from his namesake Wyoming town to the park. Just two years after Stimson's visit, Cody built a tourist lodge about halfway between the town and Yellowstone at Wapiti and another just outside the park's eastern entrance at Pahaska Tepee. Thus, Buffalo Bill's presence seems always to be lurking in Stimson's views around Cody.

The scene's basic landscape seems practically unchanged in the time between the two photos. Looking north toward Jim Mountain, Stimson's view shows wild rangelands, a few cottonwoods, the North Fork of the Shoshone, and the badlands rising up to a few snowfields on the mountain. In my view, irrigated ranchlands spread north to a line of cottonwoods along the North Fork. Beyond the river, the same badlands are there, with similar vegetation patterns leading up to the same silhouette of Jim Mountain against a blue summer sky. Most of the background, including the mountain, is within the North Absaroka Wilderness Area, where strict environmental protection measures are in effect and no machines are allowed.

The visible differences in this pair of photos are in the foreground. The barbwire fence running left to right hints at the modern closed range, while the straight dirt road and my Subaru Forester offer hints of automobile tourism and the global marketplace. Most telling is the large white sign to the right (just in front of an old billboard framework), advertising a local realty company that is subdividing the ranch into smaller New West ranchettes. A Google search shows individual parcels of "raw land" selling for $850,000 and houses for more than $2 million. Like many beautiful places in the American West, the Cody Road to Yellowstone now serves not only as a tourist route but also as an everyday road for "amenity migrants" seeking to own a beautiful piece of property. Globalization has transformed many parts of the West from local working lands to real estate developments selling commodified viewscapes to newcomers importing their wealth into traditional economies.

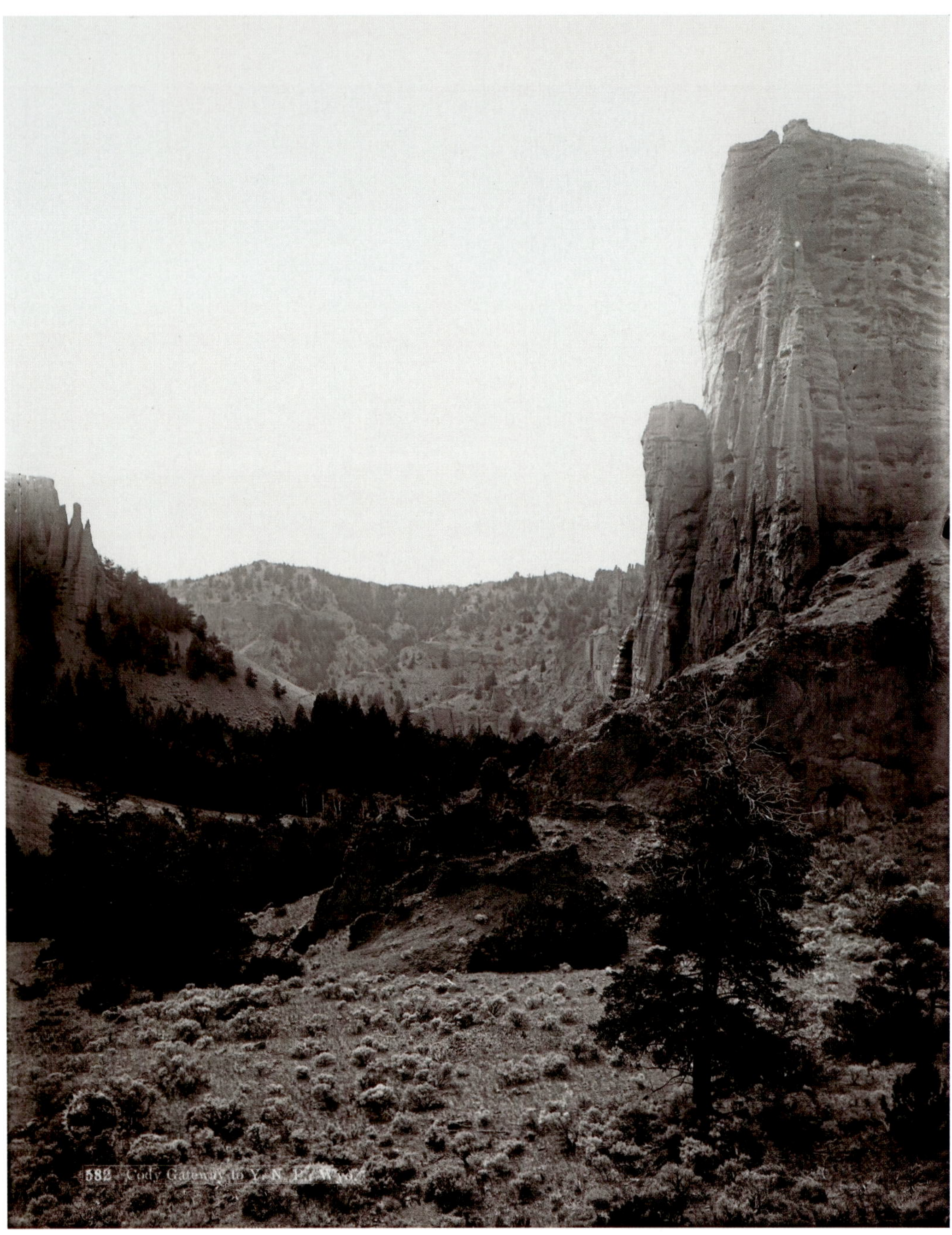

95. #582

Cody Gateway to Y.N.P., 1903, 2008
GPS COORDINATES: 44 27.338N, 109 45.738W

J. E. Stimson made four photographs of this large rock formation known as Sentinel Rock. This second vantage point was easy to find, but I did not want to get to it. Near the base of the formation is a parking pullout. I loaded up my usual assortment of gear—including a large camera bag with two camera bodies, four lenses, memory cards, batteries, chargers, a metal tripod with carrying bag, and a copy of Stimson's photograph—and crossed the modern highway (just visible in the modern photo at the left base of the hill) into the small wooded meadow slightly east of Sentinel Rock. I set up the camera and started backing toward a small rocky ridge on the steep hill behind me. Not seeing the angle I expected, I looked back toward that ridge and noticed a small break in it

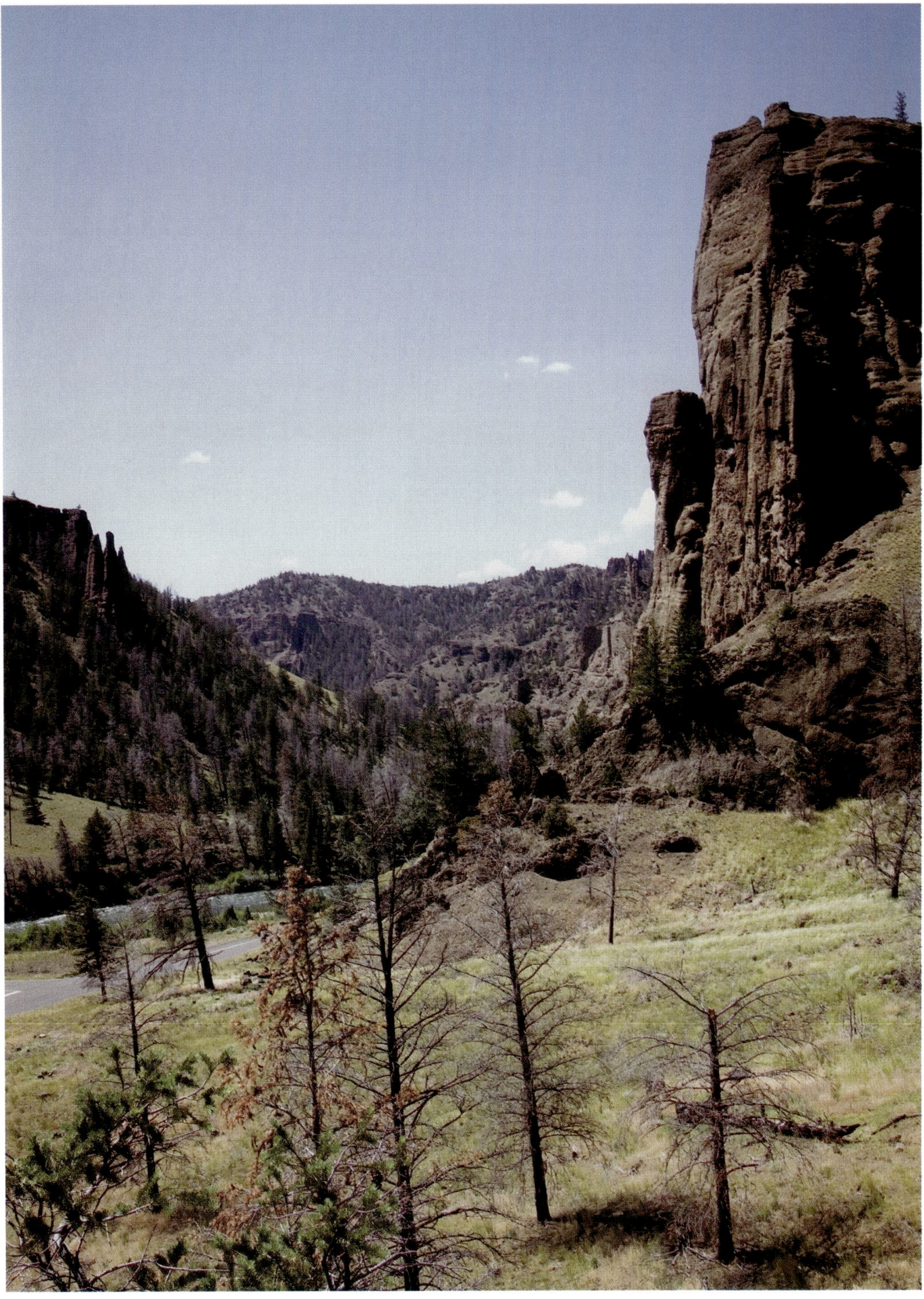

about 30 feet up the slope. I knew that it had to be the vantage point, but I did not want to climb up there with all my gear. I knew that Stimson liked to climb up on things such as water towers and buildings to get better views for his photos. So I added the GPS unit to my load, used the tripod as a sort of walking stick, and climbed up to the location. It was about 5 feet across and very uneven, but it was clearly the spot. The view to the west simply opened up as Stimson's image. The little notch at the top against the sky and the smaller rock column in relation to the spires across the valley confirmed it. I set up the camera, balanced myself, and made the photo.

A comparison of the two images further reveals that the evergreens on the far hill have thickened considerably, while those along the river have done the opposite. The trees in the foreground appear to have burned.

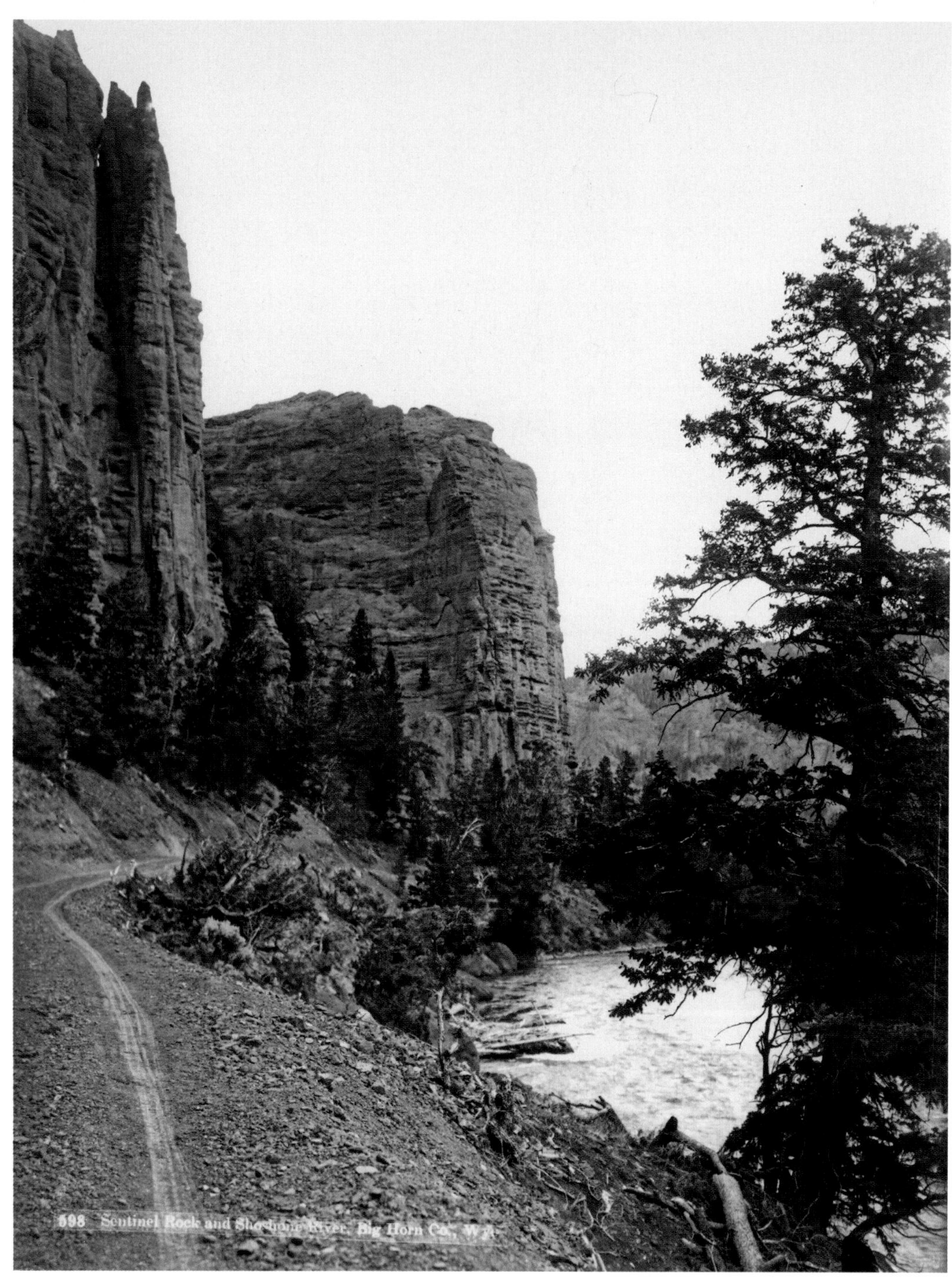
598   Sentinel Rock and Shoshone River, Big Horn Co., Wyo.

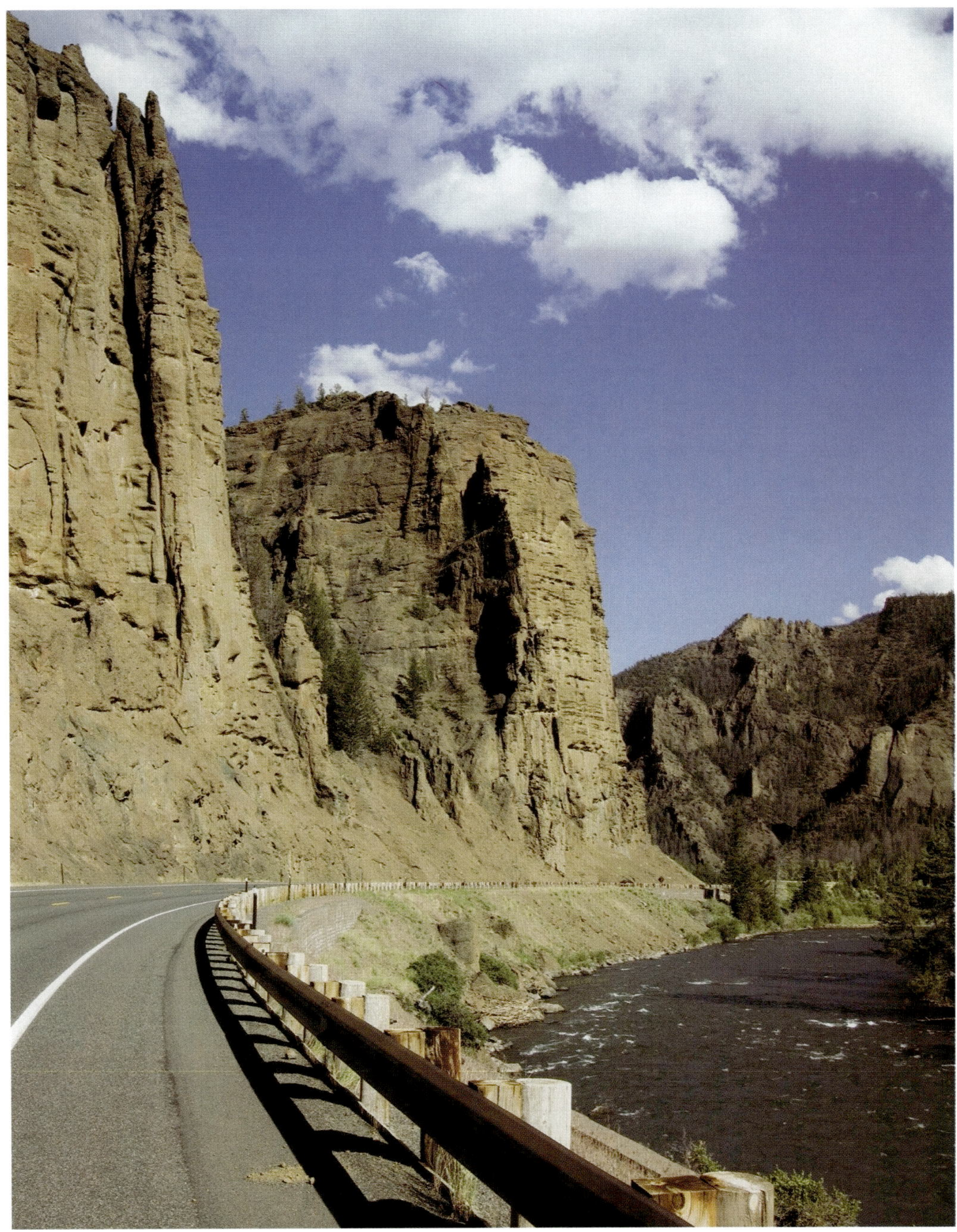

96. #598

Sentinel Rock and Shoshone River, Big Horn Co. [Park Co.], Wyo., 1903, 2008
GPS COORDINATES: 44 27.52383N, 109 46.10534W

For his fourth view of Sentinel Rock, Stimson proceeded along the road toward the park about a third of a mile and was now looking back downstream to Sentinel Rock at center. This location is just below the area known as the Palisades, for the high cliffs on the north side of the river. Stimson again expertly composed his view by placing the curving river and road between the cliffs and the tree at right.

The large tree is gone in the modern view, but the guardrail and the beautiful afternoon light have a similar positive effect on its composition. It is also a rare view in that no cars can be seen on the highway. Whether it's that sense of solitude or the soft light, the beautiful cliffs, or those two rabbit-ear–like rocks atop the cliff, this is one of my favorite pairs of images.

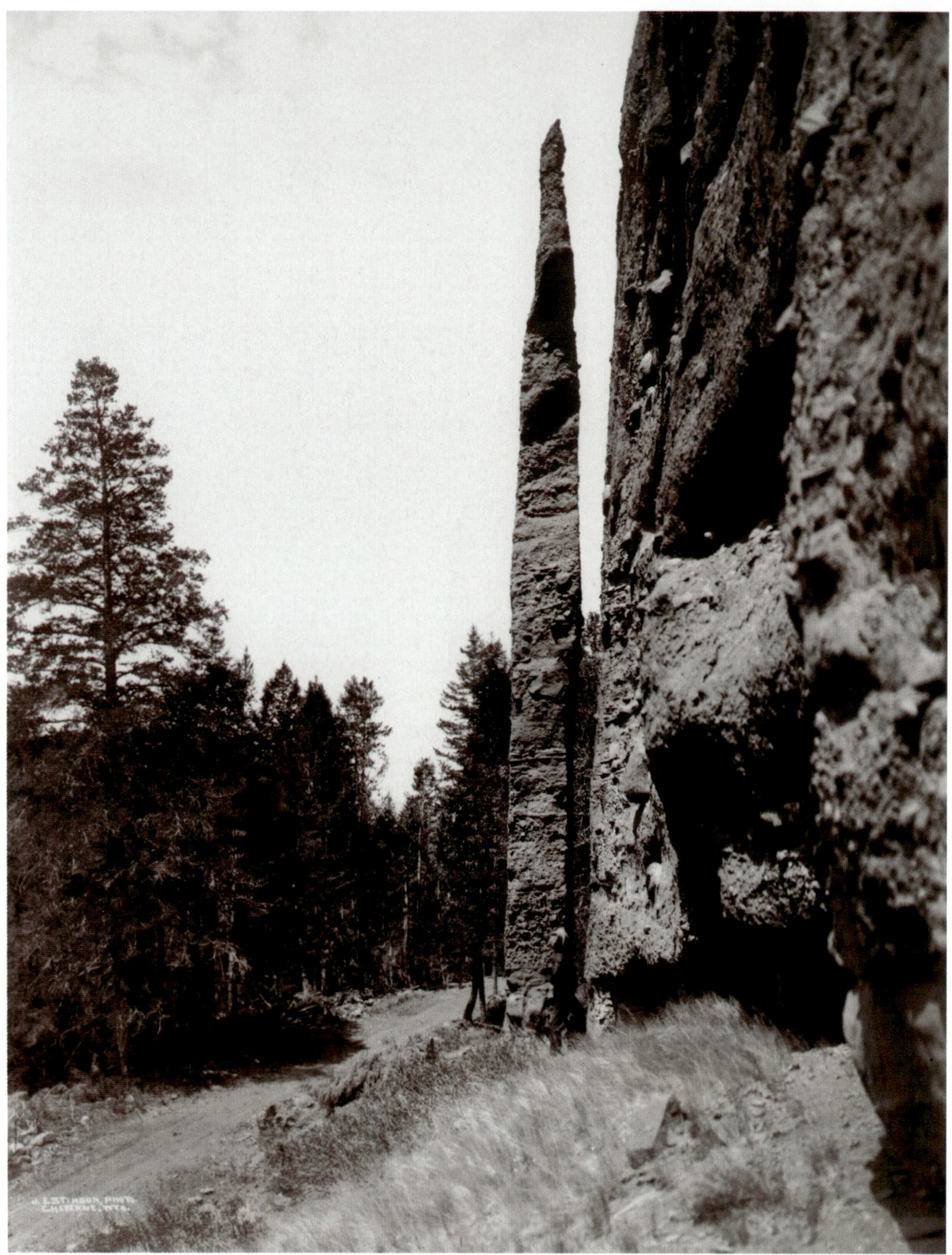

97. #573

The "Needle," Cody Gateway, 1903, 2008
GPS COORDINATES: 44 27.24283N, 109 48.8451W

J. E. Stimson called this formation the "Needle," but most guidebooks label it "Chimney Rock." In 1903 the Cody Road passed just at the base of the formation, as can be seen in Stimson's view. Today, the modern highway passes about 20 yards farther to the left. A close look reveals both of our traveling partners gazing up at the rock, Fred Chase in 1903 and Lauren in 2008. Also note the bark beetle damage present in the modern forest. A large hand-colored print of this image hangs in the Cheyenne Masonic Lodge.

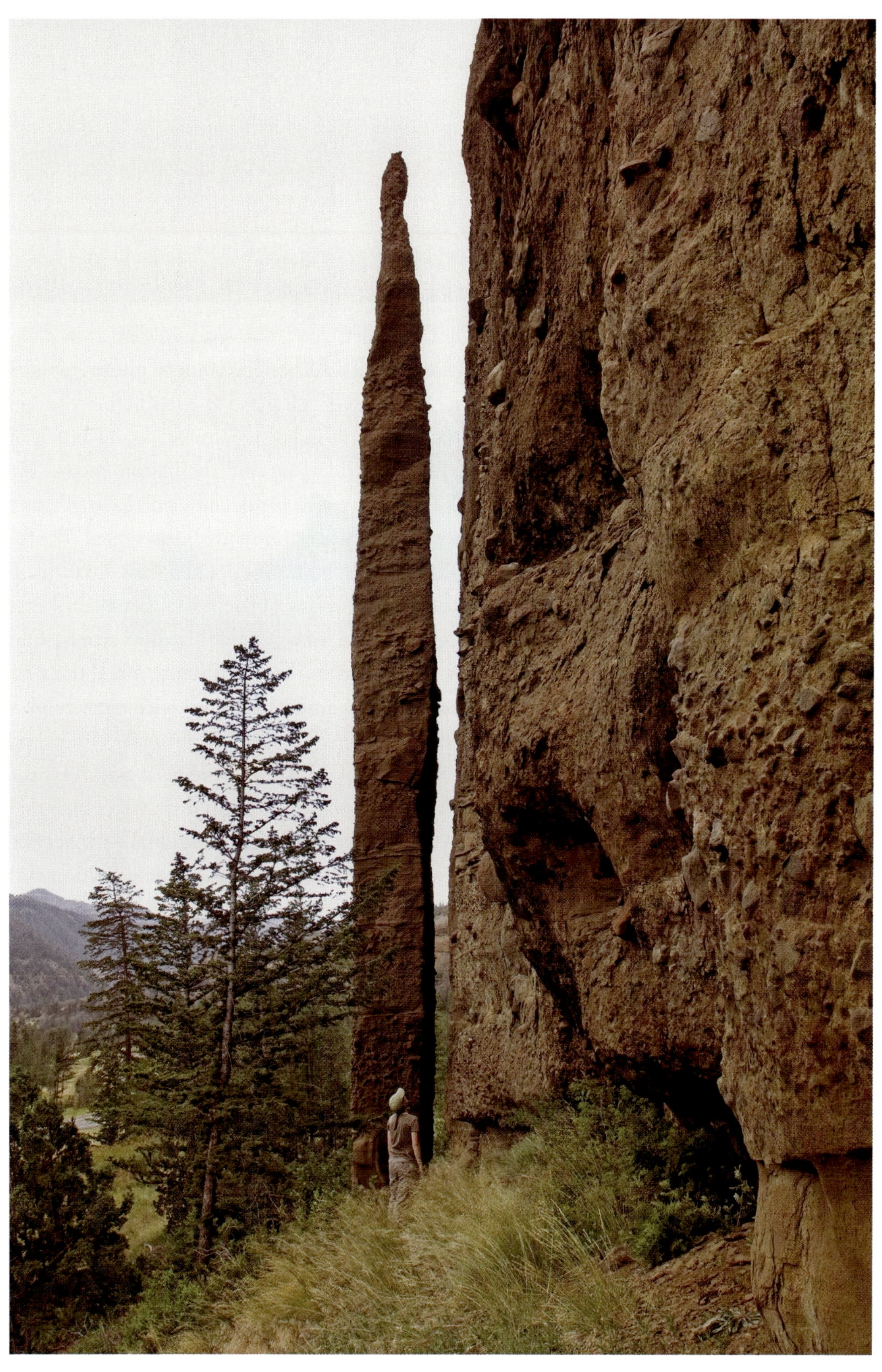

For a Wyoming promotional photographer, few places could sell as well as Yellowstone and Grand Teton National Parks. Although eminent photographers, including William Henry Jackson, had visited Yellowstone even before the US Congress set it aside as the first national park in 1872, Stimson found much of interest to sell for himself, the St. Louis World's Fair, and the Union Pacific. He first visited the park in 1902 and the following year produced a portfolio of views of Yellowstone for sale featuring twenty-five black-and-white "albertypes." The following year, Stimson traveled to the area on the newly opened East Road from Cody, Wyoming, and shot more than forty images of the route. Four years later the photographer returned and produced more views, including shots around Old Faithful Inn and the nearby Upper Geyser Basin. He also photographed the west entrance, the Lake Hotel, and West Thumb. Stimson traveled twice more to photograph the park, in 1910 and again in 1916.

Prior to that last visit, the park Stimson found would have been both very different and very similar to the one we know today. The main differences included management and travel. Until 1916, there were no familiar National Park Service rangers or automobiles. The US Army managed the park, and transportation consisted of either private horse-drawn wagons or public coaches and boats. Despite these differences, visitors such as Stimson would have found guidebooks showing many of the same trails and features we know today.

Just as Jackson had used his images of Yellowstone to help persuade the US Congress to set it aside as a national park, Stimson's promotional images of the Tetons helped in the creation of Grand Teton National Park in 1929, the creation of Grand Teton National Monument in 1943, and the eventual merger into the expanded Grand Teton National Park in 1950. Indeed, the Jackson Hole area became one of the photographer's favorite haunts. He visited for the first time in 1897, returned in 1899, again in 1916, 1924, 1925, 1927, 1928, 1930, and 1931, and for the last time in 1950, when he was eighty years old.

I first rephotographed Yellowstone and Grand Teton National Parks in July 1988. While I was in Yellowstone, several fires began that culminated in the great Yellowstone fires of 1988 that threatened most areas of the park by August, brought its first complete closure in early September, and eventually burned 36 percent of the park. Only the arrival of rain and snow in early September finally extinguished the flames. That summer became a turning point for the management of fire in national parks and a reason for me to come back and rephotograph my scenes taken just before the fires began. Although Stimson photographed Grand Teton National Park repeatedly, I took fewer photographs there, perhaps because I did not know the park as well.

When I returned in 2007 and 2008, I found Grand Teton about the same and much of Yellowstone very different, with large forests gone but smaller-tree forests growing in dense patches in their place. Although I found some new places to rephotograph, such as Dwelle's Inn and Sylvan Lake, construction projects at Artists' Point kept me from retaking that shot. All told, I retook more than fifty of Stimson's photographs, of which twenty are included here. Rephotographs that focus on the road from Cody to the east entrance can be found in my book *Passage to Wonderland*. A handful of those images are included here.

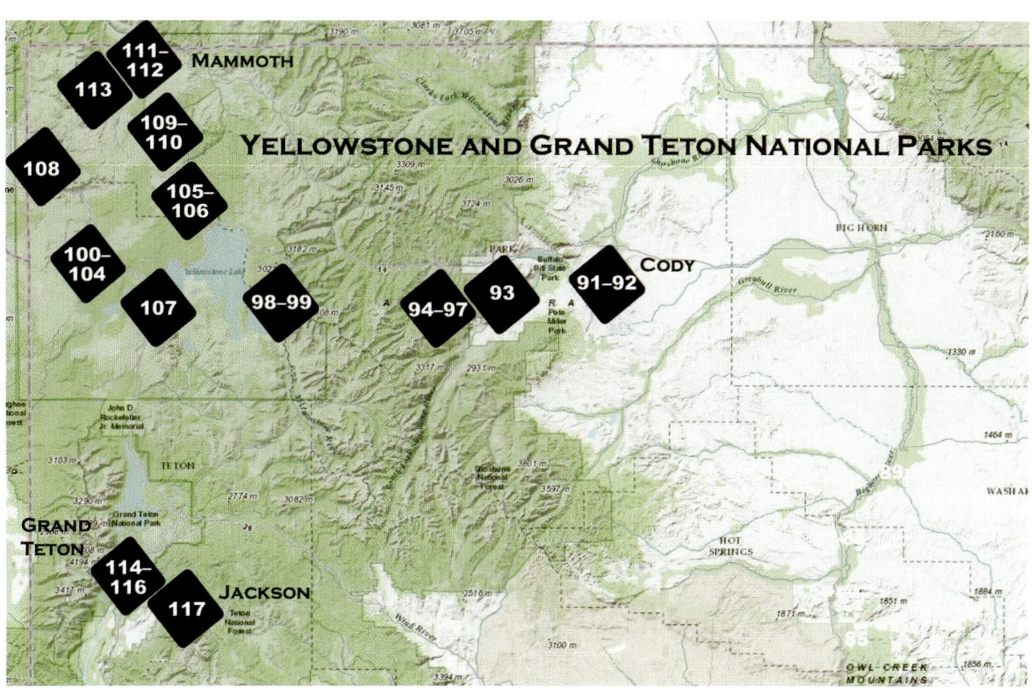

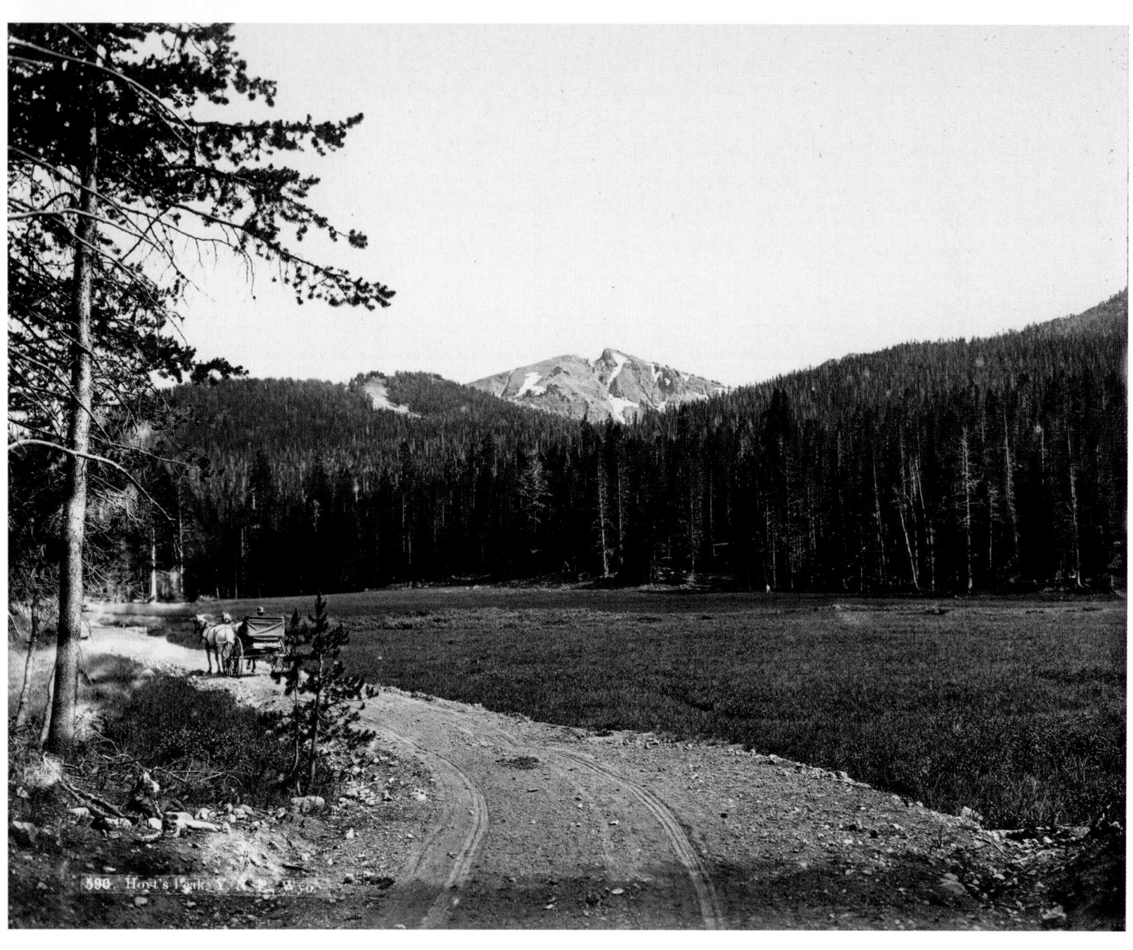

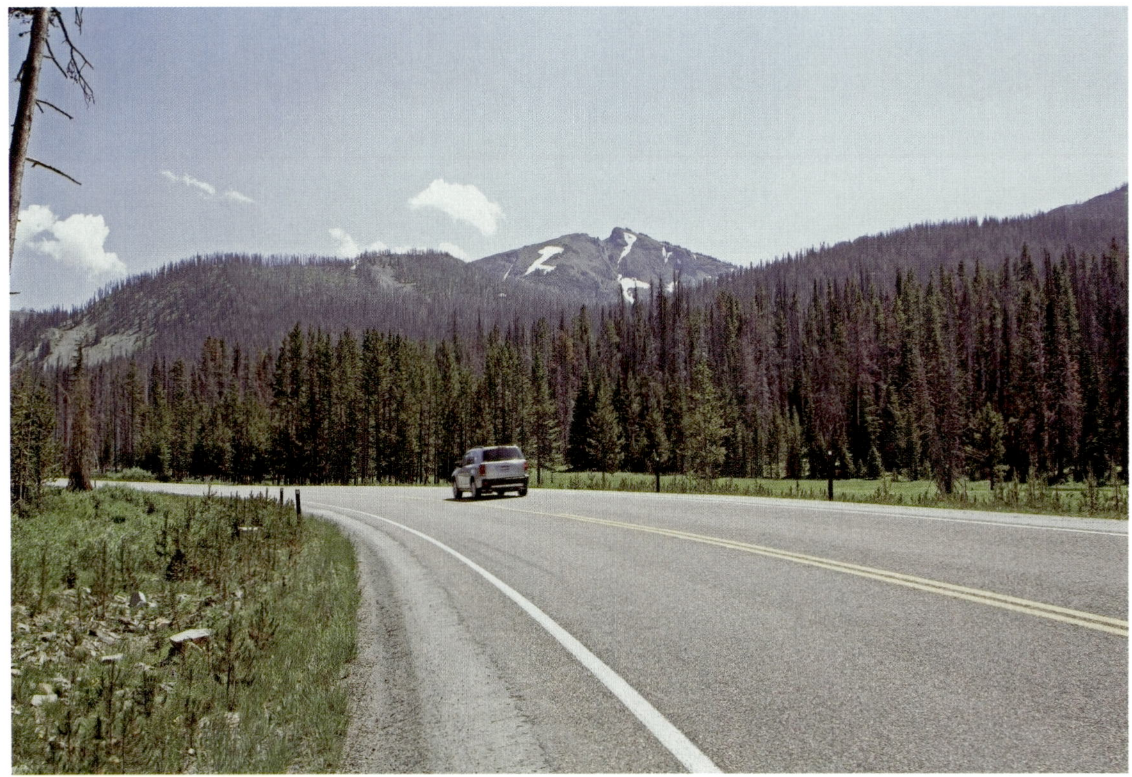

98. #590

Hoyt's Peak [Top Notch], Y.N.P., Wyo., 1903, 2008
GPS COORDINATES: 44 28.490167N, 110 9.4095W

Stimson is incorrect in calling this view Hoyt's Peak. The correct name of the mountain in view is Top Notch Peak. Hoyt's Peak is out of the camera's view to the left. This is probably an example of the photographer being confused after his return to Cheyenne following several months in the field making images.

The camera location is a little park between Eleanor Lake and Sylvan Lake. A small stream meanders through the meadow. This photograph is looking south, with Stimson's guide on the road back to Cody. Although the hillsides and open areas in the forests clearly match up, what is most amazing are the snowfields on Top Notch. Two photographs taken in July 105 years apart show nearly identical, zigzaggy patches of snow. With so many natural wonders such as geysers, waterfalls, and canyons, this little scene seems almost ordinary for Yellowstone. Millions of visitors pass over it every year never knowing they are on a historical path.

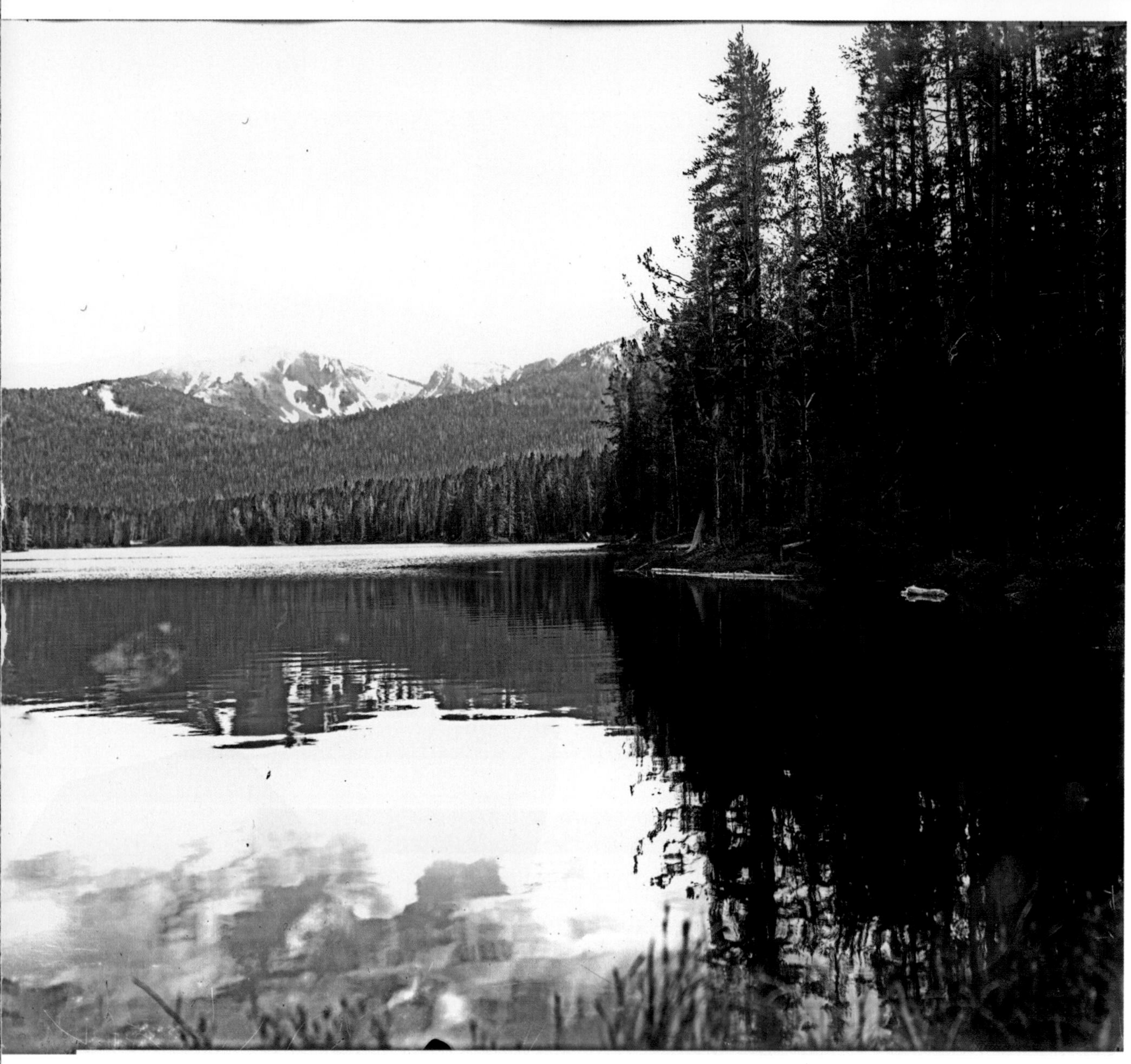

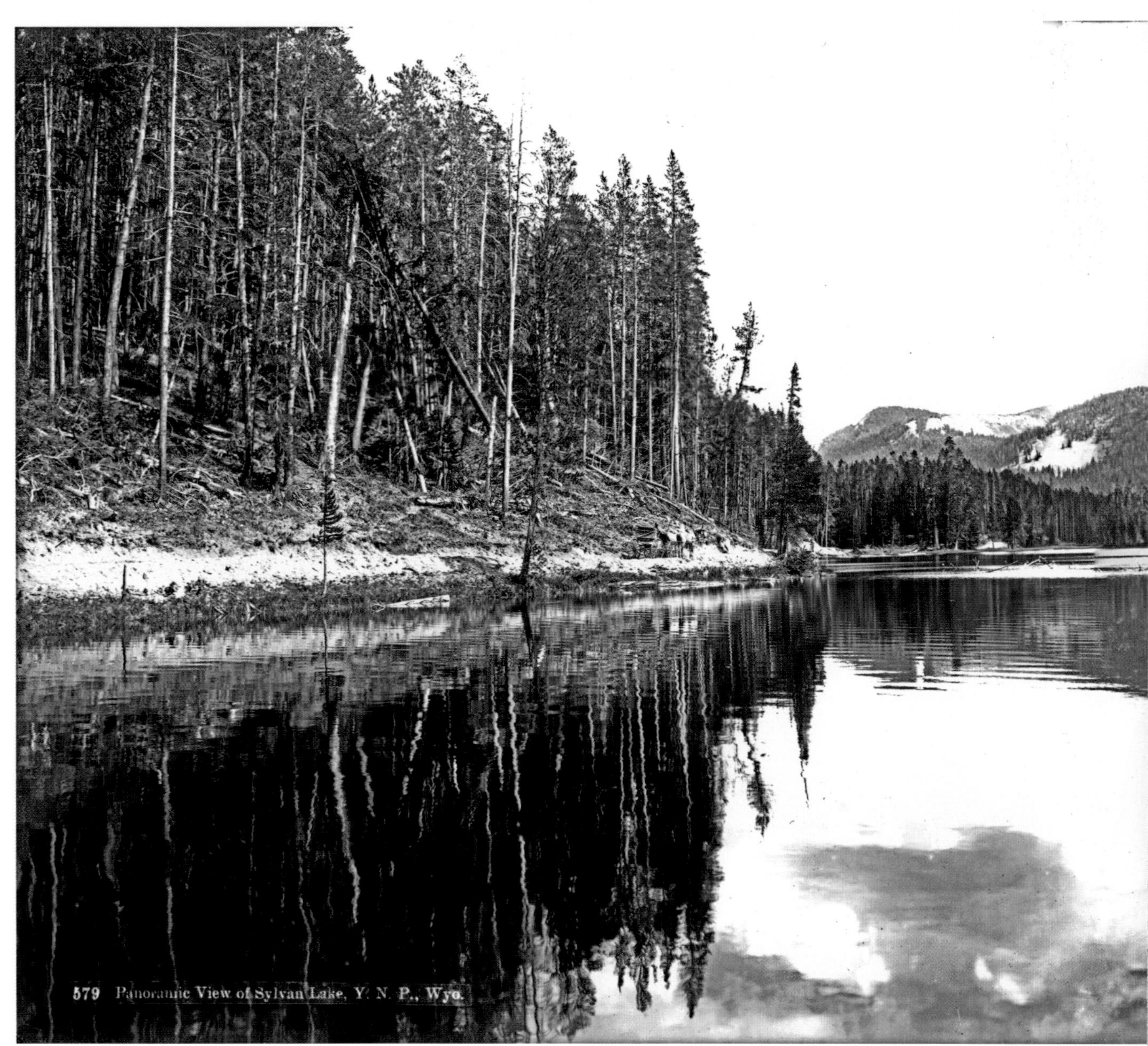

579 Panoramic View of Sylvan Lake, Y. N. P., Wyo.

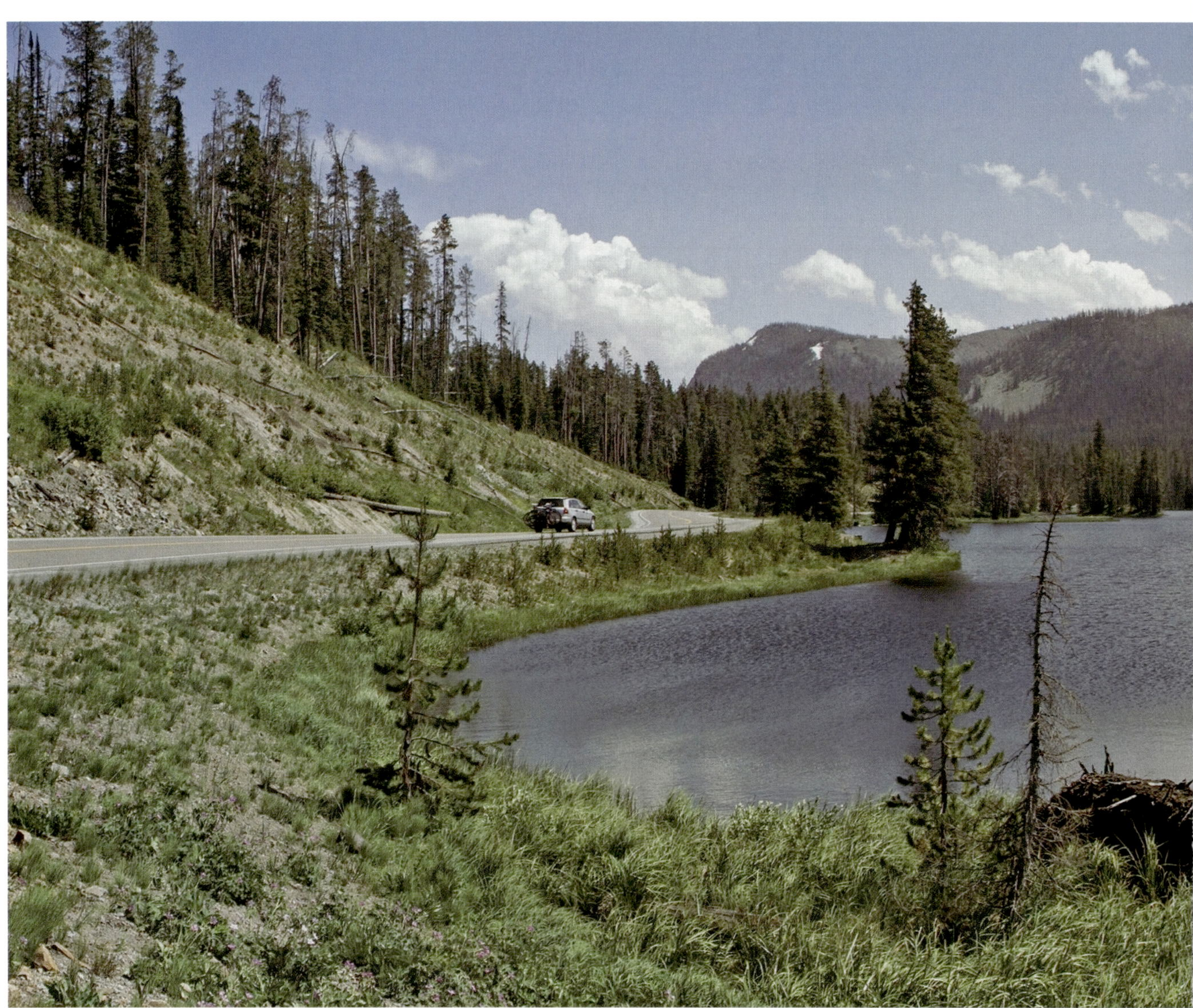

99. #579

Sylvan Lake Panorama, 1903, 2008
GPS COORDINATES: 44 28.983N, 110 09.831W

This view is from the north end of Sylvan Lake and is looking back toward Top Notch Peak and Sylvan Pass. The Cody Road can be seen skirting the lake on the left side of the photograph. Stimson's guide can also be seen, looking toward the camera. Stimson captured Sylvan Lake reflecting the distant peaks in a very picturesque manner.

Stimson made two panoramic series of Sylvan Lake from this point during that summer of 1903. After rephotographing both of them, I learned that they were both made from this very point and the only difference was a slight shift of the camera left or right. This one incorporates two separate images, #579 and #579a. For this view, I used several tools in Adobe Photoshop to stitch scans of the two images together into one continuous view.

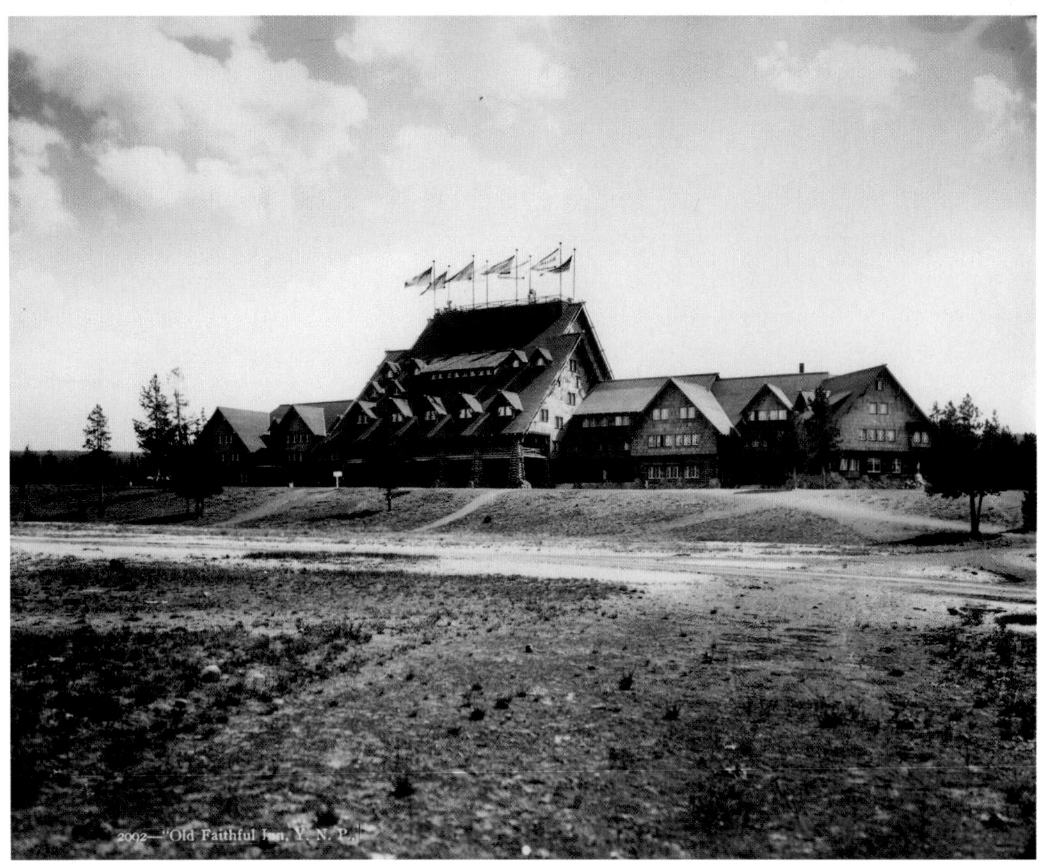
2092—"Old Faithful Inn, Y. N. P."

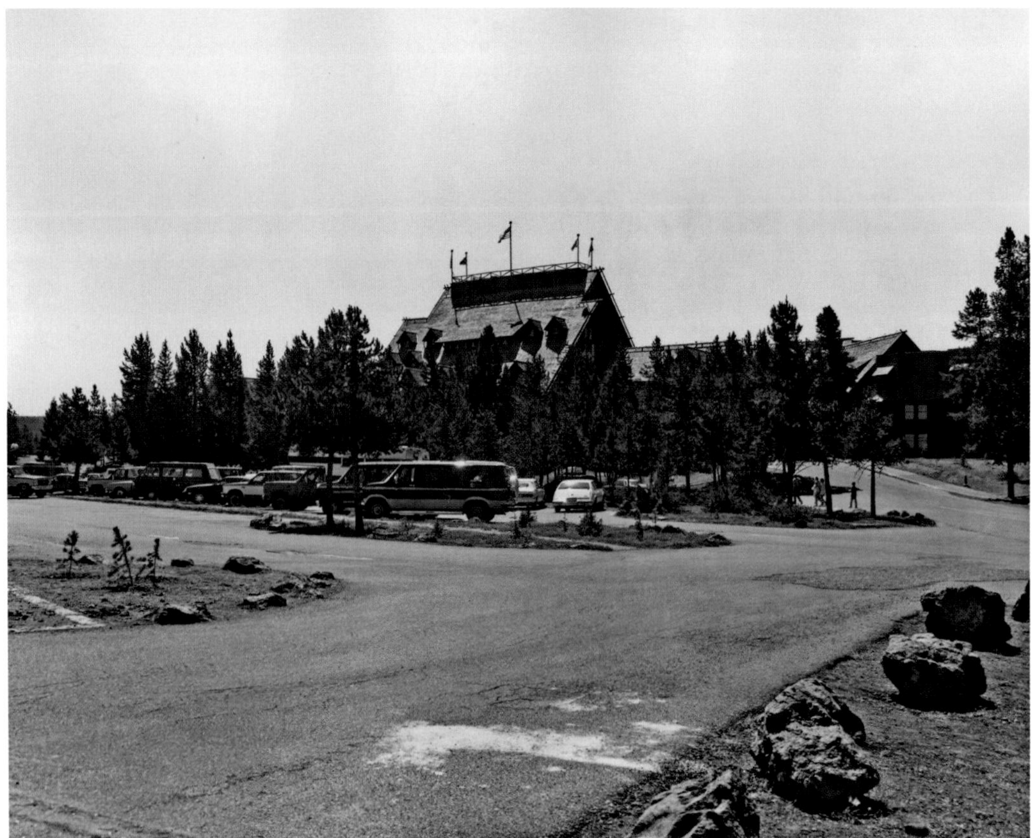

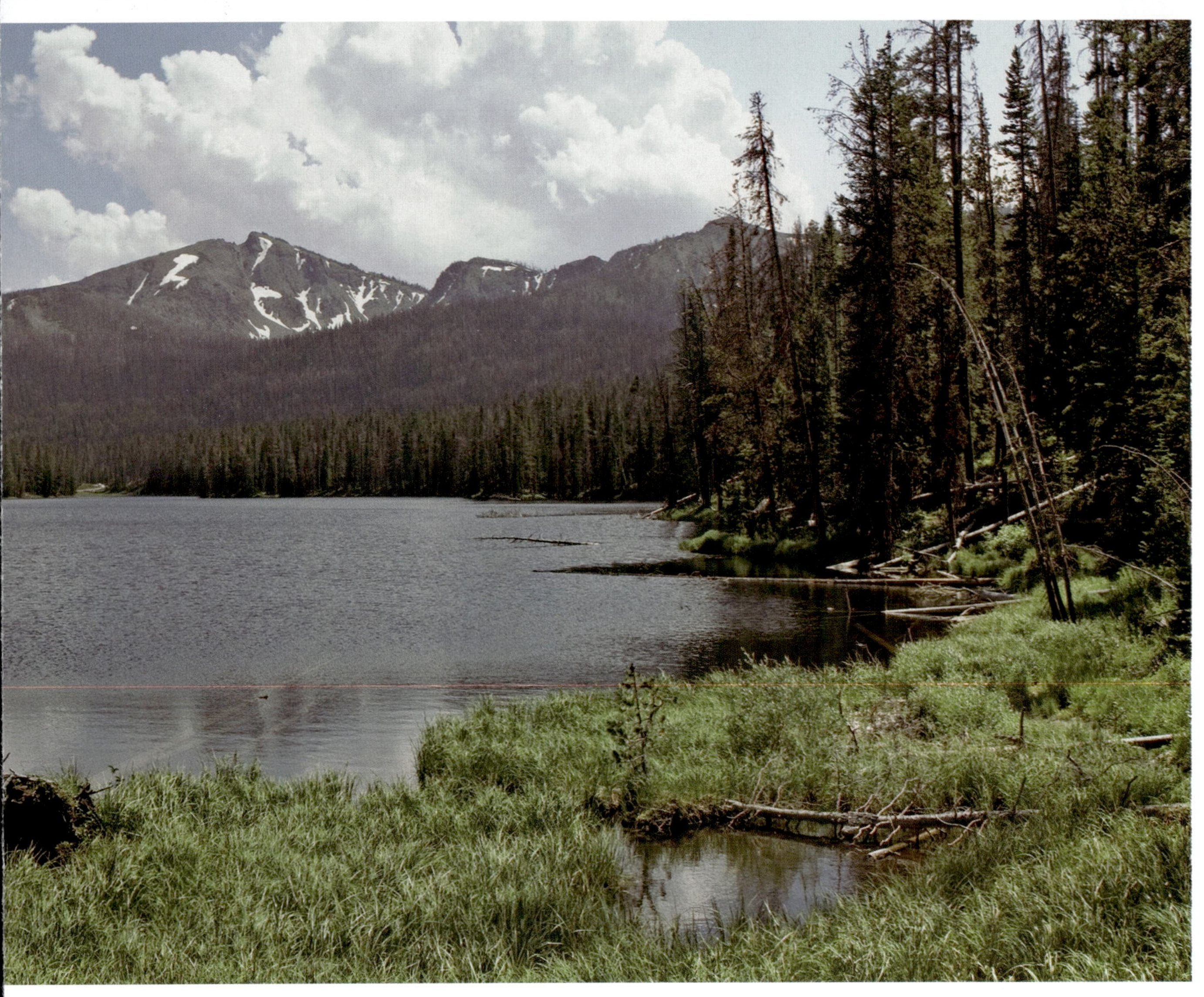

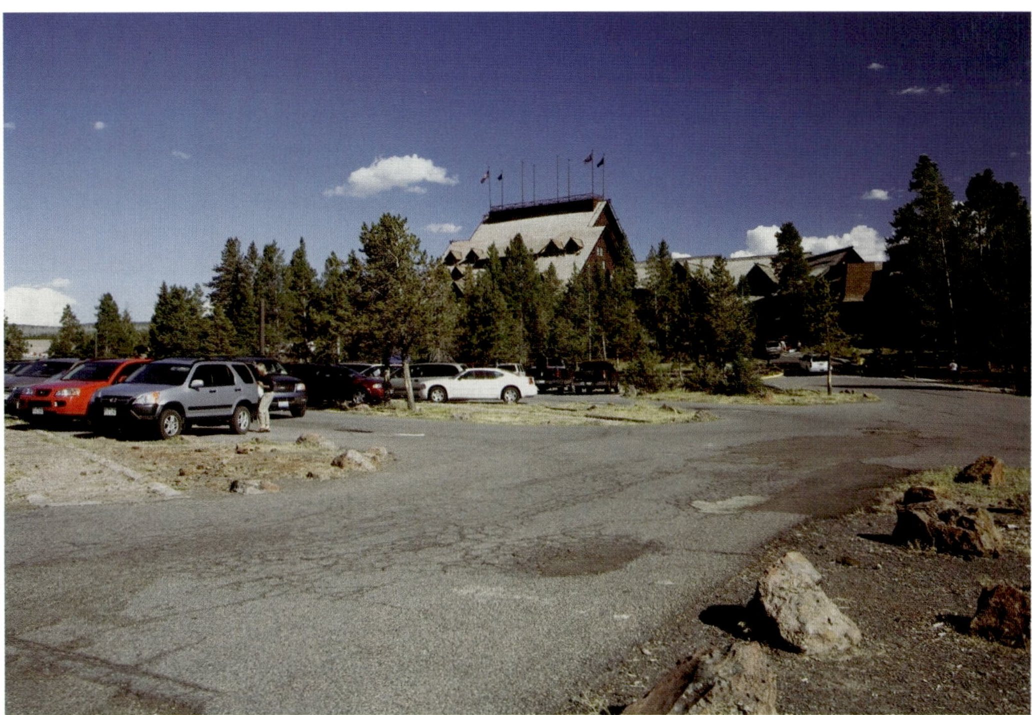

100. #2002

Old Faithful Inn, 1907, 1988, 2007
GPS COORDINATES: 44 27.65433N, 110 49.964667W

Designed by Seattle architect Robert C. Reamer and constructed by the Northern Pacific Railroad in the winter of 1903–04 at a cost of $140,000, the Old Faithful Inn is the largest free-standing log structure in the world. It is a wonderful example of Rustic architecture, rises seventy-nine feet at its highest point, and faces the original "circuit road" and not the geyser. When Stimson visited it in 1907, it was 350 feet long and had 140 rooms. Located just west of its namesake geyser, the inn had a viewing porch where visitors could watch each eruption.

Stimson's view is looking south from the southern edge of the Upper Geyser Basin. Judging by the light, the photographer made the photo in the afternoon. Although it is not a particularly stunning image, the photograph works, like many of his business images, as a slightly less than straight-on building portrait. Note the many flags flying, the stone portico, and the imbalanced number of dormers. Some speculate that because the middle row contains two dormers on the left but none on the right, the architect was suggesting that nothing in nature is perfectly symmetrical.

By the time I rephotographed it in early July 1988, the Old House, as it is known, had been through a lot. The east wing, constructed in 1913–14, added 100 rooms. The west wing, built in 1927, added another 150 rooms plus 95 bathrooms. Also in 1927, the lobby was extended outward and small gift shops were added. In 1959 an earthquake shook the inn; though extensively damaged, it held. The most noticeable change in my photograph is the added parking lot full of cars.

Within a month of making my 1988 photo, the North Fork Fire, one of hundreds in the park that summer, seriously threatened the structure. Only the gallant efforts of firefighters and volunteers saved the building. In 1998 and 1999, the east and west wings were renovated. Then, beginning in 2004 as part of its 100-year celebration, the National Park Service authorized that the entire inn be renovated. When I rephotographed it in 2007, that project had been completed. But this view, other than revealing that the inn was not destroyed in the 1988 fires, shows more about the role of tourists and their cars than it does about fire.

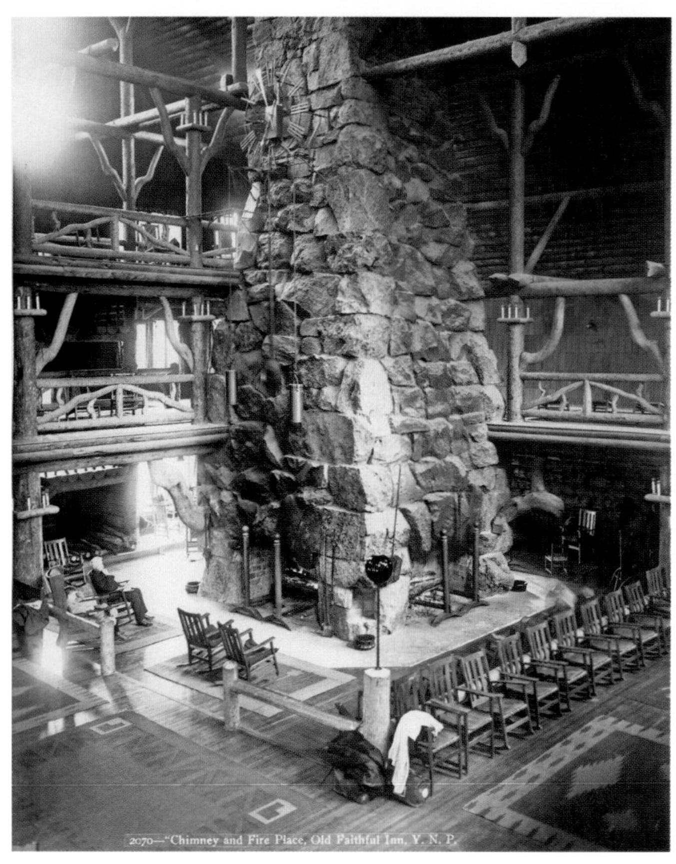
2070—"Chimney and Fire Place, Old Faithful Inn, Y. N. P.

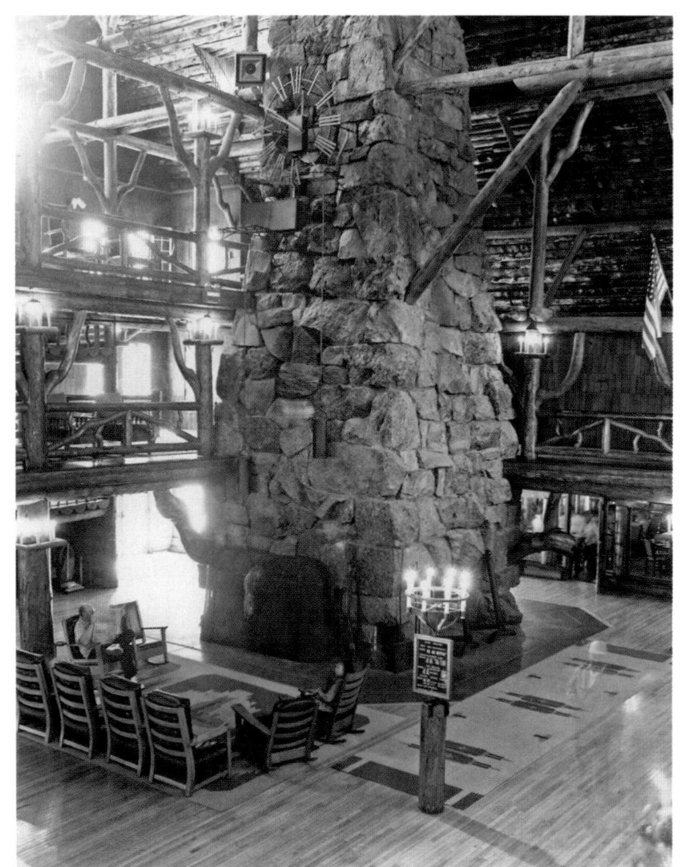

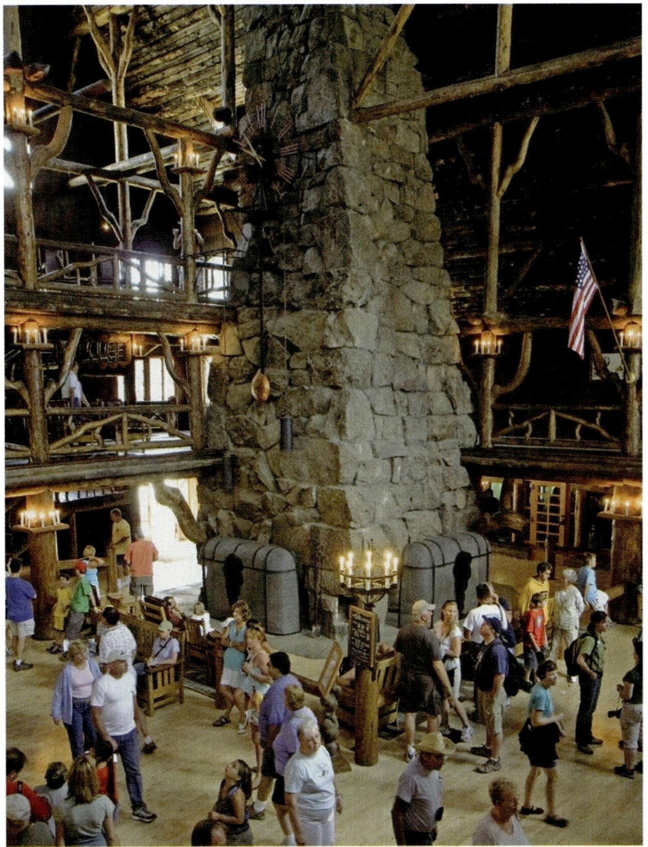

101. #2070

Chimney and Fireplace, Old Faithful Inn, 1907, 1988, 2007
GPS COORDINATES: 44 27.59133N, 110 49.8721667W

One corner of Old Faithful Inn's seven-story open-air lobby contains this massive 5-ton fireplace. It is 80 feet high, 14 feet wide at its base, and constructed of hand-quarried lava rock. It contains eight fireplaces. In Stimson's photograph, huge andirons, several rows of chairs, and a man and boy are sitting near the hearth. On its massive walls hang a giant popcorn popper and a clock, complete with 14-foot pendulum. A close examination reveals that the minute hand has moved. Of the more than 200 Stimson images I have rephotographed, only this one tells me both the time it was made (a few minutes before 7:00) and its exposure time (2–3 minutes).

In 1988, tourists filled the lobby. I noticed the chimney's large new beam, added for support after the 1959 earthquake, as well as new lights, flags, a speaker high up the chimney, and just one person sitting in the chairs and in almost the same spot as the man in Stimson's photo. I hurriedly climbed to the second floor to capture the man but worried that the crowded lobby would block my image. I set up my 4 × 5 camera on its tripod, used a light meter to figure exposure, adjusted for reciprocity (a characteristic of my film that lengthened already long exposures), and tripped the shutter for 30 seconds. When I later developed the film and printed the negative, I found an almost empty lobby! The crowd's constant movement had blurred almost everyone from the image. Although the clock's minute hand remained still, its pendulum was blurred. A man reading the newspaper in almost the same place as in Stimson's view, and a semi-stationary ghost couple, lower right, are apparent.

When I returned to the renovated inn in the summer of 2007, I was pleasantly surprised to see the lobby looking so great. The 1959 earthquake support beam had been removed and the floor changed, but nearly everything else looked about the same, including the flags, lights, chairs (Lauren, wearing a hat, is sitting with her back to the fireplace), and time of day. Twenty years apart, I took two photographs within 5 minutes of each other.

Most revealing, of course, is the crowded lobby. Modern digital cameras are far more light-sensitive than film, so I was able to expose this shot at a much faster shutter speed with flash, visually preserving the overwhelming continued tourist interest in this beautiful building.

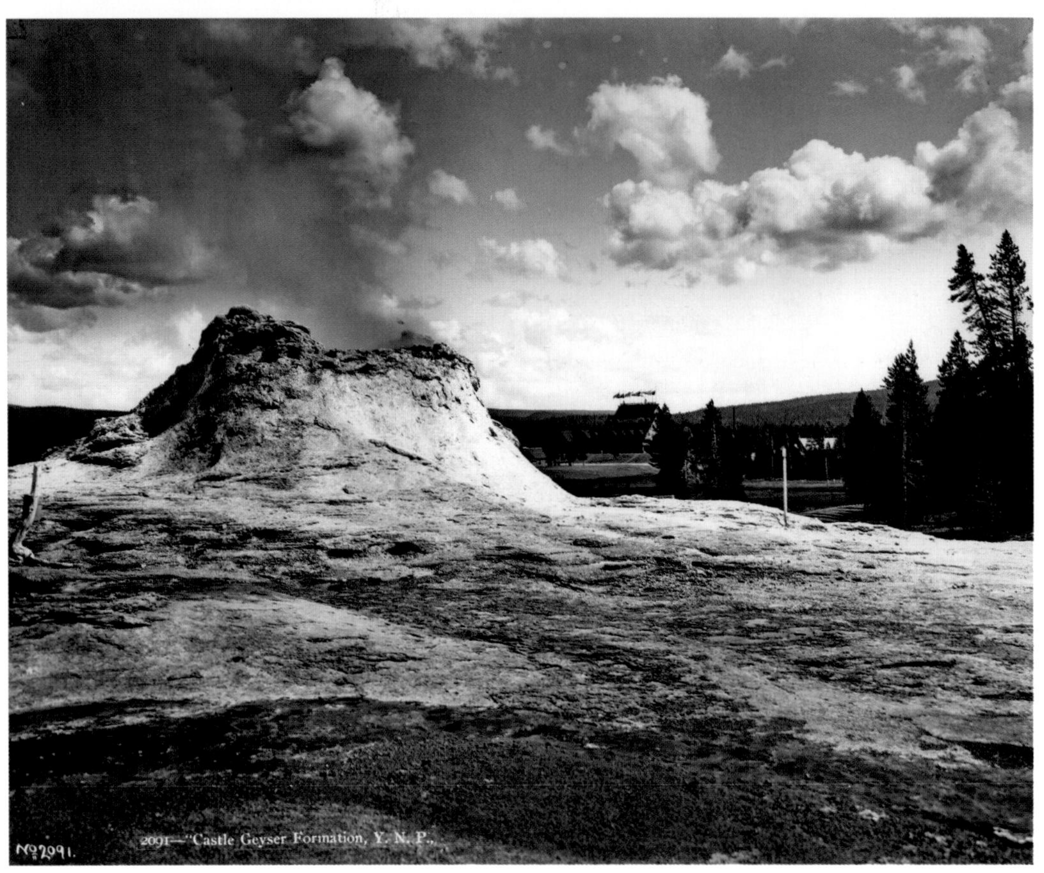
No 2991.
2991—"Castle Geyser Formation, Y. N. P.,

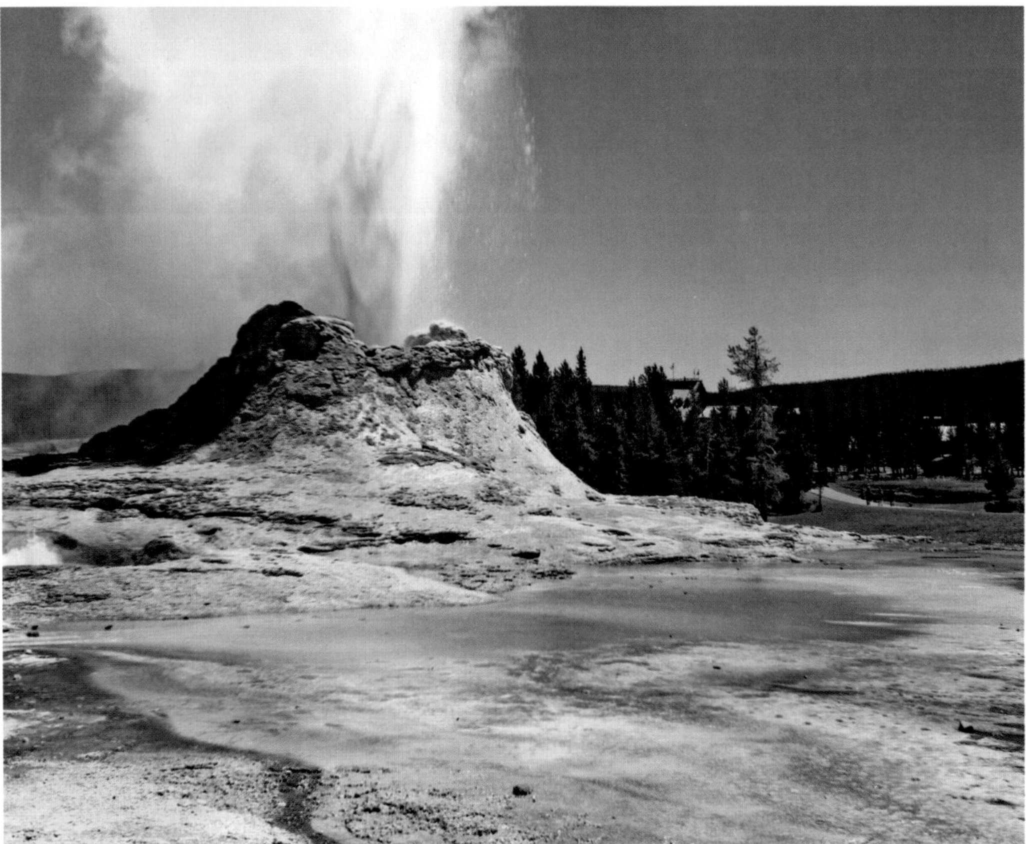

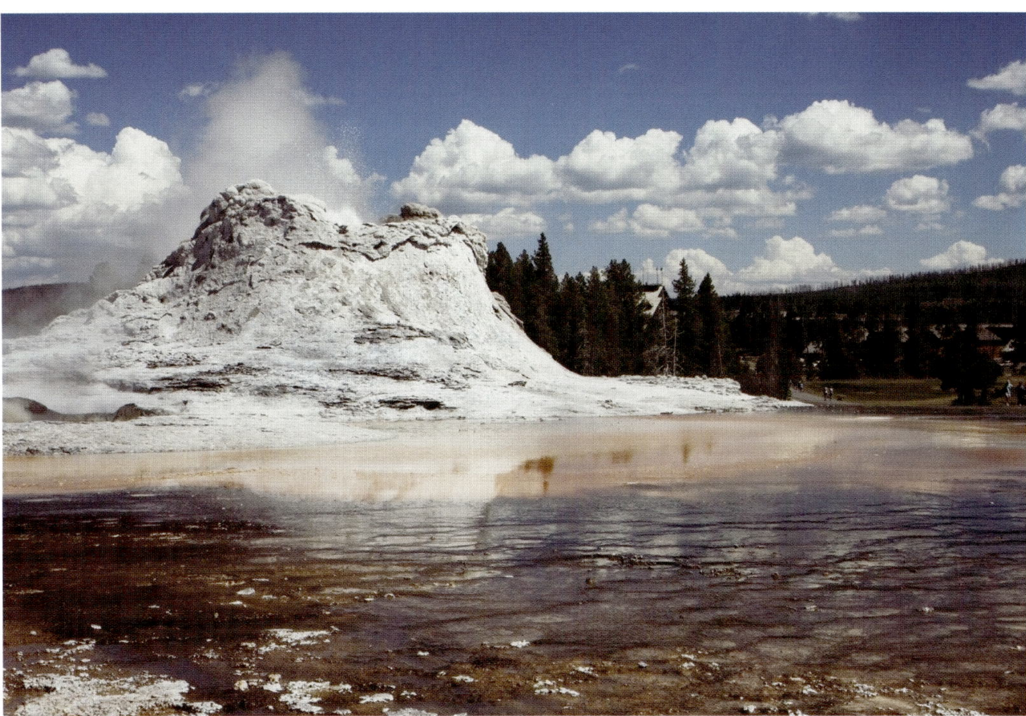

102. #2091

Castle Geyser, 1907, 1988, 2007
GPS COORDINATES: 44 27.830167N, 110 50.21967W

The next three triads of photographs show the dramatic effects of the 1988 fires on the area around Old Faithful Inn and the Upper Geyser Basin. Castle Geyser is located in the Upper Geyer Basin near Old Faithful. It was named in 1870 by the Washburn-Langford-Doane Expedition because it resembled a medieval castle. The geyser erupts to the height of about 90 feet every 10–12 hours for a duration of approximately 20 minutes. Afterward, the geyser noisily vents steam for 30–40 minutes.

In his 1907 photograph, Stimson placed his camera fairly close to the geyser, making the cone appear quite large compared to Old Faithful Inn, seen at right in the distance. Steam is venting from the top and water appears in the foreground, suggesting that the geyser had recently erupted. In the background, the flags atop the inn are blowing in the wind.

My 1988 view captures Castle Geyser in full eruption, with water spraying out of the top. Also of note in my rephotograph is the growth of the trees in the background, almost blocking Old Faithful Inn from view.

Just weeks after I made my 1988 rephotograph, the North Fork Fire began and soon threatened the Upper Geyser Basin and Old Faithful Inn. The fire began on July 22 as the result of a dropped cigarette in the Caribou-Targhee National Forest outside the park in Idaho. It soon raced northeast across the park, threatening West Yellowstone, the Madison River Valley, Norris Geyser Basin, the Grand Canyon of the Yellowstone, and, by September 5–7, the Upper Geyser Basin. Twelve hundred firefighters dug in to protect the historic structure while others dropped fire retardant on buildings in the area. Tires on nearby cars melted. On September 9 the National Park Service closed the entire park as the fire pushed on toward Mammoth Hot Springs. Only the arrival of rain and snow on September 11 brought the fire under control; then it was extinguished.

The effects of the fire are quite visible in my 2007 rephotograph. The heroic efforts of firefighters to save Old Faithful Inn are apparent because it remains, shrouded by trees between it and the geyser basin. Castle Geyser also looks about the same. Just as apparent, though, is the charred forest on the distant hillside.

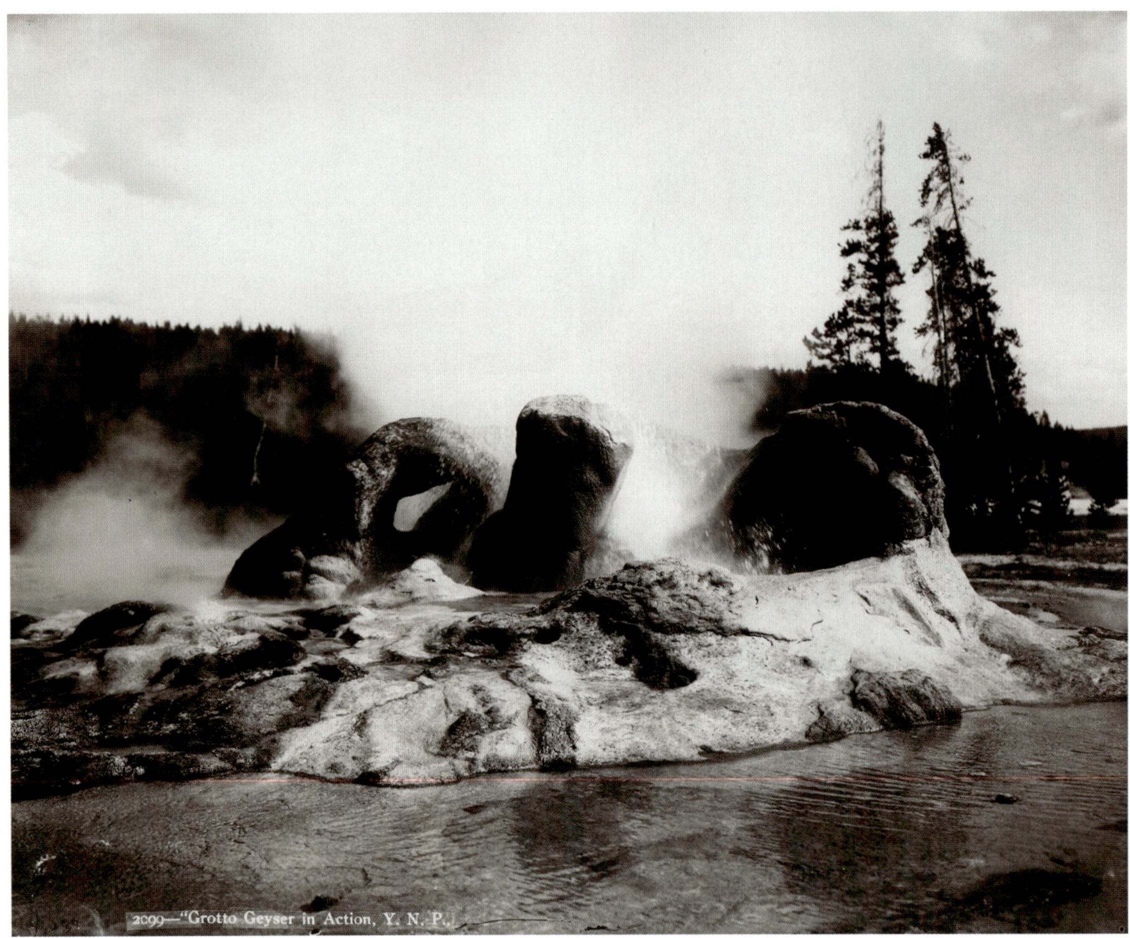

103. #2099

Grotto Geyser, 1907, 1988, 2007
GPS COORDINATES: 44 28.30667N, 110 50.531833W

Grotto Geyser, the most unusual geyser in the park, lies to the north of Castle Geyser. Named by the Washburn-Langford-Doane Expedition in 1870 for its cave-like appearance, Grotto erupts about every 8 hours, shooting water about 10 feet high for anywhere from an hour to 10 or more hours.

In his 1907 photograph, Stimson captured the geyser erupting, with water in the foreground and steam rising from its middle. Note the two large trees at right and the solid hill of forest in the background.

In my 1988 rephotograph, only a small amount of steam was venting from Grotto, providing a clear view of the formation and of the dense forest beyond. Note as well the plank sidewalk to the right of the geyser that controls tourist movement on the fragile crust.

My 2007 rephotograph also captures the formation venting only a little steam, thereby clearly showing the effects of the 1988 North Fork Fire on the background hill. Most interesting is the fire pattern. Although individual charred trees are clearly visible, the fire did not destroy the entire area. Some trees remain much as they used to be. At right, the presence of tourists on those same walkways confirms that Yellowstone is as popular as ever.

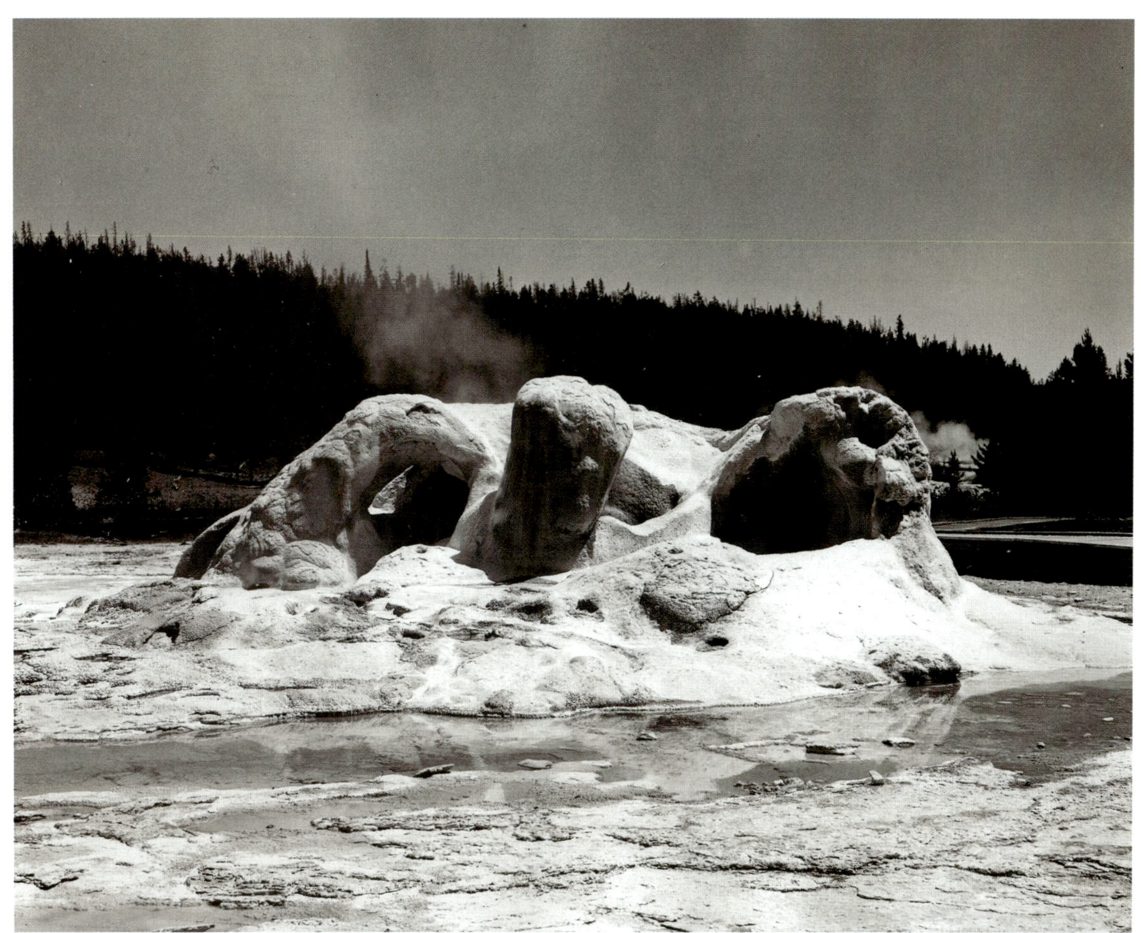

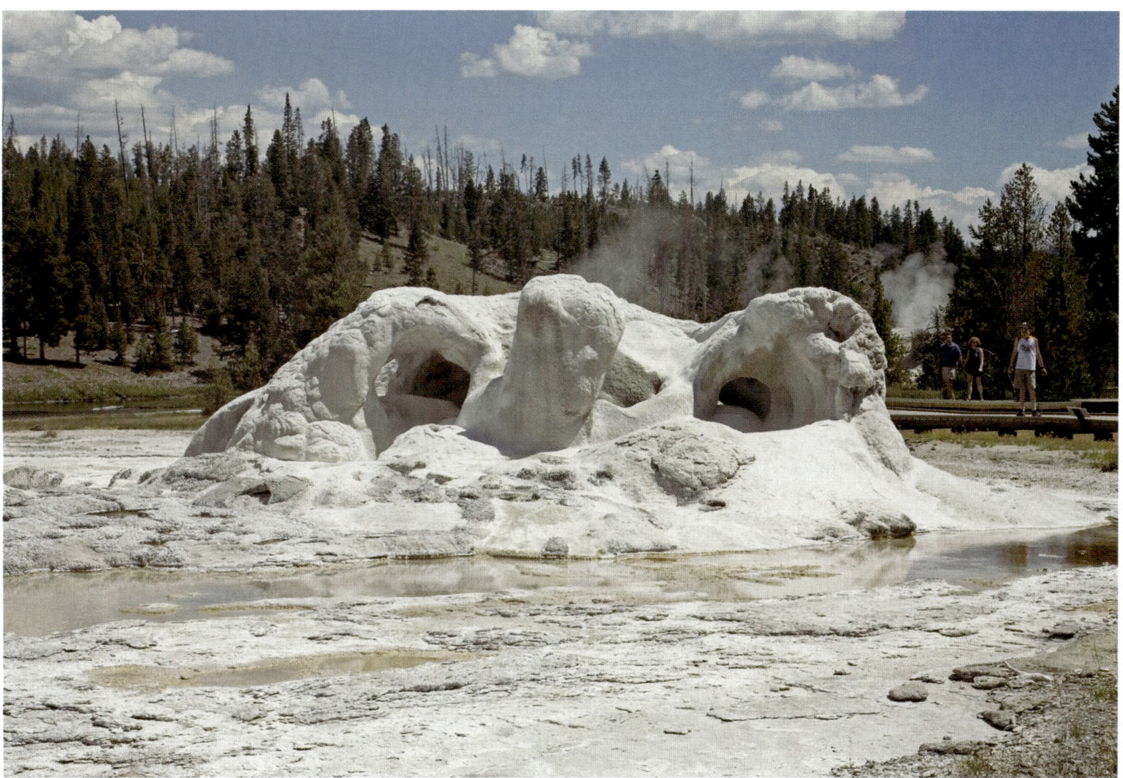

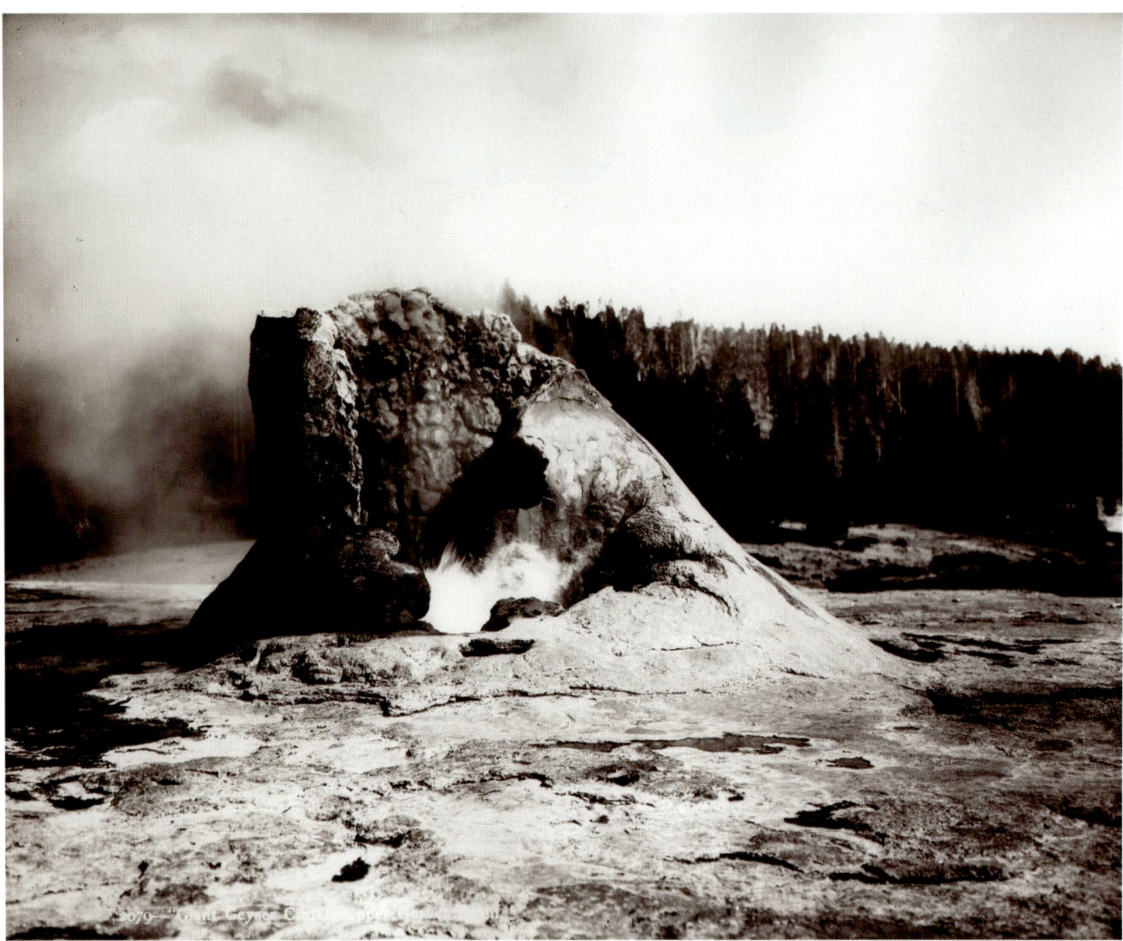

104. #2079

Giant Geyser, 1907, 1988, 2007
GPS COORDINATES: 44 28.241833N, 110 50.45W

The enormous cone of Giant Geyser is also located in the Upper Geyser Basin north of Old Faithful Inn. Standing more than 12 feet tall, Giant is the largest of a group that includes three other geysers. Also named in 1870 by the Washburn-Langford-Doane Expedition, Giant can go long periods without erupting; when it does erupt, it can be spectacular, sometimes shooting water 250 feet high.

As in his other geyser views, Stimson employed his traditional, straight-on portrait style to Giant, with the geyser situated in the center of his image. Because it is only venting steam, the dense forest beyond is clearly visible.

My 1988 rephotograph also captures only steam rising from within, so both the inner crater and the dense forest beyond are clear. As with all of these images, I am shooting from one of the plank walkways.

Like the others, the main focus of my 2007 rephotograph is not the formation but the hillside in the background. Similar to my view of Grotto, the North Fork Fire swept through the hill beyond, burning some trees but leaving others seemingly untouched. Such views are important when it comes to educating people about the "nature" of fires. Too many believe that fires are "unnatural" and must be suppressed at all times or they will completely burn down the entire forest. These photos, however, support the idea that fires are natural parts of the forest ecosystem and can produce healthier, less dense stands of trees.

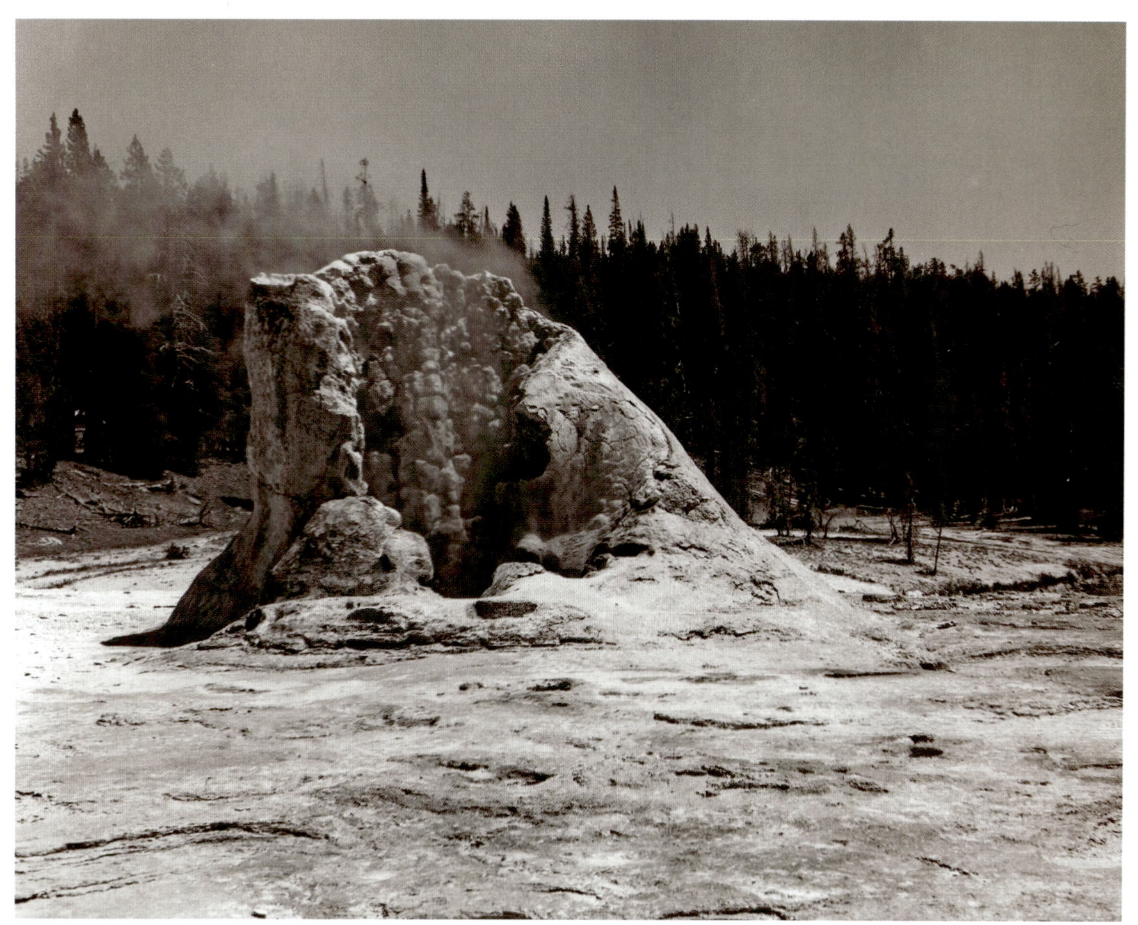

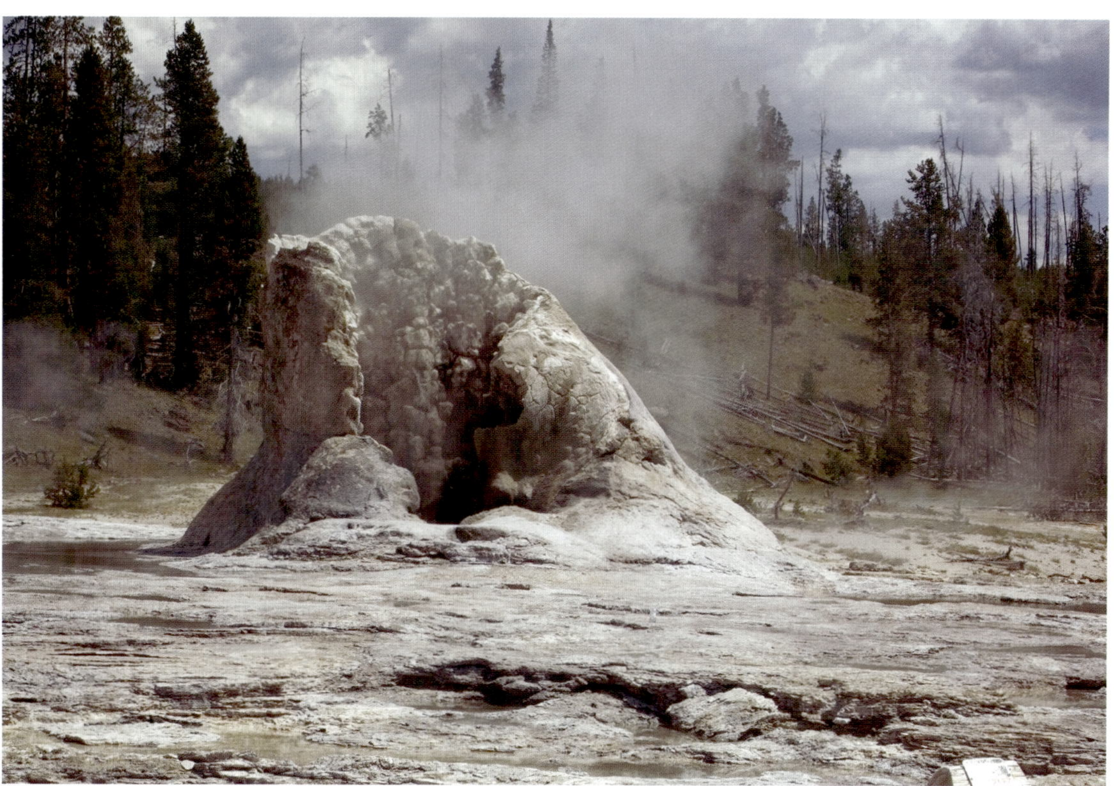

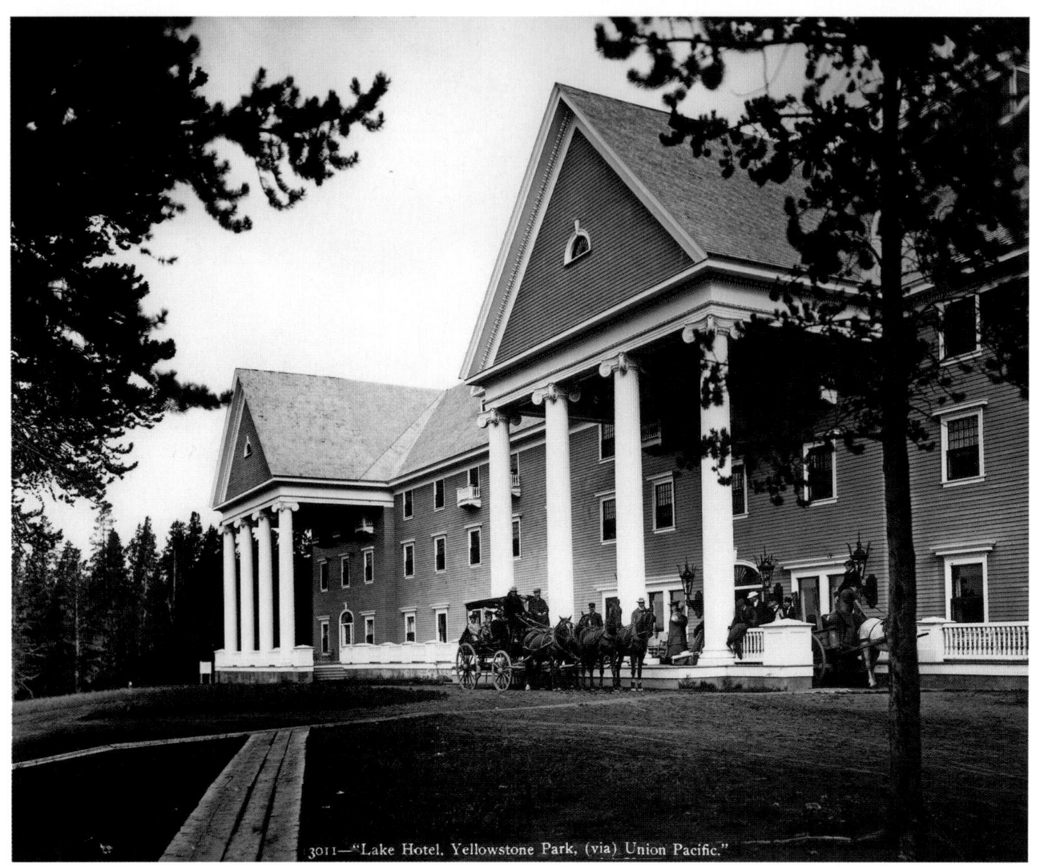

3011—"Lake Hotel, Yellowstone Park, (via) Union Pacific."

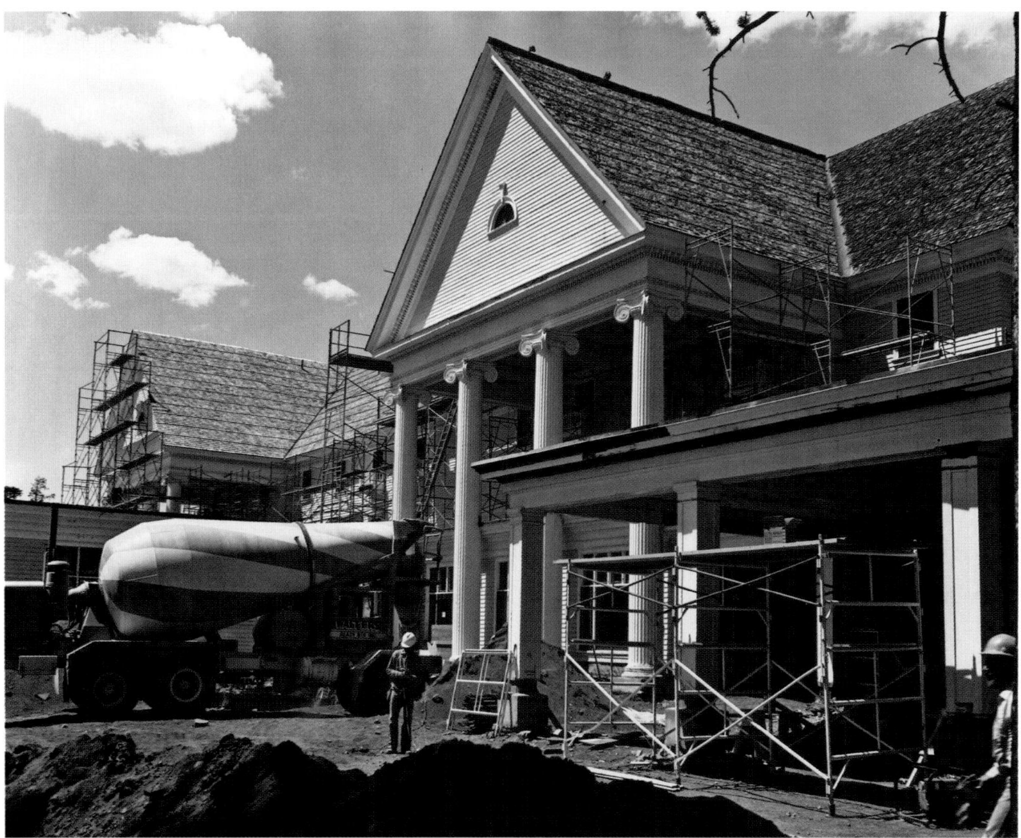

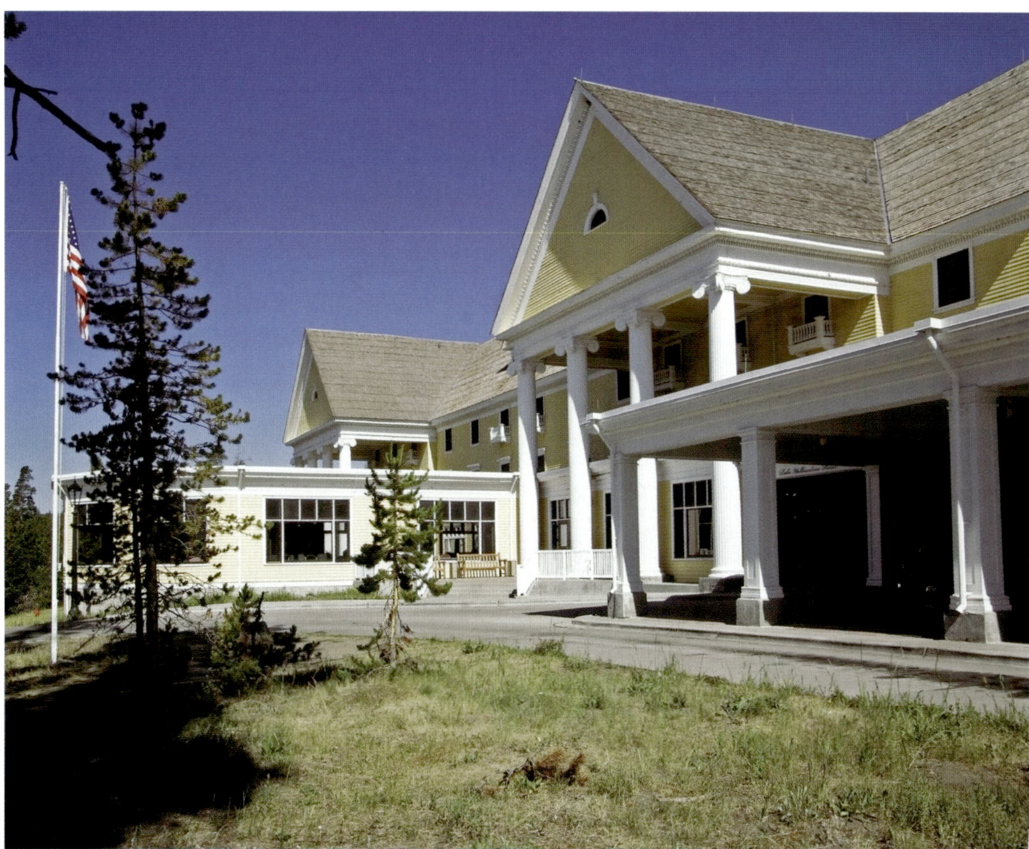

105. #3011

Lake Hotel, 1907, 1988, 2007
GPS COORDINATES: 44 32.97867N, 110 24.004667W

The Northern Pacific Railroad constructed the Lake Hotel on the northwest edge of Yellowstone Lake in 1889. At the time, it followed a traditional box design that looked like most other railroad hotels. Between 1904 and 1905, Old Faithful Inn architect Robert C. Reamer re-designed the hotel by adding gables, columns, false balconies, and fanlight windows to give the hotel a neoclassical look. The new design prompted some to rename it the Colonial, but Lake Hotel prevailed. It is the oldest surviving hotel in the park.

Stimson's 1907 view shows guests arriving at the front door. At that time, the predominant mode of travel in the park was by coach; automobiles were not allowed until 1916. Tourists tired of the dust could also take a small steamboat from West Thumb to the hotel and then a small coach up to the front door. Note the heavy coats worn by the driver and his sidekick. For this view, Stimson stepped back from the building to frame it in pine trees and was looking toward the northwest.

In the years following Stimson's photograph, the Lake Hotel faced many difficulties. After another remodel in the 1920s in which Reamer added a sun porch, a dining room, and an extended front portico, the hotel was closed during the Great Depression when tourist travel waned. The next several decades led to further decline and disrepair. Some referred to the old hotel as "bat alley." Finally, in 1981 the National Park Service and the Park Concessionaire began a 10-year remodeling project.

When I rephotographed the hotel in 1988, it was in the middle of this major renovation. Crews were pouring new concrete and working from scaffolding to repair the columns and gables. Others were working on the extended portico at right and on the sunroom just beyond the cement truck.

My 2007 color rephotograph shows the beauty of the renovated hotel, with its pale yellow exterior and white trim. When Lauren and I were planning to photograph here, we made last-minute reservations and were thrilled to book our stay. When we arrived, though, we were disappointed to learn that our reservations were for the Lake Hotel Annex, a modern motel-like structure in the back.

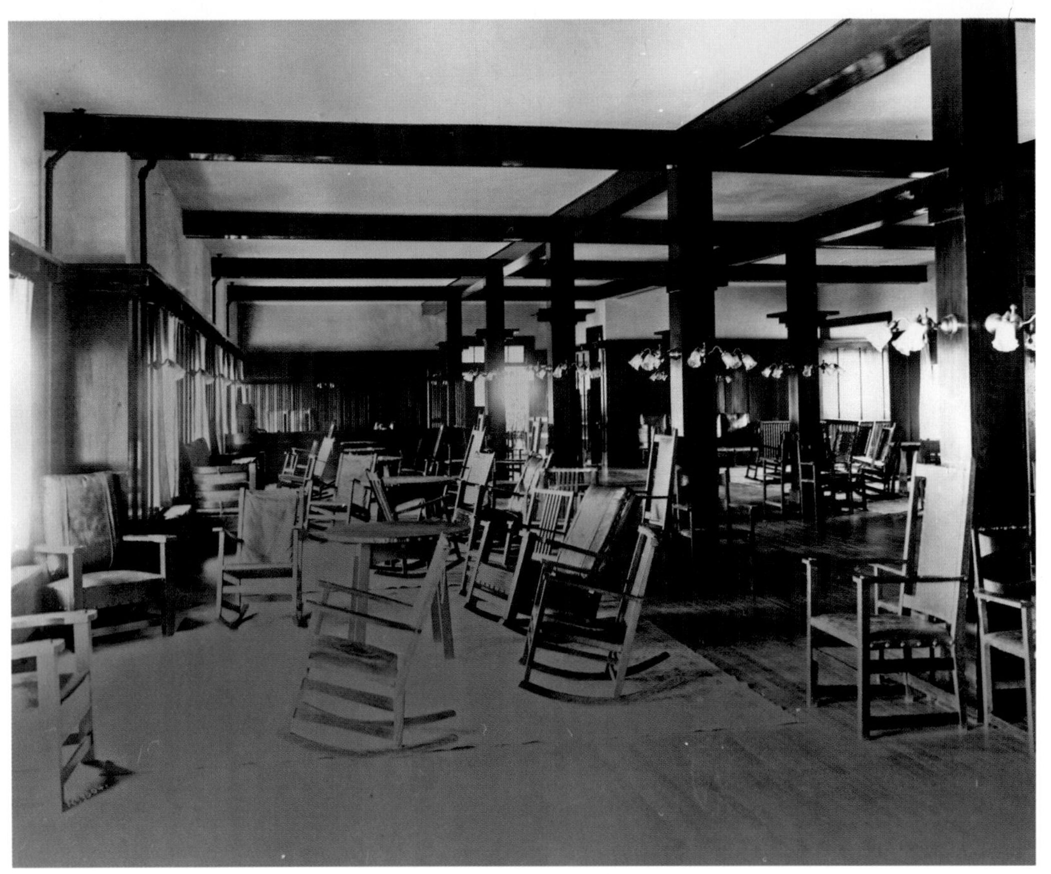

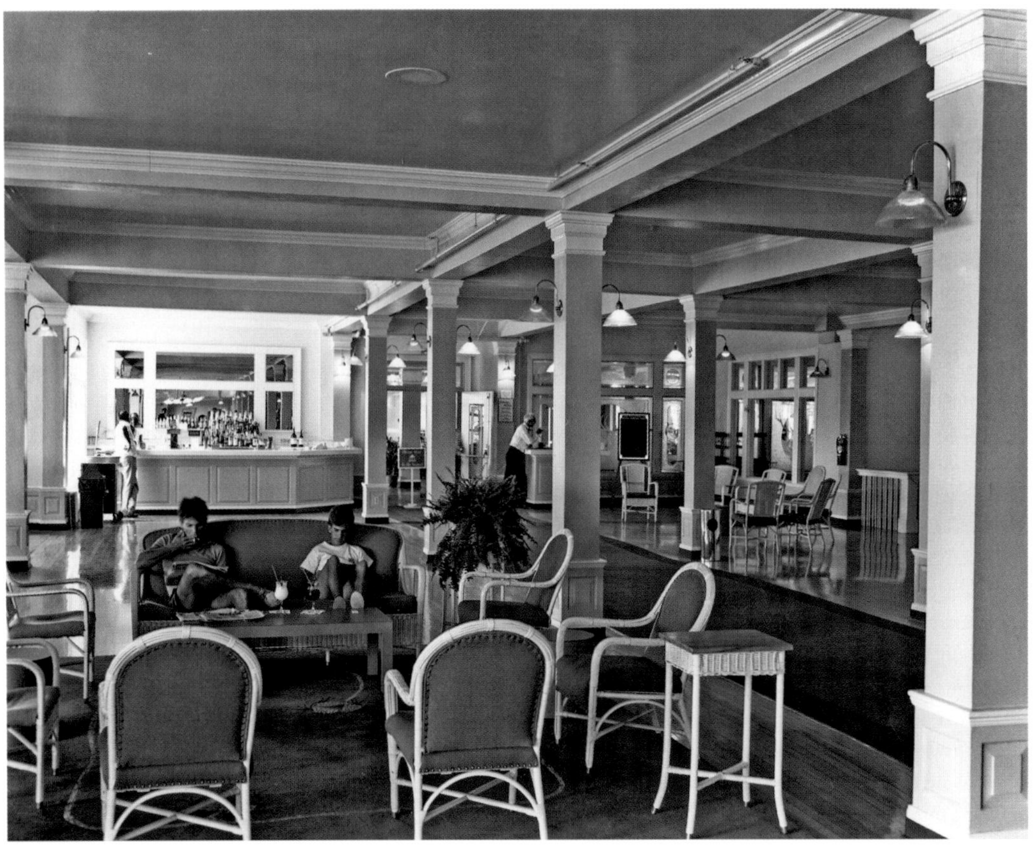

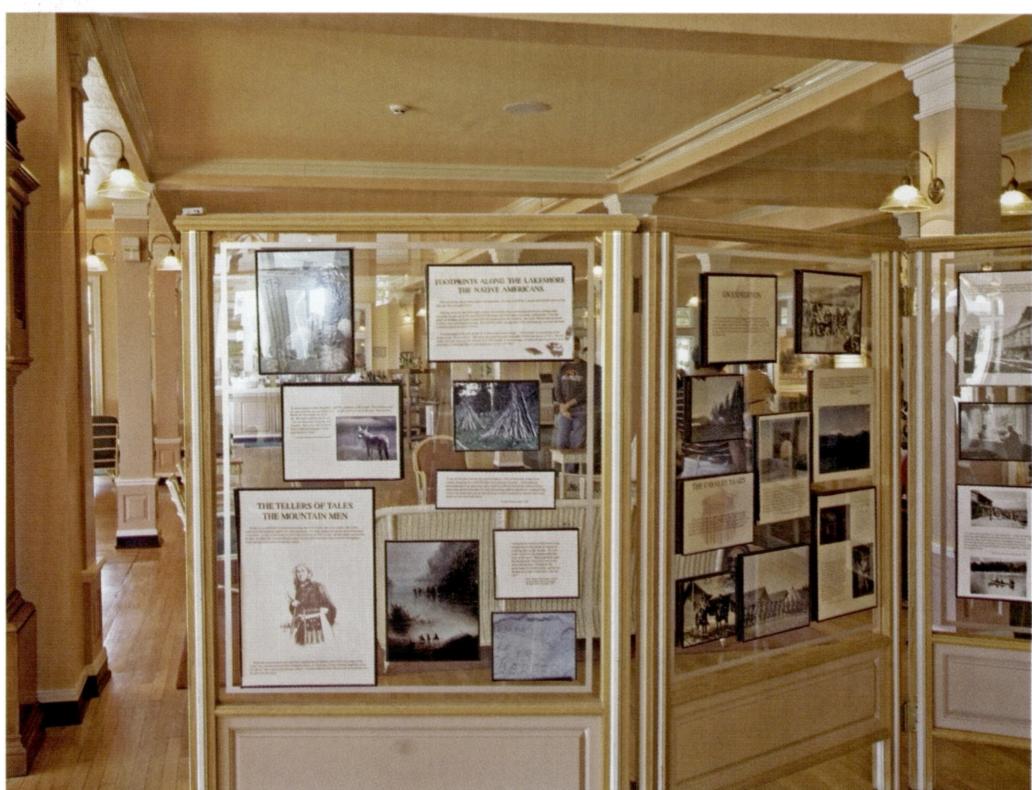

106. #3004

Lake Hotel Lobby, 1907, 1988, 2007
GPS COORDINATES: 44 32.98833N, 110 24.009167W

Robert C. Reamer remodeled the interior of the Lake Hotel in 1923–24. The redwood paneling and posts seen in Stimson's 1907 photo were painted white, and new furniture was installed. In addition, a sunroom and dining room were added.

When I rephotographed the hotel in 1988, the renovators had completed their work indoors, although construction crews still worked outside. The lobby was a delight. A new color scheme was in place, yet the basic layout seemed about the same. Sun poured in from the south. Lake views could be seen through the many windows to the left. A pianist was playing classical music. A close look even shows the same front desk at the rear.

Expecting to find essentially the same view in 2007, I was surprised to find a large, multi-panel display screen blocking my view. Somewhat ironically, the object blocking my efforts to show the history of the hotel through rephotographs was being used to show the history of the hotel! I told the hotel's manager what I was doing and asked whether it might be possible to move the screen for a few minutes so I could make my shot. I was told that the National Park Service owned the screen and that the manager worked for the Park Concessionaire and was therefore not allowed to touch it. Slightly annoyed by unwittingly having fallen into some kind of ongoing fight between the Park Service and the Park Concessionaire, I thought I would skip this rephotograph because I really could not see anything. Then I thought more about it.

I soon realized that rephotography is all about shooting something from a predetermined point and that the rephotographer should be open enough to capture whatever happened to be in the view from that vantage point at that time. Now I needed that panel in place just as it was. So rather than simply showing the same scene twenty years later, I had an image that presented insight into the ongoing relationship between the National Park Service and its concessionaire. To put it another way, I had been able to use a historical display that blocked my view as a window into the complicated history of our national parks.

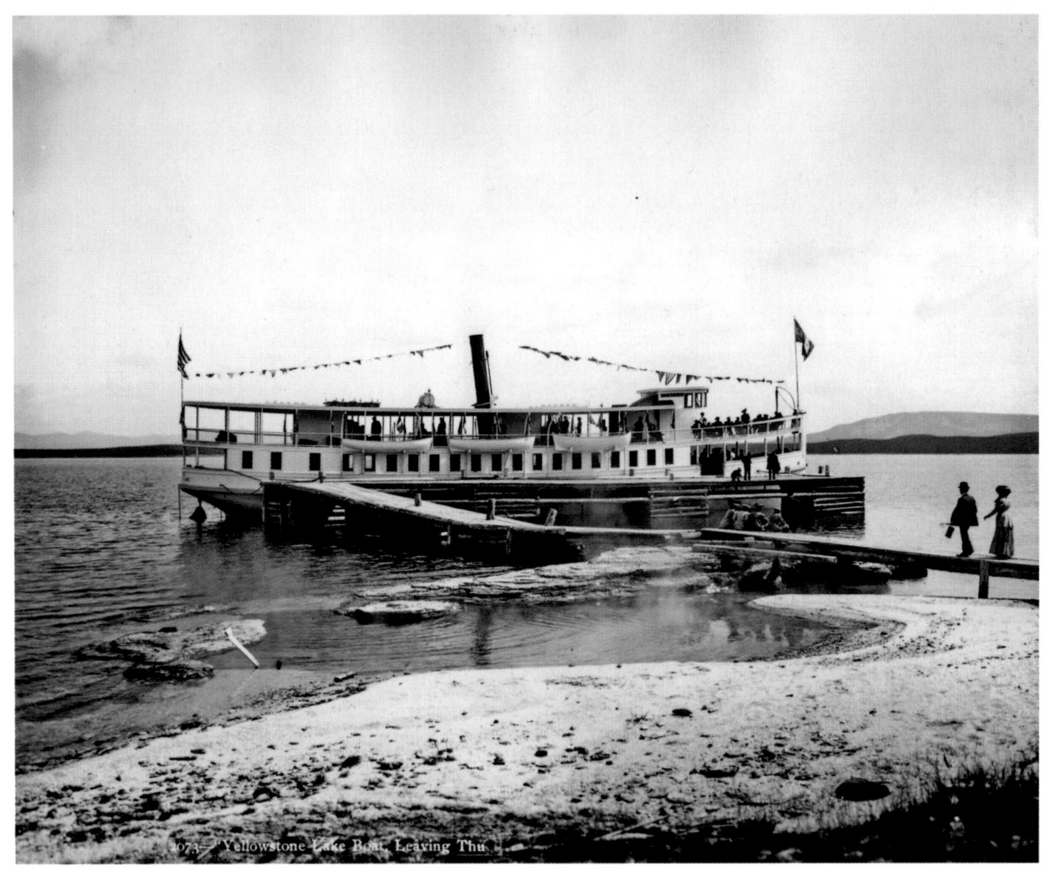
2073— "Yellowstone Lake Boat, Leaving Thu

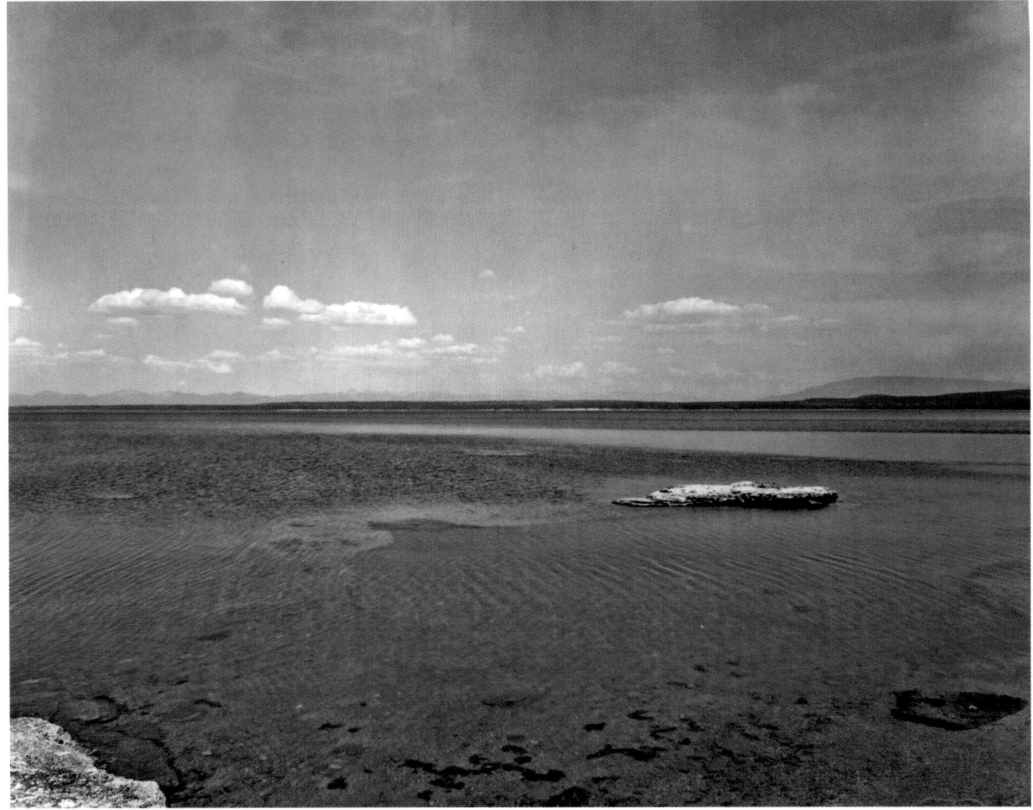

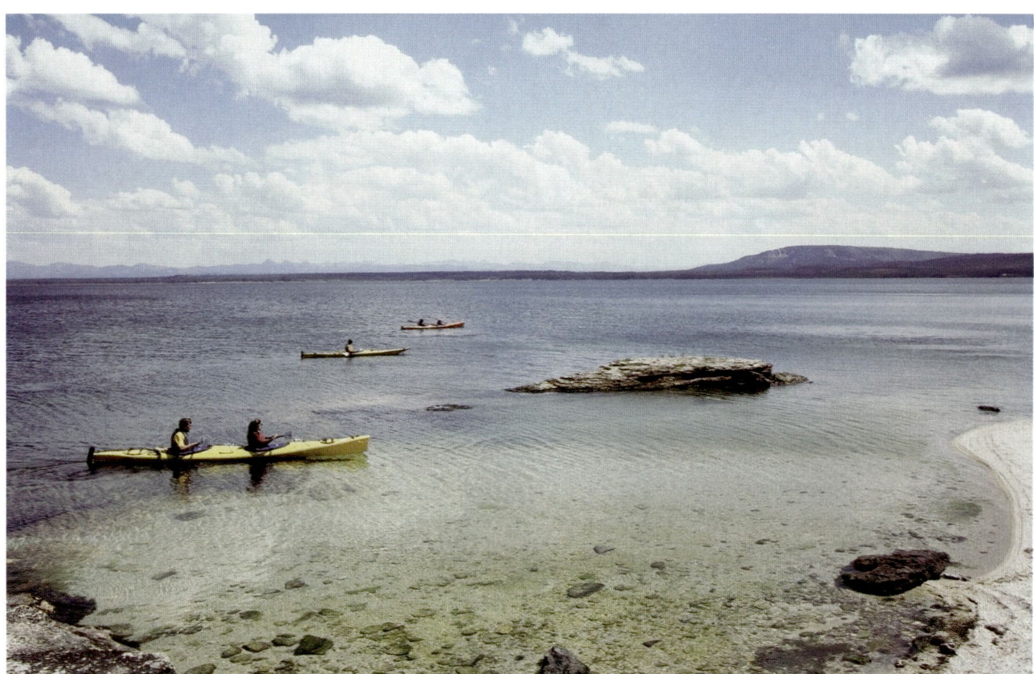

107. #2073

Yellowstone Lake Boat Leaving West Thumb, 1907, 1988, 2007
GPS COORDINATES: 44 24.9635N, 110 34.17467W

Before automobiles arrived in the park in 1916, horse-drawn coaches provided the most common form of transportation in Yellowstone. According to most accounts, these excursions were very dusty. Tourists traveling from Old Faithful could stop here at a lunch station and then continue by coach or, alternatively, take a boat trip from West Thumb to the Lake Hotel. The steamboat *Zillah* had been brought from the Great Lakes to Yellowstone in 1889 and transported up to 125 tourists at a time. Tourists could also tour the lake or go out to see a small zoo on Dot Island.

Stimson's photograph shows the boat at the West Thumb dock in 1907. A quick head count indicates about 50 people visible. This image is finely composed. Stimson used the couple walking onto the plank at right to lead the viewer to the four others sitting in front of them and then to the many people on the boat. It is also an important historical document, visually showing early-twentieth-century mass transportation in the park.

The excursion boats to the Dot Island zoo ended in 1907 when the park superintendent ordered that the animals be freed and the zoo closed. The introduction of automobiles into the park in 1916 undercut mass transportation forms like steamboats, as tourists sought freedom and independence through their own cars. The lake cruises stopped and the boat was scrapped, its boilers moved to the Lake Hotel to provide steam heat. By the time I photographed the location in 1988, the dock and gangplank were long gone. Rising lake waters had covered most of this formation, though its shape can be discerned underwater.

Nineteen years later, I again found this site at the south end of the West Thumb Geyser Basin near Lakeside Spring. As I started to take the photograph, five kayakers paddled their way through my rephotograph. I learned that visitors could rent two-person sea kayaks nearby for about $100 for a three-hour guided tour.

These images are remarkable because they show the transformation in tourism over the past century. In 1907, when Stimson visited, tourism was a group activity in which travelers used public transportation forms like coaches and the *Zillah* to enjoy Yellowstone. One hundred years later, tourism has become a personal activity—like personal computers and iPods—so travelers take small water craft on their own lake tours.

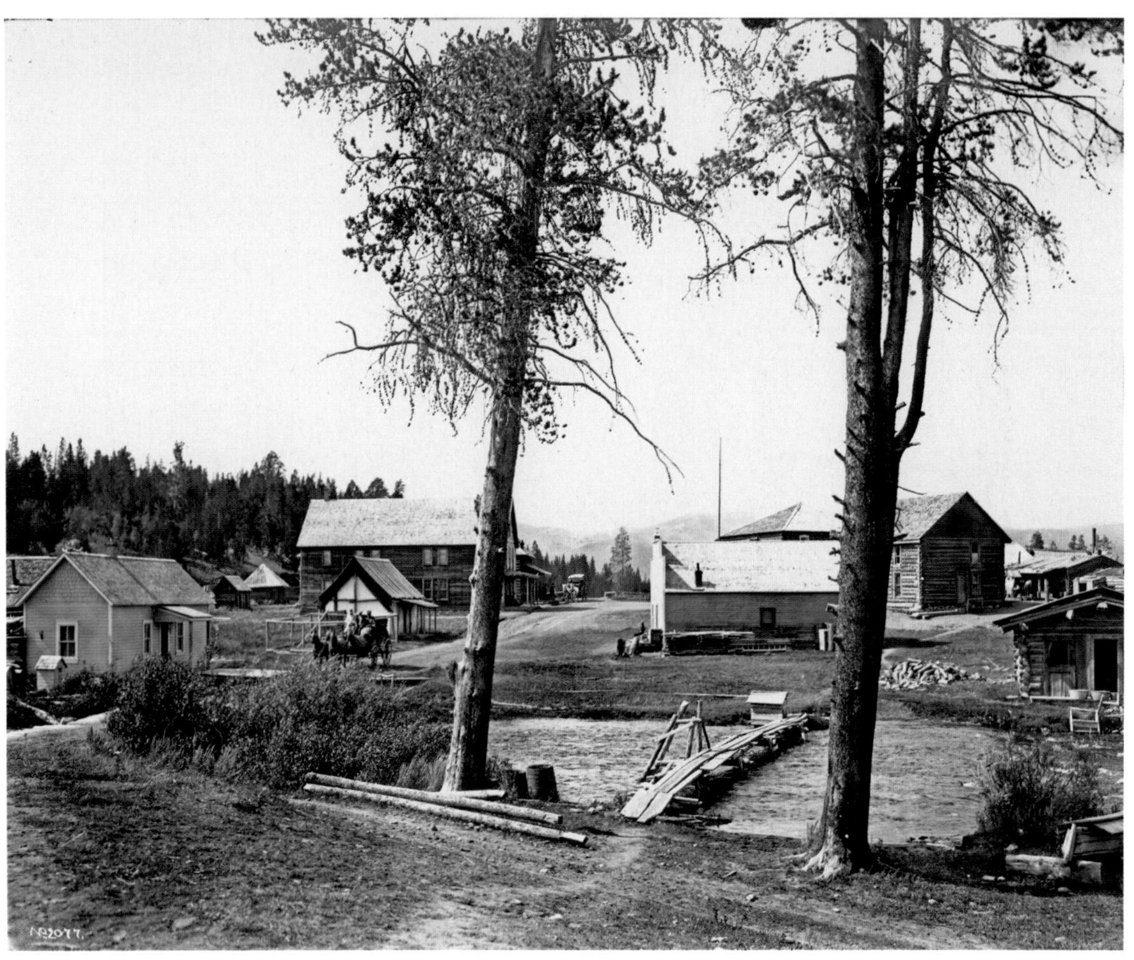

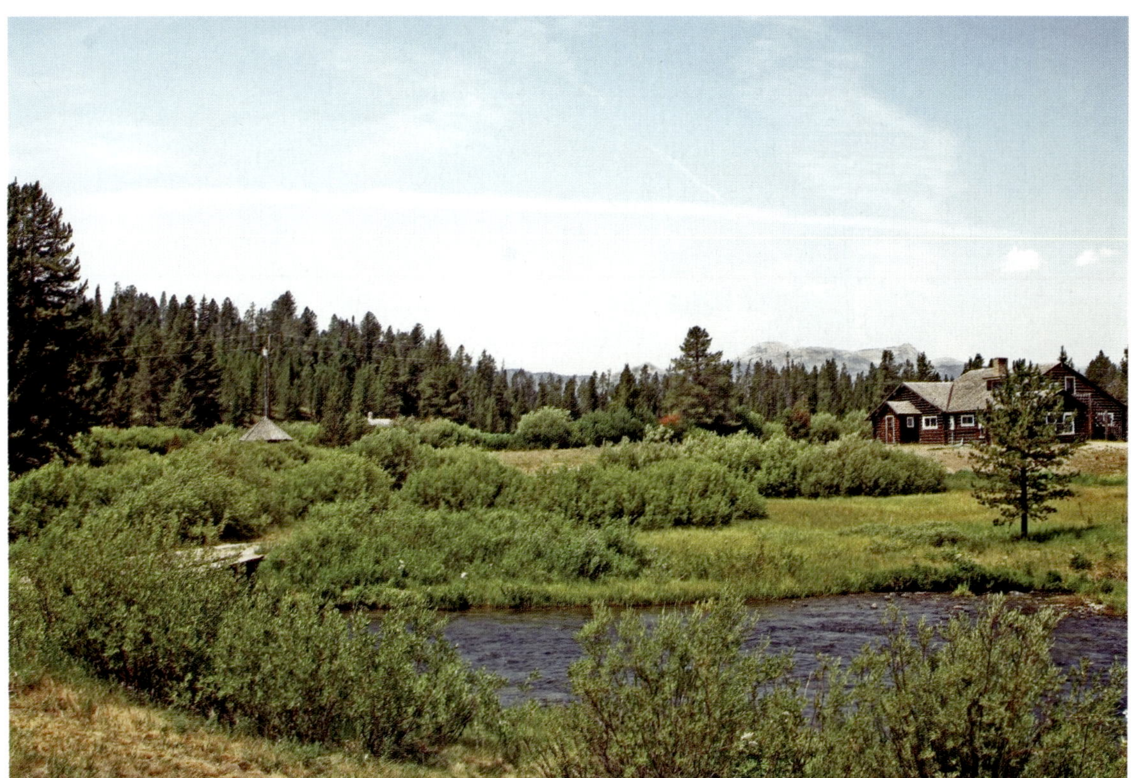

108. #2077

Dwelle's Inn, West Yellowstone, Montana, 1907, 2007
GPS COORDINATES: 44 40.435167N, 111 11.809W

Dwelle's Inn is a favorite rephotograph of mine, and it isn't even in Wyoming. In the Stimson catalog, this photograph is listed as "Devillies Inn." After some research, I learned that it was actually Dwelle's Inn and had been located on the Madison River near what is today West Yellowstone, Montana. After spending the night in West Yellowstone, Lauren and I searched for the site. Each time we got close, we found a locked gate and a "no trespassing, Madison Fork Ranch" sign. Finally finding the ranch headquarters, we passed more such signs and discovered the delightful Cici Ives, owner of the Madison Fork Ranch, the former site of Dwelle's Inn. Cici told us the history of the site and showed us around the property, helping me locate Stimson's vantage point to make my rephotograph.

Like the previous image of West Thumb, Dwelle's Inn represents one of those fascinating places, discussed in chapter 3, that transition from a sacred landscape to profane landscape almost overnight. Henry Dwelle arrived in Montana in the early 1880s and established a ranch on the Madison Fork about 5 miles west of the park. In 1884 he built a stage stop for coaches going into Yellowstone from Beaver, Idaho. In 1898, when the Union Pacific built further north to Monida, Montana, Dwelle's Inn became an overnight stop on the Monida and Yellowstone Stage Line, operated by the famous park photographer and entrepreneur Frank J. Haynes. For the next decade, Dwelle's was one of those sacred park places everyone who arrived from the West experienced. In 1908, the Union Pacific built to the park's boundary and created West Yellowstone. The following year, Dwelle's ceased operations. Several attempts were made to operate a fishing resort known as the Grayling Inn, but nothing was ever as popular as Dwelle's. It had become part of the profane landscape.

Stimson's photograph is a marvelous document of the inn at its peak. A close examination shows one coach arriving to pick up a large group of waiting tourists while another is bound for the park. It also shows Dwelle's extensive buildings, including the large two-story log building with windows behind the team of horses at center, known as "George."

In my 2007 rephotograph, the only building that remains is the small octagonal building behind "George." The ridge line (and its tall tree) and Madison Fork confirm the vantage point and the feeling of being in a ghost landscape.

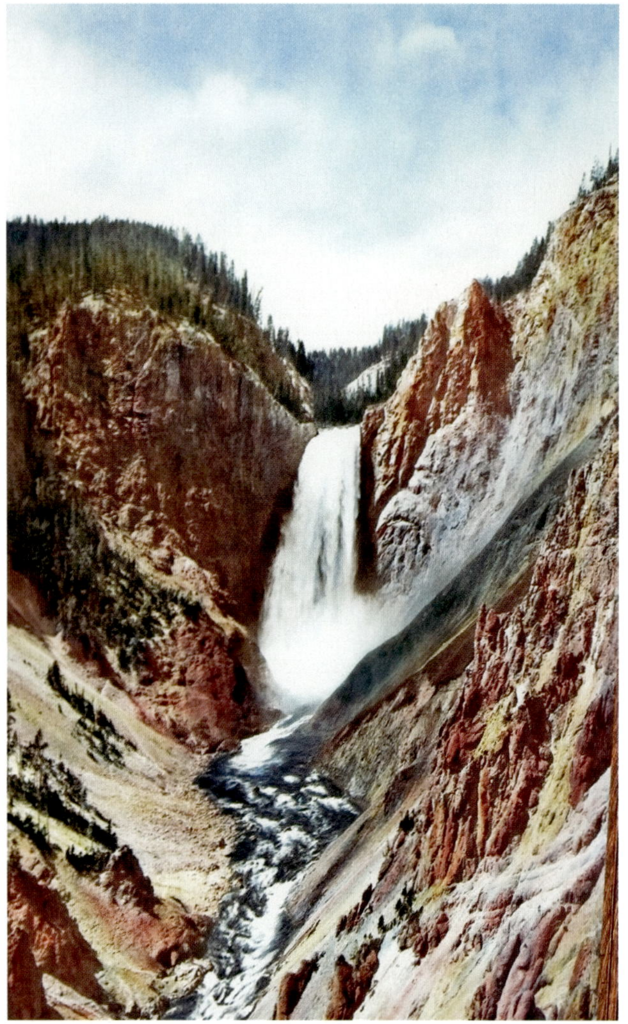

109. #308

Yellowstone Falls (Grand View), 1915, 1988, 2007
GPS COORDINATES: 44 43.16833N, 110 29.441W

The Lower Falls of the Yellowstone River is 308 feet tall—twice as high as Niagara Falls—and marks the beginning of the Grand Canyon of the Yellowstone River. The volume of water passing over the brink makes it the largest waterfall in the Rocky Mountains. With its forest background and yellow-tinted canyon, the falls is truly one of the most sublime features of the park.

Stimson first photographed the Lower Falls in 1902 and included it as the first image in his portfolio of albertypes called *Yellowstone Park* the following year. As he often did, Stimson printed numerous photographs of this image, including this enlargement, which he hand-tinted around 1915. Today it hangs in the Wyoming State Capitol Building in Cheyenne. In the photograph, Stimson is looking straight at the falls, probably from the vantage point known today as Grand View Point. His hand-tinted image, produced from memory, looks realistic, with the trees painted green, the water blue, and the canyon a combination of mostly yellows and reds.

To rephotograph from this vantage point in 1988 and again in 2007, I traveled to the north rim of the canyon and hiked down a trail to Grand View Point. I could easily discern the camera station as Stimson's and marveled at how well his colors matched the reality of the location. A close examination also shows the next vantage point, Brink of Falls, just to the right at the top of the falls. Most interesting, in 1988 I noticed a pine tree starting to grow into the viewpoint. Nineteen years later, my 2007 rephotograph confirms it and makes me wonder whether the National Park Service will eventually cut down that tree to preserve the view or allow it to grow and effectively block the view from this point. Perhaps another rephotography project in twenty years will answer my question.

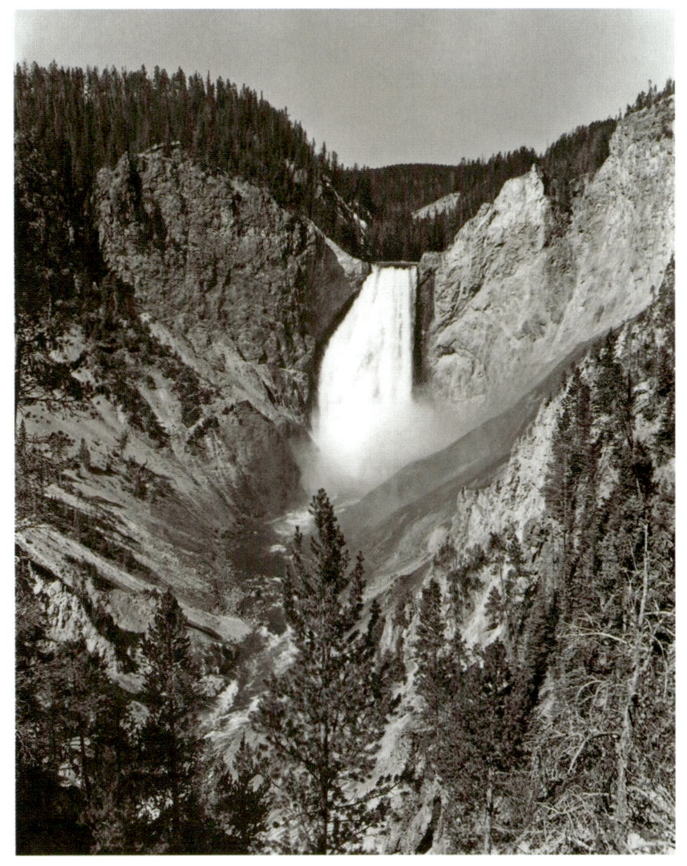

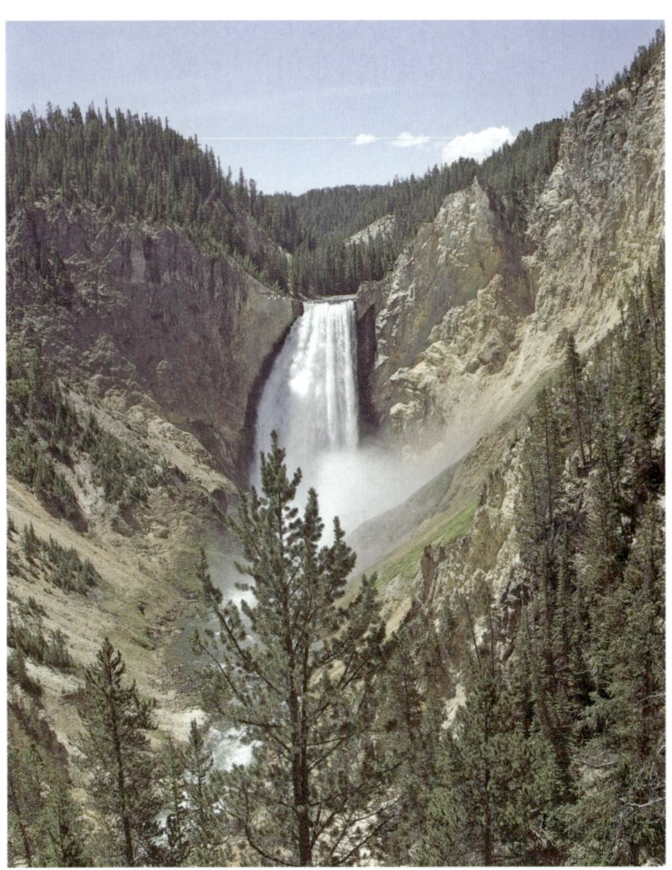

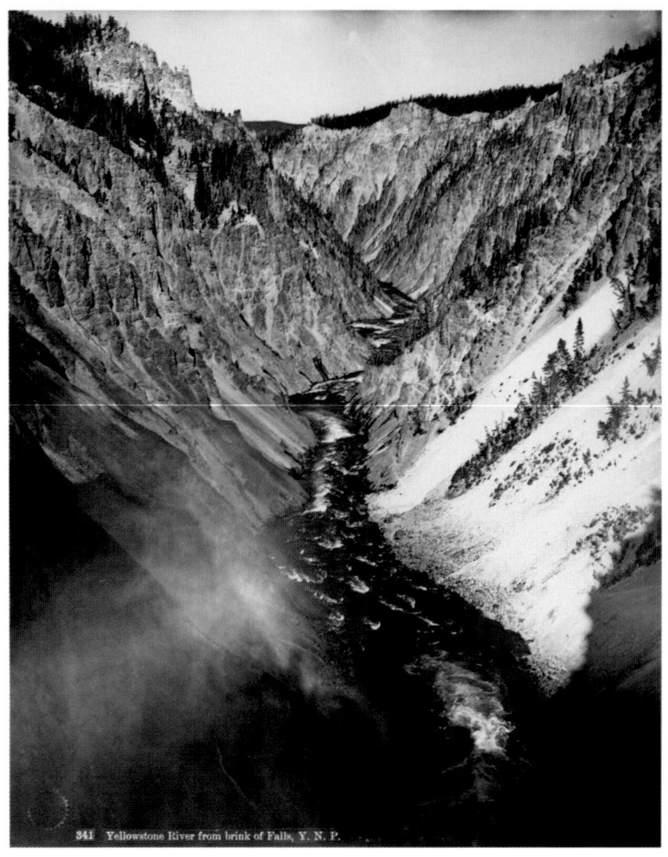
341   Yellowstone River from brink of Falls, Y. N. P.

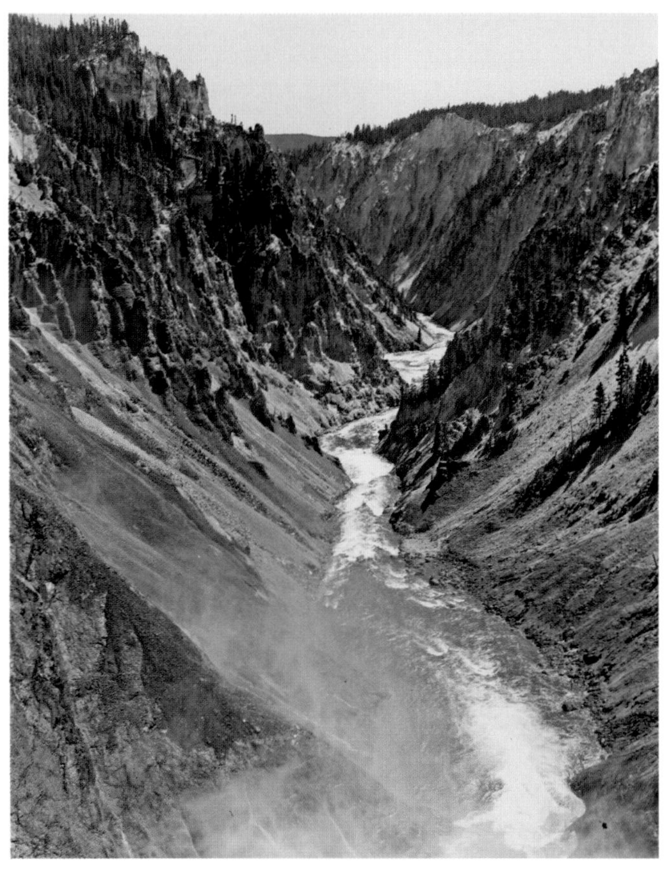

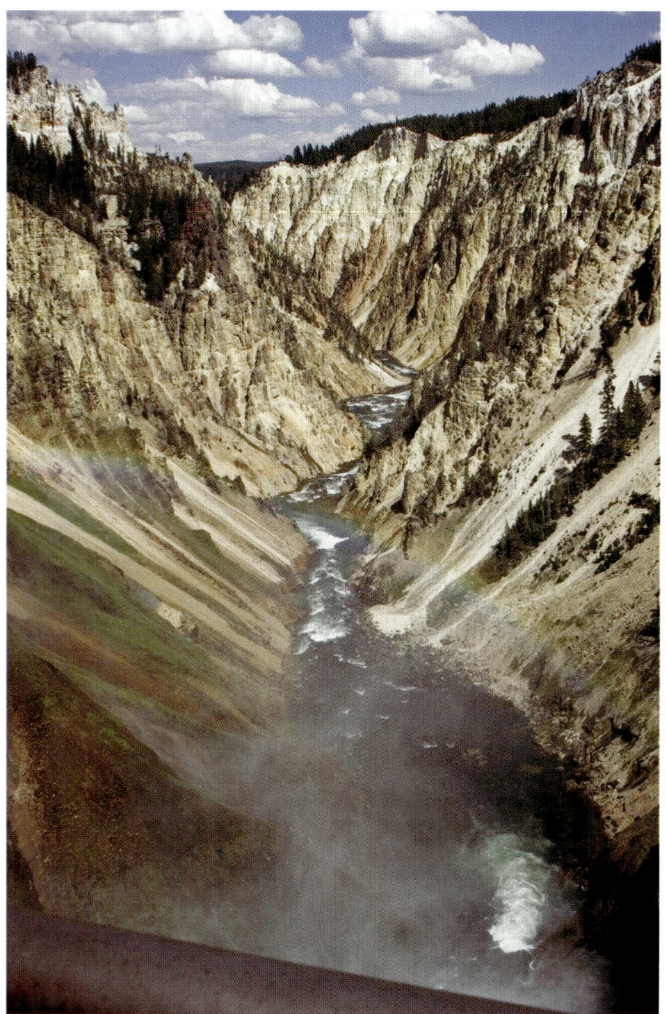

110. #341

Yellowstone River from the Falls (Brink of Falls), 1902, 1988, 2007
GPS COORDINATES: 44 43.087833N, 110 29.778833W

Brink of Falls is located on the north canyon wall at the very top of the Lower Falls. It is an amazing place to be, as anywhere from 5,000 to 63,000 gallons of water per second rush by and fall 308 feet into the canyon below, then begin working their way through the beautifully tinted Grand Canyon of the Yellowstone. To reach the spot, one has to hike down a steep, winding path that drops 600 feet in a third of a mile.

Stimson photographed this view in 1902 and included a copy of it as an albertype in his 1903 *Yellowstone Park* portfolio. I reached the spot in 1988 and again in 2007, following the same path Stimson used and landing at the same vantage point. I patiently waited my turn among the many tourists to get to the edge for my rephotograph. In many ways, this view is probably one of the easiest rephotographs I ever made because there's only one route to the location and a limited space from which to photograph. While we might also assume that it's one of the sites with the fewest changes, close examination of my two rephotographs shows several new trails and viewing locations created since Stimson made his photograph.

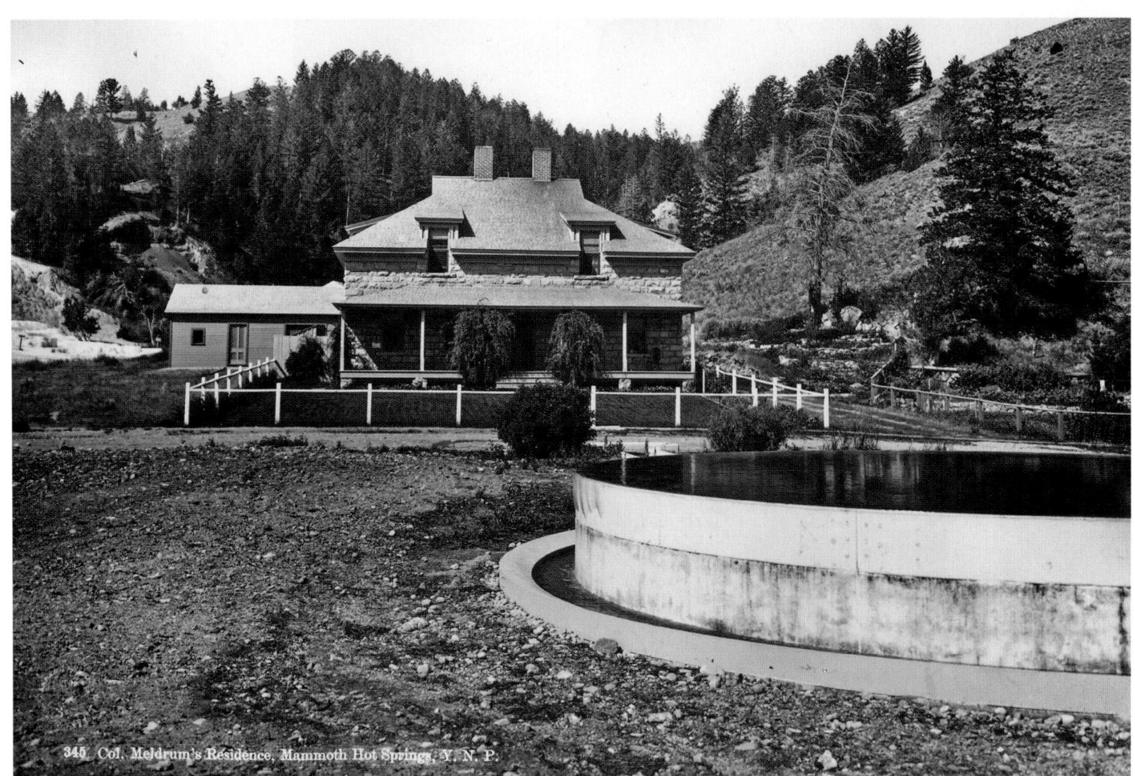

345. Col. Meldrum's Residence, Mammoth Hot Springs, Y. N. P.

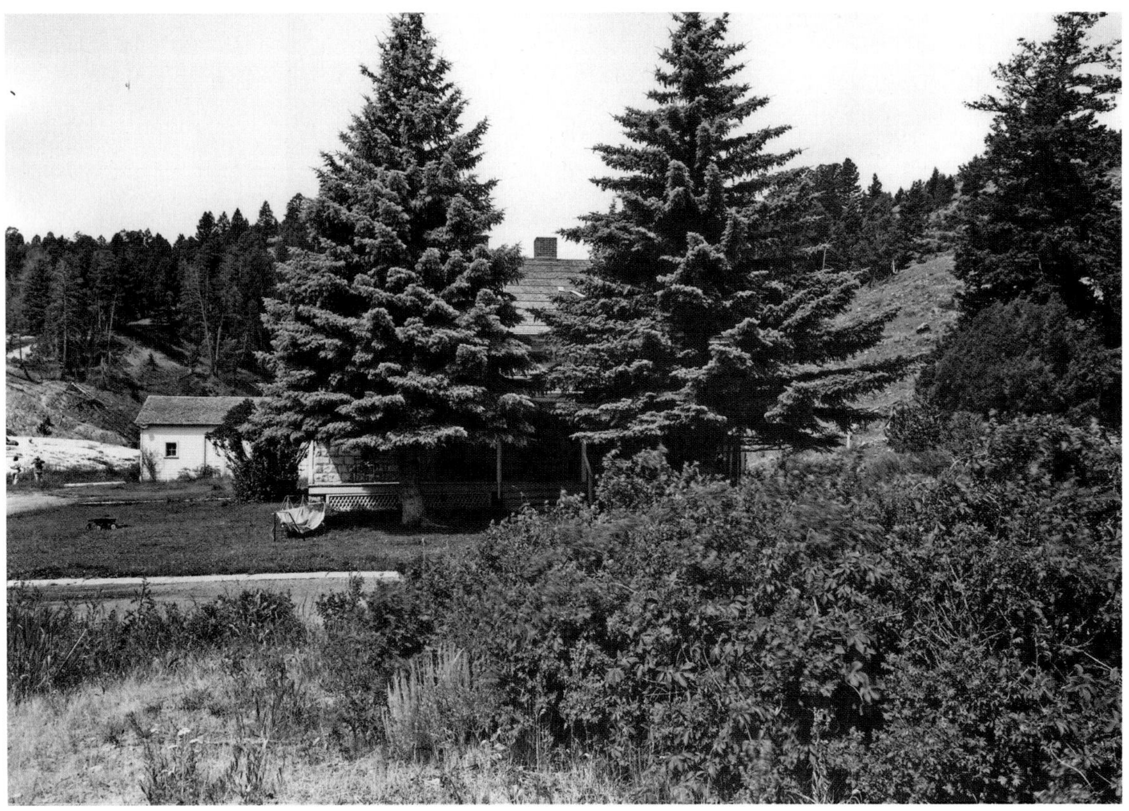

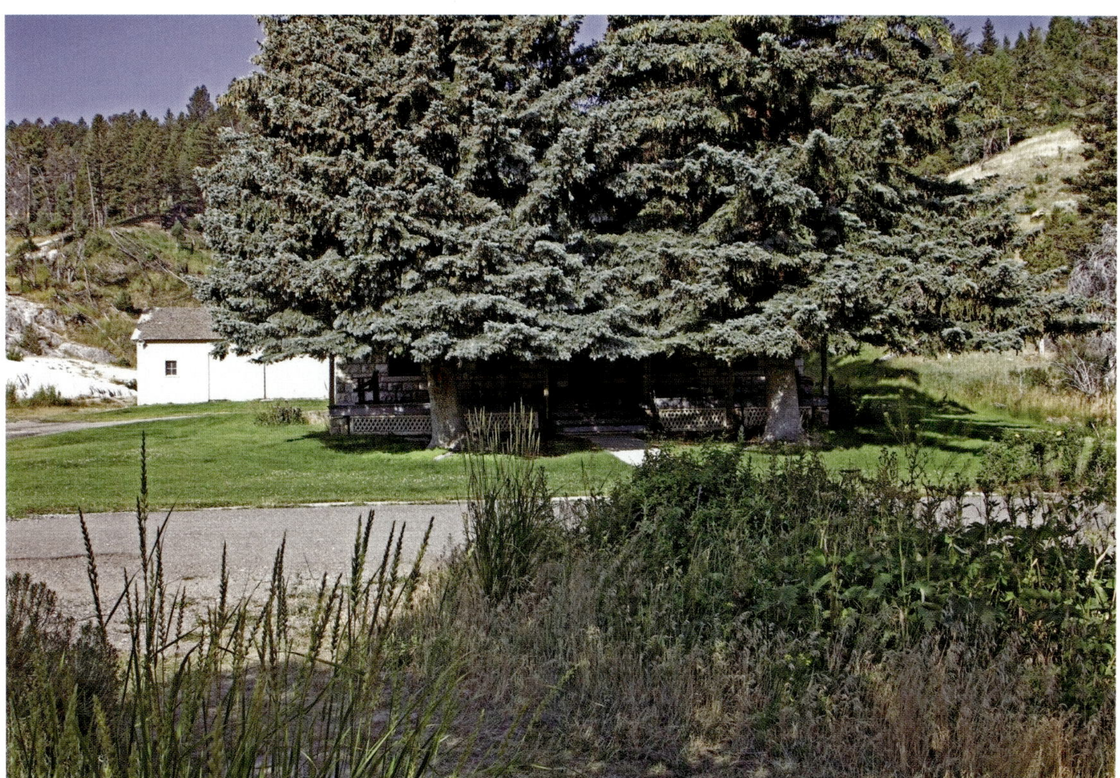

Col. Meldrum's Residence, Mammoth Hot Springs, Y.N.P., 1902, 1988, 2007
GPS COORDINATES: 44 58.425167N, 110 42.27133W

Most tourists to Yellowstone have no idea that there is a US Federal Magistrate Court with a judge whose jurisdiction is the national park. This court system hears cases involving such things as poaching, illegal trespassing, theft, illegal drug sales, and the like. In fact, Yellowstone has had such an office since the 1894 National Park Protective Act established a commissioner, now called the magistrate, to reside permanently in the park. Interestingly, in the 120 years since its creation, the park has had only eight magistrates. Apparently, they all liked their job and stayed around.

This Stimson house portrait was taken during the photographer's first visit to the park in 1902. It is described as Col. Meldrum's Residence, Mammoth Hot Springs, and represents the home, office, and jail of the first magistrate, John H. Meldrum. It is located just north of the Mammoth Hot Springs Terrace. Setting the standard for longevity in office, Meldrum was appointed to the post in 1894 and remained until 1935. The pool at right was probably a thermal spring.

My rephotographs in 1988 and 2007 show the house overwhelmed by two very large spruce trees not present in the Stimson view. In addition, the thermal spring out front has been capped and the pool removed. By 2007, a small streetlamp had been added to the area. Because its location is so close to the tourist spots at Mammoth, perhaps the large trees help hide this private residence. Each time I photographed it for this project, other tourists wandered over to where I was, took their own pictures, and often walked up to the house, assuming it was part of the tour.

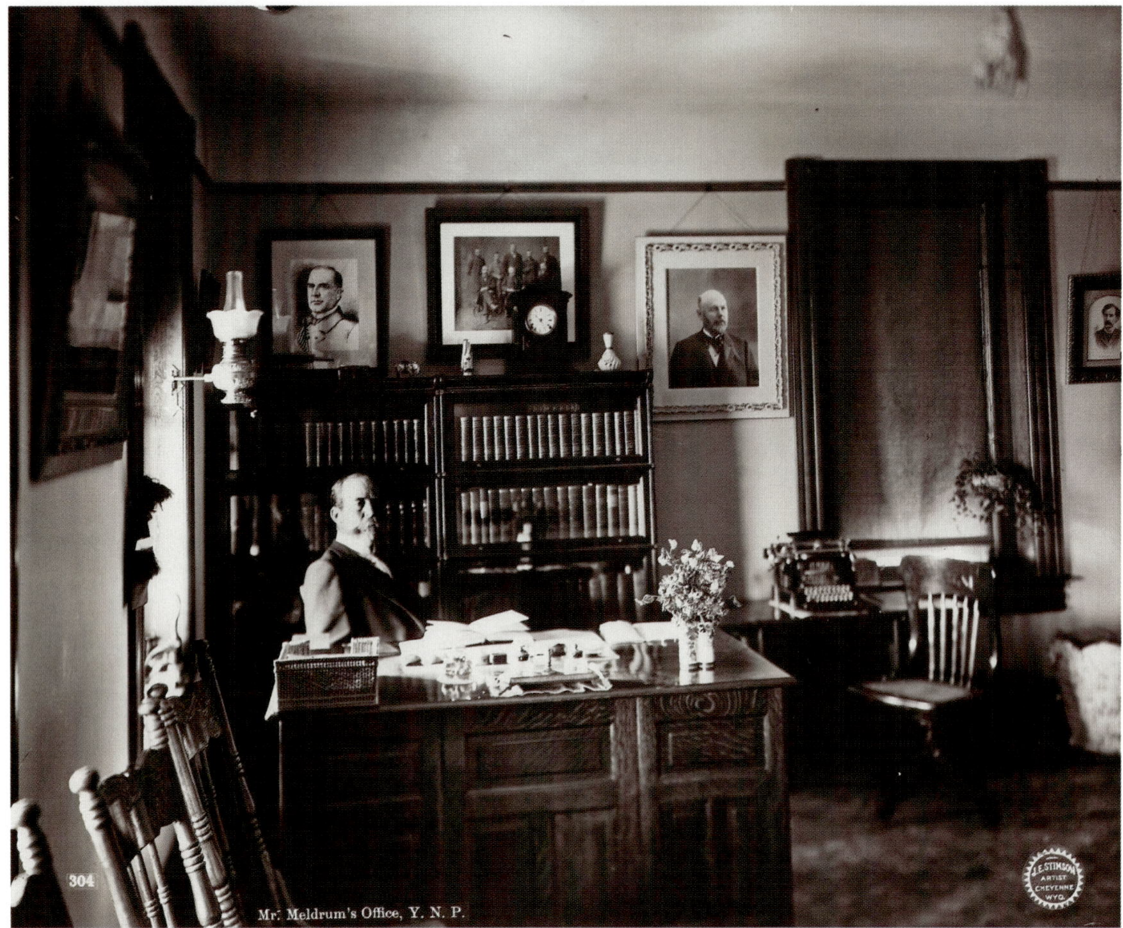

112. #304

Mr. Meldrum's Office, Y.N.P. [Magistrate Judge Stephen Cole in his den], 1902, 1988, 2008
GPS COORDINATES: 44 58.41967N, 110 42.295833W

Another of my favorite rephotographs is this set showing the interior of the magistrate's house pictured in the previous photograph. As discussed throughout this project, interior views are rare in the Stimson collection. This image shows Colonel John H. Meldrum sitting at his desk, which was located immediately to the left as one entered the house. In addition to his desk, law books, and typewriter, Meldrum has pictures of Wyoming governor Joseph M. Carey and the late president William McKinley.

When I visited the site in 1988, I walked up to the front door, rang the bell, and talked to the woman who answered about what I was doing and asked whether I could take a photograph of the office. She informed me that the office and jail had long ago been moved out of the house and that the room was used as their den. She also showed me the bathroom that had been built where the jail once stood. I marveled at the bathroom with bars on the window. Wanting to show how the scene had changed, I asked if I could repeat the photograph, and she allowed me to shoot it. My 1988 photograph shows a fairly typical late 1980s Wyoming home, complete with sofa, hi-fi, and western painting.

Before I returned to the site in 2008, I called ahead and made arrangements with Magistrate Judge Stephen A. Cole. In the post-9/11 world, such security is required. Judge Cole spent an hour showing Lauren and me around the house and answering my questions. He told me that he, too, had served a long time in Yellowstone, having been appointed to the position in 1981. He then told me that he remembered me as a University of Wyoming basketball player in the early 1980s and that his wife had let me into their house twenty years earlier to photograph their den. When I asked about the room, he told me it had since been remodeled as a small library. The Honorable Stephen A. Cole, magistrate judge, United States District Court for the District of Wyoming, then graciously posed for my rephotograph, standing in the same room in which Stimson photographed Col. John H. Meldrum more than a century earlier.

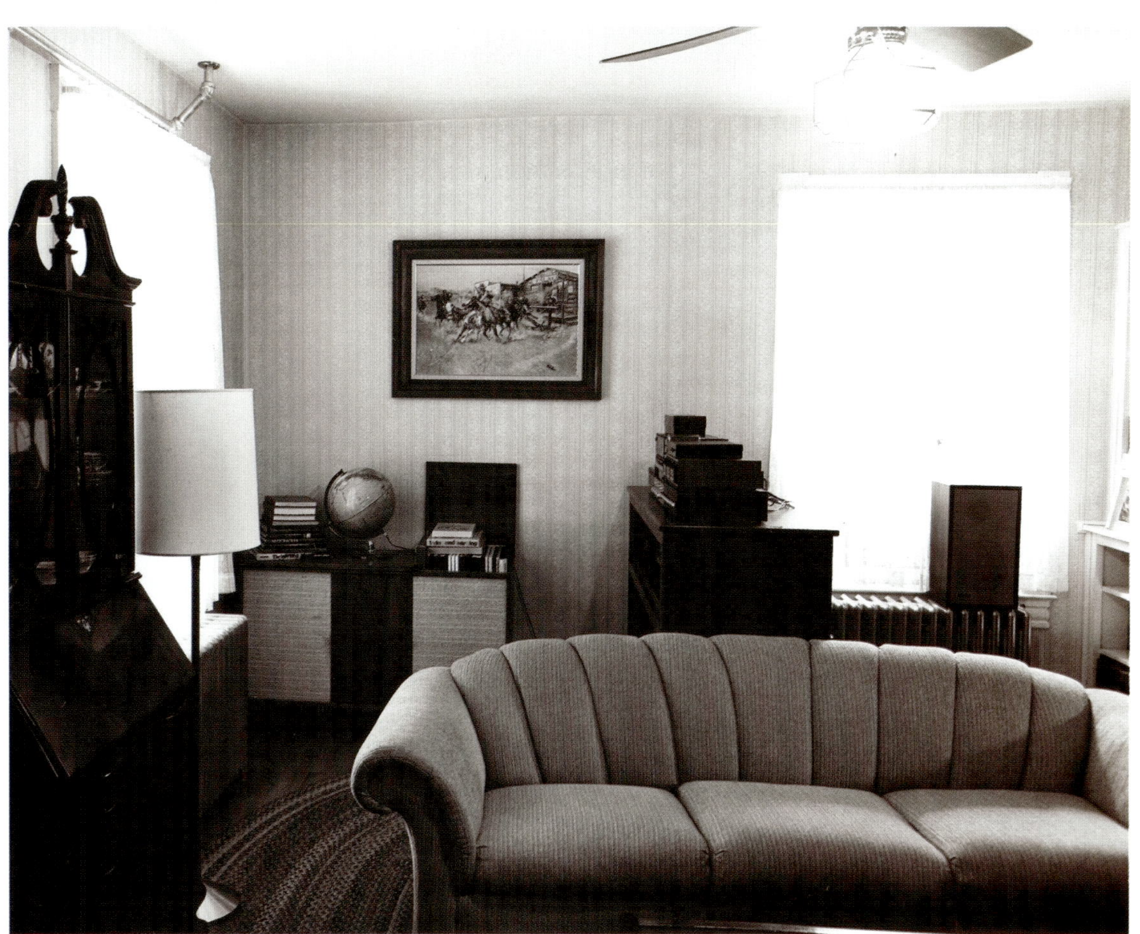

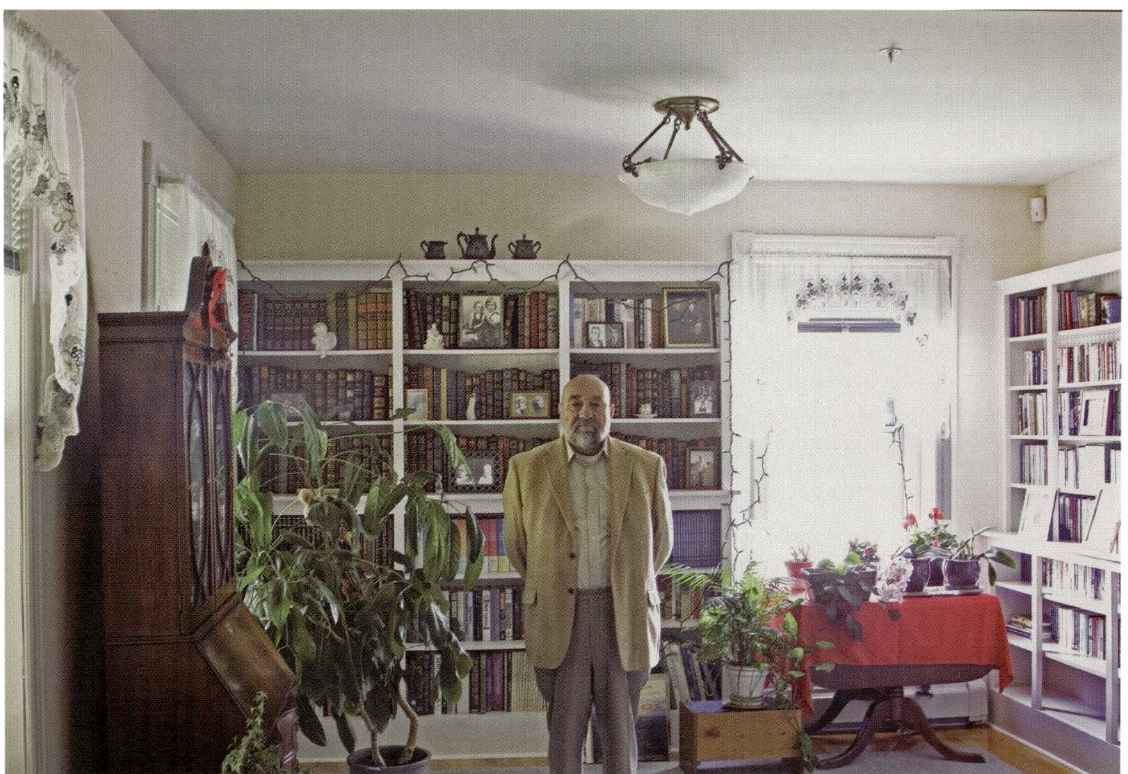

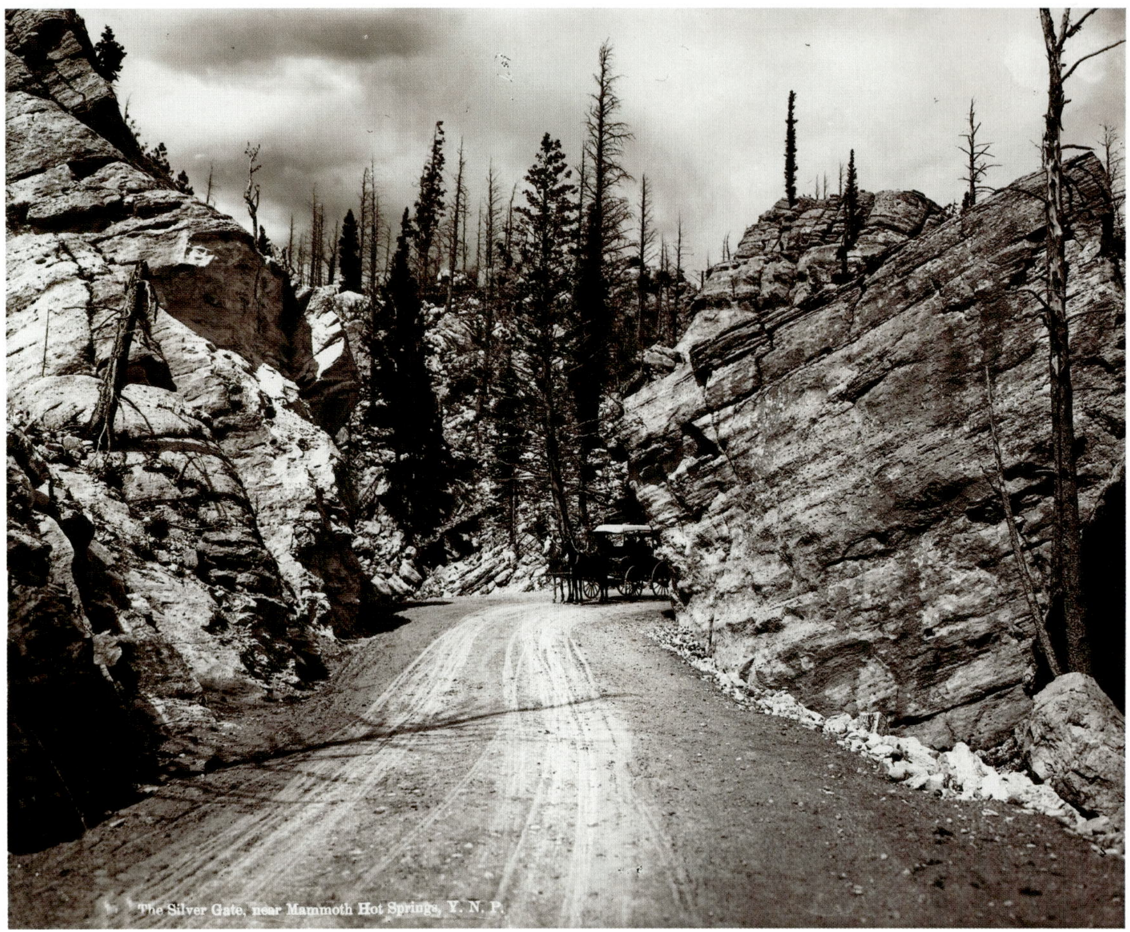

113. #363

The Silver Gate, 1902, 1988, 2007
GPS COORDINATES: 44 56.6295N, 110 43.04433W

This short road is south of Mammoth Hot Springs in a section of large tumbled rocks known as the Hoodoos. Its name, Silver Gate, refers to the drive through the large white boulders and hints at the famous nearby road called the Golden Gate. Stimson's 1902 view is a classic composition, with the large hoodoo rocks framing the road and the horse and buggy captured just as it emerges from around the bend. The burned trees in the background suggest that earlier fires had swept through the area.

I located the vantage point for my 1988 rephotograph along the Mammoth to Norris Road, about three miles south of park headquarters. This road is unnamed, one way, and less than a half mile long. Several picnic tables can be found along it. My vantage point was almost to the junction with the main road and is looking back up the one-way lane. The most important part of my rephotograph, though, is that it shows how well the background forest had rebounded since 1902.

Twenty years later, when I ventured to this spot, I was not sure what I would find. Much of the park had burned in the weeks just after I made my 1988 photographs. I was surprised to find this area seemingly untouched. I got out of the car and had Lauren slowly drive the one-way road in our Subaru Forester to mimic the horse and buggy found in Stimson's picture. It only took three laps to get it right.

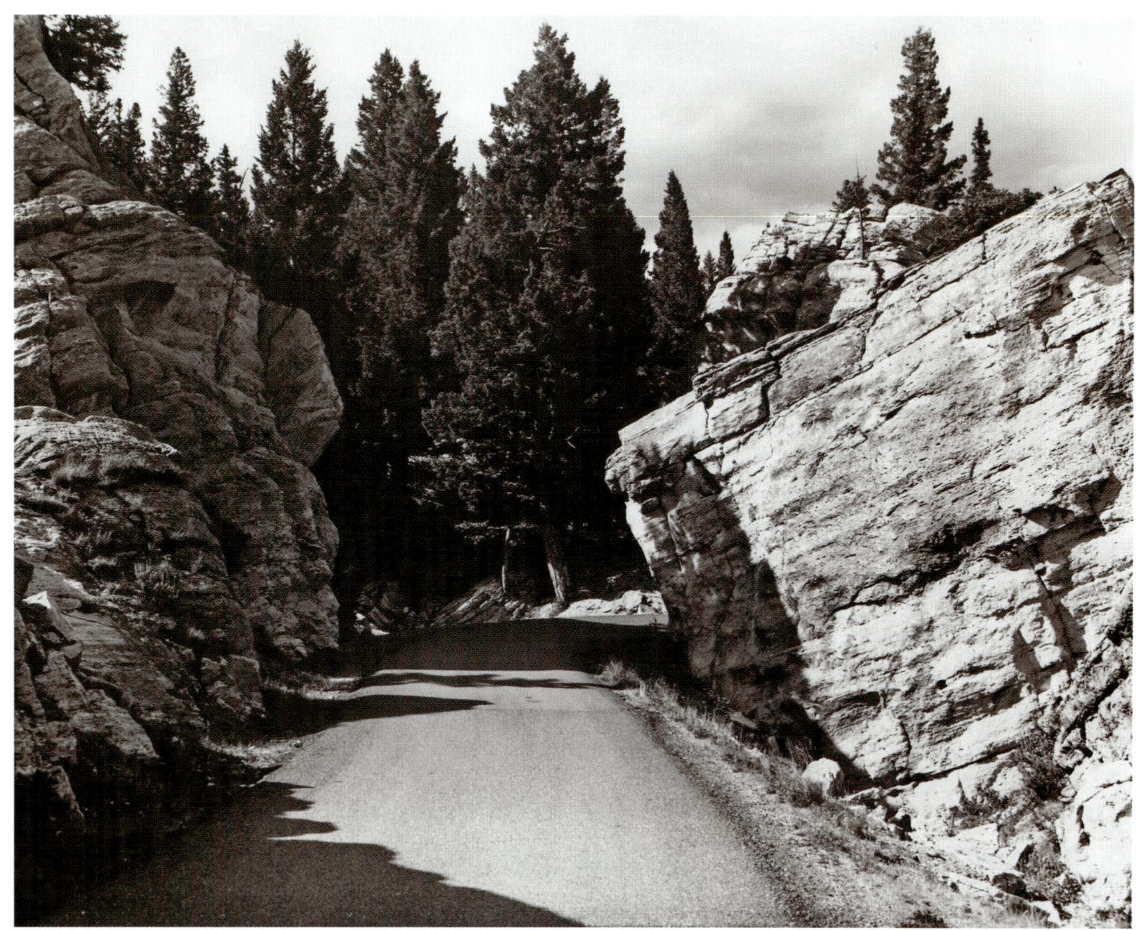

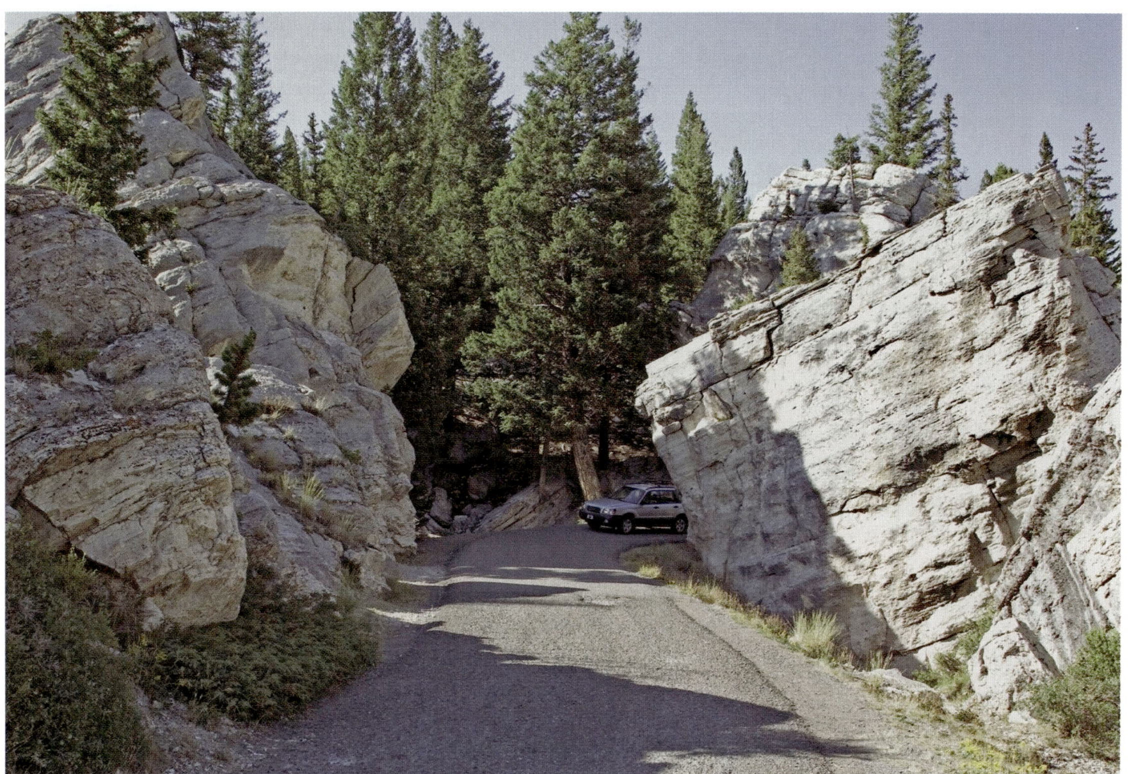

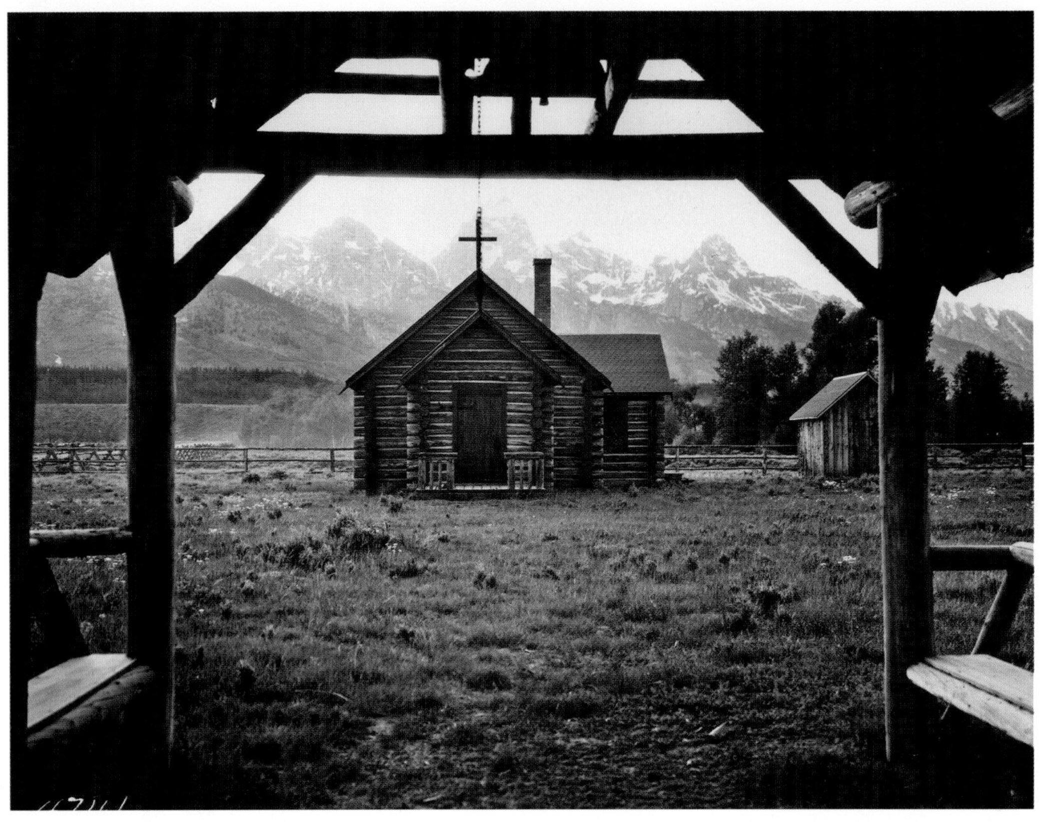

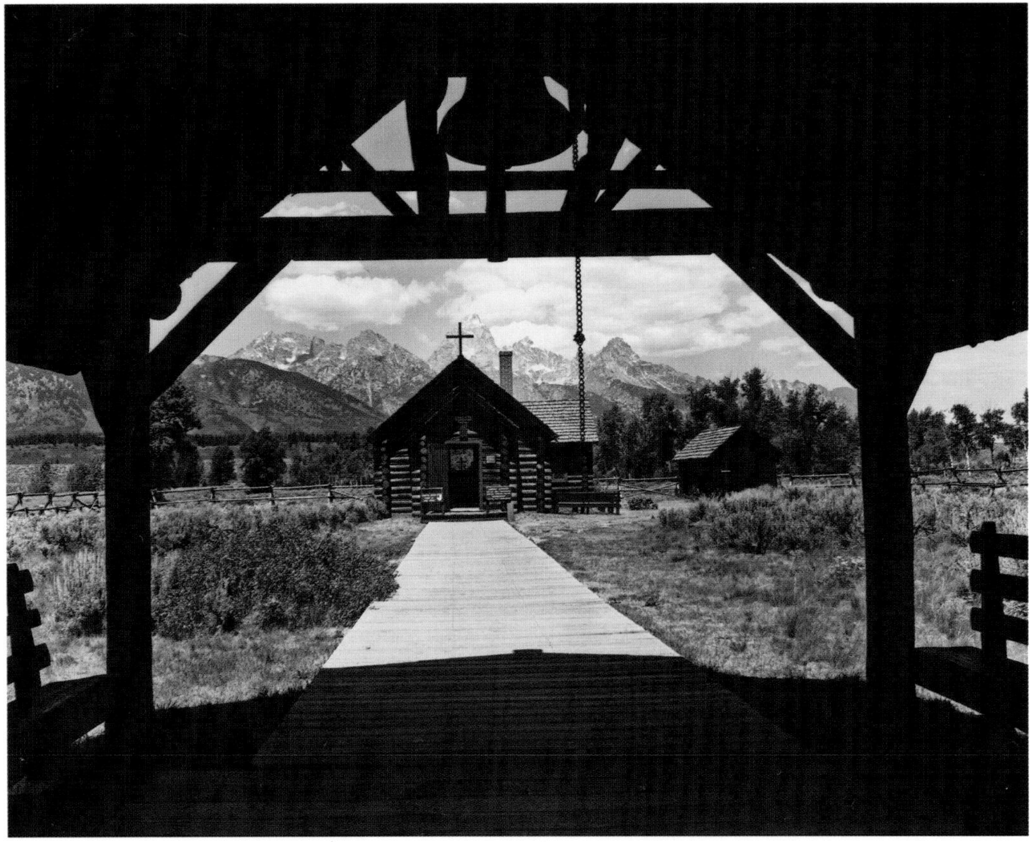

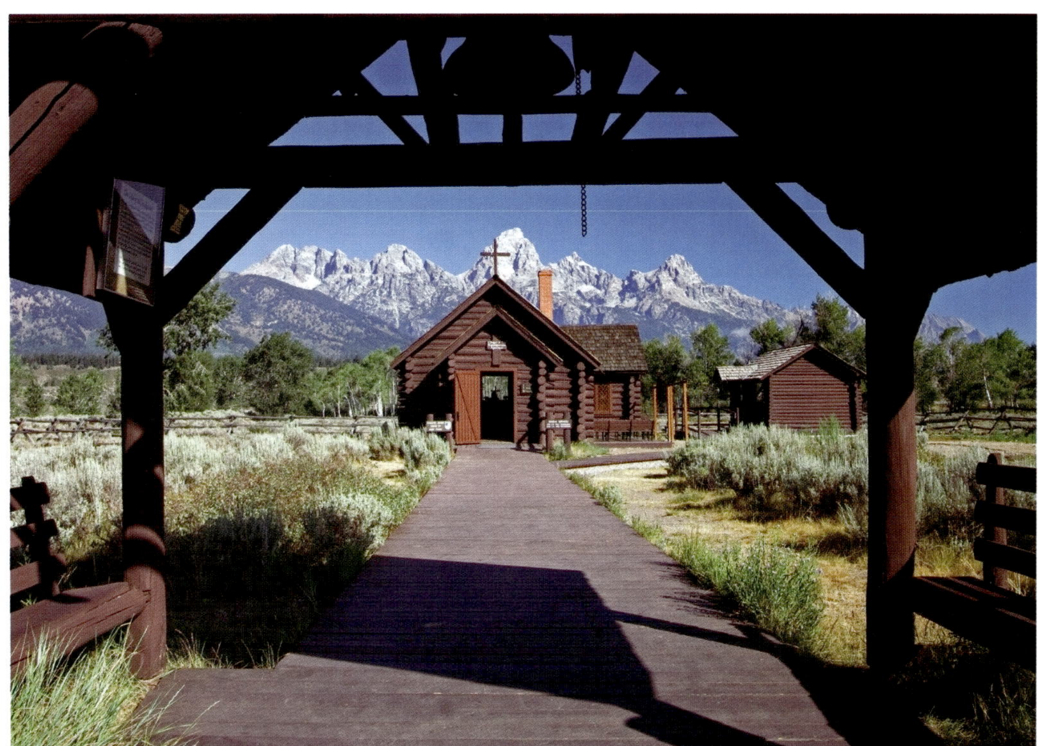

114. #4741

Chapel of Transfiguration, Moose, 1930, 1988, 2007
GPS COORDINATES: 43 39.590833N, 110 42.905W

One of the most spectacular backdrops in the world makes seeing this small log chapel near Moose an unforgettable experience. Constructed in 1924 for locals and guests at nearby dude ranches, the chapel was designed in a rustic style, sometimes called Western Craftsman. The entrance canopy protects a small bell tower and aligns the chapel with a view of the Cathedral Group, a section of peaks in the Tetons. Maude Noble, owner of nearby Menor's Ferry and an influential founder of Grand Teton National Park, donated the land.

Stimson photographed the chapel in 1930 using the entrance canopy to frame the chapel and the Tetons. The bell is visible in the tower above, and a small storage shed is seen to the right. Although he had visited Jackson Hole many times before, his 1930 visit marked the first trip since the creation of Grand Teton National Park. The original park, however, was a narrow stretch that protected only the main mountains. This area around Moose remained in private hands.

In the years after Stimson's visit, locals who wanted to preserve more of the area clamored for less development. At the same time, John D. Rockefeller Jr. began to secretly purchase lands around the park and then donated them to the government for protection. President Franklin D. Roosevelt took over this land in 1943 and created Grand Teton National Monument from it, including the lands around Moose. In 1950, Grand Teton National Park absorbed the monument, and park boundaries finally included the chapel and other nearby historic structures, including Menor's Ferry and the Bar BC dude ranch. In 1963 the chapel served as a focal point in the Henry Fonda movie *Spencer's Mountain*.

For my 1988 rephotograph, I spent almost an hour positioning my camera and tripod in an effort to match the view from the bell canopy, only to find free postcards of the same view available inside. Nineteen years later, my digital camera provided instant feedback, and I rephotographed it quickly.

Both of my rephotographs show that the chapel has been well preserved over the past eight decades. It is clearly a sacred place in every definition of the word: sacred for its religious affiliation, sacred for its glorious, sublime view, and sacred for its history. As discussed in chapter 3, even when it was not part of the national park, the chapel was a protected and sacred place.

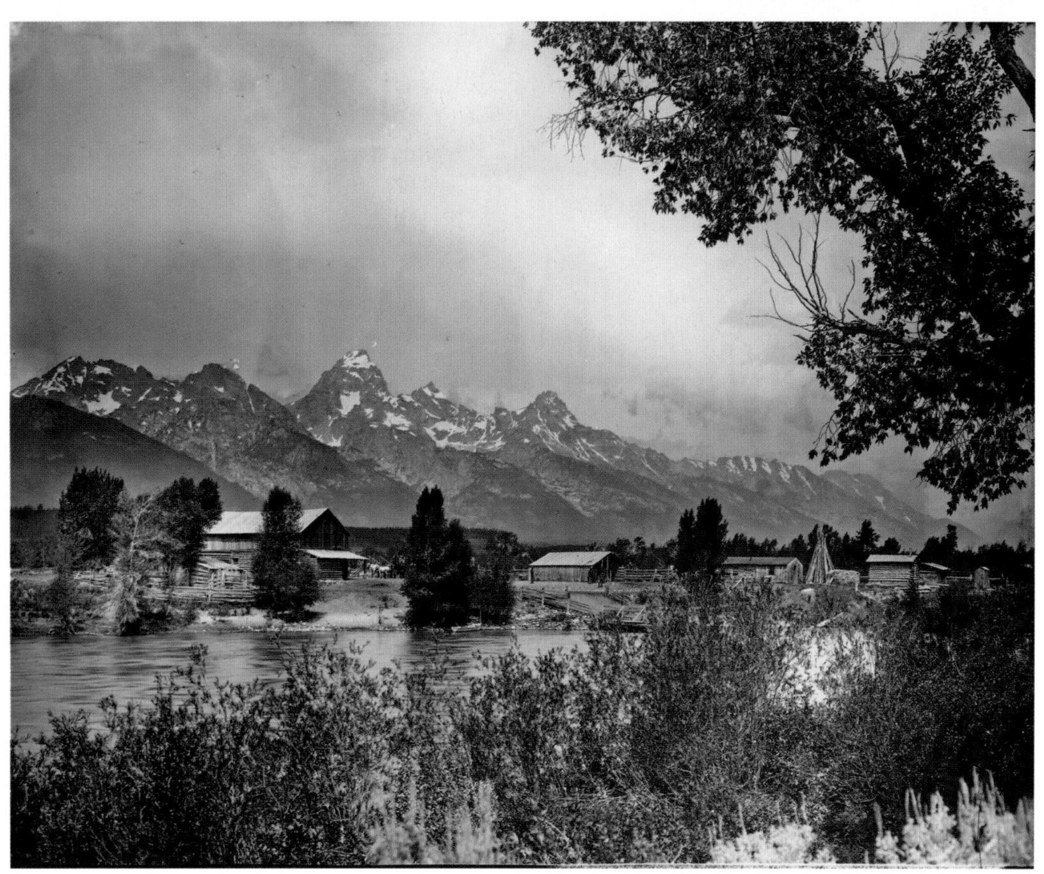

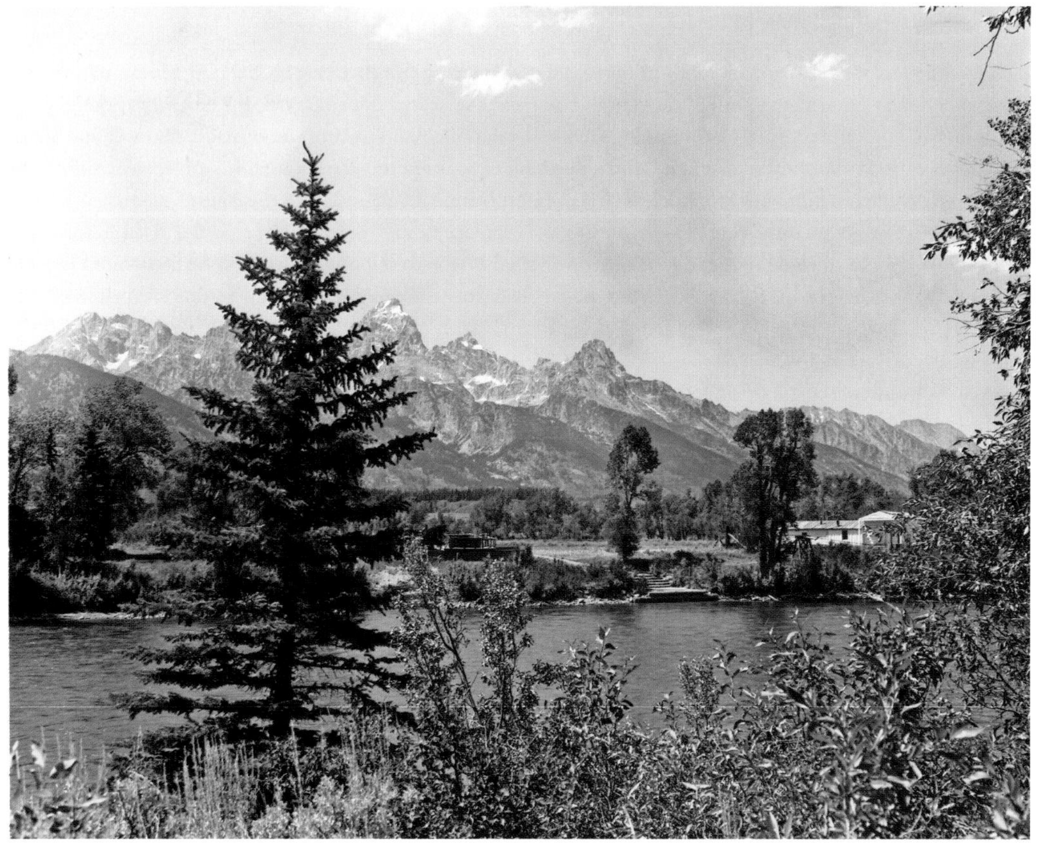

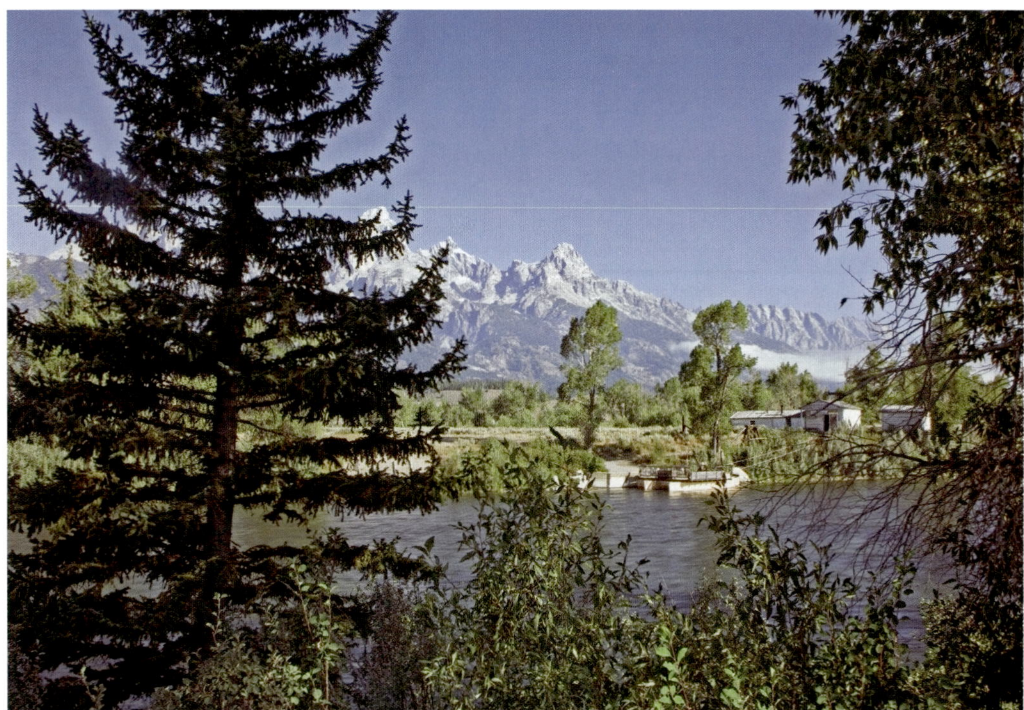

115. #E85

Menor's Ferry, Moose, 1899, 1988, 2008
GPS COORDINATES: 43 39.486N, 110 42.705W

North of Jackson Hole, the Snake River separates from a single river into many braided channels. People who wanted to cross it often found one of the historic fords where the river broke apart into shallow channels. William Menor had another idea. After locating a stretch where the braided channels combined back into one main river for about a mile, in 1894 Menor took up a homestead, intending to build and operate a reliable ferry across the Snake River. Over the next twenty-five years, Menor's Ferry became the most important river crossing in Jackson Hole. Everyone used it, so it was also a cultural symbol of the area as it existed prior to the creation of Grand Teton National Park.

Stimson's 1899 photograph, one of the earliest in his collection, was taken across the swollen Snake River from Menor's cabin. Using a tree to frame his shot, Stimson made his photograph along the river's left bank, with the water almost to eye level. The ferry can just be seen along the river's edge, while the cabins and barns on the opposite shore stand against the spectacular Teton backdrop. In a sense, by placing the human landscape in the center of a sublime natural one, he is telling us that humans can overcome the frontier.

This skilled sense of composition, used prior to Stimson being hired by either the Union Pacific or the State of Wyoming, reminds us of why these entities hired the Cheyenne photographer to promote their interests: he knew how to make good photographs.

My 1988 rephotograph shows the ferry site in Grand Teton National Park. Laurence Rockefeller restored the ferry boat in 1949, and the area became part of the park the following year. A pine tree, not present in Stimson's photograph, blocked much of the view of the barn buildings, though Menor's cabin can be seen at right.

In 2008, Lauren and I visited Menor's Ferry after touring the park's new visitor center and having a nice lunch at Dornan's. After making my rephotograph, which mostly showed the growth of that same pine from twenty years earlier but also included both Menor's cabin and the ferry, we joined a park ranger for a ride on the historic ferry over and back across the Snake River. Never one for boats, I joked with Lauren that we had now rafted the Snake River!

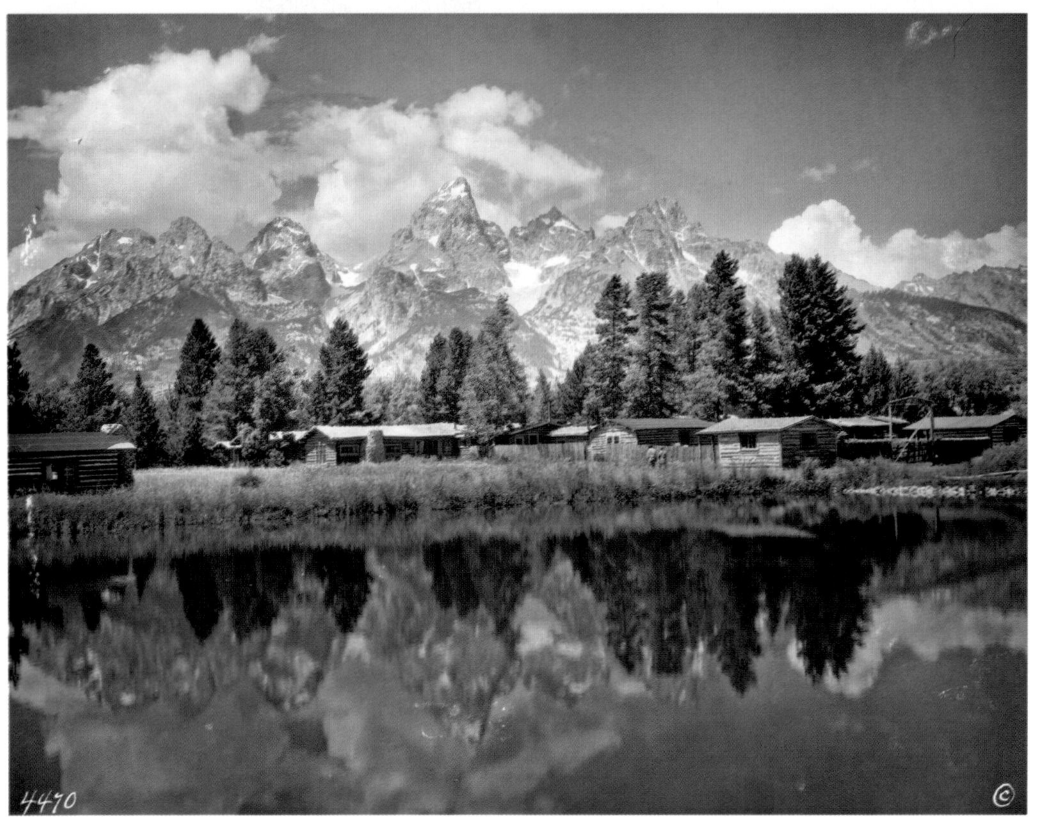

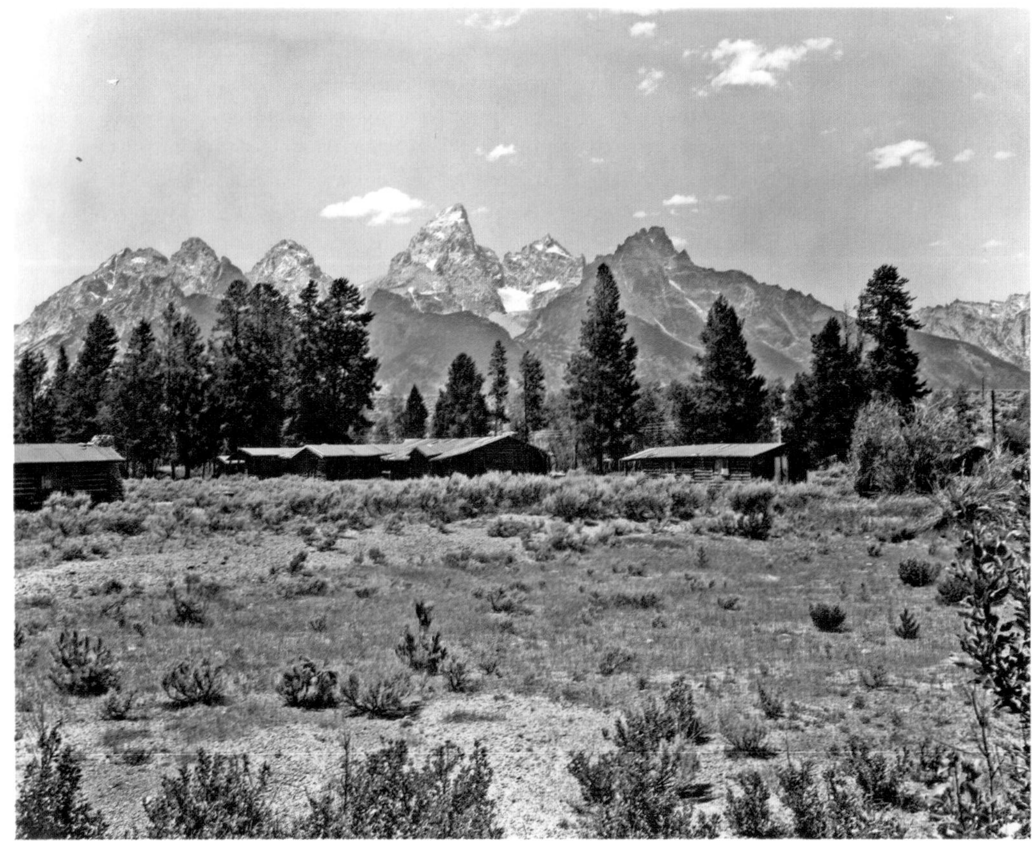

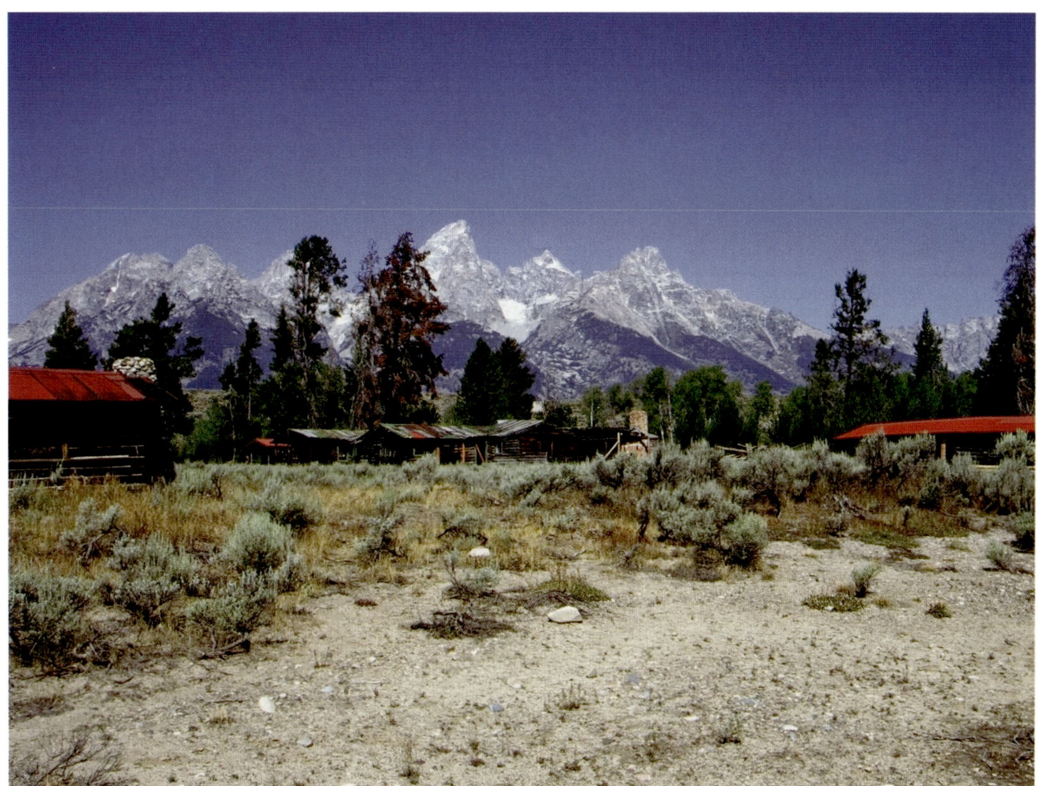

116. #4470

Bar BC, Moose, 1920, 1988, 2007
GPS COORDINATES: 43 41.691N, 110 41.662W

Struthers Burt, an eastern writer, came to Wyoming after graduating from Princeton in 1904 and founded the JY Ranch in Jackson Hole in 1908. Following a dispute with his partner, Burt opened the area's second dude ranch, the Bar BC, along the Snake River. With its Western Rustic–style architecture, the Bar BC looked like an old-time cattle ranch, even though it had been constructed for dudes.

Stimson's 1920 photograph of the Bar BC is important for a couple of reasons. First, its striking composition, with the cabins and Tetons bathed in morning sunlight and reflected in the pond, shows Stimson at the height of his craft. Just as important, though, is the year 1920 because it captures Burt's ranch just before he became nationally known for his work in Jackson Hole.

In 1924, Burt published *Diary of a Dude Wrangler*, his autobiographical account of life at the Bar BC. This book brought him national attention and encouraged writers to visit the ranch. At about the same time, he became an active advocate for federal protection of the area. After Grand Teton National Park was created in 1929, John D. Rockefeller Jr. began secretly purchasing ranches along the Snake that were then donated to the federal government for protection—first as a national monument in 1943, then as part of the park in 1950. The first ranch Rockefeller purchased was the Bar BC, though Burt negotiated a provision that allowed the ranch to continue operations. After a disagreement with his partner, Irving Corse, in the 1930s, Burt left. Corse operated the ranch until he died in the 1950s, and his widow ran it until 1985. Her death in 1988 gave the National Park Service ownership.

During my 1988 visit, the Bar BC was no longer operating and had just been given to the Park Service. My rephotograph shows most of the cabins in disrepair, the beautiful reflection pond dried up, and the site a sad reminder of better days in the past.

In 2007, when I returned to the Bar BC, a Park Service crew was stabilizing the site. I learned that plans were in place to eventually restore the ranch and remodel it into a museum. Judging from my rephotograph, the Bar BC both needs and *deserves* the attention. As a historic location of one of the places that shaped the way we think about the Tetons, the Bar BC's buildings deserve restoration and the ranch should be restored and returned to the public's view.

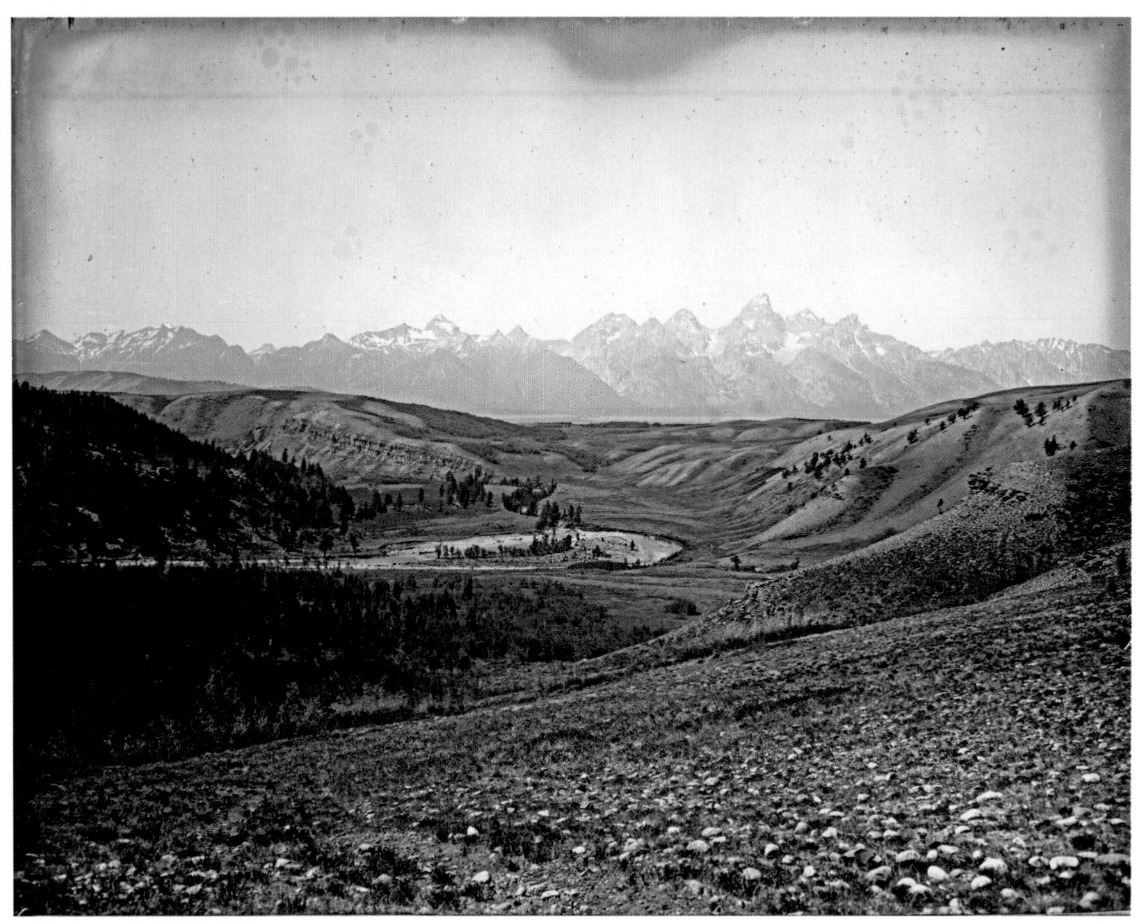

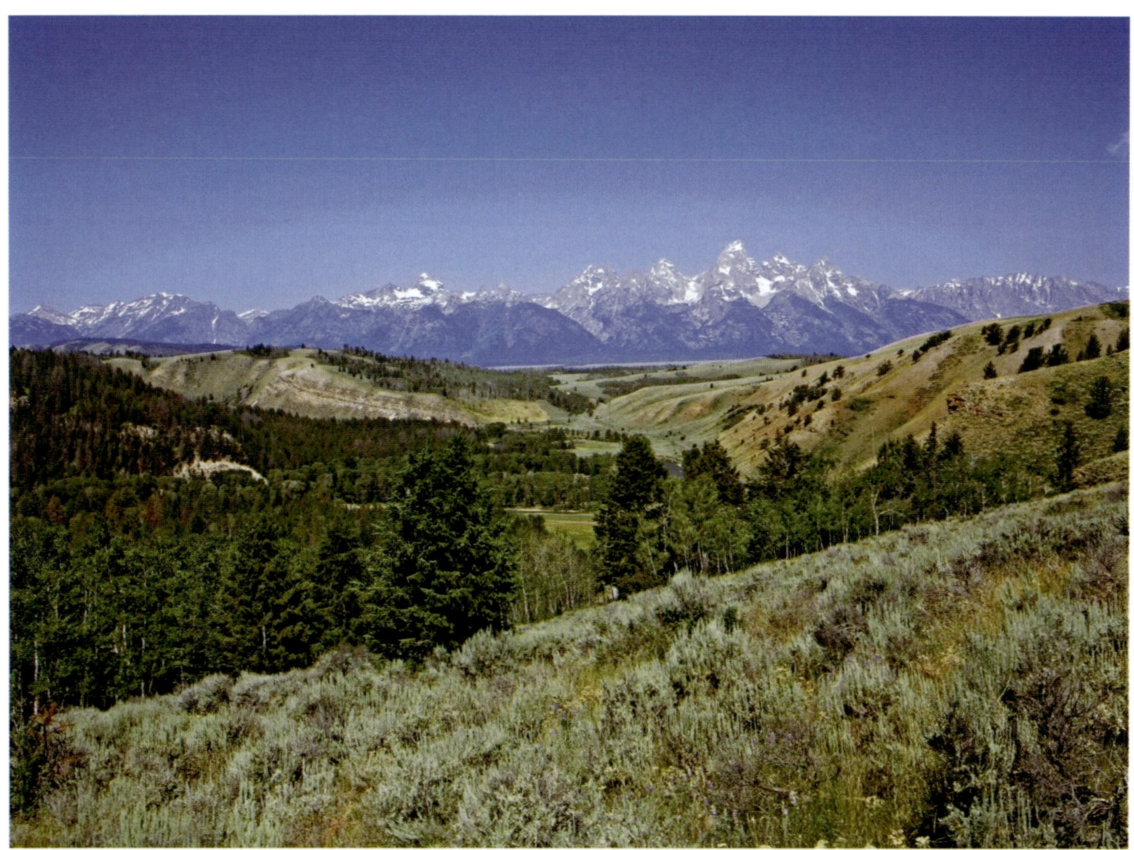

117. #E101

Tetons from Gros Ventre Butte, Kelly, 1899, 2008
GPS COORDINATES: 43 38.057N, 110 33.791W

Another of Stimson's photographs prior to his employment by the Union Pacific or the State of Wyoming was made when he was visiting Jackson Hole in 1899. Shot from Gros Ventre Butte east of Kelly, this view is looking west across a bend in the Gros Ventre River toward the spectacular Tetons. An excellent example of the photographer's early keen eye for composition, this view uses the valley's wall, right, and the dark forest, left, to frame the river bend before the viewer's eye rises upward to the faint mountains in the distance. Only light traces of a small road can be seen. It is a wonderfully sublime image.

As discussed in chapter 3, this beautiful valley became the scene of natural destruction a quarter of a century later after weeks of heavy rain in June 1925 set loose a portion of Sheep Mountain, just upstream from this vantage point, into the river valley below. An estimated 50 million cubic yards of rock slid down the mountain. The Kelly Slide, as it became known, dammed the river, creating Lower Slide Lake. Engineers determined it to be safe, but more heavy rains in 1926 and 1927, combined with heavy snowmelt, sent water over the natural dam. When residents discovered the problem, the small town of Kelly was evacuated. The dam broke, sending a wall of water 6 feet deep 25 miles downstream. The entire town of Kelly, save the church and the school, were destroyed, though only six people were lost in the flood.

When Lauren and I visited the site in 2008, we started at the bottom of this hill and carried our camera gear through sagebrush to the top, checking for the vantage point along the way. At the top, we found an old road and, just beyond that, the current Gros Ventre Road. A couple of ranches now exist along the road. Although pine trees have blocked part of the scene, the view from this hill remains spectacular, with wildflowers blooming at our feet, dark evergreens to our left, the valley floor below, and the Tetons looming in the distance. One of my last rephotographs, this sublime view was a fitting end to two more summers with J. E. Stimson.

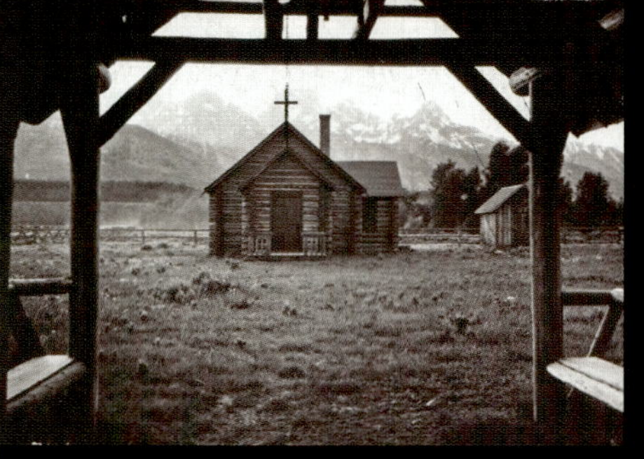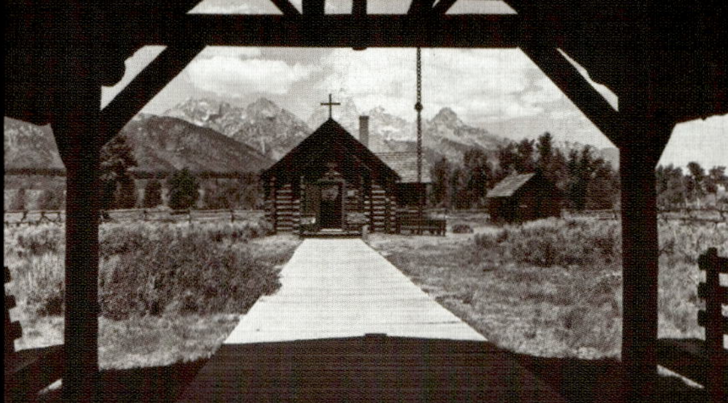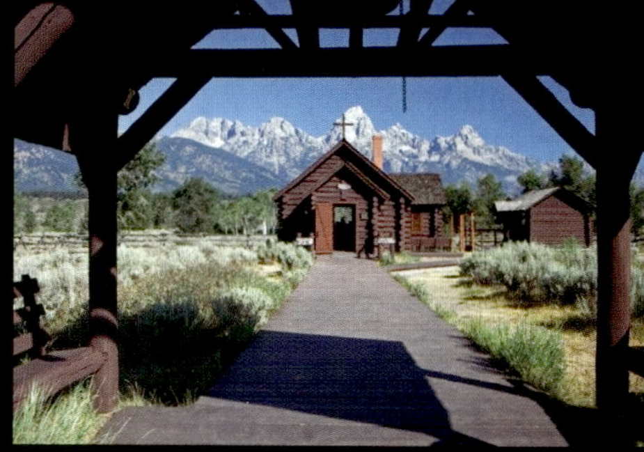

EPILOGUE

Atop the Digital Divide

DOI: 10.5876/9781607323051.c007

When I set out on this project in the summer of 2007, I thought I was making a radical shift by employing a digital camera instead of the trusted old 4 × 5 film camera. It seemed that as I loaded pictures every night from my memory card into my laptop, worked on those same pictures in the digital darkroom of Photoshop, or later printed those images on my color printer, I had indeed made an important transition. I had crossed the digital divide. But as I worked on researching, organizing, and writing this book, using computer spreadsheets, digitized online newspapers, and even faster and better computers and printers, I realized that I had been mistaken. I had not crossed the digital divide but instead sat atop it. Although I had clearly moved past the traditional chemical-film photographic approach to producing images, my methodology basically grafted digital capture, processing, and printing onto the same basic practices I had followed in the 1980s of trekking all across Wyoming, setting up a camera, and making photographs. As I finish this project and think ahead to the possibility of another rephotographic study of Wyoming sometime in the future, I can already see the downhill slope into the truly digital world and perhaps a glimpse of what digital rephotography might look like in the future. To do that, let's follow the process of rephotography through its various steps—research, capture, processing, and publishing—and then look at the effects of the new digital world on all of this.

Research for Wyoming rephotography has already moved into the digital era. The Wyoming State Archives has digitized much of the Stimson collection and included many images on its website. When I was working in the field, the state photo archivist had the capability of e-mailing images to me. This immediate access should only improve in the future, making it easier and easier to view Stimson images without having to travel to the archives in Cheyenne.[1]

Along with the archives, the Wyoming State Library's Wyoming Newspaper Project has fundamentally changed research on the state's historic newspapers. This federally funded grant project has hired hundreds of people around the state to sift through archived microfilms of the state's newspapers dating from 1849 to 1922 and index them for keyword searching. As I was researching this book, access to this service became available, and its effects were immediate. Instead of traveling to Cheyenne to read newspaper clippings or having microfilms of old papers sent through interlibrary loan and tediously reading through every one, page by page, day by day, and year by year, looking for any tidbit about Stimson, I could sit at home in Flagstaff and conduct keyword searches over the Internet, instantly finding "hits" across both the geographic expanse of the state and the temporal one of time. In several instances, for example, Stimson's images on the Cody Road or his trip to Granite Springs Reservoir, I could pinpoint his photograph to a specific date and story. By far the most important and exciting example was being able to follow Stimson's sojourns across the state during his 1903 fieldwork for the St. Louis World's Fair. From the comfort of my home office almost 1,000 miles from Cheyenne, I followed Stimson as he traversed Wyoming through the pages of the *Wheatland World*, the *Buffalo Voice*, the *Cheyenne Wyoming Tribune*, the *Sheridan Post*, the *Cody Wyoming Stockgrower and Farmer*, the *Grand Encampment Herald*, Douglas's *Bill Barlow's Budget,* and the *Laramie Boomerang.* As the newspaper project continues and grows, more and more information will be available in more and more ways, allowing researchers increasingly easier access to more materials.[2]

Along with these improved historical research avenues, access to spatial geography has been fundamentally revolutionized during the writing of this book through Google Earth. When I began in 2007, I uploaded digitized Wyoming US Geological Survey (USGS) topographical maps to my laptop computer and platted vantage points for each image from my portable GPS unit.[3] By the time I was actually writing four years later, I was taking these same GPS points, entering them into satellite images of the earth, and seeing those spots not on a map but on a zoomable satellite photograph of Wyoming. Further, the recent introduction of the "Street View" feature on Google Earth allows users to pull "Pegman" to their desired locations, and the views transform into actual 360-degree panoramic photographs taken from the road by a moving Google car loaded with digital cameras. The results are stunning. By simply knowing the GPS coordinates taken in the field, having a basic lay of the land, or comparing the original photographs to the "Street View" images, rephotographers can often now determine basic vantage points from their computers without having to step into the field. Indeed, as I was checking my vantage points for this book, I was often able to cross-reference Stimson's original view and my rephotograph via Google Earth.

At present, Google Earth only covers most major towns and streets, but the future clearly points to more and more digital saturation and ability to conduct virtual geographic fieldwork from a computer instead of in the field. In fact, a recent article in *High Country News* described how the energy bar company Nature Valley recently hired teams equipped with 360-degree cameras to hike 100 miles through Yellowstone and Grand Canyon National Parks to upload a "virtual hiking experience" for computer users who wanted a "deeper experience" than merely looking at photographs on the Web.[4]

All of this suggests that digital rephotographers of the future will, if actual fieldwork is even necessary, come to their vantage points with more and more information than was available even five years ago and—through bigger and faster computers, smart phones, WiFi, and pad technology—be able to process it more efficiently and effectively and have easier and more organized access to it at the same time. Needless to say, the way digital photographers of the future capture those historic frames will be fundamentally different from how I did so less than a decade ago and especially how Stimson did so more than a century earlier.

Digital cameras are increasingly like light-sensitive portable computers. Sensors get larger, more light-sensitive, and cheaper every year. Optics become lighter and better. Internal processors and memory cards are stronger and faster. My own history makes the point. In 1998, I used a digital camera for the first time, a 1.3-megapixel Sony that I could not afford. A couple of years later I bought a 3-megapixel "point and shoot" digital camera for $200. My first DSLR, which I used in 2007, offered 6 megapixels for about $700; the following year I doubled the quality to more than 12 megapixels for $100 less. In 2012, 18 megapixels with HD video was available for the same price. Older cameras, like old computers, now sit, hardly ever used.

Exciting new work is also developing in what is called "Computational Rephotography," which suggests new ways computers and cameras of the future will be able to assist rephotographers in finding landscapes and matching compositional elements. Developed by researchers at MIT and Adobe, Computational Rephotography utilizes a type of facial recognition software that is applied to known landscape features based on historical landscape photographs. By loading this software into laptops taken into the field, researchers have been able to guide their cameras to the desired camera stations of the original photographers. The first examples have proven worthy of continued research, with the idea that future generations of such software could eventually be uploaded to untrained rephotographers' cameras and literally guide them to the proper vantage point on the right day, select the correct lens, set exposure, and automatically take a better, more accurate rephotograph. These new images could be instantly encrypted with GIS information and automatically uploaded to Google Earth or other GIS sites.[5]

Just as the digital capture process has made revolutionary changes in the way we take pictures, smaller yet more powerful computers and software have made digital processing better and easier. Bigger and faster processors, along with ever increasing RAM memory, have combined to make the digital darkroom more than the equivalent of the chemical lab. Each generation of software, such as Adobe Photoshop, offers more and more capabilities. Rephotographers can use such tools not only to produce their own best images but also to tweak historical images to bring out more detail and better-quality images. Even Stimson's scans, already beautifully composed and properly exposed, can be processed through Photoshop to enhance their tonal quality and sharpness; in so doing, we can bring out even more detail and visual information than before.

At the same time, unscrupulous rephotographers can use such tools to purposely manipulate images to affect lighting or, worse, to fundamentally alter the original photograph or rephotograph by removing entire objects, cloning and reproducing parts of images into other areas, and thereby altering the meaning of the pairs. Indeed, digital photography has so greatly democratized the photography process and made it so easy for anyone to alter images that the phrase "photoshop a picture" suggests fundamentally altering its makeup.[6] Some critics have gone so far as to suggest that no digital image can be assumed to be real. Of course, this concept poses severe problems for rephotographers and will be dealt with more later.[7]

As much as digital technology has changed the research, capture, and processing components of rephotography, none of this compares with the revolutionary developments in the ways images are analyzed and published for the rest of the world to see. Scientists using digital rephotographs are already "counting pixels" to show vegetation change.[8] Although Photoshop and inkjet printer technology have replaced the chemistry and time of the darkroom with calibrated screens and sharp oversized images, these technologies more or less duplicate or simplify existing processes to produce images that can be mounted and framed. Far more interesting and exciting are the possibilities of interactive, hypertext images that can be viewed and linked through computers, pads, and cell phones.

These hyperphotographs are already bringing revolutionary changes to media and no doubt will continue to do so in the future. A hyperphotograph is simply one that has been "image mapped" so that parts of the photograph—or the entire picture—can be embedded with information and then linked to other images, sounds, texts, or other media. Viewers of the image can click on the part of the image they are interested in and be taken instantly to linked pieces of information. For example, a photograph of a family ranch may contain embedded links to oral histories of the people shown, architectural details on the buildings in the image, agricultural data on the crops shown in the fields, and so on. In many ways, hypertext photographs are like GIS maps, larger works that contain many smaller pieces of information embedded within themselves.[9]

Examples from my rephotography project on Stimson are the interior photos of Hardin's Ranch, discussed in chapter 5. In one of Stimson's magnificent views, each of the items on the walls—including paintings, hats, pottery, and textiles—as well as the beautiful rugs and furniture on the floor and the stack of books on the table, could have hypertext links. Then, when a viewer clicked on each item on his or her computer screen or iPad, a new window would open containing more digitized information about that item. Another could connect the image of the kind of organ in the back of one of the photographs to an Internet link showing someone playing one so modern viewers would not only see the restored instrument but hear it as well.[10] There could also be embedded links to oral histories of the Hardins and Stimson, panorama photographs, and the history of the ranch. Similarly, the rephotograph might contain oral histories of the house, its remodel, and links to texts describing the current objects in the house.

Some scholars have gone even farther, creating a visual database of known images of specific sites. When visitors to those sites capture photographs with their cell phones, they can immediately send their views to the database and other historic views of that same scene are returned, linking the visible of the present to the invisible of the past. Other applications for cell phone cameras include then-and-now photos of San Francisco available as an iPhone app so people can download the images as they are traversing the sites shown. As one critic suggests, such pictures no longer serve as individual tangible photographs but more as mosaics, ephemeral compilations of individual tiles of image and information that collectively comprise still another image. The Wyoming State Archives in Cheyenne has launched its own version of such a program based on its collections, including Stimson's. Those out in the field can enter a place name on their smart phone at the archives' Web page, and a historic image is presented to them on its screen.[11]

A fascinating reworking of rephotography into modern landscapes has been accomplished by Mark Klett. In his brilliant book *Yosemite in Time* and more recently in the amazing *Reconstructing the View*, Klett and his colleagues have first identified historic photographic vantage points and then precisely rephotographed them. Then, using digital postproduction methodology, they have taken their panoramas of Yosemite and the Grand Canyon and superimposed the historic images in their proper locations within the current views. Stunning work, the final images truly look like the Advent calendars discussed in chapter 5, with the original images resembling black-and-white doors into other times within today's color vistas.[12]

I learned of another fascinating application of computer-assisted rephotography at a July 2012 celebration of Lowell Observatory's new Discovery Channel Telescope by former astronaut Neil Armstrong. During a presentation, Armstrong narrated a multimedia show based on the work conducted by YouTube Internet sensation "GonetoPlaid." This person or persons took recent photographs made by the Lunar Reconnaissance Orbiter (LRO) that was launched in 2009 and is now circling the moon and compared them to enhanced photographs made by NASA more than four decades ago. The historic views included those made by the

Lunar Orbiter (LO) in 1967, prior to the Apollo lunar landings, and other images made by Armstrong's landing module, the Eagle, in July 1969. As Armstrong explained, by selecting specific angles from the thousands of photographs taken by the LRO, GonetoPlaid has been able to reconstruct before-and-after images of the moon. In one of these pairs, the Apollo 11 landing module is clearly visible. In another sequence compiled to recreate a movie, GonetoPlaid reconstructed the photographs made by Armstrong's Eagle as it descended to the moon in July 1969. During his presentation, Armstrong ran a computer video comparison of the images he made with those made more than forty years later by the LRO and talked about what he was thinking and doing as he made his historic descent. The comparison pictures not only prove to skeptics that the lunar landing actually happened but, moreover, represent a fascinating example of the potential for computer-aided rephotography and the future of the practice.[13]

The effects of digital research, capture, processing, and publication vary widely. Certainly, this new medium has made the rephotography process more accessible and easier to conduct. At the same time, digital work has made completed rephotography projects available to wider audiences and encouraged researchers to include more information along with their pictures. In these cases, the digital revolution has been almost *deflationary* by allowing its practitioners and fans more and more stuff for less and less cost. Digital cameras, computers, printers, and software all seem to expand in capabilities while seemingly becoming increasingly inexpensive. The actual costs of digital technology, however, might be not only extraordinary but might undermine the very processes of photography, history, and rephotography.

One interesting effect of the new digital world might be on "sense of place," which refers to the idea that some places have special meaning for people. This meaning may be derived from a history of a certain place, an intimate knowledge of its features, or a belief that a place evokes special feelings in individuals. Cultural geographer John Brinckerhoff Jackson defined sense of place as "the permanent position in both the social and topographical sense, that gives us our identity." Another way to think about sense of place is to compare it to its opposite: placelessness. Generally defined as those "cookie-cutter" places that have been repeated so many times across the country that visitors sometimes feel completely lost, placeless sites include shopping malls, fast food restaurants, housing developments, strip malls, and the like.[14]

In contrast, rephotographing Wyoming has brought me to many places that provide strong currents of the concept of "sense of place." Obvious sites include iconic landmarks like the Tetons, Yellowstone National Park, and Devil's Tower National Monument. Other places where I have lived or that I have visited many times, such as Laramie, Cheyenne, and Kemmerer—where my mother grew up— also bring a strong sense of place when I visit them. Still other places that I have studied and written about here—most notably Sheridan and its environs and the Cody Road to Yellowstone—bring about another version of this idea.

The key point is that this sense of place came to me as I was visiting these sites in person. What will happen to sense of place in the new digital world? Will having the ability to virtually visit a camera location on Google Earth provoke the same sensation? Will the multiple layers of information embedded in hyperphotographs—being able to see satellite views while listening to oral history while looking at historic maps of the place and instantly learning about native flowers and local squirrel populations—make up for not actually setting foot on a rephotographic site? I doubt it. As much as we "represent" the Tetons through art, history, geography, and photography, there is no feeling like standing on the shores of Jenny Lake and staring up at those mountains.

I have touched on another issue in the new digital world: the alteration of images using Photoshop and other computer software. The fact that the term for such changes is *Photoshop* attests to how accessible this technology has become and how widespread its practice may be. That said, altering photographs is as old as photography itself. Photographers and artists have long "retouched" portraits to make them more attractive to their customers. Before the advent of color film, photographers, including J. E. Stimson, often hand-colored prints to give them a "natural" look. Ansel Adams is famous for having compared the negative to the musical score and the print to the performance, suggesting that all photographs could be manipulated and that multiple final interpretations are not only possible but preferred. Perhaps the most drastic examples in the era of the chemical darkroom occurred in Soviet Russia. In the fascinating book *The Commissar Vanishes*, author David King shows that the Stalin government used airbrushing and other techniques to deliberately add or remove people from historic photographs for political purposes.[15]

But photoshopping goes beyond this idea. Whereas Stimson added color to make his black-and-white images more realistic and Adams dodged and burned his prints to reflect the feelings he had when he made the negative, photoshopping involves the deliberate addition or removal of elements in the photograph. Digital cameras and computer software have made the process easier and cheaper, since most "alterations" can be performed on a computer and the final product printed only when all work is completed. Leading publications such as *Outdoor Photographer* even encourage the practice, in one instance giving step-by-step instructions for removing people and walkways from a Yellowstone image to somehow "photograph these iconic spots without the inclusion of people and the heavy impact they leave behind."[16]

The ramifications of digital manipulation for rephotography are significant. For a practice that relies on matching elements of specific places against earlier versions of those same views, having the ability to selectively remove either current or past objects threatens the very core of rephotography. As has been shown in this project on Wyoming, in examples like Dietz (60) and Cambria (50), so little of the elements of Stimson's image is still visible that a viewer must trust the rephotographer that this scene is indeed showing the same vantage point. In the digital age, that trust could be negated simply because of the ability to easily manipulate the digital image. What if all the buildings in Dietz were still there and I had simply photoshopped them out?

This very idea raises bigger questions about the role of photography as a "documentary" of the past and, for that matter, the role of "truth" in history itself. In that *Outdoor Photographer* article on Yellowstone, the editors include a sidebar story called "The Ethics of Retouching." In it, they suggest that when photographs are used as "historical documents," images should be as truthful as possible. At the same time, they argue that not every photograph has that intention, that many are simply "trying to capture something of beauty for its aesthetic qualities," and that "retouching distracting elements like a boardwalk is appropriate." Author Fred Ritchin describes this another way, noting photography's "stenographic function" as a firsthand recorder of the past. But Ritchin, too, worries about how easily digital images can be manipulated and concludes that if "documentary photography cannot be trusted at least as a quotation from appearances, then photography will have lost its currency . . . [and] become a mere symbol of spin." He quotes photographer and writer Philip Jones Griffith who, in an interview with the *Digital Journalist*, reiterated the argument: "The real problem with digital is there is no reason to believe photographs any more . . . faking pictures is just so easy." Finally, Ritchin quotes filmmaker Wim Wenders, noting that "the digitized picture has broken the relationship between picture and reality once and for all. We are entering an era when no one will be able to say whether a picture is true or false. They are all becoming beautiful and extraordinary, and with each passing day they belong increasingly in the world of advertising."[17]

If indeed digital photographs are more akin to advertisements than "stenographic" recordings, then can Stimson's promotional images also be interpreted as visual documents of the past? The answer lies in how we think about the idea of history itself. For the past two or three decades, academic historians have shelved the old view of narrative history that leads to the "truth" of what happened in the past, what my colleague George Lubick liked to call the "one damned thing after another" idea. Instead, postmodern historians use analytical tools and theories to suggest that history is a cultural construction created by each generation to help it explain the past and its own future. In this view, primary sources such as photographs are never assumed to represent the "truth" of the past; instead, they are one small snippet of the conversation that helps us understand it. In this view, there is no big "truth," and therefore historians are always keenly trying to "decode" past images for what they were attempting to say in their own time and what elements those ideas bring to an understanding of the past.

For this rephotography project, such ideas are inherent in the way I approached the Stimson collection, researched his body of work, tried to understand that he was promoting a vision of Wyoming, and how he went about doing it. I then captured my own images from the same vantage points, used minimal digital processing to maintain credibility, and published the images and stories that went along with them, warts and all, in this book. As I look back at this project, I affirm that as much as I thought I had stepped out of Stimson's long shadow by going digital, in many ways I was simply bringing new technologies to old practices. Clearly not over the digital divide but instead standing firmly atop it, I can see glimpses of the digital future that includes more access to archival materials, more ubiquitous and better-detailed Google Earth images, and better Computational Rephotography software that may allow future rephotographers to identify vantage points from their homes. As they do so, they will use virtual cameras, better software programs, and bigger and faster computers that allow more manipulations and larger and more detailed hyperphotographs—embedded with increasing amounts of information, accessible across more media, and seemingly unfettered by spatial boundaries. There is no doubt in my mind that such rephotographs will help us to better understand the relationship between space and history and will no doubt imbue us with more of an understanding of the long view of history and place, knowing that such endeavors are not searching for truth but merely adding to the ever increasing conversation of history.

So, what does all this mean for Wyoming? In his book *Pushed off the Mountain, Sold down the River*, Samuel Western worries about Wyoming's future. He cites the lack of jobs for young people and their out-migration from the state in search of opportunities, continued feuding with the federal government, the ongoing power of out-of-state corporations and the subsequent boom and bust of the state's extractive economy, the growing view of the state as a place to preserve wealth rather than create it, dependence on the myth of the cowboy, and the lack of a viable agriculture sector. One of the few things he does not worry about is tourism, other than to note the increasing presence of "hobby ranchers" and second-home owners. But perhaps he should be concerned. Historian Hal Rothman famously described tourism as a "devil's bargain" that offers short-term economic gain at the expense of long-term loss of identity, as the tourist industry relentlessly remakes places to be what outsiders expect them to be rather than what residents need to sustain their communities. In short, tourism dependence creates competing "senses of place" between residents and newcomers, each of whom has their own visions of what places should be.[18]

These concerns will only grow as the state moves farther across the digital divide. More and more of the tourist experience is becoming digitized, with not only beautiful photographs of the Tetons and Yellowstone flourishing on the Internet but Web cams at Old Faithful showing real-time eruptions and YouTube clips showing Wyoming mountain bike rides, ski runs, whitewater rafting, and the like. Google Earth allows virtual tourists to scroll over scenic highways both in color and, increasingly, in 3D. As I work out on a spin cycle, I can pop in a DVD of a ride through Yellowstone or Grand Teton National Park, watch it on a very large, high-definition television, and feel as though I am riding my bike through these beautiful places from the comfort of my home more than a thousand miles away. What if the virtual Wyoming experience—free of the ever-present wind, constantly changing weather, and growing expense of travel—cuts into the Wyoming tourist economy? Or will it create greater interest and increase tourism to the state, thereby intensifying the devil's bargain?

As we move over the digital divide into the brave new digital world, about the only things we can be sure of are that images will continue to inundate us, that more and more of our sensory world will become digitized, and that more and more of our experiences will become virtual rather than real ones. In the end, only time will tell whether all this will build up our sense of place for Wyoming or frack it apart.

Notes

1. http://wyoarchives.state.wy.us/Archives/Photo.aspx [accessed March 3, 2014].

2. http://www.wyonewspapers.org/ [accessed December 12. 2011].

3. National Geographic, *TOPO! Outdoor Recreation Mapping Software: Wyoming* (Washington, DC: National Geographic Society, 2006).

4. http://www.google.com/earth/index.html [accessed December 12, 2011]; Betsy Marston, "Heard around the West," *High Country News* 43, no. 21 (December 12, 2011): 28.

5. Soomin Bae, Aseem Agarwala, and Frédo Durand, "Compuational Re-Photography," *ACM Transactions on Graphics* 29, no. 3 (June 2010: Article 24, 1-15.

6. The webpage Wiktionary, which labels itself "a wiki-based open content dictionary," defines the verb *photoshop* as "to digitally edit or alter a picture or photograph." See http://en.wiktionary.org/wiki/photoshop [accessed December 12, 2011].

7. Fred Ritchin, *After Photography* (New York: W. W. Norton, 2009), 67.

8. Laura E. Hendrick and Carolyn A. Copenheaver, "Using Repeat Landscape Photography to Assess Vegetation Change in Rural Communities of the Southern Appalachian Mountains in Virginia, USA," *Mountain Research and Development* 29, no. 1 (February 2009): 21–29.

9. Ritchin, *After Photography,* 69–77.

10. http://vimeo.com/5706735 [accessed July 22, 2012].

11. Ibid. https://itunes.apple.com/us/app/time-shutter-san-francisco/id424253488?mt=8 [accessed December 13, 2011]. For Wyoming, see http://wyoarchives.state.wy.us/ [accessed August 19, 2012].

12. Mark Klett, Rebecca Solnit, and Byron Wolfe, *Yosemite in Time: Ice Ages, Tree Clocks, Ghost Rivers* (San Antonio: Trinity University Press, 2005); Rebecca Senf et al., *Reconstructing the View: The Grand Canyon Photographs of Mark Klett and Byron Wolfe* (Berkeley: University of California Press, 2012).

13. Neil Armstrong, remarks made at Lowell Observatory's "First Light Gala Celebrating the Commission of the Discovery Channel Telescope," July 21, 2012, Flagstaff, AZ; http://www.youtube.com/watch?v=61jvslqR1cM&feature=fvsr [accessed July 22, 2012]; http://lro.gsfc.nasa.gov/mission.html [accessed July 22, 2012]; http://apollo.mem-tek.com/ [accessed July 22, 2012]; http://www.lpi.usra.edu/lunar/missions/orbiter/ [accessed July 22, 2012].

14. John Brinckerhoff Jackson, *Discovering the Vernacular Landscape* (New Haven: Yale University Press, 1984), 152; http://www.artofgeography.com/info/the-sense-of -place [accessed March 3, 2014].

15. http://www.pbs.org/wgbh/amex/ansel/filmmore/pt.html [accessed December 14, 2011]; David King, *The Commissar Vanishes: The Falsification of Photographs and Art in Stalin's Russia* (New York: Metropolitan, 1997).

16. Kevin McNeal, "Advanced Cloning," *Outdoor Photographer* 27, no. 7 (August 2011): 67–72.

17. "The Ethics of Retouching," *Outdoor Photographer* 27, no. 7 (August 2011): 71; Ritchin, *After Photography*, 31, 66, 67.

18. Samuel Western, *Pushed off the Mountain, Sold down the River: Wyoming's Search for its Soul* (Moose, WY: Homestead, 2002); Hal K. Rothman, *Devil's Bargains: Tourism in the Twentieth Century American West* (Lawrence: University Press of Kansas, 1998).

This table includes the figure number for each set of photographs from this book followed by its title and the archive number for the Stimson collection at the Wyoming State Archives in Cheyenne. Titles might be slightly altered from their original archival description. Panoramas that include multiple images are usually labeled with the same numbers followed by letters, except where noted. Persons interested in purchasing prints or digital scans of original Stimson images can contact the Wyoming State Archives in Cheyenne (http://wyoarchives.state.wy.us/) and provide the archive number. Rephotographed images may be obtained from the author by contacting him at Michael.Amundson@nau.edu.

Figure No.	Description	Archive No.
1.7	Preparing for travel	3289
1	Union Pacific Depot arch, Cheyenne	1769
2	Capital Avenue Looking South, Cheyenne	5704
3	Looking Up Randall Avenue from Capitol Dome, Cheyenne, 1910	2849
4	Nagle Residence, Cheyenne	6484
5	Telephone Building, Cheyenne	1753
6	Majestic Theater and First National Bank Building, Cheyenne	4038
7	Masonic Hall, Cheyenne	374
8	Sixteenth Street Looking East	4040
9	Hecla Mill	290
10	Interior Hecla Mill	298
11	Outing at Granite Reservoir	2233
12	Vedauwoo	6021
13	Scene in the Red Buttes Country	1423
14	The Bee Hive Rocks Red Buttes Country	1420
15	Castle Dome, Red Buttes Country	1409
16	Sphinx Rock Red Buttes District	1426
17	Old Main, University of Wyoming, Laramie	7045
18	Science Hall, University of Wyoming, Laramie	722
19	Merica Hall, University of Wyoming, Laramie	7049
20	Residence of James Mathison, Laramie	1150
21	Street Scene, Saratoga	1972
22	Panorama of Smelter, Grand Encampment	765
23	Osborne Building, Rawlins	989
24	State Penitentiary, Rawlins	992
25	Union Pacific Depot and Park, Rawlins	2659
26	The Ferris Hotel (site), Rawlins	988

continued on next page

Figure No.	Description	Archive No.
27	Panorama of Rock Springs	739
28	Panorama Green River	724
29	Brewery, Green River	726
30	Green River Depot Park from UP Gate Tower (footbridge), Green River	728
31	Panorama of Evanston	685
32	Street Scene, Evanston	996
33	Union Pacific Depot, Evanston	4050
34	Diamondville	719
35	Panorama of Kemmerer	712
36	Street Scene, Kemmerer	715
37	Cokeville, Uinta Co. [now Lincoln Co.]	705
38	Panorama of Al Bowie's Ranch	408
39	A Saturday Afternoon, Wheatland	2912
40	Old Cavalry Barracks, Fort Laramie	4690
41	Old Sutler's Store, Fort Laramie	4693
42	Hartville	1946
43	Panorama of Douglas	813
44	The Douglas Hospital (now a private residence)	821
45	Panoramic View of Natural Bridge, Converse Co.	814
46	Panoramic View of Newcastle	436
47	A Street Scene in Newcastle	439
48	Main Street Newcastle	438
49	City of Sundance and Sundance Mountain	471
50	Cambria Coal Camp	446
51	Devil's Tower from Belle Fourche River	470
52	The Red Butte, a noted landmark, Weston Co.	425
53	Panorama of Buffalo	557
54	The Occidental Hotel, Buffalo	2954
55	Panorama of Sheridan, looking east	487
56	Sheridan Inn, Sheridan	5747
57	Sheridan Inn Dining Room, early series	E22
58	Sheridan Main Street	2949
59	Officers' Quarters, Fort Mackenzie, near Sheridan	496
60	Panorama of Dietz	493
61	Dietz Street Scene	492
62	General View of Kearney Coal Camp (Kleenburn)	2593
63	Panorama of Hardin Ranch, Sheridan Co.	537
64	Panorama of Hardin Ranch, Looking North	540
65	Interior Panorama, Hardin Residence, Sheridan, Co.	534, 534a
66	Interior of Hardin Residence, Sheridan Co. (looking south)	535
67	Interior of Hardin's Residence (couple at fireplace)	533
68	Interior of Hardin Residence (looking NE)	536
69	Porch of Hardin's Residence	532
70	Dining Room Fireplace, Hardin's Residence	529
71	Panoramic View of Forbes Ranch, Sheridan Co.	525

continued on next page

Figure No.	Description	Archive No.
72	Panorama [of] Moncreiffe Ranch	483
73	Club House, Dome Lake	E49
74	Guests at Dome Lake	2635
75	General View of Dome Lake Reservoir from Club House	2630
76	Holdredge's Cabin	E6
77	West View Dome Lake Club House [Travis Cabin]	2631
78	General View of Dome Lake Reservoir	2638
79	Elk Tooth Mountain, Dome Lake, Wyo.	2641
80	At the Spillway, Dome Lake Reservoir	2633
81	South Pass [City], Fremont Co.	647
82	Panorama Carissa Mine and Mill, South Pass City	649
83	Atlantic City, Fremont Co.	650
84	View of Main Street, Lander	2939
85	Wind River Canyon	5921
86	Bird's Eye View of Thermopolis	3126
87	The Emery Hotel, Thermopolis	3131
88	Thermopolis Hot Springs Fountain	3129
89	Worland Street Scene	3143
90	Panorama of Meteetsee City	645
91	Bird's Eye View of Cody	613
92	Irma Hotel, Cody	615
93	Index Mountain at Twilight	611
94	Scene on Cody Gateway to Y.N.P., Wyo.	604
95	Cody Gateway to Y.N.P.	582
96	Sentinel Rock and Shoshone River, Big Horn Co. [Park Co.], Wyo.	598
97	The "Needle," Cody Gateway	573
98	Hoyt's Peak [Top Notch], Y.N.P., Wyo.	590
99	Sylvan Lake Panorama	579
100	Old Faithful Inn	2002
101	Chimney and Fire Place, Old Faithful Inn	2070
102	Castle Geyser	2091
103	Grotto Geyser	2099
104	Giant Geyser	2079
105	Lake Hotel	3011
106	Lake Hotel Lobby	3004
107	Yellowstone Lake Boat leaving West Thumb	2073
108	Dwelle's Inn, West Yellowstone, Montana	2077
109	Yellowstone Falls (Grand View)	308
110	Yellowstone River from the Falls (Brink of Falls)	341
111	Col. Meldrum's Residence, Mammoth Hot Springs, Y.N.P.	345
112	Mr. Meldrum's Office, Y.N.P.	304
113	The Silver Gate	363
114	Chapel of Transfiguration, Moose	4741
115	Menor's Ferry, Moose	E85
116	Bar BC, Moose	4470
117	Teton from Gros Ventre Butte, Kelly	E101

DOI: 10.5876/9781607323051.c008

Adams, Ansel. *The Camera*. Boston: Little, Brown, 1980.

Adams, Ansel. *The Negative*. Boston: Little, Brown, 1980.

Adams, Ansel. *The Print*. Boston: Little, Brown, 1980.

Along the U.P. Line: A Listing of the J. E. Stimson Photographs in the Collection of the Wyoming State Museum. March 1977: 35–40.

Amundson, Michael A. *Passage to Wonderland: Rephotographing J. E. Stimson's View of the Cody Road to Yellowstone, 1903 and 2008*. Boulder: University Press of Colorado, 2013.

Amundson, Michael A. "These Men Play Real Polo: The History of an Elite Sport in the 'Cowboy' State, 1890–1930." *Montana: The Magazine of Western History* (Spring 2009): 3–22.

Amundson, Michael A. *Yellowcake Towns: Uranium Mining Communities in the American West*. Boulder: University Press of Colorado, 2002.

Amundson, Michael A. "The British at Big Horn: The Founding of an Elite Wyoming Community." *Journal of the West* 40, no. 1 (Winter 2001): 49–55.

Amundson, Michael A. "Uncle Sam and the Yellowcake Towns: Uranium Mining Communities in the American West." PhD dissertation, Department of History, University of Nebraska, Lincoln, 1996.

Amundson, Michael A. "Home on the Range No More: The Boom and Bust of a Wyoming Uranium Mining Town, 1957–1988." *Western Historical Quarterly* 26, no. 4 (Winter 1995): 483–505. http://dx.doi.org/10.2307/970850.

Amundson, Michael A. "The Rise and Fall of Big Horn City, Wyoming." *Wyoming Annals* (Spring-Summer 1994): 10–25.

Amundson, Michael A. "Pen Sketches of Promise: The Western Drawings of Merritt Dana Houghton." *Montana: The Magazine of Western History* (Fall 1994): 54–65.

Amundson, Michael A. *Wyoming Time and Again: Rephotographing the Scenes of J. E. Stimson.* Boulder, CO: Pruett, 1991.

Amundson, Michael A. "The Mink and Manure Crowd: The History of an Elite Subculture in Wyoming." MA thesis, American Studies, University of Wyoming, 1990.

Amundson, Michael A. "Through the Lens of Stimson: Past and Present." *Annals of Wyoming* (Spring 1988): 32–45.

Armstrong, Neil. Remarks made at Lowell Observatory's "First Light Gala Celebrating the Commission of the Discovery Channel Telescope." Flagstaff, AZ, July 21, 2012.

Bae, Soomin, Aseem Agarwala, and Frédo Durand. "Computational Re-Photography." *ACM Transactions on Graphics* 29, no. 3 (June 2010): article 24.

Bartlett, Ichabod S. *History of Wyoming*, vol. 1. Chicago: S. J. Clarke, 1918.

Bowen, A. W. *Progressive Men of the State of Wyoming.* Chicago: A. W. Bowen, 1908.

Brisbin, James S. *The Beef Bonanza: Or, How to Get Rich on the Plains.* Philadelphia: J. P. Lippincott, 1881. http://dx.doi.org/10.5962/bhl.title.55439.

Burt, Struthers. *The Diary of a Dude Wrangler.* New York: Charles Scribner's Sons, 1924.

Carter, John E. "Architecture, Photography, and a Quest for Meaning." *Exposure* (Fall 1987): 16.

Chittenden, Hiram Martin. *A Western Epic: Being a Selection from His Unpublished Journals, Diaries and Reports.* Seattle: Washington State Historical Society, 1961.

Chittenden, Hiram Martin. *The Yellowstone National Park.* Cincinnati: Stewart and Kidd, 1915.

"Curious Bits of Western Scenery." *Leslie's Weekly*" 95, no. 2493 (June 18, 1903): 611, 623.

Daugherty, John, Stephanie Crockett, William H. Goetzmann, Reynold G. Jackson, Grand Teton National Park, National Park Service, Intermountain Region. *A Place Called Jackson Hole: A Historic Resource Study of Grand Teton National Park.* Moose, WY: Grand Teton National Park, 1999.

DeVoto, Bernard. "The West: A Plundered Province." *Harper's Magazine* 169 (August 1934): 355-64.

Dilworth, Leah. *Imagining Indians in the Southwest: Persistent Visions of a Primitive Past.* Washington, DC: Smithsonian Institution Scholarly Press, 1997.

Dittl, Barbara, and Joanne Mallmann. *The Story of the Lake Hotel.* Boulder, CO: Roberts Rinehart, 1987.

"The Ethics of Retouching." *Outdoor Photographer* 27, no. 7 (August 2011): 71.

Dutton, Allen A. *Arizona: Then and Now.* Englewood, CO: Westcliffe, 2002.

Fielder, John. *Colorado 1870–2000.* Englewood, CO: Westcliffe, 1999.

Fielder, John. *Colorado 1870–2000 II.* Englewood, CO: Westcliffe, 2005.

Fox, William L. *View Finder: Mark Klett, Photography and the Reinvention of Landscape.* Albuquerque: University of New Mexico Press, 2001.

Ganzel, Bill. *Dust Bowl Descent.* Lincoln: University of Nebraska Press, 1984.

Goin, Peter, *Stopping Time: A Rephotographic Survey of Lake Tahoe*. Albuquerque: University of New Mexico Press, 1992.

Griffin, Dori. *Mapping Wonderlands: Illustrated Cartography of Arizona, 1912–1962*. Tucson: University of Arizona Press.

Hales, Peter B. *William Henry Jackson and the Transformation of the American Landscape*. Philadelphia: Temple University Press, 1988.

Harvey, Thomas J. *Rainbow Bridge to Monument Valley: Making the Modern Old West*. Norman: University of Oklahoma Press, 2011.

Hatfield, William F. *Geyserland and Wonderland: A View and Guide Book of the Yellowstone National Park*. San Francisco: Press of the Hicks-Judd Company, 1902.

Hendrick, Laura E., and Carolyn A. Copenheaver. "Using Repeat Landscape Photography to Assess Vegetation Change in Rural Communities of the Southern Appalachian Mountains in Virginia, USA." *Mountain Research and Development* 29, no. 1 (February 2009): 21–29.

Hendrickson, Gordon Olaf. *Peopling the High Plains: Wyoming's European Heritage*. Cheyenne: Wyoming State Archives and Historical Department, 1978.

Hine, Robert V., and John Mack Faragher. *The American West: A New Interpretive History*. Lamar Series in Western History. New Haven: Yale University Press, 2000.

Jackson, John Brinckerhoff. *Discovering the Vernacular Landscape*. New Haven: Yale University Press, 1986.

Johnson, Kendall. *Rangeland through Time*. Laramie: University of Wyoming Agricultural Experiment Station, 1987.

Johnson, Stephen. *On Digital Photography*. Sebastapol, CA: O'Reilly Media, 2006.

Jones, Walter. *Derricks and Determination: Oil Exploration in a Portion of Southwestern Wyoming, 1847–1982*. Casper, WY: Mountain States Lithographing, 2005.

Jones, William C., Elizabeth B. Jones, and Louis C. McClure. *Photo by McClure: The Railroad, Cityscape, and Landscape Photographs of L. C. McClure*. Boulder: Pruett, 1991.

Junge, Mark. *A View from Center Street: Tom Carrigen's Casper*. Casper, WY: McMurray Foundation, 2003.

Junge, Mark. *J. E. Stimson: Photographer of the West*. Lincoln: University of Nebraska Press, 1985.

King, David. *The Commissar Vanishes: The Falsification of Photographs and Art in Stalin's Russia*. New York: Metropolitan, 1997.

Klein, Maury. *Union Pacific*, vol. 2: *1894–1969*. Minneapolis: University of Minnesota Press, 1989.

Klett, Mark, Ellen Manchester, JoAnn Verburg, Gordon Bushaw, and Rick Dingus. *Second View: The Rephotographic Survey Project*. Albuquerque: University of New Mexico Press, 1984.

Klett, Mark, and Eadweard Muybridge. *One City/Two Visions: San Francisco Panoramas, 1878 and 1990*. San Francisco: Bedford Arts, 1990.

Klett, Mark, Kyle Bajakian, William L. Fox Michael Marshall, Toshi Ueshina, Byron G. Wolfe. *Third View, Second Sights: A Rephotographic Survey Project of the American West*. Santa Fe: Museum of Santa Fe Press in association with the Center for American Places, 2004.

Klett, Mark, Rebecca Solnit, and Byron Wolfe. *Yosemite in Time: Ice Ages, Tree Clocks, Ghost Rivers*. San Antonio: Trinity University Press, 2005.

Klett, Mark, and Michael Lundgren. *After the Ruins, 1906 and 2006: Rephotographing the San Francisco Earthquake and Fire*. Berkeley: University of California Press, 2006.

Kuzara, Stanley A. *Black Diamonds of Sheridan: A Facet of Wyoming History*. Cheyenne: Pioneer Printing, 1977.

Laramie County Historical Society. *Early Cheyenne Homes*. Cheyenne: Pioneer Printing and Stationery, 1964.

Larson, Taft Alfred. *A History of Wyoming*, 2nd ed., rev. Lincoln: University of Nebraska Press, 1978.

Lears, T. Jackson. *No Place of Grace: Antimodernism and the Transformation of American Culture, 1880–1920*. Chicago: University of Chicago Press, 1994.

Le Roy, Bruce. *H. M. Chittenden: A Western Epic*. Tacoma: Washington State Historical Society, 1961.

Limerick, Patricia Nelson. *The Legacy of Conquest: The Unbroken Past of the American West*. New York: W. W. Norton, 1987.

Limerick, Patricia, Clyde A. Milner, and Charles E. Rankin, eds. *Trails: Toward a New Western History*. Lawrence: University of Kansas Press, 1991.

Lindmier, Thomas, and Cynde Georgen, eds. *South Pass City: Wyoming's City of Gold*. Virginia Beach, VA: Walsworth, 2004.

Lowenstein, M. J., comp. *Official Guide to the Louisiana Purchase Exposition*. St. Louis: Louisiana Purchase Exposition Company, 1904.

Marston, Betsy. "Heard around the West." *High Country News* 43, no. 21 (December 12, 2011): 28.

McNeal, Kevin. "Advanced Cloning." *Outdoor Photographer* 27, no. 7 (August 2011): 67–72.

McWilliams, Esther. *Eaton's Ranch*. Privately published, 1981.

Meagher, Mary, and Douglas B. Houston. *Yellowstone and the Biology of Time: Photographs across a Century*. Norman: University of Oklahoma Press, 1999.

Morton, Sam. *Where the Rivers Run North*. Sheridan, WY: Sheridan Historical Society Press, 2007.

Moulton, Candy. *The Grand Encampment: Setting the High Country*. Glendo, WY: High Plains, 1997.

Olsen, Russell A. *Route 66 Lost and Found: Ruins and Relics Revisited*. St. Paul, MN: MBI, 2004.

Peterson, Samuel E. *Tales and Trails: Stories of Atlantic City, South Pass and the Sweetwater*. Lander, WY: Jean Peterson, 1999.

Pickering, James H., Carey Stevanus, and Mic Clinger. *Estes Park: Then and Now*. Englewood, CO: Westcliffe, 2006.

Redford, Robert. *The Outlaw Trail*. New York: Grosset and Dunlap, 1976.

Righter, Robert W. *Crucible for Conservation: The Creation of Grand Teton National Park*. Boulder: Colorado Associated University Press, 1983.

Ritchin, Fred. *After Photography*. New York: W. W. Norton, 2009.

Robbins, William G. *Colony and Empire: The Capitalist Transformation of the American West*. Lawrence: University Press of Kansas, 1994.

Robbins, William G. "The Plundered Province and the Recent Historiography of the American West." *Pacific Historical Review* 55, no. 4 (November 1986): 577–97.

Rodrigues, Chris, and Chris Garratt. *Introducing Modernism*. N.P.: Totem Books, 2002.

Rogers, Garry F., Harold E. Malde, and Raymond M. Turner. *Bibliography of Repeat Photography for Evaluating Landscape Change*. Salt Lake City: University of Utah Press, 1984.

Rothman, Hal K. *Devil's Bargains: Tourism in the Twentieth Century American West*. Lawrence: University Press of Kansas, 1998.

Rydell, Robert W., and Rob Kroes. *Buffalo Bill in Bologna: The Americanization of the World*. Chicago: University of Chicago Press, 2005. http://dx.doi.org/10.7208/chicago/9780226732343.001.0001.

Scofield, Susan C. *The Inn at Old Faithful*. Crownset Associates, 1979.

Sears, John F. *Sacred Lands: American Tourist Attractions in the Nineteenth Century*. New York: Oxford University Press, 1989.

Senf, Rebecca, Stephen Pyne, Mark Klett, and Byron Wolfe. *Reconstructing the View: The Grand Canyon Photographs of Mark Klett and Byron Wolfe*. Berkeley: University of California Press, 2012.

Shea, Paul. *West Yellowstone*. Charleston, SC: Arcadia, 2009.

Stephens, Hal G. *In the Footsteps of John Wesley Powell: An Album of Comparative Photographs of the Green and Colorado Rivers, 1871–72 and 1968*. Boulder: Johnson Books; Denver: Powell Society, 1987.

Stilgoe, John R. *Metropolitan Corridor: Railroads and the American Scene*. New Haven: Yale University Press, 1983.

Stimson, J. E. *Catalogue of Wyoming Views*. Cheyenne: J. E. Stimson, 1903.

Stimson, J. E. *Yellowstone Park*. Brooklyn, NY: Albertype, 1903.

Turner, Frederick Jackson. *The Frontier in American History*. New York: Dover, 1996.

Turner, J. E. *Summer of 1932 Incorporating also Top Country*. Silver Springs, MD: Wrybolot, 1999.

Turner, Raymond M., Robert H. Webb, Janice E. Bowers, and James Rodney Hastings. *The Changing Mile Revisited: An Ecological Study of Vegetation Change with Time in the Lower Mile of an Arid and Semiarid Region*. Tucson: University of Arizona Press, 2003.

Urbanek, Mae. *Wyoming Place Names*. Missoula, MT: Mountain Press, 1988.

Warren, Louis. *Buffalo Bill's America: William Cody and the Wild West Show*. New York: Knopf, 2005.

Webb, Robert H. *Grand Canyon, a Century of Change: Rephotography of the 1889–1890 Stanton Expedition*. Tucson: University of Arizona Press, 1996.

Webb, Robert H., Diane E. Boyer, and Raymond M. Turner, eds. *Repeat Photography: Methods and Applications in the Natural Sciences*. Washington, DC: Island, 2010.

Webb, Walter Prescott, and William D. Rowley. *The Great Frontier*. Reno: University of Nevada Press, 2003.

Western, Samuel. *Pushed off the Mountain, Sold down the River: Wyoming's Search for Its Soul*. Moose, WY: Homestead, 2002.

White, Richard. *"It's Your Misfortune and None of My Own": A New History of the American West*. Norman: University of Oklahoma Press, 1993.

Whitman, Walt. "Passage to India." In *Leaves of Grass, the Collected Poems of Walt Whitman*, ed. Emory Holloway. New York: Book League of America, 1942.

Writers' Program of the Work Projects Administration in the State of Wyoming. *Wyoming: A Guide to Its History, Highways, and People*. New York: Oxford University Press, 1941.

Worster, Donald. *Dust Bowl: The Southern Plains in the 1930s.* New York: Oxford University Press, 1979.

Worster, Donald. *Under Western Skies: Nature and History in the American West.* New York: Oxford University Press, 1994.

Wyoming Recreation Commission. *Wyoming: A Guide to Historic Sites.* Basin, WY: Big Horn, 1976.

Wyoming State Historical Society. *Re-Discovering the Big Horns.* Wyoming Bicentennial Project. Cheyenne: Bighorn National Forest Volunteer Committee, 1976.

Newspapers

Bill Barlow's Budget (Douglas, WY)
Buffalo Bulletin
Buffalo Voice
Casper Star Tribune
Cheyenne Daily Leader
Cheyenne State Leader
Cheyenne Wyoming Tribune
Cody Wyoming Stockgrower and Farmer
Evanston Wyoming Press
Evanston Wyoming Times
Grand Encampment Herald
Laramie Daily Boomerang
Laramie Republican
Riverton News
Sheridan Daily Enterprise
Sheridan Post
Wheatland World
Worland Grit
Wyoming Industrial Journal (Cheyenne)
Wyoming Semi-Weekly Tribune (Cheyenne)

Interviews and Correspondence

Josephine Stimson Love, interview with author, August 3, 1988, Ranchester, WY

Mark Junge, telephone interview with author, August 24, 2010

Rebecca West, e-mail to author, January 12, 2012

Films and Other Media

Broken Trail. Motion Picture. Directed by Walter Hill. North Hollywood, CA: Butcher's Run Films, 2006.

Heaven's Gate. Motion Picture. Directed by Michael Cimino. Beverly Hills, CA: United Artists, 1980.

National Geographic. *TOPO! Outdoor Recreation Mapping Software: Wyoming.* Washington, DC: National Geographic Society, 2006.

Select Websites

Apollo 11 Mission rephotos
http://www.youtube.com/watch?v=61jvslqR1cM&feature=fvsr
http://lro.gsfc.nasa.gov/mission.html
http://apollo.mem-tek.com/
http://www.lpi.usra.edu/lunar/missions/orbiter/

Bartleby
http://www.bartleby.com/142/183.html

Black Diamond Trail Interpretive Plan
http://wyoshpo.state.wy.us/pdf/BlackDiamondTrailInterpretivePlanFinal.pdf

Demonstration of an Aeolian organ similar to the one at the Hardin Ranch
http://vimeo.com/5706735

Google Earth
http://www.google.com/earth/index.html

Historical Decennial Census Population for Wyoming Counties, Cities, and Towns
http://eadiv.state.wy.us/demog_data/pop2000/cntycity_hist.htm

Historical Society of Pennsylvania's website on albertypes
http://www.hsp.org/sites/default/files/migrated/findingaidv18albertype.pdfQ6

Historical winter wheat estimates: Wyoming
http://www.nass.usda.gov/Statistics_by_State/Wyoming/Publications/Crops
/bull-08.pdf

Itunes app for San Francisco rephotography project
https://itunes.apple.com/us/app/time-shutter-san-francisco/id411557094?mt=8

James S. Brisbin's book *Beef Bonanza: Or, How to Get Rich on the Plains*
http://archive.org/stream/beefbonanzaorhow00bris#page/n5/mode/2up

National Register of Historic Places
http://nrhp.focus.nps.gov/natreg/docs/Download.html

1904 St. Louis World's Fair Society home page
http://www.1904worldsfairsociety.org/index.htm

1905 Portland Lewis and Clark Exposition
http://www.oregonencyclopedia.org/entry/view/lewis_clark_exposition/Q7

Old Faithful Inn renovations
http://www.yellowstone-notebook.com/innrenovation.html

Phil Roberts's Wyoming home page
   http://www.uwyo.edu/robertshistory

Sacred lands
   http://www.sacredland.org/home/resources/tools-for-action/
   protection-strategies-for-sacred-sites/what-is-a-sacred-site/

Sanborn Fire Insurance Company maps at the Library of Congress
   http://www.loc.gov/rr/geogmap/sanborn/index.php

Secretary of the Interior's Standards for Historic Preservation
   http://www.nps.gov/hps/tps/standguide/overview/choose_treat.htm

Wyoming history
   http://www.wyohistory.org/

Wyoming Main Street
   http://www.wyomingbusiness.org/gateway/main-st-/1245

Wyoming Newspaper Project
   http://www.wyonewspapers.org

Wyoming State Archives
   http://wyoarchives.state.wy.us/Archives/Photo.aspx

Wyoming Tales and Trails
   http://www.wyomingtalesandtrails.com

Page numbers in boldface indicate illustrations.